PRAISE FOR *SPARTA'S THIRD ATTIC WAR*

Paul Rahe's superb series is not only a classic for specialists but also of great importance and interest to all those interested in military history and the study of international relations.

JEREMY BLACK, author of *War and Its Causes*

Accomplished historian Paul Rahe has written a deeply researched and compelling account of Sparta's triumph in the Peloponnesian War over its adversary Athens, a victory of an authoritarian militarized regime over a democracy wracked by polarized political discord. Surely, this masterly history deserves to be read as a warning about the perils confronting American democracy in today's struggles among the great powers in the international arena.

JOHN H. MAURER, U.S. Naval War College

Consider what Paul Rahe brings to his self-appointed task: a life-long immersion in the inner and public lives of these ancient peoples; a first-hand familiarity with the fields, mountain passes, and seas where they contested for survival or primacy; and a broad overarching view that makes intelligible and vivid the distinctive granularity of his evidence. Where are those others who come so fully prepared to deal with such a challenge—and do so with verve?

RALPH LERNER, University of Chicago

In his latest Sparta volume, Rahe continues to pursue a subject that hundreds of years of Classical scholarship has omitted—how Sparta, Athens, and the Persian Empire conducted a three-way rivalry. The style is succinct, the treatment sophisticated, and the effect is miraculous. Few books on strategy match this one when it comes to finding the right blend of narrative, analysis, and guarded sympathy for both Sparta and its Greek rival.

FRED S. NAIDEN, University of North Carolina

Paul Rahe is the world's leading expert on ancient Sparta. His work is indispensable if you want to understand the Peloponnesian War and its relevance today. In Sparta's Third Attic War Rahe brings together deep historical knowledge, cultural understanding, and sophisticated analysis of grand strategy and geopolitics. Simply outstanding!

ATHANASIOS PLATIAS, coauthor of *Thucydides on Strategy*

SPARTA'S THIRD ATTIC WAR

THE GRAND STRATEGY OF
CLASSICAL SPARTA, 413–404 B.C.

PAUL A. RAHE

Encounter BOOKS

NEW YORK · LONDON

© 2024 by Paul A. Rahe

First American edition published in 2024 by Encounter Books, an activity of Encounter for Culture and Education, Inc., a nonprofit, tax-exempt corporation. Encounter Books website address: www.encounterbooks.com

Manufactured in the United States and printed on acid-free paper. The paper used in this publication meets the minimum requirements of ANSI/NISO Z39.48-1992 (R 1997) (*Permanence of Paper*).

FIRST AMERICAN EDITION

LIBRARY OF CONGRESS CATALOGING IN PUBLICATION DATA IS AVAILABLE

Library of Congress CIP data is available online under the following ISBN 9781641774130 and LCCN 2024030044.

PAUL A. RAHE III

Only the dead have seen the end of war.

GEORGE SANTAYANA

CONTENTS

MAPS

Journey's End

IT TOOK DECADES to resolve the conflict that the Peloponnesians in Thucydides' day called "the Attic war" and that had, by the time of Diodorus Siculus and Strabo, come to be called "the Peloponnesian war" by the Athenocentric.[1] This should come as no surprise. When a power enjoying a supremacy on land takes on a power that rules the sea, their strategic rivalry tends to last a long time. In such circumstances, it is difficult—it may even be impossible—for either to land on the other a knockout blow.

Of course, nothing lasts forever. Sometimes, after years of struggle, the two powers reach a settlement that neither much likes but that both can abide. Sometimes, the appearance of a third power, threatening them both, forces them to resolve their differences and join forces—at least for a time. And sometimes one of the two manages to achieve a mastery on the element hitherto dominated by the other.

This, in fact, the Athenians tried to do. Lacedaemon's strength on land derived from her alliance and the number of hoplites she could muster and deploy. Athens' aim was to break up that league and use manpower supplied by Sparta's erstwhile allies to bring her down. There is reason to think that, as an exile, Themistocles son of Neocles made the attempt in the late 470s or early 460s and came tolerably close to success—and there can be no doubt that, in 418 at Mantineia, the Athenians very nearly pulled it off.

The Lacedaemonians also eventually had a go. On the eve of the second of these two powers' wars, Pericles son of Xanthippus told

his compatriots that, if Lacedaemon was the only power of consequence they had to confront, they would "win through" in that war
on condition that they kept up their fleet and avoided risky ventures
in pursuit of ulterior objects. After the plague killed Pericles in 431,
the Athenians could not contain themselves and ignored his warning. One expedition they sent to Sicily, another they dispatched to
Boeotia—all to no obvious purpose, and all at a cost. It was not,
however, until 415 that they put themselves in genuine danger by
sending an immense armada to Sicily for the conquest of Syracusa
and the island as a whole, and it was not until the following year that
they chose to double down on that commitment and put at risk the
bulk of their hoplites and their entire fleet.

The folly of the Athenians provided the Lacedaemonians with an
opening—which, spurred on by the Athenian exile Alcibiades, they
seized. First, they dispatched a single Spartiate to Syracusa to put
steel into the spines of the populace; and under his direction the Syracusans destroyed the Athenian fleet, massacred a majority of the
infantrymen dispatched, and captured nearly all of those not killed.
Then, the Spartans voted to construct a fleet of their own, to take to
the seas with the help of their allies, and rob the Athenians of their
maritime hegemony. It is the struggle that then ensued that forms
the subject of this book.

In *The Spartan Regime*, which was intended to serve as a prelude
to this series, I analyzed the character of the Spartan polity, traced its
origins, and described the grand strategy that the Lacedaemonians
first articulated in the mid-sixth century for the defense of that polity and of the way of life associated with it. In the early chapters of
the first volume in the series—*The Grand Strategy of Classical Sparta:
The Persian Challenge*—I restated the conclusions reached in that
prelude and explored in detail the manner in which the Spartans
gradually adjusted that strategy to fit the new and unexpected challenge that suddenly loomed on the horizon when the Persians first
burst on the scene. Then, in the last four chapters of the work, I
described the fashion in which they organized and managed the coa-

lition with which they confronted and defeated the invader bearing down on Hellas.

In that volume's sequel, *Sparta's First Attic War*, I charted the way in which the victorious Hellenes gradually and awkwardly worked out a postwar settlement that seemed to suit all concerned, and I paid particular attention, as in its predecessor, to neglected aspects of the story—above all, to the grand strategy pursued by the Lacedaemonians in this period, to the logic underpinning it, to the principal challenge to which it was then exposed, and the adjustments that had to be made; but also to the noiseless revolution that took place at Athens in these years and to the implications of this gradual change of regime for the rearticulation of Athens' traditional grand strategy that, in fact, took place. Then, I considered the fragility of the postwar settlement; I traced its collapse and the manner in which Sparta and Athens came into conflict; and I described the war they fought and the long-term truce they negotiated.

I began *Sparta's Second Attic War* by briefly reviewing Sparta's first Attic war with an eye to exploring two salient themes: the geopolitical logic it disclosed, and the profound impact it had on the postwar preoccupations, fears, and expectations of those who had participated in it. Then, I revisited the forging of the Thirty Years' Truce, assessed its prospects, and considered the process by which it unraveled and Athens and Sparta clashed a second time. Thereafter, I investigated their aims in this new war and the character of the military strategy adopted by each, and I examined the actual fighting; the reasons why the hopes and expectations of both sides proved erroneous; the manner in which, in response to deadlock, each city with some success adjusted her military strategy; and the fashion in which mutual exhaustion eventually gave rise to another fragile, ultimately unworkable treaty of peace. And, finally, I explored the fashion in which—despite the pretense, vigorously maintained on both sides, that Athens and Sparta were at peace and on friendly terms—the war continued and very nearly produced a decisive victory for the enemies of Lacedaemon. If I brought that volume to a close with the battle of Mantineia in 418, some sixty years after the Spartans defeated the Persian general Mardonius in the battle of Plataea, and not in 404—when Athens was forced to surrender, give up her fleet, and tear down her walls—it was because I believe that, from the perspective of the Spartans, their victory at Mantineia on this particular occasion marked the end of an epoch and paved the way for a radical shift in their grand strategy. Hitherto, they had sought to rein in the Athenians. Now, thanks to their recognition that Athens was an existential threat, they sought her destruction.

Then, in *Sparta's Sicilian Proxy War*, I turned my attention to Athens' Sicilian enterprise and to the Spartan response. As we have already had occasion to note, this conflict took place in the territory of the Corinthian colony of Syracusa, and the Spartans took advantage of this ill-advised adventure on the part of their adversaries to inflict on the Athenians a blow from which it would have been difficult for any ancient Greek community to recover. The support that the Lacedaemonians supplied to the Syracusans was the first stage in the process by which they once and for all eliminated the city of Athens as a power of great consequence. This volume traces the struggle that culminated in Lacedaemon's victory.

This series of volumes on Lacedaemon's grand strategy is meant to throw light not only on ancient Sparta; her first great adversary, Achaemenid Persia; and her initial chief ally and subsequent adversary, Athens. It is also intended as an invitation to reenvisage Greek history from a Spartan perspective, and I hope as well that these volumes will turn out to be a contribution to the study of politics, diplomacy, and war as such. As I argued in the article republished in the appendix to *Sparta's Sicilian Proxy War* and as I try in this volume and in its predecessors to demonstrate by way of my narrative, one cannot hope to understand the diplomatic and martial interaction of polities if one focuses narrowly on their struggle for power. Every polity seeks to preserve itself, to be sure; and in this crucial sense all polities really are akin. But there are also, I argue, moral imperatives peculiar to particular regimes; and, if one's aim is to understand, these cannot be dismissed and ostentatiously swept aside or simply ignored on specious "methodological" grounds. Indeed, if one abstracts entirely from regime imperatives—if one treats Sparta, Persia, Corinth, Argos, Athens, Syracusa, and the like simply as "state actors," equivalent and interchangeable, in the manner advocated by the proponents of *Realpolitik*—one will miss much of what is going on.

Wearing blinders of such a sort can, in fact, be quite dangerous, as I suggested in the preceding volumes. For, if policymakers were to operate in this fashion in analyzing politics among nations in their own time, they would all too often lack foresight—both with regard to the course likely to be taken by the country they serve and with regard to the paths likely to be followed by its rivals and allies. As I intimate time and again in this volume and in its predecessors, in contemplating foreign affairs and in thinking about diplomacy, intelligence, military strength, and that strength's economic foundations, one must always acknowledge the primacy of domestic policy. This is, as I argue in the appendix to *Sparta's Sicilian Proxy War*, the deeper meaning of Clausewitz's famous assertion that war is a continuation of policy by other means.

It is the burden of these volumes to show that in ancient Lacedaemon, Persia, Corinth, Athens, Argos, and Syracusa there were statesmen who approached the question of war and peace from a broad perspective of the very sort described in the appendix to this volume's predecessor, and that it is their presence at the helm that explains the consistency and coherence of these polities' conduct in the intercommunal arena. There is nothing known to grand strategists today that figures such as Thucydides and the statesmen he most admired had not already ascertained.[2]

When they alluded to Athens, Corinth, Syracusa, or Lacedaemon by name as a political community—and, strikingly, even when they spoke of one these *póleis* as their fatherland [*patrís*]—the ancient Greeks employed nouns feminine in gender, personifying the community as a woman to whom they were devoted—which is why I with some frequency use the feminine pronoun to refer to Sparta and other Greek cities here.

SPARTA'S THIRD ATTIC WAR

Sparta's Enduring Strategic Dilemma

Civilization is based on the organization of society so that we may render service to one another, and the higher the civilization the more minute tends to be the division of labor and the more complex the organization. A great and advanced society has, in consequence, a powerful momentum; without destroying the society itself you cannot suddenly check or divert its course. Thus it happens that years beforehand detached observers are able to predict a coming clash of societies which are following convergent paths in their development. The historian commonly prefaces his narrative of war with an account of the blindness of men who refused to see the writing on the wall, but the fact is that, like every other going concern, a national society can be shaped to a desired career while it is young, but when it is old its character is fixed and it is incapable of any great change in its mode of existence.

HALFORD J. MACKINDER

LACONIA, THE SOUTHEASTERNMOST region of the Peloponnesus, was in antiquity a world turned in on itself. Sheltered by two formidable mountain ranges, Taygetus to the west and Parnon along the Aegean coast to the east, it was cut off from the highlands of Arcadia by rough hill-country to the north. Only in the south—where the Gulf of Laconia, facing the isle of Cythera and the open Mediterranean, stretches out between the rocky peninsula to the east that ends in Cape Malea and the mountainous promontory to the west that culminates in Cape Taenarum—did the broad valley carved out by the river Eurotas appear to be easily accessible. This was, however, an illusion. For, in the face of the prevailing winds that blew from the northeast, the storms that frequently accompanied them, and the gales and turbulence characteristic of the open water below the Peloponnesus, few ancient helmsmen cared to work their way along Laconia's iron Aegean coast, to round Cape Malea, and briefly brave the high winds and waves of the open sea before slipping into this pleasing bay and making their way to the natural harbor on its shores at Gytheion—and fewer still chose to sail or row to the Gulf of Laconia from Italy, Sicily, the Adriatic, the Corinthian Gulf, or the Ionian Sea down the western coast of the Peloponnesus, around Cape Akritas, then through the open sea past Cape Taenarum—the second southernmost point on the continent of Europe.

Nonetheless, had one visited Laconia in the late ninth century B.C., one would have come upon an intrepid band of Greeks, well-versed in the Dorian dialect, settled in a handful of villages scattered along the western bank of the Eurotas. If credence is to be given the ancient legends, they had been conducted thither by twin Achaean princes descended from the demigod Heracles. Initially, they are said to have made their way on rafts from northern Hellas across the Corinthian Gulf along with two other Dorian hosts led by the uncles of these princes and, then, to have proceeded separately on foot through the Peloponnesus into the fertile, well-watered valley where Menelaus and Helen had reportedly entertained Odysseus' gallant young son Telemachus. It was on the basis of this conviction regarding the lineage of their chieftains that these intruders, who called themselves *Spartiátai*, justified their incursion into what had once constituted the kingdom of Lacedaemon and laid claim to this portion of the vast realm within the Peloponnesus said to have been accorded great Heracles. As long as the Heraclid descendants of these two princes held sway, the Spartans believed, they would themselves retain the dominion the two had seized.

In the decades that followed, we are told, these new arrivals conquered the valley in its entirety, reducing the remnants of the old Achaean population resident in the bottom lands to the status of servile sharecroppers bound to the soil and required to farm the land on behalf of their Spartiate overlords. Those who resided in the hinterlands were subdued as well. But they were left free to manage their affairs locally on condition that they supplied soldiers when called upon. The former were called helots and the latter, *períoikoi*—"dwellers-about."

On the western side of the Taygetus massif lay another, even more fertile valley. This basin, called Messenia, was watered by the Pamisos river and occupied by another Dorian band. Legend had it that this group of Dorians had crossed the Corinthian Gulf alongside the Spartiates and had done so under the leadership of an uncle of Lacedaemon's two Heraclid princes, that the claim of these Dorians to Messenia derived from this man's Heraclid status, and that in time they had forfeited this claim by overthrowing the territory's rightful prince. It was this, the Spartans told themselves in later times, that had justified their decision to cross Mount Taygetus, raid Messenia, and launch the desultory campaign of looting and conquest that eventually, in the late eighth century, culminated in a renewal of Heraclid rule and their subjection of their fellow Dorians.

How much truth there is in this collection of stories is unclear. But this much—when we compare the legends handed down with what we know concerning the archaeological record and the dialects in use in these two valleys at different times—we can with reasonable confidence affirm. The Dorian-speakers of Laconia and Messenia were, indeed, interlopers in the Peloponnesus, and they secured control at some point subsequent to the collapse of Mycenaean civilization in the twelfth century. The Spartiates were present in Laconia by the middle of the ninth century, if not before. They managed to consolidate control over the Eurotas and Pamisos valleys by the end of the eighth century. Two generations after their conquest of Messenia, the inhabitants of that fertile, well-watered region rebelled and put up a fight that persisted for a considerable span of time, and the Spartans eventually crushed the uprising and imposed helot status on most, if not all, of the surviving Messenians.

The victory achieved by the Spartiates in this later struggle took place, we have good reason to believe, in the seventh century not long after the military revolution produced by the introduction of the hoplite phalanx. This was a military formation, ordinarily eight ranks deep, in which each infantryman bore a thrusting spear, a short sword, and a concave shield called an *aspís* and might be equipped as well with a metal helmet or cap made of felt and with a corselet or cuirass and greaves made of brass.

The *aspís*—the hoplite shield—was the distinctive feature of this new formation: it had a bronze armband in the center, called a *pórpax*, through which the warrior slipped his left arm, and a leather cord or handle on or near the shield's right rim, called an *antilabé*, for him to lay hold of with his left hand. This shield might provide adequate cover for a warrior temporarily stretched out sideways in the manner of a fencer with his left foot forward as he prepared to hurl a javelin or to put his weight behind a spear thrust. But this pose could not long be sustained, for it left him exceedingly vulnerable to being shoved to the right or the left and knocked off his feet. Moreover, the minute he pulled his left foot back for any reason or brought his right foot forward while actually hurling the javelin or driving the thrusting spear home, he would have turned willy-nilly to face the enemy; and, when he was in this posture, the *aspís* left the right half of his body unprotected and exposed, and it extended beyond him to the left in a fashion of no use to him as a solo performer. Even if the hoplite ordinarily stood, as one scholar has recently suggested, in an oblique position, braced with his legs wide apart and his left foot a bit in advance of his right so that he could rest his shield on his left shoulder, his right side will have been in some measure exposed. As this analysis should suggest—when infantrymen equipped in this fashion were operating on their own—cavalry, light-armed troops, and enemy hoplites in formation could easily make mincemeat of them; and the same was apt to happen when agile light-armed troops equipped with javelins caught hoplites on rough or hilly terrain unsuited to seeking a decision by way of phalanx warfare. The hoplite was, as Euripides contended, "a slave to the military equipment that he bore [*doûlos ... tōn hóplōn*]."

When, however, men equipped with the *aspís* were deployed in close order in ranks and files on suitable ground, this peculiar shield made each hoplite warrior a defender of the hoplite to his left—for,

**Figure 1.1. Hoplite on Vix Krater,
Late Archaic Laconian Ware.**
(Vix Treasure, Musée du Pays
Châtillonnais. Châtillon-sur-Seine, France.
Photographer: Michael Greenhalgh,
Wikimedia Commons. Published
September 2024 under the following
license: Creative Commons Attribution-
ShareAlike 2.5 Generic).

as the historian Thucydides son of Olorus explains, it covered that man's right side. It is this fact that explains the logic underpinning a statement attributed to the Spartan king Demaratus to the effect that "men don helmets and breastplates for their own sake, but the *aspís* they take up for the sake of the formation which they and their fellows share."

When a substantial proportion of a community's adult male population took the field, when the available manpower was sufficient, and when everyone cooperated and their shields interlocked and formed a wall, the phalanx was a formidable instrument of war. On relatively level ground, where these heavy infantrymen could easily remain in formation, it could brush aside light-armed troops; and, thanks to the unwillingness of horses to run headlong into a wall, it could face down a frontal charge by a cavalry formation. Only on the flanks was the phalanx vulnerable to such a force; and, in the mountainous and rocky terrain predominant in most places in the Balkans, on the islands of the Aegean, and along the Anatolian coast, it could ordinarily sidestep this difficulty either by situating itself where physical obstacles obviated flank attacks or by positioning at the end of each wing a band of javelineers or horsemen of its own. It helped that, in antiquity, the cavalrymen lacked stirrups and their mounts were not shod.

Since, in infantry combat, the strength of this formation was determined by its weakest link, it left little if any room for individual heroism and imposed on everyone in the front ranks an equal responsibility for the welfare of the whole. With equal responsibility came equal respect and, in time throughout Greece, a measure of political equality and social solidarity utterly foreign to the aristocratic world so vividly depicted by Homer. The victory achieved by the Spartans over the Messenians in the seventh century flowed, at least in part, from a series of egalitarian reforms that transformed what appears to have been a relatively narrow equestrian aristocracy into a much more expansive regime of footsoldiers called *hómoioi*—equals or peers—who were united by the role they shared in fighting for and governing the *pólis* as well as by a promise, we must suspect, that, if they reconquered the Pamisos valley, each in their number would receive, as each eventually did, an equal plot of land in Messenia and helots to work it.

In later years, as a ruling order, Sparta's *hómoioi* constituted a seigneurial class blessed not only with land and laborers, but also with a leisure which they devoted to a common way of life centered on the fostering of certain manly virtues. They made music together, these Spartans. There was very little that they did alone. Together they sang and they danced, they worked out, they competed in sports, they boxed and wrestled, they hunted, they dined, they cracked jokes, and they took their repose. Theirs was a rough-and-tumble world, but it was not bereft of refinement and it was not characterized by an ethos of grim austerity, as some have supposed. Theirs was, in fact, a life of great privilege and pleasure enlivened by a spirit of rivalry as fierce as it was friendly. The manner in which they mixed music with gymnastic and fellowship with competition caused them to be credited with *eudaimonía*—the happiness and success that everyone craved—and it made them the envy of Hellas. This gentlemanly *modus vivendi* had, however, one precondition: the continued dominion of this revitalized, Dorian Lacedaemon over both Laconia and Messenia and her brutal subjection of the helots on both sides of the Taygetus massif.

The grand strategy the Lacedaemonians of this age gradually articulated in defense of the way of life they so cherished was all-encompassing, as successful grand strategies generally are. Of necessity, it had domestic consequences on a considerable scale. Its dictates go a long way toward explaining the Spartans' aversion to commerce; their practice of infanticide; their provision to every citizen of an equal allotment of land and of servants to work it; the city's sumptuary laws; their sharing of slaves, horses, and hounds; their intense piety; the subjection of their male offspring to the elaborate system of *paideía*—education, indoctrination, and character formation—known as the *agógē*; their use of music and poetry to instill a civic

9

spirit; their practice of pederasty; the rigors and discipline to which they habitually subjected themselves; the manner in which those under forty-five [the *néoi*] were consigned to a squad [*sussítíon*] of about fifteen men who resided in barracks where they shared both bed and board; and, of course, their constant preparation for war. It accounts as well for the articulation over time within this new Lacedaemon of a mixed regime graced with elaborate balances and checks—in which there were two kings who were hereditary priests and generals; an aristocratic council of elders, called the *gerousía*, that set the agenda for the assembly and provided most of the jurors who deliberated on capital cases; a board of five ephors, chosen annually from the entire citizen body by a process akin to the lot, which functioned as an executive; and a popular assembly that voted on laws and decrees and decided questions of peace and war. To sustain their dominion in Laconia and Messenia and to maintain the helots in bondage, the Spartans had to embrace the virtues of modesty, moderation, and good sense that the Hellenes summed up as *sōphrosúnē*, and they had to eschew faction; foster among themselves the same opinions, passions, and interests; and employ—above all, in times of strain—procedures, recognized as fair and just, by which to reach a stable political consensus consistent with the dictates of prudence.

Not surprisingly, this grand strategy had serious consequences for classical Lacedaemon's posture in the intercommunal sphere as well. The Spartans' perch was precarious. A Corinthian leader compared their polity with a stream, and he was right. Rivers really do grow in strength as other streams empty into them, and the like could be said of these Dorian Lacedaemonians: "There, in the place where they emerge, they are alone; but as they continue and gather cities under their control, they become more numerous and harder to fight." Even when their population was at its height, the Spartans were no more than ten thousand in number, and the territory they ruled was comparatively vast—encompassing, as it did, two-fifths of the Peloponnesus. The servile population they exploited is said to have outnumbered them in 480 B.C., when their population had declined to circa eight thousand adult males, by something like seven-to-one; and that servile population was apt to be rebellious. In Messenia, if not also in Laconia, the helots saw themselves as a people in bondage; and the geography of the southern Peloponnesus, with Mount Taygetus standing as a great obstacle between its two river basins, did not favor the haughty men intent on keeping them in that vile condition.

The Spartans could seek support from the *períoikoi*, the subordinate free population that lived in peripheral villages within Laconia and Messenia; and this, as we have seen, they did. But the latter were no more numerous than were the Spartans themselves, and it was never entirely certain that they could be relied on. They, too, had to be overawed. In the long run, the Spartiates could not sustain their way of life if they did not recruit allies outside their stronghold in the southern Peloponnesus.

It took these Lacedaemonians some time to sort out in full the implications of their position. Early on, at least, trial and error governed their approach to the formulation of policy. But by the middle of the sixth century, the ephor Chilon and others had come to recognize that, if their compatriots did not find some way to leverage the manpower of their neighbors, they would themselves someday come a cropper. And so the Spartiates embraced as their watchword his dictum—"nothing too much [*mēdèn ágan*]"—and came to practice *sōphrosúnē* abroad as well as at home. It was under his leadership that they reluctantly abandoned the dream of further expansion into Arcadia to the north, repositioned themselves as defenders of local autonomy within that populous highland region, and presented themselves to the Hellenic world as the scourge of tyranny, the champions of liberty, the friends of oligarchy, and the rightful heirs of Agamemnon. It was with this end in mind that they negotiated an alliance with the Arcadian city of Tegea, their nearest neighbor of any consequence; sidelined the Argives to the northeast, who had hitherto exercised a species of hegemony within the Peloponnesus;

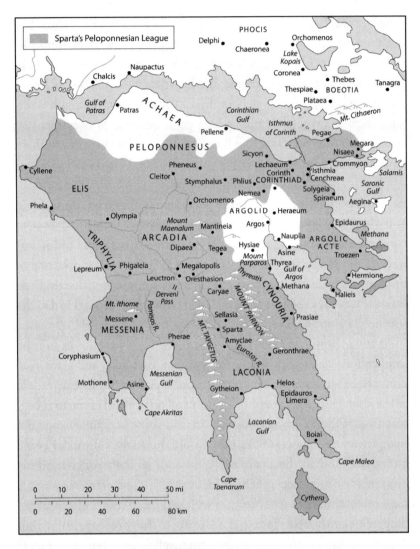

Map 1. Sparta's Peloponnesian Alliance, ca. 432

snatched from them the fertile district of Cynouria, which lay along the coast between the two communities; and then rearranged the affairs of the remaining Peloponnesians to their liking. And it was under this banner that they then founded the world's first standing alliance, which was designed to keep their formidable Argive rivals out, the helots within their own domain down, and the Arcadians, above all others, in. It was also under this banner that they arranged for the construction of a vast network of cart roads—all built on a single gauge—to unite this new coalition.[1]

Taken as a whole, the grand strategy of classical Lacedaemon was brilliantly designed for the purpose it was intended to serve. It had, however, one defect. It presupposed that for all practical purposes, the Peloponnesus was, under Sparta's hegemony, a world apart— which, to be fair, it had been for more than half a millennium and still was at the time that this strategy was first formulated. If, how- ever, there ever came a moment when a power equal to or greater than this Lacedaemon appeared in force—or even threatened to appear—at or near the entrance to that great peninsula, the Spartans would have to rethink this strategy and recast it to meet an unantici- pated challenge.

THE PERSIAN CHALLENGE

This was, of course, the situation in which the Spartans found them- selves when, in 491, the Great King of Achaemenid Persia first demanded that, as a token of submission, they give him earth and water. Moreover, if Herodotus is to be believed, they had been acutely sensitive to the danger that they might someday face from the moment, half a century before, in which the Persians seized Sardis and completed their conquest of Lydia and of the Greek cities dotted along the Anatolian coast. Indeed, there is reason to suspect that every venture the Lacedaemonians undertook in the interim— whether within the Peloponnesus, beyond it on the Greek main- land, or in the Aegean—was an oblique attempt to suppress, prevent, or counter Medism on the part of their fellow Hellenes and head off Persian expansion to the west.

Initially, the danger was not palpable. When the Persians first arrived in Anatolia, they had not yet consolidated their position in western Asia. Babylon, Afghanistan, the Indus valley, Syria, and

Cyprus still awaited them, as did Egypt in the northeastern corner of Africa and Ethiopia to the south. Moreover, they were not then a seafaring people, and they could not overcome the pertinent logistical obstacles and dispatch an army of great size to Hellas if they could not convey foodstuffs across the Aegean to feed it.

In time, however, after securing the submission of the Phoenician cities along the Levantine coast of the eastern Mediterranean, the Persians acquired a great fleet. Earlier, the ship of the line had been a double-banked galley, rowed by fifty men, called a penteconter. By the 520s, however, it was rapidly being displaced by the triple-banked trireme in much the same fashion in which the old-fashioned battleship was displaced by the Dreadnought in the early twentieth century of our own era.

The trireme was powerful, fast, and impregnable to attack by lesser craft. It rendered all previous warships obsolete, and it revolutionized warfare at sea. This graceful vessel was shaped like a wine

Figure 2.1. Double-banked [*díkrotos*] penteconter on a piratical raid closing in on a merchant *gaúlos*, painted on the outer surface of an Athenian black-figured cup, ca. 520–500, found at Vulci.
Artist unknown (British Museum 1867,0508.963).
(©The Trustees of the British Museum)

glass, and, in the manner of the pentecoters that preceded it, it sported a prow equipped with a bronze-sheathed ram. Its ram, however, had not one, but three horizontal cutting blades capable of slicing through the hull of virtually any vessel equal or smaller in mass that it struck amidships or in the stern. On the basis of what archaeologists have learned regarding the size of the ancient shipsheds in the military harbor that the Athenians eventually established in the Peiraeus, scholars generally suppose triremes to have varied in size from about one hundred seventeen to one hundred thirty feet in length and from about fifteen to eighteen feet in width, but some now think that they may have been considerably smaller.

When a trireme's full complement was on board, it was powered by one hundred seventy oarsmen facing the stern, each plying a single oar fourteen feet in length, using as a fulcrum a tholepin to which the oar was tied by a well-greased leather oarloop. These rowers, who slid back and forth on cushions of fleece so that they could leverage the muscles in their legs as they pulled the oars, were organized in three banks on three different levels—with at least two-thirds enclosed within the hull and unable to see their own oars.

In Phoenician ships, which sported majestically high bulwarks lined with shields, the remainder, called *thranítai* in Attic Greek, were also situated inside the trireme—some think, at the topwale. In the ships later deployed by the Athenians, however, they were perched on outriggers mounted above and outboard from their colleagues while the *zúgioi* were situated on the topwale and the *thalamioí*, deep within the hull. Within such a galley, there were petty officers on deck to decide on and direct the ship's course, to dictate and sustain the tempo of the oarsmen's strokes, and to convey to them the orders of vessel's helmsman or the wealthy trierarch (trireme-commander) who paid for the ship's maintenance as a "liturgy [*leitourgía*]" or public service and could choose, if he wished, to captain it. There was also a shipwright on board and a purser, and there were other specialists trained in handling the sails as well as archers and marines [*epibátai*] fully equipped for combat—enough

15

to bring the boat's full complement to two hundred men at a minimum. Its weight, when loaded with all of the pertinent equipment and personnel, was, most scholars believe, something on the order of fifty tons.

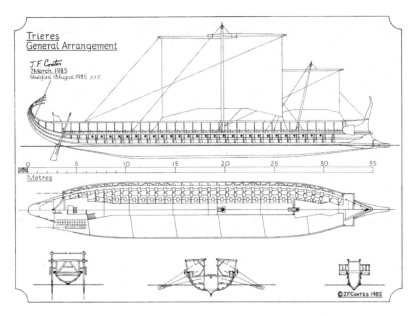

Figure 3.1. J. F. Coates' Sketch of a Trireme (1985).
(Courtesy of The Trireme Trust ©Trireme Trust)

When fully manned—as it had to be if it was not to be underpowered and slow, hard to maneuver, and unlikely to survive a contest—this newfangled ship was a formidable fighting machine. When supplemented by merchant galleys; round sailing ships [*gaúloi*] bearing grain, fresh water, and other provisions aplenty; and superannuated triremes reconfigured as horse transports, it opened up, for the first time in recorded history, the possibility that an empire could be instituted over the sea and from there project power over the surrounding lands. This, in fact, the Persians first tried to do in 490 at the behest of the formidable Achaemenid monarch Darius son of Hystaspes when they conveyed across the eastern Mediterranean and the Aegean to Marathon in Attica an amphibious force—complete with archers, spearmen, cavalrymen, and their mounts—that was capable, in principle, of conquering the most populous *pólis* in eastern Greece.

The Spartans were not present for the battle of Marathon. Although they had promised to come, they were delayed by religious obligations, a helot revolt, or, more likely, both. They must nonetheless have been heartened by the Athenians' stunning victory on this occasion. For it showed that Greek hoplites could defeat Persian footsoldiers and indicated on what condition this was possible.[2]

Of course, in recent years, it has become almost a matter of faith among scholars focused on Achaemenid Persia that the footsoldiers of the Great King were in no way inferior to the hoplites of Hellas. This claim is, however, unsustainable, for it flies in the face of what we know happened at Marathon, Thermopylae, Plataea, and Mycale. The truth is that the Persian infantry was not the strongest branch of the Great King's forces. It was ancillary and ill-equipped for a confrontation pitting an unsupported force of Greek footsoldiers against a similarly unsupported force of Persian infantrymen.[3]

Miltiades, who was the dominant Athenian commander at the battle of Marathon and who had witnessed the Persian army at war in Scythia, was admirably sensitive to this fact. Herodotus tells us that the Persians brought a substantial cavalry unit to Marathon. But when he describes the battle, he makes no mention of them at all—which strongly suggests their absence at that moment. It was almost certainly their withdrawal, preparatory to a second landing elsewhere—this time near the town of Athens—that enabled the Athenians to win.

Ordinarily, the Persians employed archers on horseback and on foot—as a species of primitive artillery—to break up enemy formations; then, these same horsemen as shock cavalry to rout and massacre the undisciplined ranks that remained; and their spearmen (most of whom doubled as archers) to clean up. At Marathon, thanks to the helmet, breastplate, greaves, and shield with which the hoplite was equipped, Persia's archers were unable to break up the phalanx; and though the archers and the dedicated spearmen sheltering behind the wicker wall set up by their front ranks greatly outnumbered the Athenians and their Plataean allies, they could not withstand the onslaught of these heavy infantrymen. Thereafter, lacking the protection ordinarily afforded by the cavalry to those in retreat, they were run down and slaughtered in droves when they gave way and fled, precisely as Herodotus insists.[4]

Ten years later, when Darius' son and designated heir Xerxes conducted in person a much more massive army into Greece, the Spartans duplicated and trumped the Athenians' spectacular feat. At Plataea, in 479, under the leadership of the Agiad regent Pausanias, they lured the forces of the Great King onto rough ground in the foothills of Mount Cithaeron where the Persian cavalry could not accompany them. There they patiently withstood the immense barrage of arrows shot. Then, they shoved their way through the wicker wall set up to shelter the archers and massacred the Persian host. On the same day, we are told, on the other side of the Aegean, at Mycale on the Anatolian shore opposite Samos, a force of Greek marines, many of them Athenians, did the same in a battle in which they took on another Persian infantry force.[5]

FROM WAR TO POSTWAR

Had the Hellenes not earlier inflicted a decisive defeat on Xerxes' fleet—as they had at Salamis the preceding year—it is exceedingly unlikely that the coalition led by Lacedaemon could have driven the Persian army from Greece. Xerxes' invasion was, after all, a combined operation. On each of the triremes in his fleet, there were thirty *epibátai*, and these galleys were accompanied by horse transports and cavalrymen as well. Had his forces established their dominance at sea, the Great King of Persia could have landed, more or less at will, an expeditionary force behind Greek lines to outflank, help surround, and crush his Hellenic foe.

The Spartans were not in a position to respond to the challenge that the maritime military revolution carried out by the Persians posed to their traditional way of war. They were landlubbers—unsurpassed at hoplite warfare. At a bottleneck, with three hundred men and reinforcements from other cities, they could, until outmaneuvered and surrounded, fend off a Persian infantry force that dwarfed theirs in size—as they did at Thermopylae. But, to sustain the effort and avoid being outflanked by a marine force landed to their rear, they needed naval support of the sort provided by their allies posted nearby at Artemisium. About armed conflict at sea as such, they knew little, if anything; and Corinth, the one city within their Peloponnesian alliance that had a great deal of experience in this sphere, was not capable of deploying a fleet of triremes large enough to counter the enormous naval armada that the Persians were preparing in the late 480s.

Mindful of their shortcomings, the Spartans amended the grand strategy they had articulated before the time when the Persians turned their attention to Greece and did so in one crucial particular: by seeking help outside the Peloponnesus—above all, from Athens, which they had tried to aid at the time of Marathon, but also from the citizens of Aegina, an island polity, adept at commerce and experienced at sea, which was situated in the middle of the Saronic Gulf. To secure the assistance required, they had to persuade the citizens of these two *póleis* to set aside the enmity that had long energized both.

This they accomplished. But it would not have sufficed had there not been a silver strike at Laurium in Attica and had a visionary Athenian statesman named Themistocles son of Neocles not persuaded his compatriots to spend the windfall on building two hundred triremes and to dedicate their efforts on the eve of the Persian invasion to becoming expert in rowing and maneuvering these magnificent galleys. The Spartan Eurybiades may have commanded the Hellenic fleet at Artemisium and Salamis in 480. But, thanks to Athens' contribution of roughly half of the galleys composing it, Themistocles exercised considerable leverage, and it was a stratagem on his part that lured Xerxes and his commanders into committing the Persian fleet to a battle in the narrows between the island of Salamis and the Attic shore where neither the superior expertise of the Phoenicians and the others who supplied ships to his fleet nor their superior numbers could be brought to bear on the outcome.[6]

The victory at Salamis that Themistocles engineered and the withdrawal of the Persian fleet that followed closely upon it came as a great relief for the Greeks, and paved the way for Sparta's defeat of the army that Xerxes left behind on Hellenic soil. But, once the Persians had fled, it also gave rise to concern on the part of the Aeginetans and almost certainly the Corinthians as well. Athens was now what it had never been before—a major maritime power—and the established naval powers in close proximity were not entirely happy with this transformation. It was their entreaties that induced the Spartans to suggest that the Athenians not rebuild the walls of Athens, which the Great King's occupying forces had torn down, and that, instead, they join with their allies in tearing down the walls of every Greek city north of the narrow isthmus linking the Peloponnesus with the rest of the mainland. Otherwise, the Lacedaemonians claimed, the Persians might return and seize a stronghold deep within Hellas.

The Athenians recognized that rendering their *pólis* indefensible in the face of a Peloponnesian invasion was the true purpose of the request. So this suggestion, on Themistocles' recommendation, they chose to reject. And they also took this great statesman's advice when he suggested that they resolve to build twenty new triremes a year and that they fortify a promontory on the Saronic Gulf, called the Peiraeus, which featured three natural harbors.

Not long before Xerxes began his march, the Athenians had gently contested the propriety of Sparta's assuming command in the maritime sphere. Then, when it became evident that no one was willing to accept upstarts as leaders on this occasion, they prudently backed off. Instead, they were forceful with their advice—both at Artemisium and Salamis in 480 and at Mycale on the Anatolian shore in 479—and thereafter they successfully pressed for a continuation of the war at sea. Moreover, when one Spartan commander, the Eurypontid king Leotychidas, demonstrated a marked reluctance regarding the proposal—advanced by the Samians, the Chians, and the communities on Lesbos—that Hellas' defensive perimeter be extended to the islands just off the Anatolian coast; and his successor in 478, Pausanias the Regent, though admirably aggressive, not only exhibited a propensity for showering contempt on and mistreating Persia's former subjects in the region but also gave every appearance of being engaged in intrigues with the Mede, the Athenian commander Aristeides son of Lysimachus, with the support of his colleague Cimon son of Miltiades, successfully maneuvered the islanders into repudiating Sparta's leadership and inviting Athens to assume the hegemony at sea. And this she did—stipulating that every member of this new maritime league either contribute ships with crews to man them or silver sufficient to support a number of ships and crews proportionate to the polity's resources.

Athens' insubordination and that of the islanders ruffled feathers at Lacedaemon, as one would expect. In the aftermath of Plataea and

Map 2. Athens' Aegean Alliance, ca. 432

Mycale, the Athenians were blunt, assertive, and anything but diplomatic. Moreover, the Spartans were used to taking the lead. This was, they thought, their right; and some in their number were ambitious, longed for glory, and wanted to greatly extend Lacedaemon's sway. There is even evidence, though its reliability has not gone uncontested, that at a moment of pique circa 475 the Spartans briefly contemplated war with Athens.

If so, cooler heads prevailed and, though annoyed, the Lacedaemonians acquiesced in Athens' seizure of the leadership of the Hellenes at sea. This they had good reason to do. There was one brute fact that had to be faced. The Persians might very well come back. They had the resources: they controlled three of the ancient world's great river-valley civilizations and, thanks to the tribute they exacted, they had amassed an immense treasure in silver and gold. They had the manpower: they ruled over millions. And they had the ambition as well: the great god Ahura Mazda demanded that the Achaemenid monarchs, who ruled in his name, bring peace and order to the world and make of it what, they were taught, it had once been—a garden or, as they put it, a *parádeisos* or "paradise." What they could not do, however, was to carry out another invasion on any great scale if they could not safely convey foodstuffs for their army by sea, and to do that they had to be supreme on that element. To prevent their return, the Hellenes had to firmly establish their dominion over the briny deep both in and beyond the Aegean.

The Spartans were ill-suited, as they knew, for shouldering this responsibility. To begin with, overextension would have been a grave danger for a community of men who derived their prosperity from the subjugation of a restive, self-conscious people greatly outnumbering them. Sparta was what Otto von Bismarck would later call "a saturated power." She had everything that a community with her character could hope for, and the pursuit of more would be likely to endanger her possession of what she already had.

This was one reason for Lacedaemonian caution. There was another. Spartan virtue was profoundly impressive, but it was also fragile. It was a hothouse flower. Its existence depended on art, which is to say: indoctrination, education, and a daily regimen. It was, moreover, rooted in shame. The chief Spartan magistrates were rightly called ephors—"overseers." For, in the absence of oversight, shame loses its force. It is not an accident that Lacedaemon did not send those under forty-five abroad. That privilege was reserved for the older men whom they called the *presbúteroi*. As the egregious misconduct of the young regent Pausanias brought home to his compatriots, those in their number who did spend time outside were notoriously susceptible to corruption.

For these reasons, it made good sense for the Lacedaemonians to stick to their original grand strategy, to practice a species of Peloponnesian isolationism, and to let the Athenians bear the burden at sea. It often makes sense for a community to rely on proxies to do its dirty work. It often makes sense for its members to welcome others willing to sacrifice lucre and life in an endeavor that happens to be supportive of their own defense. After all, the Athenians had the means—a great fleet of triremes. They had the motive: they depended for their sustenance at least in some measure on grain shipped from the Black Sea each year in mid-September. And they had the inclination: their achievements at Marathon, Salamis, and Mycale had awakened within them a quasi-Homeric love of honor and glory.[7]

Of course, for what they gained from Athens' maritime venture, the Lacedaemonians would have to pay a price. The power of the Athenians—if they were successful in fending off the Persians, in taking revenge on them, and in liberating the Greeks of the east—would grow. And they might then become a threat—which is apt to have worried some Spartans from the outset.

INTERWAR

Lacedaemon's position within the Peloponnesus was never entirely secure. The city's allies were not subjects. They were independent *póleis*. Each had her own ambitions; each, her own agenda—and these were sometimes at odds with what the Spartans thought necessary for sustaining their hegemony. Moreover, Argos—though subjected to a demographically devastating defeat circa 494—was lurking in the northeast, recovering from the loss of a generation of men and awaiting a moment when she could take revenge and regain the hegemony over the Peloponnesus that Sparta had stolen from her. The Argives had affected neutrality at the time of Xerxes' invasion, but everyone knew that they would have welcomed a Persian victory; and, ominously, the Eleans and the Mantineians had shown up for the battle at Plataea too late to be of use—weeks after they had promised to appear.

If a power of great consequence situated outside the Peloponnesus (such as what Athens might well become) were to join both with an Argos once again grown exceedingly populous and with disaffected erstwhile adherents of Lacedaemon's Peloponnesian alliance, especially if the army deployed by this coalition outnumbered the hoplites that the Spartans and their remaining allies could put into the field, Lacedaemon's very existence as a great power and the way of life treasured by the city's *hómoioi* would be at stake. This the Spartans knew. They were never oblivious to the precariousness of their situation. But in the early 460s the danger was brought home to them in an exceedingly unpleasant fashion.

In the run-up to Xerxes' invasion and while the Persians were in Greece, Themistocles had been the great proponent of Athens' alliance with the Spartans, and he had insisted that his compatriots defer to their ally. After Plataea and Mycale, however, he reversed his position, arguing that, if the Athenians fortified the Peiraeus and kept up their fleet, they had little to worry about from the Great King but very good reason to be wary of Lacedaemon. The latter, as he no doubt reminded them, had in the last decade of the sixth century mounted invasions of Attica on four different occasions.

Themistocles' reversal of course gave rise to a policy debate at Athens, which he lost—and his ostracism for ten years was, in keeping with Athenian practice, the consequence. But this setback seems not to have stopped the man. We know that he was sent into temporary exile some years after Xerxes' invasion of Greece, and we have reason to believe that this took place in or soon after 472. We know that he chose to reside for the duration in Argos. We know that he traveled through the Peloponnesus during this period. And we know that Argos and Tegea, having formed an alliance, fought a great battle against Sparta at Tegea circa 469. It is possible that Themistocles had nothing to do with this event, but that is not at all likely. There were enough Athenian volunteers fighting on behalf of Argos and Tegea at this battle to merit celebration in a poem written by Themistocles' friend Simonides.

The Argive–Tegean axis was a constellation of no mean importance. The Lacedaemonians depended for their well-being on the produce dispatched to Sparta by the helots of Messenia—and Tegea, a power of some consequence that had long been a Lacedaemonian ally, lay distressingly close to the only road suitable for carts that ran between Messenia and Laconia, where the Spartans resided. Like an umbilical cord, this well-traveled path stretched from the fertile bottom land of the Pamisos valley north through the Derveni pass, then east through south-central Arcadia around the Taygetus massif, and finally south-southeast down that mountain range's eastern flank to the Eurotas valley, where the five villages of Lacedaemon were situated. Leagued together, Tegea and Argos posed an existential threat to Sparta.

Although the Athenians as a political community played no role in the emergence of this axis, the Spartans must have pondered what would have happened had Themistocles been in charge at Athens at that time. No community relishes the prospect that its security will rest on the vicissitudes associated with another community's domestic politics.

Despite the misgivings that many Spartans entertained, Lacedaemon stuck to the policy of accommodation worked out between 479 and 475 and remained quiet as long as the *hómoioi* regarded Achaemenid Persia as a real and present danger. In 469, however, that perception almost certainly began to change. The magnificent victory over the Persians on both sea and land engineered at Eurymedon on the south coast of Anatolia by Themistocles' rival Cimon is apt to have had two effects on the Spartans. It undoubtedly relieved in some measure their fear that Xerxes might return, and it almost certainly increased their nervousness concerning the growth in Athenian power. If Plutarch is correct, as I think he is, in reporting that the Athenian diplomat Callias son of Hipponicus worked out with Xerxes a cessation of hostilities and a *modus vivendi* in the months following Cimon's victory, this will have intensified both propensities—and the role almost certainly played by Themistocles in forging the Argive–Tegean alliance and in staging the battle that followed at Tegea will have aggravated their anxieties regarding Athens.

Cimon's victory and the negotiation of a settlement of sorts with Persia's Great King no doubt heightened Athenian confidence; and this turn of events may well have occasioned, on the part of the more powerful of the *póleis* in the Aegean, a reconsideration of the utility of their alliance with Athens. This confidence helps explain why, in the aftermath, the Athenians thought that they could get away with encroaching on the extraterritorial domain on and inland from the Thracian shore that the islanders of Thasos had for many generations exploited. And a conviction that Athens was no longer needed also helps explain both why the Thasians, one of the few members of Athens' league that still supplied ships rather than silver, responded in 465 by staging a revolt and reaching out to Lacedaemon for support and why the Spartans so promptly promised to come to their rescue.

There was only one way that the Lacedaemonians could lend aid and comfort to the Thasians, and that was by leading the forces of their Peloponnesian alliance via the Isthmus of Corinth and the territory of Megara into Attica early in the spring of 464. Had they done this, it would have put the Athenians into a bind. If they did not fend off the invaders, the homes of those who lived in the countryside (a majority of the citizens)—not to mention their vineyards, their olive trees, and the grain in their granaries and their fields—

would be at risk. But Athens' hoplites were no match for such an army. They were greatly outnumbered by the heavy infantry of the Peloponnesians, and they were not as well trained as the Spartans, who formed that army's core. They could abandon the countryside and flee to the town of Athens and the port recently built nearly five miles away in the Peiraeus. Both were fortified, to be sure; and the Peiraeus could easily bring in provisions by sea. But the town of Athens was in no position to do the like, and it could not weather a siege of any duration.[8]

Had the Peloponnesians, as promised, conducted such an invasion, the Spartans could have dictated a settlement confining Athens' power. But the invasion never took place. In the winter of 465/4, a series of earthquakes struck Laconia, leveled the five villages constituting Lacedaemon, killed twenty thousand *períoikoi* and Spartiates, more than halved the number of Spartan men, and eliminated, we must suspect, an even greater proportion of the young children and women of Lacedaemon (who were more apt than their menfolk to have been inside in the daylight hours when the first and most severe of the tremors struck). The initial upheaval was immediately followed by a great helot revolt—first in Laconia and then in Messenia—and the Spartiates, who then suffered a further loss of life, were hard-pressed to contain it. So, instead of mounting an invasion of Attica, they summoned help from Mantineia, Aegina, Plataea, and no doubt a considerable number of their other allies; and they sent the vice-consul [*próxenos*] who looked after the interests of the Athenians at Sparta to ask for aid from the city whose territory they had intended to invade. Moreover, if Plutarch is to be trusted, two years after they had with the help of their allies contained and put down the rebellion in Laconia, they turned to the Athenians once again—this time for aid in eliminating a band of helots who had retreated to a stronghold on Mount Ithome in Messenia after suffering defeat in the lowlands.

In response to the Spartans' request, Cimon, their *próxenos* at Athens, led to Messenia a band of Athenian infantrymen skilled in siege warfare. But they did not stay long. For while they were trying to oust the rebellious helots from the mountain, the Thasians surrendered; and, if my reading of the evidence is correct, word of the Lacedaemonians' perfidy soon reached Athens, then the army at Mount Ithome. There was grumbling, we are told, in the Athenian ranks; and the Spartans, fearing that the Athenians would lend a hand to the Messenian rebels, sent them packing.

It was at this point that an enduring strategic rivalry between Athens and Sparta began in earnest. The Athenians carried out a democratic reform that tipped the political balance between their agrarian population and the poorer folk engaged in shipbuilding, in serving in the fleet, in guarding the walls of Athens and the Peiraeus, and in managing their league—and they did so in favor of the latter. They then repudiated their alliance with Sparta, forged an association with the erstwhile Medizers of Argos and Thessaly, and ostracized Cimon, who had long championed the connection with Lacedaemon. Thereafter, when the Megarians, who were on the losing side in a bitter border dispute with the Corinthians, sought Athenian aid, they took this Spartan ally under their protection and garrisoned the Megarians' principal town and the ports they maintained at Nisaea on the Saronic Gulf and at Pegae on the Corinthian Gulf. Then, they built walls along a corridor linking that town with the first of these two ports and posted a guard on the passes over Mount Geraneia in the southeast to monitor and, if need be, hinder or even block egress from the Peloponnesus. It was in this fashion that the Athenians launched the first of their three wars with Lacedaemon.[9]

SPARTA'S FIRST ATTIC WAR, 461–446 BC

During the first few years of this conflict, the Spartans were notable for their absence from the fray. They were preoccupied with a vain attempt to subdue the rebels ensconced on Mount Ithome; and it was not until 454, some ten years after the great earthquake and the attendant helot revolt, that the Lacedaemonians finally and with great reluctance negotiated a deal providing for the departure from the Peloponnesus of the rebels and their families. For the most part, in the interim, the Athenians had a free hand, and they used the opportunity to subdue Aegina and add it to their league, to force Troezen and Hermione into an alliance, to defeat Corinth on both land and sea, and to initiate a blockade curtailing the trade that was the lifeblood of that wealthy mercantile city. In the east, they accomplished this from Salamis in the Saronic Gulf; in the west they did so initially from the Megarian port at Pegae on the Corinthian Gulf. Later, after its subjection, they may as well have made use of the island of Aegina in the east. And, after 454, in the west, they are apt also to have employed the port of Naupactus on the north shore of the Corinthian Gulf, with its harbor located near the narrows at the entrance to that body of water—where, with the strategic importance of the settlement later called Lepanto in mind, they had settled the Messenian refugees after their withdrawal from Mount Ithome. The Athenians' ability to wreak havoc along the coastline of the Peloponnesus was limited only by the fact that, in 465, Xerxes was assassinated; that his son Artaxerxes soon thereafter repudiated the agreement negotiated by Callias; and that the Athenians took this misfortune as an opportunity to launch a breathtakingly bold attempt to hive off Egypt from the Achaemenid empire—which required a massive commitment of naval resources.[10]

In the years prior to the withdrawal of the Messenian rebels, the Spartans stirred only once. In the spring of 458, a force of fifteen hundred Spartiates and *períoikoi*, joined by a great host ("ten thousand" or more) supplied by Lacedaemon's Peloponnesian allies, slipped across the Corinthian Gulf. Their aim was to defend Doris— whence, it was supposed, the Dorians all derived—from that community's Phocian neighbors. So, at least, Thucydides was told; and this was no doubt the justification given at the time. But the Lacedaemonians surely had more in mind than the notoriously secretive authorities at Sparta let on.

If later reports are to be credited, en route to Doris, this Peloponnesian army stopped at Delphi to arrange affairs pertaining to the oracle of Apollo in keeping with the interests of the Spartans. Moreover, after settling matters with the Phocians, the army proceeded to Boeotia—according to these reports, with an eye to restoring Thebes' hegemony in that region. Thereafter, the Spartan commander conducted this army away from any plausible route home to Tanagra in southeastern Boeotia near that region's border with Attica. And there, the son of Olorus tells us, he was approached by a number of disaffected Athenians who were unhappy with Cimon's ostracism, the democratic reforms recently enacted, and the diplomatic revolution that had taken place when Athens repudiated her alliance with Lacedaemon.

These malcontents were especially upset by the fact that this change of policy was accompanied by a decision to build "the Long Walls," as they came to be called, to link Athens with her fortified port in the Peiraeus. This portended an abandonment of the coun-

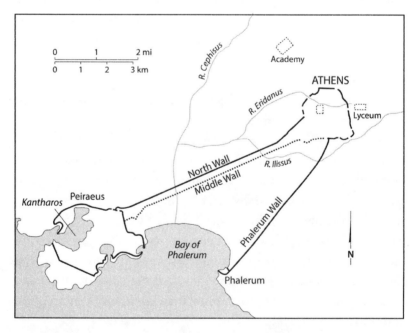

Map 3. Athens, the Peiraeus, and the Long Walls, ca. 440

tryside in the event of a Peloponnesian invasion, and these well-to-do landholders recognized as much. Their city was in the process of ceasing to be an agrarian republic and of becoming an association of tradesmen and artisans and of salarymen who derived their livelihood chiefly from what was by this time less a league of independent, autonomous, allied cities contributing ships and crews than a maritime empire called on to supply what amounted to tribute in silver—and these dissidents wanted the Spartans to intervene, effect a revolution, prevent the completion of the Long Walls, and tear down what had been built.

This suited the Lacedaemonians perfectly, and there is every reason to suspect that the authorities at Sparta had planned the expedition from the start with such a purpose in mind. If the Long Walls were completed (and that day was near), they would make Athens a virtual island capable, in an emergency, of feeding her citizens with foodstuffs imported by sea; and this would mark a dramatic shift in the strategic balance of power between the two great *póleis* of Greece—for it would mean that, even if Megara were to return to Sparta's Peloponnesian alliance, Athens would be impervious to an invasion of Attica by land. It is hard to believe that, with their population much diminished and the rebels still active in Messenia, the authorities at Lacedaemon would have dispatched so sizable an army to northern Greece solely in order to defend the Dorian metropolis.

The Athenians understood the stakes. In anticipation, they had summoned hoplites from their Argive ally and from the subject cities of the Aegean; and at Tanagra late in the summer of 458 a great battle ensued. It is said to have lasted for two long days and to have been extremely hard-fought. In time, we are told, the Spartans won a tactical victory. But it turned out to be a strategic defeat—for the Peloponnesians were allowed to return home via the Megarid, and in the aftermath the Athenians finished the Long Walls, subjugated Boeotia, and accepted the surrender of Aegina on terms.[11]

With regard to Athens, the Spartans were of two minds. They

were unhappy about the transformation of Athens' league into an empire, and they cannot have welcomed her subjection of Aegina and the pummeling that the Athenians had given the maritime communities of the Peloponnesus. But they were also aware that it was the navy of Athens' league that kept the Mede at bay; and, fearful that their compatriots would be corrupted by long service abroad, they were loath to take on such a responsibility themselves. So, when the Persians achieved a decisive victory over the Athenians and their allies in Egypt and captured or destroyed something on the order of two hundred thirty-five triremes with crews amounting to forty-seven thousand men (half again as many adult males as Athens had possessed in 480), if not more, the Lacedaemonians, though grudging, were willing to grant Athens a five-year truce. Then, when the Athenians and their allies annihilated the Persian fleet and defeated the Great King's army at Cypriot Salamis and negotiated with Artaxerxes a renewal of the arrangement worked out with his father after the battle of Eurymedon, they once again began to regard their erstwhile ally as the greater threat.

The Athenians paid a price for the truce that the Spartans accorded them. Thanks to their abandonment by Athens, the Argives found themselves forced to negotiate a thirty years' truce with Lacedaemon; and soon thereafter an enterprising and canny Spartiate named Cleandridas managed to effect an oligarchic revolution at Tegea that turned this renegade ally into a stalwart adherent of the Lacedaemonian league.

We do not know in what capacity Cleandridas accomplished this. He may have been a commander dispatched to eastern Arcadia with a considerable military force. He may have been the *próxenos* of the Tegeans at Sparta; and with the help of his guest-friends [*xénoi*] in that community he may have persuaded her citizens that, given the defection of Argos, they had no other choice. But it is also possible that Cleandridas had long been one of the three hundred *hippeîs* selected out of the *sussitía* to serve in battle as the bodyguard of the king in command—and that he had aged out of that unit when he reached forty-five; that, in accord with Spartan practice, he had then been chosen to join four other former *hippeîs* drawn from his age-class in serving for a year as "doers of good deeds [*agathoergoí*]" to whom the ephors could assign special missions at home and abroad requiring cunning, courage, prowess, subtlety, tact, and finesse; and that he had been operating at Tegea entirely on his own. In any case, this same individual is generally thought to have served as one of Lacedaemon's five ephors a few years later when—after Athens had forged a settlement with Artaxerxes, just as the truce with Sparta was about to lapse—a series of apparently coordinated events occurred that, in all likelihood, the ephors and one or more of the *agathoergoí* at their beck and call that year had engineered.

These events took place in rapid succession. Late in 447 or early in 446, a group of anti-Athenian exiles sparked a revolt in northern Boeotia at Orchomenos and the relief force sent from Athens was ambushed while on its way home—with a host of Athenians killed or captured. Later, in 446, as the Athenians were negotiating with the Boeotians a return of their men, a rebellion broke out in Histi-aea, Chalcis, and Eretria on Euboea—the nearest, largest, most important, and most valuable island in Athens' league. When the Athenians, after negotiating their withdrawal from Boeotia, inter-vened on Euboea, a group of Megarians massacred their city's Athe-nian garrison and opened their gates to a force of Corinthians, Epidaurians, and Sicyonians lurking outside. Then, when Athens sent a number of units against Megara, a Peloponnesian army—led by the young Agiad king Pleistoanax son of Pausanias with this same Cleandridas at his side—traversed the Geraneia massif, swept through the Megarid, and entered Attica, leaving a substantial Athe-nian force cut off from Athens in its rear.

Thanks to their canny exploitation of the element of surprise, Pleistoanax and his advisor had caught the Athenians off guard, and the Agiad king had them at his mercy. Due to the debacle in Egypt and their defeat in Boeotia, they were short of manpower and could ill afford to lose the men trapped behind enemy lines. Moreover, if the struggle went on, they would be apt to lose Euboea, which lay just off the Attic and Boeotian coasts and was as easily accessible from the one as from the other. There was no alternative to negotiating the outlines of a settlement on the spot.

For the Spartans, their Agiad king, and his chief counselor, this was a real accomplishment. But it was not apt to be repeated. For, had the Athenians expected an attack and had they not had a substantial force of hoplite infantrymen stranded in the Megarid behind the advancing Peloponnesian army, they would have withdrawn from the countryside, hunkered down behind their Long Walls, and imported whatever foodstuffs they needed from their subject allies in the Aegean.

In consequence, a great many of the Lacedaemonians were furious when, after this brilliantly conceived operation, Pleistoanax squandered the golden opportunity he had opened up. His failure, on the advice of Cleandridas, to inflict on the Athenians a humiliating defeat in the field and their negotiation of an armistice with Athens that required her to abandon Megara and Boeotia and evacuate from the Peloponnesus but, tellingly, left her in control of her Aegean empire—this no small number of their compatriots found it hard to forgive. And, when it was discovered that Pleistoanax and Cleandridas had accepted a handsome sweetener from the Athenian statesman Pericles son of Xanthippus, the Spartans put the Agiad king on trial, fined him, and drove him into exile; and, when his principal counselor then fled their wrath, they condemned that distinguished man to death.[12]

It is easy to see why many at Sparta were unhappy with the grand strategy that their compatriots had articulated before the Persian Wars and had revised modestly in their aftermath, and it is no less easy to see why the Lacedaemonians reluctantly stuck with that grand strategy. They had no alternative compatible with the survival of their regime and way of life. But, if Sparta was to adhere to this grand strategy, she needed an Athens strong enough to guard the sea but not so strong that she posed a threat to Lacedaemon's hegemony within the Peloponnesus—and the sneaking suspicion that sustaining so delicate a balance was beyond the capacity of Sparta and her allies gave rise to divided counsels at Lacedaemon. The Spartans were caught on the horns of an enduring dilemma. It seemed as if they would be damned if they continued to pursue their traditional grand strategy, and it seemed as if they would be damned if they abandoned it.

SPARTA'S SECOND ATTIC WAR, 431–421 BC

The treaty that put an end to Sparta's first Attic war was not, as is quite often asserted, a treaty of peace. It was a truce—with a term of thirty years—reflecting mutual exhaustion. Both parties to the truce were demographically challenged. The two agreed to delay their conflict for a generation. That is all they did. Neither side expected an enduring peace. In the meantime, both were lying in wait for an opportunity. If the citizens of either thought that the fight could be renewed on exceedingly favorable terms, they would be sorely tempted to pounce.

There were, to be sure, individuals in both camps who looked back with nostalgia on the period when they were allied and shared the hegemony. Pleistoanax was surely one of these. But his fate and that of Cleandridas tell us all that we need to know about the attitude of the majority at Lacedaemon, and we should not be surprised in the slightest that the Spartans proposed to their Peloponnesian allies a renewal of the war in 440 when the Samians, one of a handful of communities in the Aegean that still supplied ships to the Athenian alliance, launched a rebellion and secured a modicum of aid from Pissouthnes son of Hystaspes, the Persian "satrap," armed with viceregal powers, who was based at Sardis, the ancient capital of Lydia, and who was charged with governing that defunct kingdom and its environs in the interior of Asia Minor as well as the maritime regions along that subcontinent's western coast and a part of its southern shore.

The Spartan proposal was impious. It involved the breach of an oath, and the prospect must have caused considerable consternation among the intensely pious citizens of Lacedaemon. But it did make good strategic sense. What had happened in 446 was a fluke—a product of Spartan cunning—not likely to be repeated. The Long Walls made the Athenians very nearly impregnable in the face of an invasion by land. But, at sea, their hegemony was vulnerable. There were a handful of wealthy *póleis* that supplied their own ships and remained more or less fully autonomous. And, as we have seen, Samos was among them. There were also a great many cities that supplied silver alone, and within these cities—especially after Xerxes, then Artaxerxes worked out a *modus vivendi* with the Athenians—there was a great deal of resentment. A rebellion on the part of one or two of the former might well stir up a general revolt on the part of the latter.

If in 440 the Spartan initiative came to naught, it was because everything depended on Corinth, the one naval power in Lacedaemon's league capable of coming to the aid of Samos. And the Corinthians, who had recently paid a terrible price in both manpower and commercial prosperity for their adherence to Sparta, were not aching to be pummeled and deprived of access to the sea by Athens again. In 446, they had given up all hope of being a force in the Aegean, where they possessed only one colony. If they were to remain a power to be reckoned with and to retain their economic vitality (and they intended to do both), they would have to reestablish the dominance to the west—in the Corinthian Gulf, the Ionian Sea, and the Adriatic—that had in the past enabled them to found there a host of colonies. Otherwise, a blockade like the one that Athens had instituted during the first Attic war might bring them to their knees.

If there were Athenians nostalgic for the era of Cimon, when the two great Greek powers had operated like oxen in harness (as there surely were), Sparta's conduct at the time of the Samian revolt undercut their support, if it did not disillusion them entirely. The majority at Athens, as Thucydides reports, took it for granted that in the long run there would be a renewal of their war with Sparta. And Pericles, the dominant figure in that city in this period, was in their number. So, they, too, were lying in wait for an opportunity to strike a devastating blow; and, thanks to what Themistocles had very nearly pulled off during his sojourn at Argos, Xanthippus' canny son knew how this might be achieved.[13]

In the mid-430s, an occasion presented itself. The Corinthians—eager to regain ascendancy in the Corinthian Gulf, the Ionian Sea, and the Adriatic—engineered a conflict with their renegade colony Corcyra, the leading maritime power in these western waters. This enabled Pericles to make mischief with an attempt to drive a wedge between Lacedaemon and Corinth. By advertising their reluctance to be drawn into combat with the Corinthians while, nonetheless, rallying with apparent misgivings to the defense of Corcyra, his compatriots could enrage the Corinthians while perhaps appeasing the Spartans and rendering them unsympathetic to an ally that seemed to be recklessly aggressive. Then, by imposing an embargo on Megara after that city persisted in supplying ships for her neighbor's adventure in the Adriatic, they could bring home to the Corinthians the damage that they could do to a mercantile power without technically breaching their long-term truce with Lacedaemon and her Peloponnesian allies. To make it even more awkward for the Spartans to choose war, they could ostentatiously offer to submit to arbitration any complaint that the Spartans cared to lodge, as the treaty binding these two great powers required. Such seems to have been Pericles' calculation.

In the best of circumstances, the Spartans would refuse to come to the defense of Corinth and Megara, and the Corinthians would bolt from Lacedaemon's Peloponnesian alliance and in all likelihood take other cities with them—as they, in fact, threatened to do. In the worst of circumstances, the Spartans would find themselves dragged into a war, unjustified by a clear-cut breach of the existing treaty on Athens' part, which they lacked the resources to win. And when their morale sagged, when they began thinking that their difficulties were due to an act of impiety on their part and they gave up the fight, the Corinthians would make good on their threat, bolt, and take the other cities with them. At this point, an opportunity would open up for the Athenians to organize an anti-Spartan coalition within the Peloponnesus and to accomplish what Themistocles had tried to do.

Pericles had a good understanding of the character of the Spartans. He knew that they were exceptionally pious, hesitant to break pledges backed up by oaths to the gods, and slow to go to war—especially when circumstances were not unusually propitious. And the Corinthians understood the Athenians as well. When, in an appeal for help, they appeared before the Lacedaemonian assembly, they are said to have juxtaposed the two peoples in a striking fashion, asserting,

> The Athenians are innovators, keen in forming plans, and quick to accomplish in deed what they have contrived in thought. You Spartans are intent on saving what you now possess; you are always indecisive, and you leave even what is needed undone. They are daring [*tolmētaí*] beyond their strength, they are risk-takers against all judgment, and in the midst of terrors they remain of good hope [*euélpides*]—while you accomplish less than is in your power, mistrust your judgment in matters most firm, and think not how to release yourselves from the terrors you face. In addition, they are unhesitant where you are inclined to delay, and they are always out and about in the larger world while you stay at home. For they think to acquire something by being away while you think that by proceeding abroad you will harm what lies ready to hand. In victory over the enemy, they sally farthest forth; in defeat, they give the least ground. For their city's sake, they use their bodies as if they were not their own; their intelligence they dedicate to political action on her behalf. And if they fail to accomplish what they have resolved to do, they

suppose themselves deprived of that which is their own—while what they have accomplished and have now acquired they judge to be little in comparison with what they will do in the time to come. If they trip up in an endeavor, they are soon full of hope [*antelpísantes*] with regard to yet another goal. For they alone possess something at the moment at which they come to hope [*elpízousın*] for it: so swiftly do they contrive to attempt what has been resolved. And on all these things they exert themselves in toil and danger through all the days of their lives, enjoying least of all what they already possess because they are ever intent on further acquisition. They look on a holiday as nothing but an opportunity to do what needs doing, and they regard peace and quiet free from political business [*hēsuchían aprágmona*] as a greater misfortune than a laborious want of leisure [*ascholían epíponon*]. So that, if someone were to sum them up by saying that they are by nature [*pephukénai*] capable neither of being at rest [*échein hēsuchían*] nor of allowing other human beings to be so, he would speak the truth.

The Corinthian claim to the contrary notwithstanding, nature [*phúsıs*] is not apt to have had much of anything to do with the peculiar character of the Athenians. Their settled disposition was a product of their political regime and of the *nómoi*—mores, manners, and laws—to which it gave rise. To say that they were not accustomed to remaining "at rest" would be an understatement. The comparison was apt. But it is not clear that the Lacedaemonians took it to heart.[14]

Instead, rightly suspecting the intentions of the Athenians and thinking the Peloponnesian alliance that sustained them in peril, the Spartans underestimated their rivals and chose war on the mistaken assumption that it could be quickly settled in the manner in which their earlier conflict with Athens had been settled by Pleistoanax and Cleandridas. This they did against the wishes and advice of their senior statesman the Eurypontid king Archidamus son of Zeuxidamos who was keenly aware that Athens' Long Walls rendered the success of an invasion by land exceedingly unlikely, and who intimated that they could not hope to win at sea if they failed to secure financial backing from Achaemenid Persia for the construction of triremes and the remuneration of those who officered and rowed these vessels.[15]

In the first few years of the conflict, the Spartans launched repeated invasions of Attica. For a time—thanks to the damage done the morale of the Athenians by the plague, which struck Athens in 430, returned in 427, and killed a quarter, a third, or even a larger proportion of the city's population; and thanks as well to that city's dispatch, in response to the epidemic's initial onslaught, of an embassy proposing peace—they thought that annual raids and ravaging would eventually bring the Athenians to their knees. But this did not happen.[16]

The Corinthians knew better than to suppose that cursory incursions of this sort would do the job. So, in these same years—with strong support at Lacedaemon from, one must suspect, Archidamus and, one can discern, others such as Brasidas son of Tellis—they repeatedly challenged Athens' dominance in and beyond the Corinthian Gulf, hoping that, if they proved victorious in these western waters or on the nearby shores, they could drive the Athenians from the west, then turn east, and stir up a general rebellion in the Aegean and accomplish thereby what the Lacedaemonians had promised when, at the outset of the war, they had called for "the freedom of the Greeks."

Neither Peloponnesian strategy worked as planned. In Attica, the Athenians hunkered down behind their walls and toughed it out, knowing that in the allotted time there was very little that the intruders could do. Ravaging was hard work and immensely time-consuming. One could not simply burn the fields of unharvested wheat and barley. Early in the summer, these crops were too green. One had to laboriously harvest them oneself. Olive trees, for their part, were hardy and almost impervious to fire. To destroy them, one had to uproot them—which was an onerous task.

Moreover, the Athenians in these years applied against Attica's invaders a lesson that they had learned in the late 450s when they sent a hoplite army on an abortive mission to Pharsalus—which was located in Thessaly, one of the few regions in Hellas blessed with broad, well-watered plains. The walls of the town they had been unable to storm. This they had no doubt expected. The real surprise was that the cavalry of the Pharsalians managed to hunt down and kill those who dispersed for the purpose of foraging or laying waste the city's rich farmland and in the end confined the Athenians to their camp. With this unpleasant experience in mind, the Athenians subsequently raised a cavalry corps of their own not long after they completed their Long Walls. This force, which they subsidized, they then deployed to good effect in the early years of their second war with Sparta to harry Attica's Peloponnesian invaders when they left the phalanx and busied themselves with ravaging. When the Athenians were forced to abandon their countryside to the intruder, they made sure to exact a heavy price.[17]

At sea, in these years, Athens' citizens were exceedingly aggressive. The Peloponnesus they enveloped in war, imposing a blockade on Corinth and Megara, raiding the communities along that great peninsula's coast, and defending the Acarnanians, the Corcyraeans, and their other allies in the west. In the Corinthian Gulf, the modest flotilla deployed at Naupactus by the Athenians to conduct their blockade, at one point, literally ran circles around the much larger fleet deployed by Corinth and her colonists and, on another, it confronted and cowed a fleet nearly four times its size. Moreover, on the one occasion when a golden opportunity presented itself—in 428 when the citizens of the ship-providing cities of Mytilene, Antissa, Eresus, and Pyrrha on the island of Lesbos staged a rebellion against Athens and a general revolt seemed possible—the Spartans proved, as the Corinthians feared they would, to be so halfhearted and dilatory in seizing the opportunity this afforded them that, by the time that their relief expedition reached the Aegean, the moment had passed.

On the eve of the war, Pericles had told the Athenians that they would "win through," leaving it unclear whether they would be victorious or merely survive. Had it not been for the plague and the Athenians' decision early on to sue for peace, it is virtually certain that the Spartans would have quickly lost heart and done the like themselves. They had no viable military strategy. To the discerning eye, it would quickly have become evident that the invasions of Attica were not going to budge the Athenians and that the Peloponnesian fleet was nowhere near being a match for the more experienced and skillful Athenian mariners. In the event, the plague served only to sow confusion and delay the day of reckoning. In 427, the Spartans recalled Pleistoanax from exile; and, if Aristophanes' testimony can be trusted, not long before the spring of 425, they proposed that there be a cessation of hostilities and a return of the territory seized in the war.

Had Pericles been alive, he might well have seized on this occasion to press for a harder bargain—one authorizing the Athenians to keep Aegina, which they had seized and repopulated with their own citizens. He was, after all, an admirer and disciple of Themistocles, who had recognized that Sparta could only be eliminated as a rival if her league was dissolved, if she was then defeated in a hoplite battle in the southern Peloponnesus, and Messenia was liberated. It was Pericles' calculation on the eve of the war that a humiliating peace would eventuate in Corinth doing what she had quite recently threatened to do and that Athens would then be able to exploit the anarchy that this would produce within the Peloponnesus. But, of course, Xanthippus' canny son was no longer alive. He had succumbed to the plague in 430. And, in these years, there was no one else on the political stage at Athens possessed of his moral authority and strategic vision.

The Spartans understood the danger they were in. It was the threat issued by the Corinthians that had caused them to choose to break their oaths, jettison the treaty, and go to war. But, thanks to residual misgivings rooted in their experience during the Persian

Wars, they were not at this time willing to pay the price required for an alliance with the Great King. And, by 426, they were aware that neither of the two military strategies that they had pursued was viable. Moreover, they now had another matter to worry about: the thirty years' truce that they had negotiated with their perennial Peloponnesian rival the Argives was due to lapse in 421. From a strategic perspective, it is hard to say which prospect was more unnerving for the Lacedaemonians: Argos' entrance into the war on the side of the Athenians or angry mischief-making on the part of the Corinthians.[18]

Pericles, mindful of the dreadful outcome of the Egyptian expedition undertaken in the 450s, had warned the Athenians against embracing risk and attempting again to expand the empire in such a fashion while they were at war with Sparta. He understood all too well the principle of war that Alfred Thayer Mahan, the finest naval historian and geopolitical analyst that the United States has ever produced, pinpointed when—with regard to the coalition of European powers that joined together in 1778 to support the American bid for independence—he wrote,

> [I]t may be said pithily that the phrase "ulterior objects" embodies the cardinal fault of naval policy. Ulterior objects brought to nought the hopes of the allies, because, by fastening their eyes upon them, they thoughtlessly passed the road which led to them. Desire eagerly directed upon the ends in view—or rather upon the partial, though great, advantages which they constituted their ends—blinded them to the means by which alone they could be surely attained.

It was Pericles' contention that his compatriots should focus their energies on a single object—Lacedaemon's defeat; that, in the meantime, they should not pursue any ulterior object; and that they should also eschew more immediate objectives that were tangential to the business underway.[19]

The son of Xanthippus was now dead, however, and his compatriots were prone to distraction. Their control of the sea conferred on them an intoxicating freedom. It was almost the case that they could strike anywhere they wished, and the prospect fired strategic temptation. In the first half of the 420s, one of the ten *stratēgoí* they elected each year to command their forces on land and sea—an enterprising man named Demosthenes son of Alcisthenes—initiated a foolhardy invasion of Aetolia aimed ultimately at a reconquest of Boeotia. In the same years, the Athenians sent twenty, then an additional forty triremes to Sicily, ostensibly for the purpose of supporting Leontini and her allies against Syracusan aggression and of stopping the export of grain from western Greece to the Peloponnesus. But, in fact, their aim was to bring that great and immensely prosperous island within their domain. Extending Athens' dominion was, from their perspective, a worthy object in and of itself. But the risks involved should have weighed more heavily in the Athenians' deliberations. For neither undertaking, even if wildly successful, would have had any direct bearing on the outcome of their war with the Peloponnesians, and losses incurred in either theater would have reduced the city's capacity.[20]

There was, however, one initiative—this one also undertaken by Demosthenes—that really was on point. In the summer of 425, with grudging help from Eurymedon son of Thucles and another *stratēgós* tasked with conducting the reinforcements to Sicily, he managed not only to fortify Coryphasium, a towering headland on the Messenian coast immediately north of Navarino Bay, but also to garrison it with Messenian exiles from Naupactus intent on liberating their compatriots. When the Spartans rallied the Peloponnesian army and navy and mounted a full-scale assault aimed at either storming the fort or starving out its garrison, Eurymedon and his colleague, who had headed north toward Corcyra and the strait of Otranto with the galleys intended for deployment to Sicily, quickly reversed course and returned to Navarino Bay. Therein, they not only defeated the Peloponnesian fleet. They also cut off from their compatriots the garrison of Lacedaemonians that the Spartans had dispatched to the little island of Sphacteria, which stretched from north to south along the bay. Then, as a condition for negotiations, the Athenians persuaded the Spartans to hand over the remaining Peloponnesian galleys— which, on a pretext, they later refused to return. Their subsequent capture of the island, the surrender of what remained of its garrison, and the prospect that the Messenian exiles at Coryphasium might manage to stir up a helot revolt in the Pamisos valley on the western side of Mount Taygetus made the Spartans desperate to secure a peace. And when, the following year, an Athenian expedition seized the island of Cythera and began using it as a base for raiding Laconia and for stirring up the helots situated in the Eurotas valley to the east of the Taygetus massif, they became even more eager for a settlement. A helot rebellion they rightly regarded as an existential threat.

Pericles would undoubtedly have used all of this as an opportunity to elicit from the Lacedaemonians terms bound to enrage the Corinthians. But his successors pressed on, wasting resources at the urging of Demosthenes (among others) on yet another expedition against Boeotia not directly pertinent to the aims of the war; losing a great many hoplites at a battle near Delium in that region; and neglecting the only theater in which a talented and adventurous Spartan, with no galleys to deploy, might still do them real harm— Aegean Thrace and the European coast of the Hellespont, the Sea of Marmara (also known as the Propontis), and the Bosporus.[21]

Brasidas may have been the most resourceful and aggressive warrior at Lacedaemon. Now, for the first time, he was awarded an independent command. In the summer of 424, he volunteered to lead a force of seven hundred newly freed helots and one thousand mercenaries overland, through Boeotia and Thessaly, to and beyond the three-fingered peninsula in western Thrace that we now call the Chalcidice. His aim was to persuade the cities in this rich region still subject to Athens to rebel against their overlord, and he hoped thereby to spark a general revolt within Athens' imperial domain. En route, he foiled an Athenian attempt to once again seize Megara. In

Thrace, he managed to stir up a rebellion throughout much of the Chalcidice and to do the same on the river Strymon at Amphipolis— an Athenian colony of mixed population, founded in 437, of great value to Athens because of her proximity to and leverage over the highly productive gold mines of Mount Pangaeum.

Brasidas' aim was to win the war outright. After taking Amphipolis, he began building a fleet. His compatriots, however, were far more interested in recovering the men taken on Sphacteria, in securing the withdrawal of the Messenian garrison from the headland on Navarino Bay, and in regaining Cythera. He was looking for a springboard; they wanted a bargaining chip. After the Athenians sent an expedition to recover Amphipolis and Brasidas inflicted a stunning defeat on it at the cost of his life, his fellow Spartans finally managed to negotiate a cessation of hostilities and to get their men back.[22]

THE ROAD TO MANTINEIA, 421–418 B.C.

Technically, the long-term truce negotiated in 421 remained in effect for eight years, and both sides maintained the pretense by carefully refraining from attacking one another's territory. In fact, however, the truce never really came into effect. There was an exchange of prisoners, to be sure. There was even the ratification of an alliance. But Athens regained neither Amphipolis nor the tribute that the Spartans had promised that the rebel cities in western Thrace would pay, and Sparta recovered neither Cythera nor Coryphasium.

Instead, war broke out in the Peloponnesus, and Alcibiades son of Cleinias, once the ward of Pericles, talked the Athenians into sending support to the anti-Spartan coalition. It all began with the Corinthians, who sought to make good on the threat that they had issued on the eve of the great war. They persuaded the Argives to take a stab at the hegemony. They helped convince Lacedaemon's restive allies the Eleans and the Mantineians to join the Argives; and, no doubt to the Corinthians' dismay, Alcibiades then induced his compatriots, angered by the Lacedaemonians' failure to deliver Amphipolis, to join the alliance.

The Spartans did what they could to head off the threat—first, by attempting to lure the Argives into another long-term truce, then by mounting military expeditions aimed at clipping the wings of the Eleans and the Mantineians. When this proved insufficient and the Argives repeatedly ravaged the territory of their Epidaurian neighbors, they rallied their remaining Peloponnesian allies—including the Corinthians, who had returned to the fold—as well as the Megarians, who lived outside the Peloponnesus, and the Boeotians, who were quite numerous and well equipped with cavalry. Then, with a massive army, in the summer of 418, the Lacedaemonians staged an invasion of the Argolid.

The allied force was led by Agis son of Archidamus, the heir and successor of that venerable Eurypontid king. Tactically, he was adept. When the Argive coalition tried to intercept and annihilate the Lacedaemonians and their nearby allies while the latter were en route to rendezvous at Nemea with the Boeotians and Sparta's allies in the northern Peloponnesus, he deftly sidestepped their forces. When they later tried to preempt the invasion of the Argolid by marching on Nemea, he divided his army into three units—two of which slipped surreptitiously over the mountains separating Nemea from the Argolid and managed to situate themselves just north of the walled city of Argos while the third contingent followed the army of the Argive coalition back down the main road linking Nemea with the Argolid to the east and south.

The Argives, Eleans, and Mantineians were at a grave disadvantage from the outset. The Athenians, who had not reelected Alcibiades a *stratēgós*, were behindhand in coming to the Argolid's defense. The members of this coalition would have been badly outnumbered even if the Athenians had shown up. They were even worse off without them, and now Agis had his forces concentrated—and he had the army fielded by the Argives, Eleans, and Mantineians surrounded.

47

Had he been willing to follow through on this occasion, there would have been a massacre.

But he—and arguably the others in authority at Lacedaemon—had another outcome in mind. There were at Argos Laconizers, admirers of Sparta eager to overthrow the Argive democracy and put in its place, with Lacedaemonian help, an oligarchy; and there were figures at Sparta who knew these men well. One such was Lichas son of Arcesilaus, the Argive *próxenos* in that *pólis*, who was in all likelihood a member of the Lacedaemonian *gerousía*. The prospect of bringing the ancient rivalry between the two cities to an end and of adding the considerable resources in manpower and wealth of the Argives to the Spartan alliance sorely tempted the leading Lacedaemonians. And so, when that prospect was dangled before him by an Argive friend of Sparta and a sympathetic general dispatched by the Argive commanders, Agis opted—to the anger and dismay of many in his army—to negotiate a short-term truce in anticipation of there being a long-term arrangement with Argos of lasting benefit to Lacedaemon.

When, soon thereafter, a thousand Athenian hoplites arrived along with Alcibiades, who was then serving as an Athenian emissary, the Argive generals were forced by the Eleans, the Mantineians, and the popular assembly, which Alcibiades addressed, to repudiate the short-term truce and to join their allies in mounting an attempt to take on the Spartans in the southern Peloponnesus. When the news of what Alcibiades had accomplished at Argos reached Lacedaemon, Agis found himself in danger of suffering the fate meted out to Pleistoanax in 446, and he placated his compatriots by promising a compensatory victory.

There was, moreover, a clear and present danger that Tegea, a crucial ally of the Spartans, would suffer a revolution and switch sides. The army that Agis had gathered at Nemea had dispersed. At this stage, he could summon the Boeotians, the Corinthians, and Lacedaemon's other allies. But it was most unlikely that a proper concentration of forces could quickly take place and that those in the north would reach the highland valley shared by Tegea and Mantineia in time. He was fortunate, however, in one particular. The Eleans were miffed that the coalition had opted to seek a decision in Arcadia rather than in a region further west where they themselves had claims—and in a huff they had headed for home. This meant that Sparta and her allies in the south, Arcadians all, would have an army equal in size to, if not slightly larger than, that fielded by the Argives, Mantineians, and Athenians. Whether anyone was aware that, in the interim, the Eleans had reversed course and were on their way to eastern Arcadia and that another thousand Athenians were on their way as well we do not know. Agis' chief reason for wanting a quick decision is apt to have been the turmoil in Tegea.

Perhaps because of the pressure he was under, Agis was on this occasion less tactically adept. Initially, when the Argives, Athenians, and Mantineians situated themselves in an exceedingly strong defensive position on the slopes of Mount Alesion quite near the town of Mantineia, he marched on their position and was but a stone's throw away when he was dissuaded from initiating a battle in those highly unfavorable circumstances. Then, to force them to descend and fight in the plain, he marched a short distance into the territory of Tegea and began diverting a stream so as to flood a swath of farmland in Mantineia. Had he done this in the spring near harvest time, this would have elicited a quick response. But since it was high summer, the coalition army did not appear.

Instead, the Argives, Athenians, and Mantineians descended from Mount Alesion and set an ambush, deploying for battle in a spot where the Spartans could not see them—probably behind one of the two mountain spurs extending into the figure-eight-shaped valley from the east and the west at the point where the territories of Tegea and Mantineia converged. There they lurked, waiting for the Lacedaemonians to return from the territory of Tegea to their camp on the Mantineian plain. And there—alerted, one must suppose, by scouts perched atop the mountain spurs—they sprang a surprise upon the Spartans and their allies—who, thanks to intensive training over a very long period of time, managed to redeploy without a glitch from column to phalanx in time for the clash.

At this point, Agis once again proved singularly inept. He was worried that his phalanx might be outflanked on its left, as tended to happen in hoplite conflicts thanks to the plight of the heavy infantryman on the enemy right who had no one to his own right to shield his right side and who therefore tended to drift to the right out of an instinct for self-protection and thereby to draw those to his left in the same direction. So, at the very last second, Agis ordered those on his army's left flank to compensate for this propensity on the part of their foe by moving still further left. Then, he sought to shift two of the units on his right leftward to fill the hole thereby opened up. Their commanders, though trained to blind obedience, balked— thinking the maneuver impossible to effect in the time available. And, soon thereafter, the Mantineians and the elite Argive unit posted alongside them drove through the gap opened up in the Spartan line.

Had these two units been as disciplined as the Spartans, Agis would have lost the battle. But, instead of pushing through, remaining in phalanx, awaiting further orders, and then wheeling to their left to strike the Spartan units in the center from behind, they broke ranks and pursued the defeated troops on their wing to their baggage train. This gave the Spartans in the center—who had cowed the Argives opposite them and then remained in formation, awaiting further instructions—the opportunity to turn their attention to the victorious Mantineians now in disarray and to the elite Argive unit accompanying them.

It was the superior discipline of the Lacedaemonians, not the tactical brilliance of their commander, that won the day on this occasion. But won it was, and it put an end to Athens' implementation of the strategy devised by Themistocles.[23] Half a century later, that strategy would be executed against the Spartans to good effect—but not by anyone from Athens.

A NEW GRAND STRATEGY?

Politics is generational. The memory of catastrophes and crises fades with the passage of time. Recent events, however—especially, events universally experienced as a calamity or as a moment of great peril—have a way of impressing themselves not only on the minds of those who live through them but also on the imaginations of those within the generation which grows up in their shadow. The prospect that such events might be repeated concentrates the minds of such men wonderfully.

The construction of the fort at Coryphasium and the battle staged at Mantineia did not bring the enduring strategic rivalry between Athens and Sparta to an end, but they did teach the Lacedaemonians a lesson. Up to this point, it had not been fully brought home to them that, in this struggle, their existence was at stake. Now they knew better, and this realization forced many a Spartiate to think what had hitherto been almost unthinkable: that it might not be enough to defeat, humiliate, and rein in the Athenians; that the Lacedaemonians' object might really have to be what they had in 431 claimed it was—the elimination of Athens' alliance and her reduction to insignificance; and that the policy of Peloponnesian isolationism, which had long been the keystone of their city's grand strategy, might no longer be viable.

The facts that the Spartans had to face were unwelcome, to say the least. Lacedaemon was constitutionally ill-suited to an imperial venture. This, as we have seen, her citizens had learned early on. But, as long as Athens remained dominant at sea and retained her league, Sparta, her ruling order, and the way of life fostered by her regime would be in genuine peril. This the hard way the Lacedaemonians had just recently learned. And, if the Athenian alliance were to disappear and Sparta did not fill the void, the Persians would certainly do so—and then they might very well return in force to mainland Greece. This was an inconvenience of some gravity that the

Lacedaemonians could not ignore. And so the majority of the Spartiates began contemplating an imperial venture—albeit, in many cases for understandable reasons, with great reluctance and grave misgivings. It was while the Lacedaemonians were reflecting on the lessons to be learned from their experience at Coryphasium and Mantineia that an opportunity to strike a great blow presented itself.

SPARTA'S SICILIAN PROXY WAR

Restless as always and reckless as well, the Athenians opted in the spring of 415 to do the one thing that Pericles had most firmly warned them against. With their contest with Lacedaemon in abeyance but likely to be renewed when a favorable occasion presented itself to either party to the truce, they set out—with Alcibiades once again in the lead—to expand their empire on a grand scale in a fashion not directly pertinent to their quest to eliminate Sparta as a threat. This they did by launching an expedition aimed at the conquest of Syracusa and of Sicily, the island on which that city was situated. This venture was a formidable undertaking, akin to the Egyptian campaign they had launched forty-five years before—for the island in question is immense, and Syracusa was an exceedingly populous city, had long been a major power, and was a sister democracy, on occasion as energetic, innovative, daring, and ambitious as was Athens herself. With all of this in mind, the Athenians dispatched a great armada consisting of one hundred thirty-four triremes (forty of them troop transports), fifty-one hundred hoplites (fifteen hundred of them Athenians), and a horse transport carrying thirty mounts.

Apart from greed and vainglory, the Athenians had no reason for their venture in Sicily. Syracusa was, to be sure, a Corinthian colony; and she and the other Dorian cities in Sicily and Magna Graecia had promised to send a sizable navy to support the Peloponnesian cause in 432. But, as far as we know, not a single trireme had been dispatched. The risks, moreover, were great. Projecting power on such a scale at such a distance was exceedingly expensive, and it was a logis-

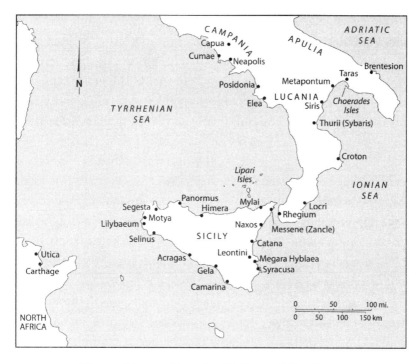

Map 4. Magna Graecia, Sicily, and Carthage

tical nightmare. Moreover, even if they were victorious, it is by no means clear that they would have had resources sufficient for holding on to what they had won.

Thanks to the terrible losses inflicted on their womenfolk and children by the plague in the early 420s, the Athenians had not in the intervening years fully recovered from the dramatic decline in manpower attendant on the spread of that pestilence, and in the late 420s they had suffered additional casualties in the battles they had fought at Delium, Amphipolis, and elsewhere. In addition, their financial reserves were very nearly exhausted. By 421, these had been reduced by almost three-quarters; and, in the aftermath, Athens had not recouped in tribute anything like what she had spent during the previous war. Given the scope and magnitude of their commitment in Sicily, if they were to lose in as thoroughgoing a way as they had lost in Egypt in 454, the Athenians would almost certainly find their city imperiled.[24]

None of this was lost on the Spartans. Of course, they were not prepared to court great danger so far afield. Though exceedingly brave as individuals, as a community, they were profoundly risk-averse, as we have seen; and, thanks to the earthquakes, the helot revolt of 464, and their losses on the field of battle thereafter, they, too, were short of manpower. So, they did what they had done when, earlier, they sent Brasidas to western Thrace. In 414, after they had become aware that the Athenians had squandered their initial advantage upon arriving in Sicily and were now bogged down at Syracusa, conducting a siege, they dispatched to Sicily a single Spartiate—Gylippus son of Cleandridas—to take command of the Syracusans and lead them to victory.

A year later, after the Athenians had indisputably broken the truce of 421 and renewed the war by raiding the Laconian coast and building a fort there on the model of the one at Coryphasium, the Spartans directed Agis son of Archidamus to respond in kind by conducting a Peloponnesian force to Deceleia, northeast of the town of Athens, to build a stronghold from which to conduct ravaging expeditions throughout Attica year round. Thereby, they intended to shut down the silver mines at Laurium and to deprive every last Athenian farmer of access to his estates and of the opportunity to sow, leave aside harvest, his crops.

These moves the Lacedaemonians made on the advice of the Alcibiades who had been responsible for Athens' involvement in forming the Argive coalition that had at Mantineia in 418 threatened their hegemony and their way of life and who had also been the chief advocate of Athens' Sicilian enterprise. This man was now an exile thanks both to factional strife at Athens and to the taste for transgression, the impetuousness, the arrogance, and self-indulgence that had opened him up to attack on religious grounds when a group of vandals mutilated the images of Hermes scattered throughout Ath-

Map 5. Athens, Attica, and Agis' Fort at Deceleia

ens, when word got out that the Eleusinian Mysteries had earlier been profaned and that Cleinias' son was implicated, and the attendant religious hysteria occasioned a witch hunt. To save his own skin, Alcibiades, who had been one of the three Athenian generals sent against Syracusa, had, when summoned home, jumped ship at Thurii; and he had then fled from western Greece to Elis. His aim, as he had openly boasted when he took to heel, was to show his compatriots that he was still very much alive.[25]

With this purpose in mind, Alcibiades did the unthinkable. He journeyed to Sparta—where, charming rogue that he was, he worked his way into the confidence of the Lacedaemonians. With regard to this near-miracle, Plutarch echoed observations of the man's near-contemporary Theopompus of Chios and of Timaeus of Tauromenium, remarking that, during his time in Laconia, the son of Cleinias

> won over the common people and bewitched them by adopting the Spartan way of life [tễ diaítễ lakōnízōn]. Seeing him with his hair in need of a trim, bathing in cold water, on terms of intimacy with barley bread, and supping black broth, they could hardly trust their eyes; and they were at a loss as to whether this man had ever had a cook in his home, had ever laid eyes on a purveyor of perfume, or endured the soft touch of Milesian wool. Among his many talents, Alcibiades possessed a singular shrewdness [deinótēs] and facility [mēchánē] for hunting human beings by suiting himself to [sunexomoioûsthai] their practices and modes of life and entering into the turn of mind and the sentiments attendant thereon [sunomopathein].

In adapting himself to a change of setting, the biographer adds, this amazing man "could effect an alteration" in his comportment and humor "faster than a chameleon.... At Sparta, he frequented the gymnasium and he was frugal and fierce of countenance; in Ionia, he devoted himself to luxury, pleasure, and ease; in Thrace, he was given to drink; and in Thessaly, he took to horse."[26]

As the Spartans learned when Gylippus succeeded and Athens lost not only the triremes, rowers, hoplites, and cavalrymen originally sent to Sicily but also the sixty-five triremes, their crews, and the twelve hundred Athenian hoplites dispatched in 413 on a relief expedition led by Demosthenes, there was more to Alcibiades than good looks and charm. Cleinias' wily son had a keen appreciation for Athens' weaknesses as well as an understanding of what, given Lacedaemon's prestige and the military preparation accorded her citizens, a single talented Spartiate could accomplish if given the opportunity to display his courage and sagacity.[27]

This turncoat's advice had proved to be strategically sound. In 480, at the time of Xerxes' invasion of Greece, there had reportedly been thirty thousand adult male Athenians. There is virtual unanimity among scholars that this number grew dramatically in subsequent decades as serving in the fleet, building and repairing triremes, jury service, and officeholding provided hitherto unknown employment opportunities for the body of impoverished Athenians classified by their city's census as "thetes." In this regard, the archaeological evidence is dispositive: by 460, what had been a village in the Peiraeus had become an urban center in its own right. Whether, by this time, there were forty, fifty, or, as some suppose, more than sixty thousand adult male Athenians is, however, uncertain. What is evident is that six years after that date the Athenians and their allies lost in Egypt upwards of two hundred thirty-five triremes and forty-seven thousand men or more. If a quarter or a third of the men captured or killed were Athenians, as seems clear enough, the catastrophe will have cost Athens at least twenty percent of her adult male population and quite possibly a quarter or even a third of that number.

When the great expedition left Athens for Sicily, there were far fewer Athenians in evidence than there had been in 460. It is likely that, between 454 and 432, Athens' adult male population for the most part bounced back. But, thanks to the plague, the number of women and children it killed, and the losses that the Athenians subsequently suffered in battle, the city was, as we have seen, far less populous in 415 than it had been at the beginning of their second war with the Peloponnesians. So, when the Athenians lost something like three thousand heavy infantrymen and cavalry in Sicily just under two decades after that conflict's inception, it mattered; and when, in addition, they lost roughly eighty-five of their own triremes, forty or more troop transports, and something like seventeen thousand mariners, it mattered enormously—for one-third to one-half of those who manned Athens' fleet were citizens of that *pólis*.

Overall, this fiasco cost Athens anywhere from a fifth to a third of her already diminished adult male population.[28]

Athens' defeat was the handiwork of the Spartiate Gylippus. But it was Alcibiades who had been responsible for his dispatch. So, it was only natural that the Lacedaemonians once again turn to the renegade Athenian for guidance when their city, this time in earnest, began prosecuting her third Attic war.

PART I

────────────

MANEUVERING
FOR ADVANTAGE

There are many kinds of maneuvers in war, some only of which take place on the battlefield. There are maneuvers far to the flank or rear. There are maneuvers in time, in diplomacy, in mechanics, in psychology.... The distinction between politics and strategy diminishes as the point of view is raised. At the summit true politics and strategy are one. The maneuver which brings an ally into the field is as serviceable as that which wins a great battle.

WINSTON S. CHURCHILL

THE SENTENCE with which Thucydides son of Olorus brings his dramatic account of his compatriots' Sicilian expedition to a close merits careful consideration. For when its author wrote, "Of the many [who went out], few made the return journey home," he was redeploying a meme that he had employed once before ... in concluding his narrative of the Athenians' Egyptian expedition.[1]

This repetition was not fortuitous. The two expeditions were alike, and Olorus' son was drawing attention to the fact. Each originated as a response to an appeal for aid. Each required a projection of power over what was, given the state of naval technology, an immense distance. Each was a high-risk, madly ambitious operation launched against a powerful foe. In both cases, an initial success was followed by a catastrophic failure. In both, the mounting of a relief expedition compounded the disaster. In both, only a few of the participants managed to escape to a nearby place of refuge and find their way back to Athens. And, on each occasion, the proportion of the city's manpower and fleet sacrificed in the course of the enterprise exceeded anything suffered by a single people in the twentieth century as a consequence of war. It beggared the imagination then. It beggars it now.

Thucydides expected those of his readers who were alert and capable of learning from the experience of others to reflect on the similarity of the two endeavors. He wanted them to ponder what it was that induced the Athenians to make the same mistake on two different occasions at a four-decade interval. He hoped that, with this in mind, they would ruminate on the peculiar character of the late fifth-century Athenian *politeía*—fashioned to a considerable degree by Pericles and his allies and celebrated in the Funeral Oration and in the speech he delivered on the eve of his death. And he was no less eager that they consider how this regime had produced the daredevil people so vividly described by the Corinthians on the eve of Sparta's second Attic war and so poignantly depicted in his own account of their Sicilian adventure.[2]

This was, however, only part of what the Athenian historian had in mind when he invited comparison. For, by this expedient, he also encouraged his readers to reflect on what had changed in the interim between Athens' two cataclysmic defeats and on why these changes had taken place. When the Egyptian disaster occurred in 454, as we have seen, Pericles arranged for the recall from exile of Cimon, who had been ostracized some years before. And the illustrious son of Miltiades then managed—with some difficulty, we must suspect, and certainly at a price—to persuade the Spartans to grant the Athenians a truce of five years' duration. Fortified by this, they could then, without fear of being attacked at home, devote their full attention and resources to the task of rebuilding their fleet, training new crews, and rowing out from the Aegean to prevent the Persians from regaining the dominion at sea that they had once possessed over the eastern Mediterranean—which is precisely what the Athenians did. In 413, however, when the catastrophe in Sicily occurred, nothing of the sort was even conceivable—and it is the reason for this change that Thucydides wants us to ponder.

The Spartiates who voted to accommodate the Athenians in 451 came from the generation that had fought the Mede at Thermopylae, Salamis, Plataea, and Mycale or from the generation that had grown up in the shadow of the invasion of Hellas mounted by the Persian Great King Xerxes son of Darius. Those battles and that epic struggle had defined these two generations. The visceral fear generated by this experience had profoundly shaped their calculations and their outlook more generally. They knew just how easily they could have lost their war with the Mede. They recognized just how dire the consequence of defeat would then have been, and they realized that it was perfectly possible and even likely that Xerxes or one of his successors would launch another, similar assault on Greece.

From the outset, the Lacedaemonians had been aware of the profound logistical obstacles that the son of Darius would encounter while marching into Hellas. None at the time anticipated the remark that an American general would make nearly two-and-a-half millennia thereafter to the effect that, while amateurs talk incessantly about strategy, military professionals tend to focus on logistics. But, had someone hazarded such an observation, the Spartans would not have been astonished. When they sent the three hundred to Thermopylae to spearhead an effort aimed at blocking the progress of Xerxes' army while the Athenians and the rest of the Hellenes positioned a naval force at Artemisium to intercept his fleet, they were attempting to exacerbate the logistical difficulties he faced and render those obstacles insuperable. Moreover, thanks to what the Hellenic victory at sea in the battle of Salamis subsequently achieved, these landlubbers from the Peloponnesus came to a fuller appreciation of the weight that, in the technological environment then per-taining, had to be accorded to war at sea. In the aftermath, as we have seen, they were even forced to acknowledge that—as long as the Athenians and their allies denied the Persians the control over the Aegean that they had once possessed—no such attack could again be mounted. For, in the absence of a transport of foodstuffs by sea, the Great King's footsoldiers would starve en route.

By the time that the Spartiates decided to send Gylippus to Sicily, however, well over six decades had passed since they had themselves tangled with the Persians, and there was no one—or next to no one—alive in Lacedaemon who had participated in any of the bat-tles mentioned above. Of course, the Spartans then in their prime were by no means ignorant of their forebears' heroic struggle against the Mede. This goes without saying. It had been their compatriots' finest hour, and the events that took place at that time were etched into their memories as a people. What the new generation did not have, however, was a close personal familiarity with and a proper appreciation of the challenge that the Persians had then posed, and for this reason the prospect that this challenge might be renewed did not loom as large in their imaginations as it had in the minds of the veterans of those engagements and their immediate offspring.

With the Athenian threat, however, the new generation was inti-mately acquainted. At Mantineia, a mere five years before the anni-hilation of the Athenian armada in Sicily, its members had been forced to fight for Lacedaemon's very existence. The numerous Spar-tan survivors of that clash knew only too well how close they had come to a defeat likely to have been fatal not just to their control of Messenia but also to their way of life—which depended both upon their possession of that fertile, well-watered province and upon their dominion over the people, native to the region, whom they com-pelled to farm it on their behalf. For them, moreover, Coryphasium was still a great irritant—and no small threat. Thanks to the possibil-ity that the Messenian exiles posted there would succeed in stirring up another helot revolt, the Lacedaemonians were always on edge and had to be even more vigilant than in normal times. If visceral fear affected their calculations, as it surely did, it was at this time directed at the Athenians, not at the Mede.

There had been moments in the past—during Sparta's first and second Attic wars and in the interlude between the two—when Xerxes' son and heir Artaxerxes had explored the possibility of reaching an accommodation with the Lacedaemonians and of lending them material backing in their recurrent conflict with Athens. Had the members of their alliance supported the Spartans' bid in the late 440s to come to the defense of Samos at the time of her rebellion, the Lacedaemonians might well have stumbled into some sort of understanding with that Great King's cousin or nephew the satrap Pissouthnes, who was making mischief for the Athenians at this juncture by supplying to the Samians aid and assistance—and in the 420s the Spartans were so sorely tempted by the prospect of such an arrangement that they had themselves initiated negotiations with Artaxerxes. But, at that time—even though they almost certainly knew that Pissouthnes, his bastard son Amorges, and a relative bearing the name of the satrap's father Hystaspes were conducting a small-scale war against the Athenians in Anatolia—they still feared the consequences of Athens' elimination as a naval power. They also knew that, in return for support, the Persians would exact a *quid pro quo*—which was a prospect that the descendants of those who had fought for Hellenic liberty at Thermopylae and Plataea found repellent. So, in making diplomatic overtures, the Lacedaemonians had displayed deep ambivalence, and vacillation on their part was the consequence. As the Athenians learned when they captured a messenger sent by Artaxerxes to Lacedaemon and translated from Aramaic the dispatch that he was carrying, each of the emissaries that the Spartans had sent in succession to the Achaemenid administrative capital at Susa in Elam, where foreign delegations were ordinarily received, had spoken in a manner contrary to and incompatible with what his predecessor had said.[3]

Now, however, yet another decade and a half had passed. The

Persian Wars had receded yet further into the past. Many a superannuated Spartiate had departed from the scene. At Lacedaemon, as we have seen, there cannot have been more than a handful of citizens left who had lived through that epic conflict—and there may have been none. Moreover, thanks to what the Athenians had attempted at Coryphasium and Mantineia, the Lacedaemonians' perceptions regarding the perils they faced had undergone a transformation; and the annihilation in Sicily of the Athenian expeditionary force had altered their expectations. In doing so, it had modified their aspirations as well.

The words that Winston Churchill wrote with an eye to the duke of Marlborough's great victory at Oudenarde—to which I have repeatedly alluded in the volumes preceding this one—once again deserve quotation in full:

> Battles are the principal milestones in secular history. Modern opinion resents this uninspiring truth, and historians often treat the decisions in the field as incidents in the dramas of politics and diplomacy. But great battles, won or lost, change the entire course of events, create new standards of values, new moods, new atmospheres, in armies and in nations, to which all must conform.

The observation that Churchill hazarded on this occasion applies not only to the battles of the Persian Wars, to Cimon's victory over the Mede at Eurymedon, to the catastrophe that struck the Athenians in Egypt, to their subsequent victory over the Persians at Cypriot Salamis, and to the clashes that took place between Athens and Sparta at Coryphasium and Mantineia. It is no less, and perhaps even more, apt when applied to the destruction of the Athenian forces in Sicily.

This Thucydides makes abundantly clear. In the winter of 413, when they first heard the news that the Athenians had suffered a great misadventure in Sicily, "the Hellenes were," he reports, "all of them *erēménoi*—jubilant and enthusiastic."

The Greeks allied with neither side—each community of citizens persuaded that, had the Athenians enjoyed success in Sicily, they would have turned on them; each supposing that the conflict to come would not last long and that their participation in it would be a thing worthy of admiration—thought that, even if uninvited, they should act on their own and launch an attack. For their part, the allies of the Lacedaemonians were united in being a great deal more eager than ever before to obtain a swift release from the considerable hardships that they had been suffering. But, most important of all, the peoples subject to the Athenians were ready to revolt, even beyond their capacity to do so, because they judged affairs in a fit of passion and would not abide the argument that the Athenians had the capacity to survive the summer to come.

And the Lacedaemonians? As a *pólis*, they were emboldened by all of this—above all by the prospect that their allies in Sicily, having been forced to increase the size of their navy, would in all likelihood be present in the spring with a great force. Being hopeful in all respects, they were disposed to take up war without even a hint of hesitation. For they reckoned that, if it ended in an admirable way, they would in the future be delivered from such perils as would have been visited on them by the Athenians if they had secured the resources of Sicily—and they judged that, after having brought the enemy down, they would in safety exercise hegemony over Hellas in its entirety themselves.[4]

Driven by fear and intoxicated by a longing for grandeur, as their Athenian opponents so often had been in the past, the Spartans responded to the good news from Sicily with an uncharacteristic vigor and dispatch. The Eurypontid king Agis son of Archidamus set out from Deceleia straightaway with an army to collect money from Lacedaemon's allies in central Greece for the construction and support of a fleet. On the Oetaeans, who had long been at odds with Sparta, he brought force to bear. On the Achaeans and the other subject allies of the Thessalians in the vicinity of Phthiotis, whom he compelled to supply hostages, he put considerable pressure. And he may also have secured Lacedaemon's dominance in the Malian Gulf and reasserted the control she had previously exercised over her colony at Heracleia Trachinia near Thermopylae.

In the meantime, his compatriots sent a missive to the Boeotians and to the cities that belonged to their Peloponnesian alliance, ordering them to join with Lacedaemon in constructing one hundred new triremes. Twenty-five of these were to be supplied by the Spartans themselves; a like number, by the Boeotians; fifteen, by the Corinthians; another fifteen, by the Phocians and eastern Locrians in tandem; ten, by the Arcadians, Pellenians, and Sicyonians; and a final ten, by the Megarians, Troezenians, Epidaurians, and Hermionaeans.

The small number requisitioned from the Corinthians might occasion surprise. Twenty years before, they had constructed sixty-seven to seventy-five new triremes in short order between the battle which they had fought against the Corcyraeans at Cape Leukimne in 435 and that which subsequently took place between these two powers at Sybota in 433. But, now thanks to the long-term damage done this once-proud naval power by the cumulative effect of the blockades put in place by the Athenians during the Peloponnesians' two previous Attic wars, Corinth no longer had the resources with which to do the like. Something of the sort can also be said regarding the Megarians, who had deployed twenty triremes against the Persians at Salamis in 480, who were maintaining forty triremes in dry dock at Nisaea late in 429, and who had suffered grievously in like fashion during the second Attic war. A lot had changed since 431, when the Lacedaemonians had hoped that their maritime allies in western Greece and those in the Greek East would, between them, put at their disposal a fleet of five hundred galleys. In the interim, sobriety had set in, and there had been a dramatic lowering of sights.[5]

As far as we can tell, the enthusiasm that Thucydides attributes to the communities that were neutral came to nothing, and the western Greeks, with the twenty-two triremes they dispatched in 412, fell far short of what the Spartans had hoped for.[6] But Lacedaemon's allies in the Peloponnesus and in central Greece were responsive, and the subject cities within Athens' imperial alliance fully lived up to expectations.

There were more than one hundred fifty of the latter. They were to be found on the islands scattered throughout the Aegean. They were located along or a short distance inland from the adjacent coasts—in Aegean Thrace and western Asia Minor; along the shores of the Hellespont, the Sea of Marmara, the Bosporus, and the Black Sea; as well as in southern Anatolia to the west of the Eurymedon river. Athens' dominion was a watery world. What Plato's Socrates says about the Hellenes more generally can be applied with even greater force to those participant in the Athenian alliance: they lived like ants and frogs around a pond.[7]

The largest and most valuable of the islands within the Athenians' sphere was Euboea, which lay just offshore from Attica and Boeotia. It was on this long, comparatively narrow isle that they lodged their herds when Attica was subject to invasion or occupation, and it was the chief source of the foodstuffs which they imported on such occasions. So, it spoke volumes about the seriousness of the perils now facing Athens that the cities on Euboea were the first to approach the Lacedaemonians.

These men lodged their appeal with Agis, who was stationed in Attica at Deceleia nearby and who, as a Spartan king in the field, had an almost completely free hand. Recognizing the importance of the island and its proximity to Deceleia, the royal son of Archidamus summoned two Spartiates from Lacedaemon to spearhead the rebellion they proposed. About one of the two—a man named Melanthus—we know nothing. His colleague, however, was the scion of an important house. His name was Alcamenes; and, in 432, it had been his father Sthenelaidas, in his capacity as an ephor, who had persuaded their compatriots to initiate Lacedaemon's second Attic war. On that occasion, his opponent in the debate, Agis' father Archidamus, had warned that their sons might well inherit that war—which is what transpired.

To Deceleia, these two Spartiates brought three hundred *neodamódeis*, but none of these liberated helots ever made it to Euboea. For, by the time that Alcamenes, Melanthus, and this band of men were ready to slip across the narrow body of water separating that island from the mainland, a delegation had arrived on an identical mission from Antissa, Eresus, Methymna, Pyrrha, and Mytilene— the five *póleis* on Lesbos, the next largest island in Athens' alliance.

A mildly contorted horseshoe-shaped isle not only sizable but quite prosperous, Lesbos was located just off the Anatolian coast below the Troad not far from the entrance to the Hellespont in a corner of the eastern Aegean settled by speakers of classical Greek's Aeolic dialect. The aspiring rebels from its five cities received firm support from the Boeotians, who spoke the same dialect of Greek and, with some justification, claimed common descent. In response to their appeal, Agis put Alcamenes in charge; gave him the title harmost, meaning "governor"; and reassigned him to that station. Agis and the Boeotians, between them, proposed dispatching with Sthenelaidas' son a flotilla of twenty triremes to support the Lesbians' revolt.[8]

This plan also came to naught. For, in the interim, emissaries from yet another large island made an appearance. This deputation hailed from Chios, an Ionian isle situated near the Anatolian coast to the south of Lesbos. Accompanying its members were envoys from Erythrae, another *pólis* where the Ionian dialect of Greek was spoken—this one situated, just across the narrow strait separating Chios from Anatolia, at the end of a large promontory, named in antiquity after Erythrae itself, which extends westward a considerable distance from the Asia Minor coast. These would-be insurgents bypassed the Eurypontid king and made a direct approach to the authorities at Lacedaemon—and what they offered was tempting in the extreme.

To begin with, the Chians were exceedingly rich. One contemporary reportedly described them as "the wealthiest of the Hellenes"; and, although he had both a motive and an aptitude for exaggeration, he may well have been right. In 494, during the Ionian Revolt, they had managed to deploy a fleet of one hundred triremes against the Persians at the battle of Lade, and Thucydides tells us that they possessed a larger servile population than any other *pólis* apart from the Lacedaemonians. There were two communities within the Athenian alliance that still supplied ships and contributed no *phóros*. Methymna on Lesbos was one; Chios was the other—and, of the two, the latter was by far the one better equipped with ships. As a Lacedaemonian *períoikos* quietly dispatched to the island confirmed, the Chians were in a position to deploy no fewer than sixty triremes in support of the cause now championed by the Spartans. Moreover, these galleys were manned not by landlubbers, but by experienced mariners adept at maritime combat and intimately familiar with the Athenian way of war.

With them, moreover, the Chian and the Erythraean notables dispatched to Lacedaemon conveyed an emissary from a Persian satrap named Tissaphernes who will loom large in the remainder of this story. Based at Sardis in Lydia, this figure was charged with governing the regions along and inland a considerable distance from the Anatolian coast to the northwest, west, and southwest of his seat—an expanse of land which abutted on a considerable stretch of coastal territory grudgingly conceded in the past to the Athenians and their allies. Perhaps with an eye to what this envoy was about to propose, the Great King had also named Tissaphernes a "military commander" with a remit extending "over the lowlands [*strategòs tōn kátō*]" along the Anatolian coast—an area considerably more extensive than his satrapy. The Lacedaemonians were not only invited by this viceroy's ambassador to take on the Athenians in the region. He

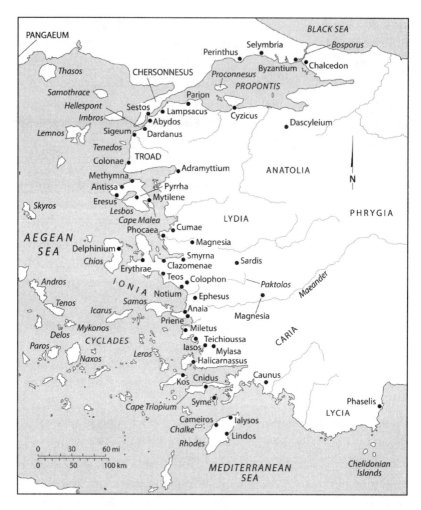

**Map 6. Western Anatolia, the Bosporus, the Propontis, the
Hellespont and the Eastern Aegean**

also promised that the satrap would provide generous financial
support.[9]

To make matters even more complicated and confusing, the
Spartans at this time also received two envoys from a counterpart
and rival of Tissaphernes named Pharnabazus son of Pharnaces—
who was the great-great-grandson of an earlier Pharnaces thought to

have been an uncle of Xerxes' father Darius. Stationed, well to the north of Sardis, at Dascyleium in Phrygia near the Propontis and the Greek city of Cyzicus, this satrap was charged—as his father, grandfather, and great-grandfather had been before him—with governing the Troad as well as the Hellespont, the Sea of Marmara, the Bosporus, and points farther east along and inland from Anatolia's Black Sea coast south all the way to and beyond the ancient Phrygian capital at Gordium. His agents were two: an exiled Megarian named Calligeitus son of Laophon and an exiled Cyzicene named Timagoras son of Athenagoras. If Plutarch is to be trusted, these men were accompanied by a delegation from Cyzicus herself. It was their task to urge the Lacedaemonians to send a fleet to the Hellespont rather than to Ionia. To support such an expedition, they had with them a sweetener: twenty-five talents, which is to say roughly fourteen hundred twenty-five pounds, of silver.[10]

The fact that both satraps approached the Lacedaemonians at this time strongly suggests what the other evidence confirms: that neither was acting on his own. Quite recently, in fact, they had both come under pressure from Persia's Great King—who kept his satraps on a short leash, as his predecessors had and his successors would. Thanks to the elaborate system of well-maintained, well-guarded, "wheel-worthy [hamáxitos]" royal cart-roads that ran from the outskirts of the empire to its various capitals and thanks also to the Persian analogue of the American Pony Express, he was in a position to have learned in a timely fashion what had happened in early October 413 in Sicily. And to the new standard of value, the new mood, and the new atmosphere produced by the great catastrophe that the Athenians had so recently suffered, this great potentate was no less responsive than were the communities in eastern Greece.

For more than thirty-five years, Persia's Achaemenid monarchs had reluctantly acquiesced in what they could never fully sanction: Athens' interference with the collection of the tribute pledged to their ancestors not only by the Greek cities dotted along the coasts within these two satrapies, but also by those situated on the islands offshore and those located on the European continent to the north and the northwest. For the first time in more than thirty years, the King of Kings was demanding that, within their satrapies, his viceroys in western Asia Minor collect the tribute owed him and even pay him the arrears built up since the amnesty occasioned by his accession to the throne—for, in his estimation and in that of the Persian people more generally, the silver in question (or its equivalent in electrum or gold) was rightly his. To this end, almost certainly after an exchange of letters with Tissaphernes concerning the manner in which this could most easily be accomplished, he had authorized his viceroys' negotiation of a working arrangement with Lacedaemon. So, at least, we must presume.[11]

When faced with these rival offers, the Lacedaemonians are apt to have paused to ask themselves what, if they accepted one or the other, they would be getting into. The Persian empire was, after all, enormous, immensely powerful, and wealthy beyond imagination—and, in the eastern Mediterranean, that kingdom was now and had long been a force to be reckoned with. No one thought its monarch bereft of ambition; and, although the Spartans had contracted a visceral fear and hatred of the Athenians, they were in no way willing to become dependents of and pawns played by the Mede.

There were, moreover, procedures in place at Lacedaemon to prevent precipitous action. Before the assembly could consider a course of action, it had to be approved by the *gerousía*. The young might be headstrong. The *gérontes* were not. They were at least sixty years in age and served until they died. In the course of their lives, like old men in every clime and time, they had witnessed considerable foolishness, and they had all too often seen things go awry. In consequence, they tended to be sober, careful, cautious, and even timid—sometimes to a fault. That there was no Spartan analogue to the expeditions that the Athenians dispatched to Egypt and Sicily is not an accident. Nor is it fortuitous that the landlubbers of Lacedaemon had never before resolutely set out to do what was required to put an end to the Athenian challenge—which was to transform

Sparta herself into a great naval power. Courageous they might well be, but audacious they were not. Thanks to the helot threat, the Lacedaemonians were instinctively risk-averse, and the leverage accorded old men within their regime reinforced this propensity.[12]

In judging how to respond to the satraps' overture, the Lacedaemonians had to consider the temperament and aspirations of the particular Great King with whom they were confronted. These in turned depended to a very considerable degree on the character of the Persian regime and on the vicissitudes of circumstance and time.

In this case, the monarch in question was, in almost every pertinent regard, a new man. Xerxes' son Artaxerxes had died a natural death in 424 after a reign as King of Kings lasting more than forty years. He had not been an especially warlike ruler; and, in later times, the Greeks remembered him as a monarch gentle in demeanor who favored peace.[13] In 413/12, however, Persia was ruled by a man of a markedly different temper. He was a son of this Artaxerxes. Originally named Ochus, he had, upon succeeding to the crown, taken as his throne-name Darius in honor of the first and greatest of Persia's Achaemenid monarchs. Artaxerxes' successor, whom scholars for convenience call Darius II, was a more formidable figure than his father, who had lucked into the throne. He was, in fact, a usurper of sorts. For he had reportedly made his way to power some eight months after his father's demise and sustained his claim—after a lengthy struggle. To understand what the Spartans had to ponder when they considered making an agreement with this man's minions, we will have to contemplate the character of the Persian *politeía*, its strengths and weaknesses, the predicament in which its ruler found himself at this time, and the regime imperatives to which he and those associated with his administration had to be sensitive.

CHAPTER ONE

PERSIKÁ

The sinews of war, funding without limits ...

MARCUS TULLIUS CICERO

I MPERIAL PERSIA was a despotism. The authority of its Great King was, in principle, absolute. According to Herodotus, there were *nómoi*—laws or customs—governing the succession. One barred bastards from eligibility if a legitimate son existed. Another stipulated that, before departing on campaign, the King name his heir and designate him as co-regent. A third, introduced in the wake of the first Darius' elevation, specified that the royal consort, the future Queen Mother, be selected from among the handful of families—constituting the highest reaches of Achaemenid Persia's aristocracy—that had been involved in securing for him the throne.[1]

In designating a successor, Cyrus, the first Darius, Xerxes, and Artaxerxes had faithfully observed the first of these requirements, and there is evidence that all four of them took care to designate a crown prince in a timely fashion. But Cyrus' son Cambyses seems not to have done anything of the kind when he marched on Egypt; and, as far as we can tell, there was no mechanism in place to prevent a Persian monarch from ignoring these or any other *nómoi*.

In fact, as Cambyses' conduct suggests, the Great King could in practice do what he thought fit. There were no formal constraints. But, of course, there were invisible impediments of another sort—

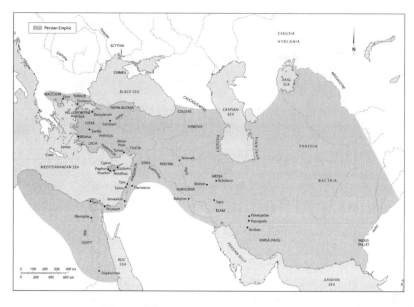

Map 7. The Persian Empire, ca. 490

for these always exist. Rulers, whatever the scope of their supposed authority may be, rely for their safety on their underlings. The same applies when it comes to the implementation of policy. These underlings have expectations of their own which cannot be entirely ignored, and this is the reason why, even in a despotism, conventions matter. The monarchs of Persia knew that, were they to eschew tradition, ignore altogether the dictates of *nómos*, and profoundly offend the body of great magnates who made up that nation's high aristocracy, they would do so at their own peril. Moreover, although the absence of a hard and fast, binding law of succession afforded the King of Kings a considerable measure of latitude in choosing his successor, there was a drawback attendant on the freedom he enjoyed. In the aftermath, there could be a great deal of second guessing on the part of his subordinates—especially if the successor he had named was a notorious weakling, an inebriate, or fool.[2]

Plato contends that the moral formation [*paideía*] afforded Cambyses, Xerxes, and most of their successors was defective. He also suggests that the spectacular achievements of Cyrus and Darius were

76

made possible by two circumstances: that neither was reared in luxury by women and eunuchs at the court, and that, when young, both knew little but the hardships of the campaign. Contemporary students of the history of ancient Iran are quick to denounce this critique of the Persian monarchy as Orientalist fantasy; and, when they describe the workings of that polity or edit a collection of translated texts meant to throw light on it, they tend to exclude observations of the sort that Plato hazarded on this occasion. This they do despite the fact the Athenian philosopher lived at the time and surely knew more about Persia than any modern scholar ever will.

There is, moreover, reason to suspect that there is something to what Plato intimates concerning unchecked rule and the corrupting influence of a despot's court. The testimony of Tacitus and Suetonius suggests that the offspring of the Roman emperors often exhibited the defects that, centuries before, Plato had attributed to the heirs of Persia's Great Kings. Moreover, in our own times, the pampered children of the rich and powerful are frequently arrogant, irresponsible, feckless, and dissolute. And, in various other ways as well, they tend to be less impressive for their virtues, talents, and achievements than for their vices, incapacity, and impunity. It can hardly be fortuitous that the death of a Persian monarch frequently gave rise to a succession crisis. If the same prospect haunted imperial Rome, it was because the circumstances were similar.[3]

Neither the first Darius nor Artaxerxes had been destined for the throne. Although he was a close relative of Cyrus' consort the mother of Cambyses; and although, in keeping with this fact, he had himself served first as Cyrus' Quiver-Bearer, then as Cambyses' Spear-Bearer, Darius son of Hystaspes was not the latter monarch's co-regent. He was not even the heir apparent—the figure called in the Akkadian in use in Babylon in this era the *mār šarri*—"the King's son." Nor was he, strictly speaking, even a member of the monarch's extended family. He was not what the Babylonian texts identify as a *mār bīt šarri*, "Son of the Royal House," or in abbreviation as a *mār bīti*—"Son of the House." He was no more than a courtier—albeit, one of the very first rank. As such, he was, in principle, ineligible for elevation. At best, if one believes his own testimony, this illustrious member of the Achaemenid clan was a very distant cousin of Cyrus— the great-great-grandson of the latter's great-great-grandfather. And one may wonder whether this self-serving claim was even true. What cannot be denied, however, is threefold: that, after the death in mysterious and suspicious circumstances of Cyrus' first-born son, designated heir, and successor, Darius mounted a successful coup d'état against Cambyses' younger brother or someone masquerading as such; that he did so in conjunction with a group of Persian nobles— Intaphernes, Otanes, Gobryas, Hydarnes, Megabyzus, and Ardumanish—who had also been quite prominent at Cambyses' court; and that, in close cooperation with four of his six co-conspirators and their descendants, Darius and his first few successors subsequently consolidated control, established the supremacy of the Achaemenid clan, and governed the realm.[4]

ARTAXERXES SON OF XERXES

In the case of Artaxerxes, who was in the fullest sense of the phrase a Son of the Royal House, the kingship had reportedly been tossed onto his lap when his father Xerxes, Darius' son and designated heir, was assassinated. In the aftermath, the King's murderers are said to have falsely blamed and executed for the deed the more senior of Artaxerxes' two elder brothers the crown prince. Then, they installed the youngest of Xerxes' three legitimate sons as Great King and no doubt saw to the elimination of his surviving brother—and this they did on the presumption that their nominee would be a mere figurehead. And, when Artaxerxes, who was then still a stripling, proved less pliant than expected, the conspirators were reportedly prepared to turn on him.

Artaxerxes' life and his kingship are said then to have been saved by an intervention on the part of one of the great magnates. His protector and benefactor was his considerably older brother-in-law—

the like-named grandson of the Megabyzus who had conspired with the first Darius. This man was a force in his own right. He was not only Xerxes' son-in-law. He had been one of that Great King's marshals on the march into Greece, and it is tolerably likely that, when Xerxes hived off Syria—"the Land-Across-the-River"—from the province of Babylonia, he was designated as its first satrap. For Megabyzus is the first figure known to have occupied that post.[5]

Some forty years after Artaxerxes' elevation to the throne, immediately following his death, there was yet another succession crisis. Concerning it, we have the report of an insider—a Greek physician from Cnidus named Ctesias, who served at the Persian court a generation thereafter and subsequently penned a book entitled *Persika* (Persian Matters). This book, which survives only in fragmentary form in an epitome made by the Byzantine scholar and patriarch Photius, is of considerable interest. For, although the salacious content of the latter's epitome has long caused scholars to look askance at and cast aspersions on the testimony of this well-placed medical doctor, the stories told therein concerning events in the second half of the fifth century do appear to be reliable. Much of the circumstantial detail that Ctesias relates concerning Persians of importance mentioned in no other Greek source is confirmed by the surviving clay tablets from Babylon. Therein, these individuals appear as great landholders, and the property belonging to those who, on his report, chose the losing side in the succession crisis under consideration here shows up thereafter in the hands of those said to have backed the winner.[6]

According to Ctesias, when Xerxes' son Artaxerxes passed away—almost certainly in Susa, where the Great Kings ordinarily resided during the winter and, one must suspect, much of the fall and spring—he left behind as his designated successor his one legitimate son: a man he named after his own father. As *mār šarri*, the younger Xerxes had no doubt been instructed in the ways of the court and in the art of governance. We know that, as his father grew old, he was made co-regent, and he may well have shared in the administration

Figure 4.1. Bas Relief at Persepolis of Artaxerxes I with his
Co-Regent Xerxes II.
Courtesy of Jona Lendering of ©LiviusOrg | Jona Lendering

of the empire. For, at Persepolis, there is a door jamb sporting a bas relief, depicting Artaxerxes enthroned with a winged disk floating above him complete with a human bust representing Ahura Mazda or, some suppose, the royal aura [*xvarnah*]. Standing behind him on a platform supported by atlantids representing the divers peoples of the empire is his son and heir apparent wearing—and this tells the tale—a crown indistinguishable from that of his father.

His preparation and experience notwithstanding, the younger Xerxes seems not have been up to the job he had been assigned— and this was presumably obvious to all concerned. It is revealing that his reign was exceedingly brief, and he never even underwent a formal investiture as Great King. For we are told that some forty-five days after his father's demise, before the obsequies at the royal burial grounds at Naqsh-e-Rustam northwest of Persepolis had even been performed, the second Xerxes was assassinated by one of his father's seventeen bastards. The perpetrator was a man named Sogdianus— who had reportedly found him in what was, we must suspect, his normal state: a drunken stupor.[7]

THE YEAR OF THE FOUR EMPERORS

This murderous act set off a civil war. For, in the absence of a legitimate heir and of an enforceable law stipulating who, in such circumstances, should inherit the office, all of Artaxerxes' surviving male offspring were, at least in principle, equally eligible. And so, two other illegitimate sons of the late Great King—including Ochus, who was the satrap of Hyrcania in eastern Iran, which stretched along the southeastern coast of the Caspian Sea—joined the assassin Sogdianus in vying for the throne. The stakes were high. We are told that he who was on the losing side was apt to be marinated in alcohol and led onto on a bed of embers where he would be transmogrified into a torch and burned to a crisp.

Though no doubt a man of considerable moxie, the figure who emerged from this contest victorious was initially, we can safely assume, in an exceedingly precarious position. Ochus was not just a bastard, which was bad enough. He was a half-breed as well, a product of his royal father's dalliance with a Babylonian concubine; and the same was true for the half-sister Parysatis whom he had wed.[8]

Ochus was, to be sure, a *mār bīt šarri*—as were, we have reason to suspect, all of the male descendants of the great Darius. As such, he had a claim of sorts. Moreover, as satrap of Hyrcania, he occupied a position of some strength. Whether he was in his satrapy when Xerxes II was killed we are not told. What we do know, however, is that he popped up in Babylon not long thereafter; and it was from southern Mesopotamia, where neither the younger Xerxes nor his assassin appears to have ever been recognized as King, that this Ochus would draw much of the support responsible for his elevation. Moreover, it was almost certainly in Babylon, rather than in Hyrcania, that he met with the Achaemenid prince Arsames, a Son of the Royal House who had been the satrap of Egypt for something like three decades, and with Artoxares, once the most influential of Artaxerxes' eunuchs, who is said to have journeyed from Armenia, where his master had exiled him. These two persuaded him not only to ignore his half-brother Sogdianus' repeated summons to the court at Susa, but also to assume the upright tiara and present himself to the world as Darius the avenger of Xerxes II.[9]

It is by no means clear what Sogdianus was doing while Ochus was busy in the western provinces. It is not likely that he remained inactive and we can perhaps presume that he tried to rally the forces of the East, but we know very little. Sogdianus did have some supporters, but their importance should not be exaggerated. Menostanes—who, as his Chiliarch, commanded the royal bodyguard and controlled access to his person—was the son of Artaxerxes' half-brother Artarios, satrap of Babylonia; and he had himself served his uncle as general—but Menostanes' inability to secure his father's province for Sogdianus suggests that his support was of meager worth. Of course, the royal bodyguard, constituted by those identified by Herodotus and other Greek writers as the Ten Thousand Immortals, would have been a formidable asset. But Ctesias tells us that Sogdianus' gifts had not mollified the wrath they harbored against the murderer of their rightful master Xerxes II. When Arbarios, the commander of the King's cavalry, fled to Ochus' side, presumably with a band of men, Sogdianus must have lost heart.[10]

Ochus' activities early in 423 are only slightly better attested. One intriguing document from the archives of the Murašû bank in Nippur reveals that the head of the firm rented a house in Babylon on 13 February 423, for an indefinite period extending to "the going-forth of the King." There was no doubt a great deal of money to be made from the preparations for the campaign in prospect.[11]

In the end, however, there was no war. Parysatis persuaded her husband Ochus to rely on trickery, and Sogdianus—against the advice of Menostanes—fell into the trap, accepting his rival's assurances at face value and in time paying for his gullibility with his life. Ctesias—who was personally acquainted with Parysatis and who discussed this and other matters with her—intimates that she was the mastermind of the entire operation that placed her husband on the throne.[12]

There is one other piece of evidence that is pertinent—for it suggests that Ochus owed a considerable debt of gratitude to a Babylonian dignitary named Bēlšunu (perhaps a relative of his mother Cosmarridene or of Andia, the mother of his wife). For he subsequently named this man to posts hitherto, as far as we can tell, reserved for Iranians—making him district governor of Babylon and, then, later appointing him governor and, one must suspect, satrap of Syria, "the Land Across-the-River," while having the man's son succeed him as district governor of Babylon.[13]

The fact that he was what we might call the Babylonian candidate would not have been a grave disadvantage for Ochus had the Persians, as a people, not been exceedingly ethnocentric and had there not been purebred Achaemenids just off-stage who had a much more plausible claim to the throne than the half-Babylonian by-blow who had seized it for himself.[14] Two facts suggest that Ochus was acutely aware that he desperately needed support from Persia's great magnates. He appointed as satrap of Babylon in place of Menostanes' father Artarios a certain Gobryas—almost certainly a descendant of the co-conspirator, Spear-Bearer, and longtime brother-in-law of the Darius whose name Ochus had assumed—and he forged a marriage alliance with the offspring of another of the elder Darius' closest associates.

In theory, as we have just seen, the Achaemenid monarchs were required to choose a consort from within the family of one of the seven conspirators responsible for the coup d'état that had eventuated in the elevation of the first Darius. In practice, they tended to adhere to the letter of this agreement while ignoring its spirit—by choosing a wife from within their own extended family. They did so because they understood what modern students of politics tend to forget: that every political regime contains within it the seeds of its own destruction. They knew that exogamous marriages on the part of absolute monarchs nearly always give rise to conflict. To avoid, on the one hand, the envy and, on the other, the sense of entitlement that such marriages tend to engender, they kept the descendants of Darius' co-conspirators and confederates—with whom they might otherwise have become dangerously entwined—at a healthy distance by the simple expedient of practicing endogamy and choosing the future Queen Mother from within the one family from among those of the seven conspirators that was the least dangerous to the family entrusted with the throne: the royal family itself. This is what Cambyses, who married two of his sisters, had done. This is what the elder Darius—who was already married to a daughter of Gobryas and who subsequently espoused a daughter of Otanes—did when he made Cyrus' daughter Atossa Queen Mother; and this may be what Ochus' father Artaxerxes did when he wed Damaspia, whose family of origin is to us unknown.

The first Xerxes was an exception to the rule—perhaps because he was not, in the beginning, the heir apparent. His consort Amestris, whom the elder Darius may well have chosen for him, was a descendant of his father's co-conspirator Otanes.[15] In selecting a wife for his firstborn son, Ochus followed this example, jettisoning the prudent strategy pioneered by the first Achaemenid monarch in choosing a consort for himself. This he did, we must suspect, because he had no choice. Mindful of the peculiar circumstances in which he found himself, he drew one important branch of the old Persian nobility quite close. This he did by marrying off his heir apparent Arsaces—the only surviving son whom he had sired with his wife Parysatis prior to becoming Great King—to a young woman named Stateira, who was herself the daughter of a satrap named Hydarnes.

This Hydarnes was, we can almost be certain, a descendant of the like-named co-conspirator of Darius; and his satrapy is likely to have been Media—which was the province that the elder Darius awarded to the first Hydarnes after that man succeeded in quelling its revolt. Stateira's father is also apt to have been a close relative—if not, in fact, a direct descendant—of the Hydarnes son of Hydarnes who commanded at the time of Xerxes' invasion of Greece the royal bodyguard identified by Herodotus and others as the Ten Thousand Immortals. That, at the same time, Ochus and Parysatis married their sole surviving daughter Amestris to Stateira's brother Teriteuchmes is further evidence for the weight given the dynastic alliance that these two great families had forged.[16]

The worries that occasioned this dynastic alliance were more than merely theoretical. Its formation seems to have been a response to a looming threat. For, after Sogdianus' bid for the throne collapsed, others soon entered the fray; and Ochus found himself required to defend his claim on the battlefield. It is this, we have reason to suspect, that explains why the records of the Murašû bank indicate that the local landowners in the vicinity of Nippur were mortgaging their property in unprecedented numbers in May and June, 423—well after Sogdianus is apt to have abandoned his bid. A mobilization order had evidently been issued, and those who held their land as a fief from the King needed silver in order to properly equip themselves for the war to come.[17]

Among the purebred Achaemenids with a better claim to the kingship than Ochus, the satrap Pissouthnes may have been preeminent. He was not just a cousin or nephew of Artaxerxes. He was the son of the elder Xerxes' full brother Hystaspes or of this Xerxes' like-named son. As such, he was, like Artaxerxes himself, a direct descendant in the legitimate line of the Persian empire's founder Cyrus and of the elder Darius. Moreover, this Pissouthnes was a man of considerable experience and acumen, who had in the past made a great deal of trouble for the Athenians, as we have seen. As of 423, he had been in command at Sardis in western Anatolia for a period verging on, if not exceeding, twenty years. Furthermore, by dint of his office and of the role he had long played in harassing the Athenians in Asia Minor and the Aegean, he had long had at his beck and call a substantial force of cavalrymen, archers, and footsoldiers armed in the Persian fashion. This force he had supplemented with a host of Greek hoplites led in 423, as it happens, by an Athenian mercenary captain named Lycon.

This particular combination of arms was by no means unusual. In the satrapies bordering on the Mediterranean, it was, in fact, the norm. It was with an army thus constituted that Artyphius, who had inherited from his father Megabyzus the province in Syria known as "the Land Across-the-River," mounted in or soon after 423 a rebellion on behalf of Ochus' full brother Arsites; and with this force he twice defeated the royal armies sent to quell the revolt. Moreover, well before the collapse of Artyphius' enterprise—in all likelihood, quite soon after its inception—Pissouthnes also launched a rebellion, almost certainly on his own behalf.[18]

To put down the latter of these two revolts, Ochus dispatched to western Anatolia two Persians of some prominence along with the future satrap Tissaphernes—who, tellingly, bore the same patronymic as Stateira and Teriteuchmes. It is by no means certain that Tissaphernes shared a father with these two. As scholars have pointed out, within the ambit of the court established by the elder Darius, Hydarnes (*Vidarna* in Old Persian) was a common enough name. But a kinship tie is more than merely possible. Indeed, given what we know of the close dynastic family alliance that Ochus had forged with the offspring of the first Darius' co-conspirator of that name, it is improbable that a figure of such high standing at this time with a father named Hydarnes was a member of a completely different lineage. Moreover, it is worth noting that, on the eve of Xerxes' invasion of Greece, "the general of the coast men" in Anatolia was a figure named Hydarnes who may well have been the Hydarnes son of Hydarnes subsequently in charge of the royal bodyguard. Tissaphernes was in all likelihood a scion of a great Persian family, exceedingly well connected at court, which had a long-standing association with and considerable property within the region to which he was sent on this occasion.[19]

OCHUS AND ATHENS

There can be no doubt that the prospects of Pissouthnes' rebellion and, for that matter, those of the revolt initiated slightly earlier by Artyphius would have been greatly enhanced had the Athenians facilitated either's hiring additional mercenaries or otherwise lent either insurgent their assistance. But from this course of action, despite the fact that at Athens they had long hosted Artyphius' brother Zopyrus, they refrained. Instead, with an eye to the exigencies they faced as a consequence of their second war with the Peloponnesians, they sagely sided with the likely victor in the ongoing succession struggle.

To this end, the Athenians dispatched in the late summer or fall of 423 an embassy, led by a man named Epilycus son of Teisander, to negotiate with the claimant by this time ensconced in Susa something more than just a continuation of the informal arrangement, occasionally honored in the breach, that Callias son of Hipponicus had originally contracted on Athens' behalf with Xerxes circa 466 and that he had later, after a hiatus, managed to renew in 449 with that monarch's son Artaxerxes. What the Athenians had in mind was

something new: a relationship of *philía*—of friendship and cooperation—confirmed by a pouring of libations [*spondaí*] and a solemn
taking of oaths, which would affirm, for the first time, that there was
amity between the two powers and bring Athens, at least notionally,
within the orbit of the King himself. This is the species of relationship that Xerxes' minion Hydarnes "the general of the coast men"
had sought to work out with the Lacedaemonians on the eve of his
master's invasion of Greece. To this end, in 423/2, Epilycus and his
colleagues almost surely offered Ochus a *quid pro quo*. For it is telling that Artyphius' rebellion and that of Pissouthnes each collapsed
when the minions of this second Darius managed to bribe the Hellenic mercenary bands arrayed against them.[20]

If, in the winter of 413/12, Darius II was prepared to jettison not
only the long-standing agreement with Athens renewed just ten
years before but also the newly established relationship of *philía*, it
was not, as many scholars assume, because the Athenians were then
sponsoring the resistance to Tissaphernes' rule as satrap being carried on from the Carian highlands by Pissouthnes' illegitimate son
Amorges. To begin with, it is not at all clear that the Athenians were
supplying the latter with aid *prior to* the Great King's issuance of
instructions to Tissaphernes, and it seems unlikely that they did so.
Moreover, even if they were engaged in such shenanigans, this
breach of the spirit of their new relationship will have been regarded
as, at most, an excuse for what the younger Darius for other reasons
wished to do.

In distant Susa, Amorges' activities were surely looked on as no
more than a petty annoyance. There were peoples all over the empire,
living in hilly or mountainous regions, whom the King did not
directly rule but dealt with in the manner of his Assyrian and Chaldaean predecessors—through diplomacy, gift-giving, and mutual
exchange—and otherwise for the most part left to their own devices.
The Mysians and Pisidians of western Asia Minor were among those
whom the Achaemenid monarchs ordinarily handled in this fashion.
Moreover, as we have seen, the borderlands in western and south-

western Anatolia had long been an arena for skirmishing between the Athenians and the Mede. Although Tissaphernes had been ordered to put an end to Amorges' depredations, this was largely a matter of local concern, for nothing in this regard seems to have been communicated to Pharnabazus. If, at this time, the younger Darius was prepared to abandon altogether the long-standing arrangement between Athens and Persia and to repudiate the tie of *philía* and the accord confirmed by *spondaí* and a taking of oaths that had at least nominally governed their relations for more than a decade, it was surely because he discerned in the new situation a god-given invitation to recover what, everyone in Persia agreed, was rightly his: the lands that Cyrus, Cambyses, and Darius had acquired and that his father and grandfather had lost.[21]

Persia's Great King no doubt longed for more than what he expressly demanded on this particular occasion—and not solely because aggrandizement tends to be the aim of those who wield tyrannical power. Although—in conquering Anatolia and subduing Ethiopia in addition to Iran, Mesopotamia, Syria, Egypt, and eastern Libya—Cyrus and Cambyses had united the Near East to a far greater degree than the most successful of their Assyrian and Babylonian predecessors; and although the elder Darius had extended the empire's boundaries even further—to Afghanistan and the Indus valley in the east and to Aegean Thrace and the northwest coast of the Black Sea in the west—Achaemenid Persia was by no means a saturated power. That it could never be, and the reasons were religious.

The inscriptions in Old Persian, Akkadian, and Elamite posted by the elder Darius and by Xerxes, Artaxerxes, and the younger Darius make it clear that the kingship of the Achaemenids was—like the Sumerian, Babylonian, Assyrian, Elamite, and Median monarchies that had preceded it—a sacral regime and that the rule of the Persians and of their Great King was rooted in and justified by a political theology stipulating that their monarch was the chosen one of their great god. Whether this was true as well for the Achaemenids' Teipsid predecessors we do not know. That the investiture ceremony initiated by Cyrus took place at Pasargadae is clear, and there is reason to connect these proceedings with the goddess Anahita. The elder Darius and his successors did not neglect this ceremony, and they were buried on that site. Indeed, with an eye to their legitimacy, they went out of their way to assert a continuity between Teipsid and Achaemenid rule. It is nonetheless striking that, in the Bisitun inscription, Darius hints at the opposite, stressing quite emphatically, in a way that raises questions about the status of his Teipsid predecessors, that he and his co-conspirators are all Persians, and it is no less striking that Anahita passes unmentioned in the inscriptions posted by the elder Darius and his first three successors.

Darius' father Hystaspes bore the name of Zoroaster's patron and, when he is first mentioned, we find him serving in Parthia in eastern Iran, not far from the region where that prophet is known to have resided. This is telling, for the inscriptions which the first Darius and his first three successors posted mention by name no god apart from the Ahura Mazda championed in the first Zoroastrian texts. Moreover, these inscriptions espouse a faith that verges on—if it does not, in fact, embrace—monotheism. In them Ahura Mazda is represented as the creator of the universe and of all that is in it (including, one must suspect, "the other gods that are," mentioned therein), and there he is also depicted as a deity who has imposed on his king a universal mission—to propagate "the Truth" and suppress "the Lie," to stamp out chaos wherever it reigns, and to bring order, beauty, justice, and happiness to a divided world hitherto consigned to commotion, ugliness, injustice, and misery. If the Achaemenid monarchy associated itself with rational public administration, domestic tranquillity, irrigation, and gardening, it was because of its divinely imposed *mission civilisatrice*.

The monumental task assigned the Persian king within this cosmological scheme was rooted in the theological dualism that characterizes Zoroastrianism to this very day. Its necessity arose from the power exercised by the Evil Spirit Ahriman—the propagator of the Lie, the father of chaos, the instigator of division, the promoter of commotion, and the source of injustice and unhappiness. This god's appellation, found in Plutarch and in later Zoroastrian writings, is an elision of Angra Mainyu, the name assigned the satanic fomenter of opposition to Ahura Mazda described in the Gathas and elsewhere in the Avesta—the earliest of the Zoroastrian writings. According to Plutarch, Artaxerxes regarded Hellas as a part of the domain ruled by this Ahriman, and we can be confident that this was the opinion propagated by the first Darius, by Xerxes, and, in time, by Artaxerxes' son and successor Darius II. If, as seems to have been the case, the agreements negotiated with Xerxes, Artaxerxes, and the second Darius by Callias, Epilycus, and their fellow Athenian ambassadors never took the form of a proper treaty between equal and independent powers to which the King, as well as the Athenians, deigned to swear adherence, it was because, even when driven to despair and forced to back off, the chosen one of the great god Ahura Mazda could not solemnly sanction a boundary limiting the realm that was rightly his—for, at least in principle, he really was what he always said he was: the King of Kings, the rightful ruler of the earth in its entirety.[22]

Of course, none of this prevented the younger Darius from facing reality and working out a *modus vivendi* with the Lacedaemonians. There is always a yawning gap between political aspirations and achievement. In any case, the elder Xerxes had set a precedent justifying such a compromise. Moreover, although that monarch's acquiescence in defeat is said to have occasioned his assassination, his successor Artaxerxes—after himself suffering a defeat at Cypriot Salamis no less devastating than the one inflicted on his father at Eurymedon—had eventually found himself forced to swallow his pride and follow suit; and this time the notables of Persia had—no doubt with great reluctance—gone along. On the interpretation adopted by these two potentates and in time sullenly accepted by their underlings, the political theology underpinning the legitimacy of the Achaemenid monarchy did not require that the Great King accomplish or even try to accomplish immediately what it clearly lay beyond his power to do. But, although this concession to time and circumstance evidently secured a grudging acceptance within the Persian realm, everyone remembered the astonishing feats of conquest accomplished by Cyrus, Cambyses, and the elder Darius; and none in their number could help but think that those who had come after had somehow fallen short. Furthermore, the peculiar species of Zoroastrianism adopted by these Achaemenids dictated that a *modus vivendi* of the sort embodied in deals of the kind forged by Xerxes, Artaxerxes, and the younger Darius be regarded as regrettable and as no more than a temporary expedient. The situation of the King of Kings differed from that of the ruling order in a Greek *pólis* in two crucial particulars: he could not even pretend that Persia was a saturated power and that by means of a genuine peace treaty he had provided for amity and peace; and he could never acknowledge that he was negotiating with an equal.[23]

The awkwardness of this situation may have weighed more heavily on the Ochus who called himself Darius than it had on his father. After all, he resembled Gylippus son of Cleandridas, the lone Spartiate whom the Lacedaemonians had dispatched to Syracusa. He, too, was a half-breed and a bastard—and, like the original Darius, he undoubtedly felt the need, as a usurper, to prove his worth. The disaster suffered by the Athenians in Sicily is apt to have looked to this Great King like a golden opportunity to do something reminiscent of the great-grandfather whose name he had made his own.

From the perspective of the younger Darius, the war about to take place in the eastern Aegean was what the conflict in Sicily had been for Sparta. It was a proxy war—from which he could greatly profit without taking any serious risks and without committing much in the way of manpower. It would bleed Persia's longtime foe Athens. It would reduce her prestige. It might even break the stalemate between the power dominant at sea in the eastern Mediterranean and the power dominant on land in western Asia that had, much to the dismay of successive Great Kings, made of the Athenian–Persian conflict an enduring strategic rivalry. All that was required was silver and gold, and the younger Darius had plenty of that.

AN ENTANGLING ALLIANCE

The Spartans were by no means ignoramuses. They were well-practiced in diplomacy before the Persians even came on the scene; and they had become close observers of the Mede well before the Athenians had. If, on the advice of the Athenian turncoat Alcibiades son of Cleinias and his faithful *xénos* Endius son of Alcibiades (who just happened to be an ephor in 413/12), the Lacedaemonians embraced the cause of the Chian and Erythraean insurgents and accepted Tissaphernes' promise of assistance, it was not because they were hopelessly naive and had succumbed to the blandishments of their Athenian guest and his Spartan guest-friend. They recognized the danger inherent in such an enterprise, and not a few in their number were nervous about the consequences of such an entanglement with the Mede. But, although the Lacedaemonians had not believed Agis' father Archidamus when, on the eve of their second Attic war, he had told them of the hitherto unpalatable arrangements that they would have to make if they were to reduce the Athenians to submission, they now knew the score. From bitter experience in that armed conflict, they had learned that the subjection of Athens was for them an existential necessity and that it could no longer be accomplished by a military campaign conducted simply and solely on land. This could be achieved, they were now fully aware, only by a coalition that wrested from that enterprising people the dominion they had established over the sea some sixty-five years before.[24]

The Lacedaemonians had promised to produce twenty-five new triremes. They had requisitioned another seventy-five from their allies in the Peloponnesus and Boeotia; and, as we have seen, quite a few in their number entertained the hope that the western Greeks would supply a great many more. But those who knew something of maritime warfare must have strongly suspected that, even if the latter set of galleys actually appeared, the fleet they deployed might prove insufficient. The sixty triremes of the Chians with their veteran crews were likely to prove invaluable; and the financial support on offer from the satrap of the Great King ensconced at Sardis was apt to be indispensable. This they believed. And, as we shall soon see, they were right to do so.[25]

Lacedaemon was not awash in precious metals, to say the least. Unlike the Athenians, the Spartans had no silver mines; and, since they were isolated and more or less self-sufficient economically, they were not a commercial polity able to exact much in the way of harbor fees. Nor did they at this time possess an empire from which they could draw *phóros*. In fact, happily embracing autarchy, they had long eschewed even the minting of coins. To say that they were in no position to fund a great war at sea would be a gross understatement, and their friends at Corinth, the only commercial power of any real significance in their Peloponnesian alliance, were no longer wealthy enough even to try.[26]

It took well over a talent of silver and, at times, considerably more to produce and equip a single trireme; and, at a drachma a day per mariner, it cost another talent and sometimes more to keep it and its crew of two hundred on station for a single month. Moreover, this was just the beginning—for hoplites and light-armed troops would also be needed; and, when sent across the Aegean, they, too, would require maintenance and pay.[27] To secure a decisive victory over the longtime lords of the sea might well require hundreds of triremes, thousands of infantrymen, and hard labor far from home over a great many months. Where else, if not from Persia, could funding on a sufficient scale be secured?

CHAPTER TWO

SKIRMISHING IN IONIA

In battle, other things being equal, the more numerous
legions win.

HALFORD J. MACKINDER

I F THE HISTORIAN Thucydides son of Olorus is to be trusted,
there were a great many in Hellas who took it for granted that the
war being mounted against Athens' hegemony would take next
to no time, and there are scholars who suppose that the Persians
entertained similar illusions.[1] That some did so goes without saying.
Desire is all too frequently the mother of delusion. But it is not clear
that the younger Darius, Tissaphernes son of Hydarnes, and Pharnabazus son of Pharnaces were among those who succumbed to this
propensity. Although they were—all three—recent arrivals at the
helm, they were the heirs of men who had learned the hard way that
one should never underestimate the Athenians, and there were
surely some among the advisors of the King and his viceroys who
harbored and gently voiced grave doubts.

The argument applies with no less force to the Lacedaemonians.
Their forebears had witnessed the Athenian performance at Artemisium, Salamis, and Mycale; and, though not present, they were aware
of what the Athenians and their allies had achieved at Eurymedon
without Peloponnesian support. The *gérontes* had all, moreover,
been of age when Athens had bounced back from the catastrophe in

Egypt and annihilated the Persian fleet at Cypriot Salamis. A great many Spartiates still in the ranks remembered how well the Athenians had weathered the calamity that they had suffered at the time of the plague. Although, in the spring of 412, a majority at Lacedaemon were blinded by ambition and hope, there were surely more than a few who suspected that the war at sea about to be launched would be hard-fought.

After all, victory at sea depended then, as it depends now, on expertise; and the Athenian mariners had been honing the requisite skills for something like three-quarters of a century, as everyone knew. No community within the Spartan coalition—not the Syracusans, for sure, nor even the Corinthians—had helmsmen, specialists, and rowers as capable of performing the elaborate maneuvers in open water that the Athenians had been practicing for just under seven decades. The number of proficient veteran seamen that Athens could muster and deploy was, of course, much reduced. But this had also been true after the Egyptian debacle—and a few years thereafter the Athenians were more formidable at sea than ever before. Only the foolhardy can have supposed that they could not and would not put up a terrific fight.

Needless to say, the news that reached Athens from Sicily in mid- or late October 413 came as a great shock. At first, Thucydides tells us, it provoked outright disbelief—even in the face of testimony from those, known to have been eyewitnesses of the calamity, who had themselves narrowly escaped death and enslavement and had made their way home. The Athenians were not inured to defeat. They had encountered setbacks from time to time—most recently, at Delium, Amphipolis, and Mantineia. But they had not suffered a genuine catastrophe on the battlefield or at sea in forty years, and the destruction of their forces in Egypt at that time was the first such disaster they had ever experienced.

Naturally, in 413, when incredulity gave way to dismay, the Athenians assessed their losses—the triremes, the nautical specialists, the rowers, the hoplites, the cavalry, and, more generally, the men in the prime of life (whom, for understandable reasons, they deemed irreplaceable). At the same time, they counted the galleys in their dockyards, the money in their treasury, the naval crews at their disposal—and they judged them grossly insufficient. Initially, we are told, they despaired as they never had before, fearing that the Sicilians would soon descend upon the Peiraeus, that their enemies nearer home would redouble their efforts and join the Sicilians in attacking them on both land and sea, and that the members of their confederation would revolt. At first, they blamed others but not themselves, turning their anger on the orators who had advocated the venture (Alcibiades among them) and venting their rage on the oracle-mongers, the seers, and the other diviners who had predicted its success.

Then, if Thucydides is to be trusted, his compatriots regained their composure, resolved not to give in, and began soberly making preparations for the great onslaught to come. First and foremost, they concentrated their attention on their fleet, gathering timber and collecting money wherever they could, as they would continue to do throughout the war. They also acted to make sure of their allies—above all, the cities on the island of Euboea—and, in the civic arena, they adopted an uncharacteristic posture of moderation with regard to public expenditures.

In addition, the Athenians did something unprecedented, suggesting a precipitous decline, if not a complete collapse, in the trust they had hitherto reposed in their political institutions and a deep nostalgia for the species of statesmen who had guided them in bygone days as well as a willingness to modify or jettison the institutions of the radical democracy and a genuine openness to rumination of a practical sort concerning a change of regime. The comic poet Eupolis caught the mood of the time when, at the City Dionysia in 413, 412, or 411, he resurrected the *stratēgós* Myronides along with Solon, Miltiades, Aristeides, and Pericles; put them on stage; and publicly lamented the poor leadership accorded the city in his own time.[2]

In this mood, the Athenians voted, with the Spartan *gerousía* in

97

mind, to create a new magistracy: a probouleutic council of ten elders called *próbouloi*—one representing each of Athens' ten tribes. Its member were not to be chosen in the traditional democratic manner by lot. They were to be directly elected, and they had to be at least forty years old. In practice, however, if we are to judge by the citizens known to have been chosen, those actually selected were men at least twenty years older than that. This council was supposed to be a repository of wisdom. Its members were charged with providing timely counsel pertinent to the city's present circumstances. To this end, they were authorized not only to convoke a meeting of the Council of Five Hundred—on which the exceptionally wealthy men whose estates produced at least five hundred measures of grain, olive oil, or wine [*pentakosiomédimnoi*]; those rich enough to be able to keep horses [*hippeîs*]; and the *zeugítai* smallholders were eligible to serve—but also to summon thereafter the city's general assembly, which included the propertyless thetes as well. It was, we must presume, the task of the *próbouloi* to set the agenda for these two bodies.

Among those whom the Athenians elected to what was in effect a second probouleutic council were two elderly men of great distinction, men who had known Cimon and who had served on the board of *stratēgoí* alongside Pericles. The first was the celebrated tragedian Sophocles son of Sophillus and the second, Hagnon son of Nicias—who had founded Amphipolis a quarter of a century before and who had been in 421 a signatory of both the Peace of Nicias and Athens' abortive alliance with Sparta. "In a panic with regard to the immediate circumstances," Thucydides concludes, the Athenians "were ready to put things in good order, as the common people are inclined to do."

It is not fortuitous that the two words—*eutakteîn* and a cognate of *sōphrosúnē*—which the Athenian historian deploys in describing his compatriots' resort to good order and their turn to economizing evoke qualities that oligarchies tended to claim as exclusively their own. With considerable justification, Aristotle in his *Politics* associates the institution of *próbouloi* with that species of government.[3]

THE FIRST CAMPAIGNING SEASON

The story that Thucydides tells about the initial stages of the maritime conflict that followed tends to leave readers unsatisfied. This is no doubt in part due to the premature death of its author and the unfinished character of his draft of the eighth and final book of his history, which ends abruptly in mid-sentence in the year 411, some seven years prior to the date at which the son of Olorus intended to bring his account to a conclusion. Within book eight, there are summaries of some of the arguments that were made, but no full-blown speeches as such. At times, it reads like a random collection of episodes. It is as if we have been presented with an unpolished fragment; and some scholars think that it consists of an incoherent series of undigested, overlapping narratives sketched out at different times on the basis of intelligence culled from different informants.[4]

While the eighth book surely is an incomplete draft, it is by no means as unpolished and undigested as some suppose. If Thucydides' account elicits frustration, there is another and more telling reason. As in the fifth book of his history, he is here describing a world in which an intercommunal order that was always fragile has given way to anarchy. If it seems as if he is relating an unconnected series of events, it is because disconnect and disarray had become the norm in the eastern Aegean—and what leaves us baffled and unsatisfied today was even more frustrating and confusing for those who lived through it. Only, for them, it was a nightmare to boot—a nightmare ongoing and so unpleasant that many of the cities in the Aegean that withdrew from the Athenian alliance in and after 412 eventually swallowed their misgivings and joined with Athens in establishing a second league with a similar purpose in 377, a century after the foundation of the first. It is their bitter experience with intercommunal anarchy that Thucydides, by way of his narrative technique, is attempting to bring home to his readers—especially in the first half of his history's eighth book.[5]

The struggle that ensued in the spring of 412 was, indeed, chaotic. Neither party to the conflict had the naval resources ready to hand that would have been required for a quick and decisive victory. The vessels promised by Syracusa and the other cities in the Greek West had not yet made an appearance, and the Peloponnesians were still in the process of building a fleet. Athens should have been better prepared, but she was not. So, the two sides scrambled to build triremes and assemble and train crews. Then, as galleys became available, they were sent off to the eastern Aegean.[6]

On the eve of their second war with the Peloponnesians, the Athenians had voted to set up an emergency fund of one thousand silver talents (ca. 23.5 tons)—not to be touched, upon pain of death, unless an attack on the city was in the offing. At the same time, no doubt at Pericles' urging, they had decided to set aside each year as a force in reserve the one hundred best triremes in the fleet with their trierarchs and not to deploy these except with that money against that peril and to impose the same penalty on anyone who proposed using this force in any other circumstance. The only way around this entrenchment clause was for the assembly—in all likelihood, an assembly with a quorum of six thousand—to pass a decree conferring legal immunity [adeía] on the citizen proposing to employ the emergency fund or deploy the fleet in reserve and on those who put the question to the assembly and voted to proceed in this fashion.

The emergency fund was still in existence, but the second element within this sensible scheme the Athenians had at some point jettisoned—perhaps when they were called upon to send a relief expedition to Sicily in 413, perhaps when the Peace of Nicias was ratified in 421, perhaps earlier yet when their finances first began to suffer strain. Precisely when they did so we do not know. All that we can say is that there was no such reserve fleet available when the news of the disaster at Syracusa reached Athens and it was most needed. Had the Athenians possessed a first-rate fleet of such a size in the spring of 412, they might well have been able to head off rebellions and inflict a crushing blow on the gradually emerging Peloponnesian fleet.[7]

The Spartans had a plan. It appears to have been the product of a compromise rendered necessary by the division of authority that was to bedevil strategic decision-making at Sparta early in the Ionian War. Worked out at a conference of the Lacedaemonian alliance held at Corinth and presided over by the Eurypontid king Agis son of Archidamus, this compromise was an attempt to reconcile the desires of the authorities at Lacedaemon, who had one set of priorities, with those of Agis himself, who had another. This fact notwithstanding, the agreement made excellent geopolitical sense—at least in theory.

The Spartans intended, as they had ever since the demographic crisis brought on by the great earthquake of 465/4, to be exceedingly parsimonious in the expenditure of citizen manpower. They no doubt remembered with pride what Brasidas as a solo performer had accomplished in Thrace in the 420s, and they surely marveled at what Gylippus had quite recently achieved in Sicily. If a half-breed could succeed in so magnificent a fashion, they are apt to have thought, purebred Spartiates could surely do the like or even better if they were dispatched to each of the principal places that Lacedaemon hoped to wrest from her foe. They proposed, therefore, to send a flotilla from the Peloponnesus to Chios under the command of a full citizen named Chalcideus and there raise a rebellion in accord with the decision reached by the authorities at Sparta. Then, they resolved to have Alcamenes son of Sthenelaidas proceed to Lesbos with an armada encompassing the Peloponnesian galleys originally sent to Chios as well as those of the Chians, where he would raise another rebellion of the sort that Agis had at first intended.

Finally, they planned to have a Spartiate named Clearchus son of Ramphias, who enjoyed the favor of Agis and just happened to be the *próxenos* of the Byzantines at Lacedaemon, conduct this combined fleet on to the Hellespont, the Sea of Marmara, and the Bosporus, where he in turn would make mischief for the Athenians. This Clearchus had one thing in common with Alcamenes. His father had played a prominent role on the eve of Sparta's second Attic war. As a diplomat in 431, Ramphias had helped deliver to Athens Lacedaemon's final ultimatum. Later, in 422, on the eve of the negotiations that produced the Peace of Nicias, he had been one of the three men sent on an abortive mission to conduct reinforcements to Brasidas in Thrace.

In the early stages of this enterprise, the Spartans and their allies no doubt hoped that Chalcideus and perhaps the son of Sthenelaidas could secure from Tissaphernes the support promised. Later on, the son of Ramphias would presumably look to Pharnabazus. The larger point was not, however, the number of talents of silver on offer from each of the two satraps—though, given the enormous costs apt to be incurred and the limited resources available to the Spartans and their allies, this was more than a mere inducement. The principal aim underpinning the plan worked out at Corinth under Agis' presidency was to gain control of the trade route by which cereals from the Black Sea were conveyed to the markets of the Aegean.

As Xenophon later tells us, the son of Archidamus was alert to the fact that grain was what we would now call a strategic substance, and he knew that this was especially the case at this stage in Sparta's enduring struggle with Athens. In ordinary circumstances, the route that ran from the Euxine through the Bosporus, the Sea of Marmara, and the Hellespont to the Mediterranean served as an umbilical cord of sorts for the Athenians and for the numerous cities within their domain that were incapable of fully making provision for themselves from their domestic agricultural resources. In the circumstances pertaining in 412, the Peloponnesian presence at Deceleia made the Athenians far more dependent on foodstuffs imported from the Black Sea and elsewhere than was the norm. To this, Agis was particularly sensitive. From his perch on the slopes of Mount Parnes at Deceleia, we are told, he watched every day with increasing frustration as a parade of merchant ships bearing grain from the Euxine arrived at the Peiraeus.[8]

To carry out the plan outlined by Agis and the conferees, the Spartans had to shift the Peloponnesian fleet, which at this point numbered thirty-nine triremes, from the Corinthian to the Saronic Gulf and do so with alacrity. The need for speed and a concern for safety militated against a circumnavigation of the Peloponnesus. So, they dispatched three unnamed Spartiates—quite possibly the three assigned the Chian, Lesbian, and Hellespontine commands—to the Isthmus of Corinth where it was possible to cart the requisite triremes laboriously, one by one, overland from the former body of water to the latter via the *díolkos*, a paved trackway just a few miles in length.

To avoid greatly alarming the Athenians, the three Spartiates opted to divide their fleet into two squadrons, which would depart at separate intervals; and, after they had managed to transfer twenty-one of the galleys across the Isthmus, they were ready and even eager to set out for Chios with the first of these units. But the Corinthians balked because it was time for the Isthmian Games and the attendant truce was already in effect; and Agis, sensitive to the opportunity this afforded him, intervened on their behalf and personally took charge of the expedition.

The celebration of these games and the truce associated with them occasioned a considerable delay damaging to the endeavor. During this hiatus, the Athenians, who had grown suspicious, sent to Chios to lodge an accusation a *strategós* of some prominence named Aristocrates son of Scellias, who had been—like Nicias, Demosthenes, and Hagnon—a signatory to both the Peace of Nicias and the abortive alliance with Sparta that followed it. When the authorities on the island, who had not taken the multitude into their confidence, firmly denied the charge, he requested as a pledge of their continued commitment to the Athenian alliance a contingent of triremes—no doubt with an eye to having hostages in hand—and the Chians dispatched seven galleys. In the meantime, the Athenians in attendance at the Isthmian Games cottoned more fully on to the conspiracy then underway. In consequence, when the twenty-one Peloponnesian galleys set out for Chios from Cenchreae, the main Corinthian port on the Saronic Gulf—tellingly with Agis' nominee Alcamenes (and not Chalcideus) in command—the Athenians were

on watch, and they managed to intercept these vessels with thirty-
seven triremes of their own and to chase the enemy squadron back
to a deserted harbor called Spiraeum some distance further southeast along the coast of the Corinthiad. There they attacked the flotilla, killed Alcamenes, and established a blockade.[9]

This sequence of events disheartened the authorities at Lacedaemon, who had been on the verge of dispatching to Chios five triremes
of their own with Chalcideus on board. Had it not been for the persistence of Alcibiades son of Cleinias, Thucydides intimates, they
might well at this point have abandoned the enterprise altogether.
But it was well known that this Athenian turncoat enjoyed close connections with the notables dominant on Chios and Lesbos; at Ephesus, Miletus, and Cyzicus; and in the other cities of consequence
scattered throughout the eastern Aegean and along both shores of
the Hellespont, the Sea of Marmara, and the Bosporus. And so, with
strong support from his guest-friend Endius, he managed to convince the board of five ephors to persevere and to send him along
with Chalcideus to the eastern Aegean. Then, no doubt to the chagrin of Lacedaemon's Eurypontid king, these two took charge of the
expedition he had planned; and, with a tiny squadron of galleys,
they set out to persuade the Chians and their neighbors to revolt.[10]

The situation faced by Chalcideus and Alcibiades was by no
means hopeless. As the latter surely knew, the cities in Ionia were
virtually defenseless thanks to the policy pursued by his compatriots. Long before, presumably at some point after 449 when Artaxerxes agreed to the accommodation pressed on him by Athens'
envoy Callias son of Hipponicus, the subject allies of Athens situated on the Aegean islands and along the Anatolian coast had been
told to tear down their walls, presumably so that they could not easily mount a rebellion against their hegemon. Moreover, in the long
and lovely period of peace that they had enjoyed subsequent to Callias' diplomatic achievement, very few of these cities had felt the
need or a desire to train and maintain on any scale a civic militia of
hoplites. Next to no one in the interim had imagined that, in the

foreseeable future, anyone would challenge the Athenians at sea, launch a naval assault on any of her allies, attack by land the *póleis* in Anatolia, or otherwise take advantage of the fact that the cities in the region were now unfortified.

In Ionia, there had once been a number of island communities that were exceptions to this rule. But, thanks to the rebellions launched by the Samians in the late 440s and by the Mytilenians and all but one of the smaller cities on Lesbos in 428, there were, as we have seen, only two such communities left—Methymna on Lesbos, which had remained doggedly loyal to Athens in 428, and Chios. These two *póleis* not only continued, as before, to supply ships to the Athenian alliance rather than *phóros*. They also retained their autonomy, their laws, and their walls. Of the two, as we have seen, Chios was by far the larger, the wealthier, and the more important.[11]

If, then, Chalcideus and Alcibiades could win over Chios, the rest would be relatively easy (or so it may have seemed). And, of course, they were well-positioned to persuade the Chians if they moved quickly before word reached Ionia about the fleet trapped at Spiraeum. It was, after all, the authorities in that *pólis* who had initiated this scheme. Moreover, on the part of these islanders, more than mere ambition was involved. None of the citizens of Chios can have been happy about the grave losses they had suffered as a consequence of being dragged into Athens' foolhardy venture in Sicily; and, thanks to the damage that the Athenians had inflicted on themselves while there, the Chians were no longer as afraid of their hegemon as they had been hitherto.

Care was taken, nonetheless, to stampede the members of the council [*Boulé*], which appears to have been Chios' principal governing body. In concert with the authorities in charge on the island, Alcibiades and Chalcideus sprung a surprise on its inhabitants, by staging a sudden and unexpected arrival of their flotilla at a time when, they knew, the governing council would actually be in session. There, in a manner reminiscent of the approach taken by Brasidas just over a decade before in Thrace, they both made rousing

Map 8. Ionia and the Eastern Aegean

speeches, promising that a great many more ships were on the way; and they carried the day. In short order, Erythrae then joined the rebellion, and Clazomenae, which was situated nearby, was induced to follow suit. It may have been in this connection that the Chians first began issuing electrum staters on a standard allowing forty of them to be exchanged for a single Persian gold daric.[12]

It would be hard to exaggerate the significance of this turn of

106

events. The Lacedaemonians were, as we have seen, risk-averse, even timid—especially with regard to overseas commitments—and, on this occasion, they had already begun to lose heart. Had it not been for Alcibiades' recruitment of the Chians and for the wealth and the sixty triremes manned by experienced mariners that they were willing to devote to the cause, Sparta's venture in the Aegean might never have gotten off the ground.

The Athenians, for their part, had squandered the bulk of their reserves on the Sicilian expedition, and they were now desperately short of cash. Already in 413, as Demosthenes was preparing to conduct the relief fleet to Syracusa and as Agis arrived to build the fort at Deceleia, they were feeling the pinch. At that time, they scrapped the assessment and collection of the *phóros* and substituted in its place a five percent tax on all seaborne trade. This would, they hoped, produce more revenue.[13]

Whether the new tax actually brought in more revenue we do not know. All that can be said is that, in 412, the Athenians' intake was not enough to meet their most pressing needs. So, upon learning of the rebellion of Chios, the Athenians, fearing the worst, voted to tap for the very first time the emergency fund they had set aside in 431, and they then set out to build and deploy a genuinely substantial fleet. At first, the numbers involved were quite small. Without delay, they dispatched Strombichides son of Diotimos with eight vessels to squelch the revolt, and soon thereafter they sent a further twelve under a commander named Thrasycles. Then, to replace the seven Chian ships and the Athenian triremes they had been forced to withdraw from the squadron maintaining the blockade at Spiraeum, they manned another ten galleys, and they also resolved to deploy in due course an additional thirty.

Strombichides quickly established himself on the island of Samos. From there, he made an attempt to solidify Athens' position at Teos, which was situated on the Anatolian shore a short distance to the south of the Erythraic peninsula. At this point, however, the Peloponnesians had the advantage, thanks to the size of the Chian fleet. So, Chalcideus set out from that island *pólis* with twenty-three triremes supported by an infantry force supplied by the Erythraeans and Clazomenians, which marched south along the Anatolian shore. Badly outmatched, Strombichides then found himself forced to retreat back to Samos. It was, moreover, at Teos that we first hear of a military intervention on the part of the Mede—when a hyparch of Tissaphernes named Stages appeared to provide assistance to the Teians busy tearing down the wall that Strombichides and his Athenians had built on the landward side of their city. Later, Tissaphernes himself, intent on guaranteeing that community's subjection, would show up with a larger force to complete the job.

In the meantime, Chalcideus and Alcibiades armed the crews of their five vessels as hoplites and left them as a garrison on Chios and substituted for them as rowers men from the island. Then, manning these ships and twenty more supplied by the Chians, they jettisoned the plan worked out by the conference at Corinth over which Agis had presided and rowed off, not to Lesbos in the north, but to Miletus in the south—where, among the local notables who exercised great sway within that *pólis*, Alcibiades had a considerable number of friends. There they raised that once great city in revolt, and they began building fortifications. According to Thucydides, the aim of Cleinias' ambitious son was to bolster his own prestige, that of the Chians, and that of Chalcideus and Endius by accomplishing as much as possible before the arrival of reinforcements. This he achieved by getting to the city a short while before Strombichides— who, after being joined by Thrasycles and his naval squadron, had set out for the same destination and was now anchored at the little island of Lade, just off the Milesian coast.[14]

Another *stratēgós* named Diomedon eventually arrived from Athens with an additional ten triremes, and in time a commander named Leon showed up with a like number. There was further skirmishing of no real consequence along the Anatolian coast near Anaia— where, in the Samian *peraía* at the base of Mount Mycale, a collection of embittered, exiled Samian oligarchs had established themselves in the wake of the abortive Samian revolt nearly three decades before. There was also skirmishing in the vicinity of Teos, her southern neighbor Lebedos, and Aerae to the north.

Eventually, the twenty Peloponnesian triremes bottled up at Spiraeum launched a successful surprise attack against the blockading squadron and then, while under the command of a Spartiate named Astyochus who had been appointed navarch by the authorities at Lacedaemon, they slipped out of the trap they were in. In the aftermath, after being refitted at Cenchreae, these vessels set out in separate squadrons for Ionia, where Astyochus, who was to be the supreme allied commander in that theater, had preceded them with a handful of ships.

There was even an attempt, undertaken by the Chians on their own, to raise Lesbos in revolt with an eye to moving on from there to the Hellespont in fulfillment of Agis' original scheme. For this purpose, they dispatched thirteen triremes to the island. At the same time, an infantry force, made up of local contingents and of the Peloponnesian rowers whom Chalcideus had armed, slipped across to the mainland and marched resolutely along the Anatolian shore in the direction of Clazomenae and Aeolian Cumae under the command of a Spartiate named Eualas. Once the cities on Lesbos had cast off the Athenian yoke and the Chian fleet was ready to enter the Dardanelles, Eualas and his men were to proceed there on foot.

Soon thereafter, another flotilla, this one led by a *períoikos* named Diniades, rowed first to Methymna, which was centrally located on the north coast of Lesbos within sight of the Troad, and then to Mytilene, which was situated on the island's east coast in the south, to bring over the two principal Lesbian cities. Then, Astyochus, who may have been instructed to pursue the plan worked out at the conference at Corinth presided over by Agis, arrived on the scene. First, he presented himself on Lesbos at Pyrrha on the Gulf of Pyrrha (now known as the Gulf of Kalloni). Then, he visited Eresus on the south coast in the formidably mountainous, western reaches of the island. Thereafter, he dispatched a Spartiate named Eteonicus with a hoplite force to rally Antissa on the island's north coast in the west; and finally, with a handful of ships, he proceeded himself to Methymna—the second largest *pólis* on the island.

This effort quickly came to naught. For Diomedon and Leon soon appeared, and they managed to retake Mytilene, then in detail the rest of the island. Clazomenae, just off the Erythraic peninsula, and Polichne, her stronghold on the mainland, they also seized.[15]

The pattern thus far evident persisted through the remainder of the summer as reinforcements arrived for this side, then the other; and a see-saw struggle ensued. Thus, for example, the contingent at Lade, commanded by Strombichides and Thrasycles, made a descent on Panormus a short distance to the south of Miletus and killed Chalcideus while Leon and Diomedon, who were enterprising sorts, staged a three-pronged landing on Chios and defeated the Chian infantry in three different hoplite battles. Then they had their soldiers ravage the countryside with its well-stocked farms, which had gone untouched since the defeat of the Persians at Mycale in 479— and, by means of this operation, the two very nearly secured the city's return to the Athenian alliance.

In the meantime, a force of forty-eight Athenian warships, many of them transports, conducted by Phrynichus son of Stratonides and by Onomacles and Scironides reached Ionia, touched at Samos, and disgorged on the peninsula where Miletus was situated a thousand Athenian hoplites, fifteen hundred Argive infantrymen, and another thousand hoplites drawn from Athens' alliance. There—although the Milesians routed the Argives—the Athenians and the hoplites drawn from among their allies defeated the Peloponnesians as well as the infantry and cavalry supplied by Tissaphernes, then forced the Milesians back behind their walls, and set about investing the town. Athens would no doubt have recovered Miletus had it not been for the unexpected arrival of yet another Peloponnesian fleet—this one intended for Astyochus, but commanded for the nonce by a Spartiate named Therimenes. It consisted of thirty-three triremes supplied by the members of Sparta's alliance and of another twenty-two Sicilian ships commanded by the Syracusan statesman Hermocrates son of Hermon.

When this armada anchored at Teichioussa in the territory of Miletus well to the south of the town, Alcibiades rode over to implore the newcomers to hasten to that city's relief and prevent its circumvallation, warning them that otherwise Ionia would be lost. This they resolved to do. But before they could act, Phrynichus, for whom Thucydides has high praise, overcame the reluctance of his fellow commanders and persuaded them that, given the restricted character of Athens' resources, they should for the time being avoid unnecessary risk and withdraw to Samos—whence they could come to learn what sort of force they were up against and intelligently calculate what tack to take.

Although scholars are, for the most part, now inclined to criticize severely the decision Stratonides' son persuaded his colleges to take, in the circumstances this decision made very good sense. The Spartans and their allies were in a position to deploy eighty triremes against the Athenians' sixty-eight, and the Peloponnesian fleet appears to have been made up entirely of battleships while a quarter to a half of the galleys within the Athenian fleet were transports. Given the financial strain that Athens was under, most, if not all, of these transports are apt to have been superannuated triremes, no longer well-suited to warfare at sea. Moreover, if previous Athenian conduct when the city was in straitened circumstances is any guide, these vessels will have been rowed, for the most part, not by experienced mariners, trained to carry out complicated maneuvers, but by the hoplites being conveyed. The superiority at sea that the Athenians had once possessed could no longer be taken for granted.[16]

On the next day, the allied fleet presented itself, cleared for battle, at Miletus and then, when it became evident that the Athenians had withdrawn, returned to Teichioussa to retrieve the ships' tackle. There Therimenes and his subordinates encountered Tissaphernes who persuaded them to conduct their galleys south to Iasos in Caria, where Amorges, the bastard son of Pissouthnes, was holed up.

The Spartans and their allies had the advantage of surprise. Amorges and his adherents, who were certainly by now aligned with Athens, took it for granted that her mariners still controlled the seas. The son of Pissouthnes the Lacedaemonians captured alive, and they turned him over to Tissaphernes, who sent the man on to be disposed of by the Great King. Amorges' mercenaries they enrolled in their own infantry. Iasos they sacked. Its inhabitants, both slave and free, they handed over to Tissaphernes at the bargain basement price of a daric (ca. twenty drachmas) a head—which was less than one-eighth of what a slave sold for at Athens—and to the citizens in their number he restored their city. In the winter that followed, this satrap made arrangements for the future defense of Iasos and, we have reason to believe, took possession of Caria, if not also Lycia, in southwestern Anatolia. Then, he journeyed to Miletus, where he distributed a month's pay to the crews of every galley at the agreed-upon rate of a drachma a day, as his emissary seems to have promised at Lacedaemon.[17]

WINTER WARRIORS

During the first campaigning season, there were no great fleet actions. In fact, early on, there were no great fleets deployed; and later, when the number of galleys on station had grown, the two sides were inclined to husband their resources. What the Peloponnesians and the Chian allies accomplished, they achieved by establishing local superiority at the critical moment, and the like can be said regarding the Athenians. As Alfred Thayer Mahan would later observe, a timely concentration of forces can work wonders.

The events of 412 were a prelude to the mayhem to come. Each side had established a base—the Athenians at Samos, and the Spartans at Miletus—and it was from these two strongholds in the heart of Ionia that each force expected to launch future operations.

The Greek word for winter—*cheimṓn*—also means storm. As this suggests, the weather in the Mediterranean is frequently tempestuous in the colder months. Prior to the age of steam, all species of seagoing vessels—galleys and sailing ships alike—had to exercise extreme caution. For, when the wind came up and blew from an unexpected quarter, they were apt to be driven into and shattered on a lee shore. In classical antiquity, triremes, which were shallower in draft than sailing vessels and apt to be swamped in high seas, were especially vulnerable when caught in a storm. Ordinarily, this restricted campaigning at sea to the summer months. But this was no ordinary time—not, at least, for those engaged abroad, and not, to be fair, for their anxious compatriots back home. So, the great struggle continued in the first few wintry months as each side gathered resources and maneuvered for advantage.[18]

Fairly early in this period—in October or early November, 412—another fleet reached Samos from Athens. Consisting of thirty-five triremes, it was led by Strombichides, who had returned home, and by Charminus and Euctemon. The squadron occupied at Chios they summoned to Samos, and then the *stratēgoí* in the field drew lots. Strombichides, Onomacles, and Euctemon took thirty ships to Chios along with a unit of hoplites drawn from among the one thousand who had served in the summer at Miletus. The other commanders instituted a blockade of the latter city with the seventy-four vessels at their disposal.[19]

In late summer, Astyochus had retreated from Lesbos to Chios, which was, as we have seen, beleaguered. There, at about the time that Strombichides and his colleagues reached Samos, he got word of Therimenes' arrival at Miletus with a sizable fleet. Intent on reaching Miletus and taking up his command as navarch, Astyochus then set out from Chios with a fleet of ten Peloponnesian and ten Chian galleys. He did not make haste. With this force, he launched an abortive attack on a member of Athens' league, sometimes subject to Erythrae but otherwise unknown to us, named Pteleum. Then, he took a detour. And, with the help of an Egyptian named Tamos, whom Tissaphernes had made hyparch of Ionia, he tried in vain to recover Clazomenae, which had switched sides. In the process, he was caught up in a great gale that drove his trireme and perhaps several others to Phocaea, then Cumae, and forced the rest of his ships to seek shelter in the little islands in the vicinity of Clazomenae—where, while the winds blew, they hunkered down for eight full days.

Thereafter, a delegation crossed from Lesbos to ask Astyochus to help them renew their rebellion. Perhaps because of his instructions, he displayed interest. His subordinates—those dispatched by the Corinthians and Lacedaemon's other allies—were more than merely reluctant. They had witnessed the first attempt, and that was enough. And, when the fleet came back together again at Chios, after being scattered by a second storm, he was no more successful in his attempts at persuasion.

There was a new harmost on the island. His name was Pedaritus son of Leon. He had been sent out with Therimenes as Chalcideus' replacement, and he had subsequently marched from Miletus to Erythrae and crossed to Chios, bringing with him the mercenaries hitherto employed by Amorges. When Astyochus approached him, he flatly refused even to allow Astyochus to use the remaining Chian galleys for this purpose. Before finally heading off to Miletus with a small flotilla made up of the triremes from Corinth, Hermione, and Laconia, Astyochus lashed out at the Chians and told them not to expect any further assistance from him. There were further delays, involving a visit to Erythrae, but Astyochus did finally make it to Miletus.[20]

While Astyochus was en route to take up his command, further reinforcements reached the Anatolian coast. A Spartiate named Hippocrates had conducted a small flotilla, made up of a single Laconian galley, a second from Syracusa, and ten more from Thurii, where the faction hostile to Athens was now once again in charge. The Thurian triremes were commanded by a celebrated pancratiast from Ialysos on Rhodes, who was descended from a long line of renowned Olympic victors, and who was arguably the greatest athlete of his time. At the Olympic games, he had been thrice victorious, and he had done the like on eight occasions at the Isthmian Games, on seven at the Nemean Games, on four at the

Pythian Games, and on yet another four at the Panathenaic Games. The name of this aristocrat was Dorieus son of Diagoras. Thanks to a democratic revolution that had taken place in his native *pólis* more than a decade before, he was *persona non grata* in his homeland. But he was now more than just another refugee residing abroad. He was a naturalized citizen of Thurii in Magna Graecia. Hippocrates had presumably chosen the southern route from the bay of Laconia via Melos and perhaps even Crete. For these vessels fetched up some miles east of Triopium, the southwesternmost point in Anatolia, at Cnidus—a Spartan colony where Tissaphernes, from what was now his Carian redoubt, had sparked a rebellion.

When word of their arrival reached Miletus, Hippocrates was instructed to use half of these ships to guard Cnidus, which was at this time located quite near the site occupied today by the Turkish city of Datça. Like the other towns in the region, it was unfortified and vulnerable to attack. The remaining triremes were to cruise about Triopium at the end of the peninsula. There Hippocrates' galleys could seize the merchant ships on their way from Egypt—bearing, one must suspect, grain to Athens and to the cities dotted about the Aegean as well as papyrus and perhaps Phoenician linen and flax suitable for the rebuilding of Athens' fleet and for conducting repairs. To this the Athenians at Samos responded by sending a fleet to capture the triremes stationed at Triopium, which they did, and to recover Cnidus, a feat they very nearly pulled off.[21]

In the meantime, Strombichides, Onomacles, Euctemon, and their fleet of thirty galleys had reached Lesbos. Using it as a base, they had then landed on Chios the hoplites accompanying them. And there, at a well-situated place called Delphinium, which boasts of two harbors and is located on the east coast of the island some nine miles north of the main town, they began constructing fortifications. It was their aim to do to their renegade allies what the Peloponnesians were doing from Deceleia to their compatriots in Attica.

The Chians, having been defeated thrice in the summer, put up no resistance; and Pedaritus—who had with him not only the

Map 9. From Chios to Rhodes

Peloponnesian rowers armed by Chalcideus, but also the mercenaries once employed by Amorges—did not think the infantrymen under his command sufficient for an engagement. So, an appeal was sent to the navarch Astyochus at Miletus; and, when out of pique he did not respond, Pedaritus wrote to the authorities at Lacedaemon to lodge an accusation of misconduct, specifying that his petulant denial to the Chians of the support they required was an unjust (and perhaps treasonous) act.

Eventually, to be sure, Astyochus relented. But he did not do so until after the entrenchment of the Athenians at Delphinium had induced an immense number of the slaves on Chios to flee to that fort and then give the Athenians guidance as to how they might do the most damage to their former masters' estates.[22] Nor did Astyochus' change of mind have any immediate consequence. For, as he was preparing to send a force to the island, he received a request from Caunus on the border between Caria and Lycia that took precedence.

In December 412, at about the time of the winter solstice, a fleet of twenty-seven galleys had set out from the bay of Laconia for the eastern Aegean under the command of a Spartiate named Antisthenes. Their principal mission—made possible by the twenty-five talents of silver brought to Lacedaemon by Pharnabazus' emissaries Calligeitus and Timagoras—was to convey Agis' associate Clearchus to the post he had been assigned in the Hellespont and to help him wrest the cities in that strategically vital region from Athenian control.

On these ships, Antisthenes also carried a board of eleven *súmbouloi* or "advisors." Ordinarily, *súmbouloi* were not dispatched unless misconduct or cowardice on the part of a commander was suspected. The mission these eleven men had been assigned was twofold. They were to examine the conduct of the navarch Astyochus, whose performance on Lesbos and at Clazomenae had been lackluster and against whom Pedaritus had lodged a complaint. They had the authority to replace him with Antisthenes if this seemed appropriate—and they were also tasked with overseeing the conduct of the war more generally. At Sparta, where the resilience of the Athenians had by many been greatly underestimated, there was evidently discontent with regard to the lack of progress in the Ionian theater.

To avoid interception, this fleet took the southern route, rowing south past Cythera to Melos. Then, after unexpectedly encountering a flotilla of Athenian triremes, Antisthenes conducted the twenty-seven galleys further south to Crete, and ultimately they ended up on the southern coast of Anatolia—where they paused at Caunus, which had been a Persian stronghold since the early 420s, to send a messenger to Miletus requesting from the navarch a convoy.[23]

Astyochus then redirected the expedition meant for Chios to Caunus, taking with him, we have reason to suspect, something on the order of sixty-four triremes. En route, he paused briefly to sack the city of Meropis on the northeastern coast of Kos and to ravage the countryside. When he reached Cnidus in the middle of the afternoon, he was warned that there was an Athenian fleet lurking in the vicinity with an eye to intercepting the Peloponnesian force now docked at Caunus, and he was pressed to do something about it.

Immediately, Astyochus headed back out to sea where, as the late-afternoon winter light quickly faded, he encountered heavy rain and an overcast sky but found no Athenians. In the morning, however, when the light returned, the sky cleared, and Astyochus managed to reunite the scattered galleys in his fleet, there was an encounter off the little island of Syme, where some of the Athenian ships were anchored. In this skirmish, the Spartans and their allies lost three ships and the Athenians, six of the twenty vessels they had dispatched to the region. It was in the wake of this exchange that the two Peloponnesian fleets came together at Cnidus. While some of the galleys belonging to the Spartans and their allies were being repaired, Astyochus, anticipating the inquisition that he was about to undergo, made the most of his inconsequential victory by returning with the combined fleet to set up on Syme what the Greeks called a *tropaîon*—a trophy of sorts commemorating his fleet's defeat of a flotilla a good bit less than a third its size. Trifling though this exchange may have been, it was the very first time that a Peloponnesian fleet had inflicted on the Athenians a genuine defeat.[24]

From Cnidus, almost certainly at the suggestion of Dorieus son of Diagoras, the combined fleet then descended upon the nearby island of Rhodes where there were three *póleis* of substance—Cameiros, Lindos, and Ialysos. Like the other towns in the region, the urban areas associated with these three communities were bereft of fortifications. Their seizure the Spartans and their allies accomplished, apparently without encountering resistance, at the invitation of some of the leading men on the island—a number of of whom appear to have been Diagorid kinsmen of Dorieus. One of the aims of the Lacedaemonians was to recruit the host of experienced mariners residing on the island and to profit more generally from the manpower fit for infantry service that these *póleis* could supply. But, at this stage, their main concern was with money—for they were understandably nervous about their dependence on the Mede— and they were beginning to think that, like their longtime rival, they would have to extract *phóros* on a considerable scale from the communities in the Aegean.

The Athenians had gotten intelligence regarding the intentions of the Spartans and their allies. But, as usual, they arrived too late and could do no more than launch raids on Rhodes from Kos and the nearby island of Chalke. After collecting thirty-two talents of silver from those resident on Rhodes—a pittance in comparison with their needs—the Peloponnesians settled down on the island for eighty full days, from mid- or late January well into April, to wait for the campaigning season to begin. Their beleaguered Chian allies they left to the mercy of the Athenians at Delphinium, who managed in the interim to kill Pedaritus and a great many Chians and to reduce the city to famine.[25]

SOURCES OF DIVISIVENESS

As should be clear, the first half of this first winter was, from a strategic point of view, an extension of the summer. Once again, although the number of vessels stationed in the eastern Aegean had grown, there were no great fleet actions. Instead, there was a slow, gradual build-up of forces on both sides; and, for the most part, the Peloponnesians had the initiative. Thanks in part to the fact the cities located on the islands and the Anatolian shore were unfortified and generally lacked a disciplined infantry, neither side encountered much in the way of resistance.

Apart from Samos—which was, as we shall soon see, a special case—there does not seem to have been a single *pólis* zealously committed to the Athenian cause. There is, moreover, evidence suggesting that a considerable number of cities not singled out by Thucydides for close attention were perfectly willing to provide aid and comfort to the Peloponnesians. Thus, for example, in 412, when Peloponnesian galleys were threatened by the Athenians or caught in a storm, Ephesus, Phocaea, and Cumae on the Anatolian coast were prepared to afford these interlopers refuge. This fact notwithstanding, it would be inaccurate to say that the *póleis* in Athens' league were as one in seeking liberation from her hegemony. Although the smaller communities—Clazomenae and Teos, for example—were by no means fiercely loyal to Athens, they do not seem to have been fiercely hostile either. In the conflict taking place, their principal aim appears to have been to secure their own safety, and it is a reasonable guess that, throughout Ionia, zeal was soon less in evidence than consternation. The long peace these *póleis* had enjoyed under Athens' domination had had on them as polities a corrupting effect. It had been decades since anyone in a great many of these communities had given serious thought to civic defense.[26]

Moreover, even in cities that were zealously engaged, such as Chios and Miletus, there was dissent. The former *pólis* could be— and was—described as a *kósmos*. She was, as the word implies, well-ordered. She had almost always been well-governed. Thucydides remarked that, apart from the Chians, no people other than the Lacedaemonians had managed to combine the success, the prosperity, and the general well-being that the Greeks called *eudaimonía* with an avoidance of *húbris* and *manía* and an embrace of the modesty, moderation, and good sense that they termed *sōphrosúnē*. This no doubt had something to do with the fact that Lacedaemon and Chios both had abnormally large servile populations, treated them harshly, and had to cope with runaways who fled to the wild, wooded, mountainous regions in their territory, as Thucydides intimates. Of course, the slaves on Chios, as chattel purchased from here and there, were less of a menace than the helots of Messenia—who, as a people in bondage, shared a common language, cults, and history and who were, as a consequence, capable of cooperation and political *práxis*. But, this fact notwithstanding, the servile population on Chios was dangerous enough to be perceived as a threat, and it remains the case that, in a polity, there is nothing as effective in promoting fellow-feeling and civic unity and in discouraging arrogance, recklessness, and audacity as the permanent presence of a potential enemy.

Chios was governed by an oligarchy. But the rich slaveholders who seem to have filled the city's high offices were, nonetheless, careful to safeguard the interests of the city's substantial merchant population, and they went to considerable lengths to promote the species of consensus and civic solidarity that the Hellenes called *homónoia*—"being of the same mind." The effort the authorities put into making it easy for Alcibiades and Chalcideus to persuade their less wealthy fellow citizens that it was time for them to abandon the Athenian alliance is a case in point.[27]

Their machinations notwithstanding, there were those on Chios who thought this course of action imprudent and wrong. The city had been a stalwart, vitally important, and much appreciated ally of Athens for sixty-five years, and she had grown immensely wealthy in that span of time. There were, moreover, those in her ruling order who had reveled in the role that their compatriots had played within Athens' league. Ion son of Orthomenes—known to scholars as Ion of Chios—had been one such. A celebrated lyric poet, philosopher, tragedian, and man-about-town, he had spent many months at Athens in the company of Cimon son of Miltiades and the like, and the surviving fragments of his memoir *Epidēmíai* or *Sojourns* show that he remained a close observer of developments there for decades after that great man's death.

It is not, then, at all surprising that, when the infantrymen led by Diomedon and Leon thrice defeated the Chians and began ravaging their farmland, Ion's son Tydeus should have been prominent among those who were suspected of plotting a return to the Athenian fold. Nor is it astonishing that the authorities on the island wanted to handle these suspects "in as measured a manner as possible [*hópōs metriótata*]." It was their moderation and their sense of proportion that had made the *pólis* of the Chians a genuine *kósmos*. It stands to reason, then, that it would be a Spartan navarch and not Tydeus' fellow Chians who saw to seizing him and his associates as hostages and that the Spartan harmost subsequently assigned to the island would respond to what was for Lacedaemon a worsening situation not just by executing Tydeus and his supporters, but also by imposing on their surviving compatriots a much narrower oligarchy than the one that had existed prior to this time.

It is also no surprise that this turn in the direction of what the Greeks, with evident dislike, called *dunasteía* should give rise within this *pólis* to an ethos of mutual suspicion and distrust that had previously been notable for its absence. Nor is it a source of amazement that the city herself would later experience civil strife. This is what one would expect. The course of events confirms everything that Thucydides has to say about the *sōphrosúnē* that the Chians had hitherto displayed, and it is also consistent with what he intimates elsewhere regarding the instinctive brutality that Lacedaemonians so often exhibited when dealing with those outside their own community.[28]

The Samians had not in the past been as moderate and gentle in their treatment of one another as had their fellow Ionians on the island of Chios. Their regime seems never to have been a *kósmos*. They had a long history of bitter caste, class, and factional strife stretching back into the archaic age; and discord had erupted again in the late 440s when the oligarchs in control of the *pólis* staged an abortive rebellion against the Athenians. In 412, when Strombichides first arrived on Samos, this island *pólis* was governed as a democracy, as it had been since the collapse of that revolt. Not far away, however, just across the water at Anaia in the Samian *peraía*, the men who had staged the rebellion three decades before and their descendants watched and waited, eager to return home in triumph and ready to exploit any opportunity that presented itself.

In 412, the long-suffering residents of Anaia were not to have such an occasion—although there is reason to think that something of the sort may at one point have been in the offing. In anticipation of an attempt, presumably with Spartan help, to install an oligarchy on Samos, an uprising was staged, and it was carried out with the assistance of the Athenians manning the three triremes stationed there at the time. This preemptive strike was directed at the leading men of the city—"the powerful ones [*hoi dunatoí*]"—from among whom the suspected conspirators came, and it eventuated in considerable savagery. Two hundred of "those who were," Thucydides tells us, "the most powerful [*hoi dunatótatoi*]," the insurgents simply killed outright. Another four hundred they drove into exile, and the property in land and the fine homes of these *dunatoí* they then divvied up among themselves. Moreover, the victors excluded from the political community the well-born descendants of the *Geōmóroi* who had reportedly shared out the land most fit for cultivation at the time of the island's first settlement; and they outlawed intermarriage between citizens and the members of this proud aristocratic caste. It is surely no accident that, thinking the new regime reliable, the Athenians hastened to confer on it the autonomy they had hitherto denied its predecessor.[29]

COALITION TENSION

There were other conflicts of importance as well. That the Persians would pose a problem for the Spartans was a given, as we have seen. If there was anyone at Lacedaemon who entertained illusions in this regard, Tissaphernes' conduct soon dispelled his misapprehensions. One source of discord was the remuneration to be paid the trireme crews. When, in the winter following the Peloponnesian victory at Iasos and the capture of Amorges, Tissaphernes appeared at Miletus and distributed to each mariner the agreed-upon monthly wage of a drachma a head, he announced that henceforth, unless the Great King expressly agreed to that stipend, he would pay them at half that rate. When Therimenes, who would soon turn over the fleet to its designated commander Astyochus and then head home, did not object, the Syracusan commander Hermocrates son of Hermon intervened to make a great fuss, and Tissaphernes agreed to a slight increase. Between these two allied powers, the rate of pay would be an enduring bone of contention; and henceforth relations between Hermon's outspoken son and the satrap would be poisonous.

There was another serious ground for dispute. As we have had occasion to note, the Mede called himself the King of Kings. As such, he could not regard the arrangement that his minions had worked out with Lacedaemon as a proper alliance—for this would imply an equality between the two parties. He supposed, instead, that with the largess on offer his satrap had acquired for him "a friend"—which is to say, a client whose army and navy would henceforth be at his beck and call. This is evident in the tentative agreement Tissaphernes negotiated with Chalcideus when the latter first arrived at Miletus, which reads less like a treaty than like a decree handed down from on high. Its terms—especially those spelled out in its first two sentences—are, to say the least, revealing, for they state with unrivaled clarity what the patron expected the client to deliver:

> Whatever territories and cities the King holds and the forefathers of the King held, let them be his. And from these cities whatever came in regularly to the Athenians in the way of money or other goods the King and the Lacedaemonians and their allies shall act in common to prevent their carrying off.

The remainder of the document is also interesting—for it not only specifies that the two parties are to battle the Athenians and that neither will make peace unless both agree. It also stipulates that any of the King's subjects who revolt will be treated as enemies by the Spartans and their allies. Although there is another parallel sentence stating the like regarding the subjects of Lacedaemon, it is no more than a meaningless gesture. In the circumstances, genuine reciprocity was impossible. The communities that the Great King considered in rebellion at this time were very nearly countless—for the elder Darius and his son Xerxes had extended their domain westward in the Aegean to the Balkan shores and on the European mainland all the way from Thrace to Boeotia. By way of contrast, the populations subject to Sparta were few and, in practice, firmly under her control.

While, in the course of the winter, Astyochus was making his way to Miletus to formally assume his command, the first agreement was set aside as inadequate and a second was negotiated with Tissaphernes by Therimenes. Apart from stipulating that the King bear the expense for the forces he had summoned to Asia and mentioning his sons Arsaces and Cyrus as parties to the agreement, it differed in substance from its predecessor only in expressly barring the Lacedaemonians and their allies from making war against, harming, or extracting *phóros* from any "territories or cities belonging to King Darius or that belonged to his father or ancestors." In agreeing to these terms, Therimenes, like Chalcideus before him, was endorsing the Great King's claim that these territories and cities and the *phóros* to be extracted from them were rightfully his.

Needless to say, there were Spartans—some of them quite influential—who could not stomach anything of the kind; and in late winter they began to make their influence felt. Among them, the best-positioned was Lichas son of Arcesilaus, who is apt to have been one of Thucydides' informants and to have supplied him with much of the documentary evidence that appears in the fifth and eighth books of his history. This Lichas was, as we have seen, a man to be reckoned with. He was well-born; blessed with wealth, influence, and connections; and given to a lavish entertainment of foreigners who attended the Olympic Games or visited Lacedaemon. In 420, he had fielded a team in the chariot race at those games, as had his father before him and, one must suspect, his forefathers as well. He also served as the *próxenos* of the Argives at Lacedaemon. In the years following the Peace of Nicias in 421, he had played a prominent role both in attempting to lure that *pólis* into an alliance with Lacedaemon and in trying to establish an oligarchy in that city; and on one occasion, in a debate before the Argive assembly, he had proved more persuasive than his Athenian antagonist Alcibiades son of Cleinias. There is, moreover, evidence suggesting that Lichas was already in 420 a member of the *gerousía,* and we have reason to believe that he had inherited guest-friendships linking him with prominent families at Cyrene and on Thasos and Samos. The little that we can discern along these lines may, in fact, be an indication of a much wider network at this man's command. At this time, he also happened to be a *súmboulos.*

In the presence of Tissaphernes, who had journeyed through Caria to Cnidus to meet with the *súmbouloi,* this proud Spartiate repudiated the tentative agreements accepted by Chalcideus and Therimenes; and, in explaining himself, he did not mince words. "It is," he reportedly told the satrap, "an outrage that the King should claim the right to hold sway now over all of territories that he and his forebears ruled at an earlier time. This would render it possible for slavery to be imposed once again on all of the islands as well as on Thessaly, Opuntian Locris, and everything as far as Boeotia. Instead of conferring on the Hellenes liberty, the Lacedaemonians would be subjecting them to the empire of the Mede." He, then, proposed that a new and better agreement be forged, and he made it clear that the Spartans would not accept maintenance [*trophé*] from the Persians on the terms agreed to by Chalcideus and Therimenes.

It is exceedingly common now for scholars to suppose that we should ignore the plain meaning of the text in the first two accords that Tissaphernes reached with the Spartans on the grounds that the Great King and his satrap could not have had it in mind to make a claim to any territories and cities other than those in Anatolia. But this is surely an error, and Lichas, who was nobody's fool, recognized it as such. For, as the Greek diplomats sent to dicker with the Persians surely had learned by now, the mission assigned Ahura Mazda's

King was the conquest of the entire earth, and in the eastern Mediterranean the first step to be taken in that direction was a recovery of everything that Xerxes and Artaxerxes had lost. In 423/22, the younger Darius had made a vain, short-lived attempt—via *philía*—to turn Athens into an instrument of Persian policy. It was now his fond hope that by the same expedient he might acquire Lacedaemon as a client and thereby induce the Spartans to do his bidding in this and in other regards. It is no surprise, then, that Tissaphernes should respond to Lichas' rant by immediately departing from Cnidus in a rage. What he had hitherto thought within his grasp had just been snatched back and what he had no doubt in triumph reported earlier in the winter to his master in Susa had been proven premature and ultimately erroneous.

Nor is it a surprise that this same satrap should reappear late in the winter—probably at the very end of March—at Caunus to supply the allied fleet with pay, to encourage it to return to Miletus, and to negotiate an accord restricting to "the King's territory, as much of it as there is in Asia," the territorial claims that the Lacedaemonians had to honor and all but promising that the younger Darius would soon dispatch a Persian fleet to the Aegean. It is, moreover, telling that this accord was not formalized until some weeks later, at the very end of winter, when there had been time for the negotiators on both sides to consult their principals back home; that the King and his sons were not themselves parties to the final agreement; and that the formalities, which took place at a gathering held in the Maeander valley near Miletus, were performed on the Persian side by Tissaphernes himself, by Pharnabazus and the other sons of Pharnaces, and by the younger Darius' brother-in-law Hieramenes, who had also been present for the parley at Caunus. Whether this Hieramenes was, like his fellow signatories, a satrap in, say, Lycia, in Cappadocia, or elsewhere in the interior of Anatolia or he had been dispatched on a special mission with instructions from the court—this we do not know. All that can be said is that the terms on which the two parties to this agreement settled at this time had been implicit in the bargain from the start. As the Spartans surely understood from the moment in which the war in the Aegean began, this was the minimum for which the King would settle, and it did not matter whether they liked it or not.

However hostile to the Mede Lichas and those of his compatriots who shared his misgivings may have been, they had in the interim discovered by a painful process of trial and error, via their foray onto Rhodes, that, at least in the short term, they could not persevere without Persian financial support. And however disappointed the Great King may have been when he learned of Lichas' repudiation of the tentative agreements reached with Chalcideus and Therimenes, it was not in his interest that the Spartans lose their war with Athens or win it without Persian help—and this he surely knew.

Codified in the agreement formalized in 411, as the campaigning season was about to begin, was a working arrangement apt to be a dead letter the moment the Athenians suffered a decisive defeat. This the Spartans recognized from the start; and there was a revealing occasion not long thereafter when Lichas publicly intimated as much after preaching to the Milesians a patience in their dealings with the Persians in their midst that they did not at all relish. Of this danger, Tissaphernes, Pharnabazus, and their master can hardly have been unaware—for when the King's viceroys established garrisons in cities such as Miletus, Cnidus, and Antandrus, the citizens were not hesitant to drive them out, and on at least one occasion the Peloponnesians lent these recalcitrant Greeks their aid. The upshot was that, in the eastern Aegean, professions of *philía* notwithstanding, coalition management was going to be an exceedingly delicate and onerous task.[30]

PART II

———————————————

THE CENTER
CANNOT HOLD

Things fall apart; the centre cannot hold;
Mere anarchy is loosed upon the world,
The blood-dimmed tide is loosed, and everywhere
The ceremony of innocence is drowned;
The best lack all conviction, while the worst
Are full of passionate intensity.

WILLIAM BUTLER YEATS

THUCYDIDES' HISTORY is more than just a narrative account of what I distinguish here as Sparta's second Attic war, her Sicilian proxy war, and her third Attic war.[1] It is also an extended philosophical meditation on war and on peace as such—on what the Athenian historian calls "motion [*kínēsis*]" and on what he calls "rest [*hēsuchía*]"—and it traces the dialectical relationship between these opposites. Thucydides' *War between the Peloponnesians and the Athenians* was, he claims, "the greatest *kínēsis*" in human history. In the first twenty-three chapters of his book (in what was termed, even in antiquity, his "archaeology," his *lógos* concerning matters ancient [*tà archaîa*]), he intimates that what made so great a war possible was an extended period in which *kínēsis* on a universal but petty scale gradually gave way to *hēsuchía* as political order replaced anarchy at home and, to some degree, abroad—as piracy on land and at sea was for the most part suppressed, as civilization supplanted chaos, and Hellenism emerged from barbarism.

Thucydides regarded the emergence of *hēsuchía* by way of what we might term the civilizing process as a magnificent but fragile achievement apt to be reversed, if men are careless, by the great *kínēseis* that the attendant buildup of resources (both moral and material) makes possible. In his seventh book, he gives us a fleeting glimpse of the potential for savagery lurking beneath the veneer of civilization, and he does so by means of a brief but poignant discussion of a massacre that took place in 413 at a little town called Mycalessus.

As Thucydides explains, in that year, some Thracian mercenaries, sought by Demosthenes, had reached Athens too late to accompany that *stratēgós* on the relief expedition dispatched to Sicily. The Athenians at the time were under financial pressure and appointed a commander to conduct the Thracians back home. En route, they were told to do whatever damage they could to those of Athens' enemies living near the coast. It was this that occasioned their landing in Boeotia near Mycalessus, whose inhabitants they caught completely off guard with the gates of the town unguarded and its walls in disrepair:

> The Thracians burst into Mycalessus, sacked the houses and temples, and butchered the inhabitants, sparing neither the young nor the old, but methodically killing everyone they met, women and children alike, and even the farm animals and every living thing they saw. For the Thracian race, like the most bloodthirsty of the barbarian kind [*toû barbarikoû*], is at its most murderous [*phonikótaton*] when most caught up in audacity [*tharsésẹ*]. So now there was confusion on all sides and death in every shape and form. Among other things, they broke into a boys' school, the largest in the place, into which

the children had just entered; and there they killed every one of them. Thus, disaster fell upon the entire city, a disaster more complete than any, more sudden and more horrible.

Thucydides does go on to discuss the Theban counterassault on the retreating Thracians; and in characteristic fashion, he takes care to remark on the effectiveness of the tactics used by these light-armed troops against the Theban cavalry, for we are clearly meant to recognize that they would have been useful against the horsemen of Syracuse. But his main emphasis falls on the fruits of civilization—on animal husbandry, on families, on children, and on the education that in every age distinguishes the fully civilized from the savage— and at the end of his narrative he returns to the losses at Mycalessus: "It was a small city. But, in the disaster just described, its people suffered calamities as pitiable as any that took place during the war." It is only after reading an account such as this that one can fully appreciate the significance of Thucydides' decision to conclude his proof for his claim that the "war between the Peloponnesians and the Athenians" described in his history was the greatest movement or commotion [*kínēsis*] in the history of the Greeks by noting that it produced "sufferings [*pathémata*] without precedent."²

Thucydides is even more interested in the moral damage that a great and long-lasting war can inflict on and within a community. He prepares the way for this assessment by examining the impact on "human nature [*anthrōpeía phúsis*]" of the plague that first struck Athens in 430; and to this end he explores the manner in which that epidemic instilled in human beings a "spiritlessness [*athumía*]" which subverted the influence of honor and eliminated the capacity of convention [*nómos*]—whether sanctioned solely by custom or by force of law—to restrain human conduct. As Thucydides puts it,

Overpowered by the violence done by the evil [*huperbia- zoménou gàr toû kakoû*] and not knowing what would become of them, human beings became neglectful of things alike sacred and profane. All the *nómoi* that they had formerly observed with regard to burials were confounded and each conducted the rites as best he could. And many, lacking what was required because of the number of those who had died before, resorted to the most shameless methods in disposing of the deceased. To funeral pyres piled up by others, some would add the corpses of their own relatives and, getting in ahead, they would set them afire; others would hurl the bodies they were carrying on top of other corpses already burning—and then go away.

In this regard and in others, the plague first gave rise to a marked increase in *anomía*—in lawlessness and a flouting of social convention. Seeing the abrupt changes—the unforeseen demise of those who were flourishing and the manner in which the propertyless suddenly came to possess the substance of those who had died—the individual more readily dared [*etólma*] to do what he had previously kept hidden and had done in a manner contrary to the dictates of pleasure. And so they thought it worthwhile to reap the fruits quickly with an eye to their own gratification since they regarded their bodies and their money alike as ephemera. And no one was enthusiastic about persisting in what was deemed beautiful and noble [*kálon*] since they thought it unclear whether they would die or not before achieving it. So, whatever gave immediate pleasure or seemed conducive to it in any way was regarded as as both noble [*kálon*] and useful. No fear of the gods and no human law [*anthrópōn nómos*] held them back. With regard to the former they judged that it was the same whether they were reverent or not—seeing that all were equally likely to die; with regard to the latter no one expected lives to last long enough for anyone to come to trial and pay the penalty for his offenses since a much greater penalty had been passed on him and was impending—so that it was only fair and reasonable that he enjoy life a bit before that penalty befell him.[3]

The collapse of morals and manners described in this remarkable passage, the emancipation of individual daring [*tólma*], and the attendant disappearance of all respect for *nómos* (whether human in origin or putatively divine) deserve special attention because Thucydides uses the same sort of language when describing the events that took place at Corcyra in and after 427 and the violence done to human nature by the war itself.

The civil strife on that island originated in a dispute between the partisans of democracy and the wealthy individuals who had been captured by the Corinthians at the battle of Sybota on the eve of Sparta's second Attic war and held hostage at Corinth for a time thereafter. The details need not concern us here. What deserves attention is what Thucydides calls "the savage [*ōmḗ*] manner in which this revolution [*stásis*] progressed" and its subversion of the conventions governing the relationship between words and deeds.

In light of what, in the circumstances, seemed justified [*dikaíōsis*], the evaluation [*axíōsis*] customarily given particular deeds by names underwent a transformation. A daring devoid of calculation and impervious to speech [*tólma mèn alógistos*] was now regarded as the courage [*andreía*] one would expect to find in a loyal member of one's upper-crust drinking and dining club [*hetaireía*]; forethought for the future [*méllēsis dè promēthḗs*] was a fancy phrase for cowardice; moderation [*tò dè sôphron*] was a disguise for a lack of manliness; the ability to consider a question in all its aspects meant that one was incapable of doing anything. A stunning quickness was identified with possessing a manly portion in life; to conspire from a position of safety was excused and praised as prevention. The one intent on brutality was deemed trustworthy always; the one speaking against it came under suspicion. Someone engaged in plotting was judged intelligent if fortune favored his plan, and the one suspecting such a plot was thought cleverer yet. To take counsel so that nothing of the sort would be necessary was to dissolve the fellowship and to panic in the face of those opposed. In a word, the one anticipating someone about to do something wicked was praised in the same fashion as the one encouraging another who as yet had no such wickedness in contemplation.[4]

The linguistic lawlessness described in this passage is as disturbing as the more substantive *anomía* generated by the plague, for language is a prerequisite for the articulation of *nómos*, and linguistic conventions are as crucial to the maintenance of civilization as are the customs and laws which normally govern human conduct. As a consequence of the inconstant evaluative significance of words, speech and reason [*lógos*] lost their purchase on reality and traditional communities collapsed altogether:

Ties of kinship were less close [*allotrióteron*] than those based on one's membership in a *hetaireía* since those in the latter were readier, without hesitation, to engage in daring action [*tolmân*]. Such associations were of use not within the context of the established laws [*nómoi*] but for aggrandizement contrary to them. And their members confirmed their trust in one another not by an appeal to the divine law [*theîos nómos*] but by a common project of breaking the social conventions and the law [*paranomêsai*]. Things nobly said by opponents were greeted, if one had a start on them, not with the generosity of the well-born [*gennaiótēti*] but by guarding against the deeds that might follow. To take revenge on someone was preferable to avoiding suffering in his stead. And if there were oaths of reconciliation, they were exchanged with regard to an immediate difficulty and remained in force as long as the parties lacked support [*dúnamis*] from elsewhere. And when the opportunity arose, the one anticipating became bold if he caught the other off guard, and he took greater pleasure in exacting vengeance because of the prior establishment of

trust than if the deed had been openly done—and he calculated that it was safe because he had gained victory by deceit
and in addition had won a contest for intelligence [*sunéseōs
agónisma*].[5]

In one particular, the civil strife at Corcyra was quite different from
the plague at Athens. The *anomía* associated with the former was not
rooted in *athumía*. If anything, those who engaged in *stásis* evidenced an excess of spiritedness [*thumós*]. As Thucydides puts it,

The cause of all these things was rule [*archē̂*] pursued out of
greed [*pleonexía*] and the love of renown [*philotimía*]. From
these prevailing passions arose as well a keen desire for victory [*philonikía*]. The leading figures in the cities claimed to
be serving the common good—with each of the two sides
adopting an attractive slogan, the patrons of the multitude
expressing a preference for political equality [*isonomía*] and
their opponents expressing one for a moderate [*sóphron*]
aristocracy—but they were in fact seeking prizes for themselves. In their desire to prevail, they dared [*etólmēsan*] to
conduct their struggle with one another with no holds barred
and proceeded against one another in a terrible fashion and
took a revenge greater still, not setting forth as a limit the dictates of justice and the city's advantage but limiting themselves always, on both sides, with an eye to their own pleasure.
And they were ready to overpower their opponents either by
condemning them on an unjust vote or by seizing them with
their own hands and so sought to satisfy immediately their
love of victory [*philonikía*]. And so neither side thought in
terms of piety, and they listened more readily to decency of
speech on the part of those who found in it the opportunity
to do something odious. Those of the citizens in the middle
were destroyed by both either because they had not joined in
the struggle or by jealousy at their survival.[6]

If this passage were simply an account of events at Corcyra, it would not be all that pertinent to the larger history of this war. But we have already been told that civil strife played a crucial role in the unprecedented suffering that made this the greatest of wars, and Thucydides treats the revolution on that island as an *exemplum*. It was merely, he tells us, "the first to break out." Later, he adds, virtually "the entirety of Hellas was subject to commotion [*ekīnéthē*] with rival parties in every city—the patrons of the common people trying to bring in the Athenians, and the few trying to bring in the Spartans." In time of peace, he insists, there would have been no opportunity for intervention: it was the war that occasioned the plague of civil strife. "In peace and when matters go well," Thucydides remarks, "cities and individuals are better-minded because they have not fallen into the necessity of doing what they do not wish. But war is a *bíaios didáskalos*—a violent teacher, a teacher of violence. In depriving individuals of the means for easily satisfying their daily wants, it assimilates the thinking of the many to their present circumstances."

At Athens, it was this "violent teacher" that had brought Cleon son of Cleaenetus, "the most violent of the citizens," to the fore in the 420s and that had then enabled demagogues, such as Cleon and Hyperbolus son of Antiphanes, as well as sycophants, adept at exploiting envy for the purpose of prosecuting and fleecing the prosperous, to launch within Athens a civil war under the color of law. It was this "violent teacher" that had instructed Peisander, Charicles son of Apollodorus, Androcles, and the like in the ways in which, for the purpose of eliminating their political rivals, they might capitalize on the religious hysteria engendered by the Herms and Mysteries Scandals. It was "the greatest movement" or "commotion" in the history of the Greeks that produced such a "movement" or "commotion" within the cities. In the process, a species of brutality that had once seemed "savage and excessive [*ōmòn … kaì méga*]" to Athenians confronting rebellious subjects became the rule within communities.[7]

Thucydides' employment of the adjective *ōmós* to characterize the revolution that took place at Corcyra deserves attention. Literally, the word means not "savage" but "raw." This is what the Athenians, upon reflection, thought of their initial decision to execute the Mytilenians after their revolt in 428; and this is what, Thucydides believes, characterized the *stásis* that, as a consequence of the war, ran through Greece much in the manner of a contagious disease. Elsewhere, the historian uses a cognate of this adjective only once— in describing an Aetolian tribe so uncivilized that, although technically Greek, its members "are said to be unintelligible when they use their tongues [*agnōstótatoi dè glōssan*] and to eat their meat raw [*ōmophágoi*]." It is a revealing passage, for the Greeks discerned in the inability to communicate in speech and in the consumption of uncooked meat a close connection: these two characteristics distinguished animals from men. Consequently, one finds *ōmós* employed by a character in Euripides to denounce Sparta, where the citizens were notably taciturn and notoriously brutal in their treatment of outsiders; and the word is similarly used in a rhetorical treatise to single out and condemn human beings who resemble wild beasts [*thēriódeis*] in conducting their affairs in a manner contrary to the dictates of reasoned speech [*lógos*].[8]

In short, Thucydides is intimating in his description of the revolution at Corcyra that this protracted war tended to reverse the process described in his "archaeology" by which a world in constant motion came to enjoy a measure of rest [*hēsuchía*] and peace emerged from war, civilization from chaos, and Hellenism from barbarism. Put bluntly, the greatest movement or commotion [*kínēsis*] in history subjected the cities of Hellas to a species of internal movement or commotion [*ekinéthē*]; and, by subverting the linguistic, social, and political conventions [*nómoi*] which distinguish men from beasts, this *kínēsis* hurled the Greeks from their exalted status as political animals back to their primordial condition as barbarians— subhuman animals never at rest [*hēsuchía*], subject to frenzy, and inclined to fall prey to a form of daring [*tólma*] which leads them to commit raw and savage deeds and renders them irrational and inarticulate [*alógistos*], incapable of forethought for the future [*méllēsis promēthḗs*], and unable to employ *lógos* in deliberating together as a community concerning the advantageous, the just, and the good.[9] It was Cleon, Hyperbolus, Androcles, Peisander, Charicles, and the like—whatever their professed partisan loyalties might have been at any given time—who introduced *kínēsis* into Athens and gradually reduced the *pólis* from a *kósmos* to a *cháos*.

It did not take much to overturn the existing order at Corcyra. For, from the outset, that *pólis* had lacked cohesion. It took considerably longer at Athens—which, since 490, had advanced from strength to strength. Even after the plague, the Herms and Mysteries debacle, the catastrophe in Sicily, and the occupation of Deceleia, the Athenians had managed to maintain a modicum of solidarity. It was the tension generated by the ongoing conflict in Ionia, by the dearth of funds, and the prospect of defeat that upended Athens.

Even then, however, it took a catalyst to set things in motion and complete the job—and the catalyst was there. Within Hellas, there was one man—an Athenian with a Spartan name—who had an interest in turning everything upside down.[10] This is what, from exile, he had achieved in the course of Athens' foray into Sicily; and in 411, as everyone would soon learn, this man's capacity for meddling and maneuver, for charming and persuasion beggared the imagination. Looking back some two millenia after this Athenian's departure from the scene, the French *philosophe* Montesquieu would in passing describe him as "the wonder [*admiration*] of the universe."[11] This, without a doubt, he was—as we shall soon see.

CHAPTER THREE

NAKED CAME THE STRANGER

Among his many talents, he possessed a singular shrewdness
and facility for hunting human beings by suiting himself to
their practices and modes of life, entering into the turn of
mind and the sentiments attendant thereon, and altering his
humor and manners faster than a chameleon.... At Sparta, he
frequented the gymnasium and he was frugal and fierce of
countenance; in Ionia, he devoted himself to luxury, pleasure,
and ease; in Thrace, he was given to drink; in Thessaly, he
took to horse. And when he kept company with Tissaphernes,
he surpassed in both pretension and extravagance the magnif-
icence of the Persians.

PLUTARCH

WITH REGARD TO Spartan–Persian relations, there
was a source of conflict and confusion as yet unmentioned, which needs close attention—for it had consequences of great moment, and it derived from Alcibiades. Cleinias'
son was a breathtakingly handsome man, possessed of great charm and
magnetism and blessed with a first-rate intellect, who attracted—
wherever he went—admiration and envy in equal measure. As we
have seen, he tended to operate on impulse; he savored transgression and had a great liking for forbidden fruit—and he was all too

heedless of the consequences. *Húbris* had gotten him into trouble at Athens, and the experience had not taught him *sōphrosúnē* or even instilled in him a calculating caution born of a schooling in the world of hard knocks. And so, in short order, the man's *húbris* produced similar results at Lacedaemon.

In 413, the Eurypontid king Agis son of Archidamus had conducted the forces of Sparta's Peloponnesian alliance to Attica, where they had built a fort at Deceleia—and there, on post, supervising the devastation of Athens' territory, he had for the most part remained.[1] Behind him at Lacedaemon he had left unattended a frisky and mischievous young wife named Timaea. If ever there was forbidden fruit, she was it.

Upper-class women in other Greek cities lived for the most part in seclusion. Their sphere was the household, and they tended to be difficult of access. As Pericles had occasion to reveal, the general opinion was that it was best that women not be spoken of—whether for good or ill. At Sparta, however, women of high status were out and about—thanks, one must suspect, at least in part to the fact that their men, who spent much of their time in the company of their messmates in the *sussitía*, were rarely at home. The women of Lacedaemon were also renowned throughout Hellas for their beauty and athletic strength, for wearing skirts slit up the sides in a manner that Greek men from elsewhere found deliciously provocative ... and for a certain adventurousness. Agis' much younger sister Cynisca not only rode horses. Like Alcibiades, she bred them and raced them. In time, she, too, would win the chariot race at the Olympic games, and she would outdo Sparta's stunningly attractive visitor by having her teams come home victorious not once but twice. As this would suggest, the relations between the two sexes were not at Sparta what they were at Athens ... or, for that matter, anywhere else (then or now). It was not unknown for a Spartiate to do what was unthinkable elsewhere—which was to lend his spouse to a friend for the purpose of procreation. Given the homoerotic ethos that was predominant in Lacedaemon, it would be odd if marital fidelity on the

Figure 5.1. Bust of Alcibiades.
(Capitoline Museum, Palazzo dei Conservatori,
Hall of the Triumphs, Rome. Photographer: Marie-
Lan Nguyen. Published unchanged 2024 under the
following license issued by Marie-Lan Nguyen:
Creative Commons Attribution 2.5 Generic)

part of a man's wife was not, in many circles, less prized there than it was in the other Hellenic *póleis*.[2]

All that we can really say is that, in the case of Alcibiades, temptation presented itself and that he was not the sort of man to turn his nose up at such an opportunity—especially when it was an occasion for one-upsmanship on a truly magnificent scale. If, as is likely, Agis, who was no longer young, had earlier sired a son, that manchild was in 412 no longer alive. So it was, we are told, Alcibiades' aim to supply him with an heir and covertly substitute his own lineage for that of the Eurypontid clan.

To attempt this was not just a personal affront. At Sparta, bedding a king's wife was a criminal act, and Timaea's misconduct verged on treason. The Lacedaemonians were an exceedingly pious lot, and the well-being of the political community and the legitimacy of her hold on Laconia in the eyes of the gods was thought to depend on the rightful claim to that territory possessed by their Heraclid chieftains. It was in keeping with this conviction that the ephors watched over the birth of prospective heirs to the two thrones.[3]

About this scandal, Thucydides is, as usual, reticent. He tells us only that Agis nursed a deep-seated hatred for the Athenian. To learn why the royal son of Archidamus so loathed the man, one must first consult Xenophon, who makes no mention of Alcibiades in this regard but does allude to the fact that there was compelling evidence that someone other than Agis was the father of Timaea's son Leotychidas. Then, one must read Plutarch, who mangles Xenophon's story somewhat but identifies the malefactor by name and describes his motive.

The tale told by Xenophon is a gossip-monger's delight. There was an earthquake—quite likely the one known to have taken place in Laconia in late February or early March 412. It forced the Lacedaemonians to bolt from their homes, which were in such situations threatened with collapse. On this occasion, a man other than Timaea's husband was spied emerging from the women's quarters in the absent Agis' house, and nine months later the Eurypontid king's wife gave birth to a bouncing baby boy.[4]

There was almost certainly more to Alcibiades' conduct on this occasion than immediately meets the modern eye. The two kings had been taught that Lacedaemon was theirs. Alcibiades they are apt, from the outset, to have regarded as an upstart, and they can hardly have failed to resent deeply the profound influence that this outsider, this renegade charmer, this outlaw, this man without a country exercised in the *pólis* that by hereditary right belonged to them—and in no way to him. Agis, for one, is said to have taken umbrage at being outshone; and this sentiment was shared, we are told, by many another leading Spartan.[5]

The indignation felt by Agis from the start may have been greatly intensified by the fact that he and Alcibiades shared a history. Just over five years before, in the immediate aftermath of his Argolid campaign, he had been outmaneuvered by the slippery Athenian, as we have seen—and his tenure as king had, for a brief but, for him, unforgettable moment, hung in the balance. This requires a full discussion: for to grasp the full depth of the Eurypontid king's resentment, one must understand what it meant to be a *basileús* at Lacedaemon and one must reconsider what Agis had suffered at the hands of Cleinias' son in light of the significance of the office he held.

BASILEÍA

One of the qualities that the *agōgē* instilled in young Spartiates was *philotimía*—the love of honor. Of course, as Heraclids, the two kings were not, strictly speaking, Spartiates themselves. As a consequence, as we have seen, their heirs apparent were not subject to the civic *paideía* accorded lesser men. But this did not alter the fact that the ethos dominant in the world in which the young men so situated grew up was honorific and that it profoundly shaped their outlook as well. After all, these two were in a privileged position. Even before they succeeded to the throne, they were very much in the public eye. Once one of them assumed the kingship, it was, in principle, his for life; and the prerogatives associated with the office were extensive.

The two kings exercised a sacral function, for they were hereditary priests and they chose the *Puthíoi* responsible both for the embassies dispatched to Delphi and for the preservation of oracles. They were expected to provide leadership—above all, on the battlefield, but off it as well. Thus, for example, they had responsibility for the upkeep of the system of cart roads, constructed on a single gauge, that the Lacedaemonians had built within their own domain and that, under their direction, their allies within the Peloponnesus had constructed throughout that peninsula. They oversaw adoptions and the marriage of unbetrothed heiresses, which put them in a position to influence the distribution of private wealth. When sent abroad, they controlled the assignments given individual infantrymen. In this setting, they could confer the opportunity for achievement on some and deny it to others. They also played a prominent role in foreign affairs—for they selected the *próxenoi* who looked after Lacedaemon's interests in foreign parts and they oversaw the appointment of Spartiates as *próxenoi* at Lacedaemon for foreign powers. In short, the patronage at their command was immense.

The two kings were also involved in the most important decision-making. *Ex officio*, they served as members of the *gerousía*, which set the agenda for the assembly. Within this aristocratic probouleutic council, there was a great deal of turnover, as well-born men over the age of sixty were elected, served, and soon thereafter died. But a man such as Agis or his Agiad counterpart Pleistoanax son of Pausanias could join that body while in his twenties and serve for four decades or more. For a man in such a position to be outshone in his own city by an interloper was as intolerable as it was unprecedented.

Of course, had there been but one king at Lacedaemon, no foreigner could ever have done what Alcibiades did. For, had there been only one man graced with the prerogatives shared at Sparta by the heads of the Agiad and the Eurypontid houses, that figure would have become a despot, and a stranger visiting would have been at his mercy. But, thanks to the rivalry that their situation kindled in the city's two *basileîs*, the Spartans had no experience with tyranny—and other magistracies emerged early on that further restricted the sway of the two kings and ordinarily forced them to work in harness.[6]

The first of these was the *gerousía*. Had there not been a dyarchy at Sparta, the size of this council, the family pride it drew on and reinforced, and the seniority possessed by the twenty-eight *gérontes* who served on it alongside the kings might not have been sufficient to insure its independence. But, in the circumstances, there always seems to have been a majority able to stand aloof.[7]

The second such magistracy was the ephorate. As it existed in the classical period, this board was a democratic institution. It had five members. They served for a single year; they were ineligible for iteration in office; and they were chosen by a process, described as childish by Aristotle but nowhere sketched out in detail, that Plato tellingly compares with a lottery. As one would then expect, the ephors were normally distinguished, as Aristotle tell us, by their lack of distinction—and, strangely enough, their ordinariness was among the chief virtues of this magistracy. Among other things, it guaranteed the participation in the city's governance of Sparta's commoners and encouraged their loyalty to the community. Even more important, during their year in office, these five for the most part ordinary men exercised by majority vote an arbitrary, almost unchecked power that it would have been dangerous in normal circumstances to confer on anyone but nonentities. It was only at the end of their period in office that they were called upon to account for their deeds and that they were subjected by their successors to a formal, judicial inquiry [eúthuna] of the sort employed in other Greek cities to guarantee that magistrates remained responsible to the political community. But the prospect that they would be judged and might be found wanting was for such men without a doubt sobering.[8]

In the period before that day of reckoning, the ephors played a predominant role in the making and implementing of public policy. They were empowered to summon both "the little assembly," which appears to have been constituted by the board of ephors and the city's *gerousía*, and the "common assembly" of the Spartiates. They could introduce laws, decrees, and declarations of war and peace in the latter through the *gerousía*; and when the "common assembly" met—whether on an extraordinary occasion or at the regular monthly time—it was they who decided who would present a particular proposal. One of their number then presided, put the question, and determined whether those shouting for the measure outnumbered those shouting against it. It is an indication of their central importance that Xenophon—the ancient writer most intimately familiar with Spartan practice and parlance—thrice ascribes important decisions to "the ephors and assembly." It would not be an exaggeration to say that the ephors administered the government at Sparta with the advice and consent of the *gerousía* and the assembly. For Aristotle rightly observes that a magistracy empowered to convene a city's assembly, set its agenda, and preside over it is virtually "authoritative within the regime."[9]

The ephors were particularly influential in the sphere of foreign relations. It was within their prerogative to determine when and for how long a foreigner might visit Sparta and a Spartan might go abroad. They ordinarily received embassies, conducted negotiations with foreign powers, and decided when to place matters before the *gerousía* and assembly. They had influence, if not control, over the appointment of the harmosts who administered communities under Sparta's dominion, and they may have played a similar role in the selection of the navarchs who commanded the city's navy. They were certainly competent to issue these officials directives. Moreover, in time of war or civic emergency, the ephors called up the army, and ordinarily they determined who was to command and which age groups were to march. In foreign affairs, there were few functions that these magistrates did not perform—other than serve as Sparta's commanders in the field.

At home, the ephors' chief task—as the title of their office suggests—was oversight. They enforced the sumptuary laws and determined which pieces of music and poetry would be tolerated within the community. They kept tabs on the *néoi*, checking each day to see that the "young men" in the *sussítia* observed the regulations regarding clothing and bedding and subjecting them every tenth day to a physical examination. Ultimately, they appointed three outstanding members of this age-category who had reached their prime to select from among their fellow *néoi* and command the three hundred *hippeîs* that formed the royal bodyguard. Likewise, the ephors controlled the treasury, disbursing the necessary funds, overseeing the collection of taxes, and receiving the proceeds from the sale of prisoners and of the other booty captured in war. They also manipulated the calendar, intercalating months when this was deemed necessary. At Sparta, the ephors controlled virtually every aspect of daily life.

Each year, when these "overseers" took office, they declared war on the helots, employing the young men of the *krupteía* to eliminate the obstreperous and those menacingly robust. At the same time, Aristotle tells us, they reissued the famous decree calling on each Spartiate to obey the law, to comply with the customs of the land, and to observe the ancient practice of shaving his upper lip. According to Plutarch, this last injunction was intended as a reminder to the *néoi* that they were to obey the city even in the most trivial of matters.[10]

The importance of the ephors is perhaps most obvious from their relationship with the two kings. Here, they had clearly defined prerogatives designed to make manifest and to enforce the sovereignty of the political community as a whole. They alone remained seated in the presence of a king; they alone had the power to summon the kings, to jail them, and even to fine them for misconduct; and in and after the fifth century, if not before, when one of the kings led out the army, two of their number ordinarily accompanied him to observe his every action and to give advice when asked.

One Eurypontid king is said to have remarked that "the magistrate rules truly and rightly only when he is ruled by the *nómoi* and ephors." His coupling of the rule of custom and law with the rule of the ephors is not an accident. At the time of his institution, the Spartan *basileús* made a compact with the *pólis* in which he swore to maintain her *nómoi*. Each month thereafter, the ephors exchanged oaths with the kings, the latter swearing to reign in accord with "the established *nómoi* of the city," the former pledging to "keep the kingship unshaken" as long as the latter abided by their "oath to the city."[11]

There was a threat implicit in the ephors' part of the bargain, and they had the power to make good on it. If they judged that a king or regent had acted against the interests of the city, they could arrest him and bring him to trial on a capital charge as if he were an ordinary Spartiate. In the course of the turbulent fifth century, they were to exercise this prerogative time and time again. Of the fifth-century kings, only three are not known ever to have been tried for a capital crime, and even this statistic may be misleading. Two of these three bore the full weight of royal responsibility for periods so brief that their escape could not be deemed significant. And neither of their reigns nor that of the third is sufficiently well attested to justify our being certain from the silence of the sources that none of them was ever in danger. The only reasonably safe conclusion is that none of them was ever convicted of a capital crime.[12]

It might, then, seem that the kings were virtual prisoners of the ephors. One circumstance precluded this. As we have seen, the ephors held office for only a year and apparently could never again do so. So, as board after board of ephors served, then retired, and as the *gérontes* slowly died off, a strong king endured, exercised his prerogatives, and worked the political and social system to benefit his friends and to impose a burden of gratitude on those judged politically prominent. In a given year, a particular king might find himself in difficulties and might deem it prudent to remain quiet, but he knew that the annual game of chance by which the ephors were chosen always offered the hope for a board more favorable to his cause or more easily influenced.

The institution of the ephorate would not alone have staved off tyranny. The fact that the kingship was dual was essential for accomplishing this feat, and it explains why political conflict at Lacedaemon tended to revolve around the two kings and the following each attracted. When the two were united, the ephors may not have had the moral authority to withstand them.

Of course, this rarely happened. The rivalry between the Agiad house and its Eurypontid counterpart, which was a central feature of the regime, generally ruled out the two kings' working in concert. In any case, had Agis enjoyed this advantage, it would not have made much of a difference. His colleague Pleistoanax lived under a cloud. In 446, when, as a very young man recently installed on the Agiad throne, he had cornered the Athenians and had them at his mercy, he had—on the advice of Gylippus' father Cleandridas—eschewed inflicting on them a defeat that would have guaranteed their subsequent subservience. Instead, as we have seen, he had negotiated a truce, preparatory for a treaty of peace, requiring their withdrawal from the Peloponnesus and the Greek mainland outside Attica but allowing them their sphere of influence in and beyond the Aegean. This had provoked fury at Lacedaemon and had occasioned his indictment for bribery and a trial that had eventuated in his withdrawal into exile. In the mid-420s, to be sure, he had been recalled. But he had then championed the negotiations that eventuated in the Peace of Nicias, which was followed by the partial dissolution of Sparta's Peloponnesian alliance, the formation of a rival coalition, Athens' support for it, and the struggle for Lacedaemon's very existence that took place in 418 at Mantineia.[13]

Pleistoanax' disgrace had left Agis more or less alone and in charge, but he had not handled the opportunity especially well. For, as we have seen, in 418 he had tried vis-à-vis Argos something comparable to the gambit Pleistoanax had attempted with regard to Athens in 446. Had it come off, it would have been a genuine triumph. But it, too, had ended in tears. So, as we have also observed, he in turn was tried on a capital charge, and he was very nearly himself deposed. It was to the machinations of Alcibiades son of Cleinias that he owed this humiliation.

AGIS AND ALCIBIADES

From 451 to 421, relations between Lacedaemon and her age-old rival Argos had been governed by a truce of sorts slated to last for thirty years. As its term approached, the Spartans, exhausted and beleaguered as a consequence of their second Attic war, had gone to great lengths to achieve the accord's renewal—with Lichas son of Arcesilaus, the Argive *próxenos* at Lacedaemon, no doubt in the lead. Had it not been for the machinations of Alcibiades at Athens, Lichas and his colleagues might well have succeeded. But the Athenian managed by his signature combination of eloquence, charm, and chicanery to thwart their efforts and to forge an alliance between Athens and the Peloponnesian *póleis* Elis, Mantineia, and Argos that posed an existential threat to Lacedaemon.

In response, as we have seen, the Spartans rallied their remaining allies and succeeded in drawing together an enormous hoplite army, which greatly outnumbered the force deployed by the Argive coalition. In a campaign marked by tactical brilliance on his part, Agis then maneuvered the Argives and their allies into a position in which they were surrounded and in danger of suffering annihilation.

Had the Eurypontid king used this opportunity to massacre the enemy army, he would have been regarded as a hero. But instead—presumably on the advice of Lichas and the other Lacedaemonian diplomats involved in Sparta's previous negotiations with the Argives—he chose to make a truce with the Argive generals, who pledged that it would eventuate in a long-term peace and perhaps even an alliance between their city and that of the Lacedaemonians.

In the aftermath, it was Alcibiades who persuaded the Argives to repudiate the pledge made on their behalf and to march off with their allies toward Laconia itself, and it was this that induced the Spartans, who were already disgruntled, to turn with a vengeance on their Eurypontid *basileús*. If Agis escaped losing the kingship on this occasion, it was only by begging for time to make up for his blunder. Then, saddled with *súmbouloi*, he led a much-reduced force north to confront the Argives, Mantineians, and Athenians in a battle at Mantineia between two armies nearly equal in size. And there—thanks to an ill-thought-out, last-minute maneuver he attempted to execute—Agis very nearly lost.[14] When Alcibiades bedded Timaea, he was rubbing salt into a wound that would never heal—and he surely knew it.

It is not then surprising that, early in the winter of 413/12, there was already a certain tension evident as to who should manage the upcoming struggle in Ionia—which put Agis in Attica, who had initially asserted the authority lodged in him as a king in the field, at odds with Endius and his fellow ephors back home, who had the ultimate say and who were listening closely to Alcibiades. What was at issue formally was whether Ionia fell under Agis' purview or would be treated as a separate theater of war managed by the ephors and their nominees. But, of course, there was much more than this at stake.

Not long after the earthquake in late February or early March 412, word is apt to have reached Archidamus' royal son that the Athenian had made of him a cuckold. This he cannot have taken lightly; and the antipathy that was initially rooted in political rivalry, jealousy, and a desire for revenge appears to have turned into an animus fueled by something far more potent. It cannot have eased matters that Agis' wife soon showed signs of being pregnant, and it can only have made things worse that in due course she gave birth to a son apt to become his heir. Moreover, if Duris of Samos and Plutarch are right in claiming that, in private among her servants, Timaea eschewed the name Leotychidas, which was given the boy in honor of his putative great-great grandfather, and, instead, referred to the child as Alcibiades, and if word of this also reached Agis, as may well have happened, it can only have further fed his fury.

The change in the political atmosphere at Lacedaemon that almost certainly ensued was enough to persuade Alcibiades, if he needed persuasion, that it was high time for him to leave Laconia and that it made sense for him to accompany Chalcideus on his voyage to Chios. Moreover, when, shortly before or after the end of the campaigning season in 412, Endius' term as ephor reached its conclusion, Alcibiades' position among the Spartiates in the eastern Mediterranean became untenable.

Among the Peloponnesians, we are told, disappointment reigned. Athens had not turned out to be the pushover they had expected. The anti-Athenian alliance had suffered a setback on Lesbos; Chios had come under great pressure; and the Athenians had very nearly retaken Miletus. If at Lacedaemon, when discussing the upcoming Ionian campaign, the son of Cleinias had, true to form, promised more than he could deliver, the Athenian resurgence will have greatly eroded, if not extinguished, his popularity; and it will have rendered him as a foreigner quite vulnerable. But it was almost certainly at the instigation of Agis and his associates that the new board of ephors sent a message to the navarch Astyochus instructing him to execute the man thought to have sought to substitute his progeny for the Eurypontid branch of Laconia's rightful proprietors.[15]

We do not know how Alcibiades learned of the fate in store for him. Pompeius Trogus, if Justin's epitome is reliable, reported that Timaea, who was apparently still smitten, tipped him off—which may have been the tale told by the fourth-century historian Ephorus of Cumae.[16] It is also possible that Endius got wind of what was in the offing and himself sent word. But it is more than merely conceivable that Astyochus—who may well have owed his original appointment as navarch to the board of ephors on which Endius had served—sent the Athenian a message urging that he flee. Unlike the other two, he was without a doubt in the know, and Thucydides' phrasing suggests that Alcibiades did not learn of the order of execution until it reached Astyochus.

That there was a political struggle underway at Lacedaemon between Agis and his associates, on the one hand, and the supporters of Endius and Alcibiades, on the other, and that it had a personal dimension is obvious. That there was a genuine policy difference between the two factions is less certain, but it is likely. Idealism tends to shroud personal antipathy. Personal rivalries, whatever their origin, are apt to eventuate in political disagreement; and this quarrel seems not to have been an exception. Agis' faction—to which Lichas, who had almost certainly worked closely with the Eurypontid king in 418, is likely to have belonged—was clearly less happy with the Persian connection forged in 412 than were the allies of Endius and his Athenian *xénos*. Even more to the point, Agis and his supporters can hardly have been satisfied with the decision that Alcibiades and Chalcideus had made to concentrate their resources on acquiring Miletus rather than on securing Lesbos and the Hellespont. It is surely pertinent that the expedition dispatched in late December 412 under the command of Antisthenes was sent to convey to the eastern Aegean not only the *súmboul01* charged with reviewing the conduct of the war and relations with Persia but also Agis' associate Clearchus son of Ramphias, who was tasked with seizing for Sparta and her allies Byzantium on the Bosporus and the Hellespont.

As we have seen, the contest between the two groups almost certainly determined some of the appointments that were made that year. We should be open to the possibility that it decided them all. If Pedaritus was named harmost of Chios almost immediately after Endius left office, factional conflict may help explain not only his shocking insubordination and refusal to cooperate with Astyochus, the overall commander in the Aegean theater—but also the latter's retaliation, the harmost's subsequent attempt to secure the navarch's ouster, and the appointment of *súmboul01* by the ephors of 412/11 to judge the latter's conduct in office and renegotiate the terms of Lacedaemon's arrangement with the Mede.

Of course, this is by no means certain. Our knowledge is sadly incomplete. But what we do know about the subsequent relations between Alcibiades and Astyochus is highly suggestive. For, after being tipped off, the wily Athenian—as always, fleet of foot—not only made his way to the court of Tissaphernes son of Hydarnes at Sardis, where he joined the satrap's entourage. He also met on occasion thereafter with the navarch instructed to secure his execution; and, in a fashion that has baffled many modern historians, Astyochus, whose close relations with Tissaphernes and his underlings caused him to be suspected at this time of having become a recipient of the satrap's largess, is said to have twice gone to considerable trouble to alert the son of Cleinias to the machinations of an Athenian adversary. Alcibiades was a man who had a knack for acquiring friends— which was a good thing for him. He was now wanted dead or alive both at Athens and at Sparta. His compatriots had even put a price on his head. A talent of silver—fifty-seven pounds of that precious metal—awaited the man or men who brought him in or saw him off.[17]

ALCIBIADES IN SARDIS

We do not know precisely when Alcibiades made the transition from Miletus to Sardis. The only chronological indicators we are given are a claim that he first came under suspicion after the death of Chalcideus and a report that he was still with the Peloponnesians a week or two thereafter when Therimenes reached the environs of Miletus. The odds are good that he was present also for the sack of Iasos, which took place immediately after the Athenian withdrawal from the territory of Miletus—although he is not expressly mentioned in connection with that event. It was presumably not long thereafter, as winter set in and the new board of ephors began to assert itself, that he is likely to have received a warning and to have made the switch.

Alcibiades may, in fact, have been behind Tissaphernes' announcement—made early in the winter months after he had paid the Peloponnesian crews—that henceforth, unless commanded otherwise by the King, he would pay the rowers and the other mariners only three obols a day. According to Thucydides, who appears to have interviewed the exiled Athenian,[18] Alcibiades had urged such parsimony and had even encouraged the satrap to say something closely akin to what he reportedly said on this occasion: that, if more was to be paid, it would have to come from the King. He is also apt to have been in Tissaphernes' entourage at Cnidus in late January or early February 411 when, confronted by Lichas, the satrap angrily departed. For, in the interim, the slippery Athenian had managed to charm the Persian viceroy and to work his way into the man's confidence. There may even have been a homoerotic dimension to their relationship. Herodotus tells us that the Persians picked up the practice of pederasty from the Greeks; and Tissaphernes, who may have been smitten, is said to have named after the devastatingly handsome Athenian the most beautiful of the parks or gardens—parádeisoi—that he, in keeping with the practice of Achaemenid Persia, had had constructed in his domain.[19]

The advice that Alcibiades reportedly proffered upon arriving at

Sardis was as sound as the advice that he had marketed earlier at Lacedaemon, and it was in no way ambiguous. It was not, he reportedly told Tissaphernes, in Persia's interest that Sparta win the war. According to Thucydides, the Athenian exhorted the King's viceroy

> neither to be in too much of a hurry to put an end to the war nor to be willing to confer power over both land and sea on a single power by bringing in the Phoenician fleet that he was making ready or by providing pay to a greater number of Hellenes. Instead, he would be well-advised to leave to each of the two powers a sphere of control and to enable the King to deploy against the community that had become vexatious to him the other community. For if dominion over both land and the sea were to fall into the hands of one of the two, the King would not know with whom he might join in putting down those exercising this dual dominion, and he would be at a loss unless he was willing to rise up and at great expense and peril undertake the fight himself. This would be the cheaper policy: at a small proportion of the outlay otherwise required and, at the same time, with safety for himself to induce the Hellenes to wear one another down.

Alcibiades appears to have been aware that, in normal circumstances, it was Persian policy to operate on the fringes of the empire through "friends"—which is to say, through client princes or polities. So, to this advice, he added something not immediately obvious: that, if Tissaphernes' master preferred to have a partner, "the Athenians would be more serviceable [*epitēdeióteroi*] to him as sharers in dominion [*koinōnoì ... tês archês*]" than the Lacedaemonians, "for they were less desirous of possessions on land." In consequence, he suggested, his compatriots would be willing to concentrate on the sea and to abandon to the King's discretion the Hellenes who resided in the territory on the Asian shore that he claimed as his own. The opposite could be expected from the Spartans, he told

Tissaphernes, "for it is unlikely that those who had set out to liberate Greeks from domination by other Greeks would refrain from liberating them from domination by the barbarians as well." In short, the Great King should wear down both sides, weaken the Athenians as much as he could, and then usher the Peloponnesians out of the territory that he regarded as his own.[20]

This was sage advice—borne out in time by events.[21] Whether, however, Tissaphernes was himself genuinely persuaded, we cannot be certain—although, as Thucydides points out, Lichas soon thereafter confirmed, at least in part, the truth of Alcibiades' argument when, at Cnidus, he not only repudiated the tentative agreements reached between the satrap and the Lacedaemonian commanders Chalcideus and Therimenes but did so on the very grounds mentioned as dispositive for the Spartans by the son of Cleinias. Nor can we be certain that Alcibiades' advice was ever conveyed to the King for his consideration, although Thucydides was persuaded that this had taken place.

All that the son of Olorus was in a position to confirm was that the satrap continued to consult his Athenian guest; that at this time his conduct conformed to what Alcibiades had urged; that, on occasion, he employed the son of Cleinias as his interlocutor with the Greeks who came as suppliants to his court; and that, in the presence of the Athenian exile, he later met with a delegation dispatched from Athens and explored just how much in the way of territory both in Anatolia and offshore they were willing to concede to his master. The Lacedaemonians and their allies, moreover, he continued to keep on short rations; and the silver he supplied to them he dispatched at irregular intervals. He is also said to have dissuaded them from vigorously taking to the sea by the simple expedient of speaking frequently about the imminent arrival of a Phoenician fleet—and on this promise he never delivered, although the fleet in question actually made it as far as the city of Aspendus in Pamphylia, a few miles up the Eurymedon river from Anatolia's southern coast. To this we can add the testimony of Xenophon, who reports that a few years after these events Tissaphernes, in his dealing with a representative of the Great King, advocated the policy that Alcibiades had pressed on him when he first came to Sardis.[22]

Of course, at this time, Tissaphernes no doubt had reasons, all his own, of an entirely different sort for following the course recommended by Alcibiades. The size of the fleet deployed by Sparta and her allies had grown. At Rhodes alone, not to mention Miletus and Chios, there were nearly one hundred galleys. If the crews there were paid at a drachma per man per month, keeping a fleet of one hundred triremes on station for a year would run the satrap in silver at least twelve hundred Attic talents—which is to say, something like thirty-four tons of that precious metal. Even at half that wage, he would have to come up with a very considerable sum; and that sort of expense his satrapy, though quite prosperous, simply could not sustain. At this stage, the question of wages was, of necessity, a matter for the King—especially if the war was apt to drag on—and, needless to say, it was for the King to decide whether and, if so, when there would be a deployment of the Phoenician fleet.[23]

As for Alcibiades, his real object lay elsewhere—where, in fact, it had lain all along. He not only wanted to show his compatriots that he was still very much alive. He wanted to persuade them that, if they wished to survive, they would have to recall him from exile and put him in charge. Everything that he had done since jumping ship at Thurii and joining the Lacedaemonians had been done with a single objective in mind: he wanted to reduce his fellow Athenians to desperate straits—but without fully doing them in. It is this that explains his preference that the war at sea take place in the vicinity of Chios and of Miletus further south rather than in the environs of Lesbos to the north and in the strategically vital region of the Hellespont. The choices that the exiled Athenian and his Spartan allies made in this regard were surely prominent among the concerns that galvanized Agis and his supporters and provoked suspicions among the Peloponnesians more generally. In comparison with the Hellespont, Miletus and cities to her south were strategically insignificant—and this was no secret.[24]

The objective that Alcibiades pursued now that he was ensconced in Sardis was to make himself seem indispensable for Athens' recovery. Tissaphernes, like the Spartans before him, was to be deployed as a pawn in a larger game being played by his guest—and, as the campaigning season in 411 approached, it began to look as if Alcibiades might actually succeed. For whatever any given group of Athenians may have thought about this particular exile, they were on one thing agreed—that they could not keep up the struggle for long without a copious and steady stream of precious metals from a reliable source. When it seemed clear that Alcibiades was now a man of influence at the satrap's court, the rowers, the specialists, and the infantrymen with the fleet on Samos began entertaining the hope that they could somehow persuade him to use his influence to secure the funds they required; and the son of Cleinias did what he could to encourage them in this supposition by sending letters to the *dunatótatoi* within the force on the island, urging them to spread the word there among "the best men [*béltistoi*]" that he would be willing to rejoin his compatriots and use his influence to make Tissaphernes friendly to the Athenians—but only if, in turn, they were prepared to effect a change of regime and replace with an oligarchy "the villainous democracy that had banished him" in the first place.

According to Thucydides, this revolutionary project was enthusiastically embraced on the island—above all, by the wealthy trierarchs who bore the considerable burden of maintaining the triremes that they commanded on station there and by the other *dunatótatoi* in their midst. In part because of what Alcibiades promised, but in part out of inclination, "they were eager to overthrow the democracy."[25]

REGIME ANALYSIS

Pertinent to the thinking of those who responded positively to Alcibiades' overture were the disasters that had taken place in the years immediately preceding the war in Ionia. In 415, there had been the decision to intervene in Sicily with a massive force, the religious panic occasioned by the mutilation of the Herms and the news that the Eleusinian Mysteries had been profaned, and the executions and banishments attendant on that panic. The following year, the Athenians had gratuitously provoked a renewal of the war with Lacedaemon. Then, in 413, there had been the dispatch of a relief force to Syracusa and the catastrophe that followed. All of this had produced (especially among the well-to-do and the educated) a widespread disillusionment with the form of government at Athens under which the crucial decisions had been made. This disillusionment is apt to have been reinforced by a trend that emerged among the cognoscenti in the second half of the fifth century. For this trend, there is incontrovertible evidence in the pages of Herodotus, in the pages of a pamphlet found among the works of Xenophon but penned by someone else in this period, and elsewhere as well.

When the historian from Halicarnassus composed his *Inquiries*—which he published in or soon after the 420s—he included within it an utterly implausible account of a debate that, he insisted, really took place among the soon-to-be Great King of Persia Darius son of Hystaspes and two of his six fellow conspirators. It turned on a question that, thanks to the vast geographical extent of the Persian empire and to the absence in antiquity of the idea of representation, could not have come up in such a company—to wit, what regime should be adopted for the empire's governance. The options said to have been considered by these three men were those distinguished by the Theban poet Pindar decades before: monarchy, oligarchy, and democracy. The debate's value to the modern historian is that it is testimony of the emergence of regime analysis in fifth-century Greece and to the sophistication achieved in that analysis prior to 413.

The advocacy of democracy that Herodotus attributes to the Persian notable Otanes and the critiques of that regime that he ascribes to Megabyzus and Darius record lines of thinking with which educated Athenians were surely familiar. Otanes' argument for democratic government had purchase. *Isonomía*—equality under the law—is, after all, attractive, and the same thing can be said for the *eúthuna*, the requirement that magistrates submit to an audit and give an accounting of their conduct in office before they lay it down. The use of the lot to fill most of the magistracies does lessen rivalry, and majority rule has this great virtue: all laws and decrees are decided upon by those who are apt to be most affected by them.

By the time of Sparta's second and third Attic wars, these arguments and others like them had found their way into the rhetoric deployed in tragedy and in the public assemblies at Athens and elsewhere. In his *Suppliants*, for example, Euripides had Theseus praise the Athenian democracy for its promotion of a rotation in office and for the freedom and equality it conferred on its citizens. In his Funeral Oration, Pericles is said to have singled out as praiseworthy not only equality under the law but also the fact that the elective offices were open to merit and that poverty was not an obstacle to public service and political advancement. At Syracusa, Athenagoras reportedly had a ready answer for those who argued that "democracy is by nature neither intelligent [*xunetón*] nor equitable [*íson*]" and that "those hold property are best-suited to ruling well." The rule of the few he denounced as unjust, suggesting that oligarchies tended to share out the dangers to everyone, but not the advantages that accrued. It was conceivable, he conceded, that the rich were the best guardians of property and that the intelligent [*xunetoí*] were the best at providing counsel. But he insisted that "the many are preeminent in judging what they hear."

By the same token, however, the criticism leveled at the direct democracies of ancient Hellas was not without merit. It might well be excessive to say, as this Megabyzus purportedly did, that "nothing is more lacking in intelligence [*axunetatóteron*] and more prone to *húbris* than the useless throng." But it was true that the common folk enjoyed little in the way of education, and *húbris* on the part of the Athenian demos was certainly on display in the period stretching from 416 to 413. Euripides has the herald dispatched to Athens from Thebes by the monarch Creon make a similar argument in his *Suppliants*, and Thucydides reports that, in the speech that he delivered at Sparta, Alcibiades remarked that it was generally "acknowledged that democracy is foolishness [*anoía*]." Moreover, a reading of the plays that Aristophanes penned in and after the 420s would lend credence to the supposition that there is something to Darius' contention that, where the demos rules, corruption [*kakótēs*] is inevitable, that corrupt politicians tend to form alliances and jointly manage in a corrupt fashion the public business, and that it takes a quasi-monarchical patron and protector of the common people [*prostás ... toû dēmou*] to wrest control from these men. A close observation of the record of the Athenian demos in the years immediately preceding Alcibiades' arrival at Tissaphernes' court might also lead one to say of the ordinary democratic citizen what Darius had reportedly said: that "he pushes and hurries the public business on violently and without reflection [*áneu nóou*] like a swollen stream." When, in the wake of the religious hysteria to which Herms and Mysteries Scandals had given rise and of the catastrophe that had taken place in Sicily, educated Athenians read these passages in Herodotus or listened to someone reading them out loud, they may well have been induced to ruefully contemplate their own situation.

Something similar is apt to have happened for a different set of reasons when these Athenians perused the brief analysis of democracy limned in the anonymous pamphlet found among Xenophon's works. In that essay, the pamphleteer expresses his disdain for democracy. It puts power, he charges, in the hands of those who suffer from poverty [*penía*] and a lack of education [*apaideusía*] and who, as a consequence, exhibit not only ignorance [*amathía*] but also disorderliness [*ataxía*], and a propensity for disgraceful conduct [*ponēría*]. At the same time, however, the author of this tract expresses a grudging admiration for the regime. From one perspective, he acknowledges, the Athenian *politeía* is well-organized: it systematically favors the poor, as opposed to the rich; the class from which the mariners come, as opposed to the class from which the hoplites are drawn; and those who look to the sea and the empire for their livelihood, as opposed to the country folk who farm the land.

In the courts, he remarks, the advantage of those favored by the regime "is a greater concern than is justice." The impecunious people at Athens profit more, he contends, from "the ignorance, propensity for disgraceful conduct, and good will [*eúnoia*]" of the scoundrel [*ponērós*] than they would from "the virtue [*areté*], wisdom [*sophía*], and ill-will [*kakónoia*] exhibited by the man of worth [*ho chrēstós*]."[26]

The frustration felt by the trierarchs and the other *dunatótatoi* on Samos was intensified by the decidedly unpleasant situation in which they as individuals found themselves. They were well-to-do, and that had made them marks. Thanks to the introduction of jury pay by Pericles in the 450s, the city's tribunals—equipped as they were with juries of one hundred, five hundred, or even one thousand— were dominated by propertyless men who resided in the town of Athens, in the Peiraeus, or nearby; and a new, combative style of politics—pioneered by the demagogue Cleon son of Cleaenetus and taken up with a vengeance by Hyperbolus son of Antiphanes, by Peisander, and by Charicles son of Apollodorus, Androcles, and the like—gave rise not only to charges of treason directed at *stratēgoí* who failed in the field. It also engendered lawsuits, brought by a class of men who came to be labeled "sycophants [*sukophántai*]," which were aimed at those in Athens and in the cities in her alliance whose wealth and standing earned them popular envy—and blackmail became commonplace.

Cases of this sort were, in effect, political; and there were no safeguards against abuse. The time allotted the two sides was brief; there were no rules governing the admission of evidence; and there was no judge trained in the law who was in a position to dismiss a defective case. Moreover, unanimity was not required for a conviction. Nor was a supermajority. Instead, the verdict and sentence were each in succession decided by a simple majority vote.[27]

There was also another dimension to the irritation felt by these men. They were for the most part landowners—as were a great many Athenians less well-off. In the 450s, as we have had occasion to observe, their forebears had rightly foreseen that the construction of the Long Walls portended Athens' abandonment of her countryside in time of war, and they had not been at all happy about the prospect that their property would then be sacrificed. Some in their number had, in fact, been so dismayed that on the eve of the battle of Tanagra, before these walls were completed, they had actually engaged in treasonous correspondence with the Lacedaemonians.[28]

In the end, of course, this came to nothing. But the event had alerted the Spartans to divisions at Athens that they might later exploit; and, at the inception of Sparta's second Attic war, Agis' father had set out quite deliberately to drive a wedge between the tradesmen and artisans and the landless thetes who labored in the dockyards, unloaded ships in the commercial harbor, and rowed in Athens' fleet, on the one hand, and the *pentakosiomédimnoi*, *hippeîs*, and *zeugítai* for the most part concentrated in the country districts, on the other. This he attempted by ravaging early every summer the lands that the members of these three juridically defined wealth-classes owned and rented out or farmed themselves. According to Thucydides, the Eurypontid king hoped thereby to set the landed and the lacklands against one another and "introduce strife [*stásis*] into the public counsels" at Athens.[29]

Although Archidamus' stratagem did not in the short run pro-duce the desired result, a number of the plays of Aristophanes that were performed in the 420s—*The Acharnians*, for example, and his *Peace*—presuppose the existence at Athens of a large rural popula-tion with a vested interest in bringing the war to an end by one means or another. The discontent with Athenian public policy that Aristophanes exploited and stoked in those years was, however, nothing in comparison with the unhappiness felt by the city's farm-ers and landowners in the wake of the year-round occupation of Deceleia instituted by Archidamus' son Agis in 413. In the early 420s, Archidamus and those who followed suit after his departure from the scene had been able to do some damage. But their visits to Attica had been brief; and, despite Cleon's attempt to abolish the subvention that underpinned it, the cavalry corps formed after the construction of the Long Walls had remained intact and had been tolerably effective in obstructing the Peloponnesians' efforts at ravaging. In and after 413, however, Agis was able to shut down Athenian agriculture altogether and to close down the mines at Laurium as well. Moreover, something on the order of twenty thousand Athenian slaves subsequently found refuge at Deceleia. Attica's landowners, including the men subject in these years to the levy on their capital known as the *eisphorá* and expected also to perform expensive *leitourgíai* as trierarchs, had been deprived of their livelihood. It appears to have been at this time that well-to-do Athenians of reduced wealth first began forming syndicates to share the trierarchy and the attendant expenses.[30]

Governments are founded for various purposes. Among them, however, the protection of life and livelihood always looms large. The fact that Athens failed to safeguard the property of the city's farming population was, we have good reason to suppose, a source of increasing bitterness on their part. It must have intensified the anger felt by the trierarchs and the other *dunatótatoi* on Samos when they reviewed in their minds the decision made in Athens' public assembly to mount the raid on Laconia that had brought the Spartans back into the war and then pondered the consequences for them: a dramatic loss of the income they received and a no less dramatic increase in the economic burdens they bore. This, too, helps explain why these men were ready to overthrow Athens' democracy, and it casts considerable light on the willingness of a substantial part of the city's population to follow their lead. What had been an academic discussion in the time of Pindar, Herodotus, and the nameless pamphleteer discussed above now impinged on political practice.

DESPERATION AND DELUSION

When directly approached by some emissaries from the camp on Samos in December 412 or very early January 411, Alcibiades added another argument to what he had communicated hitherto—intimating that, absent a shift from democracy to oligarchy, the Great King would not regard the Athenians as worthy of trust. Upon returning to the island, these emissaries drew into their conspiracy those whom they thought "serviceable [epitédeioi]," and then they broached their revolutionary project to the "mob [óchlos]" of mariners and hoplites—who, though unenthusiastic or even quite wary, were nonetheless willing to go along with an eye to the prospect of receiving wages from the King.[31]

When the leading men gathered in private thereafter to discuss in detail Alcibiades' proposal, Thucydides reports that all but one of them regarded it as "easy to implement and worthy of trust." This individual, whom he had earlier described as "not lacking in intelligence [ouk axúnetos]," was the stratēgós Phrynichus son of Stratonides, a man in his sixties who had stood up to his fellow commanders and had rescued the Athenian force besieging Miletus from a likely disaster the previous year. Now he tried again to do the like—for he alone saw through the exile's subterfuge and recognized the damage that his scheme was apt to inflict on Athens.

Alcibiades seemed to him to be no more desirous of oligarchy than of democracy (which was, in fact, the case) and to have nothing in mind other than to dislodge the city from the well-ordered condition [kósmos] now pertaining so that he could be recalled from exile via the efforts of those belonging to his hetaireíai. As for his own colleagues on Samos, it is this on which they should focus their attention: that the city not descend into faction and civil strife [hópōs mè stasiásōsin].

Nor would such a project be easy for the King to pursue— for the Peloponnesians were now on a par with the Athenians at sea, and they held cities (and not the least important of these) which lay within his empire. In any case, it made no sense for him to make trouble for himself by preferring the Athenians when he could befriend the Peloponnesians who had never done him any harm.

If anyone supposed, as some evidently did, that the establishment of an oligarchy at Athens and the prospect that the new regime would encourage her allies to do the like would make the city more popular in these *póleis*, Phrynichus thought him misguided. As he put it, the peoples in the Aegean "are not going to prefer being enslaved under a democracy or under an oligarchy to being free under whichever of these regimes happens to govern them." Nor would these peoples be likely to think that those at Athens "who called themselves the noble and the good [*kaloí k'agathoí*]" would be less irksome than the common folk of Athens. For the former were the ones who took the lead in spurring the people on to the crimes they committed; this privileged class profited more from oppressing the allies than anyone else; and, if things were left to them, Athens' allies would suffer more violence, and the people in the allied cities would be "executed without trial." The cities within Athens' league were more likely to seek and secure solace from the common lot than from men of this sort.

It says much about the desperate straits the Athenians were in and about their lack of confidence in Athens' democracy that, after making what was a compelling case, Phrynichus found himself still isolated or very nearly so. It says even more that the leading men on Samos decided to proceed with the project proposed by Alcibiades and that later, when an opportunity presented itself, they saw to it that Stratonides' all-too-perceptive son was cashiered as a *stratēgós*.[32]

In the meantime, out of desperation—no doubt fearing, as Thucydides claims, that Alcibiades' recall would mean his own demise, but also, surely, with the interest of his *pólis* still in mind—Phrynichus then resorted to a political stratagem. In an attempt to put an end to Alcibiades' intrigue, he sent a letter to Astyochus at Miletus, spelling out in detail what his former associate was up to. But, as we have had occasion to note, the Spartan navarch did not seize upon this as an opportunity to punish or at least thwart the son of Cleinias. Instead, he journeyed to Magnesia on the Maeander to present the letter to the Athenian renegade and to Tissaphernes; and Alcibiades responded with a stratagem of his own by writing to his associates on Samos a letter specifying what the son of Stratonides had done and requesting that he be executed.

To this maneuver, Phrynichus, who was now in great peril, responded with a second stratagem, writing again to Astyochus to upbraid him for betraying his confidence and to provide him with proof of his own reliability—proof that took the form both of an invitation to attack and of full and accurate information regarding the inadequate defenses of the Athenians on Samos, where there were, as yet, no fortifications. This he did, we can be confident, in the full expectation that Astyochus would once again pass the letter on to Alcibiades and that the latter would write to his associates on Samos accusing him a second time. To head this off and cast suspicion on Alcibiades himself, the son of Stratonides then drew attention to the weakness of the Athenian defenses on the island and insisted that these defects be remedied by the immediate construction of fortifications. But, although this maneuver caused Alcibiades— when he, in fact, dispatched a second letter of accusation—to be suspected of harboring a personal animus against the son of Stratonides, it did not prevent the implementation of Alcibiades' plan by Phrynichus' fellow commanders and the other leading men on the island.[33]

Nor did Phrynichus' intervention and Astyochus' handling of it drive a wedge between Tissaphernes and Alcibiades. That his comely guest dicker with the Athenians was as much in the interest of the satrap as it was in that of the exile. It might, after all, lead to an arrangement far more favorable to the Mede than anything on offer from the Spartans. In any case, the news that he was negotiating with the Athenians was apt to have on Lichas and his fellow *súmbouloi* a salutary, sobering, chastening effect—and this it surely did. For when, near the end of winter, they journeyed from Rhodes to Caunus to meet once again with the Great King's viceroy, these eleven Spartiates had not only learned the hard way that they could not function without Persian financial support. They had also had it brought home to them that, in his quest to regain what Xerxes and Artaxerxes had conceded to the Hellenes, the younger Darius had options other than Lacedaemon.[34]

Tissaphernes and Alcibiades were well worthy of one another, and the relationship between the pair, though ephemeral, was a trial marriage made in heaven. The two were cut from the same cloth: each was to good effect using the other as a pawn in the larger game that he was playing, and they admired one another's agility and guile.[35]

Cleinias' nimble son was a high-wire performer. He courted peril. He positively enjoyed the risk—and, in the course of his time in exile, he really did manage by dint of his charm, his audacity, and his penetration to turn everything in Hellas upside down. As we have seen, when he was driven into exile as a consequence of the Herms and Mysteries Scandals, Alcibiades had breathed defiance, boasting that he would soon demonstrate to his compatriots that he was not in any way dead. In 411, as the spring approached, no one could deny that this Athenian turncoat was still alive ... although by that time a host of men, who might otherwise have been indifferent, greatly regretted this fact.

CHAPTER FOUR

STÁSIS

There were all types of things in here, books on typography, epigraphy, philosophy, political ideologies.... Books like .... Thucydides' *The Athenian General*—a narrative which would give you chills. It was written four hundred years before Christ and it talks about how human nature is always the enemy of anything superior. Thucydides writes about how words in his time have changed from their ordinary meaning, how actions and opinions can be altered in the blink of an eye. It's like nothing has changed from his time to mine.

BOB DYLAN

W HEN ALCIBIADES son of Cleinias encouraged the *dunatôtatoι* within the Athenian force on Samos to overturn "the villainous democracy that had banished him," it was as if he had hurled a burning brand into a thick forest suffering from an enduring drought. As we have seen, the wealthy men whom he addressed were already eager for a change of regime, and the soldiers and mariners on Samos as well as the common people at Athens were acutely aware that the city desperately needed financial support. To the former, he had given an argument that could be used both to persuade a majority of the latter and to silence those inclined to object.

The driving force behind the initiative dreamed up by Alcibiades was, of all people, the much-mocked demagogue Peisander—the figure most responsible for instituting the witch hunt that had taken place in the wake of the Herms' mutilation. He was, on the face of it, a most unlikely oligarch, and he cannot have been a long-time partisan of the son of Cleinias.

Peisander is not known to have been rich. But, like the other prominent popular leaders, he must have possessed a competence. For none but the well-to-do had the leisure required if a man was to devote his time to public life, and in 411 he appears to have been among the trierarchs stationed at Samos. That said, he cannot have been of noble birth. For, although his conduct is discussed by various contemporaries, no one even bothers to mention his patronymic. It is as if he was no one from nowhere.

Moreover, although Peisander seems not to have joined his fellow demagogue Androcles in obsessively singling out Alcibiades and his associates for attack, there is not a shred of evidence to suggest that in 415 he came to the man's defense. He is apt, in fact, to have had the blood of a number of wealthy and well-born young Athenians on his hands—among them, in all likelihood, some of the boon companions of Cleinias' ambitious son.[1]

We do not know whether Peisander was among those who visited Sardis in December 412 or very early January 411 to listen to Alcibiades' pitch, but the odds are good that he was a member of the delegation. For, had he not been present to hear and report on what the son of Cleinias had to say, it is highly unlikely that he would have been one of those chosen to journey back home and present the exile's proposal to the *próbouloi*, the Council of Five Hundred, and the assembly.

There is reason to suspect that a considerable period of time passed between the decision on Samos to dispatch Peisander and his fellow envoys to Athens and their actual departure. The *stratēgoí* and everyone else on the island are apt to have been preoccupied at this time. The initial visit with Alcibiades and the subsequent maneuvers of Phrynichus son of Stratonides took place not long before the second week in January 411, when Astyochus left Miletus with the better part of his fleet and made his way down the Anatolian coast to effect a rendezvous with Antisthenes' flotilla at Caunus. Thereafter, for six weeks or even two months, the trierarchs and the military commanders based on Samos found themselves busy not only on Chios but also in the waters about Cnidus and, then, Rhodes.

Fortunately—at least from the perspective of Peisander and his colleagues—there was no need for hurry. In the interim, the Athenians would grow even more desperate, and rumor would do much of the preliminary spadework that needed doing. By the time— quite early in March—that the envoys from Samos arrived, the citizens were prepared for a showdown and eager to listen to the arguments on offer.[2]

PEISANDER IN ATHENS

It was in the assembly, where he had long been a force, that Peisander in due course took the lead. His colleagues had made the case for Alcibiades' recall and for making adjustments of a mildly oligarchic sort to the political practices of their compatriots. This they presented as a prerequisite for securing the friendship of Tissaphernes son of Hydarnes, an alliance with the Great King, and victory over the Peloponnesians. As one would expect, opposition quickly erupted—voiced by the resolute partisans of democracy, by those scandalized by Alcibiades' comportment, and by the Eumolpidae and the Ceryces, the two priestly families that officiated at celebrations of the Mysteries at Eleusis.

In response, Peisander came forward to address each group in turn, stating the facts, then posing a simple question. First, we are told, he drew attention to the advantages enjoyed by the Peloponnesians, who possessed as many triremes as the Athenians, who had more support than Athens did in the cities that had hitherto been her allies, and who were in receipt of generous funding from the Mede. Then, he outlined Athens' plight and asked whether any of the objectors had a plan for saving the *pólis* other than the one that his colleagues had just presented. When no one had anything to say in reply, he asserted, "This we cannot achieve unless we govern ourselves in a manner more in keeping with *sōphrosúnē* and place the magistracies into fewer hands in order to gain the trust of the King. This we cannot accomplish unless, in the present crisis, we cease taking counsel more concerning the city's regime [*politeía*] than concerning her safety and unless we recall Alcibiades who, alone among those now alive, can engineer this." It was this statement of the putative facts, this question, and this exhortation that silenced the leading opponents of the program Peisander's colleagues had presented.

It was, however, the presenter himself who persuaded the multitude. Over the years Peisander had gained the trust of Athens' tradesmen, artisans, and salarymen; and he could hardly have been considered a partisan of Alcibiades. If he, of all men, regarded adjustments in the direction of oligarchy as the price of survival, if he also thought Alcibiades' recall an urgent necessity, then, the majority of those in attendance at the assembly that day apparently thought, there really was no choice—at least for the nonce. For the time being, Peisander remarked, resorting to euphemism, it was fine that Athens be "democratically governed," but the city's governance should "not" be conducted "in the same manner" as in the recent past. Later on, he intimated, once the *pólis* had reached a safe haven, the reform of Athens' democracy that he had in mind could be revisited and reversed.

In response, the Athenians voted to send Peisander and ten others to reach an accord with Tissaphernes and Alcibiades. Then, when—to get the one fierce opponent of this scheme out of the way—Peisander attacked as treasonous the decision to bring the siege of Miletus to an end and accused Phrynichus of betraying Amorges and Iasos thereby, they dismissed the man from his position as *stratēgós* and they cashiered his colleague and presumed associate Scironides. Thereafter, to replace the two, they sent out the sometime military commanders Diomedon and Leon. That the latter were known to be amenable to working with Alcibiades and inclined to hope that the scheme outlined in the assembly by Peisander and his colleagues would succeed we can be confident.³

The fact that, apart from Scironides and the son of Stratonides, the *stratēgoí* whom the people of Athens had entrusted with high office and dispatched to Ionia appear to have been in accord with Peisander and his fellow envoys no doubt reinforced the persuasiveness of the case these men made—and, although Thucydides names very few names in the course of describing the oligarchic movement, it is clear that many former military commanders and other prominent individuals were also supportive. Among the former *stratēgoí* expressly identified were Laespodias, who had helped conduct raids along the Laconian coast in 414 at Athens' behest; his colleague in that endeavor Pythodorus, who had been a signatory of the Peace of Nicias in 421 and of the abortive alliance with Lacedaemon adopted soon thereafter; Dieitrephes, who had been dispatched in 413 to conduct the force of light-armed Thracians back to their homeland; and Aristocrates son of Scellias, who had also been a signatory of that peace and that alliance, who could be mentioned in a Platonic dialogue alongside luminaries such as Nicias and those who belonged to the house of Pericles, who was dispatched in 412 to try to head off the Chian revolt then suspected, and who would later serve as a subordinate commander under Alcibiades at the latter's invitation. To this group of notables, we can add prominent figures not known to have been elected to high office—such as Archeptolemos son of the urban planner and naturalized Athenian citizen Hippodamus of Miletus; the son of Pericles' old rival Thucydides son of Melesias, on whom his father had conferred his own father's name; and the intellectually prominent admirer of the sophist Thrasymachus Cleitophon son of Aristonymos. That there were a great many other figures of note involved goes without saying.⁴

Before leaving for Anatolia, Peisander turned to the very people whom he and his colleagues on the Commission of Inquiry had subjected to investigation in 415 at the time of the Herms and Mysteries

Scandals. In the process, he paid visits to some of the *hetaireíai*— those that had been transformed by the political crisis then underway from mere drinking and dining clubs made up of boon companions into *sunōmosíai*, associations for achieving victories in the courts and in magisterial elections composed of men bound together as co-conspirators of a sort [*sunōmótai*] by a solemn oath requiring of them secrecy and loyalty.

These "sworn confederacies" had been in evidence in 416 at the time of the ostracism of the demagogue Hyperbolus son of Antiphanes. Now, however, almost certainly as a consequence of the misfortune that had befallen a great many of the members of the *hetaireíai* in 415, political *práxis* seems to have become a focus for a great many more of what had hitherto been little more than social clubs. Peisander's aim was to forge these disparate, rival *sunōmosíai* into a single political unit. To this end, he spoke much more frankly to them than he had to the assembly, revealing the full extent of the political transformation that he had in mind and urging that they join together, take counsel regarding the destruction of the democracy and the establishment of an oligarchy, and implement the stratagems they devised.[5]

There can hardly be doubt that Peisander meant business. As we have seen, he was not the sort of man to let a crisis go to waste, and he put the same energy and determination into this endeavor that he had devoted to stoking the panic that had gripped Athens in the wake of the Herms' mutilation. His motives remain a mystery, and this fact has given rise to a great deal of scholarly speculation. Why would a man hitherto as devoted to democracy as he seems to have been now turn coat?

It is conceivable that the events of the preceding years had instilled in Peisander a profound disillusionment with the existing form of government. Zealots do sometimes change their minds, and Athens' recent experience with democratic government had been a profound disappointment.

It is also possible, however, that Peisander had never been a true believer and that he had always been driven solely by a lust for pre-eminence and power. He was not a Christian taught to regard ambition as morally suspect. He operated in a political culture shaped by Homer's *Iliad* and *Odyssey*. As one would then expect, the ancient Greeks were often unabashed and, therefore, uninhibited in their pursuit of honor and glory; and Peisander was no exception. Moreover, in republican settings, both then and now, politicians tend to be flexible. Rarely do they sacrifice popularity, advancement, office, and dominion for the sake of principle; and on the rare occasion when an individual does so it leaves a powerful impression. This was as true then as it is now. Peisander's response to the mutilation of the Herms tells us a great deal about the man. At that time, he had his eye on the main chance and on nothing else. Scruples were certainly no restraint, and he was by no means loath to seize an opportunity when it came his way. He was an adept at what its advocates now call lawfare.

There is, moreover, yet another possibility that cannot simply be dismissed. It is conceivable that Peisander believed what he had said when he spoke to the assembly at Athens—that he really was persuaded that, absent a subvention from the Mede, the Athenian *pólis* was doomed and that, if the Athenians complied with Alcibiades' wishes, the son of Cleinias could and would deliver the requisite funding.

Of course, two or even all three of these motives could have been in play. Ambition and public-spiritedness are not always at odds. In any case, if the last of the three really did play a role in Peisander's calculations, as seems likely, he was in for a profoundly unpleasant surprise. For, in mid-March 411, when he and his colleagues reached Anatolia, they and the others who had entertained such hopes discovered that desperation has one thing in common with desire. It, too, is quite frequently the mother of delusion.[6]

DISILLUSIONMENT AND DESPERATION

In the meeting that took place, Tissaphernes was present, but Alcibiades spoke on his behalf. What ensued was, in effect, a solicitation of bids. As a *quid pro quo*, Peisander and his fellow envoys initially offered the Mede the Hellenic cities in Asia Minor. But, apparently, this did not suffice. So, in the second of their meetings, they offered in addition the islands off the coast. Then, in their third conference with the satrap, Alcibiades, acting on Tissaphernes' behalf, upped the ante, demanding that the Athenians agree to allow the Great King to patrol with his fleet not only the coasts of the lands they had conceded to him but also the nearby seas. At this point, with Athens' dominion over the Aegean at stake, Peisander and his colleagues withdrew in a fury—persuaded, rightly, that the son of Cleinias had deceived them—and, not long thereafter, Tissaphernes proceeded on to Caunus to forge the agreement with Lichas son of Arcesilaus and the Peloponnesians that would be ratified in the plain of the Maeander at winter's end.[7]

Peisander and the champions of oligarchy, both on Samos and at Athens, were left in a quandary. They had made their case to the Athenian people on a false premise—that Alcibiades could and would deliver—and now they were committed. The die was cast. Even if they wanted to do so, they could no longer safely back off— especially since, back at Athens, the politicized *hetaireíai* were doing exactly what they had been instructed to do.

To begin with, some of the younger men had banded together to kill Androcles, the preeminent popular leader of the day. This they did, Thucydides reports, not only to put an end to the man's "demagogy [*dēmagōgía*]," but also to please his enemy Alcibiades, who would, they presumed, soon be recalled and render Tissaphernes friendly to Athens. Others, almost certainly men of some standing within the body politic, whom the young *hetaîroi* thought similarly "*anepitēdeíoi*"—unserviceable, inconvenient, ill-suited to their plans, and in the way—they treated in the same brutal fashion. These murders they carried out behind the scenes while openly proposing a simple and straightforward political program consisting of two mea- sures: one stipulating that henceforth no one receive public pay [*místhos*] other than those on active service in the city's navy or army, and the other prescribing that the authority to deal with pub- lic affairs [*prágmata*] be entrusted to no more than five thousand Athenians and that these be drawn from those best situated to serve the city with their money and their lives.[8]

In describing the motives of political players, Thucydides sometimes exaggerates for rhetorical effect the role played by self-interestedness while understating the influence of highmindedness. This is what he does in his treatment of the political program announced by the *het- aîroi*. It was, he says "specious [*euprepés*]," a dodge designed to deceive the gullible masses—for "the very people who were pushing the change were going to take possession of the *pólis*."

That ambition was involved goes without saying. It lurks behind every species of idealism and frequently deceives thereby even the highminded—and, as we have seen, there was nothing in the politi- cal culture of Athens to serve as a restraint. That this was not the whole story, however, and that a great many of those involved in this revolutionary project took this program seriously, Thucydides later concedes—and rightly so. For there is every reason to believe that the catastrophe in Sicily intensified what had hitherto been for the most part academic ruminations regarding the merits and defects of the various species of democracy and oligarchy; that, in raising as a serious matter the possibility of regime change on his first visit to Athens, Peisander set off a great debate of practical significance con- cerning these questions; and that some Athenians then looked abroad for superior models of self-government while others grounded their reflections on the political tradition of their own *pólis*, disputing the character of Athens' ancestral laws [*pátrioi nómoi*] and that of her ancestral constitution [*pátrios politeía*].[9]

The first of the two measures pressed in the period following Pei- sander's departure for Anatolia—that concerning public pay—was intended to ensure that Athens' revenues and what remained of the city's reserves would be devoted to the war. But it had another dimension as well. It promised to put an end to the decades-long domination of the juries by Athens' tradesmen, artisans, and salary-men. In this particular, like the second measure, it was a logical extension of what the Athenians did when they elected the ten *próbouloi*. The reform project was, in fact, a systematic attempt to redress the grievances of the city's farming population, to put an end to sycophancy, and to promote moderation and prudence in the framing of public policy by reconstituting the Athenian *politeía* on the agrarian foundations that Athens had in effect abandoned when the assembly voted to build the Long Walls. If this program were adopted, where the Athenians content to shelter behind the Long Walls had for decades reigned supreme, dominating the city's juries and her assembly, the men who tilled the soil of Attica and served as cavalrymen or as hoplites in the ranks would once again rule.

This narrowing of the city's ruling order required a sharp break with a mode of governance nearly a century old and with inclusive practices older yet. Had there been as many impoverished citizens at Athens at this time as there had been in 432, such a transformation would have been unthinkable. But, as we have seen, nearly all of the thetes dispatched to Sicily in 415 and 413 as rowers and nautical specialists had lost their lives, and many of the surviving members of the wealth-class soon to be dislodged from power were in 411 serving as rowers and specialists in the fleet deployed in Ionia. These facts notwithstanding, the conspirators realized that so radical a change could not be implemented in Athens absent a reign of terror. It is this recognition that occasioned their murder of Androcles and of the others judged *anepitēdeíoi*.

According to Thucydides, there was not at this point a departure from the long-established forms. The Council of Five Hundred still met, as did the assembly. But they deliberated on no measures other than those approved by the conspirators. Moreover, those who stood up to speak were drawn solely from among the would-be oligarchs and what the speakers said had been reviewed *in camera,* amended, and approved in advance.

"As a consequence of fear and of an awareness that the conspiracy was extensive," Thucydides reports,

> no one else rose to object. For, if anyone did speak up in opposition, an expedient was promptly found for his elimination. Afterwards, there was neither an inquiry into who had committed the murder nor, if someone was suspected, was there a trial to set things right. And so the people remained quiet and at rest, amazed and anxious, thinking it a gain if, by silence, they themselves avoided suffering violence. Supposing the conspiracy much more extensive than it really was, they were defeated in spirit. Thanks to the magnitude of their city and of their unfamiliarity with one another, they were unable to discover what was going on. For the same reason, it was impossible for a man to express that which vexed him to anyone else with an eye to taking counsel for the purpose of self-defense, for he would either have to speak to someone he did not know or to someone he knew but did not trust. Suspicion governed the relations of the adherents of the popular cause with one another—lest one of them be a participant in what was underway, there being those among the conspirators whose embrace of oligarchy no one would ever have forecast.

It evidently mattered a great deal that Attica was large, that Athens was populous, and that she was not a face-to-face community in which everyone knew everything about everyone else—for anonymity can all too easily fuel estrangement, and the attendant sense of alienation inhibited both confidence and cooperation. It mattered even more, however, that among the revolutionaries there were well-known demagogues like Peisander and other men who had long curried popular favor—among them at this stage, if not earlier, his former fellow inquisitor the sometime *stratēgós* Charicles son of

Apollodorus. It was the presence of these men and of others like them within the ranks of the conspirators, Thucydides tells us, "that contributed the most to the safety of the few by establishing within the ranks of the common folk a firm distrust of one another."[10]

At Athens, Peisander and his associates did something comparable to what the Spartiate Pedaritus' successor as harmost would later accomplish when he executed Tydeus and his supporters and imposed a narrow oligarchy on that once-well-ordered island *pólis*. In the process, these Athenian conspirators unwittingly completed by means of violence the work that Cleon son of Cleaenetus, "the most violent [*biaiótatos*] of the citizens," had begun at Athens quite early in the previous decade. They, too, pitted their fellow citizens against one another; and, by jettisoning even the appearance of legality, they did so to even greater effect than he had. The Athenian practitioners of lawfare—Cleon, Hyperbolus, Peisander, and Androcles—and the sycophants who had prosecuted and blackmailed the well-to-do were now powerfully seconded by the members of the *sunōmosíai*, subsequently rallied by this same Peisander. Between them, the demagogues, the sycophants, and the oligarchic conspirators destroyed the *homónoia*—the solidarity, the likemindedness—that had given Athens as a community a unity and strength that had set her apart from the vast majority of *póleis*. They took a flawed but relatively stable political order—a *kósmos* in which one could hope that deliberative reason would for the most part hold sway—and they shattered it. The situation was dire. For within a *pólis*, once fellow-feeling, the ethos of mutual trust, and the sense of being one has been fully destroyed, it is exceedingly difficult to reestablish a stable political order.

THE FOUR HUNDRED

After Peisander and his fellow envoys returned to Samos from their parley with Tissaphernes and Alcibiades, the conspirators took stock and decided to abandon altogether further cooperation with Alcibiades and to concentrate, instead, on establishing an oligarchy at

Athens and on sustaining the war with the resources in their posses-sion.[11] It was an act of desperation. For, in comparison with the city's needs, those resources were anything but ample.

The conspirators were, nonetheless, resolute; and they began by doing something on Samos that is powerful testimony of the fluidity of political commitments at this time. They persuaded a sizable cohort of the wealthy Samians who had supported the democratic coup d'état that had taken place on their island the year before to turn coat and establish an oligarchy there under Athenian sponsor-ship. Then, on the false presumption that it would strengthen sup-port for the Athenian cause, they dispatched half of the envoys to the islands and coastal communities of the Aegean to do the like and the other half to Athens to support the revolutionary cause at home. The latter were instructed to topple democracies and establish oli-garchies while en route—and this they did over the course of a handful of weeks, while pausing at islands such as Paros, Naxos, Andros, Tenos, and Euboea.[12]

When they finally made it to Athens—in, one must suspect, late April or early May—Peisander and his associates moved quickly to capitalize on the climate of fear that the *sunōmosíai* had produced. First, they called an assembly. Then, in the absence of a concerted opposition, they secured the selection of a board of draftsmen [*sun-grapheîs*] not only authorized as *autokratóres* to frame a proposal specifying how the city could best be governed but instructed to do so. This was to be presented not to the Council of Five Hundred, as was the norm, but directly to the people of Athens, and this was to be done soon thereafter on a day specified.

Thucydides reports that there were ten such *sungrapheîs* chosen. Aristotle—who followed the Atthidographer Androtion or his suc-cessor Philochorus, who had himself drawn on Androtion—claims that the assembly elected twenty men each over the age of forty. These were to serve alongside the ten *próbouloi* selected late in 413 as a board of thirty *sungrapheîs*; and, in doing their work, they were instructed to consult "the ancestral laws [*pátrioi nómoi*]" constituting the democracy established by Cleisthenes in the late sixth century, which did not specify that there be jury pay.

Although the difference between these two accounts is immaterial, Aristotle is apt to be right on the details. The fact that he specifies the name of the man who drafted and moved the decree, that of its principal proponent in the assembly, and that of another man who intervened to propose an amendment suggests that, behind the report that he consulted, there was not only a documentary foundation of the sort often provided by the Atthidographers but also eyewitness testimony. Moreover, the eyewitness in question and the source for the documents is apt to have been Androtion's own father Andron—an erstwhile student of the sophist Hippias. At this stage, he was a supporter of the revolution underway, and he had almost certainly been present that day in the Athenian assembly.[13]

When the day appointed for the presentation of the *sungrapheîs'* report arrived, the assembly was summoned but not to its customary seat on the Pnyx within the confines of the town. Instead, Thucydides reports, its meeting was held within the sacred precinct enclosing the temple of Poseidon Hippios at Colonus about a mile north of Athens. This site seems to have been chosen for two reasons. With Agis and a Peloponnesian force stationed at Deceleia, the thetes then present at Athens were much less likely than their hoplite compatriots to venture outside the area enclosed by the community's system of walls; and the cult site itself was associated with the Athenians who served as cavalrymen. The great majority of the latter will have been landholding members of the juridically defined wealth-classes of *pentakosiomédimnoi* and of *hippeîs*. As such, they will have been subject to the *eisphorá* and to the requirement that, from time to time, each perform a liturgy as a trierarch; and in the circumstances pertaining in 411 this is apt to have rendered them sympathetic to the oligarchic movement. At Colonus, the conspirators would encounter little, if any, resistance.[14]

At this gathering, if Thucydides is to be trusted, the *sungrapheîs* did not perform their assigned function—perhaps because there was no consensus as to the proper answer to the question they were asked to address. Instead, they advanced a single resolution, stipulating that the prytanies, drawn from the Council of Five Hundred, who presided over the assembly put to a vote all proposals pertinent to Athens' safety and that legal immunity [*adeía*] be conferred on everyone involved in effecting the constitutional changes Peisander and his colleagues thought requisite. Mindful, moreover, that someone might try to impede the actions of the assembly by lodging against a prospective reformer what was called a *graphế paranómōn*, a lawsuit asserting that the proposal was contrary to established law, or by seeking a legal remedy in the courts in some other fashion, they proposed that such a citizen be brought before the *stratēgoí* and, if found guilty of interfering, be turned over to the Eleven for execution.[15]

When this proposal was adopted and the way was clear for the consideration of measures hitherto considered almost unthinkable, Peisander once again stepped forward—and, as was his wont, he took the lead. He moved that the city's dwindling reserves and her revenues be spent on the war alone; that, apart from the archons and the prytanies, no magistrates be paid; and that the ones paid receive three obols a day. He proposed a decree stipulating that for the remainder of the war the political rights associated with citizenship be restricted to those best able to perform *leitourgíai* for the city with their persons and property and that these men number no fewer than five thousand; that they be authorized to make treaties with anyone they wished; and that one hundred men over the age of forty, ten from each of the ten tribes, be elected to serve as "registrars [*katalogeîs*]" authorized to draw up a list of the *pentakosiomédimnoi*, *hippeîs*, and *zeugítai* who would be accorded full political rights.

Peisander also moved that a probouleutic Council of Four Hundred be established in place of the old Council of Five Hundred and that it consist of forty members drawn from each of the ten tribes. According to Thucydides, he urged that this body not be chosen by lot from an elected pool, as had been the case with the old probouleutic council under the democracy, but that it be constituted in the following fashion: five presiding officers [*próedroi*] should be elected by the assembly; they should then select one hundred men (presumably ten men per tribe); and each of the hundred should in turn choose three colleagues. This council would then be fully authorized [*autokrátoras*] to rule as its members thought best and to convene as an assembly, whenever it seemed to them appropriate, the body of *pentakosiomédimnoi, hippeîs,* and *zeugítai* that came to be called the Five Thousand. In effect, Peisander was asking that, at least for the time being, the Council of Four Hundred be entrusted with Athens' governance; and his request was accepted by the assembly. Thanks to fraud and force, as Aristotle expressly points out and Thucydides implies, Athens had now become an oligarchy.[16]

Aristotle reports that, on the same day, the assembly passed another measure providing for the selection of one hundred "recorders [*anagrapheîs*]" tasked with proposing how the changes made should be implemented in detail—i.e., with drafting a constitution [*politeía*] to govern the operations of the Four Hundred and the Five Thousand. The fact that the peripatetic ascribes the passage of this measure to the Five Thousand and then admits that the Five Thousand had not yet been appointed reflects the confusion generated by the revolution. For, from the perspective of those involved, the body of *pentakosiomédimnoi, hippeîs,* and *zeugítai* assembled at Colonus that day was for all practical purposes indistinguishable from the Five Thousand slated for listing and formal registration by the *katalogeîs*. Aristotle then goes on to specify that soon thereafter the *anagrapheîs* presented two proposals to a similar assembly presided over by a man named Aristomachos—one sketching out the constitutional arrangements that should be followed in "the time to come," and the other one specifying the procedures that should be put into effect immediately.

Of these two proposals and of the *anagrapheîs* said to have framed them, Thucydides makes no mention at all. His silence should not, however, deter us from taking Aristotle's report seriously. Nor should we jump to the conclusion that neither proposal was ever in any way implemented. The historian's silence may simply be a reflection of the fact that the lack of interest in constitutional detail evident in his tendency to ignore the operations of the Athenian Council of Five Hundred under the democracy extended with equal force to the workings of the new oligarchic regime.[17]

What can be said with some assurance is that, if Aristotle is to be trusted, the conspirators moved with alacrity in the aftermath of the assembly at Colonus—selecting the Four Hundred, eliciting proposals from the *anagrapheîs*, and securing their approval. If the peripatetic's report is accurate, it was only thereafter (and, we must assume, quite soon thereafter) that they staged a coup d'état with the help of the three bodies of armed men whom Thucydides mentions: Athenian hoplites summoned from the settlement established on Aegina at the beginning of the second of Athens' three wars with the Peloponnesians; hoplites from Andros, Tenos, and Carystus whom Peisander and his associates had collected while en route to Athens from Samos; and a gang of one hundred twenty young men armed with daggers.

In the process, these would-be oligarchs reportedly overawed, then paid off, and expelled from the Bouleuterion the members of the democratic Council of Five Hundred and assumed office in their place. Aristotle dates the expulsion of the councilors to the fourteenth day of the Attic month of Thargelion (ca. 11 June in the modern Gregorian calendar), and he dates the Four Hundred's formal assumption of office to the twenty-second day of that lunar month, five weeks prior to the inception of the 411/10 archon year. Not long after performing the customary sacrifices and casting lots to determine which of the ten tribal contingents would serve as prytanies in residence at the Bouleuterion morning, noon, and night during the first bouleutic month, Thucydides adds, the Four Hundred began to rule "imperiously, jailing some of their compatriots, banishing others, and executing certain individuals, though not many (those whom it seemed convenient [*epitédeioi*] to remove from the scene)."[18]

Thucydides and Aristotle both tell us that in short order the Four

Hundred dispatched an embassy to Agis at Deceleia, proposing that peace be made on terms stipulating that the Spartans and the Athenians each continue to hold what was currently in their possession. Although this approach was no doubt later regarded by many as an act of treason, it was surely not unexpected. For there is reason to believe that an argument was made by Peisander or by someone else in the assembly at Colonus in favor of just such a resort to diplomacy and that its proponent contended that the Lacedaemonians were apt to be more open to negotiations with an oligarchy than with a democracy.[19]

From an Athenian point of view, such an overture made excellent sense. In antiquity, as we have seen, when it came to naval warfare, money really was the sinews of war. At this juncture, the financial resources of Athens and of her citizens were meager. Those of the Persians were in comparison very nearly unlimited, as they long had been. In the short run, Athens could mount a determined resistance to the Peloponnesian onslaught, and they could hope to enjoy considerable success—though this was by no means guaranteed. In the long run, however, if Sparta and her allies remained adamant and if the Mede remained willing to finance their effort, the Athenians' cause was doomed. Their opponents had staying power. They did not. Their only hope lay in driving a wedge between these two ill-sorted allies. They had tried to reach an accommodation with Tissaphernes and his master; and, despite the fact that Lichas' outburst at Cnidus had given their argument a considerable measure of credibility, they had failed. It was now time to feel out the Lacedaemonians.

THE TURN TO LACEDAEMON

Peoples tend to have a short-term horizon, and this observation applies, although with less force, to those who lead them as well. The species of foresight possessed by statesmen like Pericles son of Xanthippus and the Syracusan Hermocrates son of Hermon is rare, and that possessed by visionaries like Themistocles son of Neocles is rarer still. Persia's Great King and his satraps were fully informed concerning the danger posed by Athens. But they had no direct experience of Lacedaemon as a menace. So, in the absence of other considerations, they were inclined to think the clear and recently present danger posed by the Athenians greater than the distant and largely speculative threat posed by the rival coalition.

The Spartans were similarly positioned. There had been a period when the Mede had seemed a genuine menace, and they had acted accordingly. Now, however, thanks to the passage of time, the sustained containment of Persia, and what the Athenians had so recently done at Coryphasium and Mantineia, Athens seemed to a majority of the Lacedaemonians a far greater source of peril.

Agis, who had been a signatory of the Peace of Nicias and of the abortive alliance with Athens that followed it and who had led his compatriots against the Athenians and their Peloponnesian allies at Mantineia, is apt to have been particularly sensitive to the threat posed by Athens; and unpleasant experience may have caused him to harbor a personal animus against that *pólis*. According to Thucydides, when the envoys from Athens tried to persuade him that with an oligarchy in charge she would be less untrustworthy and more reliable as a partner in peace, Agis would have none of it. He had had enough, we must suspect, of what he and the majority of his compatriots are apt to have considered Athenian treachery; and, in any case, his bitter experience with the Argives made him doubt that such an oligarchy would long endure. In his opinion, we are told, the domestic strife besetting Athens was not at an end; the city was not likely "to remain at rest [*hēsucházein*]"; and the Athenian demos "would not so quickly surrender its ancient liberty."

Moreover, Agis suspected that, even if Athens was not already caught up in turmoil, the sight of a sizable army near the town would produce a commotion. So, instead of attempting to negotiate a mutually acceptable arrangement with the envoys, he told them more or less what Tissaphernes had conveyed to the envoys who had visited him: that, if the Athenians wanted peace, they would have to give up their dominion over the sea.

When the envoys proved to be unwilling to accept this, Agis summoned reinforcements from the Peloponnesus. When these arrived, he led them and the garrison posted at Deceleia to the very walls of Athens, hoping that the Athenians, thrown into confusion and disorder, would either submit to the harsh terms his compatriots had in mind or surrender without a blow in response to the uproar, both within and without, that his approach would generate. In any case, he thought, he would not fail to seize the Long Walls, which would be bereft of defenders.

Agis' calculations turned out to be wrong. When his army marched up to the walls, there was no *kínēsis*. The citizenry remained at rest; and, instead of submitting, the Four Hundred dispatched a force of cavalrymen, hoplites, light infantry, and archers to pick off those Peloponnesians who in their confidence came too close— which they did. This unexpected setback and the attendant bloodshed induced Agis to withdraw to Deceleia; and, after a few days, he sent the reinforcements back to the Peloponnesus.

Thereafter, when the oligarchs in charge at Athens renewed their suit, Agis, who now had a more accurate grasp of the situation, received the embassy they dispatched. It was, in fact, on his advice and with his encouragement and support that the Four Hundred soon thereafter sent to Lacedaemon to discuss terms of peace three envoys—a Melesias, apt, as we have seen, to have been the son of Pericles' last serious rival Thucydides son of Melesias; an Aristophon otherwise unknown; and the Laespodias who, as a *stratēgós* in the summer of 414, had helped conduct the raid on the Laconian coast that had provided the Spartans with a proper *casus belli*.

We do not know what would have happened had these three men reached Sparta. The Lacedaemonians had a marked predilection for oligarchy, as we have seen; and long experience had taught them that oligarchies dependent on their support tended to be pliable. It is conceivable that, if such a regime were in place, they would have been open to working with the Athenians and that a compromise could have been reached, conceding Sparta a role in the Aegean, otherwise leaving Athens' overseas dominion intact, and consigning the Mede once again to the interior of Asia Minor. It is also, however, perfectly possible—and, in the circumstances, a good deal more likely—that the Spartans would have bluntly demanded, as Agis originally had, that the Athenians surrender their supremacy at sea. Like their Eurypontid king, they had learned a lesson from the Argive debacle.

There is no reason to think that, at this time, those in command in Athens were any readier to accept an offer tantamount to surrender than they had been when their envoys first met with Agis. But a compromise that left the city's empire for the most part intact and that left her in control of the route, essential to the city's security and independence, that ran through the Hellespont, the Sea of Marmara, and the Bosporus to the Euxine—this would surely have been acceptable. In the long run, moreover, as the homebodies of Lacedaemon tired of the responsibilities that drew them overseas and as they found the cost of sustaining a fleet without a Persian subvention prohibitive, Athens—with a mixture of patience and chicanery—might well have regained what she had lost.

In the end, however, this exploratory diplomatic effort came to naught. For the oarsmen assigned to the trireme tasked with carrying the envoys to Laconia arrested them instead and turned them over to the Argives, charging the three with being among those most responsible for the overthrow of the Athenian democracy. Then, the trireme conveyed an Argive delegation to Samos—where in the interim, as these oarsmen knew only too well, those unhappy with the oligarchic enterprise had seized control of Athens' fleet.[20] It is to this development that we now must turn.

ALCIBIADES ON SAMOS

Shortly after Peisander and his fellow envoys left Samos for Athens, the oligarchic conspiracy on the island collapsed. That conspiracy had drawn strength from the presumption that, if democracy gave way to oligarchy at Athens, Alcibiades would be able to persuade

Tissaphernes and the Great King to provide the funds necessary for Athenian naval operations. Absent hope on this score, the oarsmen in the fleet and the others who found the prospect of living under an oligarchy unattractive no longer had any reason to acquiesce in Peisander's enterprise. There were also individuals on the island who had embraced the scheme because they admired Alcibiades' acumen and supposed that none but he could lead them to the victory they craved. At the moment in which the would-be oligarchs turned on the son of Cleinias, these men were inclined to turn on the conspirators.

When Peisander and his companions headed off to Athens, the Samian democrats-turned-oligarchs were poised to carry out a coup d'état. In preparation and to bolster their trust in one another, the three hundred involved in this conspiracy murdered the Athenian demagogue Hyperbolus son of Antiphanes, who had settled on the island some five years before to wait out the term of his ostracism and who is apt to have been an outspoken opponent of the enterprise launched by Peisander and his fellow trierarchs. Others who seemed to be in the way they also then killed. These assassinations the would-be Samian oligarchs accomplished with assistance from the *stratēgós* Charminus and from some of the Athenian conspirators.

When a group of prominent Samians not party to the coup attempt nonetheless got wind of what was in the offing, they approached four Athenians whom they knew to be hostile to oligarchy—a trierarch named Thrasybulus son of Lycus, a hoplite named Thrasyllus, and the *stratēgoí* Diomedon and Leon. These in turn approached the Athenian rowers and hoplites one by one and solicited their help, and when the crucial moment arrived the men they recruited rallied in support of the Samians under attack. Thirty of the three hundred conspirators the Samian democrats killed. The three leaders they exiled. Under an amnesty requiring that past misconduct be forgotten and that bygones be treated as bygones, the remainder were allowed to live on as citizens under the Samian democracy.[21]

It is worth pausing to ask how the Samians intent on heading off this coup knew that these four Athenians would be particularly sympathetic to their effort. Neither Thucydides nor any other surviving ancient source provides us with a definite answer. But, as one scholar has pointed out, the judgment of these counterrevolutionaries must have been grounded in some sort of prior experience, and there had been one occasion the year before when Thrasybulus and Thrasyllus may have forged a close relationship with the Samians most committed to sustaining democratic rule.

When the first conspiracy to overthrow the democracy was thwarted in 412, there were no more than thirty Athenian triremes in the eastern Aegean. Strombichides son of Diotimos and Thrasycles had situated themselves at Lade near Miletus with nineteen of the twenty vessels they had conducted to the eastern Aegean. Diomedon, who had conducted another ten galleys to the region, appears to have been on patrol off the Anatolian coast near Teos, and Leon was en route with an additional ten from Athens but had not yet arrived.

At the critical moment in 412, there were, as far as we can tell, only three triremes stationed at Samos. They had been posted there—presumably for the purpose of guarding the island and of alerting the other Athenian forces nearby should there be a surprise attack. One of these was presumably the twentieth of the vessels originally assigned to Strombichides and Thrasycles. The other two are apt to have been left behind by Diomedon or sent back from Teos. As we have seen, the crews of these three galleys rallied in support of the Samians who thwarted this—the first—coup attempt by would-be oligarchs. If at this time, as was perfectly possible, Thrasybulus was one of the three trierarchs in command of the triremes present and if Thrasyllus was among the hoplites serving as *epibataí* on these vessels, the two could easily have established a close relationship with some of the more stalwart defenders of the Samian democracy, and it would be their performance on this occasion that explains why they were the men approached in 411 when this particular set of Samian democrats needed help of a similar sort against their errant erstwhile allies on the island.

Of course, this hypothesis does not explain how Diomedon and Leon came to be involved. But if in the fifth century, as in the fourth, the Athenian commander assigned a particular task was free to select from among those eligible for the trierarchy the captains with whom he wished to work, Thrasybulus might well have had a prior connection with Diomedon close enough to justify his resort to him for assistance at the time of the second coup attempt in 411, and Leon was too frequently associated in command with Diomedon for us to doubt that the two were friends and allies. Moreover, these two *stratēgoí* and Thrasybulus were like-minded in at least one other particular. As we have already had occasion to note, Diomedon and Leon would not have been chosen as replacements for Phrynichus and Scironides had they been unfriendly to Alcibiades; and, as we shall soon see, Thrasybulus was among that controversial figure's preeminent partisans.

The conduct of these three men on Samos at the time of the second coup attempt may also have been inspired by their awareness of the breach that had just opened up between the son of Cleinias, on the one hand, and Peisander and his colleagues, on the other. Diomedon and Leon were in Athens and not on Samos when the oligarchic project was first seriously mooted; and, like many another trierarch assigned to the eastern Aegean, Thrasybulus may have been absent from the island—on Chios, for example—at that time as well. There is no compelling reason to suppose that any of these men was ever party to the oligarchic plot. Moreover, it was one thing to accept modest moves in the direction of oligarchy as the price for Tissaphernes' support and Alcibiades' return. It was another to join Peisander and his associates in embracing oligarchy as a positive good.[22]

The *Paralus*, the second of Athens' two messenger galleys, happened to be stationed at Samos at the time of the second coup attempt; and its crew, free citizens all, played a prominent role in blocking the coup d'état. When the dust settled, the Samian democrats and the Athenian soldiers and oarsmen dispatched the *Paralus* to Athens with word of what had happened on the island. With the trireme, they sent the avid democrat Chaereas, son of the Archestratus son of Lykomedes who had, on the eve of the previous war, commanded an Athenian expeditionary force sent to Potidaea. And, upon arrival, this Chaereas and the crew of the *Paralus* discovered that, at Athens, there really had been an oligarchic coup.

When this trireme entered the Peiraeus, Peisander and his associates arrested two or three of the crewmen and transferred the rest into a vessel tasked with guarding the island of Euboea. Later they foolishly assigned these men to convey Melesias, Aristophon, and Laespodias to Laconia. For his part, Chaereas dodged arrest and slipped quietly away, then managed to get passage back to Samos, where he grossly exaggerated the misconduct of the oligarchs: charging that at Athens everyone was being whipped, that one was not allowed to criticize those in control of the *politeía*, that the wives and children of those stationed on Samos were being abused, and that the oligarchs intended to seize as hostages the relations of those on Samos who were not of their persuasion and to kill them if those with the fleet did not submit.[23]

Thucydides reports that it took an effort on the part of "those in the middle" to dissuade the oarsmen and infantrymen on Samos from venting their wrath on the erstwhile promoters of oligarchy still in their midst and that they managed to bring home to everyone the need for unity in face of the Peloponnesian threat. Thereafter, Thrasybulus and Thrasyllus induced all of the Athenians still on the island, the erstwhile conspirators first and foremost, to take a solemn and weighty oath pledging that they would govern themselves democratically, be of the same mind, pursue the war against the Peloponnesians with vigor, regard the Four Hundred as enemies, and not treat with them—and the Samians took the very same oath. Thereafter, the Athenians on Samos held an assembly in which they deposed their former military commanders—including, apparently, Diomedon and Leon—as well as the trierarchs suspected of disloyalty and then elected Thrasybulus, Thrasyllus, and others unnamed in place of the men deposed. At this gathering, they are said to have offered one another words of encouragement, arguing that they were better positioned than their compatriots in the city—with some even expressing hope that, if Alcibiades were offered legal immunity from arrest and prosecution [*adeía*] and if he were recalled, he could arrange an alliance with the Great King. The fleet stationed on Samos had assumed all of the functions of a *pólis*. It was the view of those assembled that it was the town of Athens that was in rebellion.[24]

Not long thereafter, Thrasybulus, who professed to be hopeful that Alcibiades could negotiate an arrangement for his compatriots with Tissaphernes, managed—no doubt, with some difficulty—to persuade the rowers and infantrymen on Samos to recall him from exile and to confer on him the *adeía* that he required. From Samos he then journeyed to the court of Tissaphernes to issue the invitation, and Alcibiades returned with him to the island.

There, this infinitely flexible man reportedly spoke at length, mesmerizing his listeners. His treasonous cooperation with the Spartans he shamelessly blamed on his having been forced into exile. His ascendancy in the counsels of Tissaphernes he greatly exaggerated. The satrap had promised support to the Athenians, he claimed. He had even offered to bring into battle on their behalf the Phoenician fleet then lodged at Aspendus. But this he would do if and only if they were led by someone, such as Alcibiades, whom he could trust.

According to Thucydides, in staging his return and in framing his remarks, the son of Cleinias had in mind an audience more diverse than those within earshot. His aim was to strike fear into the oligarchs at Athens, to trigger a dissolution of the *sunōmosíai*, and to encourage the men stationed on Samos. He was also aware, we can assume, that his remarks would be bruited abroad; and with them he hoped to intensify the Peloponnesians' resentment of and hostility to Tissaphernes, to subvert their sense of self-confidence, and leave them unnerved.

As usual, Alcibiades' presentation was intoxicating; and, on the oarsmen and soldiers in his immediate audience, it had a prompt and palpable effect. Without hesitation, they elected him a *stratēgós*, and, Thucydides tells us, "they put him in charge of all public business." For their foe, these mariners and hoplites now expressed disdain; and they proposed rowing at once to the Peiraeus. From this foolhardy enterprise, Alcibiades—with some difficulty—dissuaded them; and, having done so, he headed back to Tissaphernes' court. His purpose was to use the sway that he now exercised over the Athenians to overawe the satrap and to use his apparent influence over Tissaphernes to do the like to his compatriots.[25]

Politics resembles courtship. In both, appearances matter, and fantasy frequently reigns supreme—as long as the requisite illusions can be sustained. Alcibiades, for all of his defects as a statesman, understood this better than almost any man alive in his time. As we have had ample opportunity to observe, Cleinias' eloquent son was a master of deception, and he had an uncanny ability to make men forget that he had hoodwinked them in the past. His task at this point was to hold the Athenian expeditionary force together and to drive Peisander and his associates from power in Athens. Via political legerdemain, he had conjured what amounted to a junta into existence in that *pólis*. Not long thereafter, Peisander and the other would-be oligarchs in attendance at the conference at Tissaphernes' court had discerned the illusory character of his claim to ascendancy in the counsels of the satrap, and they had turned on him with a vengeance. So now they had to go, and from his perch on Samos Alcibiades had to conjure the same junta out of existence. This he did in his customary fashion—by managing appearances.

In mid-June 411, when the Four Hundred formally assumed office, they immediately dispatched an embassy to Samos. Peisander and those who had accompanied him from the island to Athens were not unacquainted with the oarsmen and infantrymen posted there. They suspected—correctly as we have seen—that the former in particular would refuse to accept the new oligarchic order, and they feared that opposition concerted on Samos would eventuate at Athens in a counterrevolution and in their removal. With this in mind, they instructed the envoys to reassure those in Athens' expeditionary force that the oligarchy had been instituted to safeguard the city, not to harm her or her citizens. They were to tell the rowers and hoplites that the new government was constituted by five thousand Athenians, not just the four hundred who made up its council. And they were to remind them that, under wartime conditions, the assembly had never in practice brought together as many as five thousand Athenians.[26]

By the time that this embassy reached Delos, however, Thrasybulus, Thrasyllus, Diomedon, and Leon had thwarted the conspiracy fostered by Peisander to carry out a coup d'état and establish an oligarchic government on Samos. By this time, moreover, Chaereas had journeyed to Athens and had returned to report on and, in some measure, misrepresent developments there; Thrasybulus and Thrasyllus had reconstituted the expeditionary force on a democratic basis; and the possibility of Alcibiades' recall was being bandied about. Learning of this, the oligarchs' emissaries paused—no doubt in anticipation of receiving further instructions from home.[27]

By the time that the oligarchy's envoys had finally made their way to Samos, Alcibiades was in charge, and he leapt upon their presence as an opportunity to foster division within the Four Hundred at home. Thanks in part to Chaereas' somewhat misleading report, these emissaries were initially met with fury. As the son of Cleinias looked on, the rowers and soldiers shouted them down and urged the execution of those who had overthrown the democracy. Eventually, we are told, the crowd quieted down, and the delegates from Athens made their pitch, denying Chaereas' claim that the relatives of those in the expeditionary force had suffered or would suffer harm; asserting that—in keeping with what Aristotle would later describe as the constitutional arrangements for "the time to come"— everyone in the Five Thousand would, in rotation, have their share in the government; and pointing to the resistance mounted on the occasion of Agis' approach to the walls of the town as proof that the oligarchy's aim was Athens' preservation, not her destruction. None of this mollified their listeners, who once again strongly urged that the fleet head for the Peiraeus.[28]

With strong support from Thrasybulus, the son of Cleinias handled the situation with great aplomb. Initially, he allowed his compatriots on the island to vent their rage, for he knew that this would strike fear into the delegation dispatched by the Four Hundred and leave on its members an indelible impression. Then, he intervened—aware that if the expeditionary force abandoned its post on Samos, made its way to Athens, and launched a full-scale civil war, Ionia and the Hellespont would fall to the enemy. "It was," Thucydides pointedly tells us, "the very first occasion in which Alcibiades appears to have done the city a service, and in doing so he performed in an outstanding fashion. No one else had the capacity to restrain the mob and put a stop to the enterprise; and, railing at them, he turned from their wrath those enraged against the envoys on personal grounds."[29]

Then, having displayed to all concerned that he was the one in control of the situation, the son of Cleinias spoke bluntly to the Four Hundred's emissaries and sent them away, telling them that he would not prevent the Five Thousand from ruling. He insisted, however, that the Council of Four Hundred be eliminated and that the probouleutic council as it had existed in the past be reconstituted. He encouraged frugality, and he urged those in Athens to hold out and concede nothing to the city's enemies. "For," he reportedly added, "if the *pólis* is saved, there is also good reason to hope that the two bodies at odds will come to terms with one another. But once either is tripped up—either the one in Samos or the other—there will be no one left with whom to reconcile."

By staging this confrontation as he did, by bringing home to these envoys the pressing necessity that those in control in Athens conciliate the men at the front, and by suggesting a way that this could be done that was consistent with the rhetorical posture assumed by the instigators of the revolution from the outset, Alcibiades virtually guaranteed the collapse of the Four Hundred and the constitution of a regime, called the Five Thousand, in which Athens would be ruled by those with the wherewithal to provide their own armor—the *pentakosiomédimnoi, hippeîs,* and *zeugítai.* What he did on this occasion was not just another bravura performance. It was an act of statesmanship on a very high plane.[30] But there was much more to what Alcibiades had in mind than what statesmanship required.

FROM THE FOUR HUNDRED
TO THE FIVE THOUSAND

When Herodotus penned his *Inquiries* and inserted into the work the debate regarding the best regime that purportedly took place between Darius son of Hystaspes and his fellow conspirators Otanes and Megabyzus, he did not limit their purview to the advantages and defects of democracy. To this Megabyzus and this Darius, he also assigned a treatment of oligarchy. Like the remarks that Otanes, Megabyzus, and Darius were said to have made regarding democracy, their observations regarding oligarchy can hardly have been peculiar to the historian, and the line of thinking that they articulate—or something of the sort—may well have shaped the calculations of Alcibiades and those of others.

There surely is a case for conferring authority on "the best men," as Megabyzus urges—for those who are educated and apt to bring reflection to bear on public policy are less apt to blunder. That is why the democracies of modern times resort to representation, make no use of the lot, and adopt what the ancients considered an aristocratic practice: the election of public officials.[31]

But Darius' critique of rule by "the best men" has no less force than the praise conferred on that form of government by Megabyzus:

In oligarchies, where many men toil at excellence in service to the community [*areté … es tò koinón*], ferocious personal enmities tend to emerge. Each one wishes to lead the chorus, so to speak, and to have his judgment prevail. As a consequence, they fall into great enmities. From enmities, then, factions [*stáseis*] arise; and from factions, the shedding of blood.

According to Thucydides, this is exactly what happened at Athens when the envoys dispatched to Samos by the Four Hundred returned home. It is as if Alcibiades' handling of these emissaries was based on a shrewd calculation with regard to what was most apt to engender quarrels and strife within the clique that dominated the Four Hundred. It is hard to believe that this master manipulator had no idea of the mayhem he was likely to cause.[32]

The junta's inner circle consisted of four men. So Thucydides tells us. Peisander was, as we have seen, the front man. If it was the temptation initially on offer from Alcibiades that started the process, it was Peisander's grit and determination that got it off the ground. But he was no longer the brains behind the operation. That role, the Athenian historian reports, had been in due course taken up and played by a man named Antiphon son of Sophilus, whose exceptional intellectual acumen he stresses. It is a reasonable guess that this notorious backstairs operator was the mastermind behind the maneuvers that took place at Colonus and the proposals advanced in turn by the *sungrapheîs*, Peisander, and the *anagrapheîs*.

That Sophilus' son was the Antiphon who pioneered the speech-writing business in Athens is clear. He was also the first to publish speeches that he wrote, and he was a teacher of rhetoric. That the speechwriter and teacher of rhetoric was also the now well-known Athenian sophist of the same name stands to reason—for this is expressly asserted in the biographical tradition; the two fields of study were often linked in this period; and, while Antiphon was a tolerably common name in Athens, Antiphons of surpassing intelligence cannot have been all that numerous. To this one can add that the self-assurance which made the revolution possible derived from a philosophical conviction: that those who are naturally superior have a right to rule. Hinted at by Hippias in Plato's *Protagoras* when he draws a sharp distinction between those who are fellow citizens

by nature [*phúsis*] and those are fellow citizens solely because of custom or law [*nómos*], openly voiced by Callicles in Plato's *Gorgias* when
he contrasts what *phúsis* teaches regarding justice with what *nómos*
dictates, enthusiastically embraced by Thrasymachus in the first book
of Plato's *Republic*, and eloquently defended by Glaucon therein
immediately thereafter, this claim was explored—though not, as far
as we can tell, endorsed—in the works of the sophist Antiphon.

Sophilus' son, who owed his livelihood to the democracy's law
courts and assembly and who had earlier broadcast the contempt
and loathing he harbored for both Laespodias and Alcibiades, was
surely a latecomer to the oligarchic fold; and Phrynichus son of Stratonides, the third central figure mentioned by Thucydides, must for
similar reasons have been a late arrival as well. He is known to have
been associated with Antiphon in the late 420s. Moreover, as we
have seen, he shared his friend's distrust of and antipathy for Cleinias' wily son, and he had done everything in his power while stationed on Samos to obstruct the plans hatched by Alcibiades,
Peisander, and the would-be oligarchs on the island. Neither of these
figures had a future in an Athens dominated by Alcibiades. When
Peisander and his fellow conspirators turned resolutely against the
man, Stratonides' son found himself forced to ally with the conspirators whose machinations he had once so vigorously opposed and
to embrace the very men who had deprived him of his command—
and something of the sort may well have been true for Sophilus'
son as well.

The fourth figure on Thucydides' list was Theramenes son of
Hagnon. His father was, as we have seen, a well-respected senior
statesman who had been one of Pericles' closest allies. It was he who
had been chosen to found the Athenian colony at Amphipolis; and,
as one of the *próbouloi*, he had acquiesced in the oligarchic enterprise, if he had not also lent it strong support.

Like Phrynichus, Antiphon was in his sixties. Peisander—who
had been prominent enough to be noticed for nearly two decades—
was in his fifties and quite possibly older than that. Theramenes, who

was a relative newcomer on the political stage, was almost certainly a much younger man—junior, one must suspect, to Alcibiades, though not by many years; and roughly contemporaneous with his fellow demesman Thrasybulus son of Lycus.[33]

Of the foursome who dominated the junta, Hagnon's son was the only one apt to be acceptable to Alcibiades and his supporters—for, as far as we can tell, he had never crossed the man. He it was who took the lead, after the envoys returned from Samos to report what they had seen and what Alcibiades had said, and he it was who began agitating within the Four Hundred for a registration of the Five Thousand.

Theramenes' situation may have been quite delicate. For there is reason to suspect that, upon their return, the envoys spoke frankly with the inner circle of the oligarchic junta about Alcibiades' speech and then—after taking counsel with that circle's members—spoke in a more circumspect fashion when they made their formal report to the Four Hundred. For, if Thucydides' account of what they said to the latter is correct, the emissaries omitted from that report Alcibiades' demand that the Four Hundred give way to the Five Thousand and that a new Council of Five Hundred be established.

It was incumbent on Theramenes to be careful not to reveal everything that he knew to anyone he could not fully trust. If he shared what he had learned about Alcibiades' demands with anyone outside the inner circle, it was with the distinguished once and future *stratēgós* Aristocrates son of Scellias. For it was in cooperation with this prominent member of the Four Hundred that he managed to bring down the junta.[34]

In depicting these two figures and the other men with a public profile who sided with them on this occasion, the son of Olorus is scathing. They purported to be public-spirited, to be concerned about developments on Samos, and to be worried that an embassy to Lacedaemon might do the *pólıs* irreparable harm by negotiating an agreement that would not pass muster. But in the historian's view, most, if not all, of these men were opportunists driven solely by *philotimía*—ambition and the love of renown. They had taken the measure of Alcibiades' position on Samos. They were persuaded that the oligarchy could not and would not endure, and they had no desire to suffer political eclipse, exile, or execution when it collapsed. Each was, in fact, ultimately intent, so Thucydides claims, on establishing himself as the "preeminent patron and protector of the common people [*prôtos prostátēs toû dḗmou*]," and each acted accordingly.

All of this is surely true—for these were ambitious men, and the son of Cleinias had them in a corner. But one may doubt that a hankering for preeminence and prestige and a dread of dishonor and death exhausted the motives of Theramenes, Aristocrates, and those who supported them. It is perfectly possible that they were among those who had favored a broad-based, agrarian oligarchy from the outset and that they were genuinely wary of what an agreement with Lacedaemon, negotiated by those who had the most to fear from Alcibiades' ascent, would involve.[35]

So effective were Theramenes, Aristocrates, and the other prominent figures who joined them in pressing their case that it soon became evident to the three enemies of Alcibiades at the center of the oligarchic junta and to fierce opponents of democracy such as the military commander Aristarchus that they would soon be outmaneuvered, that Alcibiades' demands would be met, and that in time there would be a reconciliation between the government formed on Samos and the one existing in Athens that would not only exclude them but also hold them responsible for the crimes they had instigated or actually committed themselves. This realization, in turn, induced these men to redouble their efforts to forge a peace with Sparta; and so they dispatched to Lacedaemon Antiphon, his old friend Phrynichus, and ten others, including the former *stratēgós* Onomacles and Archeptolemos son of Hippodamus of Miletus—instructing them to make peace on any terms that could be endured.[36]

In the meantime, Peisander and the other diehards who remained at Athens began having fortifications built on the promontory of Eetioneia, which formed the northwestern boundary of Kantharos, the city's commercial port. Their aim thereby, or so they said, was to defend this—the largest and most important of the three natural harbors on the Peiraeus peninsula—against any attack that might be mounted by the expeditionary force at Samos. Of course, there was already a wall on Eetioneia's landward side; and, as one would expect, it reached all the way to the entrance of the harbor—where, on the promontory's southeastern tip, a tower had been constructed. What Peisander and his closest colleagues—above all, Aristarchus, Melanthius, and Aristoteles—sought to add was a second wall facing the port, designed to prevent attacks initiated from inside the harbor, and they set out as well to include within the fortified space a large stoa in the northeastern corner of the harbor, which functioned as a warehouse. It was at this stoa, which ran from east to west and was surrounded by water on three sides, that the grain ships were then unloaded, and it was there that the Four Hundred had Athens' grain stored.[37]

This enterprise, which was pursued with great vigor and speed, caused Theramenes and his supporters to fear that the real aim of the diehard oligarchs was to be in a position to let the Peloponnesians seize Athens' port and introduce an army within the expanse protected by the Long Walls. When Phrynichus, Antiphon, and their colleagues returned from Lacedaemon, apparently empty-handed, to report that they had been unable reach "an agreement encompassing everyone [*toîs xúmpasi xumbatikón*]," Hagnon's ambitious son—who seems no longer to have fully enjoyed the confidence of his colleagues in the inner circle—interpreted the cryptic language the envoys chose as an indication that an agreement had been reached that encompassed a much narrower body of Athenians; and he privately warned his associates that the fortifications being built along Eetioneia's southeastern shore might soon be Athens' undoing.

Then, word came in that an enemy fleet, consisting of forty-two triremes, had just anchored off Las in the bay of Laconia. Commanded by a distinguished Spartiate named Agesandridas, whose father Agesander had played a prominent diplomatic role on the eve of Sparta's second Attic war alongside Clearchus' father Ramphias,

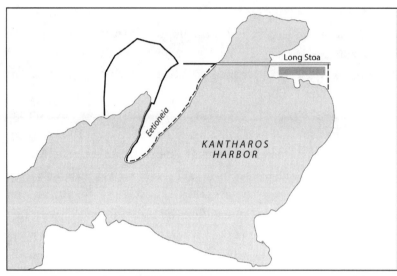

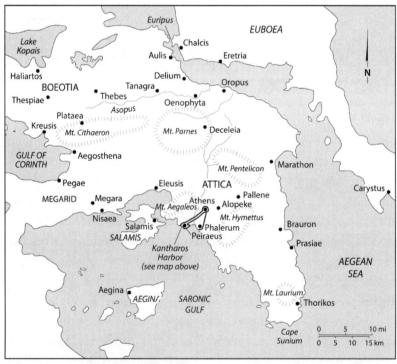

Map 10. Attica (with the Peiraeus) and Euboea, 411

its mission was to spark a general rebellion on Euboea—or so it was said. Theramenes harbored doubts. To his associates, he suggested that its true assignment was to aid those busy walling in Eetioneia, and he privately urged that precautions be taken lest Athens be surprised and seized.[38]

Thucydides, for his part, believed that Theramenes' suspicions were fully justified, and he intimates what he does not openly say: that the envoys had made treasonous arrangements with the authorities at Sparta. He did not doubt that Peisander, Antiphon, Phrynichus, and the other diehards preferred that there be peace on terms allowing Athens to retain her empire or at least her fleet, her walls, and her autonomy. But he was also convinced that, rather than be the first to fall prey to a restored democracy, these three men and their closest associates were prepared to bring in Athens' foe and to sacrifice the walls, the ships, and everything else possessed by the city in return for a pledge of legal immunity [adeía] guaranteeing the preservation of their lives. If Thucydides' suspicions are correct, these men thought that desperate times called for desperate measures. None of them can have welcomed the prospect of suffering what the Athenians called an *apotumpanismós*—whereby the man convicted was stripped of his clothes, bound hand and foot with four iron clamps to an upright pole dug into the ground; then, an iron collar, affixed to the pole, was run around his neck—and thereafter he was left, exposed to the elements, the insects, and the vermin, until in agony he expired.[39]

In the event, it took an incendiary deed to trigger resistance. This catalyst was supplied, Thucydides reports, by a nameless young *perípolos* of the sort in better times assigned to guard the borders but in this period tasked with patrolling Athens and the Peiraeus and with manning the city's complex system of walls—and he was not acting alone. Prior to this time, we are told, there was murmuring and there were even meetings among the man's colleagues, but to date no one had done anything. Without warning, we are told, this *perípolos*, assisted by an unnamed Argive and no doubt others as well, suddenly presented himself in the marketplace with a knife in his hand, which he employed to stab and kill Phrynichus shortly after Stratonides' son, who appears to have been the driving force behind the attempt to reach an accommodation with the Lacedaemonians, had left the Bouleuterion. Regarding this development, Thucydides may be in error. For other writers mention in this connection two foreigners—Thrasybulus of Kalydon in Arcadia and Apollodorus of Megara—and there is an inscription, dated to 409, honoring this Thrasybulus and a number of others; mentioning honors already conferred on Apollodorus; and recording the fact that, at the beginning of the City Dionysia, this Kalydonian was to be named a civic benefactor and awarded a gold crown and citizenship by the people of Athens in recognition of his services.[40]

It was Phrynichus' assassination that is said to have emboldened Theramenes, Aristocrates, and their supporters and spurred them to act. By this time, Agesandridas and his forces had overrun Aegina; and the Peloponnesian fleet, which included triremes from Sicily and from western Locris and Taras on the Italian boot, was anchored at Epidaurus. The fact that the Peloponnesians had actually entered the Saronic Gulf was interpreted as an indication that Euboea was not their true goal. And so, with this in mind, Aristocrates, who, as a taxiarch, was overseeing the hoplites from his tribe who were busy constructing on Eetioneia the wall facing the harbor, saw to their arrest of the *stratēgós* in charge of the enterprise—a man named Alexicles, who was closely associated with the *sunōmosíai*. Aristocrates is said to have had help from a man named Hermon, who commanded the *perípoloi* assigned to guard Munychia in the Peiraeus. When the news reached the Four Hundred, who were in session at the Bouleuterion, those especially suspicious of Theramenes threatened the man, but he pleaded ignorance and offered, as *stratēgós*, to proceed to the Peiraeus and rescue his colleague Alexicles. So he was dispatched, along with another military commander who, in fact, sympathized with his position; and, perhaps as a consequence of distrust, Aristarchus with some of the younger cavalrymen followed in their wake.

Upon arrival, Theramenes is said to have railed at the hoplites, and Aristarchus and those with him also expressed their fury. For their part, the heavy infantrymen on Eetioneia were unfazed and stalwart in the face of this criticism, and one brazenly asked Theramenes whether it would not be prudent to destroy the fortifications. When he seized on the occasion to express his concurrence, they started to do so; and someone from the crowd called out that anyone who wanted the Five Thousand to rule, rather than the Four Hundred, should join in. What those in the crowd that had gathered really wanted, Thucydides asserts, was popular rule. But they dared not say so at this time.[41]

The following day, having demolished the fortifications along Eetioneia's eastern shore, the hoplites in the Peiraeus released Alexicles, held an assembly in the theater of Dionysus there, and resolved to march on Athens—where they were met by some delegates dispatched from the Bouleuterion where the Four Hundred were meeting. These envoys successfully urged quiet and restraint and promised that the names of those in the Five Thousand would be made manifest and that the Four Hundred would henceforth be drawn from the Five Thousand in rotation in the manner stipulated by this latter body. A date was then set for an assembly to be held in the theater of Dionysus in Athens for the purpose of restoring *homónoia*.[42]

On the appointed day, word came that Agesandridas and his fleet were making their way from Megara along the shore of the island of Salamis, and everyone then hurried to the defense of the Peiraeus. Whatever his intentions may initially have been, the Spartan commander chose not to pause just outside the entrance to Athens' harbor—perhaps, if there really was a conspiracy to betray the city, because the agreed-upon signal was not given.

Instead, he conducted his fleet past the Peiraeus, rounded Sunium, anchored briefly between Thorikos and Prasiae on the eastern coast of Attica, and then moved on to Oropus on the border between Attica and Boeotia—which, thanks to treachery the previous campaigning season, had come into the possession of the

Thebans. His immediate aim was to stir up a rebellion among the Eretrians on the nearby island of Euboea, who had asked for Peloponnesian aid immediately after the Theban seizure of Oropus.[43]

In a panic, the Athenians then manned the ships in their possession and, under the command of Thumochares, headed for Euboea—which was, as we have seen, the largest and most important of the islands in their possession and a major source for the foodstuffs they now consumed. It suggests incompetence or at least negligence—on the part of both the *stratēgoí* chosen by the Four Hundred and those, selected under the democracy, whom they had displaced—that the Athenians were ill-prepared for a projection of power in their home waters and that the crews of the triremes deployed on this occasion had never even trained together.

The Spartans were an exceptionally pious lot, as we have seen. Their commanders tended to rely heavily on the seers who accompanied them when they went abroad; and, for understandable reasons, these seers tended often to be men of military as well as religious expertise. The son of Agesander, who commanded the Peloponnesian fleet in question, is not apt to have been exceptional in this regard, and we have information suggesting the identity of the seer [*mantís*] on whom he relied. When this campaign was over, we learn from an inscription that happens to have survived, the Eretrians singled out a man named Hegelochos of Taras and voted to make him their *próxenos* in that distant city and to honor him as a "benefactor [*euergétēs*]" of their own community, specifying, by way of explanation, that he had "helped liberate their *pólis* from the Athenians."

We cannot be certain of Hegelochus' identity, and we do not know what he did on this occasion, but it is clear that he played a prominent role in the events that took place on the day in question. Moreover, given his name, which was unusual and had a certain provenance, it is reasonable to speculate, as one scholar has, not only that Hegelochus was a scion of the justly famous Iamid clan descended from the celebrated Elean *mantís* Teisamenos to whom the Spartans had granted citizenship early in the fifth century but also that he held dual citizenship at Lacedaemon and at her colony Taras, that he devised the stratagem adopted by Agesandridas on this occasion, and that the Eretrians were fully aware of the role that he played.

The son of Agesander and those in his entourage may have been aware of the deficiencies that would bedevil the Athenians. If, as seems likely, there really was a conspiracy to betray Athens and if the last set of envoys dispatched to Lacedaemon were party to the plot, the Spartans are likely to have been well-informed regarding the state of the city's defenses. What no one can doubt is that Agesandridas and his advisors planned with care the operation in which they were about to be engaged, that they had done so in close cooperation with the Eretrians who had summoned them, and that everyone involved knew what he was about.

In the event, the Spartan commander left the Athenians almost no time in which to organize themselves. His crews he had take their mid-day meal. Then, upon receiving a signal from their Eretrian allies, the Peloponnesian fleet set out straightaway from Oropus on the mainland toward the territory of Eretria some seven miles away—where the Athenians had come to shore. Thanks to a stratagem devised by the Eretrians—who were itching for the Athenians' defeat—the rowers, officers, and specialists in the Athenian fleet found themselves in the situation that had bedeviled their compatriots at Syracusa two years before. For these were unable to secure food for their mid-day meal in a timely fashion from their supposed allies. In consequence, the thirty-six Athenian triremes found themselves forced to set out in disarray with incomplete, poorly trained crews who were, in most cases, insufficiently fed.

Just off the harbor of Eretria, in the channel separating the Euboean isle from the mainland, the two fleets met. For a short time, we are told, the Athenians held their own. Then, they broke. Fourteen of their triremes found refuge at Chalcis up the Euboean coast. The twenty-two galleys remaining hastened to the Euboean shore, where they were captured by the Peloponnesians. The crew members who fled overland to the fort established by the Athenians in the territory of Eretria survived. Those who sought safety in the town itself the Eretrians slaughtered without remorse.

In their eagerness to throw off Athens' yoke, the Eretrians may have been especially ardent. But, in what they desired, they were by no means peculiar. As we have seen, the various *póleis* on the island had for some time been angling for Spartan support. So it is no surprise that, in the aftermath, Agesandridas found it easy to bring over every community on the island—apart from Oreus in the northwest where, three decades before, after expelling the Histiaeans native to the place, the Athenians had settled their own citizens. Within short order, at the instigation of the Eretrians, there would be a Euboean League, and it would issue coinage on the Aeginetan standard in use in much of the Peloponnesus.[44]

There is a case to be made that, in the aftermath of the battle, Agesander's victorious son should have left the peoples of Euboea to their own devices. His direct intervention may well have hastened the rebellions, but they would have taken place in any case. The son of Olorus intimates that, had this Spartiate immediately capitalized on his triumph and conducted his fleet without delay to the Peiraeus, he might have brought the war to an end right then and there.

In the aftermath of the battle, Thucydides reports, the Athenians were caught up in a panic more severe than any they had ever known. It was worse than it had been when they first learned of the Sicilian catastrophe. The expeditionary force on Samos was in revolt. In the Peiraeus, they had hardly any galleys left and next to no crews with which to man them. They were themselves at odds with one another, and armed conflict was apt to break out at any moment. Now, to boot, they had lost Euboea, and they were terrified that their foe would descend on the Peiraeus.

Had the Peloponnesians suddenly presented themselves at the mouth of Athens' harbor, Thucydides tells us, their appearance would have intensified the divisions within the city. If this did not

yield the results desired and Agesandridas found it necessary to initiate a siege, he adds, the fleet at Samos would have been forced to
come to city's rescue and to leave the Hellespont, Ionia, and the
Aegean more generally undefended and apt to be scooped in short
order up by Athens' foe. In the event, however, Agesander's son
adopted neither expedient—for audacity was in short supply at
Lacedaemon, as the Corinthians had pointedly observed two decades
before; and Agesandridas and his advisors, although more than
capable of planning out and executing a brilliant operation, were,
like most of their compatriots, overly prone to caution. Rarely in this
war did the Spartans miss an opportunity to miss an opportunity.[45]

It was this hesitation on the part of the Lacedaemonians that
gave the Athenians the time they needed in order to pull themselves
together, to man twenty galleys, and hold an assembly on the Pnyx—
which voted to eliminate all pay for public office, to depose the Four
Hundred, and to hand affairs [*prágmata*] over to the Five Thousand,
defined as those providing their own hoplite armor. Moreover, in
the days that followed, the Athenians held frequent assemblies,
selected commissioners charged with revising the city's laws [*nomo-
thétai*], and spelled out the character of their new *politeía*. Had they
simply implemented the arrangements set out by the *anagrapheîs* for
"the time to come," as one scholar supposes, they would not have
needed to meet multiple times. What transpired was a constitutional
convention of sorts—informed by the loss of confidence in democratic institutions produced by the catastrophe in Sicily and reflec-
tive of the ruminations concerning self-government that this disaster
had inspired.[46]

Thucydides tells us that when this change of government
[*metabolé*] took place, Peisander, Alexicles, and many of those
closely associated with them slipped off to Deceleia "in short order
[*euthús*]"—while Aristarchus, who was a *stratēgós*, conducted a host
of barbarian archers to the fort at Oenoe on the Boeotian border and
betrayed the place to the Corinthians.[47] The Athenian historian does
not, however, specify at what stage in the gradual transformation

that took place these diehards made their departure, and there is reason to suspect that their decision may have been prompted by one or more events staged with an eye to hastening their withdrawal.

Theramenes was, as we have seen, eager to effect a reconciliation with the Athenians on Samos, and to this end he favored having the Five Thousand vote to recall Alcibiades from exile. To achieve everything that he wanted without encountering fierce opposition, however, he needed to capitalize on the panic that had taken place and to remove the diehards from the scene—and to accomplish this he appears to have made use of an agent.

Among his friends and among the longtime companions of Cleinias' son was a man—well-known to readers of the dialogues of Plato and the *Memorabilia* of Xenophon—named Critias son of Callaeschrus. This figure had in all likelihood been a member of the Four Hundred, but he had not, as far as we can tell, hitherto played a prominent role in Athenian public life. Now, however, perhaps prompted by Theramenes, he came forward and addressed the new Council of Five Hundred established by the Five Thousand.

Critias' purpose was to seek an *eisangelía* that was certain to strike fear into the hearts of the surviving diehards. His proposal was simple, straightforward, and ingenious: that Phrynichus be tried for treason so that, if he was found guilty, his bones would be dug up and removed beyond the borders of Attica, his house demolished, and his property confiscated. Critias suggested as well that the verdict and penalty be inscribed on a bronze stele and be displayed for all to see.

The diehards were not slow to get the point—for, if Phrynichus was judged a traitor, the same verdict was likely to be in store for them as well. It is surely this that explains why Alexicles and Aristarchus saw to the dead man's defense and came forward in court to testify on his behalf.[48]

In the interim, a second figure may have come before the new Council of Five Hundred to introduce yet another *eisangelía*. His name was Sophocles son of Sophillus. As a *próboulos*, this tragedian was complicit in the establishment of the oligarchy, and he may have wanted to distance himself from the diehards. The evidence we have is sparse and by no means dispositive—though it is highly suggestive. There are three prose passages in the *Rhetoric* in which Aristotle quotes the man: one of them a war of words between Sophocles and Peisander in which the latter is clearly on the defensive; and two other, apparently well-known, remarks that would make excellent sense if the poet had uttered them in the same context. It is not easy to imagine any other situation in which such a confrontation between Sophocles and Peisander could have taken place.[49]

It appears to have taken a threat of this sort to persuade Peisander, Alexicles, Aristarchus, and the diehards most closely associated with them to leave for Deceleia. But it was not the case that everyone in their position made the same calculation. Strange to say, at least three of the diehards remained in Athens—Antiphon, Archeptolemos, and the sometime *stratēgós* Onomacles. It was presumably their supposition that the shift from the Four Hundred to the Five Thousand was not a genuine counterrevolution and that under the latter they would themselves be safe. They had all served on the last embassy dispatched by the Four Hundred to Lacedaemon, and they could perhaps plausibly claim that, in contrast with their colleague on that embassy the son of Stratonides, they had not themselves been party to the fortification of Eetioneia.

What cannot be denied, however, is that the three miscalculated. For, not long after Phrynichus' condemnation, Theramenes and Androtion's father Andron brought a charge of treason against all three of these men, asserting that, on their embassy, they had made an arrangement with the authorities at Lacedaemon for the city to be betrayed to Agesandridas. Onomacles fled—while the other two remained in Athens to answer the charges. In the event, however, their two accusers prevailed in court; and, after their execution, a stele recording the verdict was set up next to the one dishonoring Stratonides' son. Antiphon's *apologia pro vita sua* on this occasion— with its focus on matters such as the overthrow of the democracy, the establishment of the oligarchy, and the executions, imprisonments, and banishments in which Theramenes was also complicit— may well have been, as Thucydides reports, the most impressive defense speech that he ever perused. But it did not save its author. For, at this time, the erstwhile members of the Four Hundred labored successfully to focus the attention of the jurors and their compatriots more generally on the question of treason and on that alone.[50]

The regime of the Four Hundred was short-lived. According to Aristotle, in four short months, it arrived on the scene and it was gone. He implies that the hoplite regime that succeeded the oligarchy had greater longevity; and it may, in fact, have survived for eight full months. Among the accomplishments of the Five Thousand was a reconciliation with the rival Athenian polity on Samos. It was on the motion of Theramenes that the Athenians voted to recall Alcibiades and the others with him. To the son of Cleinias and to the expeditionary force on Samos that he commanded with Thrasybulus son of Lycus, Thrasyllus, and others unnamed, they also sent word urging them to continue to take an active part in public affairs [*prágmata*].[51]

In his history, Thucydides does not ordinarily pay close attention to domestic politics in Athens or, for that matter, anywhere else. But when internal developments impinged on the war or threatened to do so, he could treat affairs internal to a city in great detail—which is what he did in describing the rise and fall of the Four Hundred. About the Five Thousand and what was later called "the *Politeía* of Theramenes," he had less to say—largely, one must suspect, because he died before he had occasion to fully trace its trajectory. Aristotle might have done the like but he refrained; and Xenophon, the one continuator of Thucydides whose work survives intact, never mentioned this short-lived regime at all—not even to report its ultimate dissolution and the restoration of the radical democracy.

We are left, then, to ponder the significance of Thucydides' final assessment. Looking back, some years after the new regime's demise, the son of Olorus wrote regarding the brief span of time when Athens' cavalrymen and hoplites were in charge: "For the first time—at least while I was alive—the Athenians appear to have governed themselves in an admirable fashion. For there was a mixing of the few and the many in their proper proportions [*metría súnkrasis*], and it was this regime that first raised the city up from the parlous state of her affairs."[52]

PART III

A LUNGE FOR
THE JUGULAR

In sketching out a blueprint for war, one's first focus of attention [*Gesichtspunkt*] should be on a discovery of the centers
of gravity [*Schwerpunkte*] on which the enemy's power rests,
and, where possible, one should trace these back to a single
Schwerpunkt. One's second focus of attention should, then, be
on uniting for the main business at hand [*Haupthandlung*] the
forces that ought to be deployed against that center of gravity.

CARL VON CLAUSEWITZ

T
HE PELOPONNESIANS landed on the island of Rhodes in
late January or very early February 411. There, we are told,
they remained, cooling their heels, for eighty days—until the
middle or the latter part of April after winter in those parts had given
way to spring and the storms had abated.

At this point, on the eve of the campaigning season, the Spartans
and their allies rowed off from Rhodes to go to the relief of their
long-suffering Chian allies. Soon after their departure from the
island, however, they spied the Athenian fleet then based at Chalke,
which was on station at Triopium; and, although eager to reach
Chios, Astyochus and, no doubt, the *súmbouloi* assigned to advise

him were not yet willing to risk a decision at sea. The Athenians, who were no less inclined to caution, then returned to Samos while the Peloponnesians rowed on to Miletus—and it was from there that Astyochus traveled up the Maeander river, in all likelihood to the satrapal palace on that stream at Magnesia, to ratify the agreement thrashed out at Caunus with Tissaphernes son of Hydarnes some weeks before.[1]

Fortunately for the Chians, at some point in the wintry season when seaborne travel is apt to be especially dangerous, a Spartiate named Leon had made his way from Rhodes to Miletus, where he had taken command of twelve of the triremes left behind to guard the town. With these, he had then journeyed further up the Anatolian coast, and he had slipped through the Athenian blockade and into the fortified harbor of the city where Pedaritus son of Leon, his predecessor as harmost on Chios (and quite possibly his father), had lost his life. The task assigned the younger Leon was to revive the morale and fortunes of the Chians—who were cowed by repeated defeats on land, who had for some time been under siege, and who were now suffering from famine. And so, after executing Tydeus son of Ion and Athens' other Chian friends and imposing a narrow oligarchy on the isle, this is precisely what he did.

It helped that, when they learned of the Peloponnesians' departure from Rhodes and of Astyochus' decision to tarry at Miletus, the surviving citizens of Chios had, out of desperation, decided to take matters into their own hands. Under their new harmost's command, these men bravely marched out from their city and positioned themselves for battle—and, at the same time, they deployed thirty-six triremes against the thirty-two Athenian galleys stationed on the island to the north at Delphinium. Nothing is said in our sources regarding a battle on land. But, in the conflict at sea, the Chians not only held their own. They also won a modest victory and dealt the Athenians a genuine setback, damaging their morale and depriving them of their hitherto unchallenged command of the waters nearby.[2]

While this struggle was going on, a Spartiate named Dercyllidas

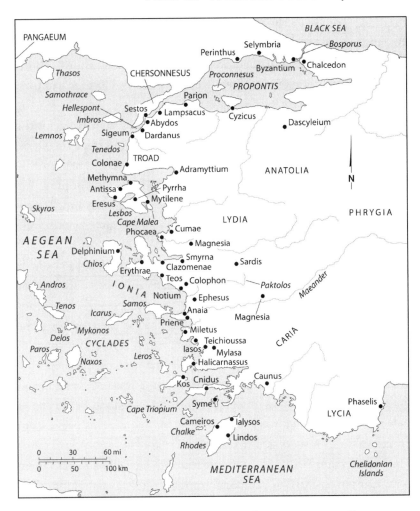

Map 11. The Eastern Aegean and Western Anatolia

set out by land from Miletus with a small infantry force, intent on reaching the Hellespont. His mission was to raise a rebellion in the Milesian colony of Abydos and elsewhere along that body of water's Asian shore. In this endeavor, he was so successful—both at Abydos and Lampsacus—that the Athenian *stratēgós* Strombichides son of Diotimos felt compelled to row up from Chios to the Hellespont with twenty-four triremes (a number of them transports loaded with

219

hoplites) to squelch these revolts. At Lampsacus, he succeeded, but the citizens of Abydos were made of sterner stuff; and he ultimately withdrew to the well-fortified port at Sestos on the European shore, which, in days gone by, the Great Kings Darius and Xerxes had used as their principal base in the region.[3]

The success of the Chians and Strombichides' departure for the Hellespont buoyed up Astyochus, who gathered the ships on Chios, brought them back to Miletus and rowed out to challenge the Athenians on Samos. By this time, it was close to the middle of June. The conspirators had overthrown the democracy at Athens; and, Thucydides tells us, the Athenians on Samos were so suspicious of one another that they did not answer the challenge.[4]

By the time that the democrats on Samos had effected a counterrevolution on the island, the Peloponnesians at Miletus, sparked by the Syracusans in their midst, had lost all patience with Astyochus and Tissaphernes. They were furious that in the months since the ratification of the treaty with Persia they had received such meager pay and that it had appeared at irregular intervals. They suspected that the Phoenician fleet so often promised was a chimera; and Astyochus, whose apparent fecklessness had occasioned criticism in the past, they blamed for keeping them waiting for this evanescent force and for not successfully staging a battle.

These expressions of discontent spurred Astyochus to act. There was, moreover, intelligence concerning the upheavals taking place on Samos—and the time seemed ripe. But once again, when challenged, the Athenians refused battle. And the very next day, when Strombichides, whom the Athenians had summoned from the Hellespont, arrived from Sestos with his flotilla, they in turn rowed out to challenge the Peloponnesians lodged at Miletus, who in turn demurred.[5]

Astyochus was in a bind. At one hundred ten triremes, his fleet was exceedingly large; and the funds supplied by Tissaphernes were insufficient for its support. With this in mind, he finally dispatched Clearchus son of Ramphias on the mission which he had been assigned a year before. This Spartiate then set out with forty triremes for the satrapy of Pharnabazus son of Pharnaces, the westernmost part of which ran along the Hellespont, the Sea of Marmara, and the Bosporus. His aim was to raise in rebellion the city of the Byzantines, and he had good reason to think this possible. As the *próxenos* at Sparta of that *pólis*, he was well-connected in that community; and there were prominent citizens there who had invited the Lacedaemonians to intervene.

Clearchus' journey was not, however, an easy one. To avoid being noticed by the Athenians on Samos, he conducted his flotilla from Miletus west into the open sea with an eye to making a roundabout approach to the Hellespont. There it was caught in a storm—as happens from time to time, even in high summer—and a majority of the vessels were driven to Delos, whence they returned to Miletus. Thereafter, landlubber that he was, Clearchus made his way to the Hellespont on horseback or on foot; and there, upon arrival, he assumed command. In the meantime, ten of the forty triremes assigned to him—those under the immediate command of a citizen of Byzantium's mother city Megara named Helixus—actually made it to their destination; and, by the time of Clearchus' arrival, they had already effected the rebellion sought.

This was an event of some importance. From Byzantium on the European shore or from the territory of Chalcedon, opposite it on the Asian shore, one could not only monitor and control all of the traffic that went back and forth between the Euxine and the eastern Mediterranean; one could also impose taxes on the goods in transit. Even more to the point, although cattle, slaves, honey, wax, and salted fish were conveyed from the former body of water to the latter, the bulk of the trade that passed from the Black Sea through this choke point consisted in the transport of what was for the Hellenes of the Aegean basin, as we have noted, a strategic substance: grain. These Greeks exchanged what they possessed in surplus—above all, wine of quality, figs, and olive oil—for the wheat and barley that they could not produce in their mountainous homeland in sufficient amounts and that the Greeks and the others who lived in the Crimea and elsewhere on the shores of the Black Sea—where, thanks to the colder climate, olive trees could not be grown—harvested in great abundance. In the best of circumstances, the Athenians and many of the island and coastal communities within the Aegean were dependent on imported cereals. At this time, deprived of access to Attica (and soon to be barred from Euboea as well), the former were doubly dependent on the commerce they conducted with the Euxine. That the Athenians on Samos responded to the rebellion of Byzantium by dispatching a mere handful of ships to the Hellespont is a sign of the degree to which they were at this point preoccupied by the revolution then underway at Athens.[6]

It was at about this time that Thrasybulus son of Lycus managed to engineer on Samos Alcibiades' recall; and this, too, had repercussions for Astyochus. For obvious reasons, it intensified the distrust that the Peloponnesians directed at Tissaphernes, and it did not help that, after the refusal of the Spartans at Miletus and their allies to accept the most recent Athenian challenge, Tissaphernes further curtailed his subvention for the Peloponnesian forces.

The Syracusans and the Thurians, nearly all of them free men, were especially angry; and the proximate focus of their fury was Astyochus. Hermocrates son of Hermon and Dorieus son of Diagoras were the men most outspoken in these altercations, and when Astyochus raised his staff of office [baktēría] to strike the latter, the violent response elicited from the trierarchs, specialists, rowers, and epibátai in attendance was such that he found himself forced to seek refuge at an altar of the gods. It was at this time that the fort built by Tissaphernes at Miletus was captured by the Milesians and the garrison driven out; and, although the timetable is uncertain, the like may by then have taken place at Cnidus as well.

It says much about Spartan policy that it was Lichas son of Arcesilaus who chastised the Milesians for their conduct on this occasion. Thanks to their experience on Rhodes, the súmbouloi dispatched from Lacedaemon were now united with Astyochus in their desire to accommodate the viceroy of the Great King. Absent his subventions, there was no hope. This they now knew.[7]

Reflections of this sort did not, however, mollify the leading figures in the Peloponnesian force. In August, when a Spartiate named Mindarus arrived to take up the navarchy, Astyochus headed for home. Accompanying him was a multilingual Carian named Gaulites who had been sent by Tissaphernes to denounce the Milesians and defend his master's comportment. For their part, the Milesians dispatched a delegation to Lacedaemon to lodge charges against the satrap; and the Syracusan Hermocrates son of Hermon, who had been at odds with the man from the outset, journeyed there to do the like.

Hermocrates is apt to have had more than one reason for taking this trip. In Syracusa, Diocles, the successor to the demagogue Athenagoras with whom he had tangled on the eve of the Athenian invasion of Sicily, was by this time fully in control; and Hermon's distinguished son was far too savvy to be unaware that he was now a marked man. A figure as formidable as he was this demagogue could not allow to return. There is some confusion in the reports that have come down to us, but one thing is clear. If Hermocrates had not yet been relieved of his command and had not yet been rendered a man without a country, he soon would be; and, if this had already happened or was in store, it was not safe for him to remain in the satrapy ruled by Tissaphernes.

When faced with these mutual recriminations, the authorities at Lacedaemon gave heed. What we are told is this: that Hermocrates lodged accusations against Tissaphernes; that Astyochus, who had hitherto been almost infinitely patient with the satrap, backed him up; and that those listening concluded that Hermocrates spoke the truth.[8] They can hardly have regarded the Peloponnesians' first full year of campaigning in Ionia as an unmitigated success. At best, the forces deployed by the Lacedaemonians and their allies could be said to have achieved a stalemate. In all fairness, the satrap cannot alone have been judged responsible for the deadlock. But the *súmbouloi* had exonerated Astyochus; and, if any other individual was to be singled out for blame, Tissaphernes was surely the one. It was the Spartans' frustration with him that paved the way for a change in strategy and a direct attack on the Athenians' center of gravity wholly in keeping with what the Eurypontid king Agis had intended from the start.

CHAPTER FIVE

THE HELLESPONT

In the Thracian Bosporus, when the current rushes down with real violence from the Black Sea, the crabs, wishing to proceed upstream, force their way against the current. As one would expect, the current is even more violent when it rips and tears about the headlands. In consequence, if the crabs try to push forward against the current at such a place, it will force them back altogether and even turn them upside down. This, however, they anticipate. So, whenever they approach such a headland, each slips into the bay behind it and awaits the others. Once they have collected at this location, they creep up onto the land, then clamber up and over the cliffs; and so on foot they work their way past the point where the sea's current is most violent. Finally, having slipped past the headland, they descend again into the sea.

CLAUDIUS AELIANUS

NEW MEN generally introduce new measures. Their self-regard virtually ensures it. In this regard, Mindarus was no exception. At first, to be sure, he exercised forbearance. In the Peloponnesian camp, Tissaphernes son of Hydarnes was gener-ally regarded as a turncoat and a secret ally of the Athenians who was intent on crippling the Peloponnesian effort. To prove that this was not so, he proposed journeying to Aspendus and taking Lichas son of Arcesilaus with him so that the Spartiate could see that there really was a Phoenician fleet. Lichas, who is apt to have been unwell and who seems to have died at this time or soon thereafter, did not himself go. Instead, a Spartiate named Philippos was instructed to make his way by sea along the Anatolian coast south, then east, to and then up the Eurymedon river with two galleys—one of them no doubt a fast ship used for the rapid conveyance of messages.

Thucydides reports that there really was a fleet, that at the time it consisted of one hundred forty-seven triremes, and that it never entered the Aegean. Had it joined the fray, it would have settled the war. This he did not doubt. What needed explanation was its failure, after being deployed within a few hundred miles of the theater of combat, to appear on the scene. Thucydides did not pretend to know what Tissaphernes had in mind. But he was prepared to speculate, and he was impressed by the fact that, all along, the viceroy's actual conduct had conformed to the advice on offer from Alcibiades son of Cleinias and that it was consistent with a desire on his part to wear out both sides. Moreover, the son of Olorus observed, the excuse offered by Tissaphernes for the fleet's failure to engage made no sense. He told the Peloponnesians that the Phoenician force could not proceed until it reached the number ordered by the Great King, which, if the testimony of Diodorus Siculus is any indication, may have been as many as three hundred triremes—at least twice what was needed for the purpose envisaged in the agreement worked out at Caunus.

The suspicions harbored by the Peloponnesians worried that Tissaphernes had switched sides were no doubt aggravated by the fact that Alcibiades ostentatiously showed up at Aspendus after promising the Athenians on Samos, whose *stratēgós* he now was, that he would either bring the fleet into the Aegean to support them or, at least, prevent its coming. Thucydides suggests that he knew already that Tissaphernes would not be dispatching the fleet to support the Peloponnesians, and this might or might not be true. All that can be said is that Mindarus gave sufficient credence to the claims being bruited about by Alcibiades that, when he dispatched

Philippos to Aspendus, he sent his "secretary [*epistoleús*]" and second-in-command—a Spartiate named Hippocrates—to Phaselis nearby. If word got out that Tissaphernes had had Philippos seized and that he had ordered the fleet to prepare for departure under Alcibiades' command, this Hippocrates would be in a position to hightail it back to the Aegean and alert the navarch.[1]

Given the enormous cost involved in assembling such an armada, training the crews, and supporting it while on station at Aspendus, and given the fact that its point of origin lay in Phoenicia, well outside the region under Tissaphernes' command, the disposition of this fleet cannot have been a matter for the satrap. Nor, as I have already suggested, is it plausible to suppose that the overall strategy being followed by the Persians in Anatolia was a thing for Tissaphernes to determine. He could, of course, propose; and this he surely did. But the larger decisions fell within the purview of his master. If Tissaphernes acted in accord with Alcibiades' advice, it was because the King was amenable.

It is easy to believe that Darius II wanted to keep the Peloponnesians on short rations. He was by no means the only Great King to shortchange his clients in this fashion. Moreover, as a policy, it made good sense. It would remind them at every turn of their utter dependence on him. If this is what he in fact intended, as a stratagem it worked brilliantly—initially with Astyochus and later as well with Lichas and the other *súmbouloi* dispatched by the authorities at Lacedaemon. It is also easy to believe that the younger Darius had no desire to see the Peloponnesian fleet on its own win a decisive battle against the Athenians. Such an event might well result in the substitution of one power hostile to Persia for another. If this Darius was as canny as he seems to have been, he will have taken to heart Alcibiades' warning to Tissaphernes—that a land power dominating the Aegean would be a greater danger to Persia than Athens had ever been or would ever be. Lichas' outburst at Cnidus he will not have forgotten.

It is nonetheless hard to believe that Darius II would have gone to the trouble and expense of assembling a great fleet at Aspendus just to frustrate, enrage, and temporarily hobble the Lacedaemonians. He must have intended its use. Had he, in fact, deployed an armada of one hundred forty-seven or more triremes in the Aegean alongside the large but considerably smaller force deployed by the Peloponnesians, the victory that the latter celebrated after Athens' defeat would, in fact, have been his. For, in the aftermath, the smaller fleet would not have been in a position to contest Persian supremacy at sea within the northeastern Mediterranean. Had it done so, it would in all likelihood have suffered defeat; and, in any case, it would have evaporated soon after the Mede had cut off the requisite funds. Once firmly ensconced within the Aegean, the Great King's forces might well have once again become dominant there.[2]

Darius was presumably miffed, as Tissaphernes surely was, at the expulsion of the Persian garrison from Miletus; and if the expulsion at Cnidus took place in time to be a consideration, the news would have intensified their annoyance. But Lichas' rant at Cnidus earlier in the year had surely been sufficient to dispel any illusions that either Persian may have entertained regarding the prospects for Spartan subservience. They needed these Greeks to help usher the Athenians off the stage; and, after reaching an accommodation with Lichas and his fellow *súmbouloi*, they were not apt to jettison their chief source of leverage as a consequence of trivial infractions of that agreement.

There must have been something else—something genuinely compelling—that occasioned the withdrawal of this massive force. In a passage replete with confusion, Diodorus Siculus gives us an inkling of what may well have been involved when he reports that the Persian fleet was redeployed because of trouble in a corner of the empire—Syria, Phoenicia, and Egypt as well—which we know to have been more important to the Great King than the Aegean ever was. There is, moreover, papyrological evidence in the form of correspondence suggesting that there was at least one rebellion during the long tenure of Arsames as Egypt's satrap. Whether the pertinent letters can be dated to 410 or soon thereafter is, however, uncertain.[3]

If the story told by Diodorus is accurate, this news escaped the notice of the Lacedaemonians. They were supposed to be satisfied with Tissaphernes' lame excuse. But, in late August or early September 411, when word came in from Philippos at Aspendus and Hippocrates at Phaselis and they learned that the fleet was not coming, they were anything but content. When Tissaphernes had departed in early August, he had told the Spartans and their allies that the hyparch Tamos would see to it that their subvention was paid. In the interim, however, they had received nothing at all. It is this that explains why Mindarus called a halt to the attempts to reach an accommodation with Tissaphernes and decided to accept the repeated invitations the Spartans had received from Pharnabazus son of Pharnaces and shift his forces to Hellespontine Phrygia where this satrap held sway. That he did so with support from the authorities at Lacedaemon, who had listened to the testimony of Hermocrates and Astyochus, we need not doubt. Everyone understood the strategic significance of the Hellespont, the Sea of Marmara, and the Bosporus.[4]

MINDARUS' DASH TO THE HELLESPONT

Earlier, in the summer, sixteen Peloponnesian vessels had been dispatched to the Hellespont, where they had overrun the Thracian Chersonnesus. Another thirteen were now sent to Rhodes under the command of Dorieus son of Diagoras to prevent an uprising in contemplation there. Then, fearful that the Athenians would get wind of his plans and obstruct his passage to the north, Mindarus imposed tight discipline on his men and set out from Miletus abruptly, without prior notice, and headed for the Hellespont with a force of seventy-three triremes. His aim was to do in the Hellespont what Clearchus son of Ramphias was attempting to do from Byzantium on the Bosporus—which was to block the passage of the grain ships that made their way in great numbers from the Crimea to the Mediterranean in mid-September.

September is by no means the worst month in the year to be out on the water in the Aegean. But it is transitional, and the jet stream's seasonal shift south has an impact throughout the Mediterranean. In later times it was the practice of the Ottoman galleys to return to port in late August or early September. Thus, it is in no way surprising that in this season, as Mindarus headed west with his fleet to slip around Samos and then make voyage to the north, the Spartans and their allies encountered a violent storm and were driven to seek refuge further west at Icarus and that it took them five or six more days to make it northward to Chios.

This storm gave the Athenians, who set out from Samos not long after Mindarus' departure, the opportunity to get to the Hellespont first. When, however, Mindarus paused at Chios to secure supplies and extract funds, Thrasyllus, who commanded the fifty-five Athenian ships initially dispatched, settled down on the north coast of Lesbos opposite the Troad, after posting scouts on the continent and on the Lesbian coast facing Chios. There, if promptly alerted by these lookouts, he would be in a position to intercept the Lacedaemonian fleet should it head for the Hellespont either via the open sea to the west of Lesbos or by way of the channel running between the offshore islands and the coast of Asia Minor. And there he began collecting ships and gathering supplies in the hope that his fleet might be able to take the initiative and preempt by attacking the Peloponnesians on Chios. For a time, however, he allowed himself to be diverted by a rebellion staged in Eresus on Lesbos' south coast in the west.

This last move was a grave blunder. Eresus was a small *pólis* with a grim mountainous hinterland of volcanic origin which was for the most part unsuited to agriculture and animal husbandry. There was little to be gained in resources of any kind from its recovery, and it was a considerable distance from the route along the Anatolian coast

Map 12. The Northeastern Aegean and the Hellespont

that the Spartan navarch was most likely to follow if he made a dash for the Hellespont—which is what he did.

While Thrasyllus was busy besieging that diminutive town with the help of Thrasybulus son of Lycus, who had anticipated his arrival there with five additional triremes in tow, Mindarus, who was an enterprising commander, made his move. First, he slipped across with his fleet from Chios to Karteria in the territory of Phocaea on the Anatolian coast. Then, at a breakneck pace, he conducted this force stealthily from port to port along the inland passage. Northward his mariners rowed, then westward, and finally northward again. Initially, they made their way past Aeolian Cumae and across the bay of Elaea to the Arginusae isles, which ran parallel to the Anatolian coast opposite the southeasternmost point of Lesbos at Cape Malea. Then, they sped across the bay of Adramyttium and followed the southern coast of the Troad to the village of Harmatus opposite Methymna. Eventually, they reached the village of Lectum and, from there, they rowed up the coast of the Troad past the villages of Hamaxitus and Larisa, the island of Tenedos, and the neighboring villages and towns.

In the process, Mindarus and the galleys under his command managed to slip unnoticed past the Lesbian cities of Mytilene and Methymna and to arrive at the entrance to the Hellespont. This brilliant operation they accomplished—in part, under the cover of darkness—without ever attracting the attention of Thrasyllus' scouts.

In the dead of the night, Mindarus' fleet then settled down at Sigeum and Rhoeteum. The appearance of a large number of campfires on the Asian shore of the Hellespont alerted the Athenians on the opposite coast to the Peloponnesians' presence, and fire signals conveyed the news to Sestos further north. In the wee hours of the morning, the eighteen triremes posted there then made their way downstream with all due speed along the shore of the Thracian Chersonnesus to its southernmost point at Elaeus—whence the Athenians hoped to flee into the open sea. They managed to get past the sixteen Peloponnesian triremes stationed on the opposite shore at Abydos without being noticed. But, at dawn, the Peloponnesians at Rhoeteum and Sigeum spied them, and Mindarus' fleet set out in hot pursuit. In the event, all but four of the Athenian vessels made it intact to Imbros or to Lemnos—islands long occupied by Athenian cleruchies.

In the aftermath, an abortive attempt was made on the part of the Peloponnesians to take Elaeus. But the effort failed, and they rowed up the Hellespont to their stronghold at Abydos, which they made their base. It was in the harbor at Elaeus that the Athenian fleets subsequently rendezvoused. There, under the command of Thrasyllus, to whom his colleagues deferred, they prepared for the great battle—so long delayed—that, everyone knew, would now finally take place. They could not allow the Spartans and their allies to seize Athens' lifeline to the grain markets of the Euxine.[5]

BRAVING THE CURRENT

The channel running from the Black Sea to the Aegean through the Bosporus, the Sea of Marmara, and the Hellespont is a river of sorts which constitutes the only outlet from the Euxine. Elsewhere, the

Danube, the Don, the Dnieper, and a host of lesser streams bring freshwater in copious amounts from Europe to the north into that capacious body of water while, in the south, other tributaries of consequence, running from the Taurus mountains northward through Asia Minor, make their contribution to its great depth and girth. The overflow that this enormous influx produces—which in the course of a year comes to on average two hundred twenty-eight billion tons of water—then rushes rapidly through what amounts to a great gorge, separating Europe from Asia. In the late spring and early summer, when the thawing of snow maximizes the flow, its motion is frequently reinforced by the strength of that season's prevailing winds.

The Sea of Marmara is one hundred seventy-five miles in length; and, at its broadest, it is fifty miles wide. The Hellespont, which stretches some thirty-eight miles, is everywhere narrow; and the Bosporus, which is half that length, is narrower still. At their choke points, the former is no more than thirteen hundred seventy-two yards wide and the latter is under seven hundred thirty-two yards in width. By the same token, the Propontis is as much as twenty-eight hundred feet deep while the Hellespont, at a mere two hundred feet in depth on average and the Bosporus at just over half that are, by way of comparison, extremely shallow. As one would then expect, the current running from the Black Sea moves much more slowly through the Marmara sea than through the constricted channels to its northeast and southwest. The Hellespont current averages three knots (3.5 miles per hour) and, at its narrowest point, it clocks in at five knots (5.75 miles per hour). For its part, the Bosporus current averages four or five knots (4.6 to 5.75 miles per hour) and speeds up to six or seven knots (6.9–8.1 miles per hour) at the narrows. Any ship heading up either channel will have to overcome the current and, much of the time, the wind. For a galley or for a sailing ship, this is a formidable challenge.[6]

How Mindarus, on the one hand, or Thrasyllus and Thrasybulus, on the other, chose to confront this challenge we are not told. But we can hazard a half-educated guess. Seventy-five years ago, a distinguished archaeologist published an article arguing that, with the ships available to them, the Mycenaeans of the Bronze Age were unable to work their way up either channel. It was not, he argued, until the invention of the penteconter—a galley powered by fifty rowers—that this could be accomplished. In the early 1980s, a British adventurer named Tim Severin set out to test this hypothesis.

Severin's aim was to have a small wooden galley built on the Mycenaean model and to conduct it solely by oar and sail on a voyage from Volos in Thessaly to the coast of Georgia in the Soviet Union, duplicating thereby the journey said by Homer to have been completed by Jason and his Argonauts and described thereafter in some detail by others—most notably, Apollonius of Rhodes. When fully equipped and manned with a helmsman to pilot it and with twenty men at the oars, Severin's galley—which he named after Jason's vessel the *Argo*—had a draft of three feet and weighed eight tons. His experience in attempting to duplicate this legendary voyage is instructive.

In May 1984, Severin and his crew had little trouble making their way up the coast of Magnesia, around what we now call the Chalcidice, and across the open sea from there to Lemnos. Then, however, with a reduced complement of fifteen, he piloted this craft east toward Imbros, then along that island's south coast—instead of following the trajectory described by Apollonius and heading northeast to Samothrace before approaching the mouth of the Hellespont from the waters to the north and east of Imbros. Along the way, he ran into an obstacle that he had not fully foreseen, which was no doubt familiar to every ancient navigator. For the current produced within the Aegean by the water spewing out of the Hellespont flows along the southern shore of Imbros—and rowing against it proved to be a hopeless endeavor. Whatever gains his oarsmen achieved while rowing they lost when they paused to rest or sleep. It took a favorable wind to enable them to overcome this difficulty, and the same could be said not only for their journey into the Hellespont itself and up that body of water to the Sea of Marmara but also for the voyage said by Pindar and by Apollonius to have been undertaken by Jason and his men.

In late May, when Severin and his crew braved the current, the wind ordinarily blows from the northeast. With the relatively primitive, square-rigged sails available, neither the Mycenaeans nor the Greeks in antiquity's later ages could sail directly into such a wind. To make it up the channel under sail, an ancient sailor and his crew would have had to wait patiently for the relatively rare day when the wind blew from the south, the west, or the southwest.

The trierarchs commanding the triremes deployed by the Spartans and the Athenians on the occasion under consideration here were better situated than Severin in two important particulars. They were operating in late September or early October when the current is less strong and fast than in the late spring and the wind is more variable; and they possessed galleys, as shallow in draft as his *Argo*, that weighed in at fifty tons, in which they had one hundred seventy oarsmen to drive them forward. With more than eleven times as many rowers powering vessels just over six times the weight of Severin's craft, the Spartans and the Athenians could overcome the current within the Hellespont without too much strain.[7]

Mindarus was in a hurry when he reached Sigeum and Rhoeteum. He could not afford to wait for a stiff breeze from the right quarter. If he did not luck into such a situation, he is apt to have ordered his trierarchs to proceed upstream under oars. In this respect, the Athenians commanded by Thrasyllus, with the assistance of Thrasybulus and others, were better positioned. They were shamefully behindhand, as we have seen. But, by this time, the damage was already done. Mindarus had slipped into the Hellespont ahead of them, and he was, as we have also seen, ensconced at Abydos on the Asian shore. At this point, a brief, further delay could do the Athenians no harm. They could take their time—and this is what they reportedly did, tarrying at Elaeus before heading upstream. For five full days, Thucydides and Diodorus report, they practiced maneuvers in the swift current that they would have to cope with on the day of battle. We are not told that they were also waiting for a favorable wind, but this is not just possible. It is highly likely.[8]

When, on the sixth day, the seventy-six Athenian and Methymnian triremes journeyed up in line ahead along the European shore of the Hellespont toward Athens' stronghold at Sestos, which was situated upstream from Abydos on the opposite shore, they either did so in a leisurely fashion under sail; or their crews labored mightily at their oars for a number of hours, covering a distance of more than twelve long miles (i.e., eleven nautical miles) against a strong current and in the face of an adverse breeze.

For their part, the eighty-six Peloponnesian triremes, which put out from Abydos and made their way in the same formation downstream along the Asian shore to meet them, did so with a minimum of effort, quite literally going with the flow of the water and perhaps also the wind. The encounter between these two fleets took place on either side of a point, called Cynossema (the Tomb of the Bitch), which thrusts outwards from the European shore where the Hellespont is at its narrowest. It is there—where, down that great gorge, the stream runs at its greatest velocity—that strong swimmers sometimes brave the current and attempt to duplicate the feat attributed to the legendary Leander in crossing from Europe to the Asian shore.[9]

THE BATTLE OF CYNOSSEMA

In this encounter, the Athenians found themselves at a distinct disadvantage. They had fewer ships, and their oarsmen may have already expended considerable energy. Moreover, the enemy had the upper hand. They were in a position to choose the location for the clash that was in the offing, and, as we have seen, they selected the narrows— where maneuverability and the skill of the more experienced Athenian helmsmen and their crews mattered far less than it did in the open sea, and where the ability of these men to control the vessels they manned was rendered considerably more difficult by a current apt to have been running at five knots. To this one can add that, while the Peloponnesians deliberately situated themselves along the Asian shore where they would have a clear view of the way in which the engagement unfolded, the Athenians suffered from the fact that their field of vision was restricted. Thanks to the position that their galleys were forced to occupy along the European shore on either side of the point on which Cynossema was located, the Athenian helmsmen—those on the vessels upstream from that landmark and those on the vessels downstream as well—were blocked from seeing what was taking place on their fleet's other wing. When Thrasyllus focused on Eresus and allowed himself to be outfoxed by Mindarus, he conferred on the Spartans and their allies every advantage for which they could have entertained hope.

Each of the two opposed fleets extended its line with an eye to outflanking the other. The Syracusans occupied the Peloponnesian right, which was upstream, and Mindarus with the fastest galleys in the fleet occupied the left, downstream. Opposite the Syracusans at the extreme end of the Athenian left was Thrasyllus, and opposite

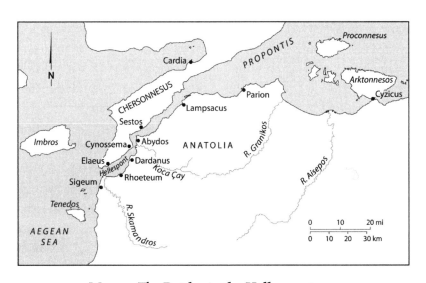

Map 13. The Battles in the Hellespont, 411

Mindarus on the extreme end of the Athenian right was Thrasybulus. The other Athenian *stratēgoí*, who pass unnamed, commanded contingents in between.

According to the son of Olorus, the Athenian line was especially thin at the center where the channel is at its narrowest, and it was in this sector that the Spartans and their allies routed the opposing galleys and forced them to the shore—where the Peloponnesian marines, who were reportedly first-rate, disembarked to seize the ships of the Athenians and pursue the crews. There were no galleys on either of the Athenian wings that could come to the rescue.

If Thucydides is correct, what decided the battle in the end was indiscipline—as was quite frequently the case in ancient Greek warfare both at sea and on land. Tempted by the flight of the Athenian triremes in the center, the vessels in the Peloponnesian fleet nearby to the south abandoned the formation, dispersed in pursuit, and fell into disorder. Hitherto, Thrasybulus had directed the triremes under his immediate command to work their way downstream in line ahead to avoid being outflanked and trapped. Now, all of a sudden, he gave the signal; and they came about and formed up in line abreast, then attacked the startled Peloponnesians opposite them and routed them before wheeling in pursuit of the scattered galleys upstream. Seeing this, the Syracusans on the other wing, who had been slowly and in an orderly fashion giving way to the assault mounted by the vessels under Thrasyllus' command, beat a hasty retreat.

Apart from Thucydides, we have one other source of information for this battle. Diodorus Siculus skips lightly over the events in the Greek East subsequent to the execution of the Athenian generals Nicias and Demosthenes by the Syracusans at the end of Sparta's Sicilian proxy war and prior to the establishment of the Four Hundred at Athens and the battle of Euboea. Moreover, his treatment of these last two developments, of Alcibiades' supposed involvement in preventing the dispatch from Aspendus of the Phoenician fleet, and of Mindarus' journey to the Hellespont is too compressed to be of much use to the modern historian. In describing the conflict on either side of the point at Cynossema, however, the Sicilian historian suddenly comes alive. This may be a reflection of his reliance at this stage on the fourth-century historian Ephorus of Cumae, who was certainly among his sources for this period. It is telling that Polybius, who is not generous in bestowing praise on his post-Thucydidean predecessors, nonetheless lauds the descriptions of naval battles he found in Ephorus' history.

Diodorus' account of the battle of Cynossema differs from that in Thucydides in two important particulars. The former attends to the importance of the current, which the latter does not even mention; and the Sicilian historian describes the conflict from the viewpoint of the men caught up in the fight while his Athenian predecessor does so from that of the commanders. Not for the last time, however, Diodorus errs. He mixes up Thrasybulus and Thrasyllus, and he attributes the Athenian victory to the arrival in the middle of the battle of an additional twenty-five triremes—of whose existence we have no prior knowledge.[10]

The battle was by no means decisive. Because the Hellespont is narrow, especially in the vicinity of Cynossema, it was easy for those who had fled to find places of refuge along the Asian shore. The Athenians lost fifteen ships; their opponents, twenty-one. In the immediate aftermath, from a material perspective, the two fleets were more evenly matched. That is all.

The battle's real importance was twofold. To begin with, the Athenians had survived. Had they suffered a grievous defeat and lost the better part of their fleet, it might well have decided the course of the war. For at home, after the disaster off Euboea, they had only a handful of ships. The battle's significance lay as well in its impact on the morale of the victors. The confidence that the Athenians had squandered in Sicily and that had eroded under the impact of a series of skirmishes in Ionia was in some measure now restored. For the first time, they understood their own capacity and the superiority of their helmsmen as well as the defects of their opponents. Moreover, the arrival of the news at Athens, shortly after the debacle off Eretria, did their compatriots there a world of good.[11]

Mindarus was, however, undaunted—and for good reason. For he retained one crucial advantage: he was free from financial worries while the enemy was justifiably obsessed with the matter. After the battle, the Athenians rowed up to Cyzicus in the Sea of Marmara, which had defected to Clearchus and Pharnabazus. Their aim was to regain the city and garner funds for the ongoing campaign. While they were preoccupied with this task, the Spartan navarch outwitted their military commanders once again—on this occasion by launching a surprise attack on Elaeus, whence he recovered the ships that the enemy had captured.

At the same time, Mindarus sent his second-in-command Hippocrates and another Spartiate named Epicles on one or more fast ships to Euboea to summon Agesandridas and the Peloponnesian fleet that had defeated the Athenians in their home waters in the battle off Eretria. His aim was to have a second go at the Athenians in the Hellespont—this time with an armada so superior in numbers that their fleet would not stand a chance.[12]

IN THE WAKE OF THUCYDIDES: XENOPHON

It is in the midst of these events that Thucydides' narrative suddenly peters out. The Athenian historian does report Alcibiades' return from Aspendus to Samos, and he pointedly draws attention to his efforts to raise money at Halicarnassus and on Kos. It is, moreover, at this point that he provides an account of the expulsion of the Persian garrison from Antandrus, and he reports as well Tissaphernes' return to Ionia, his dismay that the Peloponnesians had turned to Pharnabazus for aid, and his efforts to placate them and explain away the fact that the Phoenician fleet he had promised them never showed up. Then, while describing Tissaphernes's visit to the temple of Artemis at Ephesus and his conduct of a sacrifice there, the son of

Olorus abruptly, in mid-sentence, falls silent—almost certainly because his life had come to an end before he could finish telling his tale.[13]

It is testimony to Thucydides' stature as an historian and to the impact of his effort on his contemporaries that at least three of his younger contemporaries or near-contemporaries stepped forward to pick up the story where he left off and to carry it down to the end of Sparta's third Attic war—and beyond. Two of these were Athenians— a shadowy figure named Cratippus, who was apparently a contemporary of Thucydides, and a well-known Socratic named Xenophon son of Gryllus, who was born circa 427. The third and the last of the three to come into the world was a prominent Chian exile named Theopompus. Of these works, however, the only one that has come down to us intact is Xenophon's *Hellenica*.[14]

Our dependence on the son of Gryllus is for the modern historians of antiquity a source of frustration. Thucydides devoted thirty or more years of his life to the research underpinning his history and to its composition. Xenophon, who wrote a host of books, did nothing of the sort. To be sure, Thucydides focused his attention primarily on Athens and fell short in his account of Lacedaemon, especially where he found "the secretiveness inherent in the regime [*tês politeías tò krúpton*]" an insuperable obstacle, while Xenophon— who left Athens in 401, spent most of his life as a client of Sparta's Eurypontid king Agesilaus, and became intimately familiar with Lacedaemon in a time when, of necessity, she was more open to outsiders—paid close attention to what she did, to her leading personalities, and to her institutions and propensities (which is at times, for us, a great boon).[15] Moreover, the latter's subtlety as a writer and his discernment—much appreciated in antiquity, the Renaissance, and the early modern period and largely ignored or flatly denied throughout the nineteenth and much of the twentieth century—are now, finally, once again being given their due.[16]

Sixty years ago, Xenophon was held in contempt. Today, next to no one would endorse, as nearly everyone did then, the negative assessment of his acumen voiced by the influential German scholar

Barthold Georg Niebuhr in 1827, and next to no one would echo the words that Lord Macaulay published a year later:

> The Life of Cyrus, whether we look upon it as a history or as a romance, seems to us a very wretched performance. The expedition of the Ten Thousand, and the History of Grecian Affairs, are certainly pleasant reading; but they indicate no great power of mind. In truth, Xenophon, though his taste was elegant, his disposition amiable, and his intercourse with the world extensive, had, we suspect, rather a weak head.... Even the lawless habits of a captain of mercenary troops could not change the tendency which the character of Xenophon early acquired. To the last, he seems to have retained a sort of heathen Puritanism. The sentiments of piety and virtue which abound in his works are those of a well-meaning man, somewhat timid and narrow-minded, devout from constitution rather than from rational conviction. He was as superstitious as Herodotus, but in a way far more offensive. The very peculiarities which charm us in an infant, the toothless mumbling, the stammering, the tottering, the helplessness, the causeless tears and laughter, are disgusting in old age. In the same manner, the absurdity which precedes a period of general intelligence is often pleasing; that which follows it is contemptible. The nonsense of Herodotus is that of a baby. The nonsense of Xenophon is that of a dotard.[17]

Moreover, fewer and fewer scholars now share the conviction—expressed by Niebuhr, vigorously defended at length by Eduard Schwartz in 1889, and once almost universally held—that Gryllus' son hated the Athenian democracy and was a slavish admirer of Lacedaemon.[18]

There is, in fact, a growing and salutary willingness within the scholarly world to entertain the possibility that figures like Herodotus, Aristophanes, Thucydides, Plato, Xenophon, and Aristotle were detached observers inclined to stand apart from the fray, to regard all political regimes as being defective in one way or another, to puzzle over the virtues and defects of the various alternative modes of governance, and to consider the circumstances in which each could be sustained and would be, in fact, the best for which one could hope. It is, as scholars are beginning to realize, a mistake to project on the distant past the peculiar propensity for a rigid regime partisanship rooted in ideological commitments that has distorted modern political life for well over two centuries and to suppose that an ancient Greek who was not an unabashed admirer of Athens was a laconophile and that someone who was not an out-and-out democrat must, therefore, have been an oligarch.[19]

In consequence of the salutary shift in opinion that has taken place, Xenophon's penetration and his understanding of institutional dynamics and of character, leadership, and combat on land tends now to be for modern historians a spur to reflection.[20] All of this notwithstanding, however, no one would classify the son of Gryllus as a fully proper successor to Olorus' son, for such was not his aim. He is best understood as an admiring critic.

The key fact, explaining Xenophon's lack of the astonishing diligence displayed by Thucydides, is that he did not think the study of history a pursuit as serious and weighty as did his predecessor. The son of Olorus greatly admired foresight. Some men, he knew, needed no instruction in this regard. Themistocles achieved what he achieved "by his own native intelligence, without the help of study before or after." If, "in a future as yet obscure he could in a preeminent fashion foresee both better and worse" even "when there was little time to take thought," it was solely because of "the power of his nature." Most men, he knew, were not so blessed. But among these, he believed, there were some who possessed a capacity to profit not only from study but also from reflecting on their own experience and from weighing that of others.

It was for such men that Thucydides composed his history. It was his aim to engage their imaginations and supply them with a substitute for personal experience—a knowledge of "the things" that had happened in a particular slice of the past. The great war between the Peloponnesians and the Athenians he considered a revealing event of world-historical importance. In a justly famous passage, which helps explain the immense effort he put into achieving precision and accuracy [*akríbeía*], the historian tells us that he composed his account of the war not as "a contest piece to be heard straightaway" but as "a possession for all times [*ktêmá te es aieí*]." He was aware that the absence within his book of "the mythic" or "fabulous [*tò muthôdes*]" would render it "less delightful [*aterpésteron*]" to some than the work of Homer and Herodotus. But he did not care. It would, he confesses, satisfy his purpose if his work were "judged useful by those who want to observe clearly the events which happened in the past and which in accord with the character of mankind [*katà tò anthrópinon*] will again come to pass hereafter in quite similar ways." In short, Thucydides saw himself as a political scientist intent on discerning patterns and as an educator of use to prospective statesmen.[21]

Theopompus took the son of Olorus as his model, shared the man's estimation of the importance of history, and prided himself on his own conscientiousness and accuracy. To the period stretching from 411/10 to 395/4, he devoted twelve books of his *Hellenica*.[22] Xenophon, by way of contrast, thought four books sufficient. The latter's *Hellenica* begins with the words *metà dè taûta*—"after these things"—and it ends, pointedly, on the very same note. There is nothing within it comparable to the defense of history as an aid to statesmanship that Thucydides limns in the passage cited above. The younger Athenian appears to have doubted that events in the future would closely resemble those in the past.

Nor is there any evidence that, like Herodotus and Thucydides both, Xenophon supposed that an event, such as a great war, could give structure to a particular period. He seems, instead, to have doubted whether such structures really exist and to have regarded the overall course of events—except on those rare occasions when a leader endowed with an extraordinary capacity for persuasion and a comprehensive strategic intelligence intervenes—as one damned thing after another. It is as if the son of Gryllus deemed history to a very considerable degree irrational—an unending chronicle of occurrences that frequently defy the laws of probability and that lie largely beyond rational comprehension. In short, it is as if Xenophon anticipated the sharp criticism that Aristotle, a student of his fellow Socratic Plato, would later direct at Thucydides when, without mentioning that historian by name, the peripatetic argued that historical works are less philosophical than works of poetry in that they do not relate what is apt to take place but what actually happened—and then, to illustrate his contention, pointedly singled out a prominent Thucydidean theme: "what Alcibiades did and what happened to him."[23]

Xenophon nonetheless regarded his *Hellenica* and his other works as "a possession for all times" rather than as mere contest pieces "to be heard straightaway." As he puts it himself in a passage, squirreled away in a minor work, in which he deliberately appropriates the language deployed by his predecessor, his "purpose in writing" was not to inculcate sophistry and mere sophistication and to make men "*sophistikoí*—both cunning and clever." His aim was to render his readers "wise and good." In that sense, he wanted his work to be, and not simply to seem, "useful [*chrḗsima*]" so that it would "in all times be unquestioned and beyond reproach [*anexélegkta ê̦ aeí*]."[24]

If Xenophon thought that he could rival Thucydides in producing works of permanent importance, it was not because of the universal patterns and propensities that he supposed he had uncovered in the course of his research. It was, rather, because of the insight that he as an author brought to the task of telling what were, he did not deny, rip-roaring stories. It is this that explains why the entertaining account he provides in his *Hellenica* is far less precise, detailed, and accurate than Thucydides' monumental work; and it is why, in what might be thought a cavalier fashion, he leaves out so much that an historian on the Thucydidean, or even the modern, model would very much like to know.[25]

In short, if at times Xenophon seems careless, it is because he could not have cared less ... about the matters that most concerned Thucydides and still concern modern political historians. In consequence, his *Hellenica* is a lot like his *Anabasis* and his *Memorabilia*. None of these is from our perspective a proper history. As one classical scholar noted nearly fifty years ago, Xenophon's *Hellenica* more nearly resembles what we would call a memoir. It records the author's impressions, what he witnessed, and what, he thought, he had learned from his conversations with others. And most important, at least for our purposes here, it presumes on the part of its readers an overall familiarity with developments in the period that it covers.[26]

In consequence, when we study Xenophon, we should not expect to find a systematic analysis of the course of events. Instead, we should attend to his narration of the incidents he chooses to report; ponder his judgment of particular political regimes and of the character, skill, discernment, and tactical and strategic competence of particular individuals; and weigh his assessment of the significance of particular developments for those caught up in them. Put simply, we should be grateful for the running commentary that is on offer— even when we wish that we had been vouchsafed a chronicle.

IN THE WAKE OF THUCYDIDES: DIODORUS SICULUS

In addition to Xenophon, Cratippus, and Theopompus, there may have been another continuator of Thucydides. While working through the remains of a massive papyrus dump found at Oxyrhynchus in Egypt, scholars, active in the last century, came across three sets of fragments—two of them dealing with events that took place in Ionia and the Hellespont during the conflict under consideration here, and a third focused on developments in the mid-390s, not long after the end of Thucydides' war. The author, who appears to have composed his book in the fourth century and to have had access to eyewitness testimony for much of what he reported, has not been with certainty identified—and he has therefore been dubbed by scholars the Oxyrhynchus historian.

It is conceivable that this historian was a figure whose efforts as a continuator passed entirely unmentioned in the works from ancient times subsequent to his own that happen to survive. But this is exceedingly unlikely. For the surviving fragments of his book suggest that, as an historian, he was—if not on a par with Thucydides— at least a proper continuator intent on producing a work of comparable precision and scope; and this was clearly recognized in Egypt half a millennium thereafter, where he is known to have been read by a variety of individuals over the course of a century or two. He could, then, conceivably be Cratippus—about whom we know precious little. But the more likely candidate by far is Theopompus of Chios, who was, we now know, a contemporary or near contemporary of the events he described; who fits the profile perfectly; who is much more frequently cited by later authors than is Cratippus; and who from these authors won high praise.[27]

Be this as it may be, we are fortunate in one particular. In his own highly abbreviated account of the last years of Sparta's third Attic war, Diodorus Siculus—who composed his universal history in the last century of the pre-Christian era—preserves much of value that had its origins in the *Hellenica Oxyrhynchia*. It is possible that he discovered this material in the pages of the universal history by Ephorus of Cumae, who is thought by most scholars to have cribbed extensively from the Oxyrhynchus historian in composing his own account of the period stretching from 411 to the end of Thucydides' war and beyond. But this is by no means clear. To begin with, it is not at all certain that Ephorus read the *Hellenica Oxyrhynchia*. The evidence cited as proof for his reliance on that work comes not from any fragmentary material expressly attributed to Ephorus by any subsequent source. In its entirety, it comes from Diodorus, who is known to have consulted, compared, and puzzled over the reliability of a variety of sources. Diodorus read Ephorus. This we know. His own efforts as a universal historian may, in fact, have been inspired by the project undertaken by the historian from Aeolian Cumae; and, in the books of his history that dealt with the period stretching from the Persian Wars to Lacedaemon's demise as a great power, he sometimes drew on that man's narrative. He was not, however, uncritical, and he was not a slavish copyist. He was, in fact, perfectly capable of saying that "one should not look to Ephorus for accuracy and precision [*t'akríbés*] in every particular, seeing that with regard to many matters he gave little heed to the truth"; and, when he cites Ephorus, it is generally to criticize and reject a claim he advances or to mention him as one source of information among others. Only rarely does Diodorus treat Ephorus as an authority.[28]

We have good reason, moreover, to believe that Diodorus directly consulted the *Hellenica* composed by Theopompus of Chios, a work he mentions more than once and a work that he may—for events that took place in the Aegean world during the period stretching from 411 to 394—have relied on far more than he depended on Ephorus. In consulting Theopompus, if the conviction I share with an increasing cohort of modern historians concerning the author-ship of the *Hellenica Oxyrhynchia* is correct, Diodorus will have con-sulted the Oxyrhynchus historian himself.[29]

This likelihood notwithstanding, errors of various sorts and lacu-nae much to be regretted crept into Diodorus' narrative in the course of transmission and compression, and the attendant distortions may well have been rhetorically amplified as a consequence both of the literary ambitions, personal agendas, and propensity for moralizing of Diodorus and of the writer or writers on whose work he drew. Theopompus and Ephorus are both said to have been trained in rhetoric by Isocrates, and there is no good reason to doubt the ancient testimony. In the fourth century, history was understood as a branch of rhetoric.[30]

There is one other sign suggesting that, in writing the history of this period, Diodorus relied for the most part on Theopompus—and that is the relative dearth of chronological confusion in this part of his narrative. Ephorus eschewed the chronological schema pioneered by Thucydides and taken up by Theopompus, and he presented his account as a series of discrete vignettes, devoting each of the thirty books in his work to a single topic. Diodorus, when he followed Ephorus, selected material from his vignettes and recast it in summary form within an annalistic framework based on a false equation of the lunar calendar of Athens, which, in principle, ran from the first new moon after the summer solstice to the first new moon after the summer solstice the following year, with the consular calendar at Rome, which, in principle, ran from March to March. On occasion, this gave rise to chronological confusion, and it tolerably often resulted in Diodorus' reporting under a particular year a series of events that took place over a considerably longer span of time. That the Sicilian historian does not do the like in dealing with the period covered by Theopompus' *Hellenica* suggests that his narrative of that period is not primarily derived from Ephorus.[31]

Diodorus' errors were never, alas, confined to the chronological sphere, and they were not all due to compression or to a rhetorical amplification on his part or on that of the sources on which he relied. The fact that, in his history of the decade subsequent to the Sicilian expedition, he frequently mentions Pharnabazus when it is Tissaphernes whom he has in mind and that he no less frequently confuses Thrasybulus with Thrasyllus and vice versa is, to say the least, jarring. It suggests a certain carelessness on his part and warns us that the details that he provides should not simply be taken at face value.[32]

Diodorus' defects are an obstacle to clarity. Of this there can be no doubt. Unfortunately, however, there is a further source of confusion that the modern historian must confront. In the material devoted to the final years of Sparta's third Attic war—which is contained in the first book of his *Hellenica* and in much of the second and which may have been composed long before the rest of that work—Xenophon tended to lay out his narrative in something like the Thucydidean manner by specifying the beginning of each new campaigning season. Unfortunately for us, however, he left out one such indicator—and we have no firm, reliable information from any other source clarifying where in his account of the period stretching from the campaigning season of 410 to that of 406 the missing break between years should be situated.

In what follows, therefore, I will construct a narrative grounded in a critical assessment of what is reported in Xenophon and Diodorus, and I will insert the missing indicator of a new campaigning season where, in my opinion, the narrative requires it.[33] The testimony of Xenophon, the Oxyrhynchus historian, and Diodorus I will supplement with what can be gleaned from the surviving inscriptions and from other reports. Above all, I will look also to Plutarch, who drew on Xenophon but who profited also from reading Theopompus, Cratippus, Ephorus, and many a contemporary literary work no longer available to us.[34]

FROM THE HELLESPONT TO CYZICUS

According to Diodorus, Agesandridas responded to the order from Mindarus, conveyed by Hippocrates and Epicles, by heading out from Euboea with fifty triremes. The most direct route would have taken this force through the gap between Euboea and Andros, then north-northeast past Scyros, Lemnos, and Imbros. But to do so, he would have had to buck the current within the Aegean fostered by the influx from the Euxine. Moreover, the campaigning season had passed, the winter with its violent storms had set in, and Agesandridas was understandably wary of taking to the open sea. Although in a great hurry, he hugged the shore, as the Hellenes were apt to do; and he opted initially to have his fleet row up the lengthy sound separating Euboea from the mainland, no doubt with an eye to the fact that the island blunted the force of winter's variable winds. Thereafter, he had his galleys cruise past the iron coast of Magnesia, where there was hardly any shelter to be found; and this, perhaps because Agesandridas had gauged the weather correctly, they appear to have achieved without mishap. Then, he had them make their way along the more welcoming shores of the Thermaic Gulf to the three-fingered peninsula we now call the Chalcidice.

Upon arrival, Agesandridas' fleet worked its way successfully to the east—past Capes Castarnaeum and Amphelos, which are situated at the end of the long, thin promontories, called Pallene and Sithonia, that jut out from the Chalcidice. Then, it was faced with the third and last of that prominent geographical feature's three promontories—Acte, where many a mariner had already lost his life. At this stage, Agesandridas miscalculated, as others had before him, and things went badly wrong. As his fleet slipped past Cape Nymphaeum in the west, then rounded Cape Acrathus in the east, a Hellesponter struck from the northeast, as often happened in every season; and it shattered the Spartiate's galleys on the rugged cliffs, descending from Mount Athos, that distinguish the southernmost stretch of Acte's eastern coast.

Diodorus Siculus, who cites an inscription quoted before him by Ephorus, reports that all of the triremes were destroyed and that only twelve men survived—which is, we must suspect, a gross

Map 14. European Thrace and the Hellespont

exaggeration. We learn from Xenophon that Agesandridas' vessel, which carried a crew of two hundred mariners, reached the Hellespont, where he became Mindarus' lieutenant, and there were evidently other such galleys which made it as well. For the son of Gryllus also mentions a skirmish on their part with a tiny flotilla led by Thumochares from Athens, and Agesandridas' triremes are said to have had the better of it. This skirmish is, however, immaterial. What matters is the fact that, had it not been for the debacle at Acte and the destruction of most of this Spartan's fleet, the Athenians in the Hellespont would have been done for.[35]

In the meantime, Dorieus—no doubt having been summoned from Rhodes, where his mission had been, we know, a success—arrived in the Hellespont with fourteen triremes. Whether the Athenians, when they learned of his arrival, drove his flotilla ashore at Rhoeteum, as Xenophon reports, or at Dardanus seven miles further upstream, as Diodorus claims, we cannot tell. Either way, however, it makes more sense to join Theopompus of Chios in speaking of the conflict that followed as the second battle of Cynossema than to term it, in the modern fashion, as the battle of Abydos. Moreover, it is clear from both narratives that very little damage was done to Dorieus' flotilla; that Mindarus and the Peloponnesian fleet stationed at Abydos to the north soon came to his relief; that a full-scale naval battle subsequently took place in the lower reaches of the Hellespont; that, thanks in part to Dorieus' arrival, the Athenians were once again at a numerical disadvantage; that Alcibiades' subsequent appearance with eighteen to twenty triremes startled the Spartans and their allies and induced them to flee; and that, on land, Pharnabazus and the forces he had assembled played a prominent role in preventing the Athenians from fully exploiting their victory. In the end, they nonetheless managed to recover the triremes they had lost at Elaeus and to capture thirty of those possessed by the enemy.

Once again, thanks presumably to the narrative skill of his source or sources, Diodorus provides us with a graphic account of the fighting. After the two fleets lined up in the relatively narrow channel, he

**Figure 6.1. Warship ram on a relief showing naval tropies
and priests' emblems from Rome.**
(Precise findspot unrecorded), Augustan period (Stanza dei Filosofi,
Palazzo dei Conservatori, Rome; Photograph: Courtesy of William M. Murray
©William M. Murray).

reports, the rival commanders ordered that the *sálpinx* be blown. It
was then that the engagement in earnest began:

> In these circumstances, whenever the triremes lunged for-
> ward to ram, the helmsmen would prudently, at the critical
> moment, bring their ships about so that the blows would be
> received on the ram. When they saw their own ships with
> their sides exposed to the triremes of the approaching foe, the
> marines on deck were terrified, fearing for their lives. But
> whenever the helmsmen, as a consequence of prior experi-
> ence, managed to elude the assaults, they were again filled
> with joy and buoyed up with hopes.

Nor was the eagerness of those stationed on the decks without consequence. Some of these men, operating from a considerable dis-

tance, fired arrow after arrow so that the surrounding space was rapidly filled with projectiles. Others, whenever the galleys came near, would hurl javelins—some eagerly targeting the marines defending their ships; others, the helmsmen steering the craft. And whenever the vessels came quite close, these men would do battle with spears—and, when the triremes collided, they would jump across to the enemy galleys and have at one another with swords. Whenever a reverse took place, the victors raised the war cry, and their opponents, with a shout, came to assist—so that over the entirety of the place where the naval battle occurred a confused clamor could be heard.[36]

Whether this description is merely boilerplate, as some scholars suspect, or an accurate account attentive to the peculiarities of this particular battle we cannot be certain.

Ephorus took on a monumental task. He was an exceedingly busy man. In composing a universal history, some thirty books in length, in the middle of the fourth century, he is thought to have consulted earlier historians as well as inscriptions, collections of oracles, and the works of poets, playwrights, and pamphleteers. He was deeply appreciative of the importance of eyewitness testimony, but he is not apt to have secured a great deal of it.[37]

Ephorus or, for that matter, Diodorus may well have lifted this battle description from the work of a contemporary or near-contemporary author who was in a position to do what they, for one reason or another, could not do and who took the trouble to do it— for, as we have seen, there were at least two such authors, and Diodorus was familiar with the work of at least one of them. All that can be said with certainty is that the battle description is quite apt— for head-on collisions are far less likely when a naval engagement takes place in open water, and there we would expect reports of out-flanking maneuvers, of the *diékplous*, or even the *períplous*, which rightly pass unmentioned in an account of naval warfare within so confined a space.

In any case, on Diodorus' telling, the battle was evenly fought prior to Alcibiades' arrival. His appearance on the horizon produced in both sides an oscillation between elation and alarm until he ran up a purple pennant signaling to the Athenians that he was one of theirs. Unfortunately, however, for Alcibiades' compatriots, a storm frustrated their attempts to ram the enemy ships as they then took flight.[38]

When the battle was at an end, the Athenians withdrew to their stronghold at Sestos; and, under the cover of darkness, Mindarus conducted what was left of his fleet to Abydos. In the aftermath, both sides repaired their ships and sent out an appeal for reinforcements. Mindarus dispatched a messenger to Sparta asking for additional infantrymen and ships while Thrasyllus made his way to Athens to convey a similar plea.[39]

Forty of the Athenian triremes were left as a garrison at Sestos while the remaining galleys rowed hither and thither in the Aegean throughout the winter in a frantic search for funds. In the same period, perhaps even before Thrasyllus' arrival in Athens, Theramenes son of Hagnon set out from the Peiraeus with thirty galleys. After trying in vain to interfere with an attempt on the part of the Boeotians and the Chalcidians to build moles to narrow the channel at Eripus and then construct a bridge that would link the island of Euboea with the mainland, he headed out into the Aegean. There, with an eye to reducing or eliminating the *eisphoraí* exacted from his fellow citizens and, we are told, from Athens' allies, he not only ravaged the territory of the cities that had gone over to Lacedaemon and secured booty on a considerable scale. He also extracted funds from those known to be interested in fomenting oligarchic revolutions. On Paros, moreover, he overturned the oligarchy set up by Peisander and his colleagues, he restored the democracy, and he forced those who had participated in the oligarchy to cough up sizable sums. Thereafter, he headed to the north country where his father Hagnon had founded the city of Amphipolis. For a time, he paused to aid Athens' ally Archelaus, Perdiccas' son and successor as king of the Macedonians, who was besieging Pydna. Then, he moved on to Thrace and linked up with his fellow demesman Thrasybulus son of Lycus who was busy in that region collecting funds and shoring up support for Athens.[40]

In the meantime, Alcibiades, who appears to have been among those in charge of the forty triremes left at Sestos in the Hellespont, paid a formal visit to Tissaphernes when that satrap came on the scene—and he unexpectedly found himself imprisoned at Sardis. As Tissaphernes explained, presumably by way of excuse, the King had ordered him to fight the Athenians. Alcibiades' confinement must not have been taken all that seriously, and Tissaphernes, who was always eager to keep his options open, is apt to have connived in his escape, as Alcibiades later claimed. For, after a month, Cleinias' wily son managed to slip away on horseback to Clazomenae on the west coast of Anatolia in company with an Athenian named Mantitheus who had been captured in Caria; and, as we shall see, Tissaphernes later did his handsome Athenian guest-friend a good turn.[41]

The financial difficulties that preoccupied the Athenians left Mindarus once again free to concentrate on the war itself, and he was not behindhand in exploiting the opportunity this afforded him. With the bulk of his fleet, he rowed in stages upstream along the Asian shore. There, with the assistance of Pharnabazus, he endeavored, with considerable success, to bring into the Spartan alliance the Hellenic cities scattered along the Anatolian coast.[42]

CHAPTER SIX

THE SEA OF MARMARA
AND THE BOSPORUS

Military strategy, while one of the most ancient of the human sciences, is at the same time one of the least developed. One could hardly expect it to be otherwise. Military leaders must be men of decision and action rather than of theory. Victory is the payoff, and therefore the confirmation of correct decision. There is no other science where judgments are tested in blood and answered in the servitude of the defeated, where the acknowledged authority is the leader who has won or who instills confidence that he will win.

BERNARD BRODIE

WHEN THE WINTER was about to come to an end, Mindarus once again concentrated his forces at Abydos; and, as was his wont, he took the initiative. The sheer number of triremes that the Spartan was able to gather thanks to the Persian subventions caused the Athenian commanders still at Sestos, almost certainly with Chaereas son of Archestratus included, to do two things: to stage a withdrawal from the Hellespont to Cardia on the west coast of the Thracian Chersonnesus in the north, and to summon the scattered Athenian forces—among them, the triremes in Thrace commanded by Thrasybulus son of Lycus and

Theramenes son of Hagnon and the handful of ships at Clazomenae or Lesbos led by Alcibiades son of Cleinias. While this was going on, Mindarus had taken his fleet to Cyzicus. There, with the help of Pharnabazus son of Pharnaces, the Spartans and their allies had besieged, then seized the city.

According to Xenophon, Alcibiades was the first to reach Cardia. After taking stock, he journeyed by land across the Thracian Chersonnesus to Sestos; and, when he learned that the Peloponnesians had headed in the direction of the Euxine, he sent word for the ships at Cardia to circumnavigate the Chersonnesus and make their way back to the Hellespont. In the meantime, Theramenes and Thrasybulus reached that body of water with an additional forty ships. Their rendezvous seems to have taken place at Elaeus. Once their fleet— eighty-six triremes in number—was concentrated, the Athenian commanders were as one in thinking it time to seek a decision. As they knew, Mindarus had made a mistake. Cyzicus was on the Sea of Marmara, a body of water in which a large fleet could maneuver.[1]

Up to this point, the Athenians had been for the most part on the defensive, reacting, often too late, to what the Spartans and their allies attempted. Now, for the first time since the catastrophe in Sic-

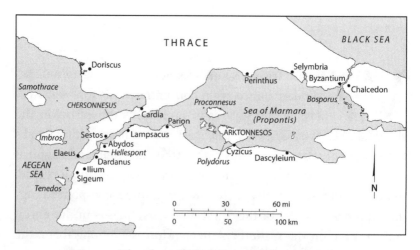

Map 15. The Sea of Marmara and the Bosporus

ily, they took the initiative and set the tempo. With an eye to hiding their numbers, the Athenian commanders had their fleet row up the Hellespont past Abydos under the cover of darkness. En route northeast, they paused briefly at Parion on the Asian shore, just beyond the point where the Hellespont gives way to the Propontis, which they apparently controlled. Then, again at night, they rowed on to the middle of the Sea of Marmara, where they established their base at Proconnesus, a community of great, but today unappreciated, geo-strategic importance that controlled the only island of any size located in the region constituted by the Hellespont, the Propontis, and the Bosporus.[2]

On Proconnesus, the Athenians took their midday meal, and, after confirming that Mindarus and Pharnabazus really were at Cyzicus, Alcibiades took the lead, summoning an assembly and telling those in the Athenian force what everyone must have suspected already—that they would soon have to fight not only on the sea but also on land and attack as well whatever fortifications the enemy had cobbled together at the hitherto unfortified city of Cyzicus. "We have no money," he explained, "and from the King the enemy has an abundance." The remainder of that day they rested, and they did so as well the day after—while Alcibiades rounded up the merchant ships or small boats in their vicinity so that no one could convey the news of their presence to the enemy. Then, surreptitiously, yet again under the cover of darkness, he had the Athenian galleys land an infantry force, under the command of Chaereas, in the territory of the Cyzicenes some distance from the city where they would not be spied.

South-southeast of Proconnesus lies a sizable peninsula called in antiquity Arktonnesos, and it may have been on its western shore that Chaereas and his hoplites waded ashore. At the base of this peninsula, on the narrow isthmus where that bulbous protrusion joins the mainland, lay at this time the prosperous Greek city Cyzicus. In these parts, in high summer, the sky is generally clear and there is next to no fog or precipitation. But as late winter gives way to early spring, in March and early April, there is with some frequency heavy fog along the Bosporus and in the Sea of Marmara, especially in the wee hours and for a time after dawn—and on occasion this impenetrable brume is accompanied by rain.[3] It was on just such a morning, some hours after landing Chaereas' force, that the Athenians in the fleet silently made their way toward Cyzicus in the darkness before dawn amidst a driving rain.

In principle, all of the *stratēgoí* were equal; in principle, when on campaign, they operated by consensus. This was the Athenian understanding. In practice, however, his colleagues deferred to Alcibiades— as men in this period were apt to do. After all, those on Samos who had elected him a *stratēgós* had, as Thucydides reports, "put him in charge of all public business." Not surprisingly, then, it was he who, on this occasion, took the lead, making his way south with a force of twenty or, perhaps, forty ships past the three small islands that lie directly to the west of the Arktonnesos peninsula, then southeast along the western coast of that prominent land mass. Thrasybulus and Theramenes, with the sixty-six or fifty-six triremes remaining, followed much the same trajectory, but lagged well behind. With his unit, Thrasybulus slipped behind the promontory that juts out from the Arktonnesos peninsula and forms the northwestern boundary of the bay of Cyzicus. There, opposite the little island of Arkte, which Diodorus dubs Polydorus, he remained—out of sight and out of mind. Theramenes appears to have lurked in the waters to the west of the path charted by Alcibiades. At least initially, all three contingents were sheltered by the thick fog. Even if Mindarus had posted lookouts on the high ground behind Cyzicus or on that atop the Arktonnesos peninsula, there was nothing that they could have seen.

The aim of the Athenian commanders was to use Alcibiades' squadron as bait. When his unit, which was presumably composed of the fastest vessels in the Athenian armada, slipped between the Arktonnesos peninsula and the isle of Polydorus and unexpectedly hove into view, Mindarus would, they hoped, set out with his armada in hot pursuit, intent on launching an attack. Alcibiades' flotilla would then flee, and the Spartans and their allies would be lured fur-

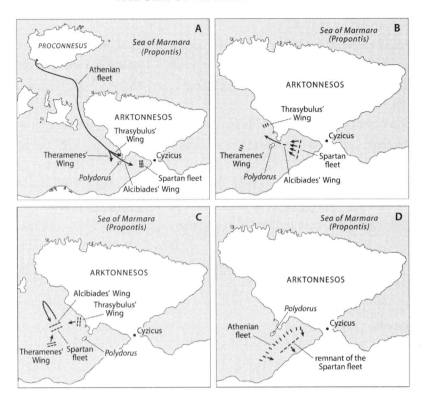

Map 16. The Sequence of Battle at Cyzicus, 410

ther and further from shore—into the open waters where the Athenians' superior skill in performing the *períplous*, the *diékplous*, the *anastrophé*, and a host of other less elaborate maneuvers would give them a decided edge. This was what Alcibiades, Thrasybulus, and Theramenes had in mind.

It was a brilliant plan, and it worked. That morning, as the fog slowly began to lift, Mindarus ventured out into the wide bay northwest of Cyzicus with sixty of his triremes. His purpose was to put them through their paces. When Alcibiades suddenly emerged from the murk, the Spartan navarch took the bait, and a chase began. At the appropriate moment—not all that long after, in flight, his squadron had once again slipped past the little isle of Polydorus— Alcibiades gave the agreed-upon signal, and the triremes under his command suddenly put about and confronted their astonished attackers. In the meantime, Thrasybulus slipped out with his division from its hideaway and suddenly emerged from the fog behind the Peloponnesian force. From this position, he then launched an assault on the enemy fleet from the rear, in order to cut it off from retreat, as Theramenes with his division appeared on the fleet's western flank. With their three squadrons, Alcibiades, Thrasybulus, and Theramenes enveloped Mindarus' force, and they rammed at the stern or amidships the galleys that their marines did not board and seize.

As was inevitable, given the size of his fleet, a fair number of Mindarus' triremes managed to slip through the net. These Alcibiades' unit pursued to the Cyzicene shore—where Pharnabazus' infantry and cavalry had their camp. There, with grappling irons, the Athenians tried to drag out to sea the triremes that had fled as well as the twenty triremes that had been left at their moorings or hauled up on the shore—presumably to effect repairs and to dry them out, scrape their bottoms, recaulk their hulls, and recoat them with pitch.

When Pharnabazus' footsoldiers came to the relief of their allies, there was, we are told, a great shedding of blood. At this point, Thrasybulus landed his *epibátai* and encouraged Theramenes to do the like and link up with the infantrymen commanded by Chaereas who had made their way past Cyzicus. When, at the urging of Mindarus, Ramphias' energetic son Clearchus led out against Thrasybulus' marines the Peloponnesian infantry and the mercenaries in the service of Pharnabazus and surrounded the Athenians, whom they greatly outnumbered, Theramenes' unit and Chaereas' forces came to their relief. After a time, Pharnabazus' mercenaries withdrew, and Clearchus and his Peloponnesians were driven off. While this was taking place, Mindarus himself, with the *epibátai* and infantrymen still at his disposal, put up, around the galleys, a stout resistance to the assault mounted by Alcibiades—and it was there that this talented, brave, enterprising Lacedaemonian navarch lost his life.[4]

Mindarus' death occasioned a panic. Had it not been for the arrival of Pharnabazus with his cavalry, there would almost certainly have been a massacre. In the event, however, the Athenians captured nearly all of the Peloponnesian galleys that they did not sink, and those that they did not capture were, in anticipation, burned by the quick-witted Syracusans. Cyzicus the Athenians soon occupied, and over the twenty days they remained in the city they gathered booty on a magnificent scale.

Thereafter, Xenophon reports, Alcibiades made his way to the northern shore of the Sea of Marmara and extracted considerable sums from Perinthus, where he was admitted into the city, and from Selymbria, which denied him entrance. Then, it is agreed, he seized Chrysopolis (the City of Gold), which was situated on a headland on the Asian side of the Bosporus directly opposite Byzantium's Golden Horn right where the Istanbul suburb Üsküdar is now located. This place he fortified, and there he posted a sizable flotilla of thirty to fifty triremes under the command of Theramenes and a *stratēgós* named Eumachos.

Their charge was threefold. Two of the responsibilities assigned them were spelled out. On the headland, which lay within the territory of Chalcedon, they were to set up a customs house whereby Alcibiades' compatriots could collect a tax of ten percent on cargoes heading from the Black Sea to the Sea of Marmara, the Hellespont, and the Aegean, if not also on those making their way in the opposite direction. This, we have reason to suspect, they had long done from Byzantium prior to her rebellion. Then, if circumstances were propitious, they were to seize Byzantium as well as Chalcedon. The third of their responsibilities was unspoken because it was universally recognized. The Athenian presence in the Bosporus with a large fleet was a guarantee—at least for the nonce—that, when the grain fleet sailed from the Euxine in mid-September, its progress would be unimpeded.

Thereafter, at Alcibiades' urging, Thrasybulus returned to Thrace with thirty additional triremes to bring the cities in that region back into the Athenian fold. In the meantime, the son of Cleinias systematically ravaged the territory of Pharnabazus and collected a great deal of booty with an eye, we are told, to relieving his compatriots of the *eisphoraí* with which they had been saddled.[5]

Needless to say, the disaster at Cyzicus inspired consternation at Sparta. At some point, Xenophon tells us, the Athenians captured an emissary dispatched to Lacedaemon by Mindarus' *epistoleús* and second-in-command Hippocrates. The message in the man's possession was suitably laconic, and it reflected the language that his compatriots tended to use when referring to triremes: "Timber lost. Mindarus dead. Men starving. At a loss what to do."[6]

AN OFFER OF PEACE

In the wake of this battle—the Atthidographer Philochorus, Diodorus Siculus, Cornelius Nepos, and a number of later authors report—the Lacedaemonians sent Endius son of the Spartan Alcibiades to Athens to sue for peace. If Androtion is to be trusted, the Athenian Alcibiades' *xénos* was not alone. Rather, in keeping with Lacedaemonian practice, he was accompanied by two other Spartiates: Philocharidas son of Eryxilaidas, who had played a prominent role eleven years before in negotiating the Peace of Nicias and in trying to sustain it; and an otherwise unidentified figure named Megillus, who may well be the Spartan interlocutor identified in Plato's *Laws* as the *próxenos* of the Athenians at Lacedaemon. The following terms were on offer: that there be an exchange of prisoners, one for one; that each side retain the cities then in its possession; and that each *pólis* withdraw the garrison or garrisons maintained on the other's territory. After stating the terms on offer, Endius is said to have spoken with great eloquence concerning what the Athenians had to gain from a cessation of hostilities and what they had to lose from continuing the war.

Although Xenophon is silent concerning this embassy and offer, there is no reason to doubt the report. Given the efforts of Thucydides' other continuators, Philochorus, Diodorus, and Nepos are apt to have been well-informed. Whether Endius actually spoke as

Diodorus firmly insists he did—this we do not know. It is perfectly possible that Diodorus, or an intermediary source, lifted the remarks Diodorus attributes to the Spartiate from the pages of a writer who was both in the know and intent, as Thucydides had been, on accurately summarizing the arguments made. It is, however, no less possible that it was a free composition thrown together by the ultimate source of this story or even by Diodorus himself. All that can be said with any degree of certitude is that the argument attributed to Endius is apt and has considerable force.

The Athenians really were in a bad way: they were denied access to their farms. What Alcibiades had reportedly said on the eve of the battle at Cyzicus was true: they had no money. The steady drumbeat of reports in Thucydides, Xenophon, and Diodorus regarding expeditions, verging on piracy, that were undertaken for the extraction of funds from the cities that had once provided Athens with *phóros* is testimony to their plight. Moreover, as Endius reportedly emphasized, in battles at sea his compatriots risked only the hulls for which they had hired crews while the Athenians risked their own lives and the very existence of their city.

According to Xenophon, Pharnabazus was of good cheer after the battle at Cyzicus. The Spartans and their allies he urged not to lose heart. In a resort to the term employed by the Lacedaemonians to denote their galleys, he said that there was plenty of "timber" in the territory of the King. All would be well if they retained, as they did, a sufficient number of men; and, saying this, he provided every one of the survivors with a cloak and cash sufficient to allow him to stave off hunger for two months. Then, he summoned their commanders and the trierarchs and instructed them to build triremes at Antandrus, which was situated below Mount Ida on the bay of Adramyttium, and he gave them money and told them to get logs from the great mountain looming over the city—where, we know, lumber fit to be turned into ship's timbers could quite easily be found.

When the Athenians and the authorities at Lacedaemon learned of Pharnabazus' largess we are not told. But it is reasonable to guess that little time intervened between his announcement of his decision and their hearing of it. There was no need for secrecy, and news of this sort traveled fast. Moreover, the Lacedaemonians, who were not themselves in any immediate danger, had no need for alacrity and were, in general, disinclined to make haste. We can be confident that there were extensive deliberations over a number of weeks before Endius and his colleagues departed for Athens, and we know from Philochorus that the delegation reached Athens before the end of the 411/10 archon year in late June or early July. By that time, if not well before, both sides are apt to have been fully informed concerning the satrap's plans.[7]

If so, the mission assigned Philocharidas, Megillus, and Endius is a sign of the degree to which a majority of the Spartans had come to regret their decision to launch the war. In many quarters, as the conduct of Lichas son of Arcesilaus shows, their alliance with the Mede had been deemed distasteful from the start; and, of course, their ignominious failure in the field was disheartening. The climb-down involved in dispatching Alcibiades' guest-friend on such an embassy must have been a real humiliation.

The Athenians were, of course, overjoyed at their victory, as they had every right to be. In short order, they responded by voting to send to Alcibiades and his colleagues an additional one thousand hoplites, one hundred cavalrymen, and thirty or more triremes— though, thanks to the time it took to construct galleys of this sort, the actual dispatch did not take place until the following spring.[8]

This victory seems also to have occasioned the restoration of Athens' radical democracy. For, although we know nothing else about the transition, we have reason to suspect that the regime of the Five Thousand lasted no more than eight months and quite possibly less, and Diodorus reports that Endius' offer, which was welcomed by "the most reasonable [epieikéstatoi] of the Athenians," was rejected by the populace—"the dêmos"—at the insistence of a demagogue named Cleophon. It is difficult to believe that this would have happened had the country folk of at least modest means, who were dominant under the Five Thousand, made the decision.

Cleophon was a man of some means. His father Cleippides had been among those who had received votes in an ostracism conducted in the late 440s, and he had been a *stratēgós* at least once—in 428/7 at the time of the Mytilenian revolt. This Cleippides' outspoken son was cut from the same cloth as Cleon son of Cleaenetus, Hyperbolus son of Antiphanes, and Peisander. He was, we are told, a lamp-maker. He was already sufficiently well-known in 416 that, at the time of the ostracism that had eventuated in Hyperbolus' withdrawal from Athens, he, too, had received a number of votes; and, like his three renowned predecessors, he had been awarded the dubious honor of being made the subject of a satirical play by Plato Comicus. On this occasion late in the spring or early in the summer of 410, he encouraged his compatriots to want more, and he persuaded them that their luck had turned.[9]

It is easy to see why Athens' salarymen and the others who treasured her empire would be reluctant to make peace. After all, the Spartans and their allies were in possession of the islands of Euboea, Chios, and Rhodes and of Abydos, Miletus, Ephesus, Byzantium, and a number of smaller *póleis* situated on *terra firma*. There were, moreover, cities in Anatolia, such as Chalcedon and Antandrus, that the Lacedaemonians shared with the Mede. Euboea had long been an important source of food for the Athenians. The income that the latter could extract from the communities at this time in the hands of the Spartans was no small matter; and, in the period in which the enemy would be bereft or at least quite short of ships, the Athenians could hope to recover at least some of the cities lost. Moreover, if one expected the war to be renewed within a year or two, it made sense to take full advantage of the opportunity that their victory at Cyzicus had afforded them. It was especially worrisome that, from Byzantium, Chalcedon, and Abydos, the Spartans and the Persians would soon again be able to obstruct the great mid-September grain shipments from the Black Sea—once they had constructed a new fleet.[10]

There was also a case to be made for peace. Athens' predicament stemmed from the alliance between Lacedaemon and the Mede. As long as that alliance was sustained, she would be in grave danger. In these circumstances, as Endius is said to have emphasized, the Spartans could afford to lose again and again while one major loss would put paid to the Athenians. Her commanders—indeed, the city herself—had recognized this. In the recent past, they had gone to inordinate lengths in an abortive attempt to drive a wedge between Athens' two enemies.

Now such a divorce was on offer, and it promised to sour relations between the Spartans and the Persians. In the absence of the subventions provided by the latter, moreover, the former would be no threat to the Athenians at sea—unless, of course, they adopted a radically new fiscal *modus operandi* based on the systematic extraction of *phóros* from the cities hitherto allied with or subject to Athens. To such a transformation, the Lacedaemonians were instinctively disinclined. It was by no means fortuitous that they had no coinage of their own. They were soldiers, members of the gentry, and communitarians. To the ethos produced by the cash nexus, they were viscerally hostile.[11]

The Spartans were, moreover, a pious lot. If the Athenians observed the terms of the agreement, they would be quite apt to do so as well. To this, one can add that the Lacedaemonians were, at heart, landlubbers. They would be instinctively reluctant to maintain a substantial presence at sea, and they did not themselves—not even with the help of their Peloponnesian and Syracusan allies—have the wherewithal with which to do such a thing.

Furthermore, the Spartans were xenophobes liable to mistreat outsiders who were under their command. In 478, as many Athenians were well aware, brutality on their part had driven the islanders into the hands of Aristeides and his colleague Cimon. In the circumstances that pertained in 410, an observer attentive to the influence over policy exercised by regime imperatives could with some force argue that the Athenians should accept the Lacedaemonian offer and then watch and wait. Rhodes, Miletus, Chios, Byzantium, and the like would soon enough rebel against their Spartan overlords and welcome back their erstwhile ally.

This consideration had weight. For it did not take long for the Lacedaemonians to wear out their welcome. Iasos is a case in point. This *pólis* had been seized from Amorges in 412. If her citizens had not already by the time of Endius' arrival at Athens expelled the Spartan harmost Eteonicus and repudiated Lacedaemon's domination, they were at this very time on the verge of doing so.[12] All that was required, if the Athenians wished to take advantage of the Spartans' ineptitude and their propensity for brutality, was the patience and determination displayed in 478 by Aristeides and Cimon.

The risks involved were, however, very considerable. Moreover, regime imperatives had as much influence in Athens as they did in Lacedaemon, and the world of Aristeides and Cimon was long gone. Patience was not a quality that the compatriots of these two statesmen still possessed in the second half of the fifth century. This the Corinthians had eloquently conveyed to the Spartans in 432. If my argument in *Sparta's Second Attic War* is sound, Pericles had understood that a peace treaty can be used as an instrument of war; and, as I suggested in that volume, this insight may have spurred on Alcibiades when he attempted to exploit the unrest occasioned within the Peloponnesus by the Peace of Nicias in and after 421. In the summer of 410, there may well have been men among Athens' *epieikéstatoi* who understood just how much damage peace could do their Lacedaemonian enemy, but they were not in charge. Cleophon was not in their number, and the salarymen of Athens, to whom he looked for support, were an especially impatient lot. Cunning indirection is not generally the strong suit of those who live from hand to mouth, and it may be telling that neither the son of Cleinias, glory-hound that he was, nor either of his close associates Thrasybulus and Theramenes is said to have weighed in on the side of the Spartan envoys and of Athens' would-be peacemakers. Alcibiades was, we know, a young man in a great hurry.

PARTISANSHIP

The restoration of the radical democracy also gave rise to a change in public policy. Fiscal discipline went by the boards. As was only natural, jury pay was restored. Cleophon also introduced a new institution—the *diōbelía*—which may have involved a distribution of two obols, one-third of a drachma, to the indigent; and by 409/8, stonecutters and the like were back at work on the Erechtheum. It was as if the emergency had passed. Moreover, as one would expect, the *eisphorá* was also reintroduced.[13]

Nor should we be surprised that the counterrevolution was accompanied by a vindictiveness largely absent in the time of the Five Thousand. If, as seems to have been the case, the decree of Demophantus was passed by the assembly in late June or early July 410, shortly after the new archon year had begun, the return to radical democracy was, in its ferocity, a grim portent indicative of what was to come. "If anyone," it read,

> brings down the democracy or holds a public office after the democracy has been brought down, let him be declared a public enemy [*polémios*] of the Athenians, let him be slain with impunity, and let his possessions become public property with a tithe set aside for the goddess. As for the one who kills a man who does this or conspires to do so, holy law shall sanction his deed [*hósios éstō*] and he will be free from pollution [*euagés*]. So let it be.
>
> All of the Athenians, articulated into tribes and demes, are to swear over an unblemished sacrifice to kill the man who does these things. Let this be the oath: "Insofar as I am able, I will slay by word, deed, vote, and my own hand whoever brings down the democracy at Athens, whoever holds a pub-

lic office after it has been brought down, and whoever attempts to become a tyrant or joins in setting up a tyranny. Moreover, if anyone else slays such a man, I shall regard him as having acted in a manner sanctioned by the gods and demi-gods [*hósion ... pròs theôn kaì daimónōn*] by killing a public enemy. And after selling all of the goods of the man slain, I will give half of the proceeds to the killer and cheat him of nothing. If anyone loses his life in the attempt to kill such a man or in the course of succeeding, I will treat him and also his children as Harmodius, Aristogeiton, and their offspring were treated. And all oaths hostile to the *dêmos* of the Athenians, which may have been sworn at Athens, in the encampment, or anywhere else, I repudiate and abandon."

In the year in which this decree was promulgated, the entire citizen body was called upon to take the oath it stipulated, and this they did at a ceremony held shortly before the City Dionysia.[14]

It is conceivable that the oath was administered to the Athenians at separate meetings of each of the city's ten tribes, as one scholar suggests. But, as another student of the subject points out, the ceremony would have been more impressive had it taken place in the theater of Dionysus at the opening of the dramatic festival. For on that occasion—in the past, if not also in 409—the Athenians had displayed the *phóros* collected from their subject allies and there had been a pouring of libations by Athens' *stratēgoí*, a parade in hoplite armor of the young men reared by the *pólis* after their fathers had died in war, and a proclamation of rewards for those responsible for slaying would-be tyrants. Even more to the point, it was at this very time in the year 409 that the Athenians appear to have instituted a new practice by singling out as a benefactor of the *pólis*, comparable to the tyrannicides Harmodius and Aristogeiton, the man recognized as responsible for the assassination of Phrynichus son of Stratonides and by awarding him citizenship and a gold crown.

We cannot be certain where the oath was administered. It would have been perfectly appropriate, as a third scholar observes, that this be done, shortly before the festival, in the Agora near the Bouleuterion. After all, it was in the Agora outside the chamber where the Council of Four Hundred was in session that Stratonides' son had been assassinated, and it was there that the Athenians posted the stele on which Demophantus' decree was inscribed.[15]

Those who took the lead in reestablishing the democracy might, with an eye to reconciliation, have done everything in their power to moderate the partisan fury apt to flare up on such an occasion. They might, for example, have enacted an amnesty on the Samian model. But, in the aftermath of the fall of the Five Thousand, they chose, instead, to stoke the flames; and so, in the courts—thanks in part to the impact of Demophantus' decree on public opinion and expectations—lawfare once again came into play, and vengeance was visited from time to time on erstwhile members of the Four Hundred.[16]

It is not, then, an accident that Alcibiades decided to remain in the eastern Aegean at this time. To the degree that it restored the self-confidence of his compatriots, the great victory at Cyzicus that he had engineered left him more, not less, vulnerable to a renewal of the wrath and resentment unleashed upon him by his fellow citizens at the time of the Herms and Mysteries Scandals in 415. Nor is it at all odd that, at Athens under the restored democracy, partisanship and political rivalry continued to get in the way of the rational conduct of policy as it pertained to the ongoing war. This was evident almost from the start, as we shall soon see.

THRASYLLUS IN IONIA

There may well have been some ugliness associated with the transition from the Five Thousand to the restored democracy; the debate concerning Endius' peace proposal is apt to have occasioned angry exchanges; and Agis may have become aware of the turmoil then besetting Athens. For, at about this time, that Eurypontid king conducted his army on an exploratory mission, almost to the walls of

Athens, comparable to the one he had undertaken in the midst of the commotion that took place in 411. There, outside the walls near the Lyceum, he was met by Thrasyllus, who was tasked with leading out the Athenian defense force and with fending the Spartan off—and, in this endeavor, the Athenian commander distinguished himself.[17]

In all likelihood, because of his success on this occasion, it was Thrasyllus who was dispatched with the impressive force that the Athenians had voted to send to Alcibiades. With him, he had not only a fleet of fifty triremes manned by ten thousand mariners but also one thousand hoplites and one hundred cavalrymen—and five thousand of his eight thousand five hundred oarsmen were equipped and trained to function as peltasts when ashore.[18]

Some scholars suppose that Thrasyllus set out early in the campaigning season of 410—quite soon after the arrival of the Spartan ambassadors in the archon year 411/10, the rejection of their peace proposal, and the skirmish near the Lyceum. For my part, I find it hard to believe that the Athenians could have organized and dispatched so substantial an expeditionary force so soon after their losses at the battle of Eretria and the departure of Theramenes with a fleet of thirty triremes manned by six thousand mariners. I find it even harder to believe that Thrasyllus could have reached the Anatolian coast in time to take advantage of the harvest that took place there early in the summer and that the Syracusans stationed at Ephesus could have had at their disposal twenty triremes within three or four months after the destruction of the Peloponnesian fleet at Cyzicus and the burning of the Syracusan galleys. There would come a time when there would be a virtual assembly line at Antandrus for the production of triremes, but that venture was at this stage in its infancy.

It makes more sense to suppose that the indicator that a new campaigning season had begun that is missing from Xenophon's text should be inserted either just before his account of the battle of Cyzicus or shortly thereafter, that the Spartan ambassadors' visit to Athens took place early in the summer of 410 not long before the

Map 17. From Rhodes to the Bosporus, 409/8

summer solstice and the end of the 411/10 Athenian archon year, and that the skirmish near the Lyceum followed later that summer. Thrasyllus' departure from Athens, which is marked off in Xenophon's text by a notice indicating the beginning of a new campaigning season, would then belong to the late spring or early summer of 409.[19]

In the Hellespont, the Sea of Marmara, and the Bosporus, help of the very sort conveyed by Thrasyllus had long been needed. The cities in this region that were scattered along the European shore were, with the notable exception of Byzantium and Selymbria, in Athenian hands. Those along the Asian shore, most of them initially unfortified in accordance with prior Athenian policy, tended at this stage to take direction from Pharnabazus and the Spartans—who could deploy against them, if need be, infantrymen and cavalrymen in ample numbers.

There is reason to suspect that, despite a serious shortfall in hoplites and horsemen, Theramenes came tolerably close to winning over Chalcedon at some point in the first two years following the Athenian victory at Cyzicus. We do not know the precise timing or any of the details. We know that Chrysopolis was situated on the territory of Chalcedon a few miles from the town, that recovering that *pólis* was part of Theramenes' remit, and that he devoted resources to ravaging the Chalcedonian territory still in her control. We also know that, while at Antandrus initiating and directing the effort to produce triremes for the Spartans and their allies, Pharnabazus suddenly found it necessary to rush to Chalcedon to provide assistance; and that, on the twenty-second day of a mid-winter month while Darius II occupied the throne, this satrap had all of the male children of the Chalcedonians castrated. What makes this last incident especially interesting is the fact that, as far as we know, this horrific punishment was reserved for peoples, subject to the Great King, who had rebelled. Had Theramenes been in a timely fashion supplied with land forces on a more substantial scale, the boys of Chalcedon might have escaped this grisly fate.[20]

What is surprising, then, and what needs explanation is that, when Thrasyllus departed from Athens early in the summer of 409 with a splendid force under his command, he headed to Ionia and not to the Hellespont and the Sea of Marmara—which was, as we have seen, a theater of far greater strategic importance. To add to the mystery, after briefly visiting Samos, this commander dallied in the region for an entire campaigning season.

Thrasyllus attacked Pygela to the south of Ephesus to no purpose. He visited the harbor town of Notium and restored Athenian control at Colophon in the interior. He marched into Lydia in late May or early June, when the grain was fully ripe and harvesting was about to begin. He systematically laid waste the countryside, and there he captured a host of slaves and collected other booty of considerable value. Then, after foolishly in this fashion forcing Tissaphernes son of Hydarnes to call out the militia made up of the fief-holders in the region and of their vassals, and after giving the satrap seventeen days in which to gather his forces, he turned his attention to Ephesus. In response, as was predictable, the satrap rallied the rural population, already mobilized, to join the Ephesians, the small Spartan contingent present, and the Syracusans and Selinuntines then lodged in the town "in defense," as he reportedly put it, "of Artemis." In his attempt to capture the place, Thrasyllus divided his forces and took great risks, and he may have come close to overrunning Ephesus. Had he succeeded, however, it would not have much mattered. The forces that Tissaphernes, the Peloponnesians, and the Syracusans and Selinuntines could bring to bear on its recovery were more than sufficient for the job. In the end, however, Thrasyllus failed, and his defeat was ignominious. For four hundred of the infantrymen in his employ lost their lives that day.

Thereafter, instead of proceeding directly to the Hellespont, Thrasyllus tarried for a time at Methymna on Lesbos, and there he did accomplish something of worth. By this time, the Syracusans posted at Ephesus had in their possession twenty brand-new triremes and five more that had recently arrived from home. Thrasyllus managed to intercept these triremes as they were on their way to the Hellespont, where they might have made mischief. Four of them he captured; the rest he forced to return to Ephesus.[21]

It is in regard to the capture of these galleys that we learn a telltale fact. The Syracusan prisoners Thrasyllus dispatched to Athens. There, they were confined to a quarry in retaliation for what had been done to the Athenians at Syracusa but they, nonetheless, man aged to escape. On the one Athenian found in their company, Thrasyllus inflicted a penalty almost unprecedented at Athens by having his soldiers stone the man to death. As it happens, the man's name was Alcibiades. He hailed from the deme of Phegous, and he was a cousin of the son of Cleinias.

That a traitor should be executed is in no way surprising. But, in Athens and everywhere else in Hellas, family mattered—often, as Sophocles' *Antigone* reveals, more than the *pólis*—and this Alcibiades had, during the Herms and Mysteries imbroglio, risked his life in a plot aimed at directing attention away from his more famous cousin's alleged misconduct. The execution of Alcibiades of Phegous was, therefore, a public affront; and it was arguably something more provocative—a barely concealed accusation. For there is no crime that this Alcibiades had committed against Athens to compare with what the like-named son of Cleinias had done; and Thrasyllus, who is—I think, pointedly—not said to have lent his support to Thrasybulus' appeal for Alcibiades' recall, was deliberately highlighting the fact. If Thrasyllus spent a summer in Ionia before making his way to the Hellespont, it was in all likelihood because he—with support from figures known to have been hostile to Alcibiades, such as Cleophon— was intent on demonstrating that the son of Cleinias was not the only Athenian *stratēgós* who could work wonders in the field.[22]

It can hardly, then, be surprising that, when winter came and Thrasyllus conducted his armada to the Hellespont, the infantrymen under Alcibiades' command greeted the newcomers with a measure of disdain. Xenophon tells us that this had to do with contempt arising from the severe defeat they had suffered at Ephesus, and this was surely part of the story. But it is hard to believe that it had nothing to do with their anger at the failure of Thrasyllus to appear in the Hellespont in a timely fashion and with the antipathy that existed between the two military commanders in charge—and this is surely what the son of Gryllus intended that we ponder when he singled out for attention the punishment meted out on Thrasyllus' orders to Alcibiades of Phegous.

SECURING THE ROUTE TO THE EUXINE

That the son of Cleinias managed to weld these two disparate bodies of men into a single force says something about his willingness to ignore an affront and about his capacity for leadership. This he did, in part, by making them work side by side throughout the winter, fortifying Lampsacus on the Anatolian shore. But there came a moment when they mounted a campaign against the stronghold of the Spartans and their allies at Abydos, and there they jointly defeated the forces of Pharnabazus and set out in pursuit. It was this shared experience that turned antagonism into comradeship.[23]

When the winter of 409/8 came to an end and the campaigning season began, Alcibiades and Thrasyllus conducted this force to Proconnesus and, from there, to the southwestern entrance to the Bosporus where they joined forces with Theramenes. Now that the *stratēgoí* in this strategically vital region finally had in their possession cavalrymen, hoplites, and peltasts in numbers sufficient to offset the advantage hitherto possessed by Pharnabazus and his Peloponnesian allies, the son of Cleinias and his colleagues intended to finish the crucial job of recovering and securing Athens' lifeline to the Black Sea by seizing Chalcedon in Asia Minor and, then, Byzantium, opposite it in Europe.

In anticipation of the struggle to come, the Chalcedonians entrusted the Thracians of nearby Bithynia with the property in their possession liable to be pillaged. When he got wind of this, Alcibiades threatened these Thracians with war, and they turned this property over to him. Then, on orders from their commander, the Athenians turned to the town itself, which was situated on the peninsula where the Istanbul suburb Kadıköy is now to be found. It they blocked off with a wooden stockade that ran across the neck of the peninsula from one spot on the Sea of Marmara to another. At some point after the battle of Cyzicus, Mindarus' former *epistoleús* Hippocrates had been made the harmost of Chalcedon—perhaps as a species of damage control after the atrocity that Pharnabazus is said to have committed there. In this capacity, he led out the infantrymen under his command, and a proper hoplite battle took place in the relatively narrow space between the town proper and the stockade, involving his troops and an infantry force under the command of Thrasyllus. It was a close-run thing; and, Xenophon reports, the struggle between the two phalanxes lasted for a considerable span of time.

When Pharnabazus sought to come to Hippocrates' assistance with his cavalry and infantrymen and mounted an attempt to slip around the stockade in the northeast where it was interrupted by a river, he found his way blocked. Then, when Alcibiades, with the Athenian cavalry and a small cohort of hoplites, intervened in support of Thrasyllus, Hippocrates was killed; and his soldiers fled back to the town.[24]

In the aftermath, Alcibiades set out for the Hellespont and the Thracian Chersonnesus to raise funds—while Theramenes and his other colleagues at Chalcedon remained behind to negotiate an arrangement with Pharnabazus. The satrap agreed to hand over to the Athenians twenty talents (well over half a ton) of silver, and he pledged that the Chalcedonians would in the future pay the *phóros* they had been accustomed to pay in the past and would hand over the arrears—one must suppose, right away. More to the point, however, Pharnabazus promised that he would conduct an Athenian embassy to the Great King, and the Athenians, for their part, vowed that they would not make war on the Chalcedonians or ravage the territory in Pharnabazus' satrapy until the return of their ambassadors, whose safety Pharnabazus formally guaranteed.[25]

The last element in this arrangement is telling. It suggests that— while the Athenians were wary of making a separate peace with the Lacedaemonians—they were still intent on driving a wedge between the Persians and their Spartan allies. Alcibiades, his colleagues in the Hellespont, and, one must suspect, his compatriots more generally appear to have regarded Persia as the lesser of the two threats they faced. As a consequence, they were still eager to work out an accommodation with the Mede. This may well be what Tissaphernes had hoped for when he provided Alcibiades with a refuge and kept the Spartans and their allies on short rations. If so, however, he had failed to persuade his master. Now it was Pharnabazus' turn to try. Or so it seemed.

The latter satrap knew which Athenian *stratēgós* was really in charge—and so he demanded that Alcibiades himself be party to the oath. The son of Cleinias was at the time at Selymbria on the north coast of the Sea of Marmara—which, at considerable risk to his own life, he had just seized with the help of the Athenian settlers who populated the Thracian Chersonnesos as well as a cohort of more than three hundred Thracian cavalrymen and a handful of supporters from within the town. By the time that he had learned of Pharnabazus' demand, Alcibiades had moved on with this force to the outskirts of Byzantium. From there, he went by sea to Chrysopolis—whence he sent word that he would swear if Pharnabazus himself did the like, which is what was done. At Chalcedon, in the presence of Alcibiades' cousin Euryptolemos son of Peisanax and an Athenian named Diotimos (who may have been the sometime *stratēgós* Strombichides' son), Pharnabazus took the oath while Alcibiades followed suit at Chrysopolis in the presence of Pharnabazus' representatives Mitrobates and Arnapes. This the two then supplemented with personal oaths binding them to one another.[26]

At Cyzicus, in due course, there was to be a rendezvous of the ambassadors, and there is in Xenophon's text a tantalizing list of those said to have gone. It mentions the Athenians Dorotheos, Philokydes, and Theagenes as well as Alcibiades' cousin Euryptolemos and his fellow prisoner at Sardis Mantitheus, and it lists as their companions on the journey to Susa the members of a delegation dispatched from Athens' ally Argos, a city that had long maintained cordial relations with the Persian court. In a separate sentence, Xenophon also mentions ambassadors [*présbeis*] drawn from among the Lacedaemonians, specifies that Pasippidas was among them, and lists as their companions the exiled Syracusan Hermocrates son of

Hermon and his brother Proxenos. The last two on this list presumably hoped, via the good offices of Pharnabazus, to present themselves to the Great King as his benefactors and to solicit help with regard to their quest to return home and set things right. The same presumption may be justified regarding the *présbeis* drawn from among the Lacedaemonians—for Xenophon has already informed us that Pasippidas, who appears to have been the immediate successor of Mindarus as navarch, was exiled not long before by his compatriots.

That there was such a rendezvous we need not doubt. That all of the individuals on this list actually showed up and set out for Susa is another matter. We have reason to believe that Hermocrates and his brother had left Anatolia for Sicily well in advance of the group's departure; and, as we will in due course have occasion to note, Mantitheus and Euryptolemos turn up elsewhere in the late spring and early summer of 407—at a time well before they could have effected their return from this mission. I suspect that the passage in question may be an interpolation—a *scholium*, an annotation penned in the margins of the manuscript by a Hellenistic or Byzantine scholar, that a later copyist mistakenly thought belonged in the text. It was not Xenophon's practice to provide such lists, and there are a number of passages in the first two books of Xenophon's *Hellenica* that are thought to be interpolations. Of course, many *scholia* supply accurate and extremely helpful information. But others are a source of confusion. This passage may be one of the latter.[27]

While Alcibiades was at Chrysopolis swearing the oath, Theramenes was at Byzantium beginning the investment of the town. When the son of Cleinias returned, the stockade was completed, and attempts were made to break down and storm the city's walls—but to no avail.

Clearchus, the *próxenos* of the Byzantines at Sparta, appears to have returned to Lacedaemon after the debacle at Cyzicus. In the September subsequent to that event, from the high ground at Deceleia, Agis had, to his great dismay, once again observed grain ships from the Euxine making their way in large numbers into the Peiraeus. To this, he had responded in characteristic fashion—by securing the dispatch of Ramphias' redoubtable son back to Byzantium on the Bosporus, where he was to be the Spartan harmost, and by having fifteen troopships, manned by the Megarians and Lacedaemon's other allies, sent with him. There, at the time of Chalcedon's defeat, Clearchus was firmly ensconced, and he had with him a sizable garrison. There were Lacedaemonian *períoikoi* and a handful of *neodamôdeis* as well as a unit of mercenaries from the Peloponnesus, a contingent of Boeotians commanded by a figure named Koiratadas, and a detachment of Megarians commanded by the Helixus who had earlier prompted Byzantium's revolt.[28]

It was in the hands of these last two figures that Clearchus left the city in order to slip across the Bosporus to Pharnabazus in search of ships and of pay for his men. His immediate aim was to secure triremes from Antandrus. He intended, then, to summon Agesandridas back from the Thraceward region where he was active with a flotilla and to gather the vessels dispatched to guard Abydos and various other cities in the Hellespont by Pasippidas when he was sent out to take up the navarchy. By attacking with this fleet the cities in the region under the Athenians' control, he hoped to force them to withdraw from Byzantium.

The son of Ramphias was a resourceful commander in no way behindhand, and this was an intelligent plan. But he erred in one particular. He thought that he had the time to do all of this, and he underestimated both the depth of the resentment stirred up in Byzantium by the harshness of his rule and the desperation felt by the citizens left to starve when he chose to reserve the food in storage for the troops in the garrison. This induced a number of the Byzantines to conspire against the new order that had been imposed on their *pólis*. If they were tempted by the prospect, it was no doubt in part because Alcibiades and his colleagues had ostentatiously refrained from sacking the towns, such as Perinthus and Selymbria, that hitherto had chosen to surrender in the face of an Athenian attack. In dealing with their allies in this region—where Pharnaba-zus and Spartans like Leon on Chios and Clearchus at Byzantium thought it best to rely on fear—the Athenian commanders appar-ently believed that gentleness and moderation would be more effective.

That Clearchus' conduct should have produced such a result was, as Xenophon intimates, an indication of the Spartiate's limitations as a leader. It was, as he also allows us to see, a sign of the magnanimity of which the Lacedaemonians were sometimes capable that later, when one of the Byzantine conspirators was tried for treason at Sparta, the court exonerated the man when he asserted, in response to the charge, that he was not a Lacedaemonian and that he had, in fact, acted as a true patriot in defense of the lives of his compatriots.

On the pertinent occasion, at night, the Athenians pretended to effect a withdrawal. Then, they sent their fleet into the Golden Horn to make a great hullabaloo in the vicinity of the commercial harbor while the conspirators broke open the Thracian gate on the city's southwestern side and let Alcibiades and his soldiers slip in. Helixus and Koiratadas were caught flat-footed and attempted to put up a fight but soon found themselves forced to surrender. They and three to five hundred others were soon thereafter dispatched to Athens—where, at the moment of embarkation, the Boeotian com-mander managed to escape into the crowd, whence he later made his way to Deceleia.[29]

According to Diodorus, not long after the fall of Byzantium, the Athenian commanders turned their attention to the Hellespont. There, step by step with the ample resources now available to them, they seized every city that the enemy controlled—apart from the Spartans' stronghold at Abydos on the Asian shore.

We do not know how much time was occupied by these exploits—at Chalcedon; at Selymbria and Byzantium; in the Helles-pont; and perhaps elsewhere nearby. It seems, however, highly likely that this endeavor required the entirety of a campaigning season and the winter months that followed, if not the early spring as well. We have reason to suspect that it was not until the end of May in 407 or early June—when the Bosporus, the Sea of Marmara, and the Hellespont were (apart from the Spartan stronghold at Abydos) more or less fully in their hands and Athens' lifeline was once again secured—that Thrasyllus and his colleagues prepared for their departure by hiving off a force adequate for the maintenance of Athenian control and by placing it under the command of Diodorus and Mantitheus.

Once this force was in place, the principal Athenian commanders—apart from Alcibiades, who appears to have headed off earlier on another errand—collected not only the prisoners seized and the spoils taken, but also the ships captured and the figureheads of the vessels disabled or destroyed (which, together, added up to two hundred or more). When all was ready, they conducted the Athenian galleys, infantrymen, and cavalrymen no longer needed in the field home where this armada was enthusiastically received.[30]

ALCIBIADES' TRIUMPHANT RETURN TO ATHENS

It was in the spring of 407 that the son of Cleinias began to think that it might be safe for him to return to the city of his birth. A decree for his recall had been passed by the Five Thousand at the urging of Theramenes—probably in the fall of 411. Now—perhaps late in 408 or early in 407—another such decree was passed. This time, it took place under the democracy at the instance of Alcibiades' old friend and boon companion Critias son of Callaeschrus.[31]

For some months, in the winter of 408/7 and the very early spring of the latter year, the son of Cleinias had tarried in the vicinity of Samos with a unit of twenty triremes. His concern—in those days, every Athenian commander's persistent concern—was money. He did what he could to extract it from the cities in Caria situated along the gulf of Keramos; and there—thanks presumably to the prestige he and his compatriots had won at Cyzicus, Chalcedon, and Byzantium and, no doubt, to his formidable skill as a diplomat and military tactician—he managed to collect a colossal sum in silver:

no less than one hundred talents, a bit under three tons of that precious metal.[32]

In the spring, a bit later than usual but well before Thrasyllus and the fleet reached Athens and almost certainly before they even headed that way, the assembly voted—so we are told by Xenophon—to make Conon son of Timotheos, who was among those then present in the town, a *stratēgós*; and then it did the same, we are told, for Alcibiades and Thrasybulus, who were in absentia. Thrasyllus appears to have been excluded, perhaps because of the mishap at Ephesus.

The fact that Theramenes' name also passes unmentioned in this account is a bit more surprising and may be significant. He had journeyed to Macedon and Thrace, then on to the Hellespont in 410 as a *stratēgós* of the Five Thousand; and, as a commander, he had done yeoman work at Cyzicus, Chrysopolis, Chalcedon, and Byzantium. But his tenure as a military commander in good standing at Athens may technically have come to an end in the summer of 409. In 411/10, as far as we can tell, Alcibiades, Thrasybulus, and Thrasyllus derived their authority solely from the soldiers and mariners in the encampment on Samos. Thrasyllus had presumably been formally designated as a *stratēgós* by the assembly at Athens for 410/9 prior to his armada's departure from the Peiraeus. But, in this year and the two years following, the status of Alcibiades and Thrasybulus was almost certainly irregular—for, otherwise, their election at Athens in the spring of 407 would not have been deemed so worthy of note and would not have weighed so heavily with Alcibiades. In the latter two years, Theramenes is apt to have joined these two in limbo— with the city and the men of the camp operating independently but, nonetheless, prudently accommodating one another. Now—except, perhaps, with regard to the status of Theramenes—the community that had its origins on Samos and the community situated in the town of Athens and in the Peiraeus nearby were once again fully one.[33]

After returning to Samos from the gulf of Keramos, Alcibiades journeyed with his flotilla of twenty triremes to Paros, then on to the bay of Laconia—where, from a distance, he could examine the thirty triremes being built in the dockyards at Gytheion and reflect on the renewed struggle likely to come. If, however, he was taking his time and followed a meandering trajectory in his trip home, it was not solely or even primarily for the purpose of seeing the places visited. It was chiefly, Xenophon informs us, because he wanted to know whether it really would be safe for him to return to the *pólis* that had turned on him and that he had turned on in return.

In the end, mindful of his election as *stratēgós* in the spring of 407 and buoyed by messages from his friends, the son of Cleinias had his helmsman steer his trireme into the Peiraeus, where he arrived, not long after Thrasyllus and the other commanders, on twenty-fifth day of the lunar month Thargelion, which appears to have fallen on this occasion in early June of our solar year. As it happens, it was on this day that the city celebrated the Plynteria.[34]

The timing of Alcibiades' arrival is a matter of some moment, and the choice made in this regard suggests a certain inattention or carelessness on his part or on the part of those at Athens who had encouraged him to stage his homecoming when he did. The twenty-fifth day of Thargelion was regarded as the most inauspicious day of the year, and on that day the Athenians ordinarily refrained from transacting public business. The reason is that, at the time of the Plynteria, the cult statue of Athena Polias was removed from its pedestal, enshrouded, and borne down to the bay of Phaleron to be washed. In the circumstances, given Alcibiades' putative past, it was, Plutarch observes, as if the veiling of the statue was the goddess' response to an affront on his part inviting retaliation—and there were at Athens men keenly aware of the impiety charges lodged in 415 against Cleinias' wayward son who took notice.[35]

Xenophon, who seems to have witnessed Alcibiades' return, emphasizes that he arrived with a modest flotilla, not, as Diodorus and Plutarch suppose, at the head of the returning armada. To Cleinias' audacious son, moreover, he attributes a certain air of diffidence. The longtime exile anchored near the shore, we are told, but he did not disembark. Instead, he spent some time eyeing the great crowd that had gathered in the harbor, looking for familiar faces. It was only when he spied his cousin Euryptolemos that Alcibiades' spirits rose. When he caught sight of others from among his kinsmen and, with them, his friends, he gathered his courage, stepped ashore, and made his way, in their company and under their armed protection, up from the harbor town to Athens proper.

There, presumably a day or two later when the auspices were more favorable, the son of Cleinias addressed the Council of Five Hundred and the assembly, denying that he had ever committed any impiety, asserting that he had been treated unjustly, and blaming everything on his ill fortune. If no one spoke up against him, Xenophon reports, it was because those assembled would not have put up with such impertinence. Instead, he was given honors that had, as far as we can tell, never been conferred on any Athenian. Like Thrasybulus of Kalydon, the metic rewarded for the assassination of Phrynichus, Alcibiades was awarded a crown of gold. He was also named "the supreme commander—*hapántōn hēgemòn autokrátōr*—in the expectation that he would be able to recover the power possessed by the city hitherto." Moreover, according to reports found in Cornelius Nepos, Diodorus, and Plutarch, the assembly also voted to have the stelae recording his condemnation hurled into the sea, to have his property returned to him, and to have the Eumolpidae and the Ceryces associated with the Eleusinian Mysteries revoke the curses they had directed at him. The Athenians even opted to allow him to choose his own colleagues for the campaign to come.

Such was the adulation that Alcibiades received; and, consummate actor that he was, he capitalized upon it in the most dramatic way possible. Ever since Agis' arrival at Deceleia, the Athenians had continued, in accord with tradition, to make their way to Eleusis to celebrate the Eleusinian Mysteries on the nineteenth day of the lunar month of Boedromion, which generally fell in late September or early October. But they had not done so in the customary fashion by processing for fourteen miles along the Sacred Way. They had journeyed, instead, by ship. As autumn approached or began in 407, however, they once again made the journey on foot as they had done in the days of yore; and this they were able to do thanks to the protection afforded them by the infantry force carefully deployed by Cleinias' now ostentatiously pious son.[36]

There would be a return to normalcy. Such was the promise Alcibiades conveyed by what he made possible on that day, and there was reason to hope that this promise would be fulfilled. By this time, after all, the two satraps in western Anatolia both appeared to have lost their enthusiasm for the struggle. Moreover, an embassy was making its way from Cyzicus to Susa along the royal road in the company of the satrap Pharnabazus. If a deal was in the offing, as seemed to be the case; if the Great King could be persuaded to abandon the war, all would be well. As their conduct after the battle of Cyzicus indicated, the Lacedaemonians were weary of war. Absent the subsidies supplied by the minions of the Persian monarch, they and their allies could hardly sustain the struggle at sea, and one could be tolerably confident that, in such circumstances, they would not even try.

Although Alcibiades knew better than to think that this goal—a consummation devoutly to be wished—had actually been achieved, he is not reported to have said one word to dampen Athenian hopes. He seems, in fact, to have been exceedingly careful not to disturb the buoyant mood. For, as we have seen, Cleinias' son lived off other men's hopes, and he had a predilection for promising more than he could deliver.

In the fall of 407, not long after Athens' celebration of the Eleusinian Mysteries, Alcibiades ventured back into the Aegean. With him went his chosen colleagues—both expert in hoplite warfare. One was the Aristocrates son of Scellias who had worked with Theramenes in effecting the transition from the Four Hundred to the Five Thousand. The other was Adeimantus son of Leucolophides, a fellow demesman of the son of Cleinias who had been caught up and condemned, alongside him, in the Herms and Mysteries Scandals. As these three conducted from Athens the force of fifteen hundred hoplites, one hundred fifty cavalrymen, and one hundred triremes they had been assigned, the city's first *hapántōn hēgemòn autokrátōr* must have been pondering what was in store for him and for his *pólis* now that he was entirely in charge. If all went well, he would not only maintain Athens' supremacy at sea. He would recover Andros, Chios, and Rhodes; and he would also succeed where Thrasyllus in 409 had so dismally failed. Along the western coast of Anatolia, his colleagues, would, city by city, force Athens' erstwhile allies back into line. What this supremely confident man did not yet know—but would soon find out—was that the Great King of Persia was now fully committed to the Spartan cause.[37]

PART IV

———————————————

THE MISSION OF CYRUS

In the struggle between the snipe and the clam,
it's the fisherman who gains the advantage.

ANCIENT CHINESE PROVERB

A T THE END of the summer or in the fall of 408, at a time
prior to Alcibiades' capture of Byzantium, Pharnabazus son
of Pharnaces set out for Susa in Elam from the satrapal
palace he maintained at Dascyleium near the Sea of Marmara in Hellespontine Phrygia. Earlier in the year, he had pledged that he would
conduct an Athenian embassy to the court of his master Darius II,
and on this journey he now embarked. In accord with his promise,
when he left Dascyleium, he paused briefly at Cyzicus nearby to collect the envoys who had rendezvoused there at his invitation.[1]

Pharnabazus evidenced no sense of urgency. He was not in a
hurry. He had put off this embassy's departure for some months;
and, as he surely knew, its members were going to have to cool their
heels for a great many more months at Gordium in central Anatolia,
roughly two hundred fifty miles east-southeast of Cyzicus.

At this stage, the town in question and its environs were a back-
water, as they are to an even greater degree right now. Once, how-

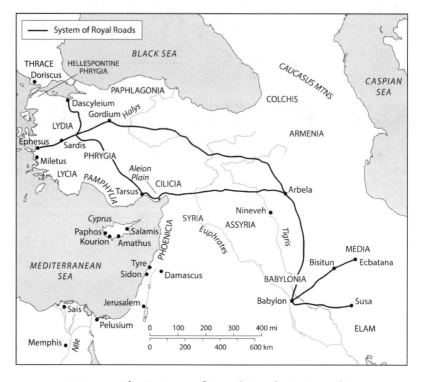

**Map 18. The System of Royal Roads in Anatolia
and Mesopotamia**

ever, Gordium had been the capital of a great kingdom. It was from here, on the border between Hellespontine and Greater Phrygia, that in the eighth century a ruler named Midas had held sway over a region of Anatolia so prosperous that legend would later assign to this king the golden touch. Shortly after the middle of the sixth century, Gordium and the surrounding territory had fallen to Cyrus son of Cambyses, the first of Persia's Great Kings; and in the fifth century, if not well before, Midas' capital had come to be governed as part of a satrapy—encompassing Hellespontine Phrygia, the Troad, Aeolis, Bithynia, Paphlagonia, and Greater Phrygia—that was assigned to the royal viceroys who had their seat at Dascyleium. So, at least, we can surmise.[2]

If Gordium was the initial destination of the party conducted by

Pharnabazus, it was because one branch of the royal road from Sardis to Susa via central Anatolia, Assyria, and Babylonia ran through that town and on to a fortified checkpoint on the Halys river a few miles beyond—before proceeding further east and then curling south toward Arbela. Moreover, as it happened, this ancient capital was a suitable place for the satrap and his entourage to winter while snow and, later, mud threatened to render overland travel through the mountains further east and south onerous, if not impossible, for a group encumbered, as they surely were, with ambassadorial baggage.[3]

A RUDE AWAKENING

In 407, well into spring when the snow had for the most part melted, the ground had dried somewhat, and the mountain passes in south-central Anatolia were more or less fully open, this party set out once again on their trek. After its members had proceeded some distance to the east and then to the southeast—quite possibly as far as Arbela—the Athenians in their number learned to their own dismay that their compatriots back home were in for a nasty and unwelcome surprise. The latter had fought long and hard. In the beginning, as we have seen, Tissaphernes son of Hydarnes had given firm and generous support to the Spartans and their allies. But after a time, under the influence of Alcibiades son of Cleinias and surely also for reasons all his own, he had inched away from that commitment; and the Athenians had begun to entertain the hope that, through his good offices, they could reach an accommodation with the Mede. When, in response to being shortchanged by Tissaphernes, the Peloponnesians shifted their focus from Ionia to the Hellespont, the Sea of Marmara, and the Bosporus, Pharnabazus had proved an enthusiastic supporter. But, after Athens' victory at Chalcedon, he, too, seemed to have changed his stance. By the end of the campaigning season in 408, it was possible to suppose that both of these satraps were ready to press their master to make peace, and the Athenians may even have imagined that an alliance of sorts was in the offing.[4]

But, as these envoys learned to their dismay on that late spring or early summer day, they and their compatriots had been snookered.

On this occasion, Pharnabazus and his entourage encountered another party of travelers traversing the royal road on which they were traveling. This company was making its way back from Susa in the direction of Sardis. It was led by a Spartiate named Boeotius. From him and from its other members, the Athenian envoys learned that—at some point subsequent to their compatriots' rejection of the peace offer conveyed to Athens by Endius son of Alcibiades and his colleagues in 410, quite possibly in the immediate aftermath of their own victory at Chalcedon and of Pharnabazus' pledge to convey an Athenian embassy to Susa—the Lacedaemonians had dispatched an embassy of their own to that ancient Elamite capital.

This can hardly have been a surprise to Pharnabazus. Boeotius and his colleagues could not have made the journey up the royal road to Susa without authorization from one of the Great King's satraps, and for this the Spartans are sure to have turned to Pharnaces' son, rather than to Tissaphernes, whom they had come to distrust. There is, in fact, every reason to suspect Pharnabazus of double-dealing. When he negotiated an armistice with Theramenes and agreed to conduct an Athenian embassy to Susa, when he demanded that Alcibiades swear to the terms of this agreement and formed a guest-friendship with the man, he no doubt informed his Spartan allies and sent word by mounted courier to Darius II. He is apt at the same time to have urged the Lacedaemonians to get the jump on the Athenians. Moreover, in delaying his own departure and that of the Athenian envoys, his aim may well have been to give the Spartans the time they needed to get matters settled in their favor before the envoys in his party arrived. To this, we can add two observations: that the news that an Athenian delegation would soon be en route to Susa will have done the Great King's bargaining position vis-à-vis the Spartan ambassadors no end of good, and that the armistice which Pharnabazus had negotiated with the Athenians would delay, if not prevent, the loss of Chalcedon and afford his territory in Hellespontine Phrygia a respite from the ravaging inflicted on it in the recent past by these same Athenians.

To make matters even more dire, the Athenians with Pharnaces' son were also told what the satrap, who was no doubt in close touch with his master, must from the outset have thought tolerably likely— that the Great King had awarded the Spartans and their allies everything they had asked—with three thousand drachmas a month pledged for every trireme that they manned. They also discovered something that is apt to have been a shock even to Pharnabazus: that Darius had decided to send his younger son Cyrus to carry out his wishes, naming him *káranos* or "lord of those who marshal in the plains of Castolus" to the east of Sardis.[5] As would soon become clear, Tissaphernes and Pharnabazus were to be relegated to an advisory role.

The returning Spartan ambassadors' report concerning Darius' commitment undoubtedly cheered the Lacedaemonians. The King's own son could hardly be less dependable than Tissaphernes, and the resources at his command were sure to be far greater than those on offer from Pharnabazus. There must, nonetheless, have been some grumbling when they discovered that the young prince about to set out for Anatolia was no more than sixteen years old, if that. His father Darius had sent a boy to do the work of a man.[6]

There was no dearth of Persian nobles of an age to manage the war and qualified by experience to do so. In view of the bitter accusations apt to have been leveled against Tissaphernes by Boeotius and his colleagues, Darius may well have been unwilling to use the man. But he could have placed Pharnabazus in charge or granted the overall military command to his own brother-in-law Hieramenes. They were both familiar with the theater of war and had worked with the Spartans before. Darius might even have raised up his elder son Arsaces who was, by this time, fully a man. The dispatch of an adolescent to govern a new satrapy made up of Lydia, Greater Phrygia, and Cappadocia and to serve as "*káranos* of those who muster in the plains of Castolus" was inappropriate as well as unprecedented.[7]

Darius' firm rejection of the policy that had so appealed to

Tissaphernes was, as we have seen, ill-advised. In counseling that satrap, Alcibiades had been self-serving, as he always was. But much of the advice he had dispensed was far from foolish. The Great King had nothing to gain and everything to lose from a Spartan victory. As the son of Cleinias had observed, it was prudent not "to entrust control of both land and sea to a single power." It was far, far better, "to leave each of the two cities with her own sphere of control [*archē*] in order to allow the Great King to summon one to his aid if the other proved troublesome." Moreover, as we have already had occasion to observe, subsequent history was to bear out the wisdom of Alcibiades' warning.[8]

It is, nonetheless, easy to imagine the arguments put forward by those of Darius' advisors who favored backing Sparta, and these arguments were not without purchase. Athens had been a thorn in Persia's side for decades. The threat posed by Lacedaemon was at this stage purely hypothetical. What most needs explaining is why Darius sent an adolescent to implement his policy.

PARYSATIS AND STATEIRA

This puzzling decision seems to have been the work of Cyrus' mother Parysatis. According to the court physician Ctesias, Darius' queen was so hostile to her eldest son Arsaces that she was quite eager to see the second Cyrus succeed to the throne of his namesake the founder of Persia's empire. This would not have been unprecedented. As Parysatis did not fail to point out, Cyrus resembled the elder Xerxes in being the first son born subsequent to his father's accession to the throne. As Darius' elder legitimate son, Arsaces was the heir apparent, but Cyrus' claim was not wholly without foundation.[9] In 407, a contest for the crown began. The final outcome would depend not only on the preference of Darius, but also on the machinations of his wily wife—though only to the extent that these enabled the younger of the two claimants to secure overwhelming military superiority when the crisis came.

As we have seen, Parysatis had long experience in matters of sibling rivalry. Moreover, she was not the first woman to exercise considerable influence at the Achaemenid court. The Great Kings generally had a number of Persian wives and a great host of foreign concubines, but each appears to have selected one from among his wives—the mother of the prospective crown prince—to be his Queen and consort. Set apart by noble birth, often by exceptional beauty and charm, and nearly always by ambition as well, this woman was well positioned to sway her husband and influence, if not dominate, her son.[10] Her power over the latter was increased by the role she had played in rearing him.

In theory, the crown prince received the traditional, military education of the Persian aristocracy; in practice, however, he seems to have been more a creature of the court than of the camp and the battlefield. While the King busied himself with matters of state, the Queen, the eunuchs of the harem, and the ambitious courtiers in attendance shaped his heir apparent to their own liking, flattering him and rendering him soft and pliable, perhaps even crippling him emotionally to make him dependent on them.[11]

This process could be quite effective. We need not believe Herodotus when he attributes "all power" to Atossa, the daughter of Cyrus the Great, wife of Darius the Great, and mother of Xerxes—but we can hardly doubt her importance. While she lived, she was apparently the preeminent figure at the Persian court—equaled only after her death by Xerxes' powerful consort Amestris.[12]

There was, one must suspect, ample occasion for rivalry between the Queen and the most prominent of her eldest son's wives. In all places and times and in every cultural milieu, the courts in absolute monarchies have tended to be snake pits—especially where polygyny is practiced and there is no hard and fast law determining succession. In such circumstances, the royal entourage is nearly always torn by ambition and by the rivalries that arise between the women within the harem, and the court is characterized by maneuver and manipulation on the part of these women and their offspring and beset with violence, poisoning, and even, on occasion, by an assassi-

nation of the monarch himself. The Persian regime was no exception. The stories that we are told regarding Atossa, Amestris, and
their successors are in no way out of the ordinary. The heirs of Cyrus
and of the first Darius were, in fact, more likely to die at the hands of
their close associates than to be killed on the battlefield or to pass
away peacefully.[13]

The trouble between Parysatis and Arsaces appears to have
sprung from a rivalry of precisely this type—one that originated, a
few years before the younger Cyrus' mission, at the time of a bizarre
conspiracy that threatened the royal family. This conspiracy—and
the circumstances which made it possible—can best be understood
in light of the challenges confronting Ochus in the early years of his
reign as Darius II and of the alliance he forged with the family of
Hydarnes in an effort to alleviate the difficulties he faced.

Initially, as we have seen, this alliance—sanctioned by custom,
dictated by prudence, and anchored by two dynastic marriages—
was contracted to help the younger Darius weather the revolt mounted
by Arsites and Artyphius and that later initiated by Pissouthnes. But
the harmony between the two families did not long survive the
death of Hydarnes and the succession as satrap of his son Teriteuchmes. Photius' epitome of Ctesias' report concerning the events that
then transpired is tantalizingly brief. Teriteuchmes was apparently a
headstrong young man with a strong distaste for the wife his father
had chosen for him. We will probably never know why. Was the
daughter of the younger Darius and Parysatis particularly ill-favored?
Was Teriteuchmes put off by the Babylonian ancestry of this Amestris? Was she arrogant to the point of being intolerable? Was her
husband simply deranged? Or did some combination of these circumstances elicit the antipathy he evidenced? We have questions
aplenty, but no answers. What is clear is that, after his father's death,
Teriteuchmes contracted a mad passion for his own half-sister
Roxana, a beautiful woman of great physical vigor, skillful with both
javelin and bow. Sometime not long before Cyrus' journey to Sardis,
Teriteuchmes—driven by eros—formed a plot to murder his wife.

Had this taken place, it would have been no ordinary homicide. Teriteuchmes cannot have expected Darius and Parysatis to tolerate the assassination of their eldest and quite possibly their only surviving daughter. What Photius' epitome of Ctesias presents as a murder conspiracy was, as he readily acknowledges, a prelude to rebellion—and this would have been no minor rebellion. For, as we have seen, Teriteuchmes' father Hydarnes, who is known to have governed a satrapy somewhere in the east, is apt to have inherited his province through multiple generations from his namesake—the elder Darius' confederate—and the satrapy in question was almost certainly Media in northern Iran. This was one of the most important provinces in the realm, and by this time it is apt to have become loyal to the satrapal family that had, if my surmise is correct, governed it for more than a century. If Teriteuchmes' conspiracy was not a threat to the younger Darius' rule, it was surely perceived as one.[14]

Of course, Teriteuchmes' royal father-in-law was by no means defenseless. By the time in which Hydarnes died, Ochus had fully secured his position. He was no longer a pretender. He was now Darius II, King of Kings, Great King of Persia—and everyone recognized as much. The authority that this man now possessed as Great King was immense; and it was at the same time charismatic, ceremonial, personal, feudal, and bureaucratic.

The Achaemenids ruled by the grace of their god Ahura Mazda, as we have seen; and affairs at the court were conducted via feasting on a monumental scale and other elaborate ceremonies aimed at inculcating a sense of hierarchy, deference, and gratitude. In practice, power derived from access to and influence with a monarch who was to most men most of the time not only unapproachable but, except on great ceremonial occasions, in effect invisible. This power was concentrated in the hands of his Chiliarch, Cup-Bearer, Spear-Bearer, Quiver-Bearer, and the like—and in the hands of those of his wives and favorite concubines; Kinsmen, in-laws, and Friends; Staff-Bearers and Table Companion; eunuchs and courtiers; Counsellors and Benefactors who ordinarily traveled with this peripatetic monarch and his royal household as that enormous body of soldiers, Magi, administrators, and clerks; of butchers, bakers, and cooks; and of retainers, servants, and camp followers made its seasonal peregrinations on horseback, in carriages, and on foot—oscillating in the cooler months by way of a royal progress between Persepolis in Persia, the great palace at Babylon in Mesopotamia, and the magnificent royal residence at Susa in Elam and then moving on, when the heat in those parts become unbearable, to his summer retreat in the mountains of Media at Ecbatana to the north.[15]

To make his will effective, the Achaemenid monarch employed an elaborate bureaucracy of satraps, hyparchs, and eparchs; of garrison commanders, royal secretaries, and judges; of tax collectors, treasurers, and scribes—all of them operating on the basis of the same protocols; all of them employing as an administrative tool Aramaic, Elamite, or both; and all paid salaries in daily rations or silver drawn from the tribute imposed on and the taxes collected in the empire's disparate provinces. This bureaucracy was held together by the complex and extended network of royal roads, which were punctuated at regular intervals by posting-places with inns where elite guides could secure bed and board for authorized travelers and where, at the end of a ride lasting a long day or night, a mounted courier could pass on his packet of dispatches to the horse and the rider next in the chain of transmission. In his province, the satrap would have been an independent potentate had it not been for the check imposed on his freedom by the royal secretary attached to his chancellery, by the garrison commanders, and by the itinerant inspectors and informers known as the Eyes and Ears of the King— all of whom reported directly to the royal court.[16]

The enormous bureaucracy was a necessary, but insufficient condition for the empire's survival. Particularly in Egypt, Babylonia, and Media, where the Persians ruled over peoples with grand imperial traditions of their own, Achaemenid rule was threatened again and again by national uprisings.[17]

These the kings sought to prevent by an intensification of the

time-tested Assyrian and Chaldaean practice of transferring populations and by settling colonies of foreign mercenaries among the
natives. There were, for example, Iranians in Syria; Hyrcanians and
Assyrians in Lydia; Aramaeans, Jews, and Phoenicians in Egypt; and
Arabs, Jews, Armenians, Egyptians, Urartians, Syrians, Lydians,
Phoenicians, and Indians scattered throughout Babylonia. If the
Babylonian evidence is indicative, these colonists were organized
into cantons according to profession, nationality, social class, military function, or mere territorial proximity. Each canton was under
the oversight of a foreman who represented the King and saw to it
that the colonists met their obligations. Graced with Bow Land,
Horse Land, or Chariot Land—which was passed, within a family,
from generation to generation but could never be sold—they provided archers, cavalry, and charioteers and paid a fixed annual rent
or tax to the royal treasury.[18]

The military colonists were by no means the only feudal vassals
to pay the King homage, wear the King's belt, and muster at gathering places such as the plains of Castolus near Sardis for the King's
annual review.[19] Much of the better land seems to have been under
the control of great magnates—Achaemenid princes, Persian gran-
dees, native dynasts, and royal favorites drawn from every nationality of the empire—who, from castles that dotted the countryside,
ruled rich tracts farmed by dependent peasants and received a steady
income from the neighboring towns. Some from this local aristocracy were exempt from taxation—but, in return for support against
unruly peasants and for protection against attack from the untamed
mountaineers and nomads who were never far distant from any corner of Persia's realm, they all contributed to the King's levy.[20]

Within this feudal nobility, the Honored Peers [homótimoi]
played a special role—serving in the elite corps of the King's foot-
guard and cavalry and drawing, in return for their services, on the
revenue of estates scattered throughout the provinces. These Honored Peers remained at court and were available to their sovereign
for virtually any task.[21]

Of course, as we have seen, the greatest privileges were reserved for the members of the handful of families from within the Honored Peers that had assisted Darius son of Hystaspes in his ascent to the throne. In the famous inscription he had had carved into the cliffs at Bisitun, this Darius had celebrated their contribution and exhorted his successors to "protect well the families of these men." The tradition that he also divided his kingdom into regions ruled over by his fellow conspirators is no doubt hyperbole. But it is certainly true that he and his successors selected most of their satraps and generals from among two bodies of men: the confederates and their off-spring, and those who were variously called in Akkadian the *mār bīt šarri*—"the Sons of the Royal House"—or simply the *mār bīti*— "Sons of the House." These offices often remained in the hands of particular individuals for decades and, in some cases, were passed from father to son for generations, as we have seen.[22]

The Sons of the Royal House and the descendants of the confederates served the King not only in person as officeholders and soldiers, but also through their retainers. They formed a class of absentee landlords with great holdings in a variety of provinces. The satrap of Egypt Arsames illustrates the situation perfectly. This protégé of Artaxerxes and supporter of the younger Darius owned large estates in Upper and Lower Egypt, in six different places on the route from Egypt to Susa, in southern Babylonia near Nippur, and no doubt elsewhere as well; and he took every opportunity to expand his holdings. Great magnates such as Arsames controlled large tracts of land and the peasants who cultivated them, and they appear also to have held authority over cantons of military colonists settled on their estates. The evidence does not justify certainty, but there are grounds for believing that the residents of these particular cantons were direct vassals not of the King, but of the estate owners. The great nobles were powerful figures in their own right.[23]

His acknowledgement throughout the empire as King brought Darius II enormous advantages. The support within the royal bodyguard which had helped him secure the crown would protect him against a coup. By selecting a trustworthy Chiliarch [*Hazarapatiš*] to command that bodyguard and control access to his person, by making himself almost unapproachable, and by including in his immediate entourage only faithful friends, eunuchs with no serious prospect of bettering their lot, and others equally dependent on his patronage, the Great King could minimize though not eliminate the possibility of assassination.[24]

The real threat was posed by the satraps and generals, particularly those Sons of the Royal House and descendants of the elder Darius' co-conspirators who had inherited or long ruled their provinces. By currying the favor of the local magnates and military colonists, these great aristocrats could become virtually independent of the court. This was particularly true of the court of Darius II. His status as a bastard and the Babylonian blood that flowed in his veins is apt to have aroused the contempt of a great many Persian nobles. Darius must have been acutely conscious of his vulnerability.

Even against the great generals and satraps, however, Darius could command impressive resources: an elaborate intelligence network; royal garrisons at Babylon, Sardis, and other strong points; and military colonists and local magnates from satrapies beyond the rebels' control, as well as the rich treasuries situated at Babylon, Susa, Ecbatana, and Persepolis. No one could mount a challenge to his authority without an army; and few, if any, of the satraps had the gold and silver to support a large enough force for a long enough time.[25]

Barring a coalition of satraps or some unrecognized advance in the art of war that rendered the King's army inferior to a much smaller force, the younger Darius could remain moderately confident. In the first few years following 423, it was essential that he place his partisans in positions of authority wherever possible and secure the loyalty of those of Artaxerxes' satraps and generals who were too well entrenched to be removed without danger.

In the event, where Teriteuchmes was concerned, Darius did not need to fall back on this apparatus. Warned by informers resident within his son-in-law's satrapy, he acted to forestall the conspiracy—chiefly, by offering one of Teriteuchmes' closest lieutenants his satrapy in return for the man's assassination. This counter-move is said to have worked, but there was apparently trouble, nonetheless. For Xenophon reports that there was a rebellion in Media that was not finally quelled until 409. Once this uprising was crushed, a general slaughter ensued in which Hydarnes' wife, two of his remaining sons, and two of his daughters followed the renegade satrap into the grave.[26]

Tissaphernes and Stateira were among the family members spared—the former presumably because of his services and perhaps because of the danger involved in trying to dislodge him from his stronghold in Asia Minor, the latter because Arsaces intervened on her behalf with his mother. According to Ctesias' report, Darius remarked at the time to Parysatis that she would rue the day that she had saved Teriteuchmes' sister. He was right: at no point did Stateira show any signs of gratitude. Moreover, she neither forgot what her family had suffered nor forgave those who had brought them down. The hatred that came to separate Arsaces' mother and her daughter-in-law no doubt spawned the contempt the mother eventually evidenced for her elder son.[27]

CYRUS' AIM

Parysatis was undoubtedly the moving force behind Cyrus' mission. His dispatch to Asia Minor two years after the uprising in Media was put down was a declaration of war. It constituted a repudiation of the policy of Stateira's kinsman Tissaphernes and his subordination to her husband's rival. Pharnabazus and Hieramenes were passed over along with Arsaces, almost certainly because they were the heir apparent's allies.[28] If Darius neglected Persia's true interests in abandoning Tissaphernes' policy and if he deserted common sense in sending an adolescent to carry out his decision, it was, at least in part, because of palace intrigue. Cyrus' arrival at Sardis marked the beginning of the struggle for power in Persia that was to end six years later with his death at the battle of Cunaxa.

If we had only the idealized portrait of Cyrus presented in Xenophon's *Anabasis*, we might assume that the young prince was but an innocent pawn in the brutal game played so skillfully by his mother. Xenophon presents his protagonist's bid for the throne as the desperate response of a man falsely accused of treason by a treacherous friend. This depiction of the relationship between Cyrus and Tissaphernes is neither plausible nor true. It is hardly likely that Cyrus failed to recognize the connection between his own rise and Tissaphernes' decline. Plutarch, who had read Ctesias, mentions that the young man took great pleasure in the charges leveled in 407 by the Spartan navarch against Tissaphernes, and there is no reason to doubt that this was the case.[29]

Cyrus' conduct makes it clear that he knew precisely what was at stake. In Xenophon's *Hellenica*, there is a passage—which some, with considerable justification, think an interpolation derived from Ctesias—reporting that in 406 Darius' younger son executed two of his own cousins, not because they had committed any crime, but because they had refused in his presence to thrust their hands into their sleeves—an honor reserved for the Great King alone. These two young men were sons of his father's sister and her husband Hieramenes, and they may well have been sent by Arsaces' supporters to keep a watchful eye on the conduct of the young prince.[30]

Far more important than the murder of Darius' nephews, however, was Cyrus' demand. In Persia, as in all traditional monarchies, protocol masked substance. The King's right to rule was founded ultimately on the formal recognition of that right in acts of ceremonial deference. By demanding such deference, Cyrus laid claim to the throne. His request was an act of treason—perhaps to be forgiven, but never to be forgotten—and it did not escape the notice of Stateira's allies.[31]

In 407, circumstances were not favorable to Cyrus' cause. He had Parysatis' good will. But he possessed few, if any, firm supporters among the great aristocrats and Sons of the Royal House who attended Darius II at the court and served him abroad as satraps, generals, and ambassadors.[32]

This should not be surprising. Like absolute monarchs in other places and times, the Achaemenids took pains to head off succession crises and prevent the civil wars that such disputes could so easily spawn. There was even, as we have seen, a *nómos* requiring that the Great King appoint one of his sons co-regent before marching off to war. The process of appointment seems to have had two stages. The local records indicate that Cambyses had already been singled out as the crown prince or heir apparent at the time of Cyrus the Great's conquest of Babylon in October 539. Subsequent to the city's fall, Cambyses assumed the Akkadian title *mār šarri* and began to perform the traditional functions of the Babylonian King's Son. This marked the first stage. The second came nine years later when, according to Herodotus, Cyrus "gave the kingdom" to Cambyses before launching his ill-fated assault on the Massagetae.[33]

The elder Cyrus' example was followed by his successors. The cuneiform tablets indicate that a new palace was being built at Babylon for Darius the Great's *mār šarri* in October 498; and Herodotus reports that, shortly before his death in 486, his father had made Xerxes "greatest after himself." The same pattern is evident in the reigns of Xerxes I, Artaxerxes I, and Artaxerxes II. There is literary or iconographic evidence that each of these monarchs eventually named one of his sons co-regent and conferred on him most of the privileges associated with the kingship.[34]

Darius II—whose hold on the throne was initially tenuous at best—had more reason than most to pick out a successor early in his reign. A King with a crown prince would be far more formidable to potential rivals than a monarch who, if assassinated or killed in battle, would leave no designated heir behind well situated to occupy the throne, rally his father's supporters, and smite his father's foes.

There was a persistent, if confused, tradition in antiquity that Darius' son Arsaces was a good bit older than Cyrus.[35] There are, moreover, cuneiform tablets in the Murašû archive which suggest that Arsaces, from the first year of his father's reign, maintained an independent household in Babylonia as King's Son [*mār šarri*] in the manner of the Achaemenid crown princes before him. When the younger Cyrus left Babylon for Sardis, Arsaces had not yet, as far as we can tell, been named co-regent. But there can have been little doubt that such an event was to be expected, given the natural course of things. In normal circumstances, Persian custom gave priority to the eldest son, and Arsaces had been singled out by his father long before. Barring a dramatic change of direction on the part of his father, Cyrus had to be prepared to see his brother assume the royal robes, receive an upright tiara identical to that of Darius, and exchange oaths with Persia's feudal nobility.[36]

It would be a mistake to underestimate the importance of the exchange of oaths which would in time take place between Arsaces and the King's subjects. The central role played in Persian politics by the concept of honor has been somewhat obscured by the Greek depiction of the Achaemenid monarchy. Where Darius the Great spoke of *mana badaka*—my subject, my vassal, my liegeman—his Greek scribe, lacking a vocabulary for feudal relations, would write *doûlos*. Following this lead, Greek writers from Aeschylus on tended to describe the relationship between King and subject as that between master and slave. There was some truth in this. In certain respects, the Persian monarchy resembled what Aristotle called an *oikonomía éthnous*—the management of a nation as a household. The Achaemenid kings were heirs to a Mesopotamia which had for millennia taken the King of the Lands to be the steward of an estate encompassing the known world and belonging to his god. Although Persia's kings apparently did not adopt this outlook in its entirety, they did rule as Ahura Mazda's anointed, and they do seem to have treated the empire as their private estate and its officials—including the high nobility—as members of the royal household subject to absolute paternal authority.[37] In consequence, there was, in practice, little check on the King's exercise of power.

This was not, however, the whole story. In theory, the King of Kings ruled also as the upholder of right and justice, the administrator of what is called in the Book of Daniel "the law of the Persians which changeth not." Persia's monarchy grew out of the hereditary tribal or village chieftainship which the Greeks with disdain called *dunasteía*—the forbearers of Darius and his successors having been the leaders of the Achaemenid clan dominant within the Pasargadae tribe of the Persian nation. The tribal ethos inherited from the Persians' nomadic and village-centered past never entirely disappeared. The King could ignore the path marked out by religiously sanctioned custom and law—but only at his own peril. Like the kings of Epirus, Macedon, and Sparta, the Achaemenid monarch was bound with his people by a covenant of sorts.[38]

From his fifth to his twentieth birthday, the King's vassal learned three things only—to ride, to use the bow, and to tell the truth. He was taught to regard mendacity as the most shameful of crimes and came to understand the term "lie" in a politically charged, even cosmic sense. In the inscription carved into the cliff at Bisitun, Darius the Great describes the rule of a usurper by announcing that "the Lie waxed great in the country both in Persia and in Media and in the other provinces." In the course of describing his own rise to power, he makes it clear that the King who departs from the path of righteousness and the vassal who breaches his oath of fealty are both "lie-followers."[39]

The elder Darius' choice of phrase was not idiosyncratic: the same motif appears in the Avestan Hymn to Mithra where Ahura Mazda addresses Zarathustra, charging,

> The knave who is false to the treaty, O Spitamid,
> wrecks the whole country, hitting as he does the
> Truth-owners as hard as would a hundred obscurantists.
> Never break a contract, O Spitamid, whether you
> conclude it with an owner of Falsehood, or a Truth-
> owning follower of the good Religion; for the contract

applies to both, the owner of Falsehood and him who
owns Truth.
To those who are not false to the contract grass-land
Mithra grants [possession of] fast horses, while Fire
[, the son of Ahura Mazda,] grants them the straightest
path, and the good, strong, incremental Fravasis of the
owners of Truth give them noble progeny....
Grass-land Mithra we worship ... [=?] ....
whose long arms reach out to catch the violators of the
contract: if [the violator is] by the eastern river he
is caught, if [he is] by the western [river] he is struck
down; whether [he is] at the source of Ranha, whether
[he is] in the middle of the earth,
Mithra [will be] seizing him still, reaching round
[him] with his two arms. The ill-fated, having forfeited
the straightest [path], is miserable in mind:
"So"—thinks the ill-fated—"[it is] not [true that]
all this ill-doing, Mithra does not see all, when his
face is not turned to [man's] trickery!"

In ancient Persia, a breach of faith was considered an attack on the
entire divine order.[40] As long as the Great King's designated heir was
attentive to the traditions of his people and honored his covenant
with them, he could depend upon the loyalty of nearly all of his
father's vassals.

If the younger Cyrus could not command the support of the
landed magnates and the military colonists who provided the Great
King with his army and if he could not sway the force identified by
Greek writers as the Ten Thousand Immortals, which functioned as
that monarch's praetorian guard, it was probably in part because
these men expected to be called upon by the younger Darius to swear to
uphold the rights of Cyrus' older brother. Unless Parysatis could persuade Darius II to alter the succession as Darius I had done, there would
be little reason for Cyrus to look for help from this quarter.[41]

Thus, when Cyrus first came to Sardis, he faced two formidable tasks: he had to carry out his father's instructions and come to the aid of the beleaguered Peloponnesians, and he had to fulfill his mother's expectations and secure for himself a base from which to repeat his father's feat in seizing the crown. The accomplishment of the latter assignment would not, however, be as easy for Cyrus as it had been for Darius: he could not expect a usurper conveniently to eliminate the rightful heir. That was something which he would have to do himself.

THE LEGACY OF MEGABYZUS

The two tasks set for Cyrus were by no means incompatible. In the years between Sparta's first and second Attic wars, western Asia had been the scene of a revolution in military tactics. In order to take full advantage of this revolution, Cyrus would need Spartan help. There was in the situation the making of a deal.[42]

The Persians had always been short of first-class heavy infantry. Apart from the royal bodyguard, there were few well-trained and disciplined contingents in the empire—and even this body of men lacked the equipment and coordination which made the hoplite phalanx so formidable. Barbarians armed with bows, javelins, and wicker shields could not stand up to Greeks arranged in closed formation; equipped with helmets, greaves, and cuirasses; and armed with thrusting spears and overlapping hoplite shields. This was the lesson taught at Marathon, Thermopylae, Plataea, Mycale, Eurymedon, and Cypriot Salamis.[43]

For control of their realm's vast plains and steppes, the Achaemenid monarchs depended less on their archers and charioteers than on their cavalry—the last including horse archers capable of firing volley after volley as they circled the enemy, knights in light armor who hurled javelins into the enemy ranks, and heavily armored and ponderous shock cavalry equipped with lances and sabers. In the open terrain of Asia, knights armed with bow, javelin, lance, and saber could defeat by a process of attrition even the Roman legions—the best of the ancient Mediterranean world's massed infantry—when the latter lacked an auxiliary cavalry force adequate to protect the army's flanks and keep the enemy's mounted archers and spear-throwers out of range.[44]

In such an environment, the comparatively primitive Greek phalanx—lacking the independent maniples which gave the Roman army its flexibility—was still more vulnerable. The hoplite shield protected its bearer's left side and the right side of the man to his left. In consequence, at the right end of the phalanx stood a soldier whose entire right side was exposed. A cavalry assault at that point could turn the flank, rout the army's right wing, and send a ripple through the infantry formation which might disrupt it altogether.[45] If the Persians lacked heavy infantry, it was probably because, in Asia, it had not in the past been required.

Except in Thessaly and, to a lesser degree, in Boeotia, the countryside of mainland Greece was for the most part too rugged for the unshod horses of antiquity. Cavalry could usually perform at best an ancillary function—picking off stray hoplites and routing those peltasts, archers, and other light-armed troops who wandered on to level ground.[46]

The effectiveness of ancient shock cavalry on the Persian model was severely hampered by the lack of a saddle with stirrups. Loaded down with chain mail and poised precariously atop his steed, the horseman kept his seat only through the pressure of his knees. It is conceivable that he compensated for the awkwardness of his position by adopting the practice attested in later times of supporting the shaft of his lance on a loop attached to the charger's neck while resting the butt end against the horse's thigh so that the animal's weight drove it home and he was not himself dislodged in the process. If so, he will nonetheless have been in serious danger of being unhorsed whenever he delivered a blow with his saber or came within reach of an enemy soldier.[47]

The addition of a saddle with stirrups would have given the

cavalryman a firmer seat and would have allowed him to couch his lance in the fashion of the medieval knights, but would not have enabled him to penetrate the phalanx. Shock cavalry can be effective in flank attack, but even there the shock it delivers is more often psychological than physical. No horse that has not gone berserk will charge into a nest of spears, smash through a wall of shields, or gallop into a solid mass of men. If properly trained and deployed in terrain preventing attack on its flanks, a phalanx of pikemen can easily withstand a cavalry charge. Only when an artillery barrage, a frontal assault by infantry, or an attack from behind or on an exposed flank has disrupted the formation and destroyed its cohesion, can the horsemen swoop down and skewer or hack away at the scattered footsoldiers.[48]

Thanks to their capacious shields and their armor, Greek hoplites were very nearly impervious to the primitive artillery rained upon them by Persia's bowmen. Moreover, thanks to the mountainous and hilly terrain in most of European Greece, a competent general could almost always find a position for his troops that would shield the flanks of his phalanx from cavalry assault. Having little use for cavalry, the Greeks put little emphasis on it—except, of course, in Thessaly and Boeotia, where there were relatively open plains. Their horses were, in any case, smaller and less strong than those of the barbarians to the East; their horsemen, ill-equipped and less agile.[49]

It was perhaps inevitable that someone sooner or later should think of combining the best of both worlds, coordinating the infantry of the West with the cavalry of the East. The addition of first-class cavalry would make little difference in mainland Greece; that of first-rate infantry could, however, be decisive in much of Asia. There, even an adequate cavalry contingent could afford hoplites the cover which the terrain provided them in Europe. Protected from flank attack and from missiles projected by enemy horsemen, the heavy infantry of Greece could not be stopped—unless, of course, they were caught in an ambush or so outnumbered by the infantry of their foe that an envelopment could be staged.

It is by no means certain who first matched Greek hoplites deployed in a phalanx with barbarian cavalry, but it is not hard to guess. The preeminent Persian general during the reigns of Xerxes and Artaxerxes was the satrap of Syria Megabyzus, the grandson of the like-named confederate. This Megabyzus crushed the rebellion of Babylon in 482, was one of the five marshals in command of the Persian army on its march into Greece two years later, married Xerxes' libidinous daughter Amytis, and played a decisive role in keeping Artaxerxes on the Achaemenid throne after Xerxes was assassinated in 465 and his first-born son Darius was in the aftermath killed.

In the 450s, after the Egyptians revolted, called in the Athenians, and killed their satrap the King's uncle Achaemenes, Artaxerxes commissioned Megabyzus to restore order. He did just that, defeating the Egyptians, bottling up Athens' fleet in the Nile Delta, and finally securing the surrender of the rebel leader and his Greek allies on promise of safe conduct.

Megabyzus' promise was not, however, fully honored. Artaxerxes' mother Amestris seems to have been particularly fond of her brother-in-law Achaemenes, who had been the satrap in Egypt; and she was enraged when he was killed. In 449, five years after the capitulation of the rebels and their Athenian auxiliaries—in the very year in which Megabyzus had negotiated a peace of sorts with the Athenians on his master's behalf—Artaxerxes finally gave way to the entreaties of his embittered mother and allowed her to execute the rebel leader and fifty of the Athenians. His honor besmirched, Megabyzus fled from the court to Syria with the remaining Athenians and launched a rebellion.

Megabyzus inflicted severe defeats on two Persian armies before negotiating a reconciliation with Artaxerxes. In his epitome of Ctesias' account of the revolt, Photius nowhere states that Megabyzus owed his victories to Greek hoplites, but it is reasonable to speculate that this was so. Hellenic soldiers of fortune were nothing new in the eastern Mediterranean. Like the Saite pharaohs of Egypt before them, western Asia's satraps normally employed Greek mercenaries as a supplement to the feudal levy of their provinces. Megabyzus had all that was required to make an advance of profound significance in the art of war—a genius for things military; long familiarity with Greek practices; close ties with Athens, which controlled the seas through which he would need to transport hoplites from the European mainland to Syria's distant shores; and, at the crucial moment, a host of Greeks who just happened to be under his protection. Had he not effected a military revolution by training Greek infantry and Persian cavalry to operate in tandem, it is hard to see how a satrap with the limited resources of his province could have proven so formidable to the King.[50]

The historical record is more substantial for the rebellions of Megabyzus' son Artyphius and Lydia's satrap Pissouthnes three decades later: they both are known to have supplemented the Persian cavalry and infantry available to them with a substantial force of Greek hoplites, and this they did to great effect. Like his father, Artyphius, who had fought alongside the man, twice defeated the King's army. If Darius' general Artasyras finally succeeded in putting down Artyphius' revolt, it was only by bribing the rebel's Greek mercenaries. Tissaphernes found it necessary to deal with Pissouthnes in similar fashion; and, as we have seen, it took the Spartan intervention in the eastern Aegean to enable him to stamp out the last embers of rebellion by capturing Iasos, the Carian stronghold of Pissouthnes' bastard son Amorges. The mercenaries taken when the city fell turned out to be Peloponnesians.[51]

In 407, when Cyrus made his journey to Sardis, the military situation was complicated by one other important fact: at least in Babylonia, the most populous of the empire's core provinces, the King's army was in an advanced state of decay. By the time of Darius II, the feudal system had deteriorated. This can best be seen in the cuneiform records of Babylonia.

In that region, the Achaemenid monarchs had originally settled their military colonists on tracts of about seventy acres—more than ample, if leased to a native entrepreneur, to provide for the well-being and equipment of a member of one of the various divisions of the royal army. In the absence of a law of primogeniture, however, these tracts had been divided and subdivided again and again over time among the descendants of the original colonists. By the time in which Artaxerxes died, some of the Great King's vassals were living on one-fifteenth of the original allotment. That allotment was still expected to help support a single trooper and, in good and bad year alike, to provide part of the means required for paying the fixed annual assessment on the original grant: nothing had changed except the number of mouths to feed. As a consequence of this added burden, the military colonists had to borrow in bad times in order to pay the King his rent. Their ability to borrow, however, was limited by their inability fully to dispose of their land: the King's law allowed the creditor to seize the crops, but not the fief.

In practice, the native entrepreneur to whom the colonist leased his land and the banker from whom he borrowed were probably the same man. In the neighborhood of Nippur, the Murašû firm domi-nated the local economy. It leased land from the great magnates, the feudal gentry, and the military colonists and canals from the King. It rented land, draft animals, farming equipment, and the use of the canals to the local farmers. The firm collected rent in dates and per-haps barley at harvest time. It marketed the produce and then paid in silver both the royal duty on the land it leased and the rent due the landowners and the King. In the economy as a whole, native entre-preneurs such as the Murašû served an essential function, mediating between the bureaucracy through which the King raised his reve-nues and the feudal retainers who provided him with his army.

In the best of times, this arrangement probably served the King very well—but the lack of a law of primogeniture had the effect over time of upsetting the delicate balance struck between the public purse and the royal army to the detriment of the latter. Without con-stant drill, the King's soldiers were useless. It was not easy for the archer to hit the mark, for the charioteer to keep his steeds under control and his vehicle upright, and for the cavalryman—particularly in an age before the invention of the saddle with stirrups—to execute complicated maneuvers without losing his seat. Impoverishment could and did deprive many military colonists of the leisure and equipment necessary for regular practice.

It is an indication of the straits they were in that some found the means to evade the law against the sale or exchange of Bow Land, Horse Land, and Chariot Land. This is evident from a cuneiform document dated to January 421, when Darius II mustered some of his troops at Uruk. Among those called up was a Jew whose father had been forced to adopt one of the Murašû in order to cover his debts. When the father died, part of his land was transferred to the firm, but, with it, went partial responsibility for providing the King with a cavalryman. When the royal summons came, the heirs struck a deal:

In the joy of his heart, Gadal-Iama the Jew has spoken thus to the son of Murašû: the planted and ploughed fields, the Horse Land of my father, you now hold because my father once adopted your father. So give me a horse with a groom and harness, a caparison of iron, a helmet, a leather breastplate, a buckler, 120 arrows of two sorts, an iron attachment for my buckler, two iron spears and a mina of silver for provisions and I will fulfill the service-duties which weigh on our lands.

The fact that Gadal-Iama had no horse of his own tells us all that we need to know about his competence as a horse archer and mounted spearman.[52]

Gadal-Iama may not have been typical of the military colonists, but the degree to which they also found themselves in great difficulty is strikingly evident from a close examination of the Murašû archives. In normal circumstances, when a local landowner mortgaged his property and subsequently paid off the debt, the record of the mortgage was destroyed. If he failed to meet the terms of the agreement, the firm retained the document and seized control of his land, but not full title. Most if not all of the mortgage records found in the Murašû archives can be taken as evidence of forfeiture and the extremely high incidence of mortgages issued in May and June 423 and never paid off is symptomatic of a crisis. The proximity of this two-month period to the time when Darius II is most apt to have been mobilizing his forces for the struggle with Arsites and Artyphius is suggestive: the military colonists in the neighborhood of Nippur to the south of Babylon apparently had to borrow substantial sums in order to equip themselves.[53] The agricultural surplus which had been put to such uses in the sixth century was nonexistent late in the fifth. A decay in the economic foundations of Persia's military strength had accompanied the advances in the art of war made by the satraps of western Asia. The Great King was still able to raise large armies. But, from among the military colonists in Mesopotamia, he could no longer expect to be able to deploy a great many archers, cavalrymen, and charioteers who were well-practiced in the military arts.[54]

The consequences of these changes can hardly have escaped the notice of the wily Parysatis and of her ambitious young son. Later, in 401, when Cyrus marched upcountry to claim what he regarded as his birthright, the core of his army was a body of more than ten thousand Greek hoplites.[55] There is every reason to believe that he was intent on securing such a force from the moment of his arrival at Sardis.

While Sparta's third Attic war continued, this was beyond Cyrus' power. In order to gather so large a hoplite army, he needed the cooperation and firm support of the power dominant in the Peloponnesus, the major source of Greek mercenaries, and the Spartans were not likely to risk losing the Persian financial subsidy essential for victory in the war against Athens merely in order to satisfy the ambitions of a sixteen-year-old.[56]

Not even a Spartan victory could guarantee support. The Great King, not Cyrus, had a claim on the gratitude of the Lacedaemonians. It was not in their interest to become deeply embroiled in the quarrel of the royal siblings. In defeat, Cyrus would earn Lacedaemon the ire of Persia. In victory, the young prince would become formidable to his allies and would be no more likely than his brother to grant freedom to the Greeks of Asia Minor. Persia had entered the war on the Peloponnesian side to recover the coastal cities wrested from its grasp long before by the Athenians and to regain as much beyond this as possible. Cyrus might promise the Asian Greeks autonomy and freedom from tribute. There was no reason to suppose that so ambitious a young man would honor so demeaning a commitment.[57] Spartan support of Cyrus' bid for power was no more rational than a wholehearted Persian commitment to the Lacedaemonian cause in the war at this time underway. But, just as the private interests of individual Persians might contribute to the pursuit of an imprudent public policy, the personal ambitions of particular Spartans might have similar consequences for the community situated on the Eurotas.

The solution to Cyrus' dilemma was simple: he needed to make Sparta his client by helping a man to power in Sparta who would remain bound to him by gratitude, interest, and fear. He needed to place a viceroy of his own choosing in charge of the affairs of Lacedaemon. He needed to find a Spartiate commander who was as ambitious as "the *káranos* of those who muster on the plains of Castolus" and who had to have Persian support as much as that Persian had to have Spartan support. Years before, we have good reason to believe, the Spartan regent victorious at the battle of Plataea had initiated through intermediaries private discussions with the Great King in a quest to become master of Lacedaemon and of Hellas itself and had for some years vigorously pursued this aim. The conspiracy of Xerxes I and the regent Pausanias had ultimately come to nought. But it had by no means been forgotten. In 407, Cyrus was looking for "a second Pausanias"; and, as Sparta's Eurypontid king Agis son of Archidamus would belatedly come to recognize, the Persian had quite quickly found his man.[58]

CHAPTER SEVEN

A Second Pausanias

In antiquity, the vestiges of servitude subsisted for some time
after that servitude was extinguished. There is a natural prejudice that induces men to despise anyone who has been their
inferior and to do so for a long time after he has become their
equal. To the genuine inequality produced by fortune or the
law there always succeeds an imaginary inequality that has its
roots in the mores of the population.

ALEXIS DE TOCQUEVILLE

THE IMMEDIATE BENEFICIARY of the dramatic shift in Persian policy was a Spartiate named Lysander son of Aristocritus. Although he may well have assumed office as navarch in
the spring of 407, he does not appear to have taken up his duties in
Ionia until late that summer—when, we must suspect, the thirty triremes that Alcibiades son of Cleinias had spied under construction
at Gytheion were seaworthy and "the *káranos* of those who muster
on the plains of Castolus" was expected to make his debut.

First, Lysander had himself conveyed from Lacedaemon to
Rhodes. Then, he collected the galleys stationed there, at Kos, and at
Miletus; slipped surreptitiously past Samos; and resituated himself
and the allied fleet at Ephesus, which is far closer than Miletus to the
Spartan stronghold on Chios and to the satrapal seat at Sardis. In
that Greek city, we are told, he busied himself with repairing his
galleys, with drying out those in danger of becoming waterlogged,
and with scraping the bottoms of the latter, recaulking their hulls,

and recoating them with pitch—and there he saw also to the construction of additional triremes.

It was in Ephesus that Aristocritus' son patiently awaited Cyrus' arrival. Finally, when all was ready, he made his way to the ancient Lydian capital to meet the younger son of Persia's Great King, and this he did in company with Boeotius and his fellow ambassadors.[1]

Cyrus' Spartan counterpart was a *móthax*. He was, we have reason to believe, a half-breed—the "bastard brat," as, in private, his political rivals may well have called him, of a Spartiate man and a helot woman. He was not the first Spartiate known to have been a *móthax*. That honor belonged to Gylippus son of Cleandridas, the hero of Sparta's Sicilian proxy war. Like Gylippus, Lysander was born in the wake of the great earthquake of 465 and the massive servile revolt that followed. Thanks to the severe shortage of manpower at Lacedaemon produced by these two catastrophes and presumably to the sponsorship of his natural father, he was, like Gylippus, reared as the messmate of a young Spartiate, subjected to the *agōgḗ*, and thereby rendered eligible for promotion to citizenship.[2]

Lysander is said to have grown up in poverty. Whether this was due to a law stipulating that a bastard had no claim on his natural father's estate or to a lack of private property on the part of Aristocritus we are not told. What we do know, however, is that, like the Agiad and Eurypontid kings, Lysander's father traced his lineage back to the demigod Heracles and that he was able to maintain a guest-friendship with the ruler of the hinterland about Cyrene in Libya—a North African prince whose name, Libys, Aristocritus gave to his other son. This suggests that Aristocritus was not himself a man without means.[3]

While nothing is known of Lysander's youth, we can hardly doubt that the privileges he enjoyed were reduced in significance by the obstacles poverty and his base origin placed in his way. The Spartiates may have referred to themselves as *hoi hómoioi*—as "the equals or peers." But, as is always the case in putatively egalitarian regimes, some were more equal than others; and at Lacedaemon the differences were pronounced. After all, the royal offices were hereditary, and only the well-born were eligible for election to the *gerousía*. To advance, Aristocritus' bastard must have done what Gylippus had no doubt done not long before. At every stage—as he progressed through the *agōgḗ*, was inducted into a *sussitíon*, joined the ranks of the *néoi*, was selected for service among the *hippeîs*, aged out of the ranks of the *néoi*, became a *presbúteros*, and was named an *agathoergós*—he must have distinguished himself for his prowess, discernment, and capacity for command; and he must have outdone the purebreds in his age cohort. Plutarch justly refers to him as a self-made man.[4]

Of course, no man is entirely his own work. No man reaches high office without the support of friends—particularly a half-breed bastard with a servile mother who has been accepted into the aristocratic family of his natural father in a community in which the hereditary principle and, with it, the right of noble birth command respect.[5]

Lysander's prospects were no doubt promoted by his father. But there is reason to suspect that he had an additional patron. We know of only one friendship predating his navarchy and linking him with another Spartiate. Plutarch mentions that he was the lover [*erastḗs*] of another Heraclid—a younger man who was exceedingly well-born but cursed with a physical defect that rendered him lame. His name was Agesilaus son of Archidamus, and the two remained close until well after the end of Sparta's third Attic war.[6]

On such a foundation, one cannot build a grand edifice. Nonetheless, the link between Lysander and Agesilaus is suggestive. The latter is known to have paid great attention to family ties and was notorious for taking great pains to benefit his friends. He is, moreover, likely to have been close to his older half-brother Agis, the Eurypontid king; and we can be confident that he exerted himself on his *erastḗs'* behalf.[7]

There is, in fact, evidence that, before 404, Agis and Lysander were on the best of terms. As we shall soon see, they vigorously supported the same foreign policy—the struggle to overturn Athens' empire and replace it with a Spartan hegemony. Moreover, while

Lysander was the commander at sea, the two took great care to pursue a mutually agreed-upon military strategy; and, in framing a proposal for a postwar settlement that they hoped Lacedaemon and her allies would adopt and be able to implement, they worked in tandem. In the course of the war, at every stage, these two men coordinated their efforts. That they were political allies we need not doubt.[8]

The little evidence that survives supports the hypothesis that Lysander's lover's half-brother Agis was the sponsor whose efforts most effectually helped secure the impoverished *móthax'* rise to prominence. To grasp the full meaning of their relationship, we need to remind ourselves once again of the central role accorded the Eurypontid king and his Agiad colleague in Spartan governance and social relations and to explore further the consequences. The leverage that Agis wielded against Alcibiades he appears to have deployed on Lysander's behalf.

BEYOND EQUALITY

In a sense, the Spartan *hómoioi*—"the equals"—really were equal. They shared in a common way of life constituted not only by education, barracks meals, and the assignment of allotments [*klêroi*] in Messenia, but also by fear—the fear that a helot uprising would bring their world crashing in on them. Fear, the great equalizer, rendered the Spartan regime conservative, stable, and—despite the economic and caste distinctions within the citizen body—socially harmonious.

The Spartans could not afford the tension between "the many" and "the few," and they knew it. They tried to suppress that tension by turning the city into a camp, the *pólis* into an army, and the citizen into a soldier. They attempted to abolish it by eliminating to the greatest degree practicable the private element in human life: by placing severe restrictions on the acquisition of property and by reducing to a minimum the influence of the family. The Spartans outlawed gold and silver coinage and encouraged homosexuality for the same reason. The *agōgē* and all that followed it were aimed at forming the completely public-spirited man—the man who would be loyal to his comrades-in-arms and who would return from every battle with his shield or on it.[9]

There were, however, two men at Lacedaemon who were not among "the *hómoioi*," two who escaped the *agōgē*, two who took their meals outside the barracks. Mere Spartiates could be elected to the *gerousía*, but, as we have seen, only a Heraclid king or his regent could serve in that venerable body before his sixtieth year. Mere Spartiates sacrificed to the gods, but only a Heraclid king or his regent could do so on the city's behalf. Mere Spartiates commanded troops, but only a Heraclid king or his regent could lead out the Spartan army and the forces of the Peloponnesian League. The Agiad and Eurypontid kings stood out from the ranks.

In a society in which military concerns predominate and in which there is a popular element in the government, generals—even hereditary generals—are men of great power and influence. A soldier's opportunity to distinguish himself on the field of the spear and the sword and to gain the admiration and support of his comrades depends more often than not on the goodwill of the commander. One need only reflect on the political consequences of replacing the consulship at Rome with a dual kingship to see the importance that the Spartan kings must have had. In Rome, the citizen was also a soldier; in Sparta, the soldier was also a citizen.

The two kings had other politically important privileges as well. As we have had occasion to note, they appointed *próxenoi* at Sparta for the various cities that had relations with her, conferring honor thereby on the men selected and securing for themselves a role in the conduct of foreign affairs. They appointed the four *Púthioi*— each naming two to keep the records of the oracles for him and to share his mess. When the city herself wished an oracle from Delphi concerning a given matter, she chose her messenger from among these four men. This practice assured royal predominance in religious affairs and made the manipulation of religion for political purposes the exclusive prerogative of the two *basileîs*. In as traditional a society as Sparta, this could have extraordinary consequences. A wily king could use religion to control the city.

The kings were also responsible for maintaining the public roads, for legalizing the adoption of children, and for securing husbands for heiresses left unbetrothed by their fathers, as we have seen. These last two functions were of an importance that needs underlining: because the Spartiates were barred from commerce and the possession of precious metals, the only legal way open to any of them for the amassing of a fortune was to inherit land or marry its owner. The rights of the kings in matters of adoption and with regard to heiresses provided them with substantial patronage.[10] Reflection on the nature of the man produced by the Lycurgan regime and on the distribution of wealth in Laconia and Messenia should clarify the importance of this.

The chief effect of Lacedaemon's attempt at a suppression of the private element in human life was to make the pursuit of wealth dishonorable. But what the Spartans disdained in public they longed for when alone. Unlike the heavenly city of Plato's *Republic*, the Spartan regime did not eliminate private property and the family altogether. The Spartiate could distinguish between the children and the estate which belonged to him and the children and the estate which did not. He had a stake in protecting and promoting those children and in increasing that estate which brought him into conflict with his peers. This was the very conflict which the banning of coinage, the encouragement of homosexuality, the *agōgē*, and the *sussitíon* were designed to expunge. The Lacedaemonian legislator sought to form a man who loved toil, victory, and honor—toil for the common cause, victory in the struggles of his people, and the honor which only his city and fellow citizens could confer on him. The lawgiver sought to redirect, transform, and harness the spirit of competition to serve the city by replacing as much as possible the love of one's own property and progeny, and the hatred of those outside the family circle implicit in that attachment, with the love of one's own city and citizens and the hatred of foreigners inherent in that commitment.[11]

Plato rightly regarded this project as a partial failure. It produced men torn between their public duties and the private wants engendered by the remnants of the distinction between mine and thine. "Men of this sort," he observed, "will desire wealth just as those in oligarchies do, and under cover of darkness, like savages, they will pay homage to silver and gold." The consequence was a Spartan disobedience of the law against the possession of gold and silver so widespread that Plato's Socrates could assert that

> there is not in all of Hellas as much gold and silver as is held privately in Lacedaemon. Through many generations, it has been entering that place from every part of Greece and frequently from the barbarians as well, but to no other place does it ever depart. As in the fable of Aesop, what the fox said to the lion is true: the tracks left by the money going into Lacedaemon are clear, but nowhere can anyone see traces of it going back out.

The Athenian philosopher speaks of the "magazines for storage and domestic treasuries" of the Spartiates, and he mentions "walls surrounding their houses," which are "exactly like private nests where they can make great expenditures on women and on whomever else they might wish"—and the evidence bears out his claim that these houses were stocked with valuables.[12]

Sparta's two kings fit the general pattern. They were the wealthiest of those domiciled at Lacedaemon. They owned choice land in many of the cities of the *períoikoi*. They benefited from a special tax levied on the Spartans; and, thanks to the political leverage they possessed, they gained more from the gold and silver that flowed into Lacedaemon from abroad than any other citizens.[13]

Aristotle shared Plato's judgment of what the latter, with an eye to its obsession with glory and honor, termed the timocratic regime.

He took note of the sumptuary laws limiting the expense and specifying the character of funerals, and he was aware of the regulations governing the comportment of the women and denying them the right to let their hair grow long, to wear jewelry in public, and to otherwise adorn themselves. But he thought these and the other similar *nómoi* grossly inadequate, and he contended that the Spartan legislator had, in fact, mixed "the love of honor" with "the love of money" and had thereby formed "private individuals covetous of wealth." Like the Halicarnassian Dionysius, the peripatetic philosopher attributed this, in part, to the absence of laws regulating the household. In particular, like Plato, he faulted Spartan institutions for their failure to bring under control "the women, who live intemperately in every kind of licence and luxury," observing that "the necessary consequence is that riches are held in honor, especially when the citizens fall under the rule of their women, as tends to happen among peoples devoted to soldiering and war.... The arrangements regarding the women not only introduce an air of unseemliness into the regime; they tend to foster avarice as well."[14]

The propensity noted by Aristotle may have been exacerbated by the aftereffects of the great earthquake of 465 and the helot rebellion that followed—for these not only halved the population and eliminated the better part of a generation of Spartiate women and children. They must also have contributed to a concentration of the existing private property in fewer hands.

In time, of course, the disproportion between the number of women and the number of men must have disappeared. But the ongoing struggle with Athens may, by eliminating men, have contributed to its return in a new and less dramatic form and to a concentration of private holdings in the hands of the Spartiates' wives, sisters, and daughters of the sort that Aristotle later noticed. These women, who lived "intemperately in every kind of licence and luxury," were no doubt much sought after by those of the surviving Spartiates who were eager to quench their thirst for wealth. Prosperous Spartiates with only daughters for heirs would naturally try to find the best possible match; and, as in other places and times, wealth tended to marry wealth. But, if a girl's father died before she was betrothed, her fate became the responsibility of the kings. We do not know whether Sparta's *basileîs* also disposed of widows—but the power to oversee adoptions and to marry off unbetrothed heiresses was power enough.[15]

Agis became king in or shortly before 426, a few years after the beginning of what must eventually have come to seem an interminable period of conflict. In the course of Sparta's second and third Attic wars and in the interlude between these two conflicts, he surely had many opportunities to secure the undying gratitude of impecunious Lacedaemonians and of others, better situated, who were burdened with a shameful passion for wealth.[16]

We do not know how Lysander overcame the disability of poverty that seems to have been his legacy as a *móthax*, but it is not hard to guess. The manner in which he won his bride did invite comment, and Agis was in as good a position to satisfy Lysander's need for personal resources as he was to whet the man's appetite for honor. As we have seen, the powers, the patronage, and the prestige that Agis had deployed against Alcibiades he had also used to enhance the prospects of men like Alcamenes son of Sthenelaidas and Clearchus son of Ramphias. If, at some point after he reached the age of forty-five, Lysander was given command of the allied fleet, it was surely in part because he enjoyed the support of his beloved *paidiká*'s older brother.[17]

It is in this context that we must understand the dispatch of Lysander as navarch late in the summer of 407 to meet the adolescent Persian prince sent down from Susa by the Great King to achieve a Spartan victory in the war against Athens. At the time, Lysander was no longer a young man. According to Plutarch, he had lived a life "more subservient to the powerful [*tôn dunatôn*] than was natural in a Spartan and was content to bear an authority heavy in weight for the sake of achieving his aims."[18] From what we know of Spartan political life and from the little that we can discern of

Lysander's ties, it is clear that the *dunatoí* to whom he had for so long been subservient included Agis and the leaders of the faction gathered about him and committed to ending the great war with a Peloponnesian victory. It is to the support of his lover Agesilaus' royal half-brother that Lysander owed his prominence.

Late in life, according to Aristotle, Lysander began to suffer from melancholia—the sadness and sullenness that was thought to characterize men of great soul such as the teacher of his younger contemporary and rival Alcibiades. Lysander shared with Alcibiades in *philotimía*—the love of honor—but differed from the Athenian and from the majority of his fellow Spartiates in being impervious to the temptations of wealth and luxury. A perverted love of honor had led Alcibiades to debauch Agis' wife. It should not be surprising that a Spartan whose love of preeminence was in no way countered, reduced, and redirected by more mundane concerns should develop black bile and find it impossible to remain forever the servant of the *dunatoí* and their leader—even if the latter was a king.[19]

CYRUS AND LYSANDER

The meeting between Cyrus and Lysander at Sardis in the autumn of 407 was cordial. Xenophon's account of their visit to a *parádeisos* and of the banquet Cyrus laid on for his guest presents a vivid picture of the warmth and conviviality that ordinarily accompanied the establishment of a relationship of guest-friendship [*xenía*] between two men. There is, moreover, every reason to suppose that sentiment seconded interest in binding together the young Persian and his Lacedaemonian colleague, and it is perfectly possible that it had a homoerotic charge. As we have had occasion to observe, the Persians picked up pederasty from the Hellenes—and Lysander was a practiced seducer of the young.

Despite initial resistance on the part of Cyrus, Lysander persisted in asking that the daily pay provided the Peloponnesian mariners by Persia be restored from three to the six obols originally on offer from

Tissaphernes. Cyrus hesitated. He had brought with him five hundred talents (14.25 tons) of silver supplied by his father—a considerable sum but not enough to pay such a wage to a great host of mariners for long. Moreover, such generosity ran contrary to the agreement that the younger Darius had negotiated with Boeotius, which had limited outlay to three thousand drachmas a month per ship (i.e., to three obols a day for each member of the crew); and it contravened the instructions Cyrus' father had issued to him. Nonetheless, at the banquet that the young man put on for his guest, when he drank to Lysander's health and wanted to know what would please him most, the Spartan asked that the rowers be paid four obols a day; and, without consulting his father, the Persian prince granted the navarch's request. If the five hundred talents proved insufficient, as might well be the case given the cost of maintaining a fleet of triremes on station month after month, he promised that he would draw on his own money, and he vowed that, if necessary, he would turn the gold and silver on his throne into coin. Of course, Tissaphernes had once made a similar commitment to the Athenians. Or so Alcibiades had claimed. But there was this difference. There can be no doubt that Cyrus really did say this, and, as we shall soon see, he meant what he said.[20]

Cyrus' willingness to accommodate his guest in this particular was a critical move, as Lysander fully understood. The Athenians were still in dire financial straits. Alcibiades knew this only too well. His voyage to Samos that autumn had been broken by an expedition against Andros, which occupied a strategic position opposite southern Euboea on the route that the grain ships ordinarily followed as they made their way from the Hellespont to Athens. There, after defeating the Andrians in a pitched battle, he failed to take their town. From there, he journeyed to the eastern coast of Anatolia, where he launched piratical expeditions against Kos, Rhodes, and the cities of Caria. When he finally reached Samos and became fully informed regarding the significance of Cyrus' arrival on the scene, he resorted to diplomacy, as was his wont; and, through the good

Map 19. Lysander in Ionia, 407/6

offices of his *xénos* Tissaphernes, he made an approach to the young Persian prince by sending an embassy to Sardis. Although the satrap is said to have urged the Great King's younger son to play the two Greek powers against one another for the purpose of weakening both, Cyrus refused to receive the Athenian delegation.[21]

As a consequence of the arrangement worked out with Cyrus, Lysander could afford to bide his time at Ephesus refusing battle while he refitted and recaulked the ships in his possession; took in more vessels as new triremes came off the assembly lines for some time up and running at Antandrus and Gytheion and now newly established at Ephesus; and lured oarsmen and specialists away from his hard-pressed opponents with the promise of higher pay. Alcibiades was less well-situated. He found it necessary to divide his forces, leaving the better part of the navy at Notium as a check on the Peloponnesian fleet stationed a short distance to the southeast at Ephesus, and proceeding with a few troopships and a substantial hoplite contingent to assist the beleaguered Clazomenians and to support the attempt of his friend and fellow *stratēgós* Thrasybulus son of Lycus to seize and fortify Phocaea. His aim appears to have been to pave the way for an assault on Chios just across the strait—where, at Delphinium, the Athenians still maintained a garrison.[22]

Alcibiades might have left Aristocrates son of Scellias or Adeimantus son of Leucolophides in charge at Notium. They were, after all, *stratēgoí*. But they had been chosen for their expertise in commanding hoplites on shore, not triremes at sea, and they may well have been posted at this time with Thrasybulus at Phocaea. So, he opted, instead, to leave an experienced mariner in charge whom he knew very well indeed and thought that he could trust—his helmsman Antiochus.

This turned to be a grave blunder—for Alcibiades underestimated the threat posed to Athens by the new Spartan navarch. In his absence and contrary to his explicit instructions, this Antiochus did not remain entirely on the defensive but attempted to achieve something worthy of note on his own hook. On the face of it, what he did was a modest departure from his orders. In the circumstances, however, it was sufficient to wreak havoc. Having noticed that Lysander sent out three triremes each day to patrol the harbor at Ephesus, Antiochus entered the harbor with a single trireme, the fastest in the Athenian fleet. His aim was to lure the galleys patrolling the harbor into an ambush in the open sea where he had stationed nine additional vessels.

Lysander is said to have been informed of the departure of Cleinias' son and to have been forewarned by deserters regarding Antiochus' intentions. He had a small contingent of fast ships ready to row out and sink the Athenian's trireme in a lightning strike. As their attack began, the nine Athenian galleys outside the harbor rowed in to come to Antiochus' defense. His trireme the Peloponnesians holed. In the process, they killed Antiochus himself; and the other galleys they routed. Deprived of their commander, alerted to the course of events, and confused by this development, of which they had apparently not been apprised, the Athenian trierarchs at Notium hastily manned their galleys, conducted them out from the harbor in an endeavor to defend their comrades, and did so in great disorder—while Lysander's fleet, in mobilizing, exhibited the discipline and close coordination that was the hallmark of Lacedaemonian operations. In the ensuing battle, the Athenians lost twenty-two of the eighty triremes stationed at Notium.[23]

The Spartan victory was for the Athenians back home and apparently also for many of those in the fleet the last straw. As was his wont, the son of Cleinias had raised their hopes sky-high and had in the end left them disappointed. From 411 on, he had repeatedly traded on the expectation that he would be able to work out an arrangement with the Great King favorable to Athens, and time and again he had failed to deliver the requisite deal.

At the insistence of Cyrus, who wished to spring a surprise on the Athenians, Pharnabazus son of Pharnaces had for some weeks or months detained the envoys he promised to conduct to Susa. When word finally reached Athens that Boeotius and his colleagues had elicited from the Great King a firm commitment to the Lacedaemonians' cause and that his younger son had arrived at Sardis intent on seeing to their victory, it must surely have occasioned profound disappointment and a great gnashing of teeth.[24] This, together with the Andrians' refusal to knuckle under and the news of the severe losses incurred at Notium, broke the spell with which Alcibiades had bewitched a majority of his fellow citizens.

As Xenophon makes clear in his description of the reception at Athens accorded Alcibiades in the late spring of 407, there had already then been a sizable minority of citizens who wanted nothing to do with the man. In the wake of Notium, they were now joined by a great many of those who had welcomed him home, and it was presumably at this time that his opponents most stridently cited as unpropitious his return to Athens while the Plynteria was being conducted.

There was also considerable discontent in the fleet. According to Plutarch, Thrasybulus son of Thraso, who hated his commander, returned from Samos to Athens to accuse Cleinias' wayward son of handing the command of the fleet over to a low-life distinguished solely by his capacity for drink and his taste for telling tales of the sea—so that he could himself wander about the region, collecting money, drinking to excess, and cavorting with the courtesans for which Abydos in particular and Ionia in general were famous. According to Diodorus, there were other returnees who charged Alcibiades with conspiracy, contending that he secretly favored the Spartans and had contracted a "friendship [*philía*]" with Pharanabazus in the expectation that at the end of the war he would be in a position "to establish a *dunasteía* over his fellow citizens [*katadunasteúein tôn politôn*]." These may have been the men, mentioned by Plutarch, who argued that it was more than merely suspicious that the Athenian *stratēgós* had built for himself a fort at Pactyes near Bisanthe in the Hellespont on the presumption that he might someday once again need a refuge.

The Athenians do not appear to have credited the charge of treason. But, in the wake of the battle, we learn from Xenophon, who was apt to have been at Athens at the time, that they did conclude that the man whom they had made *hapántōn hēgemòn autokrátōr* just a few months before had, in his role as supreme commander, demonstrated a carelessness [*améleia*] and a lack of self-control [*akrateía*] that they could not tolerate. No longer persuaded that Cleinias' son could secure for them an alliance with Persia, no longer convinced of his invincibility, and no longer willing to avert their gaze from his longstanding predilection for irresponsible conduct, a majority in the Council of Five Hundred and the assembly voted to relieve him of duty.[25]

In response, expecting that there would be worse in store for him if he returned home, Alcibiades withdrew into a self-imposed exile once again. This time he sequestered himself in the stronghold at Pactyes, just inland from the northeastern coast of the Thracian Chersonnesus, that he had prepared in anticipation of just such an eventuality. Cleinias' son was almost surely right in his calculation. When the Athenians gathered in the spring to elect a new board of *stratēgoí*, his friends and closest associates Theramenes son of Hagnon and Thrasybulus son of Lycus were not among those chosen, and it was almost certainly at this time that Cleophon son of Cleippides, who hated Alcibiades and who is said to have lodged formal charges against him, secured the exile of Alcibiades' old friend and benefactor Critias son of Callaeschrus. The financial resources afforded Lysander by Cyrus had enabled him to deprive the Athenians of their ablest commander and to relegate his exceptionally capable associates to the sidelines.[26]

Alcibiades had left Athens in the fall of 407 with more than one hundred galleys. But when Conon son of Timotheos was transferred from Andros, where he was overseeing a siege, to Samos in the spring, bringing with him twenty triremes to replace those lost at the battle of Notium, he found that he could man only seventy of the available ships—this despite the survival of nearly all of those who had crewed the boats destroyed or captured in that conflict. By this time, moreover, thanks to the intensive and ongoing work being done at Gytheion, Antandrus, Ephesus, and perhaps elsewhere as well, the Spartan fleet had burgeoned from a force of seventy triremes to an armada of one hundred forty. Demoralized by defeat, lured by the promise of higher pay distributed at regular intervals, and attracted by the prospect of a Peloponnesian victory, the mercenary oarsmen of the Athenian fleet had turned coat in droves and fled to Ephesus.[27] The intervention of Cyrus was the decisive event in the Ionian War.

LYSANDER'S LEGACY

In the course of his navarchy, Lysander had avoided unnecessary risks. He had dodged a direct confrontation with Alcibiades and his fleet—and by dint of patience, careful preparation, and cunning, he had achieved a tactical victory with strategic implications. His conduct of the war had been unimpeachable.[28]

By this time, however, if not well before, the Spartans had regularized the office of the navarch and had passed a law stipulating that the navarchy be held for only a year and that its occupant be barred from reelection. In principle, this made excellent sense. While he had all of the powers exercised by the kings on campaign, the navarch was not, as they were, accompanied by two ephors, and so he was not subject to the immediate oversight of any magistrates. In this war, Sparta's admiral sacrificed to the gods and consulted the victims; he commanded troops and delegated responsibilities; he regulated pay and disposed of booty; and he negotiated with Persia and arranged civic affairs in the Greek East. Responsible to the ephors, *gérontes*, and assembly in distant Lacedaemon and, if he was not encumbered with *súmbouloi*, to no one else, he held an office which Aristotle could term "almost another kingship." To the extent that he was free of oversight and dispensed patronage on a large scale to Lacedaemonians and foreigners alike, the navarch in a time of extensive warfare at sea was—but for the brevity of his term of office—a figure of greater stature than Lacedaemon's two kings.[29]

This was particularly true at the time of Sparta's third Attic war when what Lord Macaulay might well have described as a "noiseless" revolution began to take place. The "progress" of "noiseless revolutions" is, he writes,

rarely indicated by what historians are pleased to call important events. They are not achieved by armies, or enacted by
senates. They are sanctioned by no treaties, and recorded in no
archives. They are carried on in every school, in every church,
behind ten thousand counters, at ten thousand firesides. The
upper current of society presents no certain criterion by which
we can judge of the direction in which the under current flows.[30]

The "noiseless" revolution that took place in classical Lacedaemon
in the course of Sparta's third Attic war had its inception when the
experience of being abroad in positions of power and influence first
began to erode the self-restraint engendered in the average Spartiate
by the *agōgḗ* and the laws of his city.

The suppression of the private element in human life is, as its
chief modern proponent Jean-Jacques Rousseau once conceded, a
mutilation of human nature. It requires doing violence to the natural
impulses of men and can be sustained with rare exceptions only in a
highly controlled environment free of foreign influences. For this
reason, the Lacedaemonians barred strangers from Sparta via what
they called a *xenelasía*, prohibited *néoi* from journeying abroad
except on campaign, and allowed *presbúteroi* to do so only with the
express permission of the ephors.[31]

Sparta's enduring strategic rivalry with Athens required a departure from this regimen. Life in strange lands did nothing to temper
the antipathy for and contempt of foreigners bred in Spartans by the
exaggerated patriotism that their institutions tried to substitute for
the natural love of family. But it did liberate the Spartiate from the
sense of shame that restricted, contained, and moderated his secret
lust for wealth and for the pleasures which money could buy. The
peculiar combination of arrogance, avarice, and licentiousness that
characterized the Spartan abroad had been particularly evident in
Pausanias the Regent. In the wake of the Hellenic victory over the
Persians at Byzantium in 478, he took on Persian airs and began to
negotiate in private with the Great King, and he used his power to

gratify his most shameful appetites and treated the mariners from the allied cities with a measure of scorn and an insolence so intolerable that they broke openly with the Spartans, who had led them to victory against the hated Mede a short time before—and turned to Athens for help. According to Thucydides, the conduct of their regent so distressed the Lacedaemonians that, fearing that "those who went out would be corrupted" just as Pausanias had been, they accepted with relative equanimity the Athenian takeover of the Hellenic fleet and the hegemony at sea.[32]

On the eve of Thucydides' war between the Peloponnesians and the Athenians, the Athenian ambassadors at Sparta drew the attention of their hosts to those events then nearly half a century past, arguing,

If you were to overcome us and to take up an empire, you would swiftly lose all the goodwill which you have secured because of the fear we inspire—that is, if you hold to the pattern of conduct that you evidenced in the brief span when you were the leaders against the Mede. You have institutions, customs, and laws that do not mix well with those of others; and, in addition, when one of you goes abroad he follows neither his own customs and laws nor those employed in the rest of Hellas.

Subsequent history was to justify the warning.[33] In requiring the dispatch abroad of a host of Spartiates, Lacedaemon's third Attic war gave to many an unforgettable taste of the soft life for which Ionia was famous, increasing through familiarity the contempt in which they held strangers and unleashing, at the same time, their long-suppressed desires to share in the pleasures in which those strangers excelled.

This experience worked a predictable transformation of the Lacedaemonians, summoning into existence at Sparta a new class of men whom Xenophon described two or more decades thereafter, writing,

I am aware that in earlier times the Lacedaemonians chose to live with one another at home having modest possessions rather than to serve as harmosts in the cities and to court corruption by subjecting themselves to flattery. I am also aware that back then they feared it being discovered that they were in possession of gold while now there are those who actually make a display of its possession. To prevent this, I know, there were back then acts dictating the expulsion of foreigners [*xenelasíai*]; and to travel abroad was prohibited lest the citizens ingest *hrądiourgíai*—a slackness and sloth apt to eventuate in recklessness and crime. Now I know that those deemed first [*prôtoi*] among them are zealous that they never cease serving as harmosts in foreign parts. There was a time when they took care to be worthy of leadership. Now they exert themselves much more to exercise rule than to be worthy of doing so. Accordingly, while in former times the Hellenes would journey to Lacedaemon and ask her to lead them against those regarded as malefactors, many are now rallying with one another to prevent the Spartans from regaining dominion. There is no need to wonder why these censures are directed at them, since it is clear that they obey neither god nor the laws of Lycurgus.[34]

These men were the partisans of empire. In the waning years of Sparta's enduring conflict with Athens, when military necessity concentrated extraordinary power in the hands of the one man present in the theater of conflict, informed of every new turn in that great struggle, and empowered by law to direct affairs, the navarch was well-positioned to become the patron of the new class coming into existence—particularly if he was intent on making permanent the Spartan ascendancy that was emerging in the Greek East in the wake of Athens' decline.[35]

The only obstacle was the brevity of the navarch's tenure. This was, however, an obstacle as well to the intelligent management of the war effort. In Roman times, the need for consistent leadership in military struggles of lengthy duration and extraordinary difficulty drove the Senate to take the political risk of vesting in its ablest *imperatores* for extended periods the almost regal power of command and patronage associated with the proconsulship. The practice was to prove fatal to political liberty and to republican Rome's ruling order. It empowered overmighty subjects with a strength exceeding that of the senatorial *ordo* itself.[36] More cautious than their Roman counterparts, the Spartiates had up to this time quite consistently resolved the tension between the dictates of military necessity and those of political prudence in favor of the latter.

CALLICRATIDAS

Lysander's successor Callicratidas arrived on the scene in the spring of 406. The change in Spartan fortunes effected by Cyrus and Lysander seemed to have placed the new navarch in a position to end the war. He controlled a fleet twice the size of the Athenian force, manned by mariners flushed with victory and supported by the unbounded wealth of Persia. His opponents were demoralized, deprived of their ablest commander, and hard-pressed to pay the seamen they still had in their employ.[37]

Callicratidas was a younger man than Lysander. The dictates of the law notwithstanding, he may even have been a *néos*—a year or two under the age of forty-five. In one crucial particular, however, he resembled the son of Aristocritus. Like his predecessor, the new navarch was a *móthax*—yet another half-breed recruited into the ranks of the Spartiates thanks to the status of his father and the city's desperate need for manpower.[38]

Like Gylippus and Lysander, Callicratidas must have outdone his purebred contemporaries as he advanced through the various stages and tests of strength, endurance, courage, cunning, and aptitude for leadership that constituted the life of a young Spartiate; and he, too, is apt to have profited from the support of a patron. There is no explicit evidence linking him with the Agiad king Pleistoanax or with his son and successor Pausanias, but Callicratidas' conduct while navarch leaves no doubt whatsoever that he belonged to those at Sparta who questioned the wisdom of the crusade to deprive Athens of her empire. The coincidence between the policy he espoused and that which these two dyarchs successively pursued, when considered with regard to the tendency inherent in the Spartan constitution for there to be rivalry between the two royal houses, establishes a presumption in favor of such a link.

That, between the Agiads and the Eurypontids, there was such a contest both Herodotus and Aristotle assert. It is symptomatic of this situation that, in the fourth century, Lacedaemon's two royal houses appear to have had clients of differing political persuasion in each of the cities of the Peloponnesus.[39] If the leading men in those cities looked to the two kings for aid and comfort in their struggles against one another, the same is likely to have been true for the Spartiates at Lacedaemon. The two thrones were natural foci of power and influence. The character of the political and social organization of Lacedaemon strongly encouraged the political class to group itself into two factions around the two thrones. It is difficult to see where Callicratidas could have sought support if not from the Agiad house and those in its orbit.

This connection might serve to explain the hostility which Callicratidas incurred from the Spartans serving with the fleet. The men who remained in the eastern Aegean year after year were those most likely to have become infatuated with foreign ways, to have shed the unnatural moderation fostered among those who lived along the Eurotas, and to have emerged as the partisans of empire. It must have seemed to them intolerable to see the one naval commander of genius to have appeared in the Greek East replaced by a young and relatively inexperienced newcomer lacking in enthusiasm for the war itself. Moreover, the manner in which Xenophon describes the difficulty that this neophyte navarch faced and the linguistic terms he chose to deploy in describing this difficulty—*hupò tôn Lusándrou phílōn katastasiazómenos*—strongly suggests that "the friends of Lysander" formed a *stásis* or faction engaged in a conspiracy.[40]

These political ties could even account for the bitter exchange that occurred between the old and the new navarch when the former handed over the fleet to the latter, boasting that he was "master of the sea [*thalassokrátōr*] and victor in battle" and being told in reply that—if he was, indeed, the sea's master—he should demonstrate the fact by parading his fleet from Ephesus past the Athenian base at Samos and delivering the ships over to his successor at Miletus.[41]

Lysander's link with the Eurypontid house is, however, inadequate to explain his conduct just before his rival's arrival. The retiring navarch then acted in a manner justifying the gravest suspicions concerning his ultimate intentions—for, journeying to Sardis, he returned the unused remainder of the Persian money in his possession to Cyrus. At Ephesus, moreover, he is said to have called together the "most powerful men [*dunatótatoi*]" from the cities formerly subject to Athens and to have encouraged them to form *hetaireíai*—which is to say *sunōmosíai*—promising to make them sovereign in the various cities "if and when affairs have been set straight [*tôn pragmátōn katorthothéntōn*]."[42]

Neither deed was the work of a man who cared solely or even primarily for the victory of his city. Much more was at stake—and not merely the ascendancy of those at Sparta whose taste of rule in the Greek East had whetted their appetite for empire. Cyrus could not be certain of the military help he needed nor the conspirators of the eastern Aegean of the stable support they craved until and unless the dominion of a man was established at Sparta who would be as dependent on them as they on him. It is symptomatic of Lysander's purposes that he selected his partisans not with regard to birth or wealth, but with an eye to their influence in the cities and their loyalty to him. The "friends of Lysander" were not necessarily those whom we would be inclined to suppose the natural adherents of the Spartan cause.[43]

Soon after Lysander's departure, when Callicratidas learned that his predecessor's lieutenants were intriguing against him, he summoned them to a meeting in which he offered to return to Sparta to report on the situation in the Greek East if his subordinates thought it better that he ignore his instructions. The threat implicit in his remarks was not lost on these men. Xenophon reports that no one dared to suggest that he not carry out his orders. Given the pickle that Lysander had left him in, the new Spartan navarch had, at least for the time being, to ground his authority in fear.[44]

Callicratidas then departed for Sardis to secure money from Cyrus. There, he learned that the Persian prince was party to the conspiracy hatched by Lysander's Spartan friends—for the Great King's younger son treated the new Lacedaemonian commander with contempt and made him dance attendance at his gates. Rather than submit to a humiliating two-day delay at the Lydian capital and in all likelihood a refusal of support, Callicratidas withdrew in anger, openly observing that for Greeks to flatter barbarians for lucre was contemptible and publicly vowing that, if he returned home in safety, he would do everything within his power to reconcile the Lacedaemonians with the Athenians.[45]

After sending to Sparta for money, Callicratidas shifted his headquarters from Ephesus to Miletus. The former was, as we have seen, the Ionian city closest to Sardis, and it had long been the main center of Persian influence in the Greek East. The latter had been the scene of an ugly confrontation between Sparta's Persian and her native Greek allies in 411, as we also have had occasion to note.[46]

Contemporaries would not have mistaken the meaning of the move. The Persian connection did not command wholehearted support at Sparta. The repeated renegotiation of the treaty made in 412 by Tissaphernes and the harmost Chalcideus is evidence enough to indicate that the proponents of the war found the Persian alliance a military necessity in the Greek East, but a political embarrassment at home.[47] If Callicratidas could achieve victory without further Persian aid, the humiliating agreement, which committed Sparta to the subjection of the Greeks of Asia Minor to the Great King, could be abrogated in good faith. If, however, he was to accomplish this, he had to move quickly. He had a large fleet and no income stream.

At Miletus, when Lysander's partisans offered Callicratidas substantial financial help in return for aid in slaughtering their political foes, he indignantly refused. Instead, he turned to the popular assembly, told them of his treatment by Cyrus, reminded his listeners of their hatred of the Mede, and appealed with success for financial support from them. Even Lysander's friends then contributed. Like the Spartans supportive of Lysander who were serving in the fleet, they no doubt recognized that it was imprudent to offend a navarch so young, so forceful, and so energetic. An insurance policy could come in handy. The fleet that Callicratidas commanded was immense, and he might well be the man who brought the war to a successful conclusion.[48]

The navarch, who also received a subvention from the Chians, quickly set out against the fort at Delphinium on Chios from which the Athenians had done enormous damage to the estates of the wealthy citizens of that once prosperous isle; and, as soon as its members got a sense of the size of his armada, the garrison surrendered on terms of safe conduct and departed. Then, the Spartan navarch turned to the city of Teos on the Anatolian shore—where he managed to slip a force over the walls at night and to sack the town. It was at this point that Callicratidas focused his attention on the city of Methymna on the north coast of Lesbos, which the Athenians had also garrisoned. When the town was betrayed to him, he sacked it, allowing his soldiers to take as booty any property they found. Thereafter, to secure the money needed if he was to sustain the struggle, he sold into slavery what remained of the Athenian garrison. The pleas of his soldiers, who were eager to profit from the sale, he ignored; and, Xenophon adds, he refused to countenance the enslavement of the citizens of the town, vowing that while he was commander no such deed would be done. His last act at

Map 20. Callicratidas in the Environs of Lesbos

Methymna was to dispatch the Spartiate Thorax with the hoplites in his employ on a forced-march over the mountains to Mytilene on the island's east coast in the south.[49]

In the meantime, we are told by Diodorus, Conon had set out from Samos to come to Methymna's relief with the seventy ships he was able to man. With him, no doubt, were Leon, Archestratus, and Erasinides, who are mentioned as his colleagues by Xenophon. When, however, these commanders got word that the city had fallen, they paused for the night at one of the tiny Hekatonnesoi islands, which are scattered along the Anatolian shore opposite the northeasternmost point on the island of Lesbos. It was presumably there

that Conon received from Callicratidas the pungent message mentioned by Xenophon in which the Spartan commander resorted to a
domestic metaphor, insinuating that Sparta's hegemony over the sea
resembled the patriarchal rule of a male head of a household over his
womenfolk and boasting that he would put a stop to the Athenian
commander's engaging in *moicheía*—debauchery—with the element
that was now properly under Lacedaemon's protection and control.[50]

To make good on this boast, Callicratidas appeared at dawn on
the horizon to the west with a force twice the size of the fleet commanded by his Athenian counterpart. His purpose, Xenophon
reports, was to situate at least part of his armada between the Athenians and Samos so that they could not flee unopposed back to their
well-fortified base on that isle. In response, Conon set out straightaway southward between Lesbos and the Anatolian coast in the
direction of Samos as if to escape the trap before it was fully in place.
But he had his galleys conduct their retreat in a leisurely manner.
According to Diodorus, whose detailed account almost certainly
derives directly or indirectly from the story told by the Oxyrhynchus
historian, Timotheos' son was convinced that, if his Athenians got
into trouble, they could find refuge in one of the harbors at Mytilene
opposite the Anatolian shore. It was his hope that Callicratidas, in an
attempt to catch up with and then engulf the Athenian fleet, would
exhaust his oarsmen and that the Lacedaemonian's forces would fall
into disorder in the course of the chase so that he could suddenly
have the Athenian galleys put about and wreak havoc with the finest
ships and crews in his opponent's fleet—those that were in the lead.

Initially, Conon's stratagem worked as intended. Some of the
enemy triremes out front the Athenian's galleys rammed and holed.
In the case of others, they performed a *diékplous* and in the process,
we are told, sheared off the oars of an enemy galley as its rowers desperately backed water. Moreover, those of Conon's colleagues who
were assigned the Athenian left wing had their galleys set off in pursuit of the triremes that had fled. When the stragglers in the Spartan
fleet finally caught up, Conon conducted the forty ships under his

immediate command into the northern harbor at Mytilene as planned. The *stratēgoí* in charge of the thirty Athenian galleys originally situated on the left soon found that they had miscalculated and that their vessels were now cut off from this refuge—and so, in desperation, they ran their ships ashore. The crews from these vessels then fled on foot to the town.[51]

Callicratidas had much to celebrate. Thanks to an Athenian maneuver gone wrong, he had managed to eliminate almost half of the vessels in the Athenian fleet, and he had at the same time increased the number of triremes at his own disposal from one hundred forty to one hundred seventy. But Sparta's navarch did not pause for long to savor his victory—for, as he knew, there was more that could be done. So, Callicratidas landed additional footsoldiers on Lesbos and established a camp, where Thorax no doubt joined him. Then, after setting up a trophy in honor of his victory, he prepared to initiate a siege.

Ancient Mytilene resembled ancient Syracusa in two important particulars: the original settlement was situated on a small island just off the coast, and the town possessed two harbors joined by a channel—with one port situated outside the walls and the other within. To the north of the town lay a large bay. Today, it is not much used. But the remains of two moles, stretching out from the shore on either side of its wide entrance, testify to the importance it once had—as do the remains along its western shore of an ancient stoa and of the emporia within it that once catered to those who came down to the port to shop. In antiquity and for a long time thereafter, moles of this sort made of this bay a great harbor sheltered from storms and even, to some degree, from enemy attack. To the south, there was a smaller anchorage, which served as the city's military harbor. It was for this reason that it was enclosed within the town's fortifications. As at Syracusa, it was the channel linking the two harbors that separated the old city, which was located on the little island, from its extension onshore.[52]

Upon arrival, Conon sized up the situation and did what he could to block entry to the northern harbor. Where there was shallow water, he sank small boats loaded down with stones. Where the water was deeper and the harbor was open to the sea, he anchored large merchantmen loaded with boulders of great weight. On the merchantmen, on the breakwaters, and on a set of triremes that he stationed between the merchantmen at the harbor's entrance, he posted infantrymen. His aim with these triremes was to prevent enemy vessels from rowing into the harbor through the gaps between the merchantmen. The infantry-men on the breakwaters were tasked with preventing a landing. Those on the triremes were to fight off boarding parties, and those on the mer-chantmen were to suspend great blocks of stone from the yardarms so that they could be dropped, like the dolphins used by the Athenians at Syracusa, on vessels attempting to enter the bay.

For his part, Callicratidas led out the best of his triremes with an eye to smashing his way through into the harbor. What followed was infantry warfare on shipboard reminiscent of the final battle in 413 in the Great Harbor at Syracusa—with Callicratidas' triremes crashing into the galleys of the Athenians and his hoplites attempting to board and seize these vessels while the Athenians and their Mytilen-ian allies gallantly defended the galleys on which they were posted. The number of those who lost their lives was, Diodorus reports, considerable; and we have reason to believe that Conon's colleague Archestratus was among them. The archers and javelineers on the decks of the triremes exacted a heavy toll. Ship after ship fell prey to the great stones released from the yardarms of the merchantmen, and the marines on the galleys fought long and hard.

In time, Callicratidas called off the attack to provide his men with a respite. Then, he renewed the effort. His marines were, as it turned out, superior to their rivals in stamina and endurance. Moreover, he had more ships to throw into the fray; and so, in time, he wore down and overwhelmed the Athenians—who withdrew through the nar-row channel to the smaller harbor in the south with the triremes that remained at their disposal. The siege of Mytilene had begun in earnest.[53]

By this time, we can be confident that at least some of Lysander's erstwhile partisans had begun to regard Callicratidas with respect and to evidence a grudging admiration. It is telling that, at this point, Cyrus dispatched to Callicratidas the funds promised by the Great King and sent a personal gift signifying an offer of *xenía*. It was a belated and awkward attempt to change horses in midstream, and it was of no avail. The navarch received the money. In the circumstances, he had no choice. He was desperately short of funds, and the authorities back home would have been understandably furious had he spurned Persian support. But, in a manner that amounted to an affront, he rejected the personal gift on offer from the *káranos*, coldly replying that the public alliance existing between Persia and Sparta would suffice. Cyrus' quest to convert the friendship between the two polities into a private relationship of guest-friendship apt to secure him the aid he needed in his pursuit of the Persian crown seemed bound to fail.[54] It took an Athenian victory to restore his hopes.

THE TEST AT ARGINUSAE

The blockade initiated by Callicratidas had two purposes. One was obvious: no one was to smuggle anything into Mytilene. Otherwise, near-starvation and surrender would be indefinitely delayed. The other was no less obvious—but only if one paused to think about it. Callicratidas did not want anyone to leave Mytilene—especially, on board ship. As he was well aware, news of Conon's plight was apt to induce the Athenians to dispatch a relief expedition—and, then, everything would once again be up for grabs.

In time, the news of Conon's predicament did get out. The Athenian commander was, for obvious reasons, desperate, and he was a resourceful man. So, he devised a stratagem. For four days straight, Xenophon reports, he manned two triremes, the speediest in the fleet, with the best oarsmen in his employ and sent them out from dawn to dark to patrol the southern harbor with the marines on board concealed below deck and behind the side screens designed to protect the *thranítai* from projectiles. His purpose was to get the blockaders outside the harbor used to their presence.

On the fifth day, Conon loaded on food as well and instructed their officers and their crews to burst forth from the harbor and head for Athens and to do so at midday when the blockaders were apt to be nodding off in the heat or to be busy consuming the main meal of the day. One galley, which appears to have been commanded by Conon's fellow *stratēgós* Leon, may have been intended as a decoy. It was surely the first to leave—for, when it emerged from the harbor, sped south from Mytilene, then out to the open sea, the crews in the squadron responsible for the blockade did what one would predict: they roused themselves from their stupor, cut their anchors, and gave chase. At sunset, we are told, they finally caught up with and captured the vessel and those who manned it. It is this that explains why there is no further mention of Leon until after the war.

The second galley, which was almost certainly commanded by Conon's other surviving colleague Erasinides, seems, after a brief interval, to have followed suit. Once out of the harbor, however, it headed north, then west along Lesbos' northern shore in the direction of the Hellespont. Moreover, it got away—perhaps to the open sea, or to Elaeus in the Thracian Chersonnesus or to Imbros or Lemnos where there were Athenian cleruchies. There is no indication of pursuit. In the end, no doubt in accord with Conon's expectations, it was this messenger ship that managed to convey word to the Athenians.[55]

The Athenians may also have received further news from another source. Xenophon mentions in passing that, with a dozen triremes, Diomedon came to Mytilene to support his beleaguered compatriots; that Callicratidas caught him off guard at the northern end of the channel that separated the original settlement from its extension on the larger island and captured ten of these ships; and that Diomedon's galley and one other managed to escape. It is a reasonable guess that Diomedon, who had been elected a *stratēgós* in the spring of 406, had been among those left in charge at Samos when Conon and his colleagues set out for Methymna and that, when he heard nothing whatsoever about the fate of the Athenian fleet, he feared the worst and set out with his squadron to investigate and provide aid if aid was required. Had he had any idea of his compatriots' plight, he surely would not have pitted his flotilla against Callicratidas' armada. In any case, after his escape, he, too, is sure to have sent a message to his compatriots back home.[56]

When, in the summer of 406, they got word concerning the situation at Mytilene, the Athenians voted to dispatch a relief force; and, in the course of thirty days, they managed to scrape together a ragtag fleet and to put out to sea, we must imagine, with every ship in their dockyard that would float. That they had vessels to spare was due to the fact that late in the summer of 407—when the Athenians had first learned of the Great King's decision to back the Lacedaemonians to the hilt and to dispatch his younger son to see to their victory— they had begun melting down golden dedications from their temples and minting gold coins to pay for a crash campaign to build new triremes. Such an effort, which involved the importation of lumber on a considerable scale, cannot have been kept secret—and what of significance became known at Lacedaemon was no doubt conveyed in due course to the city's navarch in the Greek East.[57]

The galleys that the Athenians dispatched they manned, as they had manned the fleet they had deployed against the Persians at Salamis nearly three-quarters of a century before, by calling up everyone at Athens of an appropriate age—citizens, metics, and slaves— including the wealthy citizens who ordinarily served in the cavalry. To the metics and the other foreigners who volunteered they offered citizenship. To the slaves who came forward, they offered not only freedom but political rights of the sort that had been conferred on Athens' Plataean allies in 427 when their city was destroyed. This they no doubt had to do if they did not want this last class of rowers to desert to the Spartan side.[58]

Xenophon—who was almost certainly in Athens at this time and who, as a young cavalryman, is apt to have been among those called up for service with the fleet—tells us that his compatriots managed to send one hundred ten triremes to Samos on this occasion, that from the Samians they requisitioned ten more galleys, and that they extracted another thirty from their allies. Diodorus, who may well be following the Oxyrhynchus historian, reports that the Athenians fitted out sixty triremes; that, at Samos, the *stratēgoí* in command had managed to gather an additional eighty galleys; and that the Samians provided ten more.

These numbers give one pause—for it is hard to believe that the Athenians could have come up with one hundred ten triremes on short notice, and it is no less hard to fathom how the military commanders on Samos could have collected eighty galleys in Ionia. On this subject, there are, however, two things that one can say. First, Xenophon and Diodorus are in agreement on one matter—that the fleet that set out from Samos to Mytilene numbered one hundred fifty triremes—and, second, Xenophon's outlandish claim or that of Diodorus just might be true. If so, the Athenians' ability to deploy so large a fleet on short notice is an indication of the success of the crash program of trireme production that they had launched the year before when they melted down the dedications in their temples and minted gold coins.[59]

As was the norm, there were ten men on the Athenian board of *stratēgoí* at this time. Conon was preoccupied at Mytilene, and Leon appears to have been in the custody of the Lacedaemonians. But Diomedon, Pericles son of Pericles, Aristocrates son of Scellias, Erasinides, Protomachus, Thrasyllus, Aristogenes, and Lysias (who had apparently been chosen to replace Archestratus after the Athenians learned of his demise) were available, and every last one of them was dispatched. It was this group of eight men that conducted the Athenian armada northward from Samos along the Anatolian coast. When they neared their goal, they stopped at the Arginusae isles, which lie just off the mainland of Asia Minor opposite Cape Malea, the southeasternmost point on the island of Lesbos.

At his behest, Callicratidas now had, we are told, one hundred seventy triremes—what remained of his original fleet of one hundred forty galleys after the two battles at sea that had taken place near Mytilene plus the thirty vessels that the Athenians had been forced to abandon at the end of the first of these battles, the ten subsequently captured from Diomedon, and perhaps some brand new triremes produced nearby at Antandrus in the interim. To keep Conon bottled up and to prevent the thirty or so galleys still at his disposal from venturing forth and entering the fray, the Spartan navarch left fifty triremes at Mytilene under the command of Eteonicus. The remaining one hundred twenty he stationed at Cape Malea.

The Athenian fleet located on the opposite shore was larger, and this was an advantage. But the force deployed by the Lacedaemonians was more fully combat-ready. It was manned by seasoned mariners, and the crews of most of the individual ships had been operating together for some time. Moreover, many of these men had fought at Notium, and nearly all of the rest had experienced naval warfare in the two battles that took place in the vicinity of Mytilene. They knew what was required.

By way of contrast, a high proportion of the Athenian crewmembers were landlubbers who had never served at sea. What these novices had going for them, however, was determination. They were—or soon would be—citizens of one sort or another, and for them Athens' freedom and the advantages attendant on empire were at stake. They were not mercenaries like many of the men who rowed in Callicratidas' fleet. They were not inclined to prefer life and lucre to the liberty of their native land.

There are three Arginusae isles. One is a tiny speck that does not concern us here. The other two—called Garipasi and Kalemadasi—are fat fingers, parallel to one another, that stretch out from south to north just off the Anatolian coast. The Athenians camped on the former—which lay to the west of its twin. From there, when it was clear, they could see across the nine-mile-wide strait and be seen from the other side.

For a time, thanks to the Etesian winds that blow in the summer with great frequency from the north-northeast, the crews of these two fleets remained at rest, eyeing one another warily across the divide. In the middle of the night, when the wind tended to die down, Callicratidas made an attempt to put out to sea in the hope that he might descend on the Athenians at the break of dawn and catch them flat-footed. But, we are told, heavy rain and thunder put a stop to this enterprise. It was not until the morning of the second day that the two fleets had at it.

Unless the Athenian assembly stipulated otherwise, as it had when Alcibiades was made *hapántōn hēgemòn autokrátōr*, Athens' military commanders operated by consensus. Inevitably, however, one or two tended to take the lead and the others to defer; and, on this occasion, the man who took charge was, we have reason to believe, Thrasyllus. He was certainly the most experienced *stratēgós* of the lot, and he had been among the commanders in the two great trireme battles that had taken place in the Hellespont. Moreover, when there were as many *stratēgoí* on the scene as there were on this occasion, they tended to take turns at the helm—and as it happened, on the day of battle, it was Thrasyllus' turn to preside.

Although the fleet under Thrasyllus' command was the larger of the two, it was operating at an even greater disadvantage than we have thus far noted. Many of the triremes deployed by Athens are apt to have been superannuated. Others were no doubt in poor repair, and a goodly number will not have been properly dried out in some time and will not have recently had their hulls scraped, recaulked, and recoated with pitch. Moreover, as we have seen, they sported rag-tag crews unpracticed in what was a cooperative endeavor requiring considerable skill and close coordination. In consequence, these vessels were, for the most part, slow and awkward while the triremes facing them were quick and agile. The Athenians did not outclass their opponents, and they could not hope to outmaneuver them. To defeat the allied fleet, they had to outwit its commander.

Thrasyllus' record as a *stratēgós* was, as we have seen, undistinguished. He appears, however, to have been a man who learned from

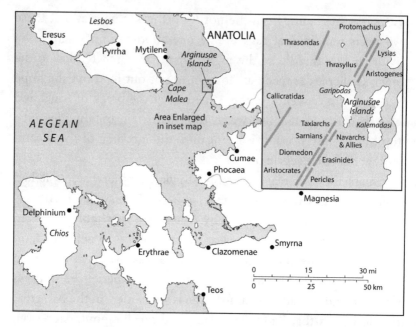

Map 21. The Battle of Arginusae, 406

experience. At Arginusae, he more than made up for his earlier bungling. On this occasion, when under his direction, Athens' *stratēgoí* deployed their ships in line abreast, they did so in two lines—one behind the other. This well-known stratagem rendered it difficult, if not impossible, for the opposing helmsmen to resort to the *diékplous*—whether it was their purpose in gliding by an enemy trireme to shear off the oars on its starboard or port side; to perform, after slipping past it, an *anastrophḗ* and, having swung around, to strike the enemy trireme in the hull or stern; or to attempt both in that order. Any ship that passed through the first of the two lines of triremes would quickly find itself beset by the galleys in the second rank.

This decision eliminated one source of danger for the Athenians but at the price of giving rise to another no less dire. It meant that— if Callicratidas had his triremes deploy in line abreast in a single line, as any naval commander in his situation would be apt to do—his fleet would outflank that of the Athenians and be in a position to engulf it and to strike it from one or both flanks. Indeed, if circumstances were propitious, it might even be able to do so from behind. To prevent this, the Athenian commanders, who were well versed in the principles of hoplite warfare, did something unprecedented. Their situation was desperate. They knew that, if the battle took place in the open sea, they would be defeated, that their fleet would in all likelihood be destroyed, and that they would lose the war, their empire, and, quite possibly, their city, their families, and their lives. So, they refused to fight on unfavorable terms. Instead, according to Diodorus, they adopted a tactic that, we know, was familiar to every infantry general and they adapted it to the maritime situation in which they found themselves.

Their fleet, no doubt at Thrasyllus' urging, the Athenian *stratēgoí* divided into two units, and they held both back from the wide channel separating the Arginusae isles from Lesbos in such a way as to include Garipasi in their battle line. In consequence, this island and the peninsula that juts out from the mainland to its north covered both flanks of the Athenians' right wing while it afforded comparable protection to their left wing on its right. In principle, of course,

**Figure 7.1. Modern Representation of Triremes
in Two Lines Abreast**
(An EDSITEment-reconstructed Greek fleet of galleys based on sources from The Perseus Project. This work is in the public domain in the United States because it is a work prepared by an officer or employee of the United States Government as part of that person's official duties under the terms of Title 17, Chapter 1, Section 105 of the US Code.) .

Callicratidas could have dispatched a unit to circle around the islands from the south and come at the Athenians from behind, but the shallowness of the waters separating Garipasi from Kalemadasi and of those separating the latter from Anatolia to the east ruled this out.

The Athenian commanders' arrangement of their ships forced Callicratidas to divide his fleet in two—for otherwise his force would have been outflanked on one side or the other. But this configuration carried with it grave difficulties. It left the Spartan navarch with four flanks exposed—none of them in any way protected by a body of land. It is no wonder that his helmsman—a Megarian named Hermon—urged him to refuse battle against a force larger than his own, and he was a fool not to heed the advice offered by that old salt.

Callicratidas had leverage. He could afford to delay. He had Conon, his crews, and the triremes still at the latter's disposition in a tight vise. Time was on his side. Absent relief, the Athenians at Mytilene would sooner or later have to surrender. There was no need for the Spartan navarch to seek an engagement. It was the Athenians who were under pressure. They had to draw the enemy fleet into an armed conflict and win, and they had to do it soon.

The Spartan navarch was, for this reason, in a position to set the terms on which the two sides would fight. What was required on his part was the quality displayed by Miltiades and the other Athenian *stratēgoí* at Marathon, by Pausanias the Regent at Plataea, and by Lysander at Notium—patience, the willingness to wait until circumstances were favorable. Callicratidas was, however, an impetuous young man ... in too much of a hurry.[60]

What followed, as Diodorus is quick to point out, was the greatest sea battle hitherto known to the Greek world. Unfortunately, neither Xenophon nor Diodorus provides a full account. But what they do have to say can for the most part be reconciled; and, on that basis, one can reconstruct what is apt to have happened.

Xenophon makes no mention of the Athenian commanders' deployment of their galleys on either side of Garipasi. But his description of their disposition of the vessels at their disposal is consistent with what we can glean from Diodorus' account. Between Garipasi and the mainland spur to its north, the span of water is restricted. To the south of this cigar-shaped island, there is open water. One would therefore expect that fewer triremes would be assigned to the Athenian right than to the Athenian fleet's other wing, and this is consistent with what Xenophon reports. The left and the center of that fleet Xenophon treats together, apparently as a single unit; and there he situates ninety triremes. The Athenian right he treats separately, as a distinct unit consisting of sixty triremes.

The two writers are also in agreement on one matter—that Callicratidas commanded the Spartan right—and, given Diodorus' description of the configuration of the Athenian forces, that is where one would expect to find the Spartan commander. For the positioning of the Athenian galleys was favorable to there being little fighting in the north. The Athenian triremes there could not advance without making themselves vulnerable to an outflanking maneuver, the triremes in the opposing fleet were in no position to mount a frontal assault, and the Spartans and their allies in this unit could not turn their attention to the Athenian unit to the south of Garipasi without rendering themselves liable to a flank attack or to an assault from behind on the part of the Athenian unit to the island's north. They were, in effect, locked in place—which is no doubt what the Athenian *stratēgoí* intended. It was in the south, where these commanders had stationed three-fifths of their fleet and where Callicratidas had situated himself, that the two fleets would be apt to clash.

The two writers are at odds on another matter, however. Xenophon reports that it was the Spartan left, in the north, that collapsed in the face of the Athenian onslaught while Diodorus reports that it was in the south, after a long struggle, that the Athenians won out and that, in the north, the Boeotians and the Euboeans held out until the victorious Athenians from the south turned on them and forced them to flee.

It is the latter narrative, which is probably derivative ultimately from the Oxyrhynchus historian, that makes sense. In the north, as we have seen, a stalemate was virtually inevitable—while, in the south, a clash was unavoidable. It is telling that Callicratidas was himself among those who lost their lives and that he reportedly did so when the trireme bearing him rammed an Athenian galley and he was either badly wounded in the melee that followed, as Diodorus reports, or hurled overboard at the moment of impact, as Xenophon claims. It is also telling that the Athenians destroyed or captured nine of the fleet's ten Laconian triremes, which surely accompanied the navarch. In the course of the day, Lacedaemon's allies lost another sixty to seventy triremes while the Athenians lost only twenty-five.[61]

Had a storm not blown up, the better part of what remained of the Athenian fleet would have descended on Mytilene and taken on the fifty triremes stationed there under the command of Eteonicus. As it happened, however, there was such a storm, and it was exceedingly violent. In consequence, the Athenians had to take shelter once again on Garipasi. In the meantime, a dispatch boat [kélēs], a small galley designed for speed, had raced up the Lesbian coast from Cape Malea to Mytilene to bring word of Callicratidas' defeat to Eteonicus, who managed to prevent a panic by persuading his crews that their navarch had, in fact, won. Then, no doubt as soon as the tempest began to abate, he dispatched the fifty triremes under his command—either southwards under the cover of night or northwards, then westward past Methymna and out to the open sea—from Lesbos to Chios, where some the triremes caught up in the battle had found refuge and where those which had fled to Aeolian Cumae and Phocaea or had been blown there by the storm eventually fetched up. Before returning to Chios himself, he took command of the hoplites stationed outside Mytilene and conducted them overland either to Methymna, as Xenophon claims, or to Pyrrha, as Diodorus reports. For their part, when the storm passed and the Spartan fleet withdrew from Mytilene, Conon and what remained of his fleet sallied forth to join the main Athenian force, and the Athenians paid a brief visit to Chios and, having accomplished nothing, withdrew to their stronghold on Samos.[62]

It is difficult, if not impossible, to achieve certitude concerning the consequences a Spartan victory at Arginusae would have had for postwar Lacedaemonian foreign policy. It is not often that a man unsympathetic to a particular war and the goals of its most ardent proponents leads his fellow citizens to victory in that very war. There is every reason to suppose that Callicratidas would have been loath to leave the Greeks of the eastern Aegean in Persian hands, but their defense would have required a policy decision long regarded as unthinkable by those who had been eager to reconcile the Lacedae-monians and the Athenians: the Spartans would have had to commit themselves to filling the vacuum left by Athens' demise.

In 478, the sentiment of Panhellenism and the fear of foreign contamination had helped allay the disgruntlement caused at Lace-daemon by her replacement by Athens as leader of the naval forces of the Hellenic League. In 406, when nearly six decades of intermit-tent strife had left the Spartiates bitterly hostile to the Athenians, it is inconceivable that anyone—even Callicratidas—would have dared to suggest a restoration of the Delian League as a counterpoise to the might of Persia. The victory would have posed a very painful dilemma for the heirs of those who had once vigorously defended Peloponnesian isolationism—whether to abandon the policy their predecessors had deemed essential for the preservation of the Spar-tan way of life and the city's long-term security, or to ignore the dic-tates of the Panhellenism born in the Persian War and long used by them to justify Athens' empire to their fellow Spartiates.

It is hard to say what Callicratidas or his friends would have done—and even harder to determine whether a victory at Arginusae would have given the defenders of tradition the political leverage they needed to counteract the influence of the partisans of empire bred by long experience in an overseas war. What might have been is an abstraction remaining a possibility only in a world of speculation. What did happen is easier to determine.

In the event, if Aristotle is to be trusted, Callicratidas' defeat set the stage for a renewed attempt at Lacedaemon, no doubt spear-headed by those who had been the young navarch's champions, to effect a reconciliation between the Athenians and the Spartans. We do not know who was dispatched to present the Lacedaemonian offer. It is perfectly conceivable that Endius son of Alcibiades was sent once again in company with his erstwhile colleagues Philocha-ridas son of Eryxilaidas and Megillus. But it is no less likely that the Spartan authorities thought it prudent in the circumstances to dis-pense with the services of the Athenian Alcibiades' *xénos*. In any case, on paper, the terms on offer were virtually identical to those in the proposal they had presented in the wake of the battle of Cyzicus.

There were, however, material differences. The Spartans still held Deceleia, but the Athenians had in the interim lost both Pylos and Nisaea. So, the only withdrawal in the offing would be on the part of the Lacedaemonians. Even more important, given the stipulation that the two parties to the peace would retain the territories that they controlled at the time in which the peace was agreed upon, the Athenians were now much better situated than they had been four years before.

Thanks to the efforts of Thrasybulus and Theramenes, they now controlled Thasos, Neapolis, Abdera, and, one must suspect, a good many other cities in Thrace. They had, as we have had occasion to note, recovered all of the cities in the Propontis and the Bosporus—including Byzantium and Chalcedon; and they exercised dominion over all of the *póleis* along both shores of the Hellespont, apart from Abydos. The city's lifeline to Athens' breadbasket in the Crimea was in their possession, and they were once again in a position to regu-late the flow of commerce between the Black Sea and the Mediterra-nean and to impose a tax upon it.

It is true that the Athenians had lost Euboea. Much of Ionia— Chios, Ephesus, Miletus, parts of Lesbos, and, in all likelihood, Aeolian Cumae, Phocaea, Kos, and Rhodes—was also in the hands of their foe, and there were no doubt a number of islands in the Cyclades that were at this stage aligned with Lacedaemon. If Andros was still among them, that, too, mattered—for the ships that brought to Athens the grain produced in the Crimea ordinarily rode the current that issued from the Hellespont and made its way past Imbros, then Lemnos, to Scyros, and on through the Doros channel between Euboea and Andros. Then, these vessels made their way around Cape Sunium and entered the Saronic Gulf. If a hostile power were to control Andros and the port of Carystus at Geraistos in southeastern Euboea just across the Doros channel, it could, with a handful of triremes, make considerable trouble for the Athenians.

Militarily, the Athenians were in a much weaker position in 406 than they had been in the wake of Cyzicus. In that earlier battle, they had destroyed the entire Lacedaemonian fleet. In this one, they had eliminated, at most, seventy-seven of the one hundred seventy Spartan triremes. At the time of their victory at Cyzicus, there was still hope that they could somehow lure the Great King into an arrangement favorable to their well-being. In 406, that pipe dream could no longer be entertained. The enemy triremes the Athenians had destroyed could and almost certainly would be quickly replaced— now that the King's younger son was present and willing to pay the cost and that a host of precision carpenters had gradually been mobilized in the wake of that earlier debacle and were on hand to do the necessary at Gytheion, Antandrus, Ephesus, and no doubt elsewhere as well. Moreover, the Spartans would have no trouble finding oarsmen and specialists to crew their ships. They had the money with which to pay them a wage that the Athenians could not hope to match.

There were other considerations as well. As we have seen, it is not likely that, if the Athenians observed the terms of the peace, the Spartans would hold onto the cities that, at this time, they controlled. The Lacedaemonians seeking peace were homebodies, not imperialists. Absent Persian support, Sparta would not be able to deploy a fleet of any size unless she collected *phóros* from the cities at this point allied with her. This, absent a lust for dominion and a conviction that nothing at home would ever go amiss, the Lacedaemonians are not apt to have done—not, at least, for any great stretch of time; and, had they done so, it would have sparked resentment and, in time, rebellion. In short, if the Athenians attended to the character of the Spartan regime and were prepared to be patient, the neglect or misconduct of the Lacedaemonians and the reinvigorated Persian threat would in all likelihood induce the cities they had lost to drift in their direction.

All in all, then, the offer presented to the Athenians late in the summer of 406 was much more attractive than the one they had considered four years before. Accepting the terms proposed on that occasion would have been a much greater risk than accepting the terms on offer at this time. In 406, it was a grave error to send the Spartan embassy back home empty-handed.

But, as we have seen, this was the sort of error to which the Athenians were especially prone. The Corinthians understood them very well. The Athenian *politeía* was what Sir Halford Mackinder would later call a "going concern." Its "character" was "fixed," and the community governed in accord with that character was "incapable of any great change in its mode of existence." Athens was still a city of salarymen eager for the pay that the *phóros* collected from a great empire made possible. Her citizens were still in the grips of the mad lust for grandeur that their achievements at Marathon, Salamis, Mycale, Eurymedon, Cypriot Salamis, and elsewhere had inspired and that Pericles had so vigorously stoked. Moreover, the victory at Arginusae, incomplete though it was, had so buoyed Athenian hopes that the demagogue Cleophon was able to convince the assembly once again to spurn the terms proposed.[63]

The Athenian assembly's rejection of the Spartan peace offer prepared the way for Lysander's recall. At the end of the winter following Arginusae, representatives from the allied cities in the Greek

East convened at Ephesus and voted to dispatch a deputation to Sparta to request that she send out again the naval commander victorious at Notium. Cyrus dispatched an emissary to echo their plea. The Lacedaemonians, mindful of their dependence on the goodwill of their Persian paymaster, responded by naming Aracus navarch while sending out Lysander as *epistoleús* to stand at his side and guide his every move.[64]

This legal fiction could not hide the facts: the Spartans had sacrificed political prudence to military necessity. Cyrus had found his second Pausanias; and, although next to no one at this point recognized the fact, Lysander was no longer the servant of the *dunatoí* and of their leader the Eurypontid king.

CHAPTER EIGHT

From Arginusae to
Aegospotami

I say, then, that the easiest way to cause a republic where the people has authority to come to ruin is to set it to mighty enterprises, since, where the people is of any importance, these enterprises are always undertaken; nor will there be any remedy for whoever is of another opinion. But if from this the city's ruin comes about, there comes about as well, and with greater frequency, the particular ruin of the citizens assigned such enterprises, for since the people had taken victory for granted, when loss comes it is blamed neither on ill-fortune nor on the impotence of the one who has governed but on his wickedness and ignorance; and most often the loss eventuates in his being killed, imprisoned, or confined, as happened ... to many Athenians.

NICCOLÒ MACHIAVELLI

WHEN LYSANDER son of Aristocritus returned to Ionia late in the winter of 406/5 with thirty-five more triremes in tow, reestablished his headquarters at Ephesus, and summoned Eteonicus and the remainder of Callicratidas' fleet from Chios, he faced a grave difficulty. In the wake of the debacle at Arginusae, the surviving Spartan leaders had run out of cash.

For a time, out of desperation, the mariners who had served with the fleet and the hoplites whom the Lacedaemonians had stationed on Chios had found employment as agricultural laborers on the island doing the farm work previously reserved for the Chians' slaves. But when the warm months came to an end and the work dried up, these men lacked the wherewithal with which to purchase clothing and footwear—and the prospect of starvation loomed. At this point, there was not just grumbling. There was talk of mutiny, and there were plans afoot to mount an attack on the town of Chios.

Eteonicus, when he learned of the conspiracy, managed by an adroit maneuver to scotch it and restore discipline. But this was, he knew, a temporary expedient. Most of these men were mercenaries. If he could not provide for them, he could not retain their loyalty— not, at least, for long. So, he turned to the Chians and persuaded them to pony up—and, from the proceeds, he then paid each man a month's wages. It was this crisis and the prospect that their city would be sacked that induced the citizens of Chios to join in the appeal for Lysander's return.[1]

In response to the situation he encountered upon arrival, the son of Aristocritus did what everyone hoped for and expected. He departed for Sardis forthwith to pay Cyrus a brief visit and to obtain the money required. The Persian prince informed him that the five hundred talents of silver sent by his father Darius had been spent. Then, as he had promised, he drew on his own resources to provide for the Peloponnesian forces. For a time, Lysander busied himself at Ephesus and saw to the construction of additional ships at Antandrus.[2]

In the meantime, Cyrus received a message from his father requesting that he come to Thamneria in Media where the aging monarch had gone to suppress a revolt of the Cadusians. Cyrus' execution of his cousins had been a grave blunder. It is improbable that Parysatis' purpose in sending her second son to Sardis had escaped the notice of Stateira and Tissaphernes, but it had been folly—the particular kind of folly to which an ambitious and headstrong adolescent is especially prone—for Cyrus to advertise his intentions.

Prior to the young prince's arrival on the scene, Hieramenes had had some sort of responsibility in Anatolia—perhaps merely as an emissary from the King, perhaps as a satrap in Lycia or Cappadocia or elsewhere in the interior of that subcontinent. There is much that we do not know. It is, however, telling that, in 411, when Hieramenes first becomes visible, he is present for the negotiations between Tissaphernes and the Spartan *súmboulo*ı at Caunus and that he then reappears at Magnesia on the Maeander alongside Tissaphernes and the sons of Pharnaces as a signatory to the agreement forged in that coastal city. His sons were no doubt tasked with keeping an eye on their ambitious cousin, and they may well have taken pains to make life difficult for the young man. They may even have made themselves an obstacle to Cyrus' exercise of the extensive authority conferred on him—an obstacle which it was essential for him to eliminate. But for him to murder the two men and to do so in the circumstances in which he did so was to play into the hands of his enemies.

The Great King was ill and not likely to live much longer, and the murder—coupled with Cyrus' inability to disguise his royal pretensions—induced Hieramenes and his wife to prevail upon her brother the younger Darius to use his own illness as an excuse to remove Parysatis' favorite from the command of the Persian forces in Anatolia. It can hardly be an accident that Arsaces' in-law and ally Tissaphernes chose to accompany Cyrus on his journey to Media. The throne was at stake, and a misstep might well be fatal for the well-placed descendants of the first Darius' co-conspirator Hydarnes.[3]

Before his departure, Cyrus took appropriate countermeasures. He summoned Lysander again to Sardis and placed him in charge of Lydia, Greater Phrygia, and Cappadocia. He assigned to him his surplus funds, he granted him the tribute owed by the cities in his province, and he promised to return with a host of ships from Phoenicia and Cilicia and begged him in the meantime not to risk his own fleet in battle. Before they parted, he pointedly reminded Aristocritus' son of the debt that Sparta owed the younger Darius' *káranos* and of the friendship that linked Lacedaemon's commander and Persia's young prince. It was then and only then that Cyrus joined Tissaphernes for the long journey ahead.

Cyrus' personal wealth, which was quite considerable, and the resources of Asia Minor, were in the hands of the one man whom he could trust. Over the sixteen months that followed, Lysander spent a colossal sum—something like seventeen hundred talents (ca. 48.5 tons) of silver—supporting the Peloponnesian fleet; and he retained as a reserve another four hundred seventy talents.[4]

LYSANDER AND HIS FRIENDS

Lysander returned from Sardis to Ephesus and made his way to Miletus—where his partisans awaited him. It was the time of the Dionysian festival, and they had arranged with him to use the occasion to do what Callicratidas had refused to countenance—which was, to massacre their political opponents. Throughout Hellas, circumstances fostered a link between religious celebrations and plots aimed at slaughter. Normally, the citizens of a *pólis* could be found scattered throughout the town and the surrounding countryside. Only at the time of a festival would they gather in one place. On this occasion, the friends of Lysander surprised in their homes and dispatched forty of their rivals; and, in the crowded marketplace, they killed another three hundred of the most prosperous [*euporōtatoi*]" of the Milesians. Among those favoring the democracy, there were, Diodorus tells us, numerous "men amply graced with taste, refinement, and education [*chariéstatoi*]," and one thousand of these fled the city.[5]

In the absence of Cyrus and Tissaphernes, the satrap Pharnabazus intervened to protect, quarter, and feed these Milesian refugees at a fortress in Phrygia near Blauda on the border of Lydia. The shoe was now on the other foot: the very Milesians who had been deeply disturbed in 411 by the Spartan decision to sell the Greeks of Asia Minor to Tissaphernes in return for financial support now found themselves entirely dependent on that satrap's colleague, sometime rival, and current political ally.[6]

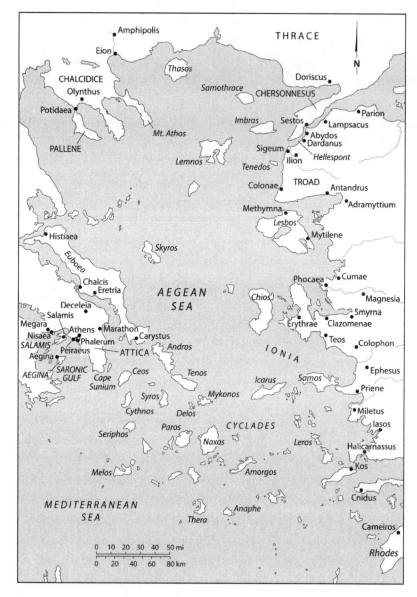

Map 22. From Ionia to the Saronic Gulf

Pharnabazus' intervention is the first unmistakable sign that the supporters of Arsaces' candidacy were aware of the symbiotic political relationship that had grown up between the Spartan commander and the Persian *káranos*. They seem to have understood perfectly the link between the factional strife affecting the Persian court and that beginning to take shape in Ionia and at Sparta. Thus, as Darius lay dying, they separated that Great King's younger son from Lacedaemon's admiral: Tissaphernes watched Cyrus and Pharnabazus, Lysander.

After the events at Miletus, the Spartan leader made his way south, pausing here and there to punish those who supported Athens. In Caria, for example, he attacked and captured Iasos—a city from which his subordinate Eteonicus, once her harmost, had been expelled— and, no doubt to the delight of that Spartiate, he plundered and razed the town, massacred the men, and enslaved the women and children. Cedreia soon suffered a similar fate.[7] Lysander spared no effort to fill the coffers of his soldiers.

In this fashion and in others, Lysander's every move seemed calculated to underline those qualities which distinguished him from Callicratidas. The headquarters which the latter had moved to Miletus, the former restored to Ephesus; the close links with Cyrus which the one had spurned, the other renewed; the Milesian conspirators whom the younger man had restrained, the older unleashed; and the enslavement of the citizens of captured Greek towns which Callicratidas had refused, Lysander carried out. The Spartan commander in charge in 405 took great pains to remind the residents of the region that he preferred his friends—Spartan and foreigner alike— to justice and decency.

The aristocratic ethic dictated that a man help his friends and do his enemies harm; the Spartan tradition, that a Lacedaemonian aid his fellow citizens and cause his city's opponents damage; and Panhellenism, that a Greek succor his fellow Greeks and wreak havoc on the barbarians. In Callicratidas, the sentiment of Panhellenism, seconded by the institutions of Sparta, formed an individual whom Plutarch could call "the best of all men and the most just," an admiral whose "leadership [*hēgemonía*]" possessed "a certain Doric simplicity and frankness." In Lysander, the aristocratic ethos, hardened by the Spartan *agōgḗ*, shaped a commander whom the biographer deemed "unscrupulous and crafty [*panoûrgos kaì sophistḗs*]," schooled in "guile [*apatḗ*]," driven by "partisan zeal [*spoudḗ*]," "devoted to his associates [*philétairos*]," and willing to commit great "injustices for the sake of his friends [*adíkiai hupèr phílōn*]."[8]

From Rhodes, Lysander made his way through the islands of the Aegean to the Saronic Gulf, overran Salamis and Aegina, and landed on the coast to meet Agis. The purpose of the voyage remains a mystery. Plutarch gives a brief account of it; Diodorus dismisses it in a sentence as uneventful; and Xenophon ignores it altogether. Some modern scholars deny that it even took place.[9]

The evidence regarding Lysander's putative voyage to the Saronic Gulf does not warrant certainty, but an educated guess is possible. Athenian morale was then at a low ebb. The victory at Arginusae had stirred joy and anger at Athens—joy sufficient to enable Cleophon son of Cleippides to secure the rejection of the Spartan peace offer; and, as we shall now see, rage with regard to something that had not been done. The details help explain Lysander's maneuver, and they bear on the outcome of the war.

THE ARGINUSAE TRIAL

In the aftermath of the battle at Arginusae, there appears to have been an attempt on the part of the victors to recover the bodies of the dead, but it had foundered. They had also failed to rescue many of the mariners who had survived the disabling of the twenty-five ships the Athenians had lost—those who had been unable to swim to shore and who, thereafter, were floating about in the water clinging to the flotsam scattered across the strait separating Cape Malea on Lesbos from the Anatolian shore to the south of Garipasi. In consequence, bloated bodies and the remains of triremes later ended up littering the coastline of the territory of Aeolian Cumae and Phocaea some ten to twenty-five miles to the south.[10]

It mattered little that the storm, which had struck this strait soon after the battle and which had prevented the fleet from proceeding immediately to Mytilene, had also rendered such a rescue and salvage operation impossible. As we have seen, an extraordinarily high proportion of those serving in the emergency fleet had been citizens, and what seemed to the unsuspecting glance to be an unnecessary loss of life and an impious failure to recover and bury the dead came to be deemed intolerable.

It is easy for us to understand the first of these concerns. No one can be indifferent to the needless death of a loved one. And—thanks, above all, to the catastrophe in Sicily but also to the skirmishing in 412 and 411 as well as to the two trireme engagements near Cynossema in the Hellespont; the clash between fleets at Eretria; the great battle at Cyzicus in the Sea of Marmara; the hoplite contest outside Ephesus; the sieges at Chalcedon, Selymbria, and Byzantium; and the two naval encounters just off the coast of Lesbos to the north of Mytilene—the Athenians had already by this time experienced a nightmarish decade of needless deaths.

We do not know how many citizens lost their lives as a consequence of the storm that descended upon the Athenians and their adversaries in the wake of the monumental clash at Arginusae. There were something like five thousand mariners on the galleys said to have been lost, and at least half of these were Athenians, if not more. When a trireme is holed, it fills with water, but, thanks to the fact that it is light, ordinarily it does not sink. Some of these crew members may have remained with the wreck and may even have survived the storm. Some of the triremes no doubt broke apart. The mariners from these ships—even those clinging to flotsam—were for the most part doomed. In one passage, Xenophon tells us that twenty-five galleys were lost with most of their crews, and regarding the number of triremes Diodorus concurs. Alcibiades' kinsman Euryptolemos son of Peisanax, who looms large in Xenophon's narrative and who had reason to minimize the losses, reduced to twelve the number of vessels whose crew members drowned. Even, however, if he was not playing fast and loose with the truth, the men who died will have been sorely missed.[11]

To us, the Athenians' second concern may seem a mystery. Burial is not for us today as weighty a matter as it was for the ancient Greeks. What we must recall to mind is the fact that the Hellenes were persuaded that those left unburied would know no rest—that they would be condemned to wander the earth forever in distress. We must also give thought to the reasons why the chorus of Thebans in Sophocles' *Antigone* comes to be so sympathetic to the protagonist of that play. As Antigone insists, burial is first and foremost a family duty. In Athens, moreover, if Aelian can be trusted, it was also recognized as a civic duty. The written law of that city reinforced the unwritten law of Hellas: it stipulated that a citizen who stumbled upon a corpse throw dirt on it—even, apparently, if the corpse belonged to a foreigner.[12]

The *stratēgoí* at Arginusae knew this only too well. According to Diodorus, when these eight men rendezvoused at Garipasi after the battle to consider what to do next, they discussed not only rowing to Mytilene—to destroy the Peloponnesian fleet besieging that city, to liberate Conon and the mariners with him, and secure what was left of his fleet—but also the recovery of the Athenian dead. Xenophon confirms this report—except that, where Diodorus refers solely to those killed, this Socratic, in keeping with the indifference regarding traditional religion that much of Athens' political class picked up from the sophists, mentions only those still alive.

The latter also adds that the *stratēgoí* resolved to divide the fleet and accomplish both tasks: the fleet's commanders were to make their way to Mytilene with most of the remaining triremes while two exceptionally experienced trierarchs—Theramenes son of Hagnon and Thrasybulus son of Lycus—and some of the taxiarchs were to set out with forty-six galleys to rescue the survivors. Diodorus reports that both parties actually embarked, that the exhausted crews on the ships assigned to pick up the corpses began to raise fierce objections when a storm came up and the sea became dangerously choppy, and that, when the storm grew more violent, both units fled back to Garipasi. That the tempest rendered a rescue operation impossible Xenophon asserts.[13]

If Xenophon's account of a speech that Euryptolemos subsequently delivered before the Athenian assembly is accurate and if Euryptolemos' claims can be trusted, when the *stratēgoí* first met after the battle, Diomedon proposed that they devote their resources to picking up the shipwrecked men. Erasinides urged, instead, that they head for Mytilene; and Thrasyllus proposed the measure ultimately agreed upon—that they divide the fleet and do both. Euryptolemos also reports that the *stratēgoí* met once again after the storm.

By this time, however, it was too late to save the lives of the shipwrecked. Moreover, it was by then impossible to find the bodies of the drowned. For up to three hours, these are apt to float. But soon enough their lungs fill with water, and they sink. Only later, after a couple of days, is the gas produced by bacteria in the abdomen sufficient to cause corpses of this sort to become bloated and bob up to the surface. By this point, thanks to the violence of the storm, these bodies will have been driven a considerable distance to the south—both by the wind and by the current running down the sound. In consequence, they will have been scattered so far and wide that they will have been, for all practical purposes, unrecoverable.

So, instead of pondering what to do, the *stratēgoí* discussed how they were to explain what they had not done—which, back home, might well be regarded as negligence and a serious dereliction of duty. It was Euryptolemos' claim that, in a fit of *philanthrōpía*, his friend Diomedon and his kinsman Pericles talked their colleagues out of dispatching a report to the Council of Five Hundred and the assembly back home blaming the failure to mount an effective rescue operation on Theramenes, Thrasybulus, and the taxiarchs; and it is clear that no such allegations were included in the official report the eight *stratēgoí* sent and that in it they contended that the storm had rendered it impossible for anyone to do anything.[14]

Xenophon also tells us that, not long after the battle, the eight *stratēgoí* participant in it were relieved of duty and that Adeimantus and Philocles were dispatched to Samos to fill in for them and share the command with Conon. The Athenian historian also implies what Diodorus tells us explicitly: that the eight were recalled to Athens. It is telling that two in their number—Protomachus and Aristogenes—ruminated on the character of their compatriots, calculated the danger that they might themselves face, and opted to ignore the summons, knowing full well that, as a consequence of their refusal, they would be exiled and condemned to death and that their property would be confiscated. The other six—Pericles, Diomedon, Erasinides, Lysias, Aristocrates, and Thrasyllus—had more confidence in the fairmindedness of their compatriots and made their way home as required.[15]

When they arrived, Xenophon reports, a popular leader named Archedemus, who administered the *diōbelía* established a few years before by Cleophon, imposed a fine of some sort on Erasinides for supposedly appropriating for his own use public money collected in the Hellespont. Then, when this *stratēgós* went to court to defend himself, this official lodged against him an additional unspecified accusation concerning his conduct as *stratēgós* and succeeded in having him remanded to jail to await trial. Whether the latter indictment had anything to do with the suggestion attributed to Erasinides that his colleagues leave the men adrift at sea to their own devices and row directly to Mytilene we are not told.[16]

When the six *stratēgoí* who answered their summons home subsequently appeared before the Council of Five Hundred, the Athenian historian adds, it was their conduct after the battle at Arginusae that they had to explain. A figure named Timocrates, about whom we know nothing, persuaded the councillors to have them all jailed and handed over to the assembly where their putative misconduct could be discussed and a decision reached as to how to proceed.[17]

In the assembly, Xenophon continues, a number of speakers

urged that the *stratēgoí* be required to undergo the *eúthuna* to which magistrates were ordinarily subject at the end of their time in office, where they would be called upon to give an official account of their failure to pick up the men shipwrecked. Among the speakers was, he tells us, Theramenes—who quoted their claim in the report that they had sent to the Council of Five Hundred that the storm had prevented the rescue of the survivors. In reply, the *stratēgoí* cited the storm again and added that, if anyone was responsible, it was Theramenes, Thrasybulus, and the taxiarchs to whom the task of rescue had been delegated.[18]

If Xenophon were our only source for this series of events, we would have to judge his account puzzling and even suspect. Theramenes and Thrasybulus were among Alcibiades' closest associates. Diomedon and Leon had been sent out to Samos as replacement *stratēgoí* in 411 in large part because these two experienced commanders were known to be a great deal friendlier to Alcibiades than were Phrynichus son of Stratonides and his associate Scironides; and, later that year, they had presumably joined Thrasybulus in urging that the mariners on the island recall the exile. For his part, Pericles son of Pericles was, like Euryptolemos, one of Alcibiades' kinsman. He had, in fact, grown up in the same household with the son of Cleinias. It is not hard to see why some of the *stratēgoí* would be eager to pin on Theramenes, Thrasybulus, and the taxiarchs the blame that they were themselves otherwise likely to incur. The factional divide at Athens was bitter. These two trierarchs and their associate Alcibiades had enemies. Moreover, as we have seen, Thrasyllus and his supporters are very likely to have been among them, and the circumstances in 406 in which he and his colleagues were chosen were conducive to the election of at least some *stratēgoí* hostile to the son of Cleinias.

It is also easy to see why others among the *stratēgoí* who were in some way tied to Alcibiades, such as Diomedon and Pericles, would come to the defense of the two trierarchs and why Aristocrates, who had worked in harness with both Theramenes and Alcibiades, is likely to have joined them. If Theramenes and Thrasybulus found themselves pitted against the likes of Diomedon, Pericles, and Aristocrates in what might well prove to be a life-and-death struggle, there must be something that Xenophon has not told us.

Fortunately, we also have the testimony of Diodorus, and he offers further information of great pertinence. Theramenes and Thrasybulus had, he tells us, reached Athens before the *stratēgoí*. When accusations were lodged against these *stratēgoí*, they—or, we must surmise, at least those in their number who had at the outset seen this event as an opportunity to eliminate Alcibiades' closest associates—assumed that Theramenes and Thrasybulus had been the instigators. In response, "letters [*epistolaí*]" were dispatched to "the people" at Athens. Whether these were sent via friends and associates or they were conveyed directly to the Council of Five Hundred and the assembly we do not know. Presumably, however, since Diodorus uses the plural, they were sent by individual *stratēgoí* acting on their own and not by the board as a whole. According to the Sicilian historian, these letters stated that Theramenes, Thrasybulus, and the taxiarchs had been assigned the salvage operation; and, at least by imputation, they attributed responsibility to them for its failure. In pointing their fingers at these two trierarchs, Diodorus observed, the authors of this accusatory correspondence had made a fatal mistake. In his view, they had turned their would-be defenders into allies of those intent on charging them.

It would, perhaps, be more accurate to say that the authors of these letters had forced the trierarchs to defend their own conduct by pointing to the official dispatch in which the *stratēgoí* took full responsibility for the decision not to carry out the rescue and salvage operation intended. By writing the letters mentioned by Diodorus, the *stratēgoí* who did so had implicitly conceded thereby that there had been gross misconduct; and, once this was granted, everyone understood that someone would have to pay.[19]

If Xenophon is correct, the six *stratēgoí* nonetheless mounted a strong defense, having the helmsmen and others who were present for the storm testify to its force and assert that it had rendered all operations impossible. Had the issues been sorted out then and there on the spot, he suggests, this testimony might have brought the inquiry to an end, and the *stratēgoí* might well have escaped condemnation. But it was late when this subject was taken up, nightfall intervened, the matter was referred back to the Council of Five Hundred, and a resolution of the question under consideration was delayed for a time while the Athenians celebrated the Apaturia.[20]

The Apaturia was a three-day festival put on each fall by the phratries, a set of ancient kinship-based brotherhoods. It was on this occasion, which ordinarily took place in October, that the boys who were born into the families included in each phratry and the young men who had come of age that year were registered and that recent marriages were acknowledged and affirmed. This festival was an affair for extended families, and, ordinarily, it was a time of jubilation. On this occasion, however, these gatherings brought home to everyone involved the losses that these families had suffered eight or more weeks before at Arginusae.[21]

When the festival was over, Xenophon reports, the council presented a *proboúleuma* to the assembly drafted by a member of that body named Callixeinos, which made no provision for a *eúthuna* or for a formal trial in court or before the assembly at which the *stratēgoí* could speak at length in their own defense. It called, instead, for there to be an immediate vote in the assembly by secret ballot as to whether, in their opinion, the *stratēgoí* present at Arginusae had done the city a wrong [*adikeîn*] by neglecting to rescue the shipwrecked men. To this, we should presumably add what Xenophon never mentions: their failure to collect the bodies of the dead and see to their burial. At this event, emotions ran high and, we are told, citizens in mourning garb with close-cropped hair presented themselves in large numbers.

Xenophon blames the outcome on Theramenes. Callixeinos was, he contends, the man's agent, and the citizens who appeared as mourners were impostors hired and deployed by his associates. There is, however, reason to doubt his testimony. Diodorus makes neither claim—and his silence in this regard is telling, for it may well reflect the opinion of the Oxyrhynchus historian, who can hardly have been unaware of the accusations directed at Hagnon's son. Even more to the point, Lysias—in a speech he later delivered denouncing Theramenes—makes no mention at all of any role he had played in the battle of Arginusae or in the subsequent trial. This last piece of evidence is dispositive. For had there been evidence that Hagnon's son had engaged in misconduct on either occasion, Lysias, who hated the man, would certainly have deployed it. Xenophon's informants had misled the future historian.[22]

What no one should doubt is that what followed was a venting of profound grief and of a religious hysteria no less intense. The Arginusae affair resembled the Herms and Mysteries Scandals in one important particular. It arose, at least in part, in reaction to the appearance of religious indifference on the part of Athens' political class. We may be able to see that there was little point in initiating a rescue and salvage operation after the storm, but those whose relatives had died and were left unburied may not have viewed the matter in this fashion.[23]

At the assembly, attempts were made by Euryptolemos and others to bring a *graphê paranómōn* against Callixeinos so that the entire proceeding would be delayed until the furor had died down and a court could judge whether the procedures prescribed in the *proboúleuma* were contrary to the *nómoi* of the Athenians, as the motion's proponents claimed. Intimidation was, however, brought to bear on these men by Callixeinos and his allies who regarded this maneuver, perhaps with justice, as an act of obstruction without legal merit. And Euryptolemos and the others backed off when the crowd began chanting that "it would be *deinón*—shocking and terrible—if the people were not allowed to do what they wished" and when they were themselves threatened with being judged then and there alongside the *stratēgoí* whom they were defending. In like fashion, when the prytanies who presided over the meeting of the assembly seemed reluctant to put to the vote a *proboúleuma* that they thought contrary to law, they were threatened with the same fate, and all but one of them—the philosopher Socrates son of Sophronicus—gave way.[24]

Thereafter, Euryptolemos is said to have given a stirring speech, defending the *stratēgoí*; insisting that the storm made a rescue operation impossible; hinting that, if anyone was guilty, it was the trierarchs and taxiarchs assigned the task; and attacking the *proboúleuma* on two separate grounds. It was, he said, contrary to Athenian law to reach a judgment without a formal trial in which the accused could defend their conduct at length, and it was no less illegal to judge the *stratēgoí* as a group, rather than as individuals.

To reinforce his argument, Euryptolemos pointed to the procedures laid out in the Decree of Kannonus, which specified how those accused of doing the city an *adikía* were to be treated, and he alluded to the procedures followed in the trials of those accused of temple-robbing and treason. It was in this context that he asserted that his friend Diomedon had actually proposed devoting the resources of the entire fleet to such a rescue operation and that his kinsman Pericles had joined with Diomedon in vetoing the proposal backed by at least some of the other *stratēgoí* that Theramenes, Thrasybulus, and the taxiarchs be blamed for the failure of an operation that had, in fact, proved impossible to carry out. Then, in a transparent attempt to save these two former generals, he proposed and very nearly succeeded in securing the passage of an amendment to the *proboúleuma* in effect severing the cases and guaranteeing to each of the defendants a separate vote.

In the end, however, thanks to the spirited resistance of Callixeinos and his associates, Euryptolemos failed, and the *proboúleuma*, as originally formulated, was adopted. Thereafter, in accord with its provisions, the assembly voted, the six *stratēgoí* who had returned to Athens and entrusted their fate to their compatriots were condemned to death—and, in due course, all six of them were executed for not doing what could not have been done.[25]

In the aftermath, we are told, the Athenians had a change of heart, recoiled in horror at what they had done, and turned with a vengeance on Callixeinos and a handful of his associates, whom they charged with deceiving the Athenian people. Whether these men were tried and convicted or merely indicted and jailed in preparation for a trial there is disagreement between Diodorus and Xenophon, and we do not know which of the two is right. What we do know is that there are two additional signs that the more extravagant claims advanced by Xenophon against Theramenes are untrue: no charge was lodged at any time against him in regard to the Arginusae affair; and, six months after the event, in the spring of 405, he was actually elected *stratēgós*. That he did not pass the scrutiny [*dokimasía*] to which elected officials were subjected in court before assuming office had nothing to do with the Arginusae trial. For our sole source for his election and rejection, Theramenes' great enemy the orator Lysias, mentions only that those who remembered 411 regarded him as disloyal to the democracy.[26]

Ultimately, of course, it does not much matter who was to blame for the execution of the *stratēgoí*—for the crucial fact is that the damage was done. At a time when the Athenians faced not only defeat but also the possibility that they would be killed, their wives and children enslaved, and their community destroyed, the *stratēgoí* convicted and executed in the aftermath of the battle of Arginusae had rallied the rag-tag forces of their compatriots and had managed by way of a brilliant maneuver to defeat an enemy fleet far superior in experience and skill and far better equipped than their own. And for this achievement—thanks to the storm, the damage it did, and the grief and rage that for a brief time had their compatriots in its grip—those in their number who did not accurately assess the Athenians' propensity for mistreating commanders and flee into exile ultimately paid with their own lives.[27]

Never before in human history and, as far as we know, never thereafter did a self-governing people inflict damage on themselves in a fashion comparable to this. First, the Athenians deprived themselves of the service of the ablest of their commanders—Alcibiades.

Then, they relegated to a secondary role his exceptionally capable associates Thrasybulus and Theramenes. And, finally, they executed or drove into exile the men of less renown who proved able, at a moment of supreme danger, to fill the shoes of these three formidable tacticians. With all of the advantages that she possessed in the wake of Athens' Sicilian catastrophe, Lacedaemon was not able to defeat Athens ... until the Athenians voted for suicide. The *stratēgoí* who assumed office early in the summer of 405 included neither Theramenes nor Thrasybulus; and they were not, as we shall soon see, up to the job.[28]

A RETURN TO THE HELLESPONT

The Arginusae trial took place in the immediate aftermath of the festival of the Apaturia in the fall of 406, as we have observed. Lysander returned to the scene the following summer. Early on in his tenure, his fleet was not large enough to take on the forces of Athens in an open fight, but it served no purpose lying at anchor in the harbor at Ephesus—and this is why Lysander set out for Attica.

One need only imagine the effect on Athenian morale at this time of the appearance of a Peloponnesian armada unopposed off the coast of Attica. As we have had occasion to note, Agis had, on more than one occasion, marshalled his troops for an attempt to take the city. It makes sense to suppose that Lysander's bold maneuver was preparatory for another such attempt. It was designed to strike panic into the citizenry and thereby to render Athens vulnerable to assault. Agis' attack either failed to materialize or it proved as unsuccessful as its predecessors and did not merit the attention of Plutarch's sources.[29]

In any event, Lysander's journey prepared the way for a meeting between the two leading Spartan supporters of the war effort. Plutarch reports that Agis marched down from Deceleia to see the naval commander. By this time, midsummer had come and gone, and the new board of archons had taken office at Athens.[30]

For at least seven years, Agis had been the principal advocate of an aggressive military strategy. It was he who had established the fort at Deceleia in Attica and who had initiated the siege of Athens. He was, moreover, one of the first to recognize that Athens' defeat in Sicily and the forging of alliance between Sparta and Persia had opened up the possibility of making that siege more effective. To this end, on the eve of Lacedaemon's intervention in the Greek East, he had begun pressing his compatriots to concentrate their efforts there on the Hellespont, the Sea of Marmara, and the Bosporus with an eye to cutting Athens' umbilical cord to the Euxine. At that time, his preferred instrument was, as we have had occasion to note, Clearchus, the son of his late father Archidamus' associate Ramphias and the *próxenos* of the Byzantines at Lacedaemon.[31]

Between them, the navarch Mindarus and this Clearchus appear to have accomplished something of the sort. But, thanks to the Athenian galleys stationed at Sestos in the Thracian Chersonnesus, to Alcibiades' annihilation of the Spartan fleet at Cyzicus, and to his establishment of a base at Chrysopolis on the Bosporus, their achievement had proved to be ephemeral. In consequence, five years prior to Lysander's voyage to the Saronic Gulf, Agis, from his perch at Deceleia, had found himself once again seething in frustration as he watched ship after ship, carrying grain grown in the Crimea, arrive at the Peiraeus after the route from the Black Sea had been reopened. It was at this time that he had reportedly remarked that there was no point in occupying Attica unless one also occupied the overseas territory from which the Athenians drew their sustenance. And so, soon thereafter, he had dispatched Clearchus once again to the Bosporus—to Chalcedon and Byzantium, the two cities controlling the narrowest point on the strait. Ramphias' son was a man of the greatest vigor. But vigor was not enough, as we have observed; and, in 408, the Athenians under Alcibiades' command subdued Chalcedon and took Byzantium.[32]

When Lysander left Attica late in the summer of 405, he took with him an added complement of infantrymen and headed for the

Hellespont. According to Xenophon, he intended "to prevent the grain ships from passing through" that body of water "and to punish the cities that had rebelled." The strategy devised by Agis in 412 was adopted and implemented by his associate and protégé Lysander seven years thereafter. It was surely this that they discussed when Lysander landed on the coast of Attica that fall.[33]

The Athenians had been ineffective, but not inactive in the meantime. The contingent based at Samos had been ravaging the countryside at Ephesus and at Chios to no real effect. The news of Lysander's arrival in the Saronic Gulf apparently induced them to set out in pursuit. But he outwitted them in the same fashion that Mindarus had outwitted Thrasyllus in 411. Escaping detection, he returned to Asia Minor by a route other than the one he had followed to Athens; and, encountering no impediment, he made his way immediately to Lampsacus in the Hellespont. The fact that the *stratēgoí* had left Athens' lifeline undefended is a sign of gross incompetence on their part.[34]

When word reached the Athenians that Lysander was in the Hellespont, besieging Lampsacus, they rushed to the same destination.

Figure 8.1. Section of Athenian trireme carved in stone; fragment of Lenormant relief, ca. 410–400

(*Acropolis Museum, Athens; Photograph: Marsyas, Wikimedia Commons, Published September 2024 under the following license: Creative Commons: Attribution Share-Alike 2.5 Generic*).

In mid-September, the ships carrying grain from the Euxine would wend their way once again through the Bosporus, the Sea of Marmara, and the Hellespont to the Aegean. This grain was for Athens a strategic substance, as we have seen. Bread was essential to the survival of the city's population. So, the grain route could not go unprotected. It was imperative that Athens' fleet prevent the Spartans from regaining control over the Dardanelles.

By the time, however, that the Athenians had gathered an armada one hundred eighty strong at Elaeus at the bottom of the Thracian Chersonnesus, Sparta's admiral had taken the Athenian stronghold at Lampsacus with the aid of an allied infantry force brought up from Abydos by his fellow Spartiate Thorax. It was a base well chosen. The city was well supplied with life's necessities, as Xenophon takes care to point out. Moreover, thanks to her agricultural hinterland and to the services she could perform for the merchants plying their trade along the route linking the Mediterranean and the Black Sea, Lampsacus was quite prosperous, and it may have been at this time that she began issuing electrum staters of her own on the Chian standard.

Even more to the point, the fortified harbor of Lampsacus lay

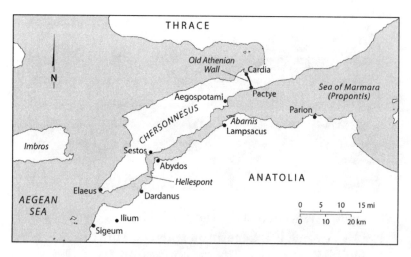

Map 23. Taking up Positions in the Hellespont

upstream twelve miles beyond the principal Athenian base at Sestos, the northernmost of the Greek settlements on the Hellespont's European shore. From it, in mid-September, Lysander could easily intercept the ships bearing grain to the Aegean from the Euxine; and this, thanks to the strength of the current and the prevailing winds, he could do without fear that the Athenians from Sestos could in force row upstream in a timely fashion and interfere.[35]

Recognizing the difficulties they would soon face, the Athenians *stratēgoí* conducted their galleys from Elaeus to Sestos and then made their way up the Hellespont to an uninviting stretch of beach called Aegospotami. Where this beach lay is a matter of controversy. Xenophon makes two incompatible statements—that it was on the coast directly opposite the Peloponnesian camp at Lampsacus (roughly three miles away from the Athenians' foe), and that it could be seen from Alcibiades' fort at Pactyes in the Thracian Chersonnesus further upstream just beyond the Hellespont a short distance inland from the Sea of Marmara. Either site is possible. Either could have accommodated the Athenian fleet. The fact that Strabo the geographer and Plutarch followed Xenophon in placing Aegospotami within the Hellespont means nothing. To become aware of the incompatibility between the Athenian historian's two claims, one must not only visit Pactyes. One must also attend to what Alcibiades could have seen from its battlements. What decides the question in favor of the site further upstream is the fact that it fits the narrative—which requires that the activity of the Athenians onshore at Aegospotami not be visible from Lampsacus, that a fleet at Lampsacus be in a position to interfere with food shipments to the Athenians from Sestos, and that a squadron in hurried flight from Aegospotami toward the Aegean pass the headland of Abarnis northeast of Lampsacus, which marks the boundary where the Propontis ends and the Hellespont begins.[36]

AEGOSPOTAMI

There was fresh water near where the Athenians appear to have camped; and, if they needed to take on the Spartans, they could draw advantage from the current and the prevailing wind. But it was exceedingly difficult for them to supply with food a fleet, manned by thirty-six thousand men, at a location well beyond Lampsacus, roughly fifteen miles north-northeast of Sestos, the nearest town of any size in their possession. So, they could not remain at Aegospotami indefinitely. Moreover, with their galleys beached on the strand, they were vulnerable to surprise attack.

By way of contrast, Lysander was comfortably situated and well-provisioned, and his fleet was lodged in a harbor fortified back in the winter of 409/8 by the soldiers and seamen deployed by Alcibiades and Thrasyllus—which the Athenians would have been ill-advised to attack. Mindful of Cyrus' instructions and aware that time was on his side, Aristocritus' son seems not to have been desperate or even eager to force an encounter. His fleet had been somewhat smaller than that of his foe when he rowed off to the Saronic Gulf. Whether, given the pace of trireme production at Gytheion, Antandrus, Ephesus, and elsewhere, this was still true later in the summer of 405 we do not know. It was, in any case, in his interest to refuse battle; to watch and wait for an opportunity, precisely as he had done at Notium; and thereby to encourage the Athenians, who were generally apt to underestimate the enemy, to suppose that he and his subordinates were afraid of a fight—and this is precisely what he did. Lysander was prepared to be daring—but only when circumstances were favorable.[37]

For what follows, we have two ancient sources. The first is Xenophon, who was apparently not an eyewitness—for he describes events for the most part from the perspective of the Spartans, with whom, in and after 401, he would become closely acquainted. The second is Diodorus Siculus, who depends ultimately, we must presume, on the Oxyrhynchus historian, and whose narrative for the most part reflects the Athenian point of view. Though different, the stories the two tell can for the most part be reconciled.[38]

According to the former, whose account is in this particular perfectly compatible with the less detailed narrative found in the latter, the Athenians rowed out every morning and, at sunrise, presented themselves for battle outside the harbor of Lampsacus while Lysander had his galleys fully manned, cleared for battle, and ready to strike but held them back. Then, when the Athenians withdrew, he sent out his fastest triremes as scouts to observe closely what the crews did once they returned to the beach at Aegospotami, and he kept his fleet ready for a fight until his scouts came back to report. This stalemate continued, the Athenian historian adds, for four straight days.[39]

While Athens' *stratēgoí* were puzzling over the dilemma they faced, Alcibiades made his move. So we are told by both Xenophon and Diodorus. From the battlements of his stronghold at Pactyes, he had been able to see both the Athenian camp on the Propontis coast nearby and Lampsacus in the distance on the Hellespont's Asian shore. Mindful of the predicament his compatriots were in, he presented himself at Aegospotami to warn the *stratēgoí* that they were exceedingly vulnerable in the position they had occupied and to urge that they withdraw to Sestos. Then, according to Diodorus, he offered to lead the armies of the Thracian princes Seuthes and Medocus (with whom he had formed an alliance) against the Peloponnesians on the Asian shore, promising to dislodge them from Lampsacus and to force them to put out to sea and accept battle. His price, the Sicilian historian adds, was a share in the command. This was, however, a price that the *stratēgoí*—with the possible but unmentioned exception of Alcibiades' fellow demesman and longtime associate Adeimantus—were simply unwilling to pay.

Some of the Athenian commanders hated Cleinias' son. According to Xenophon, Tydeus, who is apt to have been Lamachus' son and who may with some justification have blamed Alcibiades for his father's death at Syracusa, heaped insults on the man. Then,

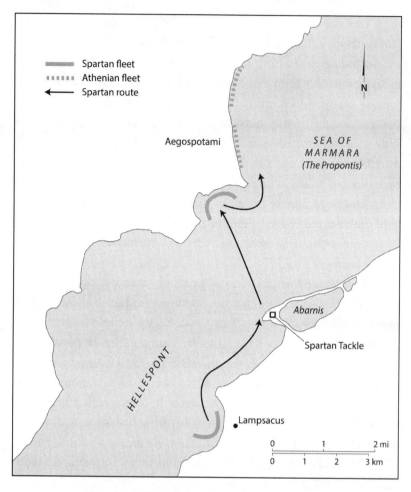

Map 24. The Battle of Aegospotami, 405

Menander, who had been appointed to serve as a *stratēgós* alongside Nicias in the later stages of Athens' Sicilian venture and who had served alongside Alcibiades prior to the attempt on Chalcedon, joined him in bluntly telling Alcibiades in no uncertain terms that they were in charge, not he, and that he should go away and not return. As Diodorus insists, the *stratēgoí* knew the score. If, after having accepted his offer, they won, the victory would be his; if they lost, the blame, their own.[40]

Finally, Diodorus reports, as the situation worsened, the dearth of food became an insuperable problem, morale and discipline declined, and everyone recognized that they could no longer remain where they were. In consequence, when Philocles' day of command arrived, he forged a consensus in the council of *stratēgoí*, instructed the trierarchs to man the triremes, and set out himself with thirty ships. Where he was going and what he was up to, Diodorus does not specify. Some scholars speculate that he was another Antiochus—that his aim, like that of Alcibiades' helmsman at Notium, was to lure Lysander's galleys out into the open water and that he expected the remaining Athenian triremes to be poised and ready to come to his rescue and to wipe out the Peloponnesian fleet. The simplest hypothesis, however, and the one most in accord with the emphasis that Diodorus places on the plight of the Athenians is that Philocles' departure was the first stage in the Athenians' withdrawal from their exposed position.

On Diodorus' telling, Lysander, forewarned by deserters concerning the Athenians' plans, was unwilling to allow them to escape the trap he had set and was eager to take advantage of their disarray. Suddenly, therefore, with his entire force, he put out to sea. Philocles' unit he caught within the Hellespont and he cut it off from Sestos. Then, he routed it, landed a hoplite detachment under the command of Eteonicus on the European shore, and swooped down on the remainder of the Athenian fleet, which was only partially manned—thanks to arrogance and carelessness on the part of the *stratēgoí* and to indiscipline on the part of the crews. The battle, if it can be called a battle, was over, for all intents and purposes, within a half hour. It ended—not with a bang but with a whimper—before it had in earnest even begun.

Xenophon makes no mention of Philocles' activity or of any Athenian initiative. On his telling, it was Lysander who took the lead. On the pertinent day, the Athenians presented themselves at the harbor, and he once again refused battle. Then, they rowed back to Aegospotami, and once again he sent out his scouts. This time, they were instructed to raise a shield if and when the Athenians on shore scattered in search of fresh water and the makings of a meal. When the officer in charge of this handful of galleys ordered that a shield be raised, Aristocritus' wily son had his triremes set out; and, while Thorax was being landed on the Hellespont's European shore with a complement of hoplites, his fleet descended on the Athenians at full speed.

The two accounts are at odds with regard to one concrete particular—the identity of the hoplite commander landed on the European shore of the Hellespont. Otherwise, they are complementary. Xenophon spells out Lysander's plan and the manner in which he implemented it while Diodorus reminds us of something Xenophon leaves out—that the Athenians, though undisciplined and inept, were not entirely passive and that Philocles and his fellow *stratēgoí* unwittingly supplied the Spartan both with the opportunity for which he was waiting and with a reason against further delay.[41]

Conon—who was far more experienced than his colleagues and, as a consequence, more alert to the danger—escaped with no fewer than eight and no more than a dozen ships. To obstruct pursuit, his contingent paused briefly on the Hellespont's Asian shore at Abarnis, the headland northeast of Lampsacus, to scoop up the masts, sails, and the other tackle that Lysander's galleys had left there when they cleared for action. Then, persuaded that the war was lost and mindful of the grim punishment so often meted out by his compatriots to defeated *stratēgoí* in the past, Timotheus' son abandoned his fatherland and headed for Cypriot Salamis with his flotilla in tow to seek refuge with that city's ruler Evagoras, who happened to be his guest-friend. Whether, in response, his compatriots voted to exile him, to confiscate his property, and condemn him to death we do not know.[42]

As Conon and his fellow escapees sped away and as the *Paralus* raced home to inform the Athenians of their fleet's fate, Lysander turned his attention to the Athenians taken prisoner in the course of the operation. As at Arginusae and for similar reasons, they had made up an unusually large proportion of the infantrymen and mariners stationed at Aegospotami.

Among the captives were Philocles, Adeimantus, and a number of the remaining *stratēgoí*, who are left unnamed. Philocles had had the crews of a captured Corinthian and a captured Andrian trireme thrown overboard to drown, and he had persuaded the Athenian assembly to pass a decree stipulating that enemy rowers apprehended be disabled by having their thumbs, if not their hands, cut off. Adeimantus had been the latter measure's sole opponent. The first of these two was questioned by Lysander, who then personally cut his throat. The second of the two was spared; and, according to Xenophon who was well-informed concerning Spartan affairs, Lysander allowed the allies serving in the fleet to determine the fate of the remaining Athenian captives—whom, in their fury, they voted to execute. Whether the number of Athenians massacred on this occasion was just over three thousand, as Plutarch claims, or nearly four thousand, as the travel writer Pausanias reports, we do not know. Nor are we in a position to judge this Pausanias' claim that Lysander left the Athenians dead unburied.[43]

It is no surprise that, in some quarters, Adeimantus was soon regarded as a traitor; that the same accusation was lodged against his longtime friend Alcibiades; and that similar claims were made, no doubt by those who had been associated with these two men, against Tydeus. It was difficult, if not impossible, for the Athenians to admit that they had themselves laid the foundation for this calamity when they cashiered Alcibiades and sidelined Theramenes and Thrasybulus, refused to make peace with Lacedaemon after Arginusae and executed the *stratēgoí* victorious in that battle, and then sent out a team of commanders for the most part made up of untried men. As Conon understood perfectly, it was far easier to pin responsibility on one or more scapegoats.[44]

In the aftermath, Lysander conducted his force down the Hellespont to take Sestos, to which, Diodorus tells us, most of the thirty-six thousand mariners and infantrymen stationed at Aegospotami had managed to flee. Then, he reversed course and conducted his fleet back up the Hellespont and across the Sea of Marmara to seize Byzantium and Chalcedon and close the strait. Having slaked the desire of his rowers and of Sparta's allies for revenge and retribution, he had the Athenians found in these cities and elsewhere conveyed back to Athens where their presence would add to the number of the besieged in need of nourishment and thereby hasten the city's surrender.[45]

The disaster suffered by the Athenians on this occasion was even greater than the defeat inflicted on the Peloponnesians by Alcibiades and his colleagues at Cyzicus a bit more than five years before. Their treasury empty and all but a few of their triremes lost, the Athenians had nothing for which to hope. The grain route was closed; the long struggle, finished. "It was at night," Xenophon reports,

> that the *Paralus* reached Athens with news of the catastrophe, and the sound of keening spread from the Peiraeus along the Long Walls to the town, as one man passed on the tidings to another; and during that night no one rested in bed. They all mourned, not for the dead only, but far more for themselves, thinking that they would suffer what they had inflicted on Sparta's colonists the Melians, when they had taken them by siege, and upon the Histiaeans, the Scionaeans, the Toronaeans, the Aeginetans, and a host of other Greek peoples.

As everyone who paused to consider the matter understood, Athens was about to be besieged by sea as well as by land.[46]

THE SURRENDER OF ATHENS

It is difficult to exaggerate the influence Lysander secured by winning at Aegospotami. When his emissary the Melian buccaneer Theopompus arrived at Sparta with the news, the jubilation must have been unprecedented. Thanks to his victory, the final outcome of the enduring strategic rivalry that had begun sixty years before was at this stage a foregone conclusion.[47]

Of course, the last of Sparta's three Attic wars was not quite over. In the wake of that great battle, after consolidating his control over the cities in the Hellespont, the Sea of Marmara, and the Bosporus, Lysander sailed to Lesbos, arranged the affairs of the five *póleis* on that island to his liking, and dispatched his lieutenant Eteonicus with ten ships to Thrace to bring the cities in that region over to the Spartan side. Everywhere the Greek *póleis* fell in line—only Samos held out. The democrats there knew all too well what the restoration of those exiled at the time of the revolutions of 412 and 411 would mean; and, with this in mind, they took occasion to complete the purge begun at that time. Samos might eventually surrender, but she would not be betrayed.

At the same time, the Athenians remained steadfast—as always. They can be accused of megalomania and folly but not of cowardice and irresolution. The day after the *Paralus* arrived, they called an assembly, voted to block up all of the harbors but one, to repair the walls, to station guards, and to prepare for a long siege. In moments of anger, under the influence of demagogues, they had committed what can only be regarded as crimes—atrocities sufficient to excuse their own annihilation. This they knew—and they were no doubt also aware of the massacre of the prisoners that had taken place immediately after Lysander's victory at Aegospotami.

Lysander tarried at Samos to invest the place, sent a messenger on to Athens to inform Agis that he would come, and followed soon thereafter with an armada two hundred strong. On the way, he stopped to restore the Aeginetan exiles and the Melian survivors to their homelands. At the same time, Pausanias brought up an army from the Peloponnesus; and, for the first time since the sixth century, the two Spartan kings were on campaign together. Nonetheless, in the face of overwhelming odds, the Athenians held out.[48]

It may have been absurd to dream, as the Athenians did dream, that Alcibiades would somehow come to their rescue. That remarkable man was still at large, to be sure. He had pulled off miracles in the past, and he could be expected to do everything in his power to

**Map 25. Attica, the Saronic Gulf, the Corinthiad, Boeotia,
and Phocis, 405/4**

do so again. But it is hard to see what Cleinias' resourceful son could
have done on this particular occasion.

This fact notwithstanding, the Athenians did have good reason
to hold out: their massacre and enslavement seemed to be in the offing. According to one ancient source, Lysander and Agis proposed
at a meeting of the congress of the allies that Athens be destroyed
root and branch and did so without consulting the authorities at
Sparta—a fact which would surely have escaped notice altogether
had there not been an uproar concerning their arrogating to themselves responsibilities and powers that belonged to others. Both

Lysander and Agis subsequently took great pains never to appear to be negotiating with the Athenians on behalf of Lacedaemon and pointedly referred all matters of substance to the ephors.[49]

It is odd that, in this context, no mention is made of Pausanias, who was present with an army in Attica at the time and who can hardly have failed to have attended the meeting. This suggests what this Agiad king's later behavior confirms: Pausanias had no more interest in extra-Peloponnesian ventures than had his father Pleistoanax. It is virtually certain that he was among those who objected to the high-handed political maneuvers of Agis and Lysander at this time. The supporters of all-out war had become the partisans of empire; the proponents of peace, the advocates of restraint. They all recognized that the elimination of Athens would create a vacuum into which Sparta would inevitably be drawn. Some welcomed the prospect; others feared the consequences.

The old argument for Peloponnesian isolationism had considerable force, as we have seen. Spartan virtue was fragile. When freed from the purview of their compatriots, the citizens of Lacedaemon were apt to engage in misconduct; and for this reason they really were unsuited to the governance of subject communities and to long service abroad.

Late fifth-century Sparta was, moreover, a city desperately short of citizen manpower. There were hordes of helots and a great many *períoikoi*. In addition, there were *neodamṓdeis*, and there must have been "inferiors [*hupomeíones*]" who had gone through the *agōgḗ* and had then been denied admission into a *sussítion*. There had never been very many Spartiates—and, after the great earthquake and the helot revolt of 465, the ratio had been altered dramatically in favor of the noncitizens. Moreover, in the six decades that had passed since that cataclysm, the population of full citizens had not fully bounced back. It seems, in fact, to have suffered further decline. Like many another dominant caste, the ruling order of Spartiates had failed to fully reproduce itself.

The demographic trend is striking: where there had been eight thousand full-fledged citizens in 480, there would be twelve hundred in 371. A city able to send five thousand Spartiates to Plataea could muster only seven hundred for Leuctra. The drop-off was steep: the best estimates concerning the Spartiate contingent at Mantineia in 418—when the Spartans risked all—point to the presence of no more than eighteen hundred *homoíoi*. At that time, the body of adult male citizens was probably not much larger than twenty-one hundred.[50]

The lower orders need not have suffered the same demographic decline as their superiors. They were not subject to the same social imperative—that forbidding the loss of economic advantage and the dissipation of wealth through an overproduction of progeny—and they did not incur the same loss of status as the sons of Spartiates who failed to secure admission into a *sussítion*.

It is impossible to be sure of the number of *períoikoi, neodamôdeis, hupomeíones*, and helots, but an estimate is possible. Plutarch claims that, at the time of the great reform attributed to the legendary law-giver Lycurgus, nine thousand allotments [*klêroi*] were set aside for Spartiates and thirty thousand for *períoikoi*. Herodotus reports that Lacedaemon sent seven helots to Plataea for every citizen she dispatched. About eighty years later, a Laconian observer could count no more than seventy-five citizens milling around in Sparta's marketplace among the four thousand other Lacedaemonians going about their business. These last two figures may be indicative of the ratio between the population of the rulers and that of the ruled in the years subsequent to Sparta's third and last Attic war. They are certainly in accord with what one would estimate in light of Plutarch's claim, Herodotus' report, our knowledge of the existence of a juridically defined order of *neodamôdeis* and of another of *hupomeíones*, the data available concerning the decline in the Spartiate population, and the likelihood that within Laconia and Messenia the lower orders remained prolific.[51]

It is no wonder that the Spartans selected the three hundred who accompanied Leonidas to Thermopylae in 480 from among those with sons to succeed them and that they were willing to make peace in 425 and later in 421 primarily in order to recover the one hundred-twenty Spartiates captured at Sphacteria. It is no wonder that they decided in 424 to murder in cold blood two thousand of the most ambitious and able helots and that they insisted in 421 on the inclusion of a clause in their treaty of alliance with Athens stipulating that aid be sent "in case of a rising of the slaves." For the Spartans, eternal vigilance was, in fact, the price of survival: the observer who counted those in the marketplace at Sparta in 400 regarded all but the citizens as eager for revolution. The others, he told the ephors, did not hide the fact when no citizens were present that they wanted to "eat the Spartiates raw."[52]

Sparta's difficulties were aggravated by her geopolitical situation, as we have had occasion to point out. A wall of mountains separated Laconia from Messenia. A messenger could traverse the narrow pass that ran between the two, and so could an army unencumbered with baggage. But, if baggage on any scale was required, it had to be conveyed along the only convenient route, which ran through the Orestheum in Arcadia, a district close to Tegea and apt to be under her control. It is an indication of this region's importance that, after the liberation of Messenia at the end of the 370s, Epaminondas of Thebes founded Megalopolis astride this route to prevent the Spartans from regaining the rich territory they had lost.[53]

This happened after the battle of Leuctra. Roughly two centuries before that fateful battle, the Lacedaemonians solved the problem posed by Mount Taygetus by reaching an accommodation with Tegea and making of her a satellite ruled by a broad-based, landed oligarchy—kept docile as the democratic wave swept over Greece by the recognition that her stability depended ultimately on the support of her more militant neighbor.

The pacification of Tegea was insufficient because of the presence of Argos. The available information concerning Argive–Spartan relations in the archaic period is scanty, but what there is confirms what common sense would suggest—that the Argives were ready and willing to help Lacedaemon's Messenian subjects against their hated overlord from the very beginning. The Spartans' success with regard to Tegea served to deprive Argos of her longtime ally, but not to reduce her hostility. Embittered by the loss to Sparta of the borderland Cynuria and waiting and watching for an opportunity to regain her lost Peloponnesian hegemony and overturn her hated rival, Argos sat poised on Lacedaemon's northeastern marches, ready to strike. The stability of the Spartan–Tegean axis and, with it, of Sparta's hold on Messenia depended upon the adherence of Mantineia, Corinth, and Elis as a counterpoise to Argos. The first two were particularly important: Mantineia lay between Argos and Tegea, and Corinth was Argos' neighbor to the north. By the end of the sixth century, the Spartans had established a system of alliances encompassing virtually the whole Peloponnesus.

It was easier for the various cities to cooperate with Sparta than to resist her. She provided the oligarchs dominant in these polities with protection against foreign attack and domestic subversion in return for their help in stabilizing the state of affairs in the Peloponnesus. Sparta was a lenient mistress: the fear of losing what she possessed restrained the natural desire to add to her possessions. Interest dictated the cooperation of the Peloponnesians with a Sparta eager to maintain the status quo and uninterested in the fruits of empire.[54]

Interest likewise dictated resistance to a Spartan policy of conquest and dominion. The establishment and maintenance of a Spartan empire would require heavy and sustained demands on Peloponnesian manpower. A Sparta able to marshal the financial and military resources of central Greece and the Aegean would so far overshadow her allies that, liberated from the fear of a helot revolt, she would not hesitate to deprive the Peloponnesian cities of the autonomy and freedom from tribute they so highly prized. In pursuing an imperial policy, Sparta risked alienating her closest allies and driving them into the arms of the Argives and those in the world beyond the Peloponnesus unwilling to submit to the Spartan yoke. The combination could be fatal.

This had almost happened on the one occasion in the past when the Spartans had made a serious attempt to extend their dominion to central Greece. After destroying the Peisistratid tyranny at Athens, the Lacedaemonians confronted the same dilemma that they were destined to face in the wake of their Attic wars: whether to withdraw to the Peloponnesus or to enlarge the sphere of their hegemony. On this occasion, Cleomenes imposed his will on Sparta and she opted for empire—only to be thwarted by the intervention of a Corinth terrified that the permanent subjugation of Athens would entail the loss of the relative liberty which her position at the gate of the Peloponnesus near the border of the political region dominated by the Spartan alliance guaranteed her. Sparta's other allies rallied behind Corinth at the time and there is clear evidence suggesting subsequent disaffection of a serious kind on the part of Tegea, Mantineia, and Elis. Her alliance in disarray, Sparta found herself forced to face Argos in 494, a helot revolt in 490, and the Persians a decade later without being able to depend on the firm support of the Peloponnesians. That she weathered the crisis was largely due to strategic sequencing: in part as a consequence of intelligent planning and in part as a consequence of dumb luck, the Argive resurgence, the helot rebellion, and the Persian assault did not coincide and the Lacedaemonians were able to deal with the challenges they faced seriatim. Given the fragility of their dominion, the Spartans had every reason to hesitate before engaging in adventures abroad.[55]

Of course, the defensive posture had its own shortcomings. As the Lacedaemonians learned the hard way time and again in the course of the fifth century, they could no longer afford to ignore the world beyond the Peloponnesus. In 480 and 479, their hesitation had very nearly made it possible for Persia to conquer Greece. In the years immediately thereafter, by withdrawing to the Peloponnesus and giving way to Athens' bid for hegemony in the Aegean, Sparta contributed to the emergence of a power able to challenge her Peloponnesian coalition. The very existence of Athens' imperial democracy gave encouragement to Argos. In the 460s and again after the Peace of Nicias—on each occasion with the collusion of certain parties at Athens—Argos intervened in the factional strife of the Peloponnesian cities, put together a coalition of democracies hostile to Sparta, and challenged her suzerainty over the Peloponnesus. Thrice Athens and Sparta formally went to war. At no time were the results a foregone conclusion. Sparta survived the storms of the fifth century not because she was invincible but because she was stable—and fortunate. Had Athens given wholehearted support to either Argive coalition, had she not suffered a disaster in Egypt and another in Sicily, Lacedaemon might well have succumbed. The Spartans had every reason to think twice before withdrawing again to their Peloponnesian stronghold: for all of its advantages, isolationism had not been a policy blessed with unmixed success.[56]

The eagerness of Lysander and Agis to destroy Athens must have seemed reckless to traditionalists like Pausanias. That king might have been willing to grant that the threat posed by Athens in 432 to Sparta's hegemony in the Peloponnesus and hence to her fragile dominion in Laconia and Messenia had justified Sparta's original decision to go to war. But, with an eye to the dwindling number of Spartiates, the growing helot threat, Lacedaemon's potentially troublesome allies, and the permanent Argive problem, he can hardly have been indifferent to Sparta's taking on the responsibilities in central Greece that the razing of Athens would have entailed.

The presence of Thebes complicated the situation. During the war, the Thebans had eliminated the threat posed by Plataea, they had consolidated their hold on a Boeotia grown rich from the plunder of Attica, and they had proved their military prowess at Delium. In 421, they had spurned the Spartan demand that they accept the Peace of Nicias. Two years later, after the tribes resident in the neighborhood of Thermopylae had inflicted a severe defeat on the Spartan colony Heracleia Trachinia, Thebes had intervened, expelled the Spartan archon, and garrisoned the place. The Spartans did nothing at the time, but nursed the grievance: when the news came to Deceleia that the Athenian force in Sicily had been annihilated, Agis marched north to restore things to their original condition. There had been excuse for the Theban intervention: Heracleia Trachinia was then in danger and the Spartans were, at the time, deeply embroiled in affairs in the Peloponnesus. But the expulsion of the Spartan archon raised the suspicion that Thebes was intent on taking over the strategically placed colony—and this was an eventuality the Spartans were not prepared to contemplate.[57]

When Lysander and Agis proposed the destruction of Athens, the Corinthian and Theban delegates expressed enthusiastic support for the idea. Because Athens did not surrender at the time, the meeting was without consequence—but the Theban enthusiasm may have caused Lysander to reconsider. Sparta could not afford to tolerate the rise of an unchecked land power in central Greece, and Thebes was better positioned to benefit from an elimination of Athens than any other city. It was wiser to preserve Sparta's ancient rival and use her as a buffer.[58]

As it became evident that the Athenians were not prepared to capitulate, Lysander returned to the eastern Aegean and famine began to take its toll. When provisions ran low and men started to die of starvation, the assembly dispatched an embassy to Agis, offering to make an alliance with Sparta if Athens could keep her walls and the fortifications at the Peiraeus. Agis took care to reply that he had no authority in the matter and the Athenians sent the ambassadors on to Lacedaemon. When the ephors learned of the terms Athens' representatives were authorized to offer, they sent them back empty-handed before they had even reached Sparta.[59]

Xenophon's narrative at this point is very curious, and it might seem to be self-contradictory. On the one hand, he reports that the ephors curtly told the Athenians "to come back having taken better counsel [*kallíon bouleusaménous*] if it was peace that they wanted." On the other hand, he claims that an Athenian named Archestratus subsequently proposed the acceptance of a Spartan peace offer stipulating that ten stades—roughly six thousand feet—of each of the two Long Walls be knocked down.[60] This may reflect a certain carelessness of composition on Xenophon's part, but there is another, more attractive alternative.

In 432, after deciding that Athens had broken the terms of the Thirty Years Peace, the Spartans sent three embassies to Athens to make demands. The second set of ambassadors commanded the Athenians to abandon the siege of Potidaea and give Aegina her liberty, but somehow conveyed the information that war could be avoided if only the Megarian decree were revoked. This makes sense if the former was the message they had been authorized to give and the latter, information passed on by one of the Spartan advocates of peace. Aristotle reports that the Lacedaemonians were in the habit of placing men of differing views on the same embassy. If Lacedaemon appeared at times to speak with two different voices, this was the cause. Something of the sort may be the reason for the oddity of Xenophon's account. The Athenian ambassadors are said to have received the ephors' message at Sellasia in Laconia. It would be altogether in accord with what we know of Spartan politics for Pausanias or one of his associates to have instructed Athens' ambassadors with regard to the concessions they would have to make if they desired peace. The Agiad king was to do just that in differing circumstances nearly two years thereafter.[61]

In any case, the Athenians, at Cleophon's urging, are said to have rejected the overture and to have sent Archestratus to jail for suggesting its acceptance. This Archestratus' identity is uncertain. He may have been related to the like-named *stratēgós* killed in 406 at Mytilene, who is known to have been a close friend of Pericles son of Pericles. He may also have been a relative of the *stratēgós* Chaereas son of Archestratus, who had played a major role in the upheaval at Samos that opened the way for Alcibiades' return and who had later worked hand in glove with Theramenes, Thrasybulus, and Alcibiades as a *stratēgós* at Cyzicus in 410. If so, it would help explain Cleophon's hostility.[62]

Not long after this, probably in December 405, Theramenes

offered to go to Lysander to find out whether the Spartans intended to enslave the Athenians and to attempt to save the city. He was sent with full powers to negotiate on her behalf. According to Xenophon, he remained with Lysander for three long months, waiting until starvation had prepared the Athenians to take any terms offered. Upon return, he pleaded that Lysander had detained him and had then directed him to go to Sparta on the grounds that only the ephors had the authority to deal with such matters. The Athenians, who had given up their hope that Alcibiades would somehow come to their rescue, responded by sending Theramenes with nine others to treat with the ephors, granting them full powers to negotiate.[63]

Xenophon reports that, in the meantime, Lysander dispatched the Athenian exile Aristoteles to inform the ephors that "the answer he had made to Theramenes was that they alone had the authority with regard to war and peace." It is obvious that Lysander and Agis had been made painfully aware of the limits to their prerogatives after the meeting of the congress of the allies at which they had proposed Athens' destruction. The exercise of power at Sparta required careful attention to constitutional niceties: not even the final and glorious vindication of their policy at Aegospotami could free Agis and Lysander from such constraints.

There was more, however, to Aristoteles' mission than meets the eye. It was not absolutely necessary to send anyone to assure the ephors that Lysander had not been arrogating their responsibilities to himself. That would have been evident enough when the embassy from Athens arrived at Sparta. Nor was it particularly appropriate to send an Athenian exile to accomplish the task. Xenophon himself casts doubt on the truth of Theramenes' claim that he had been detained—doubt which suggests what Lysias openly claims: that a conspiracy was afoot.

Before Theramenes' arrival, Lysander had favored Athens' destruction. But, according to the tactician Polyaenus, he urged in the end that a moderate settlement be imposed in order to make Athens a satellite of Sparta positioned to counter the Theban threat in central Greece. There was no one better fitted to convey this message than Aristoteles who, in 411, had attempted to betray Athens to Sparta and who had no future in 404 other than in an Athens tied securely to Sparta's apron strings. It is no accident that the Spartan peace terms required the restoration of Athens' exiles. This was part of the price which Theramenes had contracted to pay during his extended sojourn on Samos.[64]

The decree presented to Theramenes and his fellow envoys by the ephors is quoted in its entirety by Plutarch:

These things the authorities [*tà télē*] of the Lacedaemonians make known: tear down the Peiraeus walls and the Long Walls, evacuate all the cities, and stay in your own land. If you do this and receive back your exiles, you will have peace if that is what you desire. Concerning the number of ships, do what is determined there.

The Athenians had no choice but to accept. Just over sixty years had passed since the inception of the strategic rivalry that had for generations set Sparta and Athens at odds. On Thucydides' reckoning, twenty-seven years and a few days had passed since the beginning of what I have in these volumes called Sparta's second Attic war. And now, on the sixteenth of Mounichion in the Athenian year 405/4—almost certainly in March of the latter year—the great struggle was over and, as Xenophon reports, "Lysander sailed into the Peiraeus; the exiles returned; and … the victors began with great eagerness to raze the walls."[65]

Soon thereafter, the Athenians joined the Spartan alliance, agreeing to have the same friends and enemies as the Lacedaemonians and to follow them by land and sea wherever they might lead. The agreement included the normal clause by which Sparta agreed to respect her ally's autonomy—a clause stipulating that the Athenians employ their "ancestral constitution [*pátrios politeía*]."[66]

Calculations of interest had determined Lysander's decision, and his reversal of position had no doubt ended debate. But it would be an error to ignore sentiment altogether. Aelian tells us that, when the Spartans consulted the Delphic oracle concerning their wish to eliminate the *pólis* of the Athenians, they were instructed "not to remove the common hearth of Hellas," and Justin reports that the Lacedaemonians told the Athenian ambassadors that it was not Sparta's intention "to pluck out one of the two eyes of Greece." The latter remark was a nice touch: more than half a century before, Cimon son of Miltiades had led an Athenian force to Sparta's aid on the occasion of a helot revolt, justifying the action by calling on his fellow citizens "not to look on, standing idly by, while Hellas went lame and their own city became ill-matched with her yokefellow." The Spartans had not forgotten Marathon, Artemisium, Salamis, Plataea, Mycale, Eurymedon, and Cypriot Salamis. The spirit of Callicratidas had survived Aegospotami.[67]

Sparta's Imperial Venture

War in its outcome never achieves finality.

Carl von Clausewitz

T HERE WAS A celebratory atmosphere as the Spartans and their allies had the Long Walls of Athens and the fortifications about the Peiraeus torn down. There was, Xenophon reports, music "supplied by flute girls" and those victorious in the conflict regarded "that day as the beginning of freedom for Greece."[1] Through times of open warfare and armed peace, the strategic rivalry between Athens and her allies and Sparta and hers had lasted for more than six decades. Now it was over, finally over—and the victors can have felt nothing but relief. Regarding the disposition of Athens, there had been disagreement within the coalition of Greek cities, to be sure. But that was to be expected. Coalitions made up of independent powers are always a bit contentious. That day, it really was easy to forget such disputes and to suppose that a new era of peace and freedom was really at hand.

The elation had arguably been even more intense in 479 when the Mede was forced from Hellas. Xerxes' invasion had not lasted long. But the terror it had generated was far greater than that to which the enduring strategic rivalry that followed gave rise; and in that year, three-quarters of a century before the end of Sparta's third and last Attic war, there had been no storm clouds on the horizon.

Of course, the exultation had not then lasted. Soon enough, the victors began eyeing one another warily, as they had before the Persians had appeared on the scene; and, within a decade and a half, they were maneuvering against one another.

In 404, the situation was, in fact, far more troubling than it had been in 479. It was the pact with the Great King that had made Lysander's victory possible, and that arrangement was, as everyone understood, an alliance of convenience marred by an antagonism that the Spartans could neither conceal nor entirely suppress. Moreover, there was a transition underway in Persia. The old king, Darius II, was dead by 10 April; and a conflict over the succession was shaping up between his first-born son Arsaces, the *mār šarri*, and his mother's favorite, Arsaces' much younger brother Cyrus—the figure with whom, thanks to the machinations of Lysander, the Lacedaemonians were by now quite deeply entangled. Should the latter try to oust and kill his older sibling, the war between the brothers was apt with alacrity to become a war between Sparta and Persia; and, if Cyrus failed, the vast wealth hoarded by the Persians would almost certainly be redeployed against their sometime Lacedaemonian ally.[2]

Finally, there was the question of the Aegean. Hitherto, Athens had kept the peace, suppressed piracy, and provided for the defense of the Hellenes in the region. Now, Lacedaemon would have to shoulder that responsibility, and it was an open question whether she was constitutionally suited for the task. As we have already had occasion to note, on the eve of Sparta's second Attic war, an Athenian delegation at Sparta had responded to an anti-Athenian diatribe delivered by the envoys from Corinth. Among the things that its members did by way of trying to deter the Lacedaemonians from launching a war was to issue a warning apt to have irritated some Spartans and to have elicited grudging assent from others. If they substituted an empire of their own for that long maintained by the Athenians, the Spartiates were told, they would quickly squander "the goodwill" that they had secured as a consequence of the fear inspired by the Athenians. If they sustained "the pattern of conduct" they had evidenced when they led the Hellenes against the Mede, this they would surely do. After all, their "institutions, customs, and laws" set them in opposition to their fellow Greeks; and even more to the point, when sent abroad, Lacedaemonians abided neither by those nor by the "customs and laws" employed elsewhere in the Hellenic world. In 404, there were not all that many alive who remembered the deliberations held twenty-eight years before, but some members of the *gerousía* may have rehearsed in their own minds at that time the remarks made in 432.[3]

In any case, no one supposed that perpetual peace was in the offing and that history had come to an end. Such delusions are peculiar to the age in which we now live. George Santayana was by no means the first to have insisted that war is an ordinary and unavoidable part of life. In the late fifth century of the pre-modern era and for a long time thereafter, nearly everyone took for granted the opinion attributed in Plato's *Laws* to the lawgiver of Crete: "What most men call peace, he held to be only a name. In truth, for everyone, there exists by nature at all times an undeclared war among cities." This was, in fact, the common sense of the matter. In 404, from the perspective of the Hellenes, the return of armed conflict was only a matter of time.[4]

Of course, with regard to freedom and peace, there surely was a measure of wishful thinking in some quarters—but it did not last long. Within months, Lysander had imposed narrow, tyrannical juntas in Athens and in the cities scattered throughout what had hitherto been her dominion, and Sparta's imperial venture was underway. If Xenophon devoted the opening chapters of his *Hellenica* to finishing the story told by Thucydides regarding Athens' self-inflicted demise, it was to the fate of Lacedaemon's great enterprise that he devoted the remainder of the work.[5]

DATING THE DEATH OF
ARTAXERXES SON OF XERXES

T HAT THE FIRST Artaxerxes died in the Persian year 424/3 there can be no doubt. The precise timing is, however, in question. His passing is noted in three contemporary or near-contemporary sources—in Thucydides the historian, in the *Persika* of Ctesias of Cnidus, and on various clay tablets found in Babylonia. We can infer from Thucydides (4.50) that things were unsettled in the immediate aftermath of this Great King's death, but he does not relate the details. For these we have to turn to the surviving fragments of Ctesias who described at length what amounted to an interregnum.

There was a time when scholars were inclined to doubt the veracity of the last-mentioned figure's report. It is salacious, they rightly pointed out, and what he has to say about much earlier times is, indeed, fanciful. Some in the grips of a recent academic fad even charged Ctesias with the unforgivable sin of "Orientalism." Indeed, he was, we were told by one scholar, the original sinner. He was, they implied, yet another Greek bigot with a tiresome propensity for attributing serious public policy decisions to intrigues conducted by the women of the royal family. Some even doubted that Ctesias had ever even served, as he insists he had, as a physician at the court of the second Artaxerxes.[1]

There were never any grounds for dismissing Ctesias' testimony concerning the events of the second half of the fifth century. His contemporary Xenophon, who knew a great deal about the Achaemenid regime, accepted his veracity. Moreover, as we have seen, the tales that he spun concerning intrigue at the Achaemenid court are in no way fantastic. They, in fact, closely resemble what we know to have been true at the courts in absolute monarchies given to polygyny and bereft of a law of succession that existed in other places and times.[2]

This was not, however, sufficient to rein in the skeptics. If it is no longer fashionable to dismiss Ctesias' claims, that is only because we now have Babylonian evidence confirming, at least in part, his assertions. Put simply, the figures said by Ctesias to have played a prominent, if ancillary, role in the struggle for power that ensued in the wake of the first Artaxerxes' death—figures mentioned in no other surviving Greek source—have turned up as the owners of large tracts of land in southern Mesopotamia. Even more to the point, the clay tablets from the region confirm Ctesias' claims in two particulars: those said to have sided with a contender who suffered defeat in the struggle that supposedly then took place seem soon thereafter to have been deprived of their lands, and those said to have backed the ultimate victor appear to have been rewarded with generous property grants.[3]

For his part, Thucydides (4.50) tells us that, in the winter of 425/4, the Athenians captured at Eion in Thrace a Persian envoy named Artaphernes who was making his way to Lacedaemon. "Later," he adds, they sent this envoy back to the Great King with a delegation from Athens. But when this party reached Ephesus and prepared to set out for Sardis and the royal road that led from there to Susa, they got word that Artaxerxes had quite recently died, and, with this in mind, they returned home."

Ctesias' account (*FGrH* 688 F15.47–50) makes sense of Thucydides' report. The former tells us that there was an interregnum—which would explain why the news they heard at Ephesus caused the Athenian envoys to turn back. There was no point in initiating negotiations if the succession was unresolved.

According to Ctesias, when Artaxerxes died, the crown prince

Xerxes, his sole legitimate son, assumed office but he did not last long. Forty-five days later, one of Artaxerxes' seventeen illegitimate sons, a man named Sogdianus, assassinated him and assumed office in his place. He, in turn, was ousted by his half-brother Ochus, another of Artaxerxes' bastards, six and a half months thereafter.

There is a variant report in Polyaenus' *Stratagemata* (7.17.1) that is also consistent with Thucydides' account. In it, Polyaenus mentions neither Xerxes II nor Sogdianus. On his telling, Ochus concealed Artaxerxes' death for ten months, during this period he issued dispatches in his father's name, and these missives ordered Artaxerxes' subjects to acknowledge their true author as his successor and to offer him obedience.

There is much that is in dispute, but this much is clear. Ochus did become Great King, and he took the throne-name Darius. To obviate confusion, we now call him Darius II. To this we can add that we are in possession of a plausible report from the orator Andocides (3.29), specifying that soon after this Ochus came to the throne—almost certainly in 423/2—a delegation of Athenians led by a prominent citizen named Epilycus negotiated an arrangement with the man.[4]

If we had no sources other than Thucydides, Ctesias, and Polyaenus, it would make sense to suppose that Artaxerxes died at some point prior to or during the campaigning season of 424. It is, after all, exceedingly unlikely that the Athenians held Artaphernes hostage for well over a year. The natural thing for them to do after learning that the Great King was dickering with the Lacedaemonians was to dispatch an embassy to Susa forthwith—in the spring or summer of 424, at the latest—to shore up relations. The interregnum of eight to ten months would then begin at some point in the first ten months of 424 and stretch from some point prior to or during the summer to the end of that year and perhaps a month or two beyond.

To this conclusion, the Babylonian evidence—much of it deciphered, if not discovered, in recent decades—poses what might seem an insuperable challenge. This evidence consists of legal documents that are, as was the practice in that province, dated quite precisely by day and month within the particular year of the reign of a given Great King. In ordinary circumstances, documents of this sort tell us when word of the death of one king and of the succession of another reached southern Mesopotamia.

In this case, we are faced with a puzzle. None of the Babylonian tablets mentions Xerxes II at all, and none mentions Sogdianus. If we had no other source, if we were to judge solely from the tablets that have been deciphered and are now in our possession, we would have to assume that Artaxerxes was still King in late December 424, that the Ochus who assumed the kingship under the name Darius succeeded to the throne on or shortly before 10 January 423, and that there was no interregnum worth mentioning—certainly, none lasting forty-five days, leave aside eight to ten months.[5]

There is no way to reconcile the evidence now available without supposing that there is something somewhere amiss or at least something that we do not understand. If we were to take the Babylonian evidence as dispositive, as most scholars are now inclined to do,[6] we would have to suppose that the Athenians sat on Artaphernes for well over a year before making any move toward sending him him home. This is, of course, conceivable. But, in the circumstances, it is exceedingly hard to explain. The Athenians' entire strategy vis-à-vis Sparta was predicated on the presumption that the Persians would stay out of the fray. The mission of Artaphernes was for them alarming. After capturing him, they had reason to move quickly to shore up relations with the Mede.

Even more to the point, if we were to take the Babylonian evidence as dispositive, we would have to discard not only the narrative found in the surviving fragments of Ctesias but also the account supplied by Polyaenus. In ordinary circumstances, it would not be credible that Artaxerxes' sole legitimate son Xerxes ruled for more than six weeks and there was no acknowledgement of the fact in Babylonia. The latter capital was not all that far distant from the royal seat at Susa, and the Achaemenid postal system was efficient. Moreover, on Ctesias' telling, Ochus did not announce his intentions and raise his standard until well after the assassination of this Xerxes—while the Babylonian records appear to have acknowledged him as Great King within a few days of the arrival of the news of Artaxerxes' demise, if not on the very day that this news reached southern Mesopotamia.

We must choose. We must either reject or radically emend Ctesias' narrative and Polyaenus' account and suppose that the Athenians held one of the Great King's envoys hostage for well over a year. Or we must suppose that, for eight months or more in 424, the authorities in Babylonia insisted that, in their official dealings with one another, the residents of that province operate on the basis of a legal fiction—that Artaxerxes son of Xerxes was still alive.

Neither option is palatable. On the one hand, Ctesias' narrative is, in many pertinent particulars, confirmed by Babylonian evidence, as we have seen. Moreover, we have good reason to believe that it derives, at least in part, from what this inquisitive physician elicited from Ochus' consort Parysatis, a woman who was one of the principal actors in the drama that had then taken place: Ctesias *FGrH* 688 F15.51. It is, moreover, hard to believe that the Athenians, who had every reason to want to please the Persian monarch, held one of his envoys prisoner for well over a year.

On the other hand, there was, as far as we can tell, no precedent in the Achaemenid empire's sometimes stormy past for such a resort to legal fiction. Moreover, the satrap of Babylonia during the latter part of Artaxerxes' reign was his half-brother Artarios—whose son Menostanes agreed, Ctesias reports (*FGrH* 688 F15.48–49), to serve as the Chiliarch of Sogdianus. Why would Artarios refuse to acknowledge the accession of the man backed by his son?

In recent years, since the discovery of the pertinent tablets, most scholars have ignored the tale told by Polyaenus and have concluded that Ctesias' narrative must somehow be made to fit within the chronological scheme supplied by the Babylonian documents.[7] There is a way to do so that would, in fact, accommodate Polyaenus' report—though hitherto, to the best of my knowledge, it has nowhere been considered. Put simply, it is possible that the stories told by Ctesias and Polyaenus are incomplete and that Artaxerxes was alive but in a coma for some months prior to his death—that Thucydides was mildly confused and that it was news of Artaxerxes' incapacity that occasioned the premature return to Athens from Ephesus of the embassy dispatched to Susa in the summer of 424; that what is described in Ctesias as the reigns of Xerxes II and Sogdianus took place during this period; that Ochus was operating from Babylon for at least part of this time in the fashion described by Polyaenus; that in late December 424 or very early January 423, when Artaxerxes finally died, Ochus, whose allies had seized control in Babylonia, immediately asserted his claim; and that the Babylonian documents reflect the date of Artaxerxes' ultimate demise and that of Ochus' recognition as Great King in Babylonia.

There are two other alternatives. On the one hand, it is possible that unbeknownst to us, when a Great King died, there was in ordinary circumstances resort to a legal fiction—that, to avoid the legal awkwardnesses associated with an interregnum, Cyrus and his successors stipulated that the passing of a King and the end of his reign not be formally acknowledged until his burial at Naqsh-e-Rustam northwest of Persepolis and the formal investiture of his successor at Pasargadae.

On the other hand, one could suppose that something highly irregular was underway: to wit, that Artaxerxes died in the first half of 424 and that in the second half of that year there was in Babylon a resort to a legal fiction. If it was common knowledge that Artaxerxes' son Xerxes was unfit for command—which may well have been the case—Artarios may, in anticipation of his elimination, have initiated what was an unorthodox, unprecedented practice. Once, however, this Xerxes was dead, others at Babylon, who thought Sogdianus no less unfit, may well have shunted Artarios aside while maintaining the fiction that Artaxerxes was still alive.

It is important to keep in mind what Ctesias (*FGrH* 688 F15.47, 50) tells us and what we learn from the Babylonian tablets (BM 33342 with Lewis *SP*, 72): that Ochus and his consort Parysatis were both half-Babylonian; that they popped up in Babylon not long after Artaxerxes' death; that, before launching his bid for the throne, Ochus met with prominent figures, such as Arsames, the longtime satrap of Egypt, and Artoxares, who had once been Artaxerxes' favorite eunuch and who had reportedly been exiled to Armenia; and that these two men strongly encouraged the venture. Geographical considerations leave little doubt that this threesome met in Babylon. To this, we can add other evidence from the Babylonian tablets suggesting that Ochus and Parysatis had the backing of a Babylonian notable named Bēlšunu.[8] It was without a doubt in Babylon that the victor in this contest was chosen, and we should not assume that everything that took place in Babylonia following Artaxerxes' demise was done by the book.

COMMERCE WITH THE COMMUNITIES ON THE BLACK SEA, THE CURRENT FROM THE EUXINE TO THE AEGEAN, AND THE GEOSTRATEGIC SIGNIFICANCE OF PROCONNESUS

W E KNOW very little about island of Proconnesus and the like-named *pólis* located on its southern coast in the west, but there is much that we can surmise. Strabo tells us that the latter was a Milesian foundation. Herodotus names the tyrant who ruled the city on Persia's behalf in the time of the first Darius' Scythian expedition, and he reports the Proconnesians' participation in the Ionian revolt that followed. Thucydides does not have occasion to mention either the *pólis* or the island under her control, but we know from the inscriptions that make up what scholars term the Athenian Tribute Lists that the former was a *phóros*-contributing member of Athens' Delian League from 452 down to 418 (and, in all likelihood, beyond) and that it coughed up three talents of silver a year. It makes sense to suppose that Proconnesus joined that alliance soon after the Persian Wars and remained thereafter loyal to her hegemon.[1]

The silence of our sources belies the geostrategic importance of what was the only island community in the region constituted by the Hellespont, the Sea of Marmara, and the Bosporus. The *póleis* on the mainland in Europe were vulnerable to attack by the Thracians to the north; those on the mainland in Asia were similarly vulnerable to assault by the Persians to the south. As long, however, as the Athenians were dominant at sea, Proconnesus would be theirs; and, should any community on either or both of the nearby shores be conquered or revolt, this island would be the perfect staging ground for an attempted recovery.

There is more to be said. In a speech delivered in or soon after 336, Demosthenes boasted that he had seen to it that Athens' grain supply was carried along "friendly shores" from the Euxine all the way to the Peiraeus, and he singles out in this connection not only the island of Euboea but also Byzantium, Proconnesus, the Thracian Chersonnesus, Abydos on the Asian shore, and the isle of Tenedos, which is located in the Aegean immediately south of the mouth of the Hellespont. This passage strongly suggests that, in the fourth century, the Athenians provided a convoy for the grain fleet that made its way each September from the Black Sea to the Aegean and that the island of Proconnesus served as a naval base from which the Athenians were able to prevent interference with the commerce that passed through the Sea of Marmara. A glance at a map would suggest that the same is apt to have been true in the previous century, when protecting the grain trade was for Athens at least as vital strategically, if not more so.[2]

Proconnesus may have had yet another function. Long ago, Rhys Carpenter drew the attention of scholars to the difficulty involved in journeying by sea from the Aegean to the Euxine. To begin with, as he pointed out, there is a great rush of water from the latter to the former, and the current running through the Hellespont and the Bosporus is strong and swift—especially at the two straits' narrowest points. To make matters worse, the prevailing wind runs in the same direction during the season best suited to maritime travel, rendering it difficult, even today, for a sailing vessel to make its way upstream against the current. In antiquity, he argued, when such ships were dependent on square-rigged sails of the sort that rule out sailing into the wind, this was, much of the time, impossible. It was Carpenter's judgment that it was not until the introduction of the penteconter—a galley powered by fifty rowers—that ancient mariners operating from the Aegean could reach the Sea of Marmara; and, mindful that the Bosporus is not much more than half the width of the Hellespont and that the current there runs roughly twice as fast, he raised doubts as to whether commerce conducted by sea from the Propontis to the Euxine was practicable even then.[3]

Recent studies have refined and qualified Carpenter's claims. They acknowledge that the Hellespont is narrow and the Bosporus narrower still—with the former no more than thirteen hundred seventy-two yards wide at its narrowest point and with the latter at its narrowest point under seven hundred thirty-two yards in width. They add that neither of these two channels is at all deep. The Hellespont is under two hundred feet in depth while the depth of the Bosporus is just over half that. On average, they report, the Hellespont current runs at three knots (3.45 miles per hour) and, where it is at its narrowest, the current clocks in at five knots (5.75 miles per hour) while the Bosporus current averages four or five knots (4.6 to 5.75 miles per hour) and speeds up to six or seven knots (6.9–8.1 miles per hour) at the narrows.

These studies are, nonetheless, at odds with Carpenter in two regards. First, they draw attention to the fact that in the summer the wind occasionally blows from the south, and they suggest that, even in this season, travel upstream may be possible for a sailing ship with a skipper patient enough to wait for a favorable wind. Then, they observe that in the late autumn, in the winter, and the very early spring, when the current is less swift, the wind is quite variable so that it is possible, though difficult, for a sailing ship to journey to the northeast in these circumstances.[4]

None of this, however, alters the basic point that can be gleaned from Carpenter's original analysis. For one must still pause to consider not just how the grain was transported to the Aegean from the Euxine but also how the ships that bore that grain made it back to the Black Sea with the cargoes meant to pay for the cost of that grain—which cannot have been easy.

There is one further piece of evidence that may help explain how this was done, and Demosthenes' testimony underlines its significance. If Aristotle is to be trusted, in his day, a goodly proportion of the citizenry of Byzantium and Tenedos, two of the cities on Demosthenes' list of communities that were geostrategically vital vis-à-vis the grain trade, seem to have earned their living as ferrymen.[5]

We can imagine these men ferrying goods up and down the Bosporus and the Hellespont in merchant galleys equipped, as they all were, with sails enabling them to catch, on occasion, a favorable breeze, or on great barges towed by penteconters or triremes. We can imagine the employers of these ferrymen serving as middlemen; warehousing sacks of grain, amphoras of wine and of oil, and other items in their own territory; and selling them to other middlemen or directly to the merchants in command of the great freighters [*holkádes*] that plied the Aegean and the Black Sea. It is also conceivable that citizens of Proconnesus served a similar function. They were certainly well situated to do so.[6]

There are two other possibilities. These *holkádes* were sailing ships wholly bereft of oars. As the term's etymology suggests, they frequently had to be towed—in and out of harbors, for example. In the proper season, these great freighters could no doubt easily make their way under sail downstream from the Black Sea to the Aegean with grain in their holds. The return voyage—when they were loaded with wine, olive oil, and other items—was another matter. In the autumn, winter, and spring when the winds were less likely to hinder their efforts and might even provide assistance, we can imagine the ferrymen of Byzantium, Tenedos, and, if my suspicions are correct, Proconnesus using their galleys to laboriously tow these *holkádes* back from the Aegean through the Hellespont, the Propontis, and the Bosporus to the Euxine. For we know that triremes were sometimes used for towing. Alternatively, in antiquity, there might have been a tow path running along the Bosporus in the territory of Byzantium or Chalcedon, as there apparently was in later times. Gangs of men or teams of oxen might have been all that was required.[7]

What I have written here is, of necessity, speculative, and my guesswork may not be adequate. As Tim Severin discovered in the spring and early summer of 1984, when he journeyed in his modern *Argo* from Volos in Thessaly to Georgia in the Soviet Union, a galley constructed on the Mycenaean model with a shallow draft and equipped with a square sail can, with the right wind, make its way from the Aegean up the Hellespont to the Sea of Marmara. It is conceivable that, in the right circumstances, a similar sailing vessel could make its way up the Bosporus—though, thanks to the speed and strength of its current, this would be more difficult.[8]

This possibility notwithstanding, a puzzle remains. Why would Proconnesus and Tenedos be on Demosthenes' list alongside Byzantium, Abydos, and the Thracian Chersonnesus? And why should Aristotle report that a noteworthy proportion of the citizens of Byzantium and of Tenedos made their living as ferrymen? One could argue that the Byzantine ferrymen carried men and goods from Europe to Asia and back, and some of them no doubt did so. But what about Tenedos? There is surely a connection between the strength of the current that ran from the Black Sea to the Mediterranean, the difficulty involved in shipping goods from the latter body of water upstream to the former, and the fact that at the southwesternmost point on the Bosporus and just beyond the outlet of the Hellespont there were cities in which a noteworthy part of the population made their living ferrying people and goods. The supply of ferrymen mentioned by Aristotle suggests demand, and the formidable strength of the current running between the two bodies of water provides a plausible explanation for that demand.

One final observation may deserve consideration. The ancient literary evidence suggests that the grain ships tended to bring their cargo to the Aegean in mid-September—well after the grain in and near the Crimea is ordinarily harvested. For this delay, there may be an explanation. In high summer, the prevailing winds must have rendered it exceedingly difficult, if not impossible, for the *holkádes* and other sailing ships to make their way back from the Aegean to the Black Sea. In the fall, after September, however, it is far less uncommon for the wind to be blowing from the south, the west, and the southwest.

In this connection, it is also worth noting that the grain ships tended to make their journey from the Euxine to the Aegean in a large body. Piracy could be a serious threat, and there was safety in numbers—especially if the Athenians were prepared to provide a convoy.[9]

DATING THE CRISES
FACED BY DARIUS II

A CCORDING TO CTESIAS (*FGrH* 688 F15.52–55), in the years subsequent to his elevation to the kingship, Darius II faced serious challenges to his authority on at least three occasions. If we presume, as we no doubt should, that Ctesias' list is chronological, the first to make an attempt to supplant him was his own brother Arsites, who had the assistance of a satrap named Artyphius, who was the son of the younger Megabyzus and who had, in all likelihood, succeeded his father as viceroy of "the Land Across-the-Water" in Syria. The second was Pissouthnes son of Xerxes' brother or son Hystaspes, who had long governed from Sardis a satrapy in western Anatolia, and the third was Teriteuchmes son of Hydarnes, the younger Darius' son-in-law. What Ctesias does not supply is a timetable for these events.

In my narrative, I have presumed that the first two of these rebellions took place shortly after Darius had supplanted Sogdianus as the ruler of the Persian empire and that the third took place a decade or so later. I make the first presumption for a simple and obvious reason. In monarchies, when the designated successor dies and there is no obvious heir, the ambitious are not behindhand. They grab while the grabbing is good, and the efforts of one are a spur to the rest. When the elder Darius and his six confederates killed Cambyses' younger brother or the Magus masquerading as the man, there was just such an opening; and those prominent in the various nations under Persia's sway were not slow to seize the opportunity. A like pattern presented itself in the Roman empire when Nero, the last of the Julio-Claudians, committed suicide. Suddenly, it was evident that an emperor could be made in some place other than Rome, and a number of ambitious generals [*imperatores*] entered the fray. It is hard to believe that Arsites and Pissouthnes would have waited to launch their bids until Ochus had fully consolidated power; and we, in fact, have concrete evidence—often without good reason dismissed—that those dispatched to put down Pissouthnes' rebellion in western Anatolia were active there in 422 or 421.[1]

To my contention, there is, to be sure, one obvious objection. Arsites was still very much alive at the end of 417. In the second year of Darius' reign, an Arsites appears as one of the major landowners of Babylonia. The relevant cuneiform tablets (PBS II/1 nos. 48–49, 51–52, 191: BE X no. 58) identify him as the *mār bīti* Arrišittu—as the Son of the (Royal) House Arsites. In December, 417, this Arrišittu reappears as the owner of "the Estate in front of the Palace": PBS II/1 no. 137, NBRVT no. 189. It is extremely unlikely that the Arrišittu of the tablets is an Arsites other than the younger Darius' brother. The name is rare: it has not been found in the Persepolis tablets, and it appears elsewhere only with reference to the Achaemenid satrap ensconced at Dascyleium in 334.

How, an objector is bound to ask, can Arsites still be a major landowner in Babylonia some five or six years after he staged a rebellion? Although the question is a good one, it applies with no less force to Sogdianus' supporters Menostanes and Pharnakyas. They do disappear from the cuneiform documents after 424 (Lewis, *SP*, 18 n. 94, 74 n. 162). But their deaths are placed by Ctesias (*FGrH* 688 F15.52 with Lewis, *SP*, 24 n. 132, 80 n. 192) after the collapse of Arsites' rebellion, not in the immediate aftermath of Sogdianus' brief reign. In both cases, the answer is supplied elsewhere by Ctesias (F15.50–52). Thanks to the influence of Parysatis, the Ochus who became Darius was as much a fox as he was a lion; and just as he had lured Sogdianus into surrender by intimating that he would be treated mercifully, so he is apt to have attempted the same with regard to his other adversaries. Millennia before Vladimir Putin bamboozled Yevgeny Prigozhin, this aspirant recognized that it would be useful to allow these rebels to suppose that, were they to abandon their bids for the throne, they would not be severely punished.

It is, moreover, easy to imagine why Arsites might have been still at large at the end of 417. His ally Artyphius had twice defeated royal armies, and forces of this sort could not be conjured into existence overnight. Moreover, Ctesias (F15.52) tells us that, once this particular individual was in her husband's clutches, Parysatis had to press Darius and press him hard to execute his only full brother. Had she not done so, Arsites might still have appeared in the cuneiform documents at the end of his brother's reign as a major landowner in Babylonia.[2]

The circumstances pertinent to Teriteuchmes' rebellion were of another sort. He was a member of an ancient Persian family drawn by his father Hydarnes into a close alliance with the Ochus who renamed himself Darius. The forging of this alliance, which is mentioned by Ctesias (F15.55) only after he has alluded to the rebellions of Arsites and Pissouthnes, makes excellent sense as a response to the crisis occasioned by those two revolts; and thus it is only later, after Hydarnes' death and Teriteuchmes' succession to his father's satrapy, that he begins to contemplate murdering his wife and staging a rebellion.

We know that both the father and the son were satraps, and we can be confident that their satrapy lay somewhere in the east. For other men held the satrapies in the west in and after 423, and we know their names and quite a bit about them. We also know that the ancestor of Teriteuchmes and his father—the Hydarnes who was a co-conspirator of the elder Darius—was sent by that Darius to put down a rebellion in Media and subsequently served as that vitally important province's satrap, and we know of one satrapy in Anatolia that passed from father to son over a number of generations and of another in the Levant that passed from father to son. So, it makes sense to suppose that Teriteuchmes and his father served in Media and that the revolt of the former, which Ctesias describes, is identical with the uprising in Media said by Xenophon to have been quelled in 409. The removal of the offspring of the original Hydarnes from their family seat seems to have left the satrapy of Media unsettled. In the aftermath of this rebellion, not long after the younger Cyrus' arrival at Sardis, there was another uprising in Media that required the attention of the Great King—this one among the Cadusians who resided in the wilds along the western shore of the Caspian Sea in the south.[3]

WHO WAS HIERAMENES?

ITHIN THE Achaemenid hierarchy during the reign
of Darius II, Hieramenes was obviously a figure of
great importance; and, during the period after 413, he
seems to have been deeply involved in the formulation of Persian
policy in Anatolia. It is telling that he is mentioned alongside Tissaphernes on the Xanthus stele in a passage that seems to be referring
to the conference that took place at Caunus late in the winter of 411
in which arrangements were settled with the disgruntled *súmbouloi*
dispatched from Lacedaemon; and he reappears in the spring,
alongside Tissaphernes and the sons of Pharnaces, at Thuc. 8.58 as
a party to the third and most important of the early Spartan–
Persian agreements.[1]

It is an error to see in Ezra 4:8–9, 17, rescripts parallel to those in
Thuc. 8.58.1. If Hieramenes were merely the royal secretary attached
to Tissaphernes' chancellery (Hdt. 8.128.3 and Xen. *An.* 1.2.20,
which should be read with Lewis, *SP*, 25 n. 143), as some scholars
suspect, or if he were among the "associates" of Tissaphernes as others argue, he would not have been listed among those who ratified
this agreement.[2] That he is the brother-in-law of the younger Darius,
whom Xenophon or an interpolator later mentions (*Hell.* 2.1.8–9),
we need not doubt; and, if Hieramenes and Ariaramnes (Hdt. 7.11.2)
are alternative Greek transcriptions of the Achaemenid name found
in DB I.5, AmH, and AsH, as seems likely, it is reasonable to suppose that he was a Son of the Royal House. His marriage to a daughter of the elder Artaxerxes leaves little doubt that he came from the

high nobility. In this connection, note Ctesias *FGrH* 688 F13.20, who refers to an Ariaramnes who was satrap of Cappadocia in the elder Darius' time, and see Hdt. 8.90.4, who speaks of a homonymous Persian of some importance in Xerxes' entourage who was friendly to the Ionians.

There is, then, something to be said for Lewis' suggestion (*SP*, 104, 107) that Hieramenes was a special envoy from the King, who was there to ratify the document on his master's behalf. But this hypothesis leaves unexplained the presence of Hieramenes' sons in Anatolia after 407 (Xen. *Hell.* 2.1.8–9). One is left wondering whether Hieramenes was not himself a satrap somewhere in that subcontinent who was comparable to his fellow ratifiers and fully equal in status. If so, his presence at Caunus at a conference not attended, as far as we can tell, by Pharnabazus or any of the latter's brothers might be taken as evidence that his sphere of responsibility was situated in Cappadocia or along Anatolia's south coast.

It is conceivable that Krüger was right in reading *Lukíēs* instead of *Kilikíēs* at Hdt. 9.107.2, that Xerxes made Xeinagoras the governor of Lycia and not Cilicia, and that this Hieramenes was one of his successors in the post. The Xeinagoras mentioned in this passage of Herodotus as having been given a province hailed from Halicarnassus, which is quite a bit closer to Lycia (9.70.2) than to Cilicia; and, apart from Herodotus' satrapy list (3.89–97), all of the available evidence suggests that Cilicia was never a proper province and remained semi-independent under its native dynasty.[3]

GREAT MAGNATES IN THE ACHAEMENID EMPIRE

T HE CLASS OF great magnates is best attested in Mesopotamia where the financial records provide a clear picture of feudal property relations.[1] The scattered references in the ancient Greek literature and in inscriptions to property arrangements in Asia Minor and in some of the areas visited by Xenophon and the Ten Thousand corroborate the impression given by the Babylonian evidence and indicate that the social and economic system established by the Achaemenids remained intact in the Hellenistic period. Indeed, some of the evidence suggests continuity from the time of the Assyrians.

After conquering a region or suppressing a local insurrection, the Great King tended to do two things. First, he seized some of the best land and bestowed possession, but not full title, on his followers. Then, he reached an accommodation of sorts with what remained of the local elite, rewarding collaboration in a similar fashion. This gave rise to a class of rural landlords—some of them foreign, others native to the territory. In Asia Minor in the Achaemenid period, this was exemplified by the Persian Asidates and by the unknown owner of eleven parcels of land in the upper Granicus valley. For the Hellenistic period, we have the Greek or Macedonian Mnesimachus. These feudal barons built the castles and fortified towns still evident in some of the place-names of Asia Minor, and they subsisted on the product of a numerous class made up of serfs of a sort. Preeminent within this landed gentry were the satraps and their subordinates.[2]

These great magnates were expected to supply cavalry and infantry in time of need. As the case of the Persian Oeobazus and that of Croesus' fabulously wealthy grandson and heir Pythius show, the Achaemenid kings were prepared to punish with the greatest severity those who sought in any way to evade their feudal obligations. The King could, on the other hand, be extraordinarily generous to his favorites and Benefactors, granting them the use of villages and land, making them governors of or tyrants over cities, or freeing their holdings from the considerable tax burden they bore—a tax burden shared even by the Greek city-dwellers who cultivated the King's land. The onetime Spartan king Demaratus and his descendants, for example, benefited from the largess of Darius the Great; Gongylus the Eretrian and his descendants, from that of Xerxes. The case of Themistocles deserves special notice: Artaxerxes gave him Magnesia for his bread, Lampsacus for his wine, and Myos for his meat. This parallels closely the holdings of the Persian Queens. Further examples could be listed.[3]

Like the military colonists, the gentry needed the Achaemenid regime as much as it needed them. A fair proportion of these great magnates were Persians. There were others as well who were foreign to the districts they controlled. In Egypt, Babylon, Media, and elsewhere, their presence provoked resentment among the natives sufficiently bitter to occasion national uprisings against Persian domination.[4] The tension that normally existed between Persia's clients and the native population of such regions is evident enough in the response generated when the Jews began rebuilding the Temple in Jerusalem: the non-Jews settled in Palestine by its various conquerors feared that the reconstruction of the Temple was to be but a prelude to a Jewish national revolt, which would spell their own destruction.[5]

Asia Minor appears to have been relatively well pacified by the Persians. Like the Egyptians, Babylonians, and Medes, the Lydians had been an imperial people and were initially unwilling to accept the Persian yoke. We need not believe all of the details of Herodotus' account to recognize that Cyrus the Great somehow found the means to subdue them. Asia Minor remained quiet when the nations in other regions revolted at the time of Darius the Great's accession; and, when the Ionians rebelled in the 490s, the Carians were alone among the other mainlanders in joining them. It would, however, be a mistake to exaggerate the docility of the local population. Late in the second century, the region's serfs responded quickly to the call of the rebel Aristonicus. The absence of references to such uprisings in the extant ancient accounts of the Achaemenid period suggests that there were none but by no means rules out the possibility of local disturbances too paltry to be of concern to the Greek authors. Trouble was always a possibility.[6]

In any case, the gentry of Asia Minor had other reasons to look to Susa for help. From 479 to 449, they had the Athenian alliance to contend with, and the fierce mountaineers of Mysia and Pisidia were always a threat to those who farmed the flat land of the river valleys.[7]

The wild tribes of the mountains and the nomads of the desert posed problems for settled folk elsewhere as well. Indeed, in the fourth century, even the Great King found it necessary to pay tribute of a sort in order to journey through the mountains from Susa to Persepolis.[8] The first responsibility of any ruler in Asia Minor and in territories to the east was the containment of these tribes.

APPENDIX 6

ARSACES AND CYRUS:
RELATIVE AGES

THE ANCIENT EVIDENCE concerning the life span of Darius II's elder son Arsaces poses certain problems. It is clear that he died sometime between 25 November 359 and 12 April 358: BC, 19, 35. According to Plutarch (*Artax.* 30.9), who is presumably following Deinon, he was then ninety-four.

Plutarch's figure is implausible: Arsaces can hardly have been born as early as 452. His father Ochus was the son of Artaxerxes I, who was in turn the son of Xerxes I and Amestris. Ctesias (*FGrH* 688 F13.24) implies that Xerxes married Amestris only after his accession in 486: Hdt. 7.1–4; BC, 16–17. If he is correct in reporting that she died at about the same time as her third son Artaxerxes in 424 (*FGrH* 688 F14.46) and if Plato (*Alc.* I 123c4–e6) is correct in assuming that she was still alive in the early 420s just after Alcibiades reached the age of twenty and began attending the assembly (105a6–b6 and 123d6 with Peter J. Rhodes, *The Athenian Boule* [Oxford: Clarendon Press, 1985], 171–73, and Davies, *APF*, 18), Amestris will probably have been barely old enough for procreation in 486. The first son of Xerxes I and Amestris was presumably born within a year or two of the marriage. Ctesias (*FGrH* 688 F 13.24) places the birth of the second son two years later and that of Artaxerxes I sometime after that. This means that Artaxerxes I was born no earlier than 482 and was no older than seventeen when a palace coup brought him to the throne in 465: F13.33, F14.34; Diod. 11.69;

BC, 17. Artaxerxes cannot have begotten Ochus much before this and probably did so thereafter. It is perhaps biologically possible that Ochus sired Arsaces thirteen years later in 452, but it is so unlikely that we need not hesitate to abandon Plutarch's claim.

Lucan (*Macr.* 15) makes Arsaces eighty-six at the time of his death. If he is right, Parysatis bore Ochus his first son in 444. This also puts some strain on our credulity. It requires that we believe that at least twenty-one years passed between Parysatis' bearing Arsaces in 444 and her bearing his younger brother Cyrus late in or shortly after 423: Ctesias *FGrH* 688 F15.51 and Plut. *Artax.* 2.4. This is not in itself impossible, but it is incompatible with Ctesias' report (*FGrH* 688 F15.51)—on Parysatis' authority—that she bore Ochus ten more children after Cyrus.

Were it not for the fact that Arsaces was married to Stateira and begetting daughters with her by 418—in time for there to be two of marriageable age in 401 (Xen. *An.* 2.4.8, 3.4.13; Diod. 14.26.4, 15.2–3), I would be willing to abandon the tradition that he died at an unusually great age as complete fabrication. I am inclined, instead, to assume that Arsaces was about fifteen or sixteen when he married Stateira and that he did so shortly after his father's ascension to the throne. This would narrow the gap between Arsaces and Cyrus to fourteen or fifteen years. This gap need not be fatal to my hypothesis. Persian men prided themselves on the number of their sons (Hdt. 1.136.1), and both the case of Amestris and that of Arsaces' daughters suggest that the Persians, like the Greeks and the Romans, tended to marry off their daughters soon after the girls reached puberty.[1] If Parysatis gave birth to Arsaces when she was sixteen, she will—on the hypothesis advanced here—have been thirty or thirty-one when Cyrus was born. Her bearing ten more children after that is improbable, but by no means impossible, especially if there were twins in the mix. Persian women presumably underwent menopause sometime in their forties, as did their Greek and Roman counterparts.[2] Parysatis' advanced age may help explain why eight of the ten died in infancy: Ctesias *FGrH* 688 F15.51 and Plut. *Artax.* 1.1.

Darius II would have gained little from making a child crown prince in 423. For another view, see Lewis, *SP*, 135 n. 154.

It is perhaps worth adding that Plutarch (*Artax.* 30.9) exaggerates the length of Arsaces' reign as Artaxerxes II by sixteen years: cf. *BC*, 19. If we assume that he made a similar error regarding the man's age, we will arrive at a figure for his birth date consistent with the evidence for his marriage date and with the view that he was a very old man in 359/8. Plutarch's claim (*Artax.* 26.4) that Arsaces' eldest son was fifty when he was named crown prince late in his father's reign is fully in accord with the suggestions made here.

THE SELECTION OF PERSIAN
SATRAPS AND GENERALS

THE BEST EVIDENCE we possess for a tendency on the part of the Achaemenids to select satraps and generals from among two bodies of men—the Sons of the Royal House and the elder Darius' confederates and their descendants—is Herodotus' catalogue of the contingents of Xerxes' army and their commanders (7.60–98), which Burn analyzed in detail.[1] To his list of the Sons of the Royal House holding preeminent positions in the expeditionary force, we can now add Darius' first cousin Artabazus.[2]

The importance of the descendants of the confederates is evident from Herodotus' list of six marshals given overall command of the army (7.82). Among them, in addition to Gergis son of Ariazos—who had been under Darius, we now know, the satrap of Kerman, which lay some distance east of Persepolis—and to Xerxes' full brother Masistes and his first cousin Tritaikhmes, we find Xerxes' brother-in-law Mardonius, the son of the confederate Gobryas (6.43); Xerxes' first cousin Smerdomenes, the son of the confederate Otanes; and Megabyzus, the son of Zopyrus and grandson of the confederate Megabyzus (3.150–60). To the list of marshals, we should probably add Hydarnes, the son of the confederate Hydarnes, who commanded the royal bodyguard and reportedly directly to the King: 7.40–41, 83.1, 211, 215, 218, 8.113, 118.[3]

The most important of the national contingents were those equipped "with a coat of mail resembling the scales of a fish." Of these four, the Persians were commanded by Otanes, a descendant of the homonymous confederate and father-in-law of Xerxes; the Medes, by the Achaemenid prince Tigranes; the Cissians, by Otanes' son Anaphes; and the Hyrcanians, by Megapanus, who had served under Darius as satrap of Elam and who turns up later as satrap of Babylon (7.61–63).[4] The family of Intaphernes no doubt fell into disfavor when he was executed (3.118–19). Something similar may have happened to Ardumanish and his family—for, although he is mentioned on the Bisitun monument, he is entirely unknown to Herodotus and neither he nor any of his offspring show up in the tablets found at Persepolis.[5]

Our evidence for Artaxerxes' reign is much more limited but is nonetheless consistent with the impression left by Herodotus' catalogue. Consider the satrapies of the west. The satrapy with its seat at Dascyleium remains in the hands of Artabazus' descendants.[6] Lydia is governed by Pissouthnes, whose father Hystaspes is the full brother either of Xerxes (7.65) or of Artaxerxes himself (Diod. 11.69.2).[7] The marshal Megabyzus, having married Xerxes' daughter Amytis, intervenes to protect the fledgling Great King Artaxerxes ca. 465, crushes the revolt of Inarus in Egypt in the 450s, negotiates a cessation of hostilities and a *modus vivendi* with Athens in 449, serves as satrap of Syria, and leaves that province to his son Artyphius.[8] Before Inarus' revolt in Egypt, the satrap there is a figure named Achaemenes, who is either a son of the elder Darius, as Herodotus (3.12, 7.7, 97, 236–37) claims, or a half-brother of Artaxerxes, as Ctesias (*FGrH* 688 F14.36–39) contends. Afterwards, the satrap in that vitally important province is Arsames (F14.38, F15.50), who bears an Achaemenid name and who is in the Aramaic documents (*AD* nos. 2–3, 5 = *TADAE* nos. A6.3, A6.4, A6.7) identified as *br byt'* (pronounced *bar bayta*)—i.e., as a Son of the (Royal) House.[9]

In these years, as I have argued in Chapter One, there is a satrap in the east named Hydarnes who is of sufficient importance to be in a position to supply a consort to Darius II's heir apparent. He is almost certainly a descendant of the like-named confederate, and his satrapy is apt to have been Media—which the original Hydarnes was sent by the elder Darius to reconquer and where this man subsequently established his seat. The Hydarnes who had served Artaxerxes and who came to serve the younger Darius was in a position to leave his satrapy to his son—the Great King's son-in-law—Teriteuchmes. The Tissaphernes who replaces Pissouthnes in the late 420s as the satrap based at Sardis is also the son of a Hydarnes; and he, too, is apt to be a descendant of the confederate.[10]

During much, if not all, of Artaxerxes' reign, the satrap at Babylon is Artaxerxes' half-brother Artarios: Ctesias *FGrH* 688 F14.41–42. Artarios' son Menostanes is sent by Artaxerxes to put down the revolt of Megabyzus but does not succeed: F14.41. Later, during the interregnum following Artaxerxes' death, he tries to play king-maker—again to no avail: F15.49–50, 52. In the cuneiform tablets, this Menostanes is identified either as a *mār bīt šarri*, Son of the Royal House, or as a *mār bīti*, Son of the (Royal) House: BE IX nos. 75, 83–84; NBRVT no. 180.

Like the descendants of the elder Darius' co-conspirators, these Sons of the Royal House are a clearly identifiable group.[11] The Jews of Elephantine greet Bagoas the governor of Jerusalem in the seventeenth year of Darius II's reign by wishing him long life, happiness, prosperity, and "favor with Darius and the Sons of the (Royal) House [*br byt'*]": AP no. 30. Like the offspring of Saudi Arabia's Ibn Saud and his brothers in our own day, the Achaemenids of ancient Persia had by the late fifth century come to make up the bulk of a recognized ruling order. I suspect that these Sons of the Royal House are to be identified with the *suggeneîs* of Xen. *Cyr.* 8.3.13 and the *propinqui* of Curt. 6.3. Their rank would account for their being given the right to wear the royal diadem.

THE CHRONOLOGY OF

THE WAR IN 405 AND 404

THE DATING OF the events related in Chapter Eight is somewhat complicated. It is an implication of Xen. *Hell.* 2.1.10 that Lysander returned to Ephesus early in the campaigning season of 405. His victory at Aegospotami took place within that campaigning season (2.1.23–28 and context), after the midsummer Panathenaic festival when the archon Alexias (405/4) took office (Arist. *Ath. Pol.* 34.2), but before the Prometheia in November (Lys. 21.3, 9–11), and almost certainly either in September when the grain ships left the Crimea for the Aegean (Xen. *Hell.* 2.1.17 with Lotze, *Lysander,* 31) or, shortly thereafter, in October. Between the time of Lysander's return and the battle of Aegospotami falls the rebuilding of the Spartan fleet (Xen. *Hell.* 2.1.10–12), the departure of Cyrus for Media (2.1.13–14), and Lysander's voyage down the Ionian coast (2.1.15, Diod. 13.104.5–7), through the Cyclades to Athens (13.104.8, Plut. *Lys.* 9.3), and back to and then up the Ionian coast to the Hellespont to take Lampsacus (Xen. *Hell.* 2.1.17–19, Diod. 13.104.8, Plut. *Lys.* 9.4).

One note of caution is justified: the massacre at Miletus took place at the time of the Dionysia (Diod. 13.104.5) which, in Ionia, was normally celebrated during the Athenian month Anthesterion, which usually fell in January and February: Thuc. 2.15.4 with Friedrich Bilabel, *Die ionische Kolonisation: Untersuchungen über die Gründungen der Ionier, deren staatliche und kultliche Organisation und*

Beziehungen zu den Mutterstädten, Philologus Suppl. 14 (Leipzig: Dieterich'sche Verlagsbuchhandlung, 1920), 95. Diodorus (13.104.4–6) clearly places Cyrus' departure for Media before the events at Miletus, but Plutarch (*Lys.* 8.1–9.2) discusses the massacre before mentioning Cyrus' departure—albeit in a context where literary rather than chronological concerns seem to dictate the order of his narrative. I have adopted Diodorus' chronology, but not without misgivings: if the Milesian year 406/5 was not what we would call a leap year (for the Milesian calendar, see Bilabel, *Die Ionische Kolonisation*, 70, and context), it would make sense to place Lysander's visit to Miletus before his arrival at Ephesus and, thus, well before Cyrus' departure for Media. I am, however, quite prepared to believe that 406/5 was a leap year and that, at Miletus, Anthesterion came quite late that year.

Because the solar year matches neither a lunar year of twelve months nor a lunar year of thirteen months, it is impossible to synchronize a lunar calendar with the solar calendar. In consequence, to bring the lunar calendars, which were employed in the Greek cities for religious and other purposes, back into even a rough and ready agreement with the solar calendar that dictated the conduct of farmers and mariners required, from time to time, the intercalation of a month. There would be nothing surprising about Lysander's Milesian partisans using the considerable influence they obviously had to delay the coming of Anthesterion until Lysander was able to be there. In any case, Xenophon's discussion of the plight of Eteonicus' men on Chios (*Hell.* 2.1.1–5) prior to Lysander's arrival makes it clear that the latter cannot have reached Ephesus much before the beginning of spring.

ABBREVIATIONS AND SHORT TITLES

In the notes, I have adopted the standard abbreviations for texts and inscriptions, for books of the Bible, and for modern journals and books provided in *The Oxford Classical Dictionary*, 4th edition revised, ed. Simon Hornblower, Antony Spawforth, and Esther Eidinow (Oxford: Oxford University Press, 2012); *The Chicago Manual of Style*, 15th edition (Chicago: University of Chicago Press, 2003), 15.50–53; the bibliographical annual *L'Année Philologique*; Roland G. Kent, *Old Persian: Grammar, Texts, Lexicon*, 2nd edition, revised (New Haven, CT: American Oriental Society, 1953), 107–63; Pierre Lecoq, *Les Inscriptions de la Perse achéménide: Traduit du vieux perse, de l'élamite, du babylonien et de l'araméen* (Paris: Gallimard, 1997), 177–277; *The Persian Empire: A Corpus of Sources from the Achaemenid Period*, ed. Amélie Kuhrt (London: Routledge, 2007), 910–18; and https://www.livius.org/sources/content/achaemenid-royal-inscriptions/. Where possible, the ancient texts are cited by the divisions and subdivisions employed by the author or introduced by subsequent editors (that is, by book, part, chapter, section number, paragraph, act, scene, line, Stephanus page, or by page and line number). Cross-references to other parts of this volume and to the other volumes in this series refer the divisions into which the volumes are broken.

Unless otherwise indicated, all of the translations are my own. I transliterate the Greek, using undotted i's where no accent is required, adding macrons, accents, circumflexes, and so on. When others—in titles or statements quoted—transliterate in a different manner, I leave their transliterations as they had them.

For other works frequently cited, the following abbreviations and short titles have been employed:

AhW	*Aršāma and his World: The Bodleian Letters in Context*, ed. Christopher Tuplin and John Ma (Oxford: Oxford University Press, 2020).
Andrewes, *SR*	Antony Andrewes, "The Spartan Resurgence," in *CAH*, V² 464–98.
AT	John S. Morrison, John F. Coates, and N. Boris Rankov, *The Athenian Trireme: The History and Reconstruction of an Ancient Greek Warship*, 2nd edition (New York: Cambridge University Press, 2000).
BC	*Babylonian Chronology, 626 B.C.–A.D. 75*, ed. Richard A. Parker and Waldo H. Dubberstein (Providence, RI: Brown University Studies, 1956).
Bleckmann, *Niederlage*	Bruno Bleckmann, *Athens Wege in die Niederlage: Die letzten Jahre des Peloponnesischen Kriegs* (Stuttgart: Teubner, 1998).
Bommelaer, *Lysandre*	Jean-François Bommelaer, *Lysandre de Sparte: Histoire et traditions* (Athens: Ecole française d'Athènes, 1981).
Briant, *CA*	Pierre Briant, *From Cyrus to Alexander: A History of the Persian Empire*, trans. Peter T. Daniels (Winona Lake, IN: Eisenbrauns, 2002).
Buck, *Thrasybulus*	Robert J. Buck, *Thrasybulus and the Athenian Democracy: The Life of an Athenian Statesman* (Stuttgart: Franz Steiner Verlag, 1998).
Cartledge, *Agesilaos*	Paul Cartledge, *Agesilaos and the Crisis of Sparta* (Baltimore, MD: Johns Hopkins University Press, 1987).
Cawkwell, *GW*	George Cawkwell, *The Greek Wars: The Failure of Persia* (Oxford: Oxford University Press, 2005).
Debord, *AM*	Pierre Debord, *L'Asie Mineure au IVe siécle (412–323 a. C.): Pouvoirs et jeux politiques* (Bordeaux: Ausonius, 1999).
Ellis, *Alcibiades*	Walter M. Ellis, *Alcibiades* (London: Routledge, 1989).
Grote, *HG*	George Grote, *A History of Greece: From the Earliest Period to the Close of the Generation Contemporary with Alexander the Great*, 4th edition (London: John Murray, 1872).
Hatzfeld, *Alcibiade*	Jean Hatzfeld, *Alcibiade: Étude sur l'histoire d'Athènes à la fin du Ve siècle*, 2nd edition (Paris: Presses Universitaires de France, 1951).
Heftner, *Umsturz*	Herbert Heftner, *Der oligarchische Umsturz des Jahres 411 v.*

ABBREVIATIONS AND SHORT TITLES

	Chr. und die Herrschaft der Vierhundert in Athens: Quellenkritische und historische Untersuchungen (Frankfurt am Main: P Lang, 2001).
Hutchinson, *Attrition*	Godfrey Hutchinson, *Attrition: Aspects of Command in the Peloponnesian War* (Stonehouse, Gloucestershire: Spellmount, 2006).
Hyland, *PI*	John O. Hyland, *Persian Interventions: The Achaemenid Empire, Athens, and Sparta, 450–286 BCE* (Baltimore, MD: Johns Hopkins University Press, 2018).
Kagan, *Fall*	Donald Kagan, *The Fall of the Athenian Empire* (Ithaca, NY: Cornell University Press, 1987).
Kallet, *MCPT*	Lisa Kallet, *Money and the Corrosion of Power in Thucydides: The Sicilian Expedition and its Aftermath* (Berkeley: University of California Press, 2001).
Kapellos, *XPW*	Aggelos Kapellos, *Xenophon's Peloponnesian War* (Berlin: Walter de Gruyter, 2019).
Krentz, *Xenophon*	Peter Krentz, "Introduction" and "Commentary," in Xenophon, *Hellenika I–II.3.10*, ed. and tr. Peter Krentz (Warminster: Aris & Phillips, 1989), 1–15, 86–192.
Lazenby, *PW*	John F. Lazenby, *The Peloponnesian War: A Military Study* (London: Routledge, 2004).
Llewellyn-Jones, *KCAP*	Lloyd Llewellyn-Jones, *King and Court in Ancient Persia, 559 to 331 BCE* (Edinburgh: University of Edinburgh Press, 2013).
Lewis, *SP*	David M. Lewis, *Sparta and Persia* (Leiden: Brill, 1977).
Lotze, *Lysander*	Detlef Lotze, *Lysander under der Peloponnesische Krieg* (Berlin: Akademie-Verlag, 1964).
Meyer, *GDA*	Eduard Meyer, *Geschichte des Altertums*, 4th edition (Stuttgart: J. G. Cotta, 1921–58).
Munn, *SH*	Mark Munn, *The School of History: Athens in the Age of Socrates* (Berkeley: University of California Press, 2000).
OHANE	*Oxford History of the Ancient Near East*, ed. Karen Radner, Nadine Moeller, and Daniel T. Potts (Oxford: Oxford University Press, 2023).
O&R	*Greek Historical Inscriptions, 478–404 BC*, ed. Robin Osborne and Peter J. Rhodes (Oxford: Oxford University Press, 2017).
Osborne, *AAD*	Robin Osborne, *Athens and Athenian Democracy* (Cambridge: Cambridge University Press, 2010).
Ostwald, *Sovereignty*	Martin Ostwald, *From Popular Sovereignty to the Sovereignty of Law: Law, Society, and Politics in Fifth-Century Athens* (Berkeley: University of California Press, 1986).

ABBREVIATIONS AND SHORT TITLES

Rahe, *PC*   Paul A. Rahe, *The Grand Strategy of Classical Sparta: The Persian Challenge* (New Haven, CT: Yale University Press, 2015).

Rahe, *RAM*   Paul A. Rahe, *Republics Ancient and Modern: Classical Republicanism and the American Revolution* (Chapel Hill: University of North Carolina Press, 1992).

Rahe, *SFAW*   Paul A. Rahe, *Sparta's First Attic War: The Grand Strategy of Classical Sparta, 478–446 BC* (New Haven, CT: Yale University Press, 2019).

Rahe, *SR*   Paul A. Rahe, *The Spartan Regime: Its Character, Origins, and Grand Strategy* (New Haven, CT: Yale University Press, 2016).

Rahe, *SSAW*   Paul A. Rahe, *Sparta's Second Attic War: The Grand Strategy of Classical Sparta, 446–418 BC* (New Haven, CT: Yale University Press, 2020).

Rahe, *SSPW*   Paul A. Rahe, *Sparta's Sicilian Proxy War: The Grand Strategy of Classical Sparta, 418–413 BC* (New York: Encounter Books, 2023).

Rhodes, *Alcibiades*   Peter J. Rhodes, *Alcibiades: Athenian Playboy, General and Traitor* (Barnsley, South Yorkshire: Penn and Sword, 2011).

Rood, *Thucydides*   Tim Rood, *Thucydides: Narrative and Explanation* (Oxford: Oxford University Press, 1998).

Stolper, *E&E*   Matthew W. Stolper, *Entrepreneurs and Empire: The Murašû Archive, the Murašû Firm, and Persian Rule in Babylonia* (Leiden: Nederlands historisch-archaeologisch Instituut te Istanbul, 1985).

Stuttard, *Nemesis*   David Stuttard, *Nemesis: Alcibiades and the Fall of Athens* (Cambridge, MA: Harvard University Press, 2018).

Westlake, *Individuals*   Henry D. Westlake, *Individuals in Thucydides* (Cambridge: Cambridge University Press, 1968).

Westlake, *Studies*   Henry D. Westlake, *Studies in Thucydides and Greek History* (Bristol: Bristol Classical Press, 1989).

NOTES

INTRODUCTION. JOURNEY'S END

1. Cf. Thuc. 5.28.2 (*ho Attikòs pólemos*) with Diod. 13.24.2 and Strabo 13.1.39 (*ho Peloponēsiakòs pólemos*). Pausanias (4.6.1) will later refer to it as *ho Peloponnēsios pólemos*. Strabo also refers to this war in the plural as *tà Peloponnēsiaká*: 14.2.9. *Tà Persiká* could be used to refer to all "matters Persian" or, more narrowly, to "the Persian wars": Pl. *Leg.* 1.642d. For the most part, however, this conflict was called *tà Mēdiká* (Thuc. 1.14.2, Arist. *Pol.* 1303b33) or *ho Mēdikòs pólemos* (Thuc. 1.90.1, 95.7; Paus. 4.6.1). Thucydides can also speak of the Trojan war as *tà Troiká*: 1.14.1.

2. See Rahe, *SSPW*, Appendix.

PROLOGUE. SPARTA'S ENDURING STRATEGIC DILEMMA

Epigraph: Halford J. Mackinder, *Democratic Ideals and Reality* (Singapore: Origami Books, 2018), 4.

1. For a full citation of the evidence pertinent to the initial articulation of Sparta's grand strategy, a copious citation of the secondary literature, and my argument with regard to the period prior to the emergence of Achaemenid Persia, see Rahe, *SR*. Euripides on the hoplite: *HF* 190. Thucydides on the *aspís*: 5.71.1. Demaratus on the *aspís*: Plut. *Mor.* 220a. Corinthian compares Lacedaemon with a stream: Xen. *Hell.* 4.2.11–12. On the cavalry of the ancient Greeks, which I did not discuss in detail in *SR*, see Glenn R. Bugh, *The Horsemen of Athens* (Princeton, NJ: Princeton University Press, 1988); Iain G. Spence, *The Cavalry of Classical Greece: A Social and Military History with Particular Reference to Athens* (Oxford: Oxford University Press, 1993); Leslie J. Worley, *Hippeis: The Cavalry of Ancient Greece* (Boulder: Westview, 1994); and Robert E. Gaebel, *Cavalry Operations in the Ancient Greek World* (Norman: University of Oklahoma Press, 2002). Laconia: *IACP*, 569–78 with nos. 323–46. Cythera: no. 336. Gytheion: no. 333. Lacedaemon: no. 345. Messenia: 547–58 with nos. 312–22.

2. For the details, the evidence, and the secondary literature pertinent to Persia's appearance on the scene and to Sparta's measured response down to the battle of

Marathon, see Rahe, *PC*, Part I. Triremes and their crews: ibid. Chapter 1 (at notes 27–39) and Victor Davis Hanson, *A War Like No Other: How the Athenians and Spartans Fought the Peloponnesian War* (New York: Random House, 2005), 236–66, who errs only in underestimating the number of foreigners and slaves who, in ordinary circumstances, rowed in Athens' fleets. Athenian trierarch's *leitourgía*: Vincent Gabrielsen, *Financing the Athenian Fleet: Public Taxation and Social Relations* (Baltimore: Johns Hopkins University Press, 1994), 19–169. For an amusing attempt to make sense of this institution and of the conduct it inspired solely in terms of the "economic rationality" championed as an analytical tool by modern social scientists, see Brooks A. Kaiser, "The Athenian Trierarchy: Mechanism Design for the Private Provision of Public Goods," *Journal of Economic History* 67:2 (June 2007): 445–80.

3. Assertions that the Persian infantry was not inferior: see Briant, *CA*, 783–800, which should be read in light of Pierre Briant, "Histoire et idéologie: Les Grecs et la 'décadence perse,'" in *Mélanges Pierre Lévêque II: Anthropologie et société*, ed. Marie-Madeleine Mactoux and Évelyne Geny (Paris: Les Belles Lettres, 1989), II 33–47, reprinted in an English translation by Antonia Nevill as "History and Ideology: The Greeks and 'Persian Decadence,'" in *Greeks and Barbarians*, ed. Thomas Harrison (Edinburgh: Edinburgh University Press, 2001), 193–210. See also Roel Konijnendijk, "'Neither the Less Valorous Nor the Weaker': Persian Military Might and the Battle of Plataia," *Historia* 61:1 (2012): 1–17; and Jeffrey Rop, *Greek Military Service in the Ancient Near East, 401–330 BCE* (Cambridge: Cambridge University Press, 2019), 1–63. These attempts to show that the Great King's infantry was not inferior all rely on special pleading and a rejection of the ancient testimony and seem to be a defensive overreaction to the triumphalism evident in some of the Hellenic sources. The truth is that, in the course of the fifth century, the satraps of western Asia came to rely on Greek mercenaries and that, on more than one occasion, a rebellious satrap managed to defeat the forces of the Great King with an army that combined Greek hoplites with a cavalry force on the Persian model. It was this that inspired the younger Cyrus: see Paul A. Rahe, "The Military Situation in Western Asia on the Eve of Cunaxa," *AJPh* 101:1 (Spring 1980): 79–96, as well as Chapter 1 and the preface to Part IV, below.

4. On Miltiades and the Athenian victory at Marathon, see Rahe, *PC*, Chapter 4.

5. Plataea and Mycale: Rahe, *PC*, Chapter 8. Plataea: *IACP* no. 216.

6. For the details, the evidence, and the secondary literature pertinent to Xerxes' invasion of Greece, the coalition Sparta put together to resist it, and the battles of Thermopylae, Artemisium, and Salamis, see Rahe, *PC*, preface to Part II and Chapters 5–7. Corinth: *IACP* no. 227.

7. For further details, the evidence, and the secondary literature pertinent to the emergence of Athens' Delian League and to Sparta's decision to make an accommodation for it, see Rahe, *SFAW*, preface to Part I and Chapters 1 and 2. Regard-

ing Persia, see Rahe, *PC*, Chapter 1 and preface to Part II. On the persistence of the Persian threat and on the efforts of Cimon to counter it, I should have cited Cawkwell, *GW*, 126–38, who was especially alert to the situation and to the scattered evidence. Mid-September shipment of grain from the Euxine: Dem. 35.10, 50.4, 19. Grain fleet vulnerable: Philochorus *FGrH* 328 F162, Theopompus of Chios *FGrH* 115 F292. On the significance of the grain trade, see Rahe, *PC*, Chapter 3, n. 3, and *SSAW*, Chapter 3, n. 21, where I should also have cited Vincent Gabrielsen, "Trade and Tribute: Byzantion and the Black Sea Straits," in *The Black Sea in Antiquity: Regional and Interregional Economic Exchanges*, ed. Vincent Gabrielsen and John Lund (Arrhus: Arrhus University Press, 2007), 287–324 (esp. 287–97, 308–11), who makes a compelling case for the notion that the Athenians provided the grain fleet with a convoy. Samos: *IACP* no. 864. Chios: no. 840. Lesbos: 1017–21 with nos. 794–99.

8. For further detail, the evidence, and the secondary literature pertinent to Themistocles' sojourn in Argos (*IACP* no. 347), Lacedaemon's difficulties with Argos and Tegea (no. 297), Athens' victory at Eurymedon, the first Peace of Callias, the revolt of Thasos (no. 526), and Sparta's decision to offer the Thasians support, see Rahe, *SFAW*, Chapter 3. I do not find persuasive Cawkwell's arguments concerning the timing of Callias' first round of negotiations with the Great King, but I believe that he is right to note their existence: cf. Cawkwell, *GW*, 135 (with n. 13). Elis: *IACP*, 489–93 with nos. 245–63 (esp. no. 251). Mantineia: no. 281. Megara: no. 225.

9. For further details concerning the origins of Sparta's first Attic war and for the pertinent evidence and secondary literature, see Rahe, *SFAW*, Chapter 3, preface to Part II, and Chapter 4. Aegina: *IACP*, no. 358. Thessaly: 676–83 with nos. 393–417.

10. For further details and the evidence and secondary literature pertinent both to the Spartan preoccupation with the helot threat in the early years of their first Attic war and to the manner in which Lacedaemon's Peloponnesian allies suffered from the maritime machinations of the Athenians, see Rahe, *SFAW*, Chapter 5 (at notes 1–14). Messenian refugees resettled at Naupactus: Chapter 5 (esp. notes 48–52), to which I would now add Lisa Kallet, "Naupaktos, Naupaktians and Messenians in Naupaktos in the Peloponnesian War," and Phōteinḗ Sáránte, "To archaío limáni tēs Naupáktou: katáloipa kai marturíes," in *Naupaktos: The Ancient City and its Significance during the Peloponnesian War and the Hellenistic Period*, ed. Olga Palagia (Athens: D. and A. Botsaris Foundation, 2016), 15–63. Troezen: *IACP* no. 357. Hermione: no. 350. Naupactus: no. 165.

11. For further details pertinent to the stakes in the battle of Tanagra and to the consequences of its outcome and for the evidence and secondary literature, see Rahe, *SFAW*, Chapter 5 (at notes 15–45). Retrospective view of the urban–rural divide that gradually emerged in Athens in the wake of the founding of the Delian League: Xen. *Oec.* 6.6–7. Doris: *IACP*, 674 with nos. 389–92. Phocis:

397–408 with nos. 169–97. Boeotia: 431–37 with nos. 198–223. Tanagra: no. 220. Thebes: no. 221.

12. For further details and the evidence and secondary literature pertinent to the Egyptian debacle, the Five-Year Truce, the revolution at Tegea, Pleistoanax' invasion, and the so-called Thirty Years Peace, see Rahe, *SFAW*, Chapter 5 (at notes 54–68) and Chapter 6. Cypriot Salamis: *IACP* no. 1020. Boeotian Orchomenos: no. 213. Histiaea (no. 372), Chalcis (no. 365), and Eretria (no. 370) on the island of Euboea (643–47 with nos. 364–77).

13. See Rahe, *SSAW*, Chapter 1. Pissouthnes' satrapy: Debord, *AM*, 116–30. Note also Hilmar Klinkott, "The Satrapies of the Persian Empire in Asia Minor: Lydia, Caria, Lycia, Phrygia, and Cappadocia," in *OHANE*, V 592–648 (at 592–617). Samos: *IACP* no. 864.

14. Corinthian speech: Thuc. 1.70. Thucydides' confirmation: 1.118.2, 4.55.2–4, 8.96 with Rahe, *SFAW*, Chapters 3–6 (including the preface to Part II), and *SSAW*, Chapters 1–2. See Peter R. Pouncey, *The Necessities of War: A Study of Thucydides' Pessimism* (New York: Columbia University Press, 1980), 57–62, and Seth N. Jaffe, "The Regime (*Politeia*) in Thucydides," in *The Oxford Handbook of Thucydides*, ed. Ryan Balot, Sara Forsdyke, and Edith Foster (Oxford: Oxford University Press, 2017), 391–408. For extended commentaries on the Corinthians' speech, see Lowell Edmunds, *Chance and Intelligence in Thucydides* (Cambridge, MA: Harvard University Press, 1975), 7–142; and, more recently, Gregory Crane, "The Fear and Pursuit of Risk: Corinth on Athens, Sparta, and the Peloponnesians (Thucydides 1.68–71, 120–21)," *TAPhA* 122 (1992): 227–56. Corcyra: *IACP* no. 123.

15. See Rahe, *SSAW*, Chapter 2.

16. See Rahe, *SSAW*, preface to Part II, where, to n. 4, I would now add Rosalind Thomas, "Thucydides' Intellectual Milieu and the Plague," in *Brill's Companion to Thucydides*, ed. Antonios Rengakos and Antonis Tsakmakis (Leiden: Brill, 2006), 87–108.

17. See Rahe, *SFAW*, Chapter 5 (at n. 53), and *SSAW*, Chapter 3.

18. See Rahe, *SSAW*, preface to Part I and Chapters 1 and 2. Lesbos and the cities thereon: Chapter 2, note 8, below.

19. With an eye to Rahe, *SFAW*, Chapters 5 and 6, consider Thuc. 1.144.1, 2.65.7, in light of Alfred Thayer Mahan, *The Influence of Sea Power upon History, 1660–1783*, 12th edition (Boston: Little, Brown, and Company, 1943), 537.

20. See Rahe, *SSAW*, Chapter 4 (with notes 4–7, 11–12).

21. For further details, the evidence, and the secondary literature, see Rahe, *SSAW*, Chapter 3 and Part II. Corinthians on Athens and Sparta: Thuc. 1.70. For their argument in full, see Rahe, *SSPW*, Chapter 2, at note 14.

22. For further details, the evidence, and the secondary literature, see Rahe, *SSAW*, preface to Part III and Chapter 6. Chalcidice: *IACP*, 810–14 with nos. 556–626. Amphipolis: no. 553.

23. For further detail, the evidence, and the secondary literature, see Rahe, *SSAW*, Chapters 7–8 and the Epilogue—where, regarding Lichas' hospitality and his likely membership in the *gerousía*, I should have cited Critias F8 (West), Xen. *Mem.* 1.2.61, and Plut. *Cim.* 10.5–6, on the one hand, and Xen. *Hell.* 3.2.21, on the other; and where regarding his career and the role he seems to have played in supplying Thucydides with documents and with enabling him to have a remarkably precise knowledge of Spartan affairs in this period and thereafter, I should have cited the important, recent study of Robin Lane Fox, "Thucydides and Documentary History," *CQ* n.s. 60:1 (May 2010): 11–29 (esp. 13–18, 22–26). Epidauros: *IACP* no. 348.

24. See Loren J. Samons II, *Empire of the Owl: Athenian Imperial Finance* (Stuttgart: Franz Steiner Verlag, 2000), 230–48; Alec Blamire, "Athenian Finance, 454–404 B.C.," *Hesperia* 70:1 (January–March 2001): 99–126; and David M. Pritchard, *Public Spending and Democracy in Classical Athens* (Austin: University of Texas Press, 2015), 1–98 (esp. 91–98). Cf. Kallet, *MCPT*, 9–10, 148–51, who exaggerates the extent to which Athens' reserves had recovered, leaving the reader with the impression that the city was no worse off financially in 415 than she had been in 432.

25. For the details, the sources, and the pertinent secondary literature, see Rahe, *SSPW*, Part I. Alcibiades' stated aim: Plut. *Alc.* 22.3, *Mor.* 186e6–7. For an argument somewhat at odds with what I have suggested here, see Donald Kagan, *The Peace of Nicias and the Sicilian Expedition* (Ithaca, NY: Cornell University Press, 1981), 157–226.

26. Alcibiades' flexibility: cf. Plut. *Alc.* 23.3–5, where I accept the emendation suggested by Bryan, and *Mor.* 52e with Nepos *Alc.* 11 who says much the same thing and tells us that he is echoing Theopompus and Timaeus: see Theopompus of Chios *FGrH* 115 F288 and Timaeus of Tauromenium *FGrH* 566 F99. On the former, see Michael Attyah Flower, *Theopompus of Chios: History and Rhetoric in the Fourth Century BC* (Oxford: Clarendon Press, 1994). On the latter, see the secondary literature cited in Rahe, *SSPW*, Chapter 2, note 6. See also Ath. 12.534b, Ael. *VH* 4.15. Alcibiades at Sparta: Hatzfeld, *Alcibiade*, 213–14, and Stuttard, *Nemesis*, 164–66.

27. For the details, the sources, and the pertinent secondary literature, see Rahe, *SSPW*, Part II. For an argument somewhat at odds with what I have suggested here, see Kagan, *The Peace of Nicias and the Sicilian Expedition*, 226–353, 360–72.

28. Athenian demography and Athens' losses in Sicily: see Rahe, *SSPW*, Epilogue.

PART I. MANEUVERING FOR ADVANTAGE

Epigraph: Winston S. Churchill, *The World Crisis* (New York: Barnes and Noble Books, 1993), 464.

1. Cf. Thuc. 7.87.6 with 1.110.1.

2. Consider Thuc. 1.70 in light of 2.35–46 and 2.60–64, and see Rahe, *SFAW*, Chapters 4 and 6.

3. Persian overtures; Spartan calculations; Pissouthnes, Amorges, Hystaspes, and the skirmishing in the Aegean and in Anatolia; Lacedaemonian drift from refusal to ambivalence: start with Thuc. 1.109.1–3 and 115.2–117.3; then consider 1.82.1 and note 2.7.1, 67 (with Hdt. 7.137), 69, 3.19, 31, 34 (with *IG* I³ 37), and Ctesias *FrGH* 688 F14.45 (with Hdt. 3.160.2), as well as what can be learned concerning the Xanthos Stele from Peter Thonemann, "Lycia, Athens, and Amorges," in *Interpreting the Athenian Empire*, ed. John T. Ma, Nikolaos Papazarkadas, and Robert Parker (London: Duckworth, 2009), 167–94; and, finally, note Thuc. 4.50, and see Rahe, *SFAW*, Chapter 5 (with note 57), and *SSAW*, Chapters 1 (with notes 15–16), 3 (with note 62), and 6 (with notes 11–13). Note also Lewis, *SP*, 62–68. On the skirmishing in Anatolia and nearby, cf. Cawkwell, *GW*, 139–46, who dismisses its significance, with Samuel K. Eddy, "The Cold War between Athens and Persia, c. 448–412 B.C.," *CPh* 68:4 (October 1973): 241–58; Lewis, *SP*, 55–62; Kagan, *Fall*, 16–23; Debord, *AM*, 119–20; and Hyland, *PI*, 34–42, who disagree on details and even the framework within which this low-level conflict should be understood but, nonetheless, see it for what it was, and with Briant, *CA*, 579–83, who exaggerates its importance. That the Great King was behind everything that Pissouthnes cooked up in and after the 440s, there can hardly be doubt: Matt Waters, "Applied Royal Directive: Pissouthnes and Samos," in *Der Achämenidenhof/The Achamenid Court*, ed. Bruno Jacobs and Robert Rollinger (Wiesbaden: Harrassowitz Verlag, 2010), 817–28. Role accorded Susa: Hdt. 5.41 and Strabo 15.3.2 with Pierre Briant, "Susa and Elam in the Achaemenid Empire," in *The Palace of Darius at Susa: The Great Royal Residence of Achaemenid Persia*, ed. Jean Perrot (London: I. B. Tauris, 2013), 3–25, reprinted in Pierre Briant, *From Cyrus to Seleukos: Studies in Achaemenid and Hellenistic History* (Irvine, CA: UCI Jordan Center for Persian Studies, 2018), 245–82.

4. Note Rahe, *PC*, Chapters 7–8 with the Epilogue; *SFAW*, Chapters 2–3 and 5–6; and *SSAW*, Chapters 4–5 and 8 with the Epilogue. Then, consider Thuc. 8.2 and Just. *Epit.* 5.1.4–6 in light of Winston S. Churchill, *Marlborough: His Life and Times* (London: George G. Harrap & Co. Ltd., 1947), II 381, and cf. Andrewes, *HCT*, V 7–9, who misconstrues what Thucydides is up to here, with Hornblower, *CT*, III 753–56, who sees the point.

5. Spartans collect money, requisition galleys for fleet: Thuc. 8.3 with Andrewes, *HCT*, V 9–10; Kagan, *Fall*, 14–15, 24–28; Kallet, *MCPT*, 238–42; and Hornblower, *CT*, III 756–58. Dominion over the Malian Gulf: Ar. *Lys.* 1169–70. Possible reassertion of control over Heracleia Trachinia (*IACP* no. 430): cf. Thuc. 5.52.1 with Xen. *Hell.* 1.2.18. Cf. Henry D. Westlake, "Alcibiades, Agis, and Spartan Policy," *JHS* 58:1 (1938) 31–40 (at 31–38), who cites Diod. 13.9.2; suggests that Nepos *Alc.* 11.2, Ael. *VH* 4.15, and Ath. 12.534b may be pertinent; and concludes that Alcibiades was involved, with Kagan, *Fall*, 27–28 (with n. 72), and

Lazenby, *PW*, 171, who rightly harbor doubts. Corinthian trireme construction between the battles at Leukimne and Sybota: Rahe, *SSAW*, Chapter 2. Note also Lewis, *SP*, 88. Megarian triremes at Salamis in 480 and in dry dock at Nisaea in 429: Rahe, *PC*, Chapter 7, and *SSAW*, Chapter 3. Blockades: Rahe, *SFAW*, Chapter 5, and *SSAW*, Chapters 2–5. Naval expectations in 431: Thuc. 2.7.2. Oetaea: *IACP*, 684–85. Eastern Locris: 664–66 with nos. 378–88. Pellene: no. 240. Epidaurus: no. 348.

6. Flotilla of twenty-two triremes sent from western Greece: see Thuc. 8.26.1, confirmed with regard to the Syracusan contingent by Xen. *Hell.* 1.2.8, with Kagan, *Fall*, 15–16, and Hornblower, *CT*, III 823–24. Cf. Diod. 13.34.4, 61.1, 63.1, who may know of some additional ships sent later or who may simply be confused (as is often the case), and see Andrewes, *HCT*, V 61–62.

7. Athens' dominion: Meiggs, *AE*. Plato's Socrates on the Hellenes: *Phd.* 109a–b.

8. Euboean and Lesbian appeals, Agis' plans: Thuc. 8.5.1–3 with Andrewes, *HCT*, V 11–12; Kagan, *Fall*, 10–11, 28; Lazenby, *PW*, 171–72; and Hornblower, *CT*, III 760–63. Archidamus and Sthenelaidas: Rahe, *SSAW*, Chapter 2 (with notes 39–40). Later in 412, the Lesbian cities will all revolt: Thuc. 8.22.2–23.6, 100.2–3. Cities on Lesbos: Pyrrha (*IACP* no. 799), Eresus (no. 796), Antissa (no. 794), Methymna (no. 797), and Mytilene (no. 798) with Nigel Spencer, *A Gazeteer of Archaeological Sites on Lesbos* (Oxford: BAR, 1995) nos. 27, 99, 134–41, 161, 217. These sites I visited one by one while sojourning on the island from 12 to 18 April 2022, and I examined each with an eye to the role it played in Sparta's third Attic war. Lacedaemon's harmosts: Herbert W. Parke, "The Development of the Second Spartan Empire, 405–371 B.C.," *JHS* 50:1 (1930): 37–79, and Gabriele Bockisch, "Harmostaí (431–387)," *Klio* 46:1 (January 1965): 129–239. Although this marks the first occasion in which the word *harmostés* appears anywhere and the only time it appears in Thucydides, I am inclined to suspect that Salaethus, Brasidas, and possibly even Gylippus were assigned this title. See Schol. Pind. 6.154e, which suggests that the word was used to designate Spartiates who played a supervisory role in the territory held by the Lacedaemonians.

9. Chios (*IACP* no. 840), Erythrae (no. 845), and Tissaphernes: see Thuc. 8.5.4–5, 29.1, and Plut. *Alc.* 24.1 with Lewis, *SP*, 88; Andrewes, *HCT*, V 12–16; Kagan, *Fall*, 28–29; Lazenby, *PW*, 172; Hornblower, *CT*, III 763–73; Rhodes, *Alcibiades*, 56–57; and Stuttard, *Nemesis*, 179–81. Chians "the wealthiest of the Hellenes": Thuc. 8.45.4. Size of fleet deployed at the battle of Lade: Hdt. 6.8.1, 15.1. Enormous number of slaves: Thuc. 8.40.2. Note, in this connection, Arist. F472 (Rose) = 475.1 (Gigon) with Ath. 6.265b–266f. In this connection, see also Hdt. 8.105. Tissaphernes' satrapy: Debord, *AM*, 116–30. Special military command: ibid. 221–22. Overview of satrapies in Asia Minor: ibid. 19–157, 166–200, and Hilmar Klinkott, "The Satrapies of the Persian Empire in Asia Minor: Lydia, Caria, Lycia, Phrygia, and Cappadocia," in *OHANE*, V 592–648. On Tissaphernes' satrapy, note also ibid. 592–617.

10. Emissaries from Pharnabazus (Thuc. 8.6.1 and 8.1) and perhaps Cyzicus (*IACP* no. 747) as well: Plut. *Alc.* 24.1. Note Satyrus ap. Ath. 12.534d, which suggests a Cyzicene connection on the part of Alcibiades; and see Andrewes, *HCT*, V 18; Kagan, *Fall*, 28–29; Lazenby, *PW*, 172; Hornblower, *CT*, III 773–74, 779–80; and Stuttard, *Nemesis*, 180. Pharnabazus' satrapy: Debord, *AM*, 83–115 (esp. 91–104). Gordium included: *Hell. Oxy.* 24.5–6 (Chambers). Note also Klinkott, "The Satrapies of the Persian Empire in Asia Minor: Lydia, Caria, Lycia, Phrygia, and Cappadocia," 617–27.

11. Great King closely supervises his satraps: Hdt. 5.31.4, Diod. 15.41.5, Xen. *Hell.* 1.5.2–5. Achaemenid obsession with tribute: Hdt. 3.89–97 with Debord, *AM*, 41–44, 69–82, and Briant, *CA*, 357–471. Pressure in 413 from the Achaemenid monarch: Thuc. 8.5.5–6.1. For the full implications, see 8.56.4 with Briant, *CA*, 592. On what constituted the arrears, note Hdt. 6.42.2; see 6.59 and Isoc. *Pan.* 120, where we are told that arrears were forgiven at the end of a reign; and then consider Oswyn Murray, "*Ho Archaios Dasmos*," *Historia* 15:2 (April 1966): 142–56, whose analysis Lewis, *SP*, 87, and Hornblower, *CT*, III 771, endorse. In assessing the intentions of Darius II, one would err in presuming that he could not have learned of the catastrophe suffered by the Athenians in Sicily in time to be able to authorize the approach to Lacedaemon made by his satraps in Anatolia. In conveying news and directives, the Persian analogue to the Pony Express was exceedingly efficient: note Hdt. 5.52–54, 8.98; Xen. *Cyr.* 8.6.17–18 with David Graf, "The Persian Royal Road System," *AchHist* 8 (1994): 167–89; Briant, *CA*, 364–87; and Pierre Briant, "From the Indus to the Mediterranean: The Administrative Organization and Logistics of the Great Roads of the Achaemenid Empire," in *Highways, Byways, and Road Systems in the Pre-Modern World*, ed. Susan E. Alcock, John Bodel, and Richard J. A. Talbert (New York: John Wiley & Sons, 2012), 185–201, reprinted in Briant, *From Cyrus to Seleukos*, 227–44; then, see Henry P. Colburn, "Connectivity and Communication in the Achaemenid Empire," *JESHO* 56 (2013): 29–52; Amélie Kuhrt, "State Communications in the Persian Empire," in *State Correspondence in the Ancient World: From New Kingdom Egypt to the Roman Empire*, ed. Karen Radner (Oxford: Oxford University Press, 2014), 112–40; and Wouter F. M. Henkelman and Bruno Jacobs, "Roads and Communications," in *A Companion to the Achaemenid Persian Empire*, ed. Bruno Jacobs and Robert Rollinger (Hoboken, NJ: Wiley Blackwell, 2021), I 719–35. In this connection, note also Lewis, *SP*, 2–26, 56–58; Waters, "Applied Royal Directive: Pissouthnes and Samos," 817–28; and Hyland, *PI*, 45–47, who draws attention to the fact that Thucydides seems to be saying that Tissaphernes was the instigator of the decision to reach an accommodation with Lacedaemon and who rightly observes that no satrap would have done anything of the sort without royal authorization. See Just. *Epit.* 5.1.7–9. Cf. Kallet, *MCPT*, 242–46, who ignores what Thucydides leaves unsaid.

12. Role played by the *gerousía* in Spartan policymaking and its significance: Rahe, *SR*, Chapter 2.
13. Subsequent reputation of Artaxerxes son of Xerxes: Diod. 11.71, 15.93; Plut. *Artax.* 1.1; Amm. Marc. 30.8. Some scholars suspect that Ath. 12.548e is also pertinent.

CHAPTER 1. PERSIKÁ

Epigraph: Marcus Tullius Cicero, *Phil.* 5.5.

1. First two *nómoi* pertinent to the succession in Persia: Hdt. 3.2, 7.2.1. Agreement of the seven confederates that henceforth the Queen Mother be drawn from one of their families: 3.84.2. Cf. 7.2.2–3.3—where we are told that another rule, supposedly applicable also at Lacedaemon, was said to have influenced Darius' decision to prefer Xerxes to his older brother. It is, I think, telling that Herodotus thought the claim nonsense and suspected, instead, that the decision had a great deal more to do with the leverage possessed by Xerxes' mother Atossa, who was a daughter of Cyrus. In the eyes of at least some of the Great King's Iranian subjects, Darius was undoubtedly regarded as a usurper. But, as the eldest surviving grandson of Cyrus, Xerxes would surely have been deemed in these quarters a legitimate king.
2. Succession: Llewellyn-Jones, *KCAP*, 15–19.
3. Plato on the defective moral formation of Cambyses, Xerxes, and those of their successors reared by the women at court: *Leg.* 3.694c–696a. Scholars dismiss: for example, Pierre Briant, "Histoire et idéologie: Les Grecs et la 'décadence perse,'" in *Mélanges Pierre Lévêque II: Anthropologie et société*, ed. Marie-Madeleine Mactoux and Évelyne Geny (Paris: Les Belles Lettres, 1989), II 33–47, reprinted in an English translation by Antonia Nevill as "History and Ideology: The Greeks and 'Persian Decadence,'" in *Greeks and Barbarians*, ed. Thomas Harrison (Edinburgh: Edinburgh University Press, 2001), 193–210; as well as Briant, *CA*, 515–68. The pertinent passage from Plato's *Laws* is notably absent from *The Persian Empire: A Corpus of Sources from the Achaemenid Period*, ed. Amélie Kuhrt (London: Routledge, 2007), as are the similar passages from Xenophon, Isocrates, and a host of other authors whose testimony Briant rejected in the book chapter cited. With regard to the validity of what the Greeks had to say concerning the Persian court, see the more sensible observations of Lewis, *SP*, 21–22, and Llewellyn-Jones, *KCAP*, 96–148, and consider what Ibn Khaldun wrote concerning similar regimes in his *Muqaddimah*. What Briant dismisses as "ideology" is a theory of regime trajectories that was articulated and refined by Herodotus, Thucydides, Xenophon, Plato, Aristotle, Polybius, and others in ancient Greece and Rome for the purpose of making sense of the political phenomena they observed. It was not a set of ideological blinders that deter-

mined what they could and could not see. That would, in fact, be a better description for the set of presumptions that determined Briant's treatment of the ancient testimony regarding the Persian regime and dictated Kuhrt's decision that readers of her sourcebook should not be exposed to such testimony. For the ideological origins of this set of presumptions, see Edward W. Said, *Orientalism: Western Concepts of the Orient* (London: Routledge, 1979).

4. The status of the first Darius and his ascension: Rahe, *PC*, Chapter 1. For further discussion, see Matt Waters, "The Persian Empire under the Teispid Dynasty: Emergence and Conquest," and Daniel T. Potts, "The Persian Empire under the Achaemenid Dynasty, from Darius I to Darius III," in *OHANE*, V 377–510 (esp. 379–87, 402–9, 427–57). Regarding the *mār šarri* and those designated as *mār bīt šarri* or *mār bīti*, see Stolper, *E&E*, 21–22, 43, 53, 59–62, 90–91, 96, 127, and Christopher J. Tuplin, "Aršāma: Prince and Satrap," in *AhW*, III 3–72 (at 31–38). For the role accorded Darius' co-conspirators, see Appendix 7.

5. Artaxerxes' elevation, Megabyzus as protector: *SFAW*, Chapter 3 (with notes 10 and 62–63). Xerxes separates "the Land Across-the-River" from Babylonia: Kristen Kleber, "Administration in Babylonia," in *Die Verwaltung im Achämenidenreich: Imperiale Muster und Strukturen /Administration in the Achaemenid Empire: Tracing the Imperial Signature*, ed. Bruno Jacobs, Wouter F. M. Henkelman, and Matthew W. Stolper (Wiesbaden: Harrassowitz Verlag, 2017), 699–714 (at 702). Megabyzus known to have been its governor: Ctesias *FGrH* 688 F14.40–41. Note, in this connection, Peter R. Bedford, "The Satrapies of the Persian Empire: Ebir-nari/Syria," in *OHANE*, V 689–736.

6. On Ctesias, see Christopher J. Tuplin, "Doctoring the Persians: Ctesias of Cnidus, Physician and Historian," *Klio* 86:2 (February 2004): 305–47, and "Ctesias as Military Historian," in *Die Welt des Ktesias—Ctesias' World*, ed. Josef Wiesehöfer, Robert Rollinger, and Giovanni B. Lanfranchi (Wiesbaden: Harrassowitz Verlag, 2011), 449–88. Circumstantial detail concerning late fifth-century figures confirmed by Babylonian evidence: see note 10, below. This evidence proves beyond any doubt that Ctesias was well informed concerning the succession crisis and rules out the propriety of the propensity, still evident among some students of this subject, to simply dismiss his testimony: cf. for example Carsten Binder, "From Darius II to Darius III," in *A Companion to the Achaemenid Persian Empire*, ed. Bruno Jacobs and Robert Rollinger (Hoboken, NJ: Wiley Blackwell, 2021), I 457–71 (at 457–59).

7. Xerxes II made co-regent: preface to Part IV, note 34, below. Death of Artaxerxes, Sogdianus murders heir Xerxes II: Ctesias *FGrH* 688 F14.46–15.48. Obsequies and investiture ceremony: Pierre Briant, "Le Roi est mort: Vive le roi! Remarques sur les rites et rituels de succession chez les Achéménides,"in *La Religion iranienne à l'époque achéménide*, ed. Jean Kellens (Gent: Iranica Antiqua, 1991), 1–11; Carsten Binder, "Das Krönungszeremoniell der Achaimeniden," in *Der Achämenidenhof/The Achaemenid Court*, ed. Bruno Jacobs and Robert Roll-

inger (Stuttgart: Harrassowitz, 2010), 473–97; and Llewellyn-Jones, *KCAP*, 13–15. Seasonal residences of the Great King: preface to Part IV, note 15, below. I give priority to Susa here because I know of no occasion when an embassy from Greece met with the King at Persepolis, Babylon, or Ecbatana.

8. On the succession crisis that eventuated in the elevation of Ochus, see Ctesias *FGrH* 688 F15.47–53 with Val. Max. 9.2 ext. 6–7 (on the grisly fate in store for the losers), confirmed in considerable measure by the business records of the Murašû firm in Babylonia: Stolper, *E&E*, 104–24 with 54–62, 64–67, 89–93, 95–96; Veysel Donbaz and Matthew W. Stolper, *Istanbul Murašū Texts* (Leiden: Nederlands historisch-archaeologisch Instituut te Istanbul, 1997) no. 102; Matthew W. Stolper, "Achaemenid Legal Texts from the Kasr: Interim Observations," in *Babylon: Focus mesopotamischer Geschichte, Wege früher Gelehrsamkeit, Mythos in der Moderne*, ed. Johannes Renger (Saarbrücken: SDV Saarbrücker Drucherei und Verlag, 1999), 365–75 (at 372); and Matthew W. Stolper, "Parysatis in Babylon," in *If a Man Builds a Joyful House: Assyriological Studies in Honor of Erle Verdun Leichty*, ed. Ann Guinan et al. (Leiden: Brill, 2006), 463–72. The Greek evidence deserves closer attention than, in the last few decades, it has received: Thuc. 4.50; Diod. 12.64.1–65.1, 71.1; Polyaen. *Strat.* 7.17.1; and Paus. 6.5.7. See Rahe, *SSAW*, Chapter 6 (with notes 11–13). Note also Lewis, *SP*, 72–76; Briant, *CA*, 588–91; and Potts, "The Persian Empire under the Achaemenid Dynasty," 469–73. Ctesias' account of Darius II's origin receives confirmation from a tablet (BM 34787) which is dated to "the accession year of Ochus who is named Darius": Donald J. Wiseman, *BSOAS* 37:2 (1974): 450–52 (at 451). On the timing of the succession crisis, cf. Lewis, *SP*, 69–82, who has much of value to say (especially with regard to the corroboration of Ctesias' claims in the Babylonian tablets of the time), with Leo Depuydt, "The Date of the Death of Artaxerxes I," *WO* 26 (1995): 86–96, and *From Xerxes' Murder (465) to Arridaios' Execution (317): Updates to Achaemenid Chronology* (Oxford: BAR, 2008), 13–34, whose account of the chronology of the events associated with the rise of Ochus and his consolidation of power draws on important evidence unavailable to Lewis. For further discussion, see Appendix 1, below.

9. Ochus' lineage, satrap of Hyrcania: Ctesias *FrGH* 688 F15.47. Encouragement by Arsames and Artoxares; Artoxares journeys from his place of exile in Armenia; Arsames, probably from his satrapy in Egypt: F14.38, 43, F15.50. Babylon is the obvious meeting place and happens to be the locale in which the younger Darius is first attested: BM 33342 with Lewis *SP*, 72. Importance *said* to have been accorded Babylon: Xen. *Cyr* 8.6.22. Ctesias elsewhere claims that Sogdianus' reign lasted six months and fifteen days: *FGrH* 688 F15.50. In attributing two months to Xerxes II and seven months to Sogdianus, Diodorus appears to have followed Ctesias and to have rounded his figures: cf. 12.64.1 with 71.1, and see Adolf von Mess, "Untersuchungen über Ephorus: Ephorus and Ktesias," *RhM* n.f. 61 (1906): 360–407, and Jacoby, *RE* I:11 (1922), 2032–73. The later

writers who mention the two reigns appear to have done the same: see Swoboda, *RE* I:4 (1901): 2199–2205, and Weissbach, *RE* II:3 (1929): 791–93. For the evidence with regard to this Arsames, which is substantial, see *AhW*, passim. For an overview, see Tuplin, "Aršāma: Prince and Satrap," 3–72.

10. Sogdianus, Menostanes son of Artarios, Arbarios, and the royal bodyguard: Ctesias *FGrH* 688 F14.41–42, F15.48–50. For the view that Herodotus may have misnamed this body of men, see Llewellyn-Jones, *KCAP*, 37–38. Menostanes appears in four cuneiform tablets dated to the last two years of Artaxerxes' reign as Manuštanu, son of Artareme. In one, he is termed a Son of the Royal House [*mār bīt šarri*]: BE IX no. 84. In the others, he is simply called a *mār bīti*. He seems to have been in charge of the royal storehouse or treasury in Babylonia: BE IX nos. 75, 83–84; NBRVT no. 180. Menostanes' father Artarios (Artareme) is even better attested. He is named in a series of documents dated to the reign of Artaxerxes and stretching from 431 to 424: BE IX nos. 39, 48, 72, 82–84, 107; CBS no. 12961. He is mentioned in a legal context as late as the 6 October 423: PBS II/1 nos. 34, 185; *BC*, 33. But he seems to have been deposed as satrap of Babylonia sometime before 23 March 423: PBS II/1 no. 2; *BC*, 33. Arbarios (Arbareme) first appears after the younger Darius' rise to power: PBS II/1 no. 9; NBRVT no. 204. The best discussion is to be found in Stolper, *E&E*, 89–96, 102–3, 114–16. Cf. Lewis *SP*, 94 n. 18, 74 n. 162. On the Chiliarchy as an office, see the preface to Part IV, note 24, below.

11. House rented on 13 February 423 until "the going forth of the king": BE X no. 1.

12. Parysatis Ochus' principal advisor: Ctesias *FGrH* 688 F15.50. She continued to serve as his chief advisor in the years that followed: F15.51–52, 54, 56, F15b. Her importance is also evident in the Babylonian documents where she appears after the younger Darius' accession as one of the major landholders in the region: PBS II/1 nos. 38, 50, 60, 75, 119, 146–47; BE X nos. 97, 131; NBRVT no. 185 with Stolper, *E&E*, 53, 63–64, 114–16, and "Parysatis in Babylon," 463–72.

13. Babylonian mothers of Ochus and Parysatis: Ctesias *FGrH* 688 F15.50. Babylonian Bēlšunu named district governor of Babylon and, later, governor (and, perhaps, satrap) of Syria: see Xen. *An.* 1.4.10, 7.8.25; note Joachim Oelsner, "Zwischen Xerxes und Alexander: Babylonische Rechtsurkunden und Wirtschaftstexte aus der späten Achämenidenzeit," *WdO* 8:2 (1976): 310–18 (at 316–18), and Lewis, *SP*, 78 n. 184; and cf. Matthew W. Stolper, "Bēlšunu the Satrap," in *Language, Literature, and History: Philological and Historical Studies Presented to Erica Reiner*, ed. Francesca Rochberg-Halton (New Haven, CT: Yale University Press, 1987), 389–402, where Stolper suggests that Bēlšunu was given a satrapy, with Matthew W. Stolper, "The Governor of Babylon and Across-the-River in 486 B.C.," *JNES* 48:4 (October 1989): 283–305 (at 298); "The Babylonian Enterprise of Belesys," in *Dans les pas des Dix-Mille: Peuples et pays du Proche-Orient vus par un Grec*, ed. Pierre Briant (Toulouse: Presses universitaires du Mirail, 1995), 217–38; and "Achaemenid Legal Texts from the Kasr," 366–67,

369–74, where he wonders whether the title was conferred and notes that, when Bēlšunu became governor of Syria, his son replaced him as governor of Babylon. Whether Bēlšunu was, strictly speaking, a satrap or not, his elevation would appear to be unprecedented. See also Briant, *CA*, 601–2.

14. Persian ethnocentrism: Hdt. 3.134.2 with Briant, *CA*, 172–83, 349–54, confirmed by the evidence collected in Rahe, *PC*, Chapter 1, notes 58–60. Cf. Llewellyn-Jones, *KCAP*, 118, who underestimates the disadvantage conferred on Ochus by bastardy.

15. Cambyses' marriages: Hdt. 3.31–32. Darius' marriages: Hdt. 3.88.2, 7.2.1–3, 224.2. Artaxerxes' consort: Ctesias *FGrH* 688 F14.46. Xerxes' Amestris: F13.24.

16. Dynastic marriages contracted with Teriteuchmes son of Hydarnes and his sister Stateira: Ctesias *FGrH* 688 F15.55 with Briant, *CA*, 589–91. Significance: ibid. 307–10. Likely lineage of this family: Hdt. 3.70 (confirmed by DB 4.84) and 7.83.1, 211.1, 215.1, 218.2. The first Hydarnes recovers Media for Darius and ends up as its satrap: consider Hallock, *PFT* nos. 1363, 2055, V-2041, V-2349, in light of DB 2.18–28, and see Lewis, *SP*, 84 n. 14, and Wouter F. M. Henkelman, "Nakhthor in Persepolis," in *AhW*, II 193–223 (at 206–11). Descent from one of the elder Darius' co-conspirators still counted for something as late as 344: Diod. 16.47.2. On Arsaces' age at the time of his father's accession to the throne, see Appendix 6.

17. High incidence in May and June 423 of mortgages in the Nippur area: Stolper, *E&E*, 104–24. For the timing of the two rebellions that the Ochus who called himself Darius had to face after the collapse of Sogdianus' bid for the throne, see Appendix 3, below. Cf. Govert van Driel, "The Murašûs in Context," *JESHO* 32:2 (June 1989): 203–29 (at 223–24), who casts doubt on Stolper's hypothesis, and Gauthier Tolini, who suggests in his as yet unpublished dissertation "La Babylonie et l'Iran: Les Relations d'une province avec le cœur de l'empire achéménide (539–331 avant notre ère)" (Université Paris I Panthéon-Sorbonne, 2011), 554–63, that the debt crisis of 423 was a consequence of crop failure. The system of interlinked markets produced by the Achaemenid regime after Megabyzus' suppression of the Babylonian revolt that followed close upon the accession of Xerxes was not conducive to an efficient use of the resources of Babylonia: Reinhard Pirngruber, *The Economy of Late Achaemenid and Seleucid Babylonia* (Cambridge: Cambridge University Press, 2017), 35–66.

18. The timing of Pissouthnes' rebellion and of Tissaphernes' succession as satrap at Sardis can be inferred from Thucydides' report that the latter's hyparch Arsaces recruited exiled Delians from Pharnaces' satrapy for warfare in 422 or in the first half of 421 and then, for reasons all his own, murdered them: Thuc. 8.108.4–5, read in light of 8.5.1 and 32.1. The date of the rebellion is disputed: see Lewis, *SP*, 77–81; Henry D. Westlake, "Athens and Amorges," *Phoenix* 31:4 (Winter 1977): 319–29 (at 321–22), reprinted in Westlake, *Studies*, 103–12 (at 104–5); Andrewes, *HCT*, V 12–18, 356–57; Hornblower, *CT*, II 423–24, III 764–71;

Debord, *AM*, 120–21; and Briant, *CA*, 591. But, as I argue in Appendix 3, below, the evidence cited in favor of dating these rebellions after 417 proves nothing of the sort. Megabyzus, Zopyrus, Artyphius, Pissouthnes, and Tissaphernes in relation to the Persian court: Hdt. 1.160.2; Ctesias *FGrH* 688 F14.34–15.53; Diod. 12.64.1, 71.1; and Paus. 6.5.7. Note Potts, "The Persian Empire under the Achaemenid Dynasty," 474–77. On Pissouthnes more generally, see Appendix 7.

19. We learn Tissaphernes' patronymic from the Xanthus Stele: Lewis, *SP*, 83–84 (with n. 4), and Debord, *AM*, 120 n. 38. Hydarnes' office in Anatolia ca. 482: Hdt. 7.135. Whether this Hydarnes was the Hydarnes son of Hydarnes chosen the following year to lead what Herodotus calls the Ten Thousand Immortals (7.83.1) we do not know, but it does seem likely. Cf. Lewis, *SP*, 83–84, and Briant, *CA*, 978, who strongly doubt that Tissaphernes could have been a sibling of Stateira and Teriteuchmes. Both do so on the conviction that Ctesias would have said as much if it were true, but this presupposes something utterly implausible—that nothing of significance dropped out when Photius made his epitome of the *Persika*—and, if, as Briant (*CA*, 589) points out, Xenophon (*An.* 2.3.17) is correct, which seems likely, Teriteuchmes had siblings, apart from Stateira, who were not executed along with his mother, his brothers Mitrostes and Helicus, and two of his sisters when he plotted to murder his wife and stage a revolt: Ctesias *FGrH* 688 F15.55–56. Vidarna was a relatively common name at the court of the first Darius, as Lewis, *SP*, 84–85 n. 14, showed. But this does not mean that more than one clan was involved in and after 423.

20. Epilycus and *philía*: Andoc. 3.29, read with an eye to Ar. *Eq.* 478 and to what Theopompus of Chios *FGrH* 115 F153–54 emphatically denies, and *IG* I³ 227 = *ML* no. 70 = *O&R* no. 157, which strongly suggests that Theopompus is in error and that these negotiations actually took place. Date of *spondaí* and circumstances: Rahe, *SSAW*, Chapter 6 (esp. note 13). Pissouthnes' revolt may well have postdated the arrangements worked out with Epilycus, as Hyland, *PI*, 42–45 (with n. 39), contends. But, if so, it did not postdate it by much: see Kagan, *Fall*, 19–22, and Rahe, *SSAW*, Chapter 6 (with notes 11–13). Offer to the Spartans made by Hydarnes when they met him in Anatolia: Hdt. 7.135–36. A similar offer subsequently conveyed to the Athenians: 8.136, 140. Cf. Moshé Amit, "A Peace Treaty between Sparta and Persia," *RSA* 4:1–2 (1974): 55–62 (at 60), who underestimates what *philía* implies in the case under consideration here.

21. Athens and Amorges: Thuc. 8.5.5, 19.2, 28.2–4. The supposition that the Athenians were aiding Amorges *prior to* Tissaphernes' approach to the Lacedaemonians has no foundation in Thucydides; and had they acted in a manner likely to annoy the Persians while the Sicilian Expedition was underway, he would have been apt to mention it as yet another example of their recklessness. The supposition is based solely on the testimony of the orator Andocides, who was inclined to engage in special pleading and who was, like Isocrates (8.84–85) and

Aeschines (2.76), more than merely capable of chronological distortion where it served his rhetorical purpose: consider Andoc. 3.29 in light of Antony Andrewes, "Thucydides and the Persians," *Historia* 10:1 (January 1961): 1–18 (at 2–5), and Westlake, "Athens and Amorges," 19–29, reprinted in Westlake, *Studies*, 103–12; and see Moshé Amit, "The Disintegration of the Athenian Empire in Asia Minor (412–405 B.C.E.)," *SCI* 2 (1975): 38–71 (at 44–46); Kagan, *Fall*, 29–31; and Stephen Ruzicka, *Trouble in the West: Egypt and the Persian Empire, 525–332 BCE* (Oxford: Oxford University Press, 2012), 35–36. Whether *ML* no. 77.79 = *IG* I^3 370 = *O&R* no. 170.79 is pertinent is, for good reason, in dispute. Given the state of the stone on which it is inscribed, it is not clear that the Athenian *stratēgós* mentioned with regard to expenditures in 414 was stationed in Ephesus or at Hephaestia on the island of Lemnos; and, even if this inscription could be taken as proof that he was posted in the former city, it would not lend support to Andocides' claim—for Miletus, to the south of Ephesus, and Iasos on the coast of Caria were the cities within Athens' domain that lay closest to Amorges' refuge. The Great Kings' way of dealing with mountain peoples and the like: Appendix 5, note 8, below. Long-established pattern of skirmishing in western Anatolia and beyond: note 3, above. Cf. Lewis, *SP*, 85–87 (esp. n. 25); Andrewes, *HCT*, V 17–18; and Hornblower, *CT*, III 768–71, who doubt that Darius II could have learned of the catastrophe suffered by the Athenians in Sicily in time for this to have played a role in the thinking that eventuated in the approach to Lacedaemon made by his two satraps and who are therefore inclined at least to entertain the possibility that Andocides is telling the truth, with the secondary literature cited in note 11, above, which makes it clear that messages could be conveyed between Sardis and Susa in twelve days; then, cf. Briant, *CA*, 591–92; Stuttard, *Nemesis*, 179; and Hyland, *PI*, 45, who also accept the testimony of Andocides, with Just. *Epit.* 5.1.7–9; Kagan, *Fall*, 22–23, 29–33; and Lazenby, *PW*, 172–73, who rightly emphasize the opportunity opened up by the Sicilian disaster.

22. Pasagardae and Anahita: Plut. *Artax.* 3.1–2 with Fred S. Naiden, *Soldier, Priest, and God: A Life of Alexander the Great* (Oxford: Oxford University Press, 2018), 61, 144 (with 331), 159–62, 166–69, 175. On the emphatically Persian character of the Achaemenid monarchy in the time of the first Darius and on the political theology it espoused during his reign and that of Xerxes, Artaxerxes, and Darius II, see Rahe, *PC*, Chapter 1 and preface to Part II, where full annotation is provided. To the evidence collected there, I would now add Plut. *Mor.* 369d–370c, which identifies Ahura Mazda as a god who can and does create other gods. I suspect that the monotheism of the Ionian philosophers (Arist. *Ph.* 203b3–15) owes something to early Zoroastrianism. In this connection, see Xenophanes 21 B11–12, 14–16, 23–26 (DK^6). On Artaxerxes and his son Darius II, see A^{1}Pa, A^{1}Pb, D^{2}Ha, D^{2}Sa, and D^{2}Sb with Lewis, *SP*, 77–78 (esp. n. 182). The first Great King to have posted an inscription mentioning gods other than Ahura

Mazda was the younger Darius' son and heir Artaxerxes II, who added Mithras and Anahita: A²Ha, A²Hb, A²Sa, A²Sd. He certainly did not invent either cult, but for the claim of Berossos *FGrH* 680 F11 that it was the younger Artaxerxes who introduced the worship of Anahita, there is this to be said: he really does seem to be the first Achaemenid to have given it royal sanction. For a further discussion of Achaemenid political theology, see the preface to Part IV, note 15, below. For an argument concerning the political culture of the Achaemenid monarchy that is similar to the one I presented in *PC* and reiterate here, see Hyland, *PI*, 1–14. I do not, however, think—as Hyland does—that Artaxerxes, Darius II, and their advisors ever regarded the arrangement with Athens forged after Eurymedon in the 460s and renewed in 449 as anything other than a humiliation and a great embarrassment. At the very least, as Thucydides makes crystal clear, the younger Darius wanted to recover in Anatolia what his father and grandfather had lost; and the cold war that Pissouthnes is known to have conducted against Athens in the Aegean and in Asia Minor in the 440s and 420s is evidence that the elder Artaxerxes harbored similar ambitions. In the late 440s, Artaxerxes toyed with the idea of sending the Phoenician fleet into the Aegean; and later, as we shall soon see, Darius II did the same.

23. Athenian agreements with Persia: Rahe, *SFAW*, Chapters 3 (with notes 1–10), 4 (with notes 40–41), and 6 (with notes 13–18), and *SSAW*, Chapter 6 (with notes 11–13). I find it hard to believe that Artaxerxes and his courtiers could have regarded their defeat at Cypriot Salamis and their acquiescence in a postwar arrangement with Athens that differed not one whit in its terms from the post-Eurymedon agreement that had inspired Xerxes' assassination sixteen years before as anything but a profound humiliation and a severe setback: cf., however, Briant, *CA*, 573–77, 579–83, and Hyland, *PI*, 15–36.

24. Spartan alliance with the Chian and Erythraean conspirators and with Tissaphernes, role of Alcibiades: Thuc. 8.6.3–4 with Hatzfeld, *Alcibiade*, 214–17; Lewis, *SP*, 88–89; Andrewes, *HCT*, V 19; Hornblower, *CT*, III 774–77; Rhodes, *Alcibiades*, 56–57; and Stuttard, *Nemesis*, 179–83. Note also Nepos *Alc.* 4.7, Just. *Epit.* 5.1.4. Advice of Archidamus twenty years before: Thuc. 1.82.1.

25. Competing offers and Spartan reflections: Kagan, *Fall*, 32–35, and Lazenby, *PW*, 171–73. Lacedaemonian judgment correct: Isoc. 4.139–40.

26. Spartan economy: Rahe, *SR*, Chapter 1.

27. Trireme costs: Rahe, *SSPW*, Chapter 2, note 42. For an admirably detailed study of the enormous costs associated with conducting war at sea and on land at a considerable distance from home, see Margaret L. Cook, "Timokrates' 50 Talents and the Cost of Ancient Warfare," *Eranos* 88 (1990): 69–97. In this connection, see also Stephen O'Connor, "The Daily Consumption of Classical Greek Sailors and Soldiers," *Chiron* 43 (2013): 327–56, who cites the considerable secondary literature on this subject.

Epigraph: Halford J. Mackinder, *Money-Power and Man-Power: The Underlying Principles Rather than the Statistics of Tariff Reform* (London: Simkin-Marshall, 1906), reprinted in *Orbis* 63:2 (Spring 2019): 155–71 (at 162).

1. See, for example, Hyland, *PI*, 50–52.

2. Athenian response to calamity: Thuc. 8.1 and Just. *Epit.* 5.1.10 with Andrewes, *HCT*, V 5–7; Kagan, *Fall*, 1–10; Ostwald, *Sovereignty*, 337–38; Heftner, *Umsturz*, 1–6; Kallet, *MCPT*, 227–38; Robin Osborne, "Changing the Discourse," in *Popular Tyranny: Sovereignty and its Discontents in Ancient Greece*, ed. Kathryn A. Morgan (Austin: University of Texas Press, 2003), 251–72, reprinted with an addendum in Osborne, *AAD*, 267–88; Lazenby, *PW*, 171; and Hornblower, *CT*, III 749–51. Consider Eupolis *Demes* F99–146 (PCG) in light of Franco Sartori, *Una Pagina di storia ateniese in un frammento dei 'Demi' eupolidei* (Rome: L'Erma Di Bretschneider, 1975), 11–15, 31–85, and see Ostwald, *Sovereignty*, 341–42, as well as Munn, *SH*, 135–37. Note also John M. Edmonds, "The Cairo and Oxyrhynchus Fragments of the *Dēmoi* of Eupolis," *Mnemosyne* 3rd ser., 8 (1939): 1–20. Depleted reserves, desperate state of finances for the duration of the war: Loren J. Samons II, *Empire of the Owl: Athenian Imperial Finance* (Stuttgart: Franz Steiner Verlag, 2000), 230–93; Alec Blamire, "Athenian Finance, 454–404 B.C.," *Hesperia* 70:1 (January–March 2001): 99–126 (at 114–23); and David M. Pritchard, *Public Spending and Democracy in Classical Athens* (Austin: University of Texas Press, 2015), 1–99 (esp. 91–99). Note also Kallet, *MCPT*, 227–84.

3. *Sōphrosúnē* and *eutakteîn*: Thuc. 8.1.3–4. *Próbouloi*, consider Thuc. 8.1.3; Ar. *Lys.* 421, 467, *Thesm.* 808–9; Arist. *Ath. Pol.* 29.2 (where the number is specified); Harp. s.v. *sungrapheîs*, citing Androtion *FGrH* 324 F43 and Philochorus *FGrH* 328 F136; and *Lex Seguer.* 298.25, in light of Diod. 12.75.4 (where, as often happens in the case of this author, the date could well be wrong); note Ar. *Lys.* 420–23, 433–34, 441–42, 445, 449, 455, 461, where one must allow for comic exaggeration; then, see Arist. *Pol.* 1298b29, 1299b31 and 36–38, 1323a7 with François Ruzé, "La Fonction des probouloi dans le monde grec antique," in *Mélanges d'histoire ancienne offerts à William Seston* (Paris: Boccard, 1974), 443–62 (esp. 446–49); Rhodes, *CAAP*, 372–73; Andrewes, *HCT*, V 6–7; Ostwald, *Sovereignty*, 338–43; Kagan, *Fall*, 5–7; Munn, *SH*, 134–37; Heftner, *Umsturz*, 6–16; and Hornblower, *CT*, III 752–53. For a defense of the date given at Diod. 12.75.4, cf. Antony Andrewes and David M. Lewis, "Note on the Peace of Nikias," *JHS* 77 (1957): 177–80 (at 177). Hagnon: Lys. 12.65 with Thuc. 1.116.1–117.2, 2.58.1, 95, 4.102.3, 5.19.2, 24.1. Sophocles: Arist. *Rhet.* 1419a26–30 with Ion of Chios F104 (Leurini) = *FGrH* 392 F6 and Plut. *Nic.* 15.2 with Michael H. Jameson, "Sophocles and the Four Hundred," *Historia* 20:5/6 (4th Quarter 1971): 541–68 (esp. 541–57). See also Leonard Woodbury, "Sophocles among

the Generals," *Phoenix* 24:3 (Autumn 1970): 209–24; and cf. Harry C. Avery, "Sophocles' Political Career," *Historia* 22:4 (4th Quarter 1973): 509–14, with Peter Karavites, "Tradition, Skepticism, and Sophocles' Political Career," *Klio* 58:2 (January 1976): 359–65.

4. Incoherence of the eighth book, overlapping narratives: Ulrich von Wilamowitz-Möllendorff, "Thukydides VIII," *Hermes* 43:4 (1908): 578–618, reprinted in Wilamowitz-Möllendorff, *Kleine Schriften* (Berlin: Weidmann, 1935–72), III 307–45, and Andrewes, *HCT*, V 1–4, 93–95, 361–83.

5. Integrity of book eight defended: Hartmut Erbse, *Thukydides-Interpretationen* (Berlin: de Gruyter, 1989), passim (esp. 1–82). Coherence of the narrative: W. Robert Connor, *Thucydides* (Princeton, NJ: Princeton University Press, 1984), 210–30; Rood, *Thucydides*, 251–84; and Carolyn Dewald, *Thucydides' War Narrative: A Structural Study* (Berkeley: University of California Press, 2005), 144–54, who try to make sense of its strangeness in literary terms. Narrative confusion due to intercommunal anarchy: Debord, *AM*, 215. On the scholarly debate, see Hornblower, *CT*, III 1–4, 883–86, 1029–30. Cf. Rahe, *SSAW*, Chapter 7, on the fifth book of Thucydides' history. On the reconstitution of the Athenian alliance, see *R&O* no. 22 = *IG* II² 43 = *GHI* no. 123 with Jack Cargill, *The Second Athenian League: Empire or Free Alliance* (Berkeley, CA: University of California Press, 1981). The provisions of this agreement supplied safeguards against the abuses attendant on Athens' transformation of the first alliance into an instrument of imperial domination.

6. Regarding the ships available to each side at any given time in the summer of 412, see Andrewes, *HCT*, V 27–28.

7. Status of emergency funds and reserve fleet: regarding the former, consider Thuc. 8.15.1 and Philochorus *FGrH* 238 F138 in light of Thuc. 2.24.1, and see Hornblower, *CT*, III 794–96; regarding the latter, cf. Thuc. 8.1.2 with 2.24.2, and see Andrewes, *HCT*, V 6, and Hornblower, *CT*, III 751. Quorum required for assembly conferring *adeía*: Dem. 24.46 with Charles Hignett, *A History of the Athenian Constitution* (Oxford: Clarendon Press, 1952), 236. For an overview, see David M. Lewis, "Entrenchment-Clauses in Attic Decrees," in *Phóros: Tribute to Benjamin Dean Meritt*, ed. Donald W. Bradeen and Malcolm F. McGregor (Locust Valley, NY: J. J. Augustin, 1974), 81–89, reprinted in Lewis, *Selected Papers in Greek and Near Eastern History*, ed. Peter J. Rhodes (Cambridge: Cambridge University Press, 1997), 136–49.

8. Initial Spartan plan: Thuc. 8.8.2 with Hatzfeld, *Alcibiade*, 219; Andrewes, *HCT*, V 20–21; Kagan, *Fall*, 36–37; Lazenby, *PW*, 173; Hornblower, *CT*, III 780–81; and Stuttard, *Nemesis*, 182–83. Note, in this connection, Thuc. 8.8.1. The career of Clearchus' father: 1.139.3, 5.12.1–14.1. Trouble arising from divided authority: Debord, *AM*, 203–4. Dependence of Athens and other Aegean cities on grain imported from the Black Sea: Prologue, note 7, above. Impact of Peloponnesian presence at Deceleia: Rahe, *SSPW*, Chapter 5, note 1. Agis watches parade of

merchant ships: Xen. *Hell.* 1.1.35. Clearchus *próxenos* at Lacedaemon of the citizens of Byzantium (*IACP* no. 674), enjoys favor of Agis: Xen. *Hell.* 1.1.35–36. Although Xenophon's testimony pertains to the year 410, Agis surely became alert to the source of Athens' provisions soon after his arrival at Deceleia in 413, and the plan worked out at the conference held at Corinth under his presidency in 412 has his fingerprints all over it. On Clearchus' subsequent career in the course of Sparta's third Attic war, see Chapters 3 and 5–8, below. His father had been a man of consequence: Thuc. 1.139.3, 5.12.1.

9. Isthmian Games and truce, Aristocrates' assignment, Spiraeum blockade: Thuc. 8.8.4–11.2 with Hatzfeld, *Alcibiade*, 219; Andrewes, *HCT*, V 22–25; Kagan, *Fall*, 37–39; Lazenby, *PW*, 173–74; and Hornblower, *CT*, III 781–89. Hornblower's identification of the name of the pertinent refuge I accept. *Díolkos*: Rahe, *SFAW*, Chapter 1, note 3. On Aristocrates, see Thuc. 5.19.2, 24.1; Ar. *Av.* 126; Pl. *Grg.* 472a–b; and Chapters 4–8, below. On the character of the Chian government, see note 27, below.

10. Alcibiades overcomes the ephors' reluctance; he and Chalcideus voyage to Chios: Thuc. 8.11.3–12.3 with Hatzfeld, *Alcibiade*, 219–20; Andrewes, *HCT*, V 25–27; Kagan, *Fall*, 39–42; Lazenby, *PW*, 174; Hornblower, *CT*, III 789–90; and Stuttard, *Nemesis*, 183–85. Alcibiades' ties in the eastern Aegean—especially, on Lesbos, at Ephesus (*IACP* no. 844) and Miletus (no. 854), as well as at Cyzicus: Thuc. 8.17.2, Andoc. 4.30, Satyrus ap. Ath. 12.534d, Plut. *Alc.* 12.1. Role in stirring up the rebellions: Nepos *Alc.* 4.7, Just. *Epit.* 5.2.1–3.

11. Cities in Ionia (and elsewhere apart from European Thrace) without walls: Thuc. 3.33.2 with Gomme, *HCT*, II 294–95; Andrewes, *HCT*, V 35–36; and Hornblower, *CT*, I 414–15, confirmed by Thuc. 8.31.3, 35.3, 41.2, 44.2, 50.5, 62.2, 64.3, 107.1; Xen. *Hell.* 1.1.22, 5.11. Chios an exception: Thuc. 4.51. Mytilene had had walls before her rebellion: 3.2.2, 39.2. As had Samos: 1.116.2, 117.1, 3. Some cities responded to the change in circumstances at this time by constructing walls: 8.64.3, 100.5, 103.2; Xen. *Hell.* 1.1.26, 1.2.2. And the Athenians sometimes built fortifications to protect the communities they controlled: Thuc. 8.51.1–2, 108.2; Xen. *Hell.* 1.2.15; Diod. 13.66.1.

12. Alcibiades and Chalcideus raise a rebellion on Chios: Thuc. 8.14 with Hatzfeld, *Alcibiade*, 220–21; Andrewes, *HCT*, V 34–36; Kagan, *Fall*, 43–46; Debord, *AM*, 204; Lazenby, *PW*, 174; Hornblower, *CT*, III 792–93; and Stuttard, *Nemesis*, 186–87. Chios' staters silver and electrum: cf. Wesley E. Thompson, "The Chian Coinage in Thucydides and Xenophon," *NC* 11 (1971): 323–24, and Nicholas Hardwick, "The Solution to Thucydides VIII 101.1: The 'Chian Fortieths,'" *Quaderni ticinesi di numismatica e antichità classiche* 25 (1996): 59–69, with Aneurin Ellis-Evans, "Mytilene, Lampsakos, Chios and the Financing of the Spartan Fleet (406–404)," *NC* 176 (2016): 1–19 (esp. 11–14). Clazomenae: *IACP* no. 847.

13. *Phóros* scrapped, 5% tax substituted: Thuc. 7.28.4 with Andrewes, *HCT*, IV

401–2, and Hornblower, *CT*, III 594–96. Note Samons, *Empire of the Owl,* 250–54, and Kallet, *MCPT,* 195–226, and see Blamire, "Athenian Finance, 454–404 B.C.," 99–126 (esp. 112–15), and Thomas J. Figueira, "The Imperial Commercial Tax and the Finances of the Athenian Hegemony," *IncidAntico* 3 (2005): 83–133, who shows that, on the basis of the evidence currently available, there is no good reason to suppose, as many do suppose, that the *eikóstē* was abandoned and the *phóros* brought back in 410 or thereafter.

14. Athenians tap emergency fund; Strombichides and Thrasycles to Ionia; revolt of Teos (*IACP* no. 868), then Miletus, after the arrival of Chalcideus and Alcibiades; Persian intervention: Thuc. 8.15.1–17.3 and, for the timing, Philochorus *FGrH* 328 F138 with Andrewes, *HCT,* V 36–40; Kagan, *Fall,* 46–47, 51, 53–54; Kallet, *MCPT,* 246–50; Lazenby, *PW,* 174–76; Hornblower, *CT,* III 794–800; and Stuttard, *Nemesis,* 187–89. Alcibiades' role: Nepos *Alc.* 4.7, Just. *Epit.* 5.2.1–3. Strombichides son of Diotimos: Davies, *APF* no. 4386. Thrasycles: Thuc. 5.19.2, 24.1, 8.17.3, 19.2, and *IG* I³ 80. Erstwhile greatness of Miletus: Rahe, *PC,* Chapter 3.

15. Diomedon, Leon, and skirmishing; Astyochus at Spiraeum; Lesbian revolt stirred up by Chians, Hellespontine aim, rebellion supported by Astyochus, squelched by Diomedon and Leon: Thuc. 8.19–20, 22–23, with Andrewes, *HCT,* V 42–44, 49–54; Kagan, *Fall,* 56–59; Debord, *AM,* 207–8; Lazenby, *PW,* 176–77; and Hornblower, *CT,* III 802–14. Earlier history of Anaia in the Samian *peraía*: consider Thuc. 3.19.2, 32.2, 4.75.1, in light of 1.115.5, 116.1–117.3, 4.75.1, and *IG* I³ 96, note 8.19.1, 61.2, and see Ugo Fantasia, "Samo e Anaia," *Serta Historica Antiqua* 15 (1986): 113–43, and *IACP* no. 838. Lebedos: no. 850. Aerae: no. 837. Aeolian Cumae: no. 817. On the navarchy, cf. Beloch, *Gr. Gesch.,* II:2 269–89, with Raphael Sealey, "Die spartanische Navarchie," *Klio* 58:2 (January 1976): 335–58, and see Wesley E. Thompson, "Astyochos' Office," *CQ* 33:1 (1983): 293–94; Bommelaer, *Lysandre,* 75–79; and Hornblower, *CT,* III 806–7. Diomedon: Thuc. 8.54.3, 73.4; Xen. *Hell.* 1.5.16, 6.16, 7.1, 29, 34. Leon: Thuc. 5.19.2, 24, 8.23–24, 54–55, 60.3, 73.4–6, 76.2; Xen. *Hell.* 1.5.16, 6.16, 2.3.14, 39; Pl. *Apol.* 32c–d with W. James McCoy, "The Identity of Leon," *AJPh* 96:2 (Summer 1975): 187–99.

16. Death of Chalcideus, battle at Miletus, arrival of Peloponnesian fleet prevents investment, reappearance of Hermocrates: Thuc. 8.24–27, 29.2. Cf. Andrewes, *HCT,* V 54–67; Kagan, *Fall,* 60–68 (which announces a theme to which Kagan returns with some frequency in 69–105); Lazenby, *PW,* 177–78; and Hornblower, *CT,* III 814–31, who are agreed in thinking the Athenian withdrawal from Miletus a grave error, with Thuc. 8.27.5 who has nothing but praise for Phrynichus' judgment, and with Stuttard, *Nemesis,* 190–92. For a corrective to Kagan's insistence in the passages cited that, in this period, the Athenians were decisively superior at sea, see Fred S. Naiden, "Spartan Naval Performance in the Decelean war, 413–404 BCE," *Journal of Military History* 73:3 (July 2009): 729–

44. At best, they had a modest advantage, as Moshé Amit, "The Disintegration of the Athenian Empire in Asia Minor (412–405 B.C.E.)," *SCI* 2 (1975): 38–71 (esp. 53–54), contends. The Peloponnesian fleet included the twenty-five triremes conducted to Miletus by Chalcideus and Alcibiades and the fifty-five commanded by Therimenes. The Athenian fleet included the eight sent out with Strombichides, the twelve conducted to the eastern Aegean by Thrasycles, and the forty-eight commanded by Phrynichus and his colleagues. The latter bore with them 3,500 hoplites. If the transports were rowed by the hoplites they were conveying—as had been the policy adopted in 428 when Athens was suffering financial constraints at the time of the Mytilenian revolt (Thuc. 3.18.3–5, read in light of 3.19)—twenty-one of the triremes in the Athenian fleet will have had landlubbers doing the rowing. If the *thranítai* on the outriggers were mariners and the remaining rowers were hoplites, thirty-two transports will have been required. Apart from the book by Lazenby, none of the scholarly works listed above mentions the inclusion of transport ships in the Athenian fleet, and Lazenby dismisses the significance of this fact, arguing mistakenly that a trireme is a trireme.

17. Conquest of Iasos (*IACP* no. 891), seizure of Amorges, booty, pay from Tissaphernes, and the treatment of the surviving Iasians: Thuc. 8.28.1–4, 29.1 with Amit, "The Disintegration of the Athenian Empire in Asia Minor (412–405 B.C.E.)," 57–59. See also Andrewes, *HCT*, V 67–70; Kagan, *Fall*, 64, 69–70; Debord, *AM*, 209–10; Lazenby, *PW*, 178–79; and Hornblower, *CT*, III 831–36. For the value of a daric, see Xen. *An.* 1.7.18. In 414, the slaves owned by the Hermokopidae fetched one hundred seventy to one hundred eighty drachmas a head: *IG* I³ 421–30 = *ML* 79 = *O&R* no. 172. Strategic significance of victory, evidence for extension of control to Caria and Lycia: Hyland, *PI*, 57–60. Strategic considerations governing Tissaphernes' conduct: John W. I. Lee, "Tissaphernes and the Achaemenid Defense of Western Anatolia, 412–395 BC," in *Circum Mare: Themes in Ancient Warfare*, ed. Jeremy Armstrong (Leiden: Brill, 2016), 262–81 (esp. 262–69).

18. Maritime conditions in the different seasons: Jamie Morton, *The Role of the Physical Environment in Ancient Greek Seafaring* (Leiden: Brill, 2001), and James Beresford, *The Ancient Sailing Season* (Leiden: Brill, 2013). Regarding the ships available to each side at any given time in the winter of 412/11, see Andrewes, *HCT*, V 28–30.

19. Strombichides, Charminus, Euctemon conduct another thirty-five triremes to Samos; some sent to Chios; the rest blockade Miletus: Thuc. 8.30 with Andrewes, *HCT*, V 72–73; Kagan, *Fall*, 77; and Hornblower, *CT*, III 838–39.

20. Astyochus at Clazomenae; Lesbos venture thwarted; Pedaritus harmost at Chios; Erythrae fiasco; failed attack on Pteleum (*IACP* no. 862); Astyochus reaches Miletus: note Thuc. 8.28.5, and see 8.31–34; *Hell. Oxy.* 5 (Chambers); and Isoc. 6.53 with Westlake, *Individuals*, 292–95; Andrewes, *HCT*, V 69,

73–77; Kagan, *Fall*, 77–80; Lazenby, *PW*, 179–80; and Hornblower, *CT*, III 834–35, 839–47. Phocaea: *IACP* no. 859. On Tamos, see Thuc. 8.87.1; Xen. *An.* 1.1.6–8, 2.21, 4.2; Diod. 14.19.5–6, 35.3–5.

21. Hippocrates' flotilla, Dorieus' role, skirmishing at Triopium and at Cnidus (*IACP* no. 903) where Tissaphernes had sparked a rebellion: Thuc. 8.35, read in light of Plut. *Mor.* 835d-e, with Andrewes, *HCT*, V 77–78; Kagan, *Fall*, 80; Lazenby, *PW*, 180; and Hornblower, *CT*, III 847–52, whose discussion of the location of Cnidus vis-à-vis Triopium is dispositive. Importance of this trade route: Thuc. 2.69.1, Diod. 14.79.4–8, Plut. *Per.* 37.4, read in light of Xen. *Hell.* 1.5.19, Androtion *FGrH* 324 F46, and *AT*, 179–90 (esp. 184–86, 189–90). Dorieus and his forebears: consider Thuc 3.8, 8.61.2, 84.2; Xen. *Hell.* 1.5.19; Androtion *FGrH* 324 F46; and Paus. 6.7.1–7 (with *Hell. Oxy.* 18 [Chambers]), in light of Pind. *Olymp.* 7 (with the attendant scholia) as well as *IvO* no. 151; *POxy.* 2.222.2.17, 30; and *Syll.*³ 82, and see the discussion of the Diagoridae in Rahe, *SR*, Chapter 2 (with note 75); Simon Hornblower, *Thucydides and Pindar: Historical Narrative and the World of Epinikian Poetry* (Oxford: Oxford University Press, 2004), 131–42; Francis Cairns, "Pindar *Olympian* 7: Rhodes, Athens, and the Diagorids," *Eikasmos* 16 (2005): 63–91; and Nigel Nicholson, "When Athletic Victory and Fatherhood Did Mix: The Commemoration of Diagoras of Rhodes," *BICS* 61: 1 (2018): 42–63. Rhodes: *IACP*, 1196–98 with nos. 993–1000. Ialysos: no. 995.

22. Athenian fort at Delphinium on Chios, desertion of slaves, Astyochus' delays: Thuc. 8.38.2–4, 40 with John Boardman, "Delphinion in Chios," *ABSA* 51 (1956): 41–54; Andrewes, *HCT*, V 82–84, 86–87; Kagan, *Fall*, 84–85; Debord, *AM*, 209–11; Lazenby, *PW*, 180–81; and Hornblower, *CT*, III 857–62, 864–66.

23. Antisthenes' fleet, traveling via Melos (*IACP* no. 505) and Crete (1144–49 with nos. 944–92), reaches Caunus: (no. 898), *súmbouloi* aboard, Astyochus summoned for convoy duty: Thuc. 8.39, 41.1 with Andrewes, *HCT*, V 84–87; Kagan, *Fall*, 85–87; Lazenby, *PW*, 181; and Hornblower, *CT*, III 862–64, 866–67. Function of advisors: Thuc. 2.85.1, 3.69.1, 5.63.4. Astyochus' conduct: Westlake, *Individuals*, 290–307. Cf. Caroline Falkner, "Astyochus, Sparta's Incompetent Navarch?" *Phoenix* 52:3/4 (Autumn-Winter 1999): 206–21, who thinks it defensible. Caunus in the 420s: Peter Thonemann, "Lycia, Athens, and Amorges," in *Interpreting the Athenian Empire*, ed. John T. Ma, Nikolaos Papazarkadas, and Robert Parker (London: Duckworth, 2009), 167–94. This city may have become detached from the Great King as a consequence of Pissouthnes' revolt and may not have returned to Persian control until after the capture of Amorges.

24. Astyochus heads for Caunus; sacks, on the island of Kos (*IACP*, 752–55), the city of Meropis (no. 499); defeats a numerically inferior Athenian fleet in a skirmish at Syme (no. 522); sets up a *tropaîon*: Thuc. 8.41.2–42.4 and Ar. *Thesm.* 804, 836–38 with Alan H. Sommerstein, "Aristophanes and the Events of 411," *JHS* 97 (1977): 112–26; Andrewes, *HCT*, V 87–89; Kagan, *Fall*, 87–90; Lazenby,

PW, 181–82; and Hornblower, *CT*, III 867–73. See Strabo 14.2.19 with Susan M. Sherwin-White, *Ancient Cos* (Göttingen: Vandenhoeck & Ruprecht, 1978), 29–39. Cf. Caroline Falkner, "The Battle of Syme, 411 B.C. (Thuc. 8.42)," *AHB* 9:3/4 (1995): 117–24, who exaggerates the significance of the skirmish at Syme, with Olivier Chêne, "La Bataille de Symè (Thuc., VIII, 42: Janv. 411 a.C.)," *REG* 113:1 (January–June 2000): 101–30, who does not. What had taken place at Spiraeum (Thuc. 8.20.1) was no more than a skirmish.

25. Ialysos, Cameiros (*IACP* no. 996), and Lindos (no. 997) on Rhodes secured by the Spartans and their allies, role played by Dorieus' Diagorid kinsmen: Thuc. 8.44, read in light of *Hell. Oxy.* 18 (Chambers) and Paus. 6.7.1–7, with Andrewes, *HCT*, V 91–93; Kagan, *Fall*, 92–94; Debord, *AM*, 211–12; Lazenby, *PW*, 183–84; and Hornblower, *CT*, III 878–83. See also Henry D. Westlake, "Conon and Rhodes: The Troubled Aftermath of Synoecism," *GRBS* 24:4 (1983): 333–44; Ephraim David, "The Diagoreans and the Defection of Rhodes from Athens in 411 B.C.," *Eranos* 84 (1986): 157–64, which should be read in tandem with David, "The Oligarchic Revolution at Rhodes, 391–389 B.C.," *CPh* 79:4 (October 1984): 271–84; and Simon Hornblower, "What Happened Later to the Families of Pindaric Patrons—and to Epinician Poetry?" in *Reading the Victory Ode*, ed. Peter Agócs, Chris Carey, and Richard Rawles (Cambridge: Cambridge University Press, 2012), 93–107 (at 94–95, 98). For evidence suggesting (but not proving) that, from the outset, Dorieus was himself deeply involved, see Diod. 13.38.5, 45.1. Chios reduced to famine: Thuc. 8.55.2–56.1 with Andrewes, *HCT*, V 132; Kagan, *Fall*, 94; and Hornblower, *CT*, III 921–22. Regarding Chalke, see *IACP* no. 477.

26. Mix of motives, self-preservation primary: Henry D. Westlake, "Ionians in the Ionian War," *CQ* 29:1 (1979): 9–44, reprinted in Westlake, *Studies*, 113–53. Widespread desire for liberation from Athenian domination: Akiko Nakamura-Moroo, "The Attitude of Greeks in Asia Minor to Athens and Persia: The Decelian War," in *Forms of Control and Subordination in Antiquity*, ed. Toru Yuge and Masaoki Doi (Leiden: E. J. Brill, 1988), 567–72. Ephesus, Phocaea, and Aeolian Cumae: Thuc. 8.19.3, 31.3 with Andrewes, *HCT*, V 43, 74; Kagan, *Fall*, 46–47, 57; and Hornblower, *CT*, III 805, 841.

27. Chios a *kósmos*, Chian *sōphrosúnē*: Thuc. 8.24.4, which should be read in light of 40.2. Sensitivity to the opinion of "the many": 8.9.3, 14. To what degree Chios was oligarchic at this time is a matter of dispute: note 8.14.2, where one is left with the impression that the council was the city's governing body, and Hdt. 1.165.1 and Arist. *Pol.* 1291b24, which suggest the importance accorded the mercantile element in the population. Contrast between chattel slavery on Chios and the subjection of an existing population by Lacedaemon: Ath. 6.265b–266f, who cites a host of sources, including Theompompus *FGrH* 115 F122 and Nymphodorus *FGrH* 572 F4, which should be read in light of Alexander Fuks, "Slave War and Slave Troubles in Chios in the Third Century," *Athenaeum* n.s. 46

(1968): 102–11. Cf. *SIG*³ 986, as interpreted by W. G. Forrest, *ABSA* 55 (1960): 180, and Andrewes, *HCT*, V 22.23, with Trevor J. Quinn, "Political Groups in Chios: 412 B.C.," *Historia* 18:1 (January 1969): 22–30; J. L. O'Neil, "The Constitution of Chios in the Fifth Century B.C.," *Talanta* 10/11 (1978–79): 66–73; and Kagan, *Fall*, 43, who suspect that Chios was governed by a mixed regime or a nominally democratic constitution dominated, in fact, by wealthy landholders. What cannot be denied is that the common people ordinarily deferred to the city's wealthy slaveholders: see Hornblower, *CT*, III 785–86.

28. Chios and Athens: Trevor J. Quinn, *Athens and Samos, Lesbos and Chios, 478–404 B.C.* (Manchester: Manchester University Press, 1981), 39–49. In this connection, note Marcel Piérart, "Chios entre Athènes et Sparte: La Contribution des exilés de Chios à l'effort de guerre lacédémonien pendant la Guerre du Péloponnèse, *IG* V 1, 1 + (*SEG* XXXIX 370)," *BCH* 119:1 (1995): 253–82. Ion son of Orthomenes: Rahe, *SFAW*, Chapter 2 (with note 40). Activities of and penalty inflicted on Tydeus son of Ion and his associates, narrow oligarchy imposed, ethos of suspicion consequent: consider Thuc. 8.24.2–6, 31.1, 38.2–3 in light of Plut. *Mor.* 241d, and see Theopompus of Chios *FGrH* 115 F7–8, *Hell. Oxy.* 5 (Chambers), and Diod. 13.65 with Andrewes, *HCT*, V 55–58, 73, 82–84; Kagan, *Fall*, 84; and Hornblower, *CT*, III 815–21, 839, 857–61. It is apt to have been at this time that some Chians lodged a complaint at Lacedaemon against their harmost Pedaritus: Plut. *Mor.* 241d–e. Thucydides on the Spartan propensity for brutality: 1.130.2, 2.67.4, 3.32.2, 93.2, 5.51.1–52.1. See also the material collected in Rahe, *SSPW*, Chapter 6, note 16.

29. Revolution on Samos: Thuc. 8.21, which should be read in light of 63.3. Cf. Quinn, *Athens and Samos, Lesbos and Chios*, 10–23; Kagan, *Fall*, 56 n. 19; Andrewes, *HCT*, V 44–49; Martin Ostwald, "*Stasis* and *Autonomia* in Samos: A Comment on an Ideological Fallacy," *SCI* 12 (1993): 51–66; and Lazenby, *PW*, 176, who suppose that after the Samian revolt the Athenians acquiesced in the reestablishment of an oligarchy on the island, with Ronald P. Legon, "Samos in the Delian League," *Historia* 21:2 (2nd Quarter 1972): 145–58 (at 154–56); Andrew W. Lintott, *Violence, Revolution and Civil Strife in the Classical City, 750–330 B.C.* (Baltimore: Johns Hopkins University Press, 1982), 101–3; Kagan, *Fall*, 56–57; and Hornblower, *CT*, III 808–9, who read Diod. 12.28.3–4 in light of Thuc. 1.115.3 and 8.63.3 and make a compelling case that the regime in place in 412 was a democracy dominated by the leisured *Geōmóroi*. Long history of factional strife on Samos: Rahe, *PC*, Chapters 1–3, and *SSAW*, Chapter 1. Anaia: see note 15, above.

30. Persian–Spartan agreements: consider Thuc. 8.17.4–18.3, 36.1–38.1, 39, 41.1–44.1 (where, at 43.3, I have adopted Bekker's emendation as did the editor of the Oxford Classical Text), in light of 2.8.4, then see 8.57.1–59.1 with 84.4–5, where Lichas urges patience on the Milesians chafing under the Persian yoke. Every-

thing of significance referred to the King: Hdt. 5.31.4, Diod. 15.41.5. Identity of
Hieramenes: Appendix 4. On the evolution of these accords and the concerns
responsible, see Moshé Amit, "A Peace Treaty between Sparta and Persia," *RSA*
4:1-2 (1974): 55–62; Lewis, *SP*, 83–107 (esp. 90–107); Andrewes, *HCT*, V
40–42, 78–82, 84–91, 136–46; Edmond Lévy, "Les trois Traités entre Sparte et
le Roi," *BCH* 107:1 (1983): 221–41; Kagan, *Fall*, 47–50, 80–82, 90–92, 96–100;
Briant, *CA*, 592–93; Debord, *AM*, 205, 210–14; Kallet, *MCPT*, 250–67;
Lazenby, *PW*, 176, 180, 182–83, 186; Cawkwell, *GW*, 149–55; Hornblower, *CT*,
III 800–802, 852–57, 862–64, 866–78; and Hyland, *PI*, 55–69. On the geopolitical logic underpinning these agreements, see Moshé Amit, "The Disintegration of the Athenian Empire in Asia Minor (412–405 B.C.E.)," 38–71. Scholarly
consensus the Mede not seeking anything beyond Asia Minor: cf. the secondary
literature cited in Hyland, *PI*, 68 n. 106, with the more sensible observations of
Hatzfeld, *Alcibiade*, 221–23. On Lichas and his family, consider Thuc. 5.22.2,
50.4, 76.3, and Xen. *Hell.* 3.2.21–22 (where it is more than merely possible that,
in being called an *ánēr gérōn*, he is being described as a member of the *gerousía*)
in light of Hdt. 1.67.5–68.5; note Xen. *Mem.* 1.2.61 and Plut. *Cim.* 10.5–6, then
see Critias F8 (West) and Paus. 6.2.1–2. Note the Prologue, above, and see
Rahe, *SR*, Chapter 4 (with note 45), as well as Rahe, *SSAW*, Chapter 8 and Epilogue; then consider Simon Hornblower, "Lichas Kalos Samios," *Chiron* 32
(2003): 237–47 in light of Lilian H. Jeffery and Paul Cartledge, "Sparta and
Samos: A Special Relationship," *CQ* n.s. 32:2 (1982): 243–65. Cyrene: *IACP*
no. 1028. On the man's career and his likely role as an informant of Thucydides,
cf. Jean Pouilloux and François Salviat, "Lichas, Lacédémonien, archonte à Thasos et le livre VIII de Thucydide," *CRAI* 127:2 (1983): 376–403, with Paul Cartledge, "A New Lease of Life for Lichas son of Arkesilas?" *LCM* 9 (1984):
98–102, and see Robin Lane Fox, "Thucydides and Documentary History,"
CQ n.s. 60:1 (May 2010): 11–29 (esp. 13–18, 22–26). Garrisons expelled: Thuc.
8.84.4–5, 108.4–5, 109; Diod. 13.42.4; Xen. *Hell.* 1.1.26. Although the third
accord specifies that it was agreed upon in the thirteenth regnal year of Darius II,
it seems likely that this refers to the year as measured in Susa, where it began in
January or February, rather than to the year as measured in Babylon, where it
began at the end of March or in early April: see Elias J. Bickerman, "En Marge de
l'écriture, I: Le Comput des années de règne des Achéménides (Néh., I, 2; II, 1
et Thuc., VIII, 58)," *Revue Biblique* 88:1 (January 1981): 19–41 (esp. 19–23), and
note W. Kendrick Pritchett, *Thucydides' Pentekontaetia and Other Essays* (Leiden:
Brill, 1995), 183–84. Much of what has been written concerning the chronology
of this period needs adjustment in light of this fact: see Chapter 4, note 2, below.
Presence of Hieramanes with Tissaphernes at Caunus: see the Xanthus stele
(*Tituli Asiae Minoris* I.44c.11–12) with Johannes Friedrich, *Kleinasiatische
Sprachdenkmäler* (Berlin: de Gruyter, 1932), 66. Party to the agreement ratified

in the Maeander valley: Thuc. 8.58.1. Brother-in-law of the King: Xen. *Hell.* 2.1.8–9. He is apt to have been a Son of the Royal House, and it is conceivable that he was satrap of Lycia or Cappadocia: see preface to Part IV, note 30, below. Antandrus: *IACP* no. 767.

PART II. THE CENTER CANNOT HOLD

Epigraph: William Butler Yeats, "The Second Coming," 1919, in Yeats, *Michael Robartes and the Dancer* (Churchtown, Dundrum: Chuala Press, 1920), 19–20.

1. In the first few pages of this chapter, I draw on Paul A. Rahe, "Thucydides' Critique of *Realpolitik*," *Security Studies* 5:2 (Winter 1995): 105–41, reprinted in *Roots of Realism: Philosophical and Historical Dimensions*, ed. Benjamin Frankel (London: Frank Cass, 1996), 105–41.

2. Fate of Mycalessus (*IACP* no. 212): Thuc. 7.29–30 with Matthew A. Sears, *Athens, Thrace, and the Shaping of Athenian Leadership* (Cambridge: Cambridge University Press, 2013), 79–87, 250–63 (esp. 250–57). For the significance of Thucydides' inclusion of this event, see Clifford Orwin, *The Humanity of Thucydides* (Princeton, NJ: Princeton University Press, 1994), 133–36, and Trevor J. Quinn, "Thucydides and the Massacre at Mykalessos," *Mnemosyne* 4th ser., 48:5 (November 1995): 571–74. Cf. Lisa Kallet, "The Diseased Body Politic, Athenian Public Finance, and the Massacre at Mykalessos (Thucydides 7.27–29)," *AJPh* 120:2 (Summer 1999): 223–44, revised and reprinted in Kallet, *MCPT*, 121–46, whose attempt to draw a moral connection between the massacre and Athens' new tax on commerce seems to me a stretch. Cf. Edith Hall, *Inventing the Barbarian: Self-Definition through Tragedy* (Oxford: Clarendon Press 1989), esp. 101–59, with Zofia Halina Archibald, *The Odrysian Kingdom of Thrace: Orpheus Unmasked* (Oxford: Clarendon Press, 1998), 98–102. The distinction that Thucydides draws between the civilized and the barbarous may be an example of xenophobia and chauvinism, as Hall suggests. But such a cultural judgment may also simply be valid; and there is, I think, a compelling case to be made that the pride in their cultural achievement evidenced by the Hellenes was, though exaggerated, by no means unjustified. Magnitude of motion measured by magnitude of suffering: cf. Thuc. 1.1.2–3 with 23.1–3, and see Adam Parry, "Thucydides' Historical Perspective," *YClS* 22 (1972): 47–61.

3. Thucydides on the plague: 2.50–53. As Hornblower, *CT*, I 480, points out, Thucydides' description is replete with language found in the Hippocratic medical texts.

4. Thucydides on the linguistic anarchy produced by a revolution: Thuc. 3.82.1–4. For the problems posed to the translator by the first sentence in the block quotation, see John T. Hogan, "The ἀξίωσις of Words at Thucydides 3.82.4," *GRBS* 21 (1980): 139–49, and John Wilson, "'The Customary Meanings of Words Were Changed'—Or Were They? A Note on Thucydides 3.82.4," *CQ* 32 (1982): 18–20.

5. Thucydides on the power of partisanship, cunning, and ruthlessness during a revolution: 3.82.6–7.
6. Thucydides on rule pursued out of greed and on the emptiness of slogans: 3.82.8. *Stásis* and an excess of spiritedness: Seth Benardete, "Achilles and the Iliad," *Hermes* 91 (1963): 1–16.
7. War a *bíaios didáskalos* producing *stásis* and savagery throughout Hellas: Thuc. 3.82.1–3. Civil strife helps produce "unprecedented suffering": 1.23.1–2. Brutality once thought "savage and excessive": 3.36.4.
8. Thucydides' employment of the adjective *ōmós*: 3.36.4, 82.1, 94.5 with Thomas S. Engeman, "Homeric Honor and Thucydidean Necessity," *Interpretation* 4:2 (Winter, 1974): 65–78 (at 74 n. 21), and W. Robert Connor, *Thucydides* (Princeton, NJ: Princeton University Press, 1984), 82 n. 5. Its employment elsewhere: Eur. *Supp.* 187 and Arist. [*Rh. Al.*] 1420a28–1421a24 (esp. 1420a28–b1).
9. Thucydides' archaeology and civilizing process: note 1.2–21, and consider 1.3, 5–6, 17–18 in light of 12.1. War and civil war as commotion: cf. 1.1.2 with 3.82.1. Note Thucydides' use (5.25.1) of the cognate *diekínoun* in asserting a continuity between the movement or commotion that preceded and the one that followed the Peace of Nicias: 5.25–26. Cf. his use of the word *kínēsis* at 3.75.2, 5.10.5, and of the verbal form at 4.55.4. Man's potential as a political animal, the central significance of his possession of *lógos*, and his capacity to fall short: consider Arist. *Pol.* 1252b27–1253a39 in light of Paul A. Rahe, "The Primacy of Politics in Classical Greece," *AHR* 89 (1984): 265–93, and see Rahe, *RAM* I, and note the discussion of political eros in Rahe, *SSPW*, Chapter 2 (with notes 23–25).
10. Alcibiades a Spartan name: Thuc. 8.6.3.
11. See Charles-Louis de Secondat, baron de La Brède et de Montesquieu, *L'Esprit des lois* 1.5.4, in *Œuvres complètes de Montesquieu*, ed. Roger Caillois (Paris: Bibliothèque de la Pléiade, 1949–51), II 276.

CHAPTER 3. NAKED CAME THE STRANGER

Epigraph: Plutarch, *Alc.* 23.4–5.
1. Agis at Deceleia—except when on foray to central Greece: Thuc. 8.3.1, 5.1–4. It is conceivable that Alcibiades traveled with him to Deceleia, as Diod. 13.9.2 claims. If so, however, he did not stay, and the thesis that he played a diplomatic role at this time in central Greece is unproven: see preface to Part I, note 5, above.
2. Spartan mores: Rahe, *SR*, Chapter 1. Situation of Spartan women in comparison with that of Greek women elsewhere: Sarah B. Pomeroy, *Spartan Women* (Oxford: Oxford University Press, 2002). Cynisca: Xen. *Ages.* 9.6, Paus. 3.8.1–2, Plut. *Ages.* 20.1 with Stephen Hodkinson, *Property and Wealth in Classical Sparta* (Swansea: Classical Press of Wales, 2000), 102, 294–95, 310–11, 313, 316, 321–23, 327–28, and Donald G. Kyle, "'The Only Woman in Greece': Agesilaus, Alcibiades, and Olympia," *Journal of Sports History* 30:2 (Summer 2003): 183–

203. Attitude voiced by Pericles: Thuc. 2.45.2 with Plut. *Mor.* 242e, and see Gomme, *HCT*, II 142–43, and Hornblower, *CT*, II 314, who cite the pertinent secondary literature.

3. Alcibiades' intention: Plut. *Alc.* 23.8, and *Ages.* 3.2. Sparta and the Heraclid claim: Hdt. 5.43. For further allusions to the import of descent from Heracles and Zeus, see 1.7, 13–14, 91, 7.208, 8.137, 9.26–27, 33; Thuc. 5.16.2; Xen. *Lac. Pol.* 15.2. In this connection, see Walter Burkert, "Demaratos, Astrabakos und Herakles: Königsmythos und Politik zur Zeit der Perserkriege (Herodot 6, 67–60)," *MH* 22 (1965): 166–77, and Ulrich Huttner, *Die politische Rolle der Heraklesgestalt im griechischen Herrschertum* (Stuttgart: Franz Steiner Verlag, 1997), 48–58. Ephors attend birth: Hdt. 5.41. Plato reports that the ephors kept the wives of the kings under public guard in order to guarantee the purity of the blood of their offspring: *Alc.* I 121b4–8. That, at an earlier time, Agis had had a son can be inferred from the fact the his much younger half-brother, who would otherwise have been the heir apparent, did what heirs apparent did not do. He underwent the *agōgē*: Plut. *Ages.* 1.1–5. As an alternative, one could, of course, cite this fact as evidence that the ancient sources are in error and that the pertinent Leotychidas was born well before 412, as Robert J. Littmann, "A New Date for Leotychidas," *Phoenix* 23:3 (Autumn 1969): 269–77, does. But it is far less likely that the stories told by Xenophon and Duris of Samos are apocryphal than that Agis fathered a son much earlier who died at some point prior to 412 and that no surviving writer thought the man's life and death worthy of mention. Our knowledge of such matters is meager in the extreme—especially with regard to Lacedaemon.

4. Earthquake late in the winter of 413/12; Agis' hatred of Alcibiades, grounds: note Thuc. 8.6.5, and consider 12.2, 45.1 in light of Xen. *Hell.* 3.3.1–4; then, see Duris of Samos *FGrH* 76 F69; Plut. *Alc.* 23.7–9, 24.3–4, *Lys.* 22.6–13, *Ages.* 3; and Paus. 3.8.3–10, and cf. Solomon Luria, "Zum politischen Kampf in Sparta gegen Ende des 5. Jahrhunderts," *Klio* 21, n.s. 3 (1927): 404–20; Henry D. West-lake, "Alcibiades, Agis, and Spartan Policy," *JHS* 58:1 (1938) 31–40 (at 34–35); and Littmann, "A New Date for Leotychidas," 269–77, who reject the story of young Leotychidas' paternity, and Cartledge, *Agesilaos*, 110–15, who harbors doubts, with Jean Hatzfeld, "Notes sur la chronologie des *Helléniques*," *REA* 35:4 (1933): 387–409 (at 387–91), and *Alcibiade*, 217–20 (esp. 218 n. 3), 226, as well as Jacqueline de Romilly, *The Life of Alcibiades: Dangerous Ambition and the Betrayal of Athens*, tr. Elizabeth Trapnell Rawlings (Ithaca, NY: Cornell University Press, 2019), 102–3, 106–9. See also Andrewes, *HCT*, V 26–27; Kagan, *Fall*, 42; Ellis, *Alcibiades*, 66–68 (with n. 96); Hornblower, *CT*, III 789–90; and Rhodes, *Alcibiades*, 58. Cf. Stuttard, *Nemesis*, 175–78, 184–85, who accepts Plutarch's account at face value and accordingly dates the pertinent earthquake earlier. Note Ath. 13.574d.

5. Agis' resentment predates the adultery, shared by leading Spartiates: Nepos *Alc.*

5.1, Just. *Epit.* 5.2.4, and Plut. *Alc.* 24.3 with Stuttard, *Nemesis*, 194–95. I doubt that relations were ever cordial. Cf., however, ibid. 164–65, 175–76. Political consequences of the quarrel: Westlake, "Alcibiades, Agis, and Spartan Policy," 38–50.

6. Ethos of *philotimía*: Rahe, *SR*, Chapter 1. For a fuller discussion of the preroga- tives of the kings than is possible here and for an attempt at a full citation of the primary sources and the pertinent secondary literature, see Rahe, *SR*, Chapter 2 (with notes 16–35).

7. For a much fuller discussion of the prerogatives of the *gérontes* than is possible and appropriate here and for an attempt at a full citation of the primary sources and the pertinent secondary literature, see Rahe, *SR*, Chapter 2 (with notes 57–67).

8. Selection of ephors akin to lottery: Pl. *Leg.* 3.692a. Mode of selection childish: Arist. *Pol.* 1270b27–28. Ordinariness of those chosen: 1270b8–10, 20–29. See Rahe, *SR*, 170 n. 51.

9. Xenophon on decision makers at Sparta: *Hell.* 2.4.38, 3.2.23, 4.6.3. Aristotle on import of ephors' prerogatives: *Pol.* 1322b12–16.

10. Obedience to the law, shaving of upper lip: Arist. F538–39, 611.10 (Rose) = F543, 545, Tit. 143.1.2.10 (Gigon); Plut. *Lyc.* 28, *Cleom.* 9.3.

11. Ruled by laws and ephors: Plut. *Mor.* 211c. Royal oath to maintain *nómoi*: Nicho- las of Damascus F114.16 (*FHG* Müller III 459). Monthly exchange of oaths with kings: Xen. *Lac. Pol.* 15.7.

12. For a fuller discussion of the prerogatives of the ephors and of their relations with the two kings than is possible here and for an attempt at a full citation of the primary sources and the pertinent secondary literature, see Rahe, *SR*, Chap- ter 2 (with notes 37–52).

13. Pleistoanax as king: see the Prologue, above; Rahe, *SFAW*, Chapter 6 and Epi- logue; and *SSAW*, Prologue, Chapters 1, 6–8.

14. Alcibiades, Agis, and the Argive coalition: see the Prologue above, and Rahe, *SSAW*, Chapters 7–8 with the Epilogue.

15. Timaea's conduct, reasons for Alcibiades' departure from Lacedaemon, order for his execution: Thuc. 8.12.2, 45.1; Duris of Samos *FGrH* 76 F69; Plut. *Alc.* 23.7–9, 24.3–4, *Ages.* 3.1–3 with Jean Hatzfeld, "Notes sur la chronologie des Helléniques," 391–95, and *Alcibiade*, 219–20, 224–27; Westlake, *Individuals*, 298–300; Andrewes, *HCT*, V 93–96; Kagan, *Fall*, 42, 55 n. 15, 70–72; Ellis, *Alcibiades*, 67–68, 71 (with n. 7); Lazenby, *PW*, 184; Hornblower, *CT*, III 883– 87; Rhodes, *Alcibiades*, 58–59; Romilly, *The Life of Alcibiades*, 102–3, 106–9; and Stuttard, *Nemesis*, 184–85, 193–95. Note also Nepos *Alc.* 5.1–2, Just. *Epit.* 5.2.4– 5. Ephors' term of office: Thuc. 5.36.1, on which cf. Gomme and Andrewes, *HCT*, IV 38, who are not fully in accord, with Hornblower, *CT*, III 84–85.

16. Timaea said to have tipped off Alcibiades: Just. *Epit.* 5.2.5.

17. Alcibiades to Tissaphernes' court, Astyochus maintains contact and continues

cooperation, thought to be in the satrap's pay: Thuc. 8.45.1, 50.1–5; Nepos *Alc.* 5.3; Just. *Epit.* 5.2.5; and Plut. *Alc.* 24.3–25.13 with Busolt, *Gr. Gesch.*, III:2 1437 n. 6, 1469. Note Rhodes, *Alcibiades*, 59. Cf. Kagan, *Fall*, 79 (with n. 44), who thinks the evidence that Astyochus was aligned with Endius and Alcibiades too thin to build upon. On Astyochus' relations with Alcibiades after he took up residence with Tissaphernes, cf. Hatzfeld, *Alcibiade*, 233–36; Raphael Sealey, "The Revolution of 411," in Sealey, *Essays in Greek Politics* (New York: Manyland Books, 1967), 111– 32 (esp. 115–20); Mabel Lang, "Alcibiades vs. Phrynichus," *CQ* n.s. 46:1 (1996): 289–95; and Stuttard, *Nemesis*, 204–9, who are incredulous and think the entire story an invention of Alcibiades; Henry D. Westlake, "Phrynichus and Astyochus (Thucydides VIII.50–1)," *JHS* 76 (1956): 99–104 (at 103), and *Individuals*, 299–300, as well as Hornblower, *CT*, III 905, who suppose that Astyochus was so slow-witted that he continued to trust Alcibiades; Kagan, *Fall*, 79, 122–30; Ellis, *Alcibiades*, 74–78; and Edmund F. Bloedow, "Phrynichus the 'Intelligent' Athenian," *AHB* 5:4 (1991): 89–100 (at 94–99), who think that Astyochus outwitted both Phrynichus and Alcibiades and drove a wedge between the latter and Tissaphernes; Romilly, *The Life of Alcibiades*, 116–18, who suspects that Astyochus was, as alleged by his angry underlings, in the pay of Tissaphernes; and Andrewes, *HCT*, V 93–96, 117–21, who is, like Hatzfeld, Lang, and Stuttard, incredulous and who thinks that, if Astyochus had actually received an order to execute Alcibiades, he could not have acted towards him after his flight as he reportedly did. Price on Alcibiades' head: Philochorus *FGrH* 328 F134, Pollux 10.97.

18. Evidence that the son of Cleinias was himself interviewed by Thucydides: see Peter A. Brunt, "Thucydides and Alcibiades," *REG* 65: 304–5 (January–June 1952): 59–96, reprinted in Brunt, *Studies in Greek History and Thought* (Oxford: Clarendon Press, 1993), 17–46. I am not persuaded by the objections raised by Henry D. Westlake, "The Influence of Alcibiades on Thucydides, Book 8," *Mnemosyne* 4th ser., 38:1/2 (1985): 93–108, reprinted in Westlake, *Studies*, 154– 65, who speculates that one of Alcibiades' boon companions was Thucydides' informant. To his argument, we should apply Ockham's razor—which should make us hesitant to multiply witnesses otherwise unattested. The fact, rightly stressed by Westlake, that the Athenian historian was less well-informed concerning Alcibiades' activities subsequent to his departure from Tisapphernes' court than concerning those that took place before that event is more apt to be an indication that Thucydides met with the son of Cleinias shortly before that dazzling figure left Asia Minor for Samos. There is, after all, good reason to suppose that the historian spent time in Miletus in 412 and 411: Robin Lane Fox, "Thucydides and Documentary History," *CQ* n.s. 60:1 (May 2010): 11–29 (esp. 13–18, 22–26). In any case, the fact that Alcibiades was among Thucydides' informants does not mean that the latter always believed what the man told him. Nor should it be taken to mean that Alcibiades was his only informant: see Hart-

mut Erbse, *Thukydides-Interpretationen* (Berlin: de Gruyter, 1989), 75–82. The accuracy of Thucydides' description of Alcibiades' motives, which has been charted by Henry D. Westlake, "Personal Motives, Aims and Feelings in Thucydides," in Westlake, *Studies*, 201–23 (at 213–18), should be reassessed in light of Lane Fox's findings.

19. Three obols a day: Thuc. 8.29.1 with Andrewes, *HCT*, V 70; Kagan, *Fall*, 70–74; and Hornblower, *CT*, III 836. Alcibiades' advice: Thuc. 8.45.2–3. Cf. Andrewes, *HCT*, V 96–99, who suspects that the passage cited here is a doublet of the passage cited above, with Hornblower, *CT*, III 883–88. Note Rood, *Thucydides*, 265, who suspects that two different reductions in pay may have been involved. Tissaphernes charmed, names a *parádeisos* after Alcibiades: Nepos *Alc.* 5.2–3, Just. *Epit.* 5.2.5–7, and Plut. *Alc.* 24.4–7 with Stuttard, *Nemesis*, 193, 195–98. Persians pick up pederasty from the Greeks: Hdt. 1.135. Persian *parádeisoi*: Briant, *CA*, 200–203, 232–39, and Christopher J. Tuplin, "The Parks and Gardens of the Achaemenid Empire," in Tuplin, *Achaemenid Studies* (Stuttgart: Franz Steiner Verlag, 1996), 80–131, and "Paradise Revisited," in *L'Orient est son Jardin: Hommage à Rémy Boucharlat*, ed. Sébastien Gondet and Ernie Haerinck (Louvain: Peeters, 2018), 477–501. For the Persian court at Sardis, see Elspeth R. M. Dusinberre, *Aspects of Empire in Achaemenid Sardis* (Cambridge: Cambridge University Press, 2003).

20. Alcibiades' advice to Tissaphernes: Thuc. 8.46.1–4 with Andrewes, *HCT*, V 100–103; Kagan, *Fall*, 74–77; Kallet, *MCPT*, 259–62; Lazenby, *PW*, 184; Hornblower, *CT*, III 889–92; and Stuttard, *Nemesis*, 199–201. See also Nepos *Alc.* 5.3, Just. *Epit.* 5.2.5–14. Cf. Stuttard, *Nemesis*, 201–2, who interprets Thuc. 8.47.1 as implying the presence of the Great King in Sardis where others presume that Tissaphernes employed Persia's pony express to run Alcibiades' argument by him.

21. Alcibiades' advice borne out by events: Xen. *Hell.* 3.1.3–2.20, 4.1–4.2.4; *Ages.* 1.6–36, 2.16; Diod. 14.35.6–37.4, 38.2–3, 6–7, 39, 79.1–83.3; *Hell. Oxy.* 9–25 (Chambers); Paus. 3.9; Plut. *Ages.* 6–15.

22. Tissaphernes' response to Alcibiades' advice, Lichas' confirmation of the Athenian's claims, negotiations with the Athenians: Thuc. 8.45.2–6, 46.5, 52, 56 with Hatzfeld, *Alcibiade*, 227–32, 237–40; Lewis, *SP*, 98–102; Andrewes, *HCT*, V 96–100, 103–5, 121–23, 132–36; Kagan, *Fall*, 91–92, 96–97; Lazenby, *PW*, 184–85; Cawkwell, *GW*, 151–55; Hornblower, *CT*, III 887–88, 890–92, 907–10, 921–24; Rhodes, *Alcibiades*, 59–60, 63–64; and Stuttard, *Nemesis*, 200–202, 211–13. Cf. Kagan, *Fall*, 76–77, who questions whether Athens would be have made a better partner for Persia than Sparta. In my opinion, he underestimates the power of Panhellenic sentiment in Lacedaemon. Had it been as weak as he supposes, the Spartans would have been more forthcoming in their dealing with Artaxerxes in the first half of the 420s. Moreover, Kagan fails to appreciate the significance of Athens' relative lack of interest in a land empire. The Athenians would not have tried to take Anatolia away from the Mede, as the Spartans under

Agesilaus in due course did: see Robin Seager and Christopher Tuplin, "The Freedom of the Greeks of Asia: On the Origins of a Concept and the Creation of a Slogan," *JHS* 100 (1980): 141–54 (esp. 142–46); Cartledge, *Agesilaos*, 208–18; and Rood, *Thucydides*, 266 n. 52. The fact that the Persian fleet promised by Tissaphernes never advanced beyond Aspendus (*IACP* no. 1001) has given rise to considerable discussion: see Chapter 5, note 3, below. Tissaphernes' subsequent advocacy of the policy pressed on him at this time by Alcibiades: see Chapter 7 (with note 21), below.

23. At a time when the Greek cities on the western and southern coasts of Anatolia and the islands off those coasts were in Persian hands, the elder Darius reportedly hoped to extract nine hundred Babylonian talents (the equivalent of 1,050 Euboean/Attic talents) from the two administrative districts assigned to Tissaphernes by the younger Darius nearly a century later: consider Hdt. 3.89.1–90.1 in light of 95. Needless to say, Tissaphernes was in no position in 411 to collect anything even approaching a sum so large. His niggardliness a response to the enormous cost of the war: see Stuttard, *Nemesis*, 201, and Hyland, *PI*, 60–64, who thinks this Tissaphernes' sole motive. But the fact that it was a legitimate concern does not mean that Alcibiades' argument played no role in the calculations of the satrap and his master. It was one thing to want to make of Lacedaemon a loyal client; it was another to expect to succeed in the short run given the intensity of the reluctance displayed by Lichas. Even if the acquisition of a docile client was the ultimate aim, it made good sense in the short run to play the two Greek powers off against one another with the aim of reducing the power of both: cf. John O. Hyland, "Thucydides' Portrait of Tissaphernes Re-Examined," in *Persian Responses: Political and Cultural Interaction with(in) the Achaemenid Empire*, ed. Christopher Tuplin (Swansea: Classical Press of Wales, 2007), 1–25 (esp. 8–14), with Josef Wiesehöfer, "'. . . Keeping the Two Sides Equal': Thucydides, the Persians and the Peloponnesian War," in *Brill's Companion to Thucydides*, ed. Antonios Rengakos and Antonis Tsakmakis (Leiden: Brill, 2006), 657–67 (at 660–65), and note Xen. *Hell.* 4.1.32.

24. To the best of my knowledge, the only scholar to have attended to Alcibiades' motives for diverting the attention of the Spartans and their allies from the Hellespont is Hatzfeld: see *Alcibiade*, 214–17. As Debord, *AM*, 204, observes, the son of Cleinias played an oversize role throughout this period.

25. Alcibiades' con and the response of the leading Athenians on Samos: Thuc. 8.47 with Hatzfeld, *Alcibiade*, 232–33; Lewis, *SP*, 98–99; Andrewes, *HCT*, V 106–7; Heftner, *Umsturz*, 40–49; and Hornblower, *CT*, III 892–94. Note also Kagan, *Fall*, 74–77, 112–19. See also Diod. 13.37.2–3, Just. *Epit.* 5.3.1. Trierarchy a burden: Xen. *Ath. Pol.* 1.13, Ar. *Eq.* 912–18 with Moshé Amit, *Athens and the Sea: A Study in Athenian Sea Power* (Brussels: Latomus, 1965), 103–15, and Vincent Gabrielsen, *Financing the Athenian Fleet: Public Taxation and Social Relations* (Baltimore: Johns Hopkins University Press, 1994), 19–169. *Leitourgíai* more

generally: Matthew R. Christ, *The Bad Citizen in Classical Athens* (Cambridge: Cambridge University Press, 2006), 143–204, and Peter P. Liddel, *Civic Obligation and Individual Liberty in Ancient Athens* (Oxford: Oxford University Press, 2007), 262–77.

26. Herodotus' Persian Debate: consider 3.80–82 in light of Pind. 2.86–88, and see David Asheri, Alan Lloyd, and Aldo Corcella, *A Commentary on Herodotus Books I–IV*, tr. Barbara Graziosi, Matteo Rossetti, Carlotta Dus, and Vanesa Cazzato, ed. Oswyn Murray and Alfonso Moreno (Oxford: Oxford University Press, 2007), 471–76. Publication date of Herodotus' *Inquiries*: Rahe *SSPW*, Chapter 3, note 15. Debate regarding regimes in Euripides: *Supp.* 403–62. Pericles' defense of democracy: Thuc. 2.37.1 with Edward M. Harris, "Pericles' Praise of Athenian Democracy," *HSPh* 94 (1992): 157–67, reprinted with an addendum in Harris, *Democracy and the Rule of Law in Classical Athens: Essays on Law, Society, and Politics* (Cambridge: Cambridge University Press, 2006), 29–39. Athenagoras on democracy: Thuc. 6.39.1–2. Alcibiades on the acknowledged mindlessness of democracy: 6.89.6. Pamphleteer: [Xen.] *Ath. Pol.* passim (esp. 1.1–9, 13). For my purposes here, it does not matter whether one dates this work to the 440s, as Glenn W. Bowersock, "Pseudo-Xenophon," *HSPh* 71 (1967): 33–55 (at 33–38), summarized in "Introduction," in Xenophon, *Scripta Minora*, tr. E. C. Marchant and Glenn W. Bowersock (Cambridge, MA: Harvard University Press, 1968), 461–73 (at 463–65), was inclined to do, or to the time of Sparta's second Attic war, as W. G. Forrest, "The Date of the Pseudo-Xenophontic *Athenaion Politeia*," *Klio* 52 (1970): 107–16, did. For an overview, see Peter J. Rhodes, "Oligarchs in Athens," in *Alternatives to Athens: Varieties of Political Organisation and Community in Ancient Greece*, ed. Roger Brock and Stephen Hodkinson (Oxford: Oxford University Press, 2000), 118–36 (esp. 128–36).

27. Jury pay and the composition of juries: Arist. *Ath. Pol.* 27.3–4, *Pol.* 1274a8–10; Pl. *Grg.* 515e; Plut. *Per.* 9.1–3; Aristid. *Or.* 46.192 (Dindorf) with *CAAP*, 338–40, and Minor M. Markle, "Jury Pay and Assembly Pay," in *CRUX: Essays Presented to G. E. M. de Ste. Croix on His 75th Birthday*, ed. Paul Cartledge and F. David Harvey, *HPTh* 6:1/2 (1985), 265–97, reprinted in *Athenian Democracy*, ed. Peter J. Rhodes (Oxford: Oxford University Press, 2004), 95–131. For the context in which jury pay was introduced, see Rahe, *SFAW*, Chapter 6. In the mid-420s, it was increased at Cleon's instigation from two to three obols (half a drachma): Schol. Ar. *Vesp.* 88 and 300 with Meiggs, *AE*, 331 (including n. 1). The change was made prior to the production of Aristophanes' *Knights* in 424: see *Eq.* 255. The wealthy and prominent both at home and abroad become marks: see [Xen.] *Ath. Pol.* 1.14–18, 3.2–7; Ar. *Eq.* 166, 259–65, 288, 1358–60, *Vesp.* 241, 288–89, 622–30, 924, 1037–42, *Av.* 285, 1410–69; Philippides F29 (Kock); Antiph. 5.69–71; Lys. 18.9, 25.3, 16, and 26, 27.26; Xen. *Mem.* 2.9, *Symp.* 4.30, *Oec.* 11.21–25, *Hell.* 2.3.12; Pl. *Cri.* 44e–45a, *Resp.* 8.553b, 565b; Isoc. 15.159–60, 164, 313–14, 318, 18.9–14, 21.5, 8; Dem. 23.15, 24.41, 25.41, 47,

49–50, 52, 82, 58.63, 59.43; Aeschin. 2.145; Hyp. *Lyc.* 2; Arist. *Ath. Pol.* 35.3, *Rhet.* 1382a1–7, *Pol.* 1304b20–24, 1305a3–7; Plut. *Arist.* 26.2–5, *Nic.* 4.4–8 with an eye to Thuc. 1.77.1. In this connection, see Vincent Gabrielsen, "*Phanerá* and *Aphanês Ousía* in Classical Athens," *C&M* 37 (1986): 99–114. Cleon and Hyperbolus litigious: Ar. *Ach.* 377–82 (with the scholia), *Eq.* 305–6, 441–44, 1256, *Nub.* 207–8, *Pax* 505, *Av.* 39–41. Sycophants: L. B. Carter, *The Quiet Athenian* (Oxford: Clarendon Press, 1986), 1–130 (esp. 99–130). Cf. Robin Osborne, "Vexatious Litigation in Classical Athens: Sykophancy and the Sykophant," in *Nomos: Essays in Athenian Laws, Politics, and Society*, ed. Paul Cartledge, Paul Millett, and Stephen C. Todd (Cambridge: Cambridge University Press, 1990), 83–102, reprinted with an addendum in Osborne, *AAD*, 205–28, who thinks (or once thought) sycophancy on the whole a plus, with David Harvey, "The Sykophant and Sykophancy: Vexatious Redefinition?" in *Nomos*, 103–21, whose account of the damage done is dispositive—although this is not universally acknowledged: cf. Matthew R. Christ, *The Litigious Athenian* (Baltimore: Johns Hopkins University Press, 1998). Note, however, Ostwald, *Sovereignty*, 208–13; Munn, *SH*, 70–71; and Robin Osborne, "Changing the Discourse," in *Popular Tyranny: Sovereignty and its Discontents in Ancient Greece*, ed. Kathryn A. Morgan (Austin: University of Texas Press, 2003), 251–72 (at 251–56), reprinted with an addendum in Osborne, *AAD*, 267–88 (at 267–73). Then, see Edward M. Harris, "Was All Criticism of Athenian Democracy Necessarily Anti-Democratic?" in *Democrazia e antidemocrazia nel mondo greco*, ed. Umberto Bultrighini (Alessandria: Edizioni dell'Orso, 2005), 11–23, and "Cleon and the Defeat of Athens," in Harris, *The Rule of Law in Action in Democratic Athens* (Oxford: Oxford University Press, 2013), 305–44.

28. Treason on the eve of Tanagra: Rahe, *SFAW*, Chapter 5.

29. Archidamus deliberately sets out to promote *stásis* at Athens: consider Thuc. 2.20.4–5 in light of Xen. *Oec.* 6.6–7, and see Edmund M. Burke, "The Habit of Subsidization in Classical Athens: Toward a Thetic Ideology," *C&M* 56 (2005): 5–47 (esp. 5–21), and Rahe, *SSAW*, Chapter 3.

30. Symbiotic relationship between rural production, the marketing of agricultural surpluses, and the performance of expensive *leitourgíai*: Robin Osborne, "Pride and Prejudice, Sense and Subsistence: Exchange and Society in the Greek City," in *City and Country in the Ancient World*, ed. John Rich and Andrew Wallace-Hadrill (London: Routledge, 1991), 119–45, reprinted with an addendum in Osborne, *AAD*, 104–26. Syndicates: Borimir Jordan, *Athenian Navy in the Classical Period* (Berkeley: University of California Press, 1975), 70–72, and Gabrielsen, *Financing the Athenian Fleet*, 173–82. Levy on capital: Peter Fawcett, "'When I Squeeze You with *Eisphorai*': Taxes and Tax Policy in Classical Athens," *Hesperia* 83:1 (January–March 2016): 153–99.

31. Emissaries to Alcibiades at Sardis and acceptance of his project: Thuc. 8.48.1–3, Nepos *Alc.* 5.3, Just. *Epit.* 5.3.2–4 with Hatzfeld, *Alcibiade*, 233; Andrewes, *HCT*,

V 107–8; Kagan, *Fall*, 119–21; Kallet, *MCPT*, 262–65; Lazenby, *PW*, 184; Hornblower, *CT*, III 894–95; Rhodes, *Alcibiades*, 61; and Stuttard, *Nemesis*, 203–4, who misreads Thuc. 8.47.2–48.2 as a reference to the Samians as opposed to the infantrymen, rowers, and specialists on Samos. For a cogent defense of the half-truth that class had nothing to do with this development and everything that followed and that it all turned solely on the attitude taken by various individuals with regard to Alcibiades, see Sealey, "The Revolution of 411," 111–32.

32. Phrynichus' critique of Alcibiades' proposal: consider Thuc. 8.48.4–7 in light of 27.5 and 54.3, where we learn of his being cashiered; note the trajectory of Thasos (8.64.2–5 and *Hell. Oxy.* 10 [Chambers], confirmed by *ML* nos. 83 and 89 as well as *SEG* 38.851A, lines 4 and 19, and analyzed by Andrewes, *HCT*, V 156–61; Bleckmann, *Niederlage*, 216–22; and Hornblower, *CT*, III 940–43), which corroborates Phrynichus' analysis of the attitude of those in the cities long allied with Athens; and see Plut. *Alc.* 25.6 with Hatzfeld, *Alcibiade*, 233–34; Andrewes, *HCT*, V 108–16, 126–31; Heftner, *Umsturz*, 43–50; Lazenby, *PW*, 184; Hornblower, *CT*, III 895–901, 916; Rhodes, *Alcibiades*, 61; and Stuttard, *Nemesis*, 204–5. For a comparison of what Brasidas says at Acanthus (Thuc. 4.86.4–5) and what Phrynichus says here (8.48.5), see C. H. Grayson, "Two Passages in Thucydides," *CQ* 22:1 (May 1972): 62–73, and Ian M. Plant, "Thuc. VIII.48.5: Phrynichus on the Wishes of Athens' Allies," *Historia* 41:2 (1992): 249–50. Cf. Nicholas G. L. Hammond, "The Meaning and Significance of the Reported Speech of Phrynichus in Thucydides 8.48," in *Greece and the Eastern Mediterranean in Ancient History and Prehistory*, ed. Konrad H. Kinzl (Berlin: de Gruyter, 1977), 147–57, reprinted in Hammond, *Collected Studies I: Studies in Greek History and Literature, Excluding Epirus and Macedonia* (Amsterdam: Hakkert, 1993), 65–75, and Kagan, *Fall*, 122–23, who think that Phrynichus was, from the outset, at heart an oligarch no less hostile to the democracy than he was to Alcibiades, with Herbert Heftner, "Phrynichos Stratonidou Deiradiotes als Politiker und Symbolfigur der athenischen Oligarchen von 411 v. Chr.," in *Democrazia e antidemocrazia nel mondo greco*, 89–108, who shows that the evidence suggests otherwise.

33. Phrynichus vs. Alcibiades: Thuc. 8.50–51. Cf. Plut. *Alc.* 25.6–13, who misreads Thucydides' account, with Westlake, "Phrynichus and Astyochus (Thucydides VIII.50–1)," 99–104; Ulrich Schindel, "Phrynichos und die Rückberufung des Alkibiades," *RhM* n.f. 113:4 (1970): 281–97; Andrewes, *HCT*, V 117–21; and Hornblower, *CT*, III 901–7. Thucydides' account of Phrynichus' stratagem, of Astyochus' response, and of that of Alcibiades has given rise to a mix of incredulity and speculation. Cf. the secondary literature on this subject cited and described in note 17, above, as well as Westlake, "Phrynichus and Astyochus (Thucydides VIII.50–1)," 101, and Rhodes, *Alcibiades*, 61–62, who suggest that Phrynichus must have supposed Alcibiades still in the Spartan camp, with Bloedow, "Phrynichus the 'Intelligent' Athenian," 89–100, who errs only in suppos-

ing that Phrynichus' attempt to drive a wedge between Tissaphernes and Alcibiades succeeded; with Heftner, "Phyrnichos Stratonidou Deiradiotes als Politiker und Symbolfigur der athenischen Oligarchen von 411 v. Chr.," 89–94, and *Umsturz*, 50–58, whose account is quite sensible; and with Julia L. Shear, *Polis and Revolution: Responding to Oligarchy in Classical Athens* (Cambridge: Cambridge University Press, 2011), 26–39, 66–67, who goes astray only in thinking that Thucydides depicts Phrynichus as a tyrant. Magnesia on the Maeander: *IACP* no. 852.

34. Impact of Rhodian interlude and of Tissaphernes' dickering with Athens on the calculations of Lichas and his colleagues: Kallet, *MCPT*, 259–67.

35. Temporary convergence of the interests of Alcibiades and those of Tissaphernes: Lewis, *SP*, 99–107. Cf. Kagan, *Fall*, 124–30, 135–37, who joins Bloedow, "Phrynichus the 'Intelligent' Athenian," 89–100, in believing that Phrynichus drove a wedge between the two, with Stuttard, *Nemesis*, 211–13.

CHAPTER 4. *STÁSIS*

Epigraph: Bob Dylan, *Chronicles, Volume One* (New York: Simon and Schuster, 2004), 36.

1. Peisander a demagogue and inquisitor: Rahe, *SSPW*, Chapter 3, note 39. Prominence among the oligarchs in 411: Thuc. 8.49; Andoc. 2.14; Lys. 12.66, 25.9 with Hatzfeld, *Alcibiade*, 236–37; Andrewes, *HCT*, V 116–17; Munn, *SH*, 139–51; and Hornblower, *CT*, III 901. See also Lys. 7.4. Cf. Arthur Geoffrey Woodhead, "Peisander," *AJPh* 75:2 (1954): 131–46, who thinks that in 415 he must have been a supporter of Alcibiades, with Ostwald, *Sovereignty*, 331–32, 350–52. Androcles vs. Alcibiades: Thuc. 8.65.2 and Plut. *Alc.* 19.1–3, read with an eye to Andoc. 1.27. Peisander may have been the son of a certain Glaucetes, as we learn from an inscription: Rahe, *SSPW*, Chapter 3, note 36.

2. The precise timing of Peisander's first visit to Athens and of the other events that took place in the first half of 411 is disputed, and calculations are complicated by two considerations: first, that at some point between January and June, for a period of six weeks to two months, everything was put on hold; and, second, that much of what has been written concerning the chronology of this period needs adjustment in light of the fact, remarked on in Chapter 1, note 30, above, that the thirteenth regnal year of Darius II is apt to have begun in January or February 411, and not in March or April: cf. Mabel Lang, "The Revolution of the 400: Chronology and Constitutions," *AJPh* 88:2 (April 1967): 176–87, with Andrewes, *HCT*, V 131, 184–93; then, cf. Harry C. Avery, "The Chronology of Peisander's Mission to Athens," *CPh* 94:2 (April 1999): 127–46, with Colin Austin and S. Douglas Olson, "Introduction," in Aristophanes, *Thesmophoriazusae* (Oxford: Oxford University Press, 2004), xxiii–xliv; and see Nikolaos Karkavelias, "The Chronology of Pisander's Mission to Athens Revisited: Thucydides

8.53–54," *Acta Classica* 57 (2014): 53–75. Note, however, Herbert Heftner, "Die Rede für Polystratos ([Lysias] 20) als Zeugnis für den oligarchischen Umsturz von 411 v. Chr. in Athen," *Klio* 81:1 (1999): 68–94, and *Umsturz*, 93–108, as well as Alan H. Sommerstein, "Aristophanes and the Events of 411," *JHS* 97 (1977): 112–26, and Pavel Nývlt, "Sparta and Persia between the Second and the Third Treaty in 412/411 BCE: A Chronology," *Eirene* 50:1/2 (2014): 39–60. In supposing that this delay took place after the decision to send Peisander and his colleagues and before their departure for Athens, I have adopted the chronology suggested by Avery and taken up by Karkavelias. By way of contrast, Sommerstein and Nývlt suppose that, after their subsequent negotiations with Tissaphernes, Peisander and his colleagues spent a considerable number of weeks overthrowing democracies at places like Paros, Naxos, Tenos, and Carystus before proceeding on to Athens and bringing down the democracy there while Heftner—who bases his reconstruction of events on the supposition that [Lys.] 20.1–11 is a fragment of a speech delivered in 410 and that its account of events, though presented in a defense speech delivered in court, is accurate—believes that it took Peisander and his allies a number of weeks to maneuver the Four Hundred into power. My own view is that, after Peisander and his associates met with Tissaphernes the second time, speed was very much in their interest for reasons that will soon become evident; and I believe that they then moved with dispatch, as Thucydides' narrative suggests.

3. Peisander's initial visit to Athens, presentation to the assembly, deposition of Phrynichus and Scironides: Thuc. 8:53.1–54.3 with Hatzfeld, *Alcibiade*, 237; W. James McCoy, "The 'Non-Speeches' of Pisander in Thucydides, Book Eight," in *The Speeches in Thucydides*, ed. Philip A. Stadter (Chapel Hill: University of North Carolina Press, 1973), 78–89 (at 78–84); Andrewes, *HCT*, V 123–28; Ostwald, *Sovereignty*, 350–54; Kagan, *Fall*, 131–34; Heftner, *Umsturz*, 58–65, 72–74; Hornblower, *CT*, III 910–16; and Stuttard, *Nemesis*, 209–11. Note, in this connection, Ar. *Lys.* 490–91 with Sommerstein, "Aristophanes and the Events of 411," 112–26, and Andrewes, *HCT*, V 189; then, see Arist. *Pol.* 1304b10–15. There are no grounds for supposing that Phrynichus and Scironides were cashiered and replaced by Diomedon and Leon at this time because the former pair were suspected of oligarchic sympathies, as Ostwald, *Sovereignty*, 346–48, claims. Phrynichus was at the time a fierce defender of the existing political order; he was dismissed, as Thucydides makes crystal clear, because he opposed Peisander's scheme; and Diomedon and Leon must then have been on board with Peisander, as Heftner, *Umsturz*, 72–74, suggests.

4. Laespodias: consider Thuc. 8.86.9 in light of 6.105.2. Pythodorus: consider Arist. *Ath. Pol.* 29.2. in light of Thuc. 5.19.2, 24.1, 6.105.2, and see Arist. *Ath. Pol.* 35.1 and Xen. *Hell.* 2.3.1. Dieitrephes: consider Thuc. 8.64.2 in light of 7.29.1–5, and see Andrewes, *HCT*, V 156–61, and Hornblower, *CT*, III 940–43. Aristocrates son of Scellias: consider Thuc. 8.89.2, 92.4 in light of 5.19.2, 24.1, 8.9.2;

Xen. *Hell.* 1.4.21; and Pl. *Grg.* 472a–b. Archeptolemos son of Hippias: Plut. *Mor.* 833d–834b = Craterus *FGrH* 342 F5b. Melesias son of Thucydides: Thuc. 8.86.9. Cleitophon son of Aristonymus: consider Arist. *Ath. Pol.* 29.3 in light of Pl. *Resp.* 1.328b7, 340a3–b8, and *Cleitophon* passim, and see Ar. *Ran.* 967 and Arist. *Ath. Pol.* 34.3. There were, to be sure, other Athenians named Pythodorus and Aristocrates. But how many of these individuals were prominent enough to be accorded a leading role at this time?

5. Peisander and the *sunōmosíai*: Thuc. 8.54.4, read in light of 8.48.3, 65.2, and Hyp. 4.7–8, with Andrewes, *HCT*, V 128–31; Ostwald, *Sovereignty*, 354–57; Kagan, *Fall*, 135; Munn, *SH*, 139–40; Heftner, *Umsturz*, 65–67; Hornblower, *CT*, III 916–20; and Rahe, *SSPW*, Chapter 3 (with the secondary literature cited in note 16). It is—as Ostwald, *Sovereignty*, 233–34, sagely points out by way of correcting George Miller Calhoun, *Athenian Clubs in Politics and Litigation* (Austin: Bulletin of the University of Texas, 1913), 8 n. 7, 144 n. 4, and Franco Sartori, *Le Eterie nella vita politica ateniese del VI e V secolo a. C.* (Rome: Bretschneider, 1957), 75–76—a grave blunder to suppose that the *hetaireíai* of the 420s were made up of oligarchic conspirators. It is, as he notes, telling that the suspicions of Cleon and his followers, as depicted in Aristophanes, concerned tyranny and that oligarchy was not mentioned at all: see Rahe, *SSPW*, Chapter 3 (at note 16). As Ostwald, *Sovereignty*, 355 n. 73, also points out, Calhoun, *Athenian Clubs in Politics and Litigation*, 4–7, and Sartori, *Le Eterie nella vita politica ateniese*, 17–33, are less sensitive to the changing connotation of terms like *sunōmosía* in these years than is Olivier Aurenche, *Les Groupes d'Alcibiade, de Léogoras et de Teucros: Remarques sur la vie politique Athénienne en 415 av. J.-C* (Paris: Les Belles Lettres, 1974), 32–41.

6. Cf., however, Arist. *Pol.* 1304b7–14, who supposes that, with regard to the intentions of the Persian king, Peisander and his colleagues employed deceit from the outset.

7. Peisander and the delegation from Athens meet with Tissaphernes and Alcibiades: Thuc. 8.56 with Hatzfeld, *Alcibiade*, 237–41; Andrewes, *HCT*, V 132–36; Lewis, *SP*, 100–103; Kagan, *Fall*, 135–38; Heftner, *Umsturz*, 75–87; Hornblower, *CT*, III 921–24; Rhodes, *Alcibiades*, 63–64; Stuttard, *Nemesis*, 211–14; and Hyland, *PI*, 66–71, who thinks that Tissaphernes, on the King's behalf, was angling for what amounted to an Athenian surrender. That the younger Darius would have welcomed this I do not doubt; that he had any expectations in this regard seems to me highly unlikely. On the implications of the concession, sought by the Mede, of his right to deploy a fleet in the waters in question, cf. Michael Goldstein, "Athenian-Persian Peace Treaties: Thucydides 8.56.4 and 8.58.2," *CSCA* 7 (1974): 155–64, who thinks, as do I, that more was at stake than the eastern Aegean, with Lewis, *SP*, 101 n. 74.

8. Murder of Androcles and others, promulgation of political program: Thuc. 8.65.2–5 with Andrewes, *HCT*, V 161–62; Hornblower, *CT*, III 943–44; and

Stuttard, *Nemesis*, 214–15. Note, in this connection, Gianluca Cuniberti, "La Presenza ateniese a Samo e le uccisioni di Iperbolo e Androcle nell'ottavo libro di Tucidide," *Annali dell'Istituto Italiano per gli Studi Storici* 14 (1997): 53–80. If I do not follow Kagan, *Fall*, 138–44, it is because I believe that the *sunōmosíai* went into action soon after Peisander's departure for Anatolia and that backing off was no longer an option. I find it hard to believe that Peisander had no idea of what he was doing when he turned the *sunōmosíai* into a conspiracy against the democracy: cf., however, Ostwald, *Sovereignty*, 358–59.

9. Status of the revolutionary program: cf. Thuc. 8.66.1 with 97, where it becomes clear that more than mere ambition is at stake. Self-interestedness of Cleon, Brasidas, Nicias, Pleistoanax, and Phrynichus rightly noted by Thucydides, then assigned an exaggerated role: 5.16.1–17.1, 8.50.1. Whatever one makes of Arist. *Ath. Pol.* 30.1–32.1, it is evidence that there had been extensive debate and deliberation concerning the best provisions for Athenian self-government. Role played by tradition in this discussion: consider Thuc. 8.76.6 and Arist. *Ath. Pol.* 29.3 with 34.3 in light of Thrasymachus 85 B1 (DK⁶), and note the apparent sympathy for Thrasymachus' thinking attributed by Plato to Cleitophon: *Resp.* 1.340a–c. That the appeal to tradition as authoritative was not a monopoly of those who insisted that the Five Thousand should rule is clear from Thuc. 8.76.6: cf. Alexander Fuks, *The Ancestral Constitution: Four Studies in Athenian Party Politics at the End of the Fifth Century* BC (London: Routledge and Kegan Paul, 1953), 1–33, 107–10; Jacqueline Bibauw, "L'Amendement de Clitophon (Aristote, *Ath. Pol.* 29.3)," *AC* 34:2 (1965): 464–83 (esp. 474–83); Sergio A. Cecchin, *Pátrios Politeía: Tentativo propagandistico durante la guerra del Peloponneso* (Turin: G. P. Paravia, 1969), 26–63; and Moses I. Finley, "The Ancestral Constitution," in Finley, *The Use and Abuse of History* (New York: Viking Press, 1975), 34–59 (esp. 35–39), with Robin Osborne, "Changing the Discourse," in *Popular Tyranny: Sovereignty and its Discontents in Ancient Greece*, ed. Kathryn A. Morgan (Austin: University of Texas Press, 2003), 251–72, reprinted with an addendum in Osborne, *AAD*, 267–88; and Julia L. Shear, *Polis and Revolution: Responding to Oligarchy in Classical Athens* (Cambridge: Cambridge University Press, 2011), 41–60.

10. First stage of the revolution at Athens: Thuc. 8.66. Cf. Andrewes, *HCT*, V 163–64, with Heftner, *Umsturz*, 109–17, 123–30, and see Kagan, *Fall*, 141, 143–44; Munn, *SH*, 138–39; and Hornblower, *CT*, III 944–48. Charicles' affiliation at this time: consider Lys. 13.74 in light of Xen. *Hell.* 2.3.2 and Lys. 12.55. Charicles' position can also be inferred from Isoc. 16.42. For his background, see Rahe, *SSPW*, Chapter 3, note 38.

11. Conspirators on Samos resolve to proceed without Alcibiades and without Persian support: Thuc. 8.63.4 with Andrewes, *HCT*, V 156; Kagan, *Fall*, 138–40; Heftner, *Umsturz*, 87–92; and Hornblower, *CT*, III 940.

12. Oligarchies to be imposed on Samos and elsewhere: Thuc. 8.63.3, 64.1–65.1 with

Andrewes, *HCT*, V 153–61; Kagan, *Fall*, 140–41, 164–65, 168, 185; Heftner, *Umsturz*, 90–92, 211; and Hornblower, *CT*, III 938–43. Paros: *IACP* no. 509. Naxos: no. 507. Andros: no. 475. Tenos: no. 525.

13. Election of *sungrapheis*: Thuc. 8.67.1 and Arist. *Ath. Pol.* 29.1–3, who appears to be following the Atthidographer Androtion son of Andron *FGrH* 324 F43, from whom Philochorus *FGrH* 328 F136 also cribs, with Ar. *Lys.* 421. That the *próbouloi* were involved in overthrowing the democracy and setting up an oligarchy is clear from Arist. *Rhet.* 1419a26–30 and Lys. 12.65. On the role played by Andron, see Craterus *FGrH* 342 F5a ap. Harp. s.v. *Andrōn* and Craterus *FGrH* 342 F5b ap. Pl. *Mor.* 833e, and cf. Antony Andrewes, "Androtion and the Four Hundred," *PCPhS* 202 (1976): 14–25, with Robin Lane Fox, "Thucydides and Documentary History," *CQ* n.s. 60:1 (May 2010): 11–29 (at 27 n. 83), who provides an emendation needed by Andrewes' argument. See Pl. *Prt.* 315c where we find the young Andron in the late 430s associated with the sophist Hippias, who emphasizes that the members of the intellectual elite, in contrast with ordinary folk, are fellow citizens by nature and not by law (337c–d); and *Grg.* 487c, where we find the same young man in the early 420s associated with Gorgias' student Callicles, who draws a sharp distinction between justice according to the law and justice according to nature. In this connection, cf. McCoy, "The 'Non-Speeches' of Pisander in Thucydides, Book Eight," 84–88, with Andrewes, *HCT*, V 164–65, 312–16; Rhodes, *CAAP*, 369–77; Ostwald, *Sovereignty*, 359, 368–73; Kagan, *Fall*, 141–46; Munn, *SH*, 135–38; and Hornblower, *CT*, III 948–49. Cf. Heftner, *Umsturz*, 130–41, whose reordering and reinterpretation of the events pertinent to the rise and fall of the Four Hundred I think untenable for the reasons spelled out in note 16, below. That Thucydides and Aristotle are describing the same events seems to me clear and their accounts are for the most part complementary. In general, where Thucydides provides less detail with regard to the legislation passed in this period and Aristotle, more, it is because the former is writing a political and the latter a constitutional history. With this fact in mind, I have sought to reconcile the two accounts, and I have for the most part followed Thucydides' narrative of political developments and added detail from Aristotle's discussion of the legislation. Cf., however, the treatment of these two sources in Heftner, *Umsturz*, 93–108, 130–210, who thinks them less easily reconciled, with that in Andrewes, *HCT*, V 184–256; Rhodes, *CAAP*, 362–69; and Rood, *Thucydides*, 269–71 (esp. n. 61). For another view of the relationship between these two accounts, cf. Mabel Lang, "The Revolution of the 400," *AJPh* 69:3 (1948): 272–89, and "The Revolution of the 400: Chronology and Constitutions," 176–87.

14. Assembly at Colonus, not Pnyx: Thuc. 8.67.2 with McCoy, "The 'Non-Speeches' of Pisander in Thucydides, Book Eight," 88–89; Peter Siewert, "Poseidon Hippios und die Athenischen Hippeis," in *Arktouros: Hellenic Studies Presented to Bernard M. W. Knox*, ed. Glenn W. Bowersock, Walter Burkert, and Michael Put-

nam (Berlin: de Gruyter, 1979), 280–89; Andrewes, *HCT*, V 165–67; Ostwald, *Sovereignty*, 372–74; Kagan, *Fall*, 147; and Hornblower, *CT*, III 949–50. Cf. Heftner, *Umsturz*, 142–64, whose reordering and reinterpretation of the events pertinent to the rise and fall of the Four Hundred I think untenable for the reasons spelled out in note 16, below. Athens' cavalrymen were for the most part recruited from among the well-to-do, and they are apt to have been sympathetic to the oligarchic movement at this time, as they evidently were in the immediate wake of this war: Xen. *Hell.* 3.1.4.

15. Proposal that assembly be freed from impediments and inhibitions associated with the *graphē paranómōn* and with other legal actions, such as the *eisangelía*, the *prósklēsis*, the *éndeixis*, and the *apagōgé*: Thuc. 8.67.2 and Arist. *Ath. Pol.* 29.4 with David M. Lewis, "Entrenchment-Clauses in Attic Decrees," in *Phóros: Tribute to Benjamin Dean Meritt*, ed. Donald W. Bradeen and Malcolm F. McGregor (Locust Valley, NY: J.J. Augustin, 1974), 81–89, reprinted in Lewis, *Selected Papers in Greek and Near Eastern History*, ed. Peter J. Rhodes (Cambridge: Cambridge University Press, 1997), 136–49; Andrewes, *HCT*, V 167–68, 216; Rhodes, *CAAP*, 377–79; Ostwald, *Sovereignty*, 374, 377; Kagan, *Fall*, 147–48; and Hornblower, *CT*, III 950–51. Cf. Heftner, *Umsturz*, 153–64, which should be read in light of the criticism that I spell out in note 16, below. On the *graphē paranómōn*, its likely origin, and its function, note Aeschin. 3.3–8, 190–200 (esp. 191), and Dem. 58.34; then see Mogens Herman Hansen, *The Sovereignty of the People's Court in Athens in the Fourth Century* B.C. *and the Public Action against Unconstitutional Proposals* (Odense: Odense University Press, 1974), and *The Athenian Democracy in the Age of Demosthenes: Structure, Principles and Ideology*, tr. J. A. Crook (Oxford: Blackwell, 1991), 205–12. On the other legal remedies expressly set aside on this occasion, see Mogens Herman Hansen, *Eisangelia: The Sovereignty of the Peoples's Court in Athens in the Fourth Century* B.C. *and the Impeachment of Generals and Politicians* (Odense: Odense University Press, 1975), and *Apagoge, Endeixis and Ephegesis against Kakourgoi, Atimoi and Pheugontes: A Study in the Athenian Administration of Justice in the Fourth Century* (Odense: Odense University Press, 1976).

16. Constitutional proposal adopted at Colonus: Thuc. 8.67.3 and Arist. *Ath. Pol.* 29.5–30.1, which are at odds in one particular. Thucydides appears to deny what Aristotle asserts: that the proposal adopted came from the *sungrapheîs*. Also cf. Thuc. 8.63.3, where it is expected that five thousand will be the upper limit, with [Lys.] 20.13, which, if it is to be given any weight, serves to confirm Aristotle's claim that this number was supposed a minimum, that *katalogeîs* were appointed at this time to select the Five Thousand, and that the procedures involved were emergency measures meant to last until the end of the war. For another view of the manner in which events unfolded, see Heftner, "Die Rede für Polystratos ([Lysias] 20) als Zeugnis für den oligarchischen Umsturz von 411 v. Chr. in Athen," 68–94, and *Umsturz*, 93–108, 130–210, who prefers the account provided

in [Lys.] 20.1–11 to that supplied by Thucydides. There are three reasons for not sharing Heftner's preference. First, where we can test Thucydides' accuracy, we find his reputation for veracity and exactitude justified. Second, we have no idea who the author of [Lys.] 20.1–11 is and whether these paragraphs are what they purport to be—a speech or part of a speech actually delivered in 410 in defense of an erstwhile member of the Four Hundred named Polycrates and not a later rhetorical exercise. Third, if it could be established that the paragraphs in question do come from a speech delivered for this purpose in 410, they would be framed with an eye to depicting Polycrates' conduct in the best possible light, and such an exercise often requires a departure from and a concealment of the truth. For example, the tribesmen said in these paragraphs to have elected Polycrates a member of the Four Hundred could easily be the ten individuals said by Thucydides to have been chosen from his tribe for this purpose by the five *próedroi* elected at Colonus. Note also *O&R* no. 173 = *ML* no. 80 = *IG* I³ 98 lines 5–8, which seems to show the Council of Four Hundred meeting under the presidency of the five *próedroi*. In this connection, see Dieter Flach, "Der oligarchische Staatsstreich in Athen vom Jahr 411," *Chiron* 7 (1977): 9–33; Andrewes, *HCT*, V 168–69, 217–18; Rhodes, *CAAP*, 379–85; Ostwald, *Sovereignty*, 374–78; Kagan, *Fall*, 148–49; and Hornblower, *CT*, III 951–53. Role played by Peisander: Thuc. 8.68.1. Success a consequence of fraud and force: Arist. *Pol.* 1304b7–15 with Henry D. Westlake, "The Subjectivity of Thucydides: His Treatment of the Four Hundred at Athens," *BRL* 56 (1973/4): 193–218, reprinted in Westlake, *Studies*, 181–200, who does an admirable job of unearthing the historian's judgments. Whether his having opinions of this sort renders Thucydides' account more subjective is another matter. Would a failure on his part to describe force and fraud as force and fraud render a writer more objective or merely suggest that he is obtuse? The former would be true if and only if there really were no validity to moral assessments. If, as one historian has recently claimed, there is now a consensus among scholars "that the selection of as well as the interpretation of events is an essentially subjective process," it speaks ill of contemporary scholars: see Michael Attyah Flower, *Theopompus of Chios: History and Rhetoric in the Fourth Century* BC (Oxford: Clarendon Press, 1994), 187–88. For, if there were no standards by which to determine whether a given author's selection of events and that author's interpretation of them deserved praise or blame, the entire scholarly endeavor would be a waste of effort and time.

17. The *anagrapheîs*, their proposals, and the adoption of those proposals: Arist. *Ath. Pol.* 30.1–32.1. As one would expect, this passage and Thucydides' silence regarding the *anagrapheîs* has given rise to a great deal of speculation. See, for example, Andrewes, *HCT*, V 218–34; Rhodes, *CAAP*, 385–405; Ostwald, *Sovereignty*, 379–85; Kagan, *Fall*, 149 n. 71, 158–60; François Ruzé, "Les Oligarques et leurs 'constitutions' dan l'*Athènaiôn Politeia*," in *Aristote et Athènes*, ed. Marcel Piérart (Paris: Boccard, 1993), 185–201; Heftner, *Umsturz*, 177–210; and Shear,

Polis and Revolution, 41–53. I find attractive the reading of Arist. *Ath. Pol.* 30.2–3 and the emendation proposed by Edward M. Harris, "The Constitution of the Five Thousand," *HSPh* 93 (1990): 243–80 (at 247–57), which render the passage intelligible, coherent, and consistent with the claim advanced by the envoys the Four Hundred sent to Samos that is reported by Thucydides at 8.86.3, 93.2. In the absence of such an emendation, as Heftner, *Umsturz*, 183–86, points out, Thucydides' testimony and that of Aristotle cannot be reconciled.

18. Coup d'état: consider Thuc. 8.69–70 in light of 2.27.1, 7.57.2, and 8.65.1, and see Arist. *Ath. Pol.* 32.1–2 with Andrewes, *HCT*, V 178–81, 233–38; Rhodes, *CAAP*, 404–7; Ostwald, *Sovereignty*, 381–82, 385–87; Kagan, *Fall*, 156–64; and Hornblower, *CT*, III 960–64. The 14th of Thargelion, which is dated to 9 June in the Julian calendar, took place on 11 June in the Gregorian calendar: see www.skyviewcafe.com. On the inception of the archonship of 411/10, see Benjamin D. Meritt, *The Athenian Calendar in the Fifth Century* (Cambridge, MA: Harvard University Press, 1928), 98, and *Athenian Financial Documents of the Fifth Century* (Ann Arbor: University of Michigan Press, 1932), 104–6, who dates it to 25 July in the Julian calendar (27 or 28 July in the Gregorian calendar), when, subsequent to the summer solstice, there was a new moon: see www.skyviewcafe.com. Cf. Heftner, *Umsturz*, 164–76, which should be read in light of the criticism that I spell out in note 16, above. Much was later made by Theramenes' enemies of his participation both in this coup and in arranging for the executions, imprisonment, and banishment that followed: Schol. Ar. *Ran.* 541 and Ar. F563 (PCG).

19. Peace overture to Agis from Athenian oligarchs: Thuc. 8.70.2 and Arist. *Ath. Pol.* 32.3 with Andrewes, *HCT*, V 182, 239; Rhodes, *CAAP*, 410; Kagan, *Fall*, 165–67; and Heftner, *Umsturz*, 241–45. Argument reportedly made that the Spartans would be more likely to welcome negotiations with an oligarchy than a democracy: Xen. *Hell.* 2.3.45. Carystus: *IACP* no. 373.

20. Agis' miscalculations, the unacceptable terms he proposed, the failure of his march on Athens, Athenian envoys sent on to Sparta, arrested, and conveyed to Argos: Thuc. 8.71 and Arist. *Ath. Pol.* 32.3, followed by Thuc. 8.86.9, with Andrewes, *HCT*, V 182–8, 288–89; Rhodes, *CAAP*, 410; Kagan, *Fall*, 167–68, 185; Heftner, *Umsturz*, 241–42, 244–50; and Hornblower, *CT*, III 964–66, 1003. Laespodias' generalship: Thuc. 6.105.2. I see no reason why the envoys arrested (8.86.9) cannot be the envoys mentioned as having been dispatched at 8.71.3, as Andrewes and Hornblower suppose. The events on Samos and at Athens described in 8.73–75 appear to have taken place while the events at Athens described in 8.65–71 were underway. Money as the sinews of war: Cic. *Phil.* 5.5, Plut. *Cleom.* 27.1. Cf. Niccolò Machiavelli, *Discorsi sopra la prima deca di Tito Livio* 2.10, in Machiavelli, *Tutte le opere*, ed. Mario Martelli (Florence: Sansoni Editore, 1971), 159–60.

21. Samian oligarchic conspiracy thwarted, role played by the Athenians Diomedon, Leon, Thrasyllus, and Thrasybulus: Thuc. 8.73 with Andrewes, *HCT*, V

257–66; Ostwald, *Sovereignty*, 387–89; Kagan, *Fall*, 168–70; Heftner, *Umsturz*, 211–17; Hornblower, *CT*, III 968–74; and Stuttard, *Nemesis*, 215. On these Athenians, see Chapter 2, note 15, above, as well as W. James McCoy, "Thrasyllus,"*AJPh* 98:3 (Autumn 1977): 264–89.

22. Consider Thuc. 8.63.3–4 and 73 in light of 21, which should be read with 15.1, 16, 17.3, 19.2, 20.2, 23.1; note 23.1, 24.2–3, 54.3, 55.1; and see W. James McCoy, "Thrasybulus and his Trierarchies," *AJPh* 112:3 (Autumn 1991): 303–23 (esp. 303–17), who poses questions concerning Thrasybulus, Thrasyllus, Diomedon, and Leon that his predecessors failed to ask. Fourth-century *stratēgoí* select trierarchs for campaigns: Debra Hamel, *Athenian Generals: Military Authority in the Classical Period* (Leiden: Brill, 1998), 30–31. Cf. Buck, *Thrasybulus*, 19–31, who overlooks the evidence strongly suggesting that Peisander engineered sending out Diomedon and Leon to replace Phrynichus and Scironides because he knew that Diomedon and Leon favored the recall of Alcibiades and who thinks Thrasybulus a "fervent democrat" who was a rival, not a close associate, of Cleinias' son. No "fervent" democrat would have championed the recall of a man who had just recently pressed for an oligarchic revolution in Athens, and none would later have been invited to take Theramenes' place among the Thirty, as Thrasybulus was: Diod. 14.32.5–6, Just. *Epit.* 5.9.13. It is telling that, from 411 to the end of the war, he was in and out of favor in tandem with Alcibiades. The Athenians knew that he was a partisan of Cleinias' son. There is other evidence suggesting that his outlook was not decidedly at odds with that of Theramenes: see Xen. *Hell.* 2.3.42. Cf. Buck, *Thrasybulus*, 71–72, 76, who dismisses it as "unbelievable" that "a man so well known as a staunch democrat" would have been approached by the Thirty, and who rejects evidence indicating that many of those who associated themselves with Thrasybulus in 403 in his attempt to overthrow the Thirty had been close political allies of Theramenes a short time before.

23. Crew of the *Paralus*, Chaereas' lies: Thuc. 8.73.5, 74 with 1.57.6. See Andrewes, *HCT*, V 265–67; Kagan, *Fall*, 170–71; Heftner, *Umsturz*, 211–12, 217–21; and Hornblower, *CT*, III 973–75.

24. Unity on Samos, Thrasybulus and Thrasyllus elected *stratēgoí*, encouraging words, hope for help from Alcibiades: Thuc. 8.75–76 with Hatzfeld, *Alcibiade*, 241–44; Andrewes, *HCT*, V 267–71; Kagan, *Fall*, 171–73; Marta Sordi, "Trasibulo e la controrivoluzione di Samo: L'Assemblea del popolo in armi come forma di opposizione," in *L'Opposizione nel mondo antico*, ed. Marta Sordi (Milan: Vita e pensiero, 2000), 103–9; Heftner, *Umsturz*, 217–31; Hornblower, *CT*, III 975–81; and Stuttard, *Nemesis*, 215–16.

25. Alcibiades recalled, elected *stratēgós* by those on Samos: Thuc. 8.81–82 with Hatzfeld, *Alcibiade*, 244–49; Andrewes, *HCT*, V 275–77; Kagan, *Fall*, 173, 176–79; Heftner, *Umsturz*, 251–56; Hornblower, *CT*, III 988–89; Rhodes, *Alcibiades*, 64–66; and Stuttard, *Nemesis*, 216–20.

26. Envoys dispatched by the Four Hundred to Samos, instructions: Thuc. 8.72 with

Andrewes, *HCT*, V 183–84; Kagan, *Fall*, 180–81; Heftner, *Umsturz*, 173–76, 242–45; and Hornblower, *CT*, III 966–68.

27. Envoys sent from the Four Hundred to Samos tarry on Delos: Thuc. 8.77 with Andrewes, *HCT*, V 270–71; Kagan, *Fall*, 180; Heftner, *Umsturz*, 175–76, 242–43; and Hornblower, *CT*, III 981.

28. Pitch made by the Four Hundred's emissaries: Thuc 8.86.1–4 with Andrewes, *HCT*, V 285–86; Harris, "The Constitution of the Five Thousand," 247–57 (esp. 254); Heftner, *Umsturz*, 257–59; and Hornblower, *CT*, III 1000. Cf. Kagan, *Fall*, 181 (with n. 87), who wrongly supposes that the claim regarding the size of the assembly applies only to the assemblies held since the Four Hundred came to power.

29. Alcibiades, supported by Thrasybulus, allows the men on Samos to vent and prevents an expedition against the Peiraeus: Thuc. 8.86.4–5, where—for the reasons spelled out by Andrewes, *HCT*, V 286–88; Kagan, *Fall*, 180–83 (esp. n. 90); Rood, *Thucydides*, 275–76 (with n. 75); and Hornblower, *CT*, III 1001–2—I read *prôton* ("the first occasion") with the Vatican manuscript (MS B), and Plut. *Alc.* 26.6, where Thrasybulus' contribution is mentioned. Cf. Peter A. Brunt, "Thucydides and Alcibiades," *REG* 65: 304–5 (January–June 1952): 59–96 (at 61 n. 1), reprinted in Brunt, *Studies in Greek History and Thought* (Oxford: Clarendon Press, 1993), 17–46 (at 18 n. 2), who argues for the *prôtos* ("in an outstanding fashion") found in the other manuscripts. I see no reason to doubt that Thucydides took a dim view of Alcibiades' previous conduct. Indeed, as Rood, *Thucydides*, 280–82, emphasizes, the historian says only that he "appears" to have done the city a service. Cf. Kagan, *Fall*, 183, who believes, as I do not, that it would have been wiser and relatively easy for the fleet to row to the Saronic Gulf and seize the Peiraeus. Cf. also Edmund F. Bloedow, *Alcibiades Reexamined* (Wiesbaden: F. Steiner, 1973), 38–41, who supposes that the loss of Ionia and the Hellespont to the Spartans, who were at this time supported by Pharnabazus, would have brought Tissaphernes over to the Athenians, and see Stuttard, *Nemesis*, 219–20.

30. Alcibiades' exhortation to the envoys of the Four Hundred: Thuc. 8.86.6–7 with Hatzfeld, *Alcibiade*, 249–50; Andrewes, *HCT*, V 288; Ostwald, *Sovereignty*, 390; Kagan, *Fall*, 184–85; Heftner, *Umsturz*, 257–59; Hornblower, *CT*, III 1002; Rhodes, *Alcibiades*, 66–67; and Stuttard, *Nemesis*, 222–26, who rightly emphasizes its impact.

31. On this, see Rahe, *RAM* III.i–vi (esp. i).

32. Alcibiades' calculation and the defects inherent in oligarchy: consider Thuc. 8.89–90 (esp. 89.3)—along with Andrewes, *HCT*, V 298–301 and Hornblower, *CT*, III 1010–11—in light of Hdt. 3.81–82, and see David Asheri, Alan Lloyd, and Aldo Corcella, *A Commentary on Herodotus Books I–IV*, tr. Barbara Graziosi, Matteo Rossetti, Carlotta Dus, and Vanesa Cazzato, ed. Oswyn Murray and Alfonso Moreno (Oxford: Oxford University Press, 2007), 473–76.

33. Foursome leading the oligarchic junta: Thuc. 8.68 and Arist. *Ath. Pol.* 32.2 with Andrewes, *HCT*, V 169–78; Kagan, *Fall*, 150–56; Ostwald, *Sovereignty*, 358–66; Heftner, *Umsturz*, 65–71, and Hornblower, *CT*, III 953–60. Additional important sources for the biography of Antiphon son of Sophilus: Pl. *Menex.* 236a, Xen. *Mem.* 1.6.1–15, Plut. *Mor.* 832b–834b. Antiphon vs. Laespodias: Antiph. F21–24 (Thalheim). Hostility to Alcibiades: Antiphon F66–67 (Thalheim) ap. Plut. *Alc.* 3 and Ath. 12.525b. I see no reason to accept the contention of Kenneth J. Dover, "The Chronology of Antiphon's Speeches," *CQ* 44:1/2 (January–April 1950): 44–60 (at 55–56), that Antiphon's speech attacking Alcibiades is to be dated to 411: his assertion rests entirely upon the supposition that Antiphon's willingness to disparage Alcibiades in 411 was for Peisander and the like his only recommendation. It is far more likely that he was recruited because his hostility to the man was well-known and because of the keen intelligence he brought to bear on political maneuvers. Associate of Phrynichus in the late 420s: Ar. *Vesp.* 1301–2. Antiphon the speechwriter and Antiphon the sophist one and the same: cf. Gerard J. Pendrick, "Introduction," in *Antiphon the Sophist: The Fragments*, ed. and tr. Gerard J. Pendrick (Cambridge: Cambridge University Press, 2002), 1–26, who thinks otherwise, with John S. Morrison, "Antiphon," *PCPhS* n.s. 7, 187 (1961): 49–58; Harry C. Avery, "One Antiphon or Two?" *Hermes* 110:2 (1982): 145–58; Michael Gagarin, *Antiphon the Athenian: Oratory, Law, and Justice in the Age of the Sophists* (Austin: University of Texas Press, 2002), 37–52; and Michael J. Edwards, "Notes on Pseudo-Plutarch's Life of Antiphon," *CQ* n.s. 48:1 (1998): 82–92, who supplies a persuasive defense of the biographical tradition as reported in Plut. *Mor.* 832b–834b. See also Ostwald, *Sovereignty*, 359–64. *Phúsis* vs. *nómos*: Pl. *Prt.* 337c–e, *Grg.* 481b–491b, *Resp.* 1.336b–350d, 2.358b–362c; and Antiph. 87 B44 (DK⁶). On Theramenes, see Davies, *APF* no. 7234.

34. Impact of Alcibiades' speech; Theramenes, Aristocrates, and the dissident oligarchs: cf. Thuc. 8.89.1–2 with 86.6–7, and see Arist. *Ath. Pol.* 33.2 with Kagan, *Fall*, 185–89 (with n. 1, where he cites W. James McCoy, "Theramenes, Thrasybulus and the Athenian Moderates" [Ph.D. diss., Yale University, 1970], 81–82, who appears to have been the first to note the discrepancy between what Alcibiades said and what the envoys reported to the Four Hundred). See also Andrewes, *HCT*, V 294–98; Rhodes, *CAAP*, 413–14; Ostwald, *Sovereignty*, 390–93; Heftner, *Umsturz*, 260–65; and Hornblower, *CT*, III 1007–10. Aristocrates' prior career: see Chapter 2, above. For what was to come, see *IG* I³ 964; *O&R* no. 180 = *ML* no. 84 = *IG* I³ 304; Xen. *Hell.* 1.4.21, 5.16, 6.29, 7.2; Lys. 12.66; Diod. 13.74.1, 101.5; Philochorus *FGrH* 328 F142; Dem. 58.67 with Rhodes, *CAAP*, 413.

35. Motives Thucydides attributes to Theramenes, Aristocrates, and the other leading dissidents: 8.89.2–4 with Andrewes, *HCT*, V 294–301; Kagan, *Fall*, 189–90; Heftner, *Umsturz*, 261–65; and Hornblower, *CT*, III 1008–11.

36. Diehards desperate; Antiphon, Phrynichus, Onomacles, Archeptolemos, and

eight other envoys to Lacedaemon: Thuc. 8.90.1–2 and Plut. *Mor.* 833e–f with Andrewes, *HCT*, V 301–3; Ostwald, *Sovereignty*, 393; Kagan, *Fall*, 190–92; Heftner, *Umsturz*, 260–70; and Hornblower, *CT*, III 1011–13. On Archeptolemos, see Ar. *Eq.* 794–95 and *Pax* 665 along with Schol. Ar. *Eq.* 327.

37. Fortifications added on Eetioneia: Thuc. 8.90.1–5 and Xen. *Hell.* 2.3.46 with Dem. 34.37, Paus. 1.1.3, and Schol. Ar. *Ach.* 547. Cf. Andrewes, *HCT*, V 301–7, with Kagan, *Fall*, 190 (esp. n. 10); Heftner, *Umsturz*, 270–78; and Hornblower, *CT*, III 1011–16.

38. Theramenes' fears regarding the fortifications along Eetioneia's southeastern shore, expedition of Agesandridas: Thuc. 8.91.1–2 with Andrewes, *HCT*, V 307–8; Ostwald, *Sovereignty*, 393–94; Kagan, *Fall*, 192–93; Heftner, *Umsturz*, 270–78; and Hornblower, *CT*, III 1016–19. Las in the bay of Laconia: Paus. 3.24.6, Ephorus *FGrH* 70 F117, and Pseudo-Scylax 36 with *IACP* no. 337. Agesander the diplomat: Thuc. 1.139.3.

39. Thucydides on the aims of the diehards: 8.91.3–92.1 with Andrewes, *HCT*, V 307–9; Kagan, *Fall*, 192–93; Heftner, *Umsturz*, 270–78; and Hornblower, *CT*, III 1018–19. *Apotumpanismós*: Rahe, *SSPW*, Chapter 3 (with note 9).

40. Assassination of Phrynichus: cf. Thuc. 8.92.2 and Plut. *Alc.* 25.14 with Lys. 13.70–72 and Lycurg. *Leoc.* 112, and see *O&R* no. 182 = *ML* no. 85 = *IG* I³ 102 and Plut. *Mor.* 834b with Andrewes, *HCT*, V 309–10; Ostwald, *Sovereignty*, 393–95; Kagan, *Fall*, 193; Heftner, *Umsturz*, 265–70; and Hornblower, *CT*, III 1019–21. Phrynichus then dominant within the oligarchy: Arist. *Pol.* 1305b27. On the *perípoloi*, see Thuc. 4.67.2 and Ar. *Av.* 1360–71 with Henry D. Westlake, "Overseas Service for the Father-Beater," *CR* n.s. 4:2 (June 1954): 90–94.

41. Agesandridas in the Saronic Gulf with ships from Sicily, Western Locris (*IACP*, 391–92, with nos. 157–68), and Taras (no. 71); Aristocrates and the hoplites at Eetioneia arrest Alexicles; Theramenes and Aristarchus arrive; hoplites begin to tear the wall down: Thuc. 8.92.3–11 with Andrewes, *HCT*, V 311–14; Kagan, *Fall*, 193–96; Heftner, *Umsturz*, 270–78; and Hornblower, *CT*, III 1021–23. Alexicles: Lycurg. *Leoc.* 115. On Hermon, see also *O&R* no. 180 = *ML* no. 84 = *IG* I³ 304.

42. Wall along Eetioneia's southeastern shore torn down, hoplites assemble and march on the town of Athens, Five Thousand promised, assembly scheduled: Thuc. 8.93 with Andrewes, *HCT*, V 314–16; Ostwald, *Sovereignty*, 394; Kagan, *Fall*, 196–97; Heftner, *Umsturz*, 270–78; and Hornblower, *CT*, III 1023–24.

43. Agesandridas glides past Salamis and the Peiraeus and heads for Oropus (*IACP* no. 214): Thuc. 8.94.1–95.1 with Andrewes, *HCT*, V 316–17; Kagan, *Fall*, 197–99; Heftner, *Umsturz*, 272–73; Hutchinson, *Attrition*, 173–74; and Hornblower, *CT*, III 1024–26. Oropus betrayed earlier to the Thebans, Eretrians request Peloponnesian intervention: Thuc. 8.60.1–2 with Andrewes, *HCT*, V 146; Kagan, *Fall*, 95–96; and Hornblower, *CT*, III 931–32. Note also Thuc. 8.5.1.

44. Athenian fleet defeated off Eretria, Eretrian rebellion, general Euboean revolt: consider Thuc. 8.95.2–7; Arist. *Ath. Pol.* 33.1; and Diod. 13.34.2–3, 36.3–4, in

light of Thuc. 8.5.1, 91.2, and see Andrewes, *HCT*, V 317–20; Rhodes, *CAAP*, 411; Kagan, *Fall*, 198–99; Hutchinson, *Attrition*, 174–76; and Hornblower, *CT*, III 1026–28. Note also Xen. *Hell.* 1.1.1, which may or may not be a reference to this battle. Eretrian inscription recording the honors conferred on Hegelochos of Taras: *O&R* no 175 = *ML* no. 82 = *IG* XII.ix.187 with Hornblower, *CT*, III 1017–18, whose ingenious argument is more fully developed in Simon Hornblower, "What Happened Later to the Families of Pindaric Patrons—and to Epinician Poetry?" in *Reading the Victory Ode*, ed. Peter Agócs, Chris Carey, and Richard Rawles (Cambridge: Cambridge University Press, 2012), 93–107 (at 97–102, 106–7). Coinage is the only evidence we have for the Euboean League, but it is dispositive: see William P. Wallace, *The Euboian League and its Coinage* (New York: American Numismatic Society, 1956). Oreus (sometimes called by its previous name Histiaea): Thuc. 1.114.3, 7.57.2, and Theopompus *FGrH* 115 F387 with *IACP* no. 372. On the complex relationship of the cities on Euboea with Athens, see Malcolm B. Wallace (with Thomas J. Figueira), "Athens and Euboea in the Fifth Century: Toward a New Synthesis," in *Euboea and Athens: Proceedings of a Colloquium in Memory of Malcolm B. Wallace*, ed. Jonathan E. Tomlinson et al. (Athens: The Canadian Institute in Greece, 2011), 233–59, and "Karystos in Euboia and Attic Hegemony," in *Hegemonic Finances: Funding Athenian Domination in the 5th and 4th Centuries*, ed. Thomas J. Figueira and Sean R. Jensen (Swansea: The Classical Press of Wales, 2019), 79–108.

45. Agesandridas' missed opportunity: Thuc. 8.96 with Andrewes, *HCT*, V 321–23; and Hornblower, *CT*, III 1028–31. Cf. Kagan, *Fall*, 199–201, who supposes that, had the fleet been recalled from Samos, the Athenians would have achieved a great victory, and Hutchinson, *Attrition*, 175–77, who harbors doubts and rightly suspects that the Spartans' aim was to deprive the Athenians of access to Euboea, then the Euxine.

46. Establishment of a hoplite regime dubbed the Five Thousand: Thuc. 8.97.1–2, Arist. *Ath. Pol.* 33, and Diod. 13.38.1–2 with Rhodes, *CAAP*, 410–14; Ostwald, *Sovereignty*, 395–99; Kagan, *Fall*, 201–2; and Heftner, *Umsturz*, 279–80. That participation in the assembly was reserved for those able to provide their own weapons, as is asserted in the three ancient sources cited here, there need be no doubt: cf. Geoffrey Ernest Maurice de Ste. Croix, "The Constitution of the Five Thousand," *Historia* 5:1 (1956): 1–23, whose position is endorsed by Raphael Sealey, "The Revolution of 411," in Sealey, *Essays in Greek Politics* (New York: Manyland Books, 1967), 111–32 (at 124–32), and has more recently been reasserted by Ralph Gallucci, "Relations between Athens and its Fleet in 411/10 BC," in *Text and Tradition: Studies in Greek History and Historiography in Honor of Mortimer H. Chambers*, ed. Ronald Mellor and Lawrence A. Tritle (Claremont, CA: Regina Books, 1999), 183–202, who all suppose that the thetes were allowed to vote in the assembly, with Peter J. Rhodes, "The Five Thousand in the

Athenian Revolutions of 411 B.C.," *JHS* 92 (1972): 115–27; and Andrewes, *HCT*, V 323–30, who rightly think this implausible. Then, see Kagan, *Fall*, 202–5; Heftner, *Umsturz*, 280–312; and Hornblower, *CT*, III 1032–36. I do not find plausible the contention of Harris, "The Constitution of the Five Thousand," 257–76, that the arrangements for "the time to come" proposed by the *anagrapheîs* were implemented at this time. Serious constitutional deliberations: Osborne, "Changing the Discourse," 251–72 (esp. 256–72), reprinted with an addendum in Osborne, *AAD*, 267–88 (esp. 273–88), and Shear, *Polis and Revolution*, 41–60. Cf. Munn, *SH*, 146, who is inclined to credit the self-serving testimony of a son of one of the *katalogeîs* ([Lys.] 20.13) who claims that his father and his colleagues registered nine thousand Athenians as members of the Five Thousand.

47. Flight of Peisander and Alexicles to Deceleia: Thuc. 8.98.1, Lys. 7.4, and Lycurg. *Leoc.* 115 with Andrewes, *HCT*, V 340; Kagan, *Fall*, 207; Heftner, *Umsturz*, 312–22; and Hornblower, *CT*, III 1037. Aristarchus betrays Oenoe: Thuc. 8.98.1–3 (to be read with 2.18.2), Xen. *Hell.* 1.7.28, and Lycurg. *Leoc.* 112–15 with Andrewes, *HCT*, V 340–41; Kagan, *Fall*, 207; Heftner, *Umsturz*, 312, 314, 319; and Hornblower, *CT*, III 1037–38.

48. Critias vs. the remains of Phrynichus: Craterus *FGrH* 342 F17 = Schol. Ar. *Lys.* 313, Plut. *Mor.* 834b, Lycurg. *Leoc.* 113, and Plut. *Alc.* 25.14 with Ostwald, *Sovereignty*, 402–3; Kagan, *Fall*, 207–8; Heftner, *Umsturz*, 313–14, 317–22; and Stuttard, *Nemesis*, 225–26. Critias likely to have been a member of the Four Hundred: note Lys. 13.74 and Dem. 58.67; then, cf. Harry C. Avery, "Critias and the Four Hundred," *CPh* 58:3 (July 1963): 165–67, with Gabriel Adeleye, "Critias: Member of the Four Hundred?" *TAPhA* 104 (1974): 1–9, and "Critias: From 'Moderation' to 'Radicalism,'" *Museum Africum* 6 (1977/78): 64–73. Tie with Alcibiades: Pl. *Prt.* 316a, Plut. *Alc.* 33.1. Friendship with Theramenes: Xen. *Hell.* 2.3.15.

49. Sophocles' war of words with Peisander: Ar. *Rhet.* 1419a25–30. His other reported remarks: 1374b35–1375a2 and 1416a14–17. My treatment of these three passages derives from the ingenious reconstruction provided by Michael H. Jameson, "Sophocles and the Four Hundred," *Historia* 20:5/6 (4th Quarter 1971): 541–68. Note also Stuttard, *Nemesis*, 225.

50. Indictment of Onomacles, Antiphon, and Archeptolemus; trial of the latter two; charge of treason tied to embassy; Antiphon's rhetorical focus on the overthrow of the democracy: consider Antiph. F1–6 (Thalheim) in light of Thuc. 8.68.2, Lys. 12.67, and Plut. *Mor.* 833d–834b = Craterus *FGrH* 342 F5b, and see William Scott Ferguson, "The Condemnation of Antiphon," *Mélanges Gustave Glotz* (Paris: Presses Universitaires de France, 1932), I 349–66; Andrewes, *HCT*, V 197–201; Ostwald, *Sovereignty*, 401–2; Kagan, *Fall*, 208–10; Hornblower, *CT*, III 956–58, who wonders whether what passes as fragments of the speech actually given might not derive from a later rhetorical exercise; and Shear, *Polis and Revolution*, 60–67. In this connection, see Michael J. Edwards, "Antiphon the

Revolutionary," in *Law, Rhetoric, and Comedy in Classical Athens: Essays in Honour of Douglas M. MacDowell*, ed. Douglas L. Cairns and R. A. Knox (Swansea: Classical Press of Wales, 2004), 75–86.

51. Duration of the Four Hundred and the Five Thousand: Arist. *Ath. Pol.* 33.1 and Diod. 13.38.1 with Rhodes, *CAAP*, 411–13. A little about the institutions functioning during its rule can be gleaned from Craterus *FGrH* 342 F5b = Plut. *Mor.* 833d–834b. Theramenes and recall of Alcibiades, reconciliation with the force on Samos: Thuc. 8.97.3, 98.4; Diod. 13.37.5, 38.2, 42.1–2; Nep. *Alc.* 5.4; and Plut. *Alc.* 27.1 with Hornblower, *CT*, III 1033–38. Cf. Andrewes, *HCT*, V 323–41, and see Ostwald, *Sovereignty*, 364–66; Kagan, *Fall*, 206–7; Gallucci, "Relations between Athens and its Fleet in 411/10 BC," 170–84; Heftner, *Umsturz*, 279–312; and Rhodes, *Alcibiades*, 68–69. I do not believe, as do Hatzfeld, *Alcibiade*, 254–58, and Stuttard, *Nemesis*, 226, that Critias played a prominent role at this time in securing Alcibiades' recall. See Chapter 6, note 31, in context, below.

52. Thucydides' judgment of the Five Thousand: 8.97.2. The meaning of this passage has long been disputed: for a thorough review of the secondary literature prior to the late 1960s, see Guido Donini, *La Posizione di Tucidide verso il governo dei cinquemila* (Turin: G. B. Paravia, 1969). Cf. Andrewes, *HCT*, V 331–41, and Rood, *Thucydides*, 380 (esp. n. 87), with Ostwald, *Sovereignty*, 395–97 (esp. n. 199); Kagan, *Fall*, 205–6 (with n. 55); and Hornblower, *CT*, III 1033–38. *Politeía* of Theramenes: Diod. 13.38.1–2 with Ostwald, *Sovereignty*, 364–66, 395–411. On the dearth of information concerning this *politeía*, see Rhodes, *CAAP*, 411–12.

PART III. A LUNGE FOR THE JUGULAR

Epigraph: Carl von Clausewitz, *Vom Kriege* (Hamburg: Severus Verlage, 2016), 465.

1. Peloponnesian departure from Rhodes for Chios; sojourn at Miletus while Athenians at Samos: Thuc. 8.60.2–3 with Andrewes, *HCT*, V 146–49, who makes a compelling case against supposing that Thucydides defined his winters and summers in astronomical terms rather than with regard to the observable change of seasons as they pertained to campaigning on land and at sea, which will have varied somewhat from year to year, as well as Otta Wenskus, "Thukydides VIII 29–60: Die Chronologie des Kriegswinters 412/411," *Hermes* 114:2 (1986): 245–47, and Hornblower, *CT*, III 931–32, who agree. For a spirited rejoinder, cf. W. Kendrick Pritchett, "The Solar Year of Thucydides," in Pritchett, *Thucydides' Pentakontaetia and Other Essays* (Amsterdam: J. C. Gieben, 1995), 173–204 (esp. 183–94). who argues that Thucydides' text should be emended to bring it into accord with the view that the Athenian historian aimed at astronomical, as opposed to military, precision. See also Lazenby, *PW*, 186–87, who does not address this question.

2. Chian revival, victory of sorts at sea: Thuc. 8.61. Command of the sea: 8.63.1. See

Westlake, *Individuals*, 300-301; Andrewes, *HCT*, V 149-50; Lazenby, *PW*, 187; and Hornblower, *CT*, III 933-35, 937.

3. Dercyllidas and Strombichides in the Hellespont: Thuc. 8.61.1, 62 with Andrewes, *HCT*, V 149-53; Lazenby, *PW*, 187-88; and Hornblower, *CT*, III 932-34, 936-37. Sestos (*IACP* no. 672) well-fortified: Theopompus of Chios *FGrH* 115 F390 = Strabo 13.1.22. Once a Persian base: Hdt. 9.114.2-121.1, Thuc. 1.89.2, Diod. 11.37.4-5. Abydos: *IACP* no. 765. Lampsacus: no. 748.

4. Astyochus challenges the Athenians at Samos; they do not respond: Thuc. 8.63.1-2, which should be read in light of 8.63.3-72.2. See Andrewes, *HCT*, V 153, and Hornblower, *CT*, III 938.

5. Peloponnesian discontent; both sides willing to fight when at advantage; otherwise, neither willing to take the risk: Thuc. 8.78-79 with Westlake, *Individuals*, 301-2; Andrewes, *HCT*, V 271-74; Kagan, *Fall*, 173-74; Lazenby, *PW*, 188-89; and Hornblower, *CT*, III 981-85.

6. Clearchus and the rebellion of Byzantium, inadequate Athenian response: Thuc. 8.80 with Andrewes, *HCT*, V 274-75; Kagan, *Fall*, 175-76; Lazenby, *PW*, 189; and Hornblower, *CT*, III 985-87, who rightly draws attention to Byzantium's significance. Vital importance of the grain trade for Athens and for other Aegean póleıs: Prologue, note 7, above. Delos: *IACP* no. 478. Chalcedon: no. 743. Wine and olive oil from the Mediterranean traded for cattle, slaves, honey, wax, salted fish, and, first and foremost, grain: cf. Polyb. 4.38.4-5 with Fernand Braudel, *The Mediterranean and the Mediterranean World in the Age of Philip II*, tr. Siân Reynolds (New York: Harper & Row, 1966), I 230-75 (esp. 230-59), 328-32, 570-606. Taxation on goods in transit: Alexander Rubel, "Hellespontophylakes—Zöllner am Bosporos? Überlegungen zur Fiskalpolitik des attischen Seebundes (*IG* I³ 61)," *Klio* 83:1 (2001): 39-51, and Vincent Gabrielsen, "Trade and Tribute: Byzantion and the Black Sea Straits," in *The Black Sea in Antiquity: Regional and Interregional Economic Exchanges*, ed. Vincent Gabrielsen and John Lund (Arrhus: Arrhus University Press, 2007), 287-324 (esp. 287-97, 308-11).

7. Alcibiades' recall, Tissaphernes' niggardliness, Astyochus and Dorieus, the fury of those in the Peloponnesian force, Persian garrison at Miletus expelled, Lichas' chagrin: Thuc. 8.83-84, which should be read with an eye to what Plutarch (*Nic.* 9.4) reports concerning the Spartan *baktēría*. Note, in this particular connection, Xen. *An.* 2.3.11 and Plut. *Lyc.* 11, *Them.* 11.3, *Lys.* 15.7. The timetable for the garrison expulsions at Cnidus and Antandrus is uncertain—though the latter event is said to have been a reaction to Tissaphernes' failure to deliver the fleet promised: Thuc. 8.108.4-109.1 and Diod. 13.42.4. See Westlake, *Individuals*, 303-4; Andrewes, *HCT*, V 278-80; Kagan, *Fall*, 179 (with n. 79); Lazenby, *PW*, 189-90; Hornblower, *CT*, III 989-96; and Hyland, *PI*, 81-86.

8. Mindarus succeeds Astyochus; Astyochus, Hermocrates, Milesians, Tissaphernes' envoy Gaulites journey to Sparta; Hermocrates' plight: Thuc. 8.85, to be read with Xen. *Hell.* 1.1.27-31, where considerable chronological confusion is

evident, and Diod. 13.63.1, which refers back to Hermocrates' deposition and banishment in order to make sense of his subsequent conduct in Sicily. Diocles triumphant: Arist. *Pol.* 1304a27, Diod. 13.34.6. In discussing the reforms he introduced, Diodorus (13.33.2–3, 35) confuses the Syracusan demagogue with a lawgiver of that name (quite possibly a Corinthian) who lived in the archaic period. On the timetable for Hermocrates' deposition and banishment, cf. Henry D. Westlake, "Hermocrates the Syracusan," *BRL* 41 (1958): 239–68 (at 259–62, esp. 259 n. 1), reprinted in Westlake, *Essays on the Greek Historians and Greek History* (Manchester: Manchester University Press, 1969), 174–202 (at 192–96, esp. 193 n. 38), with Andrewes, *HCT*, V 280–85; Kagan, *Fall*, 180 (with n. 81); Krentz, *Xenophon*, 102–5; Lazenby, *PW*, 190; and Hornblower, *CT*, III 996–99. On the impact of the testimony delivered at Lacedaemon, see Lewis, *SP*, 110–14, and Hyland, *PI*, 85. For an examination of Thucydides' assessment of Astyochus, see Westlake, *Individuals*, 290–307.

CHAPTER 5. THE HELLESPONT

Epigraph: Aelian *NA* 7.24.

1. Mindarus' forbearance; Tissaphernes, the Spartiates Philippos and Hippocrates, Alcibiades, and the Phoenician fleet at Aspendus: Thuc. 8.87.1–89.1, 99.1; Diod. 13.36.5, 37.2–5, 38.4–5, 41.4, 42.4, 46.6 (whence comes the number three hundred); and Plut. *Alc.* 25.4. Cf. Isoc. 16.18. On the *epistoleús* as the second-in-command, see Pollux 1.96, and note Xen. *Hell.* 2.17, 6.2.25. In this connection, see Hatzfeld, *Alcibiade*, 250–54, and Andrewes, *HCT*, V 289–94 (esp. 292–93), who rightly raises the question what the Persians really wanted this fleet to achieve. Note also Kagan, *Fall*, 211–14; Briant, *CA*, 593, 596–97; Kallett, *MCPT*, 274–77; Lazenby, *PW*, 190–91; Hornblower, *CT*, III 1005–7; Rhodes, *Alcibiades*, 67–68; Stuttard, *Nemesis*, 220–21; and Hyland, *PI*, 77–81, who takes up the question posed by Andrewes. Hippocrates *epistoleús*: Xen. *Hell.* 1.1.23. He was later made harmost of Chalcedon: Diod. 13.66.2. That Lichas died at Miletus we can infer from Thucydides' report that, when he passed away, the citizens of that *pólis* refused to allow the Lacedaemonians to bury him where they wished: 8.84.5. There is an inscription from Thasos, dated to 398/7, mentioning an árchōn there named Lichas son of Arcesilaus: *SEG* 33.702. That the *súmboulos* of 411 is somehow linked to the árchōn in question—who might be a Thasian guest-friend or even a grandson—there can be little doubt. The supposition that he was the same man leaves open the question what the elderly Spartiate was doing at Miletus in or after 397. The passage from Thucydides cited above makes the most sense from both an historical and a literary point of view if Lichas' death followed not long after his chastisement of the Milesians for expelling the Persian garrison. Cf. Jean Pouilloux and François Salviat, "Lichas, Lacédémonien, archonte à Thasos et le livre VIII de Thucydide," *CRAI* 172:2 (1983):

376–403, with Paul Cartledge, "A New Lease of Life for Lichas son of Arkesi-las?" *LCM* 9 (1984): 98–102. See also Hornblower, *CT*, III 995–96. Regarding Phaselis, see *IACP* no. 942.

2. The fleet and policy more generally a question for the King, expenditures made on the fleet, advantage to be gained from its deployment: Andrewes, *HCT*, V, 292–93; Briant, *CA*, 596–97; and Hyland, *PI*, 77–79, 88–90. Notorious nig-gardliness of the Persian Great Kings: *Hell. Oxy.* 22 (Chambers) with Briant, *CA*, 594–96.

3. The fact that the Persian fleet promised never advanced beyond Aspendus has given rise to considerable discussion: cf. Thuc. 8.87 with 58.6 and 78, and see Diod. 13.38.4–5, 46.6 with *AD* nos. 5, 7–8 = *TADAE* nos. A6.7, A6.10–A6.11 (which, some think, should be read in light of *TADAE* nos A4.5 and A5.5), and see D. G. K. Taylor, "The Bodleian Letters: Text and Translation," and Christo-pher J. Tuplin, "The Bodleian Letters: Commentary," in *AhW*, I 21–49 (at 30–31, 36–39), 61–283 (at 111–30, 180–216). Then, cf. David M. Lewis, "The Phoeni-cian Fleet in 411," *Historia* 7:4 (October 1958): 392–97, reprinted in Lewis, *Selected Papers in Greek and Near Eastern History*, ed. Peter J. Rhodes (Cam-bridge: Cambridge University Press, 1997), 362–68, and *SP*, 133–34, who accords weight to Diodorus' testimony and who is inclined to read the corre-spondence cited above in this context, with Joachim F. Quack, "Zur Datierung der Aršama-Dokumente auf Leder," in *Diwan: Studies in the History and Culture of the Ancient Near East and the Eastern Mediterranean*, ed. Carsten Binder, Hen-ning Börm, and Andreas Luther (Duisburg: Wellem Verlag, 2016), 53–64, who argues that *AD* nos. 5, 7–8 = *TADAE* nos. A6.7, A6.10–A6.11 date to the after-math of Megabyzus' installation of Arsames as satrap in or soon after 454; and see Andrewes, *HCT*, V 289–93, 455–56; Lazenby, *PW*, 190–91; Stephen Ruz-icka, *Trouble in the West: Egypt and the Persian Empire, 525–332 BCE* (Oxford: Oxford University Press, 2012), 36–37 (with notes 3–8); Christopher Tuplin, "Aršāma: Prince and Satrap," in *AhW*, 3–72 (at 64–72); and Stuttard, *Nemesis*, 221–22, who suspect that Lewis is right on both counts, as do I. Cf., however, Donald Lateiner, "Tissaphernes and the Phoenician Fleet (Thucydides 8.87)," *TAPhA* 106 (1976): 267–90; Kagan, *Fall*, 212–13; Hartmut Erbse, *Thukydides-Interpretationen* (Berlin: de Gruyter, 1989), 20–22; Briant, *CA*, 596–97; Cawk-well, *GW*, 153–55; and Hornblower, *CT*, III 1004–7, who prefer Thucydides' hypothesis to the supposition, supported by Diodorus, that the fleet was needed elsewhere, as well as Hyland, *PI*, 81–91, who argues that the fleet's redeploy-ment was a response to the expulsion of the Persian garrisons at Miletus and Cnidus. As Hyland acknowledges, however, the latter expulsion may well have taken place after and in reaction to the decision to redeploy the Phoenician fleet, as Diodorus (13.42.4) asserts.

4. Fleet remains at Aspendus, subvention promised left unpaid, Mindarus decides to head for the Hellespont: Thuc. 8.87.1, 99.1, Diod. 13.38.3–7. See also 13.41.4,

42.4, 46.6. The difficulty in which Tissaphernes found himself and the apparent incompatibility between the clear thinking imputed to him by Thucydides and what he actually did is, I suspect, less a reflection of error on Thucydides' part regarding the man's aim than of the fact that the satrap was in the end, for all of his freedom of maneuver, an implementer of royal policy: cf. Henry D. Westlake, "Tissaphernes in Thucydides," CQ n.s. 35:1 (1985): 43–54, reprinted in Westlake, Studies, 166–80.

5. Mindarus heads for the Hellespont followed by Thrasyllus: Thuc. 8.99–103 and Diod. 13.38.5–39.1 (which should be read with Xen. Hell. 1.1.2). Cf. Diod. 13.38.6 with 39.3, and see Andrewes, HCT, V 341–51; Kagan, Fall, 214–18; AT, 97, 104–5; Lazenby, PW, 195–96; Hornblower, CT, III 1039–47; and Stuttard, Nemesis, 226–27. Extraction of funds: Thuc. 8.101.1, which should be read in light of the secondary literature on Chian staters cited in Chapter 2, note 12, above. Cf. Hutchinson, Attrition, 177–79, who is far too willing to make excuses for Thrasyllus. The fact that Thrasyllus was assigned fifty-five ships and Thrasybulus, five indicates that the former was in charge and not, as Buck, Thrasybulus, 31–32, asserts, the latter. Eresus I visited on 15 April 2022. It is hemmed in by mountains. The soil on the mountainsides is volcanic and unsuited to growing even scrub. Ottoman withdrawal to port in late August or early September: John Guilmartin, Gunpowder and Galleys: Changing Technology and Mediterranean Warfare at Sea in the Sixteenth Century (Cambridge: Cambridge University Press, 1980), 104–5, and Philip Williams, Empire and Holy War: The Galley and Maritime Conflict between the Hapsburg and Ottoman Empires (London: I. B. Tauris, 2014), 226. On the months fit for seaborne transit, see also the evidence collected in Rahe, PC, Chapter 4, note 45. Icarus (IACP, 740 with nos. 480–81), Tenedos (no. 793), Sigeum (no. 791), Rhoeteum (no. 790), and Elaeus (no. 663).

6. Obstacles to moving upstream in the Hellespont and Bosporus: Jamie Morton, The Role of the Physical Environment in Ancient Greek Seafaring (Leiden: Brill, 2001), 40–45, 48–51, 85–90, 152, 237–38, 242–43, 258–61, and James Beresford, The Ancient Sailing Season (Leiden: Brill, 2013), 45–52, 79–83, 101. See also Appendix 2.

7. Argument against Mycenaean ability to journey by sea from the Mediterranean to the Black Sea: Rhys Carpenter, "The Greek Penetration of the Black Sea," AJA 52:1 (January–March 1948): 1–10. The experience imputed to Jason's Argonauts: Pind. Pyth. 4.116–223 (esp. 199–206), Ap. Rhod. Argon. 1.925–35. That of their late twentieth-century imitators: Tim Severin, The Jason Voyage: The Quest for the Golden Fleece (New York: Simon and Schuster, 1985), passim (esp. 77–112). Lemnos (IACP 756–57 with nos. 502–3), Imbros (no. 483), and Samothrace (no. 515).

8. Peloponnesians at Abydos: Thuc. 8.103.1. Athenians delay at Elaeus for five days: 8.103.3, Diod. 13.39.2–3.

9. Both sides approach Cynossema: Thuc. 8.104.1 and Diod. 13.39.3 with

Andrewes, *HCT*, V 351–54; *AT*, 81–83; and Hornblower, *CT*, III 1047–49. I myself have some experience of the power of the current at Cynossema. In the summer of 1985, I accompanied my former tutorial partner Peter Simpson in a small motorboat as he attempted in vain to swim the narrows from Europe to Asia. I have also profited from conversations with my late friend Patrick Leigh Fermor, who was in magnificent condition when he managed this feat on 13 October 1984, some five months before his seventieth birthday.

On the limits to human stamina as they apply to long-duration rowing, see John Coates, "Human Mechanical Power Sustainable in Rowing a Ship for Long Periods of Time," and Harry Rossiter and Brian Whipp, "Paleo-Bioenergetics: Clue to the Maximum Sustainable Speed of a Trireme under Oar," in *Trireme Olympias: The Final Report: Sea Trials 1992–4, Conference Papers 1998*, ed. Boris Rankov (Oxford: Oxbow Books, 2012), 161–68 (especially the latter). The speed that could be sustained by triremes over a great many hours is in dispute: note *AT*, 102–6, and see Timothy Shaw, "From the Golden Horn to Heraclea: Duration of the Passage in Calm Weather" and "The Performance of Ancient Triremes in Wind and Waves," and Boris Rankov, "On the Speed of Ancient Oared Ships: The Crossing of L. Aemilius Paullus from Brindisi to Corfu in 168 BC," in *Trireme Olympias: The Final Report*, 63–75, 145–51, who think that it was possible for a well-trained crew of young men to keep up a pace of seven knots or more. Cf., however, Herman Wallinga, "Xenophon on the Speed of Triremes," in ibid. 152–54, who thinks that, even at their fastest, the triremes of the Greeks, when rowed, could not maintain anything like the speed suggested by Shaw and Rankov and who calls into question the testimony of Xen. *An.* 6.4.2. On the veracity of Xenophon's account of the journey from Byzantium to Heraclea on the Euxine, I am inclined to side with Shaw—although, as is evident in my narrative above, I am fully persuaded that Wallinga is correct in supposing that, in dashing (largely, under the cover of darkness) from Arginusae to the Hellespont, Mindarus in 411 did not follow the Anatolian shore into and around the Adramyttium bay but slipped across its mouth and thereby took the shorter of the two available routes, rowing ninety-five rather than one hundred twenty-four nautical miles in the time allotted. Moreover, the case made by Ian Whitehead, "*Tri-ereis* Under Oar and Sail," in ibid. 155–60, against the supposition of Rankov and Shaw that the language deployed in Xen. *An.* 6.4.2 rules out the use of sail as a supplement to rowing seems to me to be dispositive; and his essay has the virtue that it is sensitive to the limits of human endurance. Absent adverse winds, but without the advantage of favorable winds, the fastest trireme in Athens' fleet, manned by the strongest and best-trained of her rowers, is said to have managed to keep up a pace of six knots or slightly more over thirty-plus hours while rowing the one hundred eighty-four nautical miles that separated the Peiraeus from Mytilene: *AT*, 95–96. This Thucydides (3.49.2–4) regards as a signal accomplishment. If we entertain the possibility that the "long" or "very long day" mentioned by Xenophon at *An.* 6.4.2 extended twenty-one hours or more, the trireme that he describes will have covered the one hundred twenty-nine nautical miles separating Byzantium from Heraclea at much the same pace: *AT*, 102–4. No fleet—certainly, none made up of triremes powered by ordinary, tolerably well-trained oarsmen—could come close to such a feat, especially if the circumstances were unpropitious.

10. Battle of Cynossema: Thuc. 8.104–5 and Diod. 13.39.2–40.4 with Andrewes, *HCT*, V 351–54; *AT*, 81–83; and Hornblower, *CT*, III 1047–49. Diodorus' account of events in the Greek East subsequent to the Sicilian expedition: 13.36.1–39.1. Polybius' praise for Ephorus' naval battle narratives: 12.25.F1 = Ephorus *FGrH* 70 T20. Cf. Lazenby, *PW*, 196–98, who dwells on Diodorus' errors and denies that the two accounts can be reconciled, with Kagan, *Fall*, 218–24, who highlights the difference in perspective of the two authors and attempts, with considerable success, to effect a reconciliation, and see Hutchinson, *Attrition*, 179–82, who makes good use of both accounts. On Ephorus generally, see the secondary literature collected in Rahe, *SR*, Introduction, n. 8. On Diodorus, see Rahe, *SSPW*, Chapter 2 (with notes 5–8). For the suggestion that Diodorus' account of this derives ultimately from the Oxyrhynchus historian, see Bleckmann, *Niederlage*, 242–47. Thucydides' failure to mention the current is a genuine defect.

11. The importance of the battle at Cynossema: Thuc. 8.106 and Diod. 13.40.5 with Andrewes, *HCT*, V 353–54; Kagan, *Fall*, 224–25; Lazenby, *PW*, 198; Hutchinson, *Attrition*, 182–83; and Hornblower, *CT*, III 1049–50.

12. Cyzicus and Elaeus: Thuc. 8.107, Diod. 13.40.5. Agesandridas' fleet summoned from Euboea: Thuc. 8.107.2, Diod. 13.41.1. Pharnabazus' generosity: Hyland, *PI*, 91–92. See Kagan, *Fall*, 225; Lazenby, *PW*, 198–99; and Hutchinson, *Attrition*, 183.

13. Thucydides' final words: 8.108–9 with Andrewes, *HCT*, V 355–58, and Hornblower, *CT*, III 1050–54. Cf. Hugo Montgomery, *Gedanke und Tat: Zur Erzählungstechnik bei Herodot, Thukydides, Xenophon, und Arrian* (Lund: C. W. K. Gleerup, 1965), 93–94; John A. Wettergreen, "On the End of Thucydides' Narrative," *Interpretation* 9:1 (August 1980): 93–110; Haruo Konishi, "Thucydides' *History* as a Finished Piece," *LCM* 12 (1987): 5–7; Steven Forde, *The Ambition to Rule: Alcibiades and the Politics of Imperialism in Thucydides* (Ithaca, NY: Cornell University Press, 1989), 171 n. 43; Stewart Flory, "The Death of Thucydides and the Motif of 'Land on Sea,'" in *Nomodeiktes: Greek Studies in Honor of Martin Ostwald*, ed. Ralph M. Rosen and Joseph Farrell (Ann Arbor: University of Michigan Press, 1993), 113–23 (at 116); Gregory Crane, *The Blinded Eye: Thucydides and the New Written Word* (Lanham, MD: Rowman & Littlefield, 1996), 256; and Munn, *SH*, 323–27, who speculate that Thucydides stopped where he did deliberately, with Rood, *Thucydides*, 282–84. For a brief but pointed reflection on Thucydides' achievement, see ibid. 285–93. It is worth

noting that Diodorus (13.42.4) treats the incident at Antandrus as a response to the news that the Persian fleet had headed back to Phoenicia. Halicarnassus: *IACP* no. 886. In the next few paragraphs, I draw on Paul A. Rahe, "What Sort of Historian Was Xenophon?" in *Governing Oneself and Others: On Xenophon of Athens*, ed. Charlotte C. S. Thomas (Macon, GA: Mercer University Press, 2024), 117–50. The overlapping material is reprinted here with the permission of Mercer University Press.

14. Continuators considered: see Guido Schepens, "L'Apogée de l'archè spartiate comme époque historique dans l'historiographie grecque du début du IVᵉ siècle av. J.-C.," *AncSoc* 24 (1993): 169–204; Roberto Nicolai, "Thucydides Continued," in *Brill's Companion to Thucydides*, ed. Antonios Rengakos and Antonis Tsakmakis (Leiden: Brill, 2006), 693–719, which is useful but does not do full justice to Thucydides' impact on Xenophon, Theopompus, Cratippus, and—if, as some suppose, he is not to be identified with Theopompus or Cratippus—the Oxyrhynchus historian; Christopher J. Tuplin, "Continuous Histories (*Hellenica*)," in *A Companion to Greek and Roman Historiography*, ed. John Marincola (Malden, MA: Blackwell, 2009), 159–70; and Nino Luraghi, "Xenophon's Place in Fourth-Century Greek Historiography," in *The Cambridge Companion to Xenophon*, ed. Michael A. Flower (Cambridge: Cambridge University Press, 2017), 84–100. That, in and after the fourth century, Thucydides was far more widely read than mentioned is now evident: Roberto Nicolai, "*Ktema es aei*: Aspetti della fortuna di Tucidide nel mondo antico," *RIFC* 123 (1995): 5–26, reprinted in an English translation as " "*Ktêma es aei*: Aspects of of the Reception of Thucydides in the Ancient World," in *Thucydides: Oxford Readings in Classical Studies*, ed. Jeffrey S. Rusten (Oxford: Oxford University Press, 2009), 381–404; and Simon Hornblower, "The Fourth-Century and Hellenistic Reception of Thucydides," *JHS* 115 (1995): 47–68, reprinted in revised form in Hornblower, *Thucydidean Themes* (Oxford: Oxford University Press, 2011), 286–322. That Theopompus was, like Ephorus, a younger contemporary of Cratippus and Xenophon is now clear: Michael Attyah Flower, *Theopompus of Chios: History and Rhetoric in the Fourth Century BC* (Oxford: Clarendon Press, 1994), 11–29 (esp. 11–17, 27–29).

15. Spartan secretiveness: Thuc. 5.68.2. Xenophon and Sparta: Gerald Proietti, *Xenophon's Sparta: An Introduction* (Leiden: E. J. Brill, 1987); Christopher J. Tuplin, *The Failings of Empire: A Reading of Xenophon Hellenica 2.3.11–7.5.27* (Stuttgart: Franz Steiner Verlag, 1993); and Michael A. Flower, "Xenophon as a Historian," and Paul Christesen, "Xenophon's Views on Sparta," in *The Cambridge Companion to Xenophon*, 301–22, 376–99; as well as Noreen Humble, *Xenophon of Athens: A Socratic on Sparta* (Cambridge: Cambridge University Press, 2021).

16. Xenophon's reputation: Tim Rood, "Redeeming Xenophon: Historiographical

Reception and the Transhistorical," *Classical Receptions Journal* 5:2 (2013): 199–211, and "Xenophon's Changing Fortunes in the Modern World," in *The Cambridge Companion to Xenophon*, 435–48.

17. See Barthold Georg Niebuhr, "Über Xenophons Hellenik," *RhM* 1 (1827): 194–98, reprinted in an expanded form in Niebuhr, *Kleine historische und philologische Schriften* (Bonn: E. Weber, 1828–43), 464–82, and Thomas Babington Macaulay, "History," *Edinburgh Review* 47:94 (May 1828): 331–67 (at 342–43), reprinted in Macaulay, *Critical, Historical and Miscellaneous Essays* (New York: Hurd & Houghton, 1860), I 376–432 (at 393–94).

18. Cf. Eduard Schwartz, "Quellenuntersuchungen zur griechischen Geschichte II," *RhM* n.f. 44 (1889): 161–93, reprinted in Schwartz, *Gesammelte Schriften II: Zur Geschichte und Literatur der Hellenen und Römer* (Berlin: Walter de Gruyter, 1956), 136–74, with Leo Strauss, "The Spirit of Sparta or the Taste of Xenophon," *Social Research* 6:4 (November 1939): 502–36, who was the first to challenge the scholarly consensus in this particular; and see William E. Higgins, *Xenophon the Athenian: The Problem of the Individual and the Society of the Polis* (Albany: State University of New York Press, 1977), 99–127; Proietti, *Xenophon's Sparta*; and Christopher J. Tuplin, *The Failings of Empire*; "Xenophon, Sparta and the *Cyropaedia*," in *The Shadow of Sparta*, ed. Anton Powell and Stephen Hodkinson (New York: Routledge, 1994), 127–81; and "Xenophon and Athens," in *The Cambridge Companion to Xenophon*, 338–59. Then, consider Noreen Humble: "*Sophrosyne* and the Spartans in Xenophon," in *Sparta: New Perspectives*, ed. Stephen Hodkinson and Anton Powell (Swansea: Classical Press of Wales, 1999), 339–53, in light of Humble, "Was Sōphrosynē Ever a Spartan Virtue?" in *Sparta: Beyond the Mirage*, ed. Anton Powell and Stephen Hodkinson (Swansea: The Classical Press of Wales, 2002), 85–109, and see Humble, "The Author, Date and Purpose of Chapter 14 in the *Lakedaimoniōn Politeia*," in *Xenophon and his World*, ed. Christopher J. Tuplin (Stuttgart: Franz Steiner Verlag, 2004), 215–28; "Why the Spartans Fight So Well . . . Even in Disorder: Xenophon's View," in *Sparta and War*, ed. Stephen Hodkinson and Anton Powell (Swansea: Classical Press of Wales, 2006), 219–33; "The Renaissance Reception of Xenophon's *Spartan Constitution*: Preliminary Observations," in *Xenophon: Ethical Principles and Historical Enquiry*, ed. Fiona Hobden and Christopher Tuplin (Leiden: Brill, 2012), 63–88; "True History: Xenophon's *Agesilaus* and the Encomiastic Genre," in *Xenophon and Sparta*, ed. Anton Powell and Nicolas Richer (Swansea: Classical Press of Wales, 2020), 291–318; and *Xenophon of Athens*, passim, as well as Christesen, "Xenophon's Views on Sparta," 376–99. For exemplary expositions of the view once in vogue, see E. M. Soulis, *Xenophon and Thucydides: A Study on the Historical Methods of Xenophon in the Hellenica with Special Reference to the Influence of Thucydides* (Athens: s. n., 1972); George Cawkwell, "Introduction," in Xenophon, *A History of My Times (Hellenica)*, tr. Rex Warner (Harmondsworth: Penguin Books, 1978), 7–46, as

well as Cawkwell's annotations to the text; and Cartledge, *Agesilaos*, 55–73 (esp. 55–65), 78, 186, 190, 217, 234, 242–43, 262, 296–98, 305, 307, 328, 343, 348, 362, 379–80, 388, 400–401, 413–20 (esp. 413–18, 420). In my opinion, Ernst Badian, "Xenophon the Athenian," in *Xenophon and his World*, 33–55, errs when he goes to the opposite extreme and contends that Xenophon distorts the historical record to make his fatherland look good.

19. Cf. Arnold Hugh Martin Jones, "The Athenian Democracy and its Critics," *Cambridge Historical Journal* 11:1 (1953): 1–26, reprinted in Jones, *Athenian Democracy* (Baltimore, MD: Johns Hopkins University Press, 1957), 41–72; Moses I. Finley, *Democracy Ancient and Modern* (Brunswick, NJ: Rutgers University Press, 1973); and Josiah Ober, *Political Dissent in Ancient Athens: Intellectual Critics of Popular Rule* (Princeton, NJ: Princeton University Press, 1998), who treat all or nearly all of these figures as partisans whose criticism of the Athenian democracy is unworthy of serious consideration, with Edward M. Harris, "Was All Criticism of Athenian Democracy Necessarily Anti-Democratic?" in *Democrazia e antidemocrazia nel mondo greco*, ed. Umberto Bultrighini (Alessandria: Edizioni dell'Orso, 2005), 11–23. For exceptions to the new rule, who are still inclined to sniff out partisanship where others now discern honest criticism worthy of consideration, but who nonetheless acknowledge Xenophon's keen intelligence, see Frances Pownall, *Lessons from the Past: The Moral Use of History in Fourth-Century Prose* (Ann Arbor: University of Michigan Press, 2004), 65–112; Vincent Azoulay, *Xenophon and the Graces of Power: A Greek Guide to Political Manipulation*, tr. Angela Krieger (Swansea: Classical Press of Wales, 2018); Vivienne J. Gray, *Xenophon on Government* (Cambridge: Cambridge University Press, 2007), passim (esp. 217–21); and Anton Powell, "'One Little *Skytalē*': Xenophon, Truth-Telling in his Major Works, and Spartan Imperialism," in *Xenophon and Sparta*, 1–63, whose attempt to restore, refine, and amplify the thesis of Schwartz makes no mention of the secondary literature, critical of that thesis, cited in note 18, above.

20. On Xenophon's skill, on his subtlety as a writer, and on his political and moral discernment, see the secondary literature cited in note 18, above, and consider the later work of Leo Strauss: *On Tyranny: An Interpretation of Xenophon's Hiero* (New York: Mansfield Centre Martino Publishing, 1948), *Xenophon's Socratic Discourse: An Interpretation of the Oeconomicus* (Ithaca, NY: Cornell University Press, 1970), and *Xenophon's Socrates* (Ithaca, NY: Cornell University Press, 1972), who was the pioneer in the treatment of Xenophon as a thinker worthy of study. Then, see William P. Henry, *Greek Historical Writing: A Historiographical Essay Based on Xenophon's Hellenica* (Chicago: Argonaut, 1967); Bodil Due, *The Cyropaedia: Xenophon's Aims and Methods* (Aarhus: Aarhus University Press, 1989); Vivienne J. Gray, *The Character of Xenophon's Hellenica* (Baltimore: Johns Hopkins University Press, 1989); John Dillery, *Xenophon and the History of his Times* (London: Routledge, 1995); Christopher Nadon, *Xenophon's Prince:*

Republic and Empire in the Cyropaedia (Berkeley: University of California Press, 2001); the essays collected in *The Long March: Xenophon and the Ten Thousand,* ed. Robin Lane Fox (New Haven, CT: Yale University Press, 2004), and in *Xenophon and his World*; Vivienne J. Gray, "Le Socrate de Xénophon et la Démocratie," tr. Louis-André Dorion and G. Mosquera, *EPh* 69:2 (May 2004): 141–76; John W. I. Lee, *A Greek Army on the March: Soldiers and Survival in Xenophon's Anabasis* (Cambridge: Cambridge University Press, 2007); the essays collected in *Xenophon: Oxford Readings in the Classical Studies,* ed. Vivienne J. Gray (Oxford: Oxford University Press, 2010); Michael A. Flower, *Xenophon's Anabasis, or the Expedition of Cyrus* (Oxford University Press, 2012); the essays collected in *Xenophon: Ethical Principles and Historical Inquiry*; Eric Buzzetti, *Xenophon the Socratic Prince: The Argument of the Anabasis of Cyrus* (London: Palgrave MacMillan, 2014); James Tatum, *Xenophon's Imperial Fiction: On the Education of Cyrus* (Princeton, NJ: Princeton University Press, 2016); Paul Ludwig, "Xenophon as a Socratic Reader of Thucydides," in *The Oxford Handbook of Thucydides,* ed. Ryan Balot, Sara Forsdyke, and Edith Foster (Oxford: Oxford University Press, 2017), 515–30; the essays collected in *The Cambridge Companion to Xenophon* and in *Plato and Xenophon: Comparative Studies,* ed. Gabriel Danzig, David Johnson, and Donald Morrison (Leiden: Brill, 2018); Thomas L. Pangle, *The Socratic Way of Life: Xenophon's "Memorabilia"* (Chicago: University of Chicago Press, 2018), and *Socrates' Founding: Political Philosophy in Xenophon's "Economist," "Symposium," and "Apology"* (Chicago: University of Chicago Press, 2020); the essays collected in *Xenophon and Sparta*; and Matthew R. Christ, *Xenophon and the Athenian Democracy: The Education of an Elite Citizenry* (Cambridge: Cambridge University Press, 2020).

21. Contrast Thucydides' eulogy of Themistocles (1.138.3) with that he accorded Pericles (2.65) and compare his statement of his own aim (1.22.4) with the comparable passage in Herodotus (Proem); then, note Dion. Hal. *Thuc.* 7–8; and see Paul A. Rahe, "Thucydides as Educator," in *The Past as Prologue: The Importance of History to the Military Profession,* ed. Williamson Murray and Richard Hart Sinnreich (Cambridge: Cambridge University Press, 2006), 95–110. I doubt that Thucydides' prime concern was the instruction of historians—though this was surely a byproduct of his effort: cf. Lisa Kallet, "Thucydides' Workshop of History and Utility Outside the Text," with Peter Hunt, "Warfare," both in *Brill's Companion to Thucydides,* 335–68, 385–413.

22. Diodorus on the period covered by the *Hellenica* of Theopompus of Chios and on the number of books he devoted to that period: 13.42.5, 14.84.7. Exceptional diligence and accuracy: Theopompus of Chios *FGrH* 115 F26, T28a with Flower, *Theopompus of Chios,* passim (esp. 17–19, 63–66, 184–210). See also, from the postscript added to the paperback edition published in 2006, 257–58, and Riccardo Vattuone, "Looking for the Invisible: Theopompus and the Roots

of Historiography," in *Between Thucydides and Polybius: The Golden Age of Greek Historiography*, ed. Giovanni Parmeggiani (Washington, DC: Harvard University Press, 2014), 7–37.

23. Xenophon and history: cf. Thuc. 1.21–22 (esp. 22.4) with Arist. *Poet.* 1451b1–12, and ponder the significance of Xen. *Hell.* 1.1.1 and 7.5.27 in light of the brief remarks of Leo Strauss, "Greek Historians," *RMeta* 21:4 (June 1968): 656–66 (esp. 660–63); Proietti, *Xenophon's Sparta*, ix–xxii (esp. xvi–xviii); John Marincola, "Genre Convention, and Innovation in Greco-Roman Historiography," in *The Limits of Historiography: Genre and Narrative in Ancient Historical Texts*, ed. Christina Shuttleworth Kraus (Leiden: Brill, 1999), 281–324 (esp. 311); Ludwig, "Xenophon as a Socratic Reader of Thucydides," 515–30; and Kapellos, *XPW*. For another view, well argued and highly informative but, on this crucial point, I think wrongheaded, cf. Tim Rood, "Xenophon and Diodorus: Continuing Thucydides," in *Xenophon and his World*, 341–95.

24. Xenophon's programmatic statement: *Cyn.* 13.7.

25. For a list of Xenophon's omissions, see George E. Underhill, *A Commentary with Introduction and Appendix on the Hellenica of Xenophon* (Oxford: Clarendon Press, 1900), xxi–xxxv.

26. See Cawkwell, "Introduction," 22–46. Note also C. H. Grayson, "Did Xenophon Intend to Write History?" in *The Ancient Historian and his Materials: Essays in Honour of C. E. Stevens on his Seventieth Birthday*, ed. Barbara Levick (Westmead, Farnborough, Hants: Gregg International, 1975), 31–43; Gray, *The Character of Xenophon's Hellenica*, passim; Edmond Lévy, "L'Art de la déformation historique dans les *Helléniques* de Xénophon," in *Purposes of History: Studies in Greek Historiography from the 4th to the 2nd Centuries B.C.*, ed. Herman Verdin, Guido Schepens, and Eugénie de Keyser (Louvain: The Catholic University, 1990), 125–57; and Jean-Claude Riedinger, *Étude sur les Helléniques de Xénophon et l'histoire* (Paris: Les Belles Lettres, 1991). Although these four scholars are perceptive and pay close attention to Xenophon's subtlety as a writer, they are too prone to suppose that an author cannot display literary skill without mendacity. For a corrective, see the works of Humble and Tuplin cited in Rahe, *SR*, Chapter 1, n. 78.

27. Oxyrhynchus historian: Iain A. F. Bruce, "Introduction," in Bruce, *An Historical Commentary on the Hellenica Oxyrynchia* (Cambridge: Cambridge University Press, 1967), 1–27. On the vexed question of authorship, see Herbert Bloch, "Studies in Historical Literature of the Fourth Century B.C.: I. The *Hellenica Oxyrhynchia* and its Authorship," *HSPh* suppl. vol. I (1940): 303–41, who makes the case that the Oxyrhynchus historian was not among the historians whose names have come down to us; Bruce, "Introduction," 22–27, and Rhodes, *Alcibiades*, 73–74, who suspect that Cratippus may have been the author; and Richard Billows, "The Authorship of the *Hellenika Oxyrhynchia*," *Mouseion* 3rd

ser., 9:3 (2009): 219–38, who makes what is, in my opinion, a compelling case for Theopompus' authorship, which is dependent on his redating of the man's lifetime. The fact that the most recent comprehensive study of Theopompus independently reached a similar conclusion on the basis of the same evidence confirms Billows' redating (Flower, *Theopompus of Chios*, 11–29 [esp. 11–17, 27–29]), as does the claim of Nepos (*Alc.* 11.1) that he belonged to the generation immediately following that of Thucydides and Alcibiades. Moreover, although Flower believes, as many do, that stylistic considerations rule out Theopompus' authorship of the *Hellenica Oxyrhynchia*, his own correction of the standard depiction of the Chian historian's style belies this claim, and the two passages (Theopompus of Chios *FGrH* 115 F20, 22) that, in making his case, he juxtaposes with the surviving fragments of the Oxyrhynchus historian cannot bear the weight that he places on them: one should consider Flower, "Xenophon as a Historian," 312 (with n. 31), where Billows' argument passes unmentioned, in light of the warning issued by Peter A. Brunt, "On Historical Fragments and Epitomes," *CQ* 30:2 (1980): 477–94, and keep in mind the fact that what we think of as fragments often tell us more about the individual quoting or excerpting them than about the writer on whom he draws. In this case, they cast light chiefly on the tastes and interests of Athenaeus (12.543b–c, 14.657b–c). Our sources regarding Cratippus are few: Dion. Hal. *Thuc.* 16; Plut. *Mor.* 345d, 834c–d; Marcellin. *Vit. Thuc.* 33 = Cratippus *FGrH* 64 T1–3. Those concerning Theopompus are numerous. One sign, unmentioned by Billows, that the Oxyrhynchus historian is likely to be Theopompus is that, although much of Diodorus' narrative is ultimately derivative from the former, he lists the latter as a continuator of Thucydides and specifies the points at which his narrative begins and ends (13.42.5, 14.84.7), but never even mentions Cratippus at all. This would be even more telling if we were to suppose that Diodorus lifted this information concerning Theopompus from the pages of Ephorus (which I think unlikely)—for it would strongly suggest that, when Ephorus mentioned Thucydides' continuators, he left Cratippus off the list. The fact that the *Hellenica Oxyrhynchia* seems to have been more widely read in Egypt in the first and second centuries of the modern era than any earlier historians—apart from Herodotus, Thucydides, and Xenophon—suggests that it is highly unlikely that he is unmentioned in any of the sources subsequent to his own time, and it may be telling that both Diodorus (13.47.1) and Theopompus (*FGrH* 115 F5) treat as the second battle of Cynossema what modern scholars dependent on Xenophon call the battle of Abydos. See also Bleckmann, *Niederlage*, 19–266; and cf. Guido Schepens, "Who Wrote the *Hellenica Oxyrhynchia*? The Need for a Methodological Code," *Sileno* 27 (2001): 201–24, and Adalberto Magnelli, "Lo Storico di Ossirinco: Il più antico Continuatore delle *Storie* di Tucidide?" *RAL* 17 (2007): 41–73, with Bruno Bleckmann, *Fiktion als Geschichte: Neue Studien zum Autor der Hellenika Oxyrhynchia and zur Historiographie des vierten vorchristlichen*

Jahrhunders (Göttingen: Vanderhoeck & Ruprecht, 2006), passim (esp. 32–35, 139–43). Bleckmann, who makes a strong case for Theopompus' authorship, stands virtually alone in his low estimate of the discernment of the Oxyrhynchus historian. See Christopher Tuplin's review of *Fiktion als Geschichte*: *JHS* 128 (2008): 239–40. Bleckmann's contention that the Oxyrhynchus historian was dependent on Xenophon's *Hellenica* and wove fictions around Xenophon's account echoes an opinion regarding Theopompus' practice expressed in one passage that, in late antiquity, Eusebius of Caesarea attributed to the Neoplatonist Porphyry of Tyre: Theopompus of Chios *FGrH* 115 F21. Otherwise, it has little to recommend it. It is, of course, perfectly possible that the younger of these two historians read the *Hellenica* penned by his elder and attempted to gather evidence enabling him to improve on it, but it is by no means certain that Xenophon's composition, which was not completed until the mid-350s, entered into circulation before that of Theopompus. Although I think that the Oxyrhynchus historian often provides a more extensive and superior account of events, I would not be prepared to argue, in the spirit of Bleckmann, that the difference between the two proves that Xenophon was, at times, willing to resort to fiction, as Grayson, "Did Xenophon Intend to Write History?" 31–43, suspects. I would only suggest that Xenophon saw himself as commenting on the age in which he had lived and that Theopompus sought to treat it, in the spirit of Thucydides, comprehensively.

28. Ephorus' supposed use of the *Hellenica Oxyrhynchia*: Godfrey L. Barber, *The Historian Ephorus* (Cambridge: Cambridge University Press, 1935), 49–67, and Victor Parker, "The Historian Ephorus: His Selection of Sources," *Antichthon* 38 (2004): 29–50 (at 36–39). On the latter work's influence, direct or indirect, on Diodorus, see Gustav A. Lehmann, "Theopompea," *ZPE* 55 (1984): 19–44. Evidence that Ephorus as a universal historian may have been Diodorus' inspiration: Diod. 4.1.2–3, 16.76.5. Severe criticism directed at Ephorus: 1.39.13 = Ephorus of Cumae *FGrH* 70 F65e. See also Diod. 1.9.5 = F109, 37.4 = F65e, 39.7–13 = F65e. Cited as one source in a context in which the testimony of at least one other historian is specified or implied: Diod. 5.64.3–4 = F104, 13.54.5= F201, 60.5 = F202, 80.5= F203, 14.11.1–4 = F70, 54.4–6 = F204, 15.60.5 = F214. Cited by Diodorus as the source for a claim he adopts: 12.38.1–41.1 = F196, 13.43.3 = F199. For a welcome corrective to the scholarship that supposes that Diodorus was an uncritical and servile copyist unlikely to consult more than one source: see Kenneth S. Sacks, *Diodorus Siculus and the First Century* (Princeton, NJ: Princeton University Press, 1990).

29. Diodorus' close familiarity with Theopompus (1.1.37, 4.1.3, 7.17.1) and with his *Hellenica* in particular: 13.42.5, 14.84.7. Billows, "The Authorship of the *Hellenika Oxyrhynchia*," 219–38, suggests and Egidia Occhipinti, *The Hellenica Oxyrhynchia and Historiography: New Research Perspectives* (Leiden; Boston: Brill, 2016), 57–86, who is unaware of Billows' article, argues at length that Diodorus

had direct access to the Oxyrhynchus historian. See the review of Occhipinti's book by Christopher Tuplin, *AHB* 31 (2016): 121–30. When Diodorus cites Ephorus regarding the period addressed by Theopompus' *Hellenica*, it is either with regard to events in the Greek West or with regard to Persian conduct: 13.54.5 = Ephorus *FGrH* 70 F201, 60.5 = F202, 80.5 = F203, 14.11.1–4 = F70, 22.2 = F208, 54.4–6 = F204.

30. Isocrates trains Ephorus and Theopompus in rhetoric: Cic. *De or.* 2.13.57, 22–23.94, *Brut.* 56.204, *Orat.* 44.151, 51.172, 61.207; Diod. 4.1.3; Strabo 13.3.6; Quint. *Inst.* 2.8.11; Plut. *Mor.* 837c. Cf. Flower, *Theopompus of Chios*, 42–62, who rejects the testimony of Cicero and the other ancient writers. For my part, I am inclined to think that Cicero, who studied oratory in Athens, knew a great deal more about the history of oratory and its influence on the development of the historical craft than do modern scholars. None of this suggests that we should dismiss as merely histrionic the work of Isocrates' students: see John Marincola, "Rethinking Isocrates and Historiography," in *Between Thucydides and Polybius*, 39–61.

31. On Ephorus and his practices as an historian, note Diod. 5.1.4, 16.14.3, 76.5, and see the bibliography collected in Rahe, *SR*, Introduction, note 8, and *SFAW*, Chapter 1, note 59.

32. On distortions that can be discerned in Diodorus' narrative and their likely sources, see Christopher J. Tuplin, "Military Engagements in Xenophon's *Hellenica*," in *Past Perspectives: Studies in Greek and Roman Historical Writing*, ed. Ian S. Moxon, John D. Smart, and Anthony J. Woodman (Cambridge: Cambridge University Press, 1986), 37–66, and Vivienne J. Gray, "The Value of Diodorus Siculus for the Years 411–386 BC," *Hermes* 115:1 (1st Quarter 1987): 72–89.

33. According to Malcolm Maclaren Jr., "On the Composition of Xenophon's *Hellenica*, Parts I and II," *AJPh* 55: 2 and 3 (1934): 122–39, 249–62, the style of writing in Xen. *Hell.* 1.1.1–2.3.10 sets it apart from what follows. According to Henry, *Greek Historical Writing*, it does nothing of the sort. For the missing chronological indicator, see Chapter 6, note 19, below.

34. For a lengthy comparison and assessment of Thucydides' continuators requiring a close examination of Diodorus Siculus and the *Hellenica Oxyrhynchia* as well as of Xenophon and for considerable speculation regarding the relationship between the three, see Bleckmann, *Niederlage*, 17–266.

35. Disaster off Mount Athos: Diod. 13.41.2–3 = Ephorus *FGrH* 70 F199. Thumochares and Agesandridas reach the Hellespont, fight a skirmish: Xen. *Hell.* 1.1.1. Agesandridas becomes Mindarus' lieutenant: 1.3.17. See Kagan, *Fall*, 225–27. Cf. Lazenby, *PW*, 199, who takes Diodorus' testimony at face value. Current in the Aegean produced by the influx from the Euxine: Morton, *The Role of the Physical Environment in Ancient Greek Seafaring*, 43–44. Scyros: *IACP* no. 521.

36. Battle description: Diod. 13.45.9–46.2.

37. Ephorus' outlook as an historian and his efforts: see Guido Schepens, "Éphore sur la valeur d'autopsie (*FGrH* 70 F110 = Polybe XII 27.7)," *AncSoc* 1 (1970): 163–82, and "Historiographical Problems in Ephorus," in *Historiographia Antiqua* (Louvain: Leuven University Press, 1977), 95–118; and Pownall, *Lessons from the Past*, 113–42.

38. Dorieus, Alcibiades, Pharnabazus and the second battle in the Hellespont: Xen. *Hell.* 1.1.2–7, Theopompus of Chios *FGrH* 115 F5, Diod. 13.45–46. and Plut. *Alc.* 27.2–6 with Henry D. Westlake, "Abydos and Byzantium: The Sources for Two Episodes in the Ionian War," *MH* 42:4 (1985): 313–27 (at 314–22), reprinted in Westlake, *Studies*, 224–38 (at 225–31); Kagan, *Fall*, 227, 230–33; *AT*, 83–84; Lazenby, *PW*, 199–201; and Hutchinson, *Attrition*, 183–85, who professes a preference for Xenophon but, in fact, attempts to reconcile the two accounts. Cf. Buck, *Thrasybulus*, 33–35, who persists in assuming that Thrasybulus was in charge and who, for no good reason, attributes to him the Athenian victory produced by the timely arrival of Alcibiades, with Hatzfeld, *Alcibiade*, 264–67. For doubts as to the plausibility of the narrative found in Diodorus, see Tuplin, "Military Engagements in Xenophon's *Hellenica*," 54–55. For its outright rejection as part of a larger attempt to demonstrate that the Oxyrhynchus historian was a writer of fiction out to embroider and improve upon Xenophon's narrative, see Bleckmann, *Niederlage*, 42–56. For a defense of the Sicilian historian's account, see Peter Krentz, "Xenophon and Diodoros on the Battle of Abydos," *AHB* 3:1 (1989): 10–14; and for a vivid, imaginative, and highly plausible reconstruction of this battle, see Stuttard, *Nemesis*, 228–32. Although Xenophon is responsible for our terming this event the battle of Abydos, that phrase is a misnomer. Whether it started at Rhoeteum or Dardanus, it surely took place a considerable distance downstream from the Spartan stronghold.

39. Thrasyllus to Athens in search of reinforcements: Xen. *Hell.* 1.1.8. See also 1.1.34. Mindarus' appeal for infantrymen and ships: Diod. 13.47.2. It is important to keep in mind what Kapellos, *XPW*, 14, forgets: that triremes captured reduce the size of the enemy's fleet without adding to the size of one's own force unless one can man the hulls one has seized.

40. Garrison left at Sestos: Xen. *Hell.* 1.1.7–8. Athenian efforts at money-raising: Xen. *Hell.* 1.1.8, 12. Theramenes' endeavors: Diod. 13.47.6–8, 49.1 with Kagan, *Fall*, 233–35, and Lazenby, *PW*, 201–2. On the bridge built to link Euboea with Boeotia, see Strabo 9.2.2. Thrasybulus was—or soon became—an aficionado with regard to Thracian affairs: David F. Middleton, "Thrasyboulos' Thracian Support," *CQ* n.s. 32: (December 1982): 298–303. Pydna: *IACP* no. 544.

41. Alcibiades and Tissaphernes, imprisonment and escape: Xen. *Hell.* 1.1.9, Plut. *Alc.* 27.6–28.2 with Hatzfeld, *Alcibiade*, 267–69; Kagan, *Fall*, 235–36; Lazenby, *PW*, 202; Rhodes, *Alcibiades*, 74–75; and Stuttard, *Nemesis*, 233–34. Cf. Briant, *CA*, 593–94, and Hyland, *PI*, 94–95, who have trouble imagining Tissaphernes' collusion in the escape of Alcibiades and Mantitheus but who nonetheless

acknowledge that it is a wonder that the two could have made their way through Lydia all the way to Clazomenae unscathed and suggest that lower-level officials must have been involved. That Tissaphernes' underlings would have looked the other way on such an occasion without a wink and a nod from on high I find implausible. It is, I think, telling that Tissaphernes will later do what he can to assist Cleinias' son: Xen. *Hell.* 1.5.8-9.

42. Mindarus and the Asian shore: Diod. 13.47.2.

CHAPTER 6. THE SEA OF MARMARA AND THE BOSPORUS

Epigraph: Bernard Brodie, *Strategy in the Missile Age* (Princeton, NJ: Princeton University Press, 1959), 21.

1. Athenian flight to Cardia (*IACP* no. 665), Mindarus' redeployment at Cyzicus, Alcibiades effects a concentration of forces with an eye to staging a battle in the Sea of Marmara: Xen. *Hell.* 1.2.11-12, Diod. 13.49.2-4, Plut. *Alc.* 28.2. See Hatzfeld, *Alcibiade*, 269-70; Kagan, *Fall*, 236-37; Lazenby, *PW*, 202-3; Hutchinson, *Attrition*, 185; Rhodes, *Alcibiades*, 75; and Stuttard, *Nemesis*, 234-35.

2. Voyage via Parion (*IACP* no. 756) to Proconnesus (no. 759): Xen. *Hell.* 1.1.13 and Diod. 13.49.5-6 with Hatzfeld, *Alcibiade*, 270; Kagan, *Fall*, 237; and Hutchinson, *Attrition*, 186. The island's geostrategic importance: see Appendix 2.

3. Preparations for the battle of Cyzicus: Xen. *Hell.* 1.1.14-15, Diod. 13.49.6, and Plut. *Alc.* 28.3 with Hatzfeld, *Alcibiade*, 270-72; Kagan, *Fall*, 238; Lazenby, *PW*, 203; Hutchinson, *Attrition*, 186; Rhodes, *Alcibiades*, 75; and Stuttard, *Nemesis*, 235-36. Likely location of Chaereas' landfall: John R. Hale, *Lords of the Sea: The Epic Story of the Athenian Navy and the Birth of Democracy* (New York: Viking Penguin, 2009), 353-54. If, in teasing out the implications of Plutarch's reference to *zóphos* at *Alc.* 28.4, I posit in the narrative that follows the presence of thick fog where only driving rain, darkness, and gloom are mentioned in our sources, it is due to the fact that—from September 1984 to August 1986, when I lived in Istanbul in an apartment from which I could see the Bosporus—I frequently witnessed fog without rain on mornings in the late winter and spring but never rain without fog.

4. The battle of Cyzicus: note Xen. *Hell.* 1.1.16-18, which has Alcibiades as its focus and may for the most part be derivative from the testimony of Spartan eyewitnesses, as Krentz, *Xenophon*, 98-99, suggests. Especially for the battle at sea, see Diod. 13.50-51, Frontin. *Str.* 2.5.44-45, and Polyaen. *Strat.* 1.40.8-9, which derive from a common source; and then consider Plut. *Alc.* 28.4-9, which is an attempt to reconcile the two accounts. Note also Pl. *Menex.* 243a and Just. *Epit.* 5.4.1-3. In this connection, see Hatzfeld, *Alcibiade*, 269-73; Robert J. Littmann, "The Strategy of the Battle of Cyzicus," *TAPhA* 99 (1968): 265-72; Edmund F. Bloedow, *Alcibiades Reexamined* (Wiesbaden: F. Steiner, 1973), 46-55; Antony Andrewes, "Notion and Kyzikos: The Sources Compared," *JHS*

102 (1982): 15–25 (esp. 19–25), who suggests that Polydorus was the tiny island Arkte, which lies just off the coast of Arktonnesos opposite the promontory that marks out the northeastern boundary of the bay of Cyzicus; Kagan, *Fall*, 238–44; *AT*, 84–88; Lazenby, *PW*, 203–5; Hutchinson, *Attrition*, 186–88; and Hale, *Lords of the Sea*, 211–17. Cf. Christopher J. Tuplin, "Military Engagements in Xenophon's *Hellenica*," in *Past Perspectives: Studies in Greek and Roman Historical Writing*, ed. Ian S. Moxon, John D. Smart, and Anthony J. Woodman (Cambridge: Cambridge University Press, 1986), 37–66 (at 60–62), who entertains doubts concerning the viability of Diodorus' narrative; Vivienne J. Gray, "The Value of Diodorus Siculus for the Years 411–386 BC," *Hermes* 115:1 (1st Quarter 1987): 72–89 (at 80–84), who suspects that the Sicilian historian's account of this battle and what we find in Frontinus and Polyaenus is boilerplate derived from Ephorus; and Bleckmann, *Niederlage*, 56–72, who supposes that the Oxyrhynchus historian was Diodorus' ultimate source and thinks his reportage all too creative. If I reject their arguments, it is because the ultimate source of Diodorus' account displays a superior knowledge of the particulars—above all, the weather in the late winter and early spring, which I witnessed day after day in those seasons while residing nearby in Istanbul from 1984 to 1986, and the geography, which I examined with some care on a visit that took place in the summer of 1985. What they take to be verisimilitude I take to be an accurate report. It is now fashionable—thanks to the argument made by Kagan in the passage cited above—to suppose that Xenophon exaggerated the ascendancy of Alcibiades; to rely, instead, on a snippet from Cornelius Nepos (*Thras.*1.3), who composed biographical sketches three and a half centuries after these events; and to treat Thrasybulus on the basis of Nepos' passing remark as a more important commander than the man whose partisan he was. Cf. Buck, *Thrasybulus*, 36–39; Hutchinson, *Attrition*, 185, 188, 204; Rhodes, *Alcibiades*, 76; and Stuttard, *Nemesis*, 236–37, who echo Kagan's argument. One does not have to agree with Bleckmann's critique of the testimony of Diodorus, Ephorus, and the Oxyrhynchus historian to be impressed by the force of the case he makes for Alcibiades' preeminence in this battle: *Niederlage*, 67–72. To get a sense of the special pleading that the attempt to elevate Thrasybulus requires, note Diod. 13.49.1 in context, and cf. its interpretation in Buck, *Thrasybulus*, 38 n. 106, and Hutchinson, *Attrition*, 185, with that in Andrewes, "Notion and Kyzikos," 20 n. 12. Xenophon, who greatly admired Thrasybulus, had no doubt as to the preeminence of Alcibiades: note William E. Higgins, *Xenophon the Athenian: The Problem of the Individual and the Society of the Polis* (Albany: State University of New York Press, 1977), 122–23; then, see Gerald Proietti, *Xenophon's Sparta: An Introduction* (Leiden: E. J. Brill, 1987), 1–9. It is essential to remember that, in principle, all of the Athenian *stratēgoí* on any given campaign were equal and that they operated by consensus: Debra Hamel, *Athenian Generals: Military Authority in the Classical Period* (Leiden: Brill, 1998), 94–99. But it is also important to keep

in mind Thucydides' claim (8.82.1) that, upon electing Alcibiades a *stratēgós*, the Athenians on Samos "put him in charge of all public business." That the Athenians in this period supposed that Thrasybulus, in fact, played second fiddle to Alcibiades is crystal clear. In all likelihood, the snippet from Nepos reflects the view of a fourth-century writer, such as Ephorus, who had the good sense to admire Thrasybulus and to think less well of Alcibiades and who therefore sought, as is only natural given the human propensity for partisanship, to denigrate the accomplishments of the latter and elevate the status of the former. It is not always the best men, however, who make the most effective leaders.

5. Cyzicus, Perinthus (*IACP* no. 678), and Selymbria (no. 679): Xen. *Hell.* 1.1.18–21, Diod. 13.51.8. Chrysopolis in the territory of Chalcedon and the duties on trade that Alcibiades imposed: Xen. *Hell.* 1.1.22, Theopompus of Chios *FGrH* 115 F7, Polyb. 4.44.2–4, Diod. 13.64.2, Just. *Epit.* 5.46. Similar duties levied by the Athenians in earlier times from Byzantium: Alexander Rubel, "*Hellespontophylakes*—Zöllner am Bosporos? Überlegungen zur Fiskalpolitik des attischen Seebundes (*IG* I³ 61)," *Klio* 83:1 (2001): 39–51, and Vincent Gabrielsen, "Trade and Tribute: Byzantion and the Black Sea Straits," in *The Black Sea in Antiquity: Regional and Interregional Economic Exchanges*, ed. Vincent Gabrielsen and John Lund (Arrhus: Arrhus University Press, 2007), 287–324 (esp. 287–97, 308–11). Assignment regarding Byzantium and Chalcedon: Diod. 13.64.3, confirmed by Xen. *Hell.* 1.1.26. Thrasybulus to Thrace, Alcibiades ravages Pharnabazus' territory: Diod. 13.64.4. See Hatzfeld, *Alcibiade*, 273–77; Kagan, *Fall*, 244–45; and Lazenby, *PW*, 206. Grain from the Euxine: Prologue, note 7, above. In this connection, see Gabrielsen, "Trade and Tribute," 287–324, and Alexander Rubel, "Die ökonomische und politische Bedeutung von Bosporos und Hellespont in der Antike," *Historia* 58:3 (2009): 336–55.

6. Laconic message intercepted: Xen. *Hell.* 1.1.23, Plut. *Alc.* 28.10.

7. Endius' embassy: Philochorus *FGrH* 328 F138, Diod. 13.52.2–7, Nepos *Alc.* 5.5, Aristeid. 1.237 (Lenz-Behr), Just. *Epit.* 5.4.4 with Kagan, *Fall*, 248–49; Munn, *SH*, 154–55; Lazenby, *PW*, 206–7; Hutchinson, *Attrition*, 188; Rhodes, *Alcibiades*, 76–77; Hyland, *PI*, 96; and Stuttard, *Nemesis*, 234–39. Accompanied by Philocharidas and Megillus: Androtion *FGrH* 324 F44. On Philocharidas son of Eryxilaidas, see Thuc. 4.119.2, 5.19, 21.1, 24, with Rahe, *SSAW*, Chapters 6–7. On Megillus, see Xen. *Hell.* 3.4.6 and Pl. *Leg.* 1.642b with Herbert W. Parke, "A Note on the Spartan Embassy to Athens (408/7 B.C.)," *CR* n.s. 7:2 (June 1957): 106–7. Pharnabazus has fleet built at Antandrus: Xen. *Hell.* 1.1.24–26 with Kagan, *Fall*, 274, and Hyland, *PI*, 96–97. Mount Ida as a source of timber: Theophr. *Hist. pl.* 4.5.5 and Strabo 13.1.51 with Russell Meiggs, *Trees and Timber in the Ancient Mediterranean World* (Oxford: Clarendon Press, 1982), 108, 332, 357, which should be read in light of his more general observations regarding the sources and uses of timber in antiquity: 39–48, 116–53, 188–217, 325–70.

8. Reinforcements requested, reinforcements eventually voted: Xen. *Hell.* 1.1.8, 34,

read in light of Diod. 13.52.1, where chronological confusion has been produced by compression. Eventual dispatch the following spring: Xen. *Hell.* 1.2.1–13 with note 19, below—where I examine the disputes concerning the dating of this and subsequent events down to the battle of Notium.

9. Longevity of the Five Thousand: consider Arist. *Ath. Pol.* 23.1–24.1 and Diod. 13.38.1 in light of Andoc. 1.96–98, who quotes the decree of Demophantus; and see Rhodes, *CAAP*, 411–13. Cf. Kagan, *Fall*, 252–63, and Stuttard, *Nemesis*, 238–40, who argue that the restoration of the radical democracy followed the rejection of the peace. Cleophon and the Athenians' rejection of Endius' proffer of peace: Diod. 13.53. Cf. Antonio Natalicchio, "La Tradizione della offerte spar-tane di pace tra il 411 ed il 404: Storia e propaganda," *RIL* 124 (1990): 161–75, who claims that the Sparta peace offers reportedly conveyed in this period are a fiction invented by oligarchic propagandists, with Bleckmann, *Niederlage*, 393–404, and Munn, *SH*, 154–55. Cleophon son of Cleippides: Barry Baldwin, "Notes on Cleophon," *AClass* 17 (1974): 35–47.

10. See Kagan, *Fall*, 248–52, and Lazenby, *PW*, 207, who give these arguments great weight.

11. See Hyland, *PI*, 96, who suspects that the Lacedaemonians would have aban-doned Anatolia to the Persians and Athenians.

12. Trajectory of Iasos: consider Xen. *Hell.* 1.1.32—where I think that the reference to dereliction on the part of Tissaphernes and of Mindarus' successor Pasippidas justifies accepting the emendation suggested by Kahrstedt and endorsed by Meiggs, *AE*, 364–65, 570–78—in light of Thuc. 8.28.2–4, 29.1, 36.1. Cf. Krentz, *Xenophon*, 105, who recognizes that Tissaphernes' writ did not extend beyond Anatolia, but is nonetheless inclined to stick with the manuscript tradition, which mentions Thasos, not Iasos. See Marcel Piérart, "Chios entre Athènes et Sparte: La Contribution des exilés de Chios à l'effort de guerre lacédémonien pendant la Guerre du Péloponnèse, *IG* V 1, 1 + (*SEG* XXXIX 370)," *BCH* 119:1 (1995): 253–82 (at 277–80), and Lazenby, *PW*, 206, who do the like.

13. Jury pay: consider Arist. *Ath. Pol.* 27.3, Ar. *Eq.* 797–800, and Schol. Ar. *Vesp.* 88 in light of Rhodes, *CAAP*, 338–40, and see Ar. *Ran.* 138–41 (with the scholia). *Diōbelía*: consider Arist. *Ath. Pol.* 28.3 in light of Rhodes, *CAAP*, 355–57, and see James J. Buchanan, *Theorika: A Study of Monetary Distributions to the Athe-nian Citizenry during the Fifth and Fourth Centuries B.C.* (Locust Valley, NY: J. J. Augustin, 1962), 35–48, and Josine Blok, "The '*Diōbelia*': On the Political Econ-omy of an Athenian State Fund," *ZPE* 193 (2015): 87–102. Note Aeschin. 2.76, Arist. *Pol.* 1267b11–12. Work on the Erechtheum: *IG* I³ 474 = *O&R* no. 181. See Lacey Davis Caskey, "The Inscriptions," in *The Erechtheum, Measured, Drawn, and Restored*, ed. James M. Paton, Gorham et al. (Cambridge, MA: Harvard University Press, 1927), 277–422. *Eisphorá*: Rudi Thomsen, *Eisphora: A Study of Direct Taxation in Ancient Athens* (Copenhagen: Gyldendal, 1964), 176–77. For brief overviews, see Munn, *SH*, 156–59, and Stuttard, *Nemesis*, 239–40.

14. The decree of Demophanthus: Andoc. 1.96–98, which should be read with Eur. *Ion* 1334. That the decree—mentioned by Demosthenes (20.159) and attributed by Lycurgus (*Leocr.* 124–27) to the immediate aftermath of the Thirty—can, in fact, be dated to the first prytany of the archon year 410/9 is evident from a comparison of its prescript—as emended by Lipsius, Boeckh, Droysen, and MacDowell—with that of *IG* I³ 375.1–3. See Lazenby, *PW*, 207. Cf. Mirko Canevaro and Edward M. Harris, "The Documents in Andocides' *On the Mysteries*," *CQ* n.s. 62:1 (May 2012): 98–129 (esp. 98–100, 119–25), who conclude from the decree's departures from the language normally used in Attic legislation during this period that it is a forgery, with Alan H. Sommerstein, "The Authenticity of the Demophantus Decree," *CQ* n.s. 64:1 (May 2014): 49–57, who suggests that such departures are to be expected in a decree that is supposed to mark off emphatically a new epoch and who believes in its historicity, as do I. Cf., however, Edward M. Harris, "The Authenticity of the Document at Andocides *On the Mysteries* 96–98," *Tekmēria* 12 (2013–14): 121–53, who remains adamant. In the end, this dispute turns on a single question: whether a decree that, Harris admits in his final statement on the matter (143), was "not any routine piece of legislation" might not in its wording depart in dramatic ways from what was routine. In this connection, one might want to consider Brian M. Lavelle, "*Adikia*, the Decree of Kannonus, and the Trial of the Generals," *C&M* 39 (1988): 19–41 (esp. 34–41).

15. Demophantus' decree situated in its larger sociopolitical context: Peter Wilson, "Tragic Honours and Democracy: Neglected Evidence for the Politics of the Athenian Dionysia," *CQ* n.s. 59:1 (May 2009): 8–29, who draws attention to Ar. *Av.* 1074–75 and to *O&R* no. 182 = *ML* no. 85 = *IG* I³ 102, which records the awarding of a crown to Thrasybulus of Kalydon in the theater of Dionysus at the beginning of the City Dionysia in 409, and who argues that it is likely that the oath was administered there at the same time, with Robin Osborne, "Inscribing Performance," in *Performance Culture and Athenian Democracy*, ed. Simon Goldhill and Robin Osborne (Cambridge: Cambridge University Press, 1999), 341–58 (esp. 354–58), reprinted with an addendum in Osborne, *AAD*, 64–84 (esp. 77–81), whose discussion highlights the hyperpolitical character of the Demophantus decree and of the way in which this Thrasybulus was honored; Julia L. Shear, *Polis and Revolution: Responding to Oligarchy in Classical Athens* (Cambridge: Cambridge University Press, 2011), 1–18, 61–67, 70–111, 135–65, who suggests that the oath was administered before the beginning of the City Dionysia in the Agora; James F. McGlew, "Fighting Tyranny in Fifth-Century Athens: Democratic Citizenship and the Oath of Demophantus," *BICS* 55:2 (December 2012): 91–99; and David A. Teegarden, "The Oath of Demophantus, Revolutionary Mobilization, and the Preservation of the Athenian Democracy," *Hesperia* 81:3 (July 2012): 433–65, and *Death to Tyrants! Ancient Greek Democracy and the Struggle against Tyranny* (Princeton, NJ: Princeton Univer-

sity Press, 2014), 15–53, who argues that the oath must have been administered in meetings held by each of the ten tribes. Cf. Harris, "The Authenticity of the Document at Andocides *On the Mysteries* 96–98," who, in response to Tee-garden's claim that the oath provided a foundation for revolutionary mobiliza-tion against the Thirty, rightly points out that the oath passes unmentioned in the speeches Xenophon attributes to Thrasybulus son of Lycus and to Cleocri-tus. This may, however, say more about the outlook of these two men and about the known predilections of those whom they were addressing than about the thinking of the more ardent democrats in the Peiraeus who rallied to their stan-dard. Lycus' son had been a close associate of his fellow demesman Theramenes and of Alcibiades; and, when Theramenes was executed, he was invited to take the man's place as a member of the Thirty. He is apt to have been among those who opposed the Thirty but was known to have entertained misgivings regard-ing the radical democracy and the savage tone of the Demophantus decree.

16. Subsequent prosecutions aimed at the former oligarchs: Andoc. 1.73–79, Ar. *Ran.* 686–705. Cf. Ostwald, *Sovereignty*, 418, and Munn, *SH*, 159–60, who do not do this propensity justice, with Robin Osborne, "Changing the Discourse," in *Popular Tyranny: Sovereignty and its Discontents in Ancient Greece*, ed. Kathryn A. Morgan (Austin: University of Texas Press, 2003), 251–72 (at 261), reprinted with an addendum in Osborne, *AAD*, 267–88 (at 278), and Julia L. Shear, "The Oath of Demophantus and the Politics of Athenian Identity," in *Horkos: The Oath in Greek Society*, ed. Alan H. Sommerstein and Judith Fletcher (Liverpool: Liverpool University Press, 2007), 148–60, who recognize its importance. Cf. also Kagan, *Fall*, 253–62, who takes a far more sanguine view of the conduct of public policy under the restored democracy than I think justified.

17. Thrasyllus fends off Agis: Xen. *Hell.* 1.1.33–34 with Lazenby, *PW*, 208.

18. Departure of Thrasyllus with a formidable armada: Xen. *Hell.* 1.2.1, which should be read in light of 1.1.8 and 34.

19. Thrasyllus' departure early in a new campaigning season: Xen. *Hell.* 1.2.1. Har-vest time in western Anatolia: 1.2.4. Syracusan flotilla: 1.2.8, 12. For admirably lucid descriptions of the quandary that scholars face regarding the timetable for this period and for surveys and assessments of the various attempts to specify where the missing chronological indicator should be situated, see Lotze, *Lysander*, 72–86; William P. Henry, *Greek Historical Writing: A Historiographical Essay Based on Xenophon's Hellenica* (Chicago: Argonaut, 1967), 39–45; Antony Andrewes, "Chronological Notes," in *CAH*, V² 503–4; and Krentz, *Xenophon*, 11–14. I have rejected the chronology originally laid out by Christian Friedrich Ferdinand Haacke, *Dissertatio chronologica de postremis belli Peloponesiaci annis secundum Xenophontis historiam Graecam recte digerendis* (Stendal: n. p., 1822)—which posits, first, that the new year specified in Xen. *Hell.* 1.2.1 begins in the summer of 410 eight to ten weeks after the battle of Cyzicus; then, that 1.3.1 marks the onset of summer in 409; that 1.4.1 marks the onset of summer in 408;

that 1.5.11 marks the onset of summer in 407; that 1.6.1 marks the onset of summer in 406; and that there is a very considerable gap between the battle of Notium in 407 and the battle of Arginusae in 406. Cf. Noel Robertson, "The Sequence of Events in the Aegean in 408 and 407 B.C.," *Historia* 29:3 (3rd Quarter 1980): 282–301, who disagrees with Haacke only in placing Notium and Arginusae both in 406, in supposing that it took Alcibiades a full campaigning season to collect the one hundred talents of silver he extracted from Caria (Xen. *Hell.* 1.4.8–9), and in thinking that a full year passed between Cyrus' encounter with the Athenian ambassadors being conducted to Susa and his arrival at Sardis; Piérart, "Chios entre Athènes et Sparte," 276–77, who locates the missing indicator at Xen. *Hell.* 1.3.14, and who disagrees with Haacke only in positing that a full year passed between the return to Anatolia of Boeotius and the other Spartan ambassadors and the arrival of the younger Cyrus, in arguing that the siege of Byzantium began in 409 and did not end until 407, and in contending that otherwise nothing much happened in 408; and George E. Pesely, "The Date of Thrasyllos' Expedition to Ionia," *AHB* 12.:1–2 (1998): 96–100, who echoes Julius Beloch, "Zur chronologische Interpolationen in Xenophons *Hellenika*," *Philologus* 43 (1884): 275–95, in dismissing all of the indicators that a new year has begun as interpolations and goes one step further in rejecting as interpolations the reference to the beginning of the summer at Xen. *Hell.* 1.2.1 and the statement at 1.2.4 that the grain was ripe when Thrasyllos conducted his invasion of Lydia. That there are interpolations in the transmitted text is clear enough: Detlef Lotze, "Die chronologische Interpolationen in Xenophons *Hellenika*," *Philologus* 106 (1962): 1–13 and "War Xenophon selbst der Interpolator seiner *Hellenika* I–II?" *Philologus* 118 (1974): 216–17. It is also conceivable (but by no means evident) that Beloch was correct in suggesting that the passages indicating the beginning of a new year are among them. If so, however, it is perfectly possible that these interpolations reflect accurate information, drawn from another historian of the period such as Theopompus of Chios, regarding the beginning of a new campaigning season, and it is wrong to suppose, as Pesely does, that the references to the onset of summer at Xen. *Hell.* 1.2.1 and to the fully ripened grain at 1.2.4 have no importance for Xenophon's narrative—for there is a point to these references that any ancient reader would have noticed immediately: to wit, that this was the time of year when an invading army could live off the land and force the local population to march out in defense of its territory and the fruits of its labor. For the reasons spelled out in the text above, I have followed the argument laid out by Henry Dodwell, *Annales Thucydidei et Xenophontei: Praemittitur apparatus, cum vitae Thucydidis synopsi chronologica* (Oxford: Sheldonian Theater, 1702). As Andrewes, "Chronological Notes," 504, points out, the construction of twenty triremes takes time. See also Lotze, *Lysander*, 72–86; Bommelaer, *Lysandre*, 61–62; Kagan, *Fall*, 265 (with n. 75); Lazenby, *PW*, 208; and Rhodes, *Alcibiades*, 73, who make the same choice.

Note, however, Bleckmann, *Niederfolge*, 267–314, who embraces Haacke's analysis; Munn, *SH*, 335–39, who agrees with Piérart, whom he does not mention; and Krentz, *Xenophon*, 11–14, who endorses the argument of Robertson.

20. Ravaging of Chalcedonian territory: Diod. 13.66.1. Pharnabazus' sudden departure for Chalcedon where assistance was needed: Xen. *Hell.* 1.1.26. Castration: consider Eust. *Commentarii in Dionysium Periegetam* 803 = Arr. *Bithyniaca* F37 (Roos) = Arrian of Nicomedia *FGrH* 156 F79–80 and Plut. *Cam.* 19.9 (where I accept the emendation suggested by Unger and taken up in the Teubner and Budé editions) in light of Hdt. 6.9.4, 32, which should be read with 3.92.1; and see A. Brian Bosworth, "The Emasculation of the Chalcedonians: A Forgotten Episode of the Ionian War," *Chiron* 27 (1997): 297–313, who may be right in supposing that the expedition of Clearchus, mentioned at Xen. *Hell.* 1.3.35–36, and the assignment of Hippocrates to Chalcedon as a harmost (1.3.5–6, Diod. 13.66.2) reflect Lacedaemonian damage control in response to the atrocity that Pharnabazus is said to have committed. I do not, however, find Bosworth's more general indictment of Xenophon as a narrator persuasive. Cf. Hyland, *PI*, 100, who doubts Arrian's tale on the presumption that Pharnabazus would not have done anything that would have greatly displeased his Peloponnesian allies.

21. Thrasyllus' detour to Ionia; interventions at Colophon (*IACP* no. 848) and Notium (no. 858), in Lydia, and at Pygela (no. 863) and Ephesus; naval interchange off Methymna: consider Xen. *Hell.* 1.2.1–13 in light of 1.1.8, 34, and Diod. 13.52.1, where compression has produced chronological confusion. On the conflict at Ephesus, see as well *Hell. Oxy.* 1–3 (Chambers) and Diod. 13.64.1, and cf. Bleckmann, *Niederlage*, 149–62, who is as critical of the Oxyrhynchus historian as he is of Diodorus Siculus. On the naval skirmish near Methmyna, see also Cratippus *FGrH* 64 T2 = Plut. *Mor.* 345d. In this connection see Hatzfeld, *Alcibiade*, 277–79; Kagan, *Fall*, 265–73; Lazenby, *PW*, 208–10; Rhodes, *Alcibiades*, 78–79; Stuttard, *Nemesis*, 242–43; and Kapellos, *XPW*, 24–29.

22. Thrasyllus's disposition of the Syracusans captured at Methymna and his treatment of Alcibiades of Phegous: Xen. *Hell.* 1.2.13–14. Alcibiades of Phegous at the time of the Herms and Mysteries Scandals: Andoc. 1.65–66. Stoning not a normal Athenian penalty: Vincent J. Rosivach, "Execution by Stoning in Athens," *ClAnt* 6:2 (October 1987): 232–48. On the date of Thrasyllus' excursion, see Dion. Hal. *Hyp. Lys.* 32 and, for what it is worth, Diod. 13.54.1. Cleophon's hostility to Alcibiades: Himer. *Ecl.* 36.15=Phot. *Bibl.* 377a18. On the political background, see Hatzfeld, *Alcibiade*, 277–81, 327; Antony Andrewes, "The Generals in the Hellespont, 410–407 B.C.," *JHS* 73 (1953): 2–9; W. James McCoy, "Thrasyllus," *AJPh* 98:3 (Autumn 1977): 264–89 (esp. 271–84); and Loren J. Samons II, *Empire of the Owl: Athenian Imperial Finance* (Stuttgart: Franz Steiner Verlag, 2000), 269–70, who draws attention to pertinent evidence heretofore ignored. Cf. Kagan, *Fall*, 265–73 (with n. 105); Peter Krentz, "Athenian Politics and Strategy after Kyzikos," *CJ* 84:3 (February–March 1989): 206–15;

Bleckmann, *Niederlage*, 443–60 (esp. 457–60); and Stuttard, *Nemesis*, 242–43 (with n. 37). To sustain the thesis that Thrasyllus was on good terms with Alcibiades—which is advanced by Kagan, Krentz, Bleckmann, and Stuttard—one must resort to special pleading. One must assert that Thrasyllus' foray to Ionia made good strategic sense in the circumstances then pertaining, and one must either argue for emending Xenophon's text, substituting *apélusen* ("set free") for the *katéleusen* ("stoned to death") found in all of the surviving manuscripts (which is—as Rhodes, *Alcibiades*, 79 n. 45, points out—a real stretch), or deny that the stoning of Alcibiades' cousin had any political significance, which is hard to believe. Note Lazenby, *PW*, 210, who is puzzled by the foray and has trouble believing that Thrasyllus would have so antagonized Alcibiades.

23. Evolving relations between Alcibiades' men and those of Thrasyllus: Xen. *Hell.* 1.2.15–17, Diod. 13.64.4, Plut. *Alc.* 29.1–5 with Hatzfeld, *Alcibiade*, 280–81; Kagan, *Fall*, 275–76; Lazenby, *PW*, 210–11; Stuttard, *Nemesis*, 243–44; and Kapellos, *XPW*, 29.

24. Chalcedon besieged, hoplite battle: Xen. *Hell.* 1.3.1–7, Diod. 13.66.1–2, Plut. *Alc.* 29.6–30.2 with Hatzfeld, *Alcibiade*, 281–82; Kagan, *Fall*, 276–78; Lazenby, *PW*, 211–12; and Stuttard, *Nemesis*, 245–46. I do not think Pharnabazus' exclusion from the story plausible, but cf. Rhodes, *Alcibiades*, 79–80. I see no reason why the accounts we are given cannot for the most part be reconciled, but cf. Bleckmann, *Niederlage*, 72–80.

25. Alcibiades in the Hellespont, provisional settlement reached with Pharnabazus at Chalcedon: Xen. *Hell.* 1.3.8–9, Diod. 13.66.3, Plut. *Alc.* 30.3–31.1 with the admirably precise study of Moshé Amit, "Le Traité de Chalcédoine entre Pharnabaze et les stratèges Athéniens," *AC* 42:2 (1973): 436–57, and with Hatzfeld, *Alcibiade*, 284–85; Kagan, *Fall*, 278–81 (esp. n. 16); Krentz, *Xenophon*, 119–20; Lazenby, *PW*, 212; Rhodes, *Alcibiades*, 81–82; and Stuttard, *Nemesis*, 248–49, 251–52. Ambassadors' safe return guaranteed: Xen. *Hell.* 1.4.7. The fact that, in 405, there was an Athenian garrison in Chalcedon (Xen. *Hell.* 2.2.1) suggests that the Athenians took possession at some point after this settlement's collapse. The fact that the Chalcedonians are called upon to pay *phóros* is sometimes taken as an indication that the 5% tax on commerce was dropped and the *phóros* system restored and that the decree recording the last-known assessment (*IG* I³ 100) should be dated to 410. That the 5% tax was kept in place, however, is suggested by Ar. *Ran.* 363. On the debate, see Meiggs, *AE*, 438–39. There is no strong evidence that the *phóros* system was reinstated: see Chapter 2, note 13, above.

26. Alcibiades at Selymbria and on the outskirts of Byzantium: Xen. *Hell.* 1.3.10 and Plut. *Alc.* 30.3–10, where his capture of the former city is described in detail. Note, in this connection, Diod. 13.66.3–4, and see Hatzfeld, *Alcibiade*, 284–87; Kagan, *Fall*, 281–82; Krentz, *Xenophon*, 120–21; and Lazenby, *PW*, 213. Son of Cleinias becomes a party to the settlement with Pharnabazus: Xen. *Hell.* 1.3.11–12 and Plut. *Alc.* 31.2, with Kagan, *Fall*, 278–79, whose eagerness to deny Alci-

biades' preeminence is misplaced; Krentz, *Xenophon*, 121; Lazenby, *PW*, 212; and Hyland, *PI*, 103–4. Euryptolemos son of Peisanax: Xen. *Hell.* 1.4.19, 7.12, 16, 34. Whether this Peisanax was a brother of Alcibiades' Alcmeonid mother Deinomache or a son of Cimon and of a sister of this Deinomache, as is suggested by Schol. Aristeid. *Hypothesis to Kimon* in *On the Four* (Dindorf 3.315), we do not know: see Peter J. Bicknell, "Diomedon Cholargeus?" *Athenaeum* 53 (1975): 172–78 (at 177), and Wesley E. Thompson, "Euryptolemos," *TAPhA* 100 (1969): 583–86.

27. Supposed makeup of the embassy, Argives and Spartans included: consider Xen. *Hell.* 1.3.13 with Amit, "Le Traité de Chalcédoine entre Pharnabaze et les stratèges Athéniens," 451–55 (with n. 16). See also Lazenby, *PW*, 212–13. Argive relations with the Mede: Rahe, *PC*, Chapters 5 (with notes 58–59), 6 (with notes 1 and 4), and 8 (with note 43); *SFAW*, Chapter 3 (with note 32); and *SSAW*, Chapter 6 (with note 27), and Matthew W. Waters, "Earth, Water, and Friendship with the King: Argos and Persia in the Mid-Fifth Century," in *Extraction and Control: Studies in Honor of Matthew W. Stolper*, ed. Michael Kozuh (Chicago: The Oriental Institute of the University of Chicago, 2014), 331–36. Only on the chronological hypothesis advanced by Robertson, "The Sequence of Events in the Aegean in 408 and 407 B.C.," 286–93 (esp. 286, 290–91); Piérart, "Chios entre Athènes et Sparte," 276–77; and Munn, *SH*, 335–39, with regard to the time that passed between the Athenian ambassadors' discovery that they had journeyed in vain and the arrival of Cyrus at Sardis—which is subject to insuperable objections (see note 19, above)—would Euryptolemos and Mantitheus have had time to go on the embassy; proceed overland to Gordium; winter there; journey to a point further south and east; be detained by Pharnabazus for three years, three months, or even three weeks; and then pop up where and when, as we shall see, they later appear. For an untenable, if understandable, attempt to dodge the chronological difficulties, cf. Michal Podrazik, "Cyrus the Younger, Greek Envoys, and the So-Called Treaty of Boiotios (409–408 BC)," *Anabasis* 6 (2015): 78–83. Report that Pasippidas was exiled: Xen. *Hell.* 1.1.32. Evidence suggesting that he had succeeded Mindarus as navarch: 1.1.32, 3.17. Timing of Hermocrates' return to Sicily: Diod. 13.63 with Jakob Seibert, *Die politischen Flüchtlinge und Verbannten in der griechischen Geschichte: Anmerkungsteil und Register* (Darmstadt: Wissenschaftliche Buchgesellschaft, 1979), 238–41, 558 n. 124, and David M. Lewis, "Sicily, 413–368 B.C.," in *CAH*, VI² 120–55 (at 130). Suggestion that the plight and purpose of Pasippidas were analogous to those ascribed to Hermocrates: Amit, "Le Traité de Chalcédoine entre Pharnabaze et les stratèges Athéniens," 454–55, and Piérart, "Chios entre Athènes et Sparte," 281–82. Rhodes, *Alcibiades*, 82–83, suggests the possibility that Pasippidas had switched sides and that those on this embassy were all hostile to Lacedaemon, but he also draws attention to difficulties posed by the lineup and the timetable. For the view that Pasippidas had been recalled from

exile, that he and his unnamed colleagues represented Lacedaemon, that Boeotius was one in their number, and that they made up the embassy known to have left for Susa well before the departure of Pharnabazus with the Athenians and Argives: see Lotze, *Lysander*, 9–10. In this connection, note Beloch, *Gr. Gesch.*, II:2 256–57; Bommelaer, *Lysandre*, 62–70; and Krentz, *Xenophon*, 121, who adopt a similar hypothesis. On Pasippidas, see also Hyland, *PI*, 100. Likely interpolations: Xen. *Hell.* 1.1.37, 2.1, 19, 3.1, 5.21, 6.1, 2.1.10, 2.24, 3.1–2, 9.

28. Agis again dispatches Clearchus to the Bosporus: Xen. *Hell.* 1.1.35–36. Cf. Krentz, *Xenophon*, 28, with Olivier Chêne, "Xénophon, *Helléniques*, I, 1, 36 et l'envoi de Cléarque à Byzance aprés la bataille de Cyzique," *REG* 111:2 (July–December 1998): 481–502. Garrison at Byzantium: Xen. *Hell.* 1.3.15.

29. Alcibiades' treatment of the Selymbrians: Plut. *Alc.* 30.7–10, confirmed by *IG* I³ 118 = *ML* no. 87 = *O&R* no. 185 with Kagan, *Fall*, 282; Lazenby, *PW*, 213; Rhodes, *Alcibiades*, 80–81; and Stuttard, *Nemesis*, 246–48. Byzantium invested, Clearchus' plans, the town betrayed, Alcibiades' stratagem, the garrison's surrender, citizens spared, conspirator tried and acquitted at Lacedaemon: Xen. *Hell.* 1.3.14–21; Diod. 12.66.4–67.7; Nep. *Alc.* 5.6; Frontin. *Str.* 3.11.3; Polyaen. *Strat.* 1.40.2, 47.2; Plut. *Alc.* 31.3–8 with Hatzfeld, *Alcibiade*, 287–88; Henry D. Westlake, "Abydos and Byzantium: The Sources for Two Episodes in the Ionian War," *MH* 42:4 (1985): 313–27 (at 322–27), reprinted in Westlake, *Studies*, 224–38 (at 231–34); Kagan, *Fall*, 282–84; Krentz, *Xenophon*, 121–24; Lazenby, *PW*, 213–15; Rhodes, *Alcibiades*, 81–82; and Stuttard, *Nemesis*, 249–51. Cf. Gray, "The Value of Diodorus Siculus for the Years 411–386 BC," 87–89; Bleckmann, *Niederlage*, 80–91; and Tuplin, "Military Engagements in Xenophon's *Hellenica*," 48–49. There is other evidence, suggesting a deliberate policy on the part of Athens at some point, that may well be an endorsement of the approach taken by Alcibiades more generally at this time: consider *IG* I³ 17 in light of Nikolaos Papazarkadas, "Athens, Sigeion and the Politics of Approbation during the Ionian War," in *Athēnaiōn Episkopos: Studies in Honour of Harold B. Mattingly*, ed. Angelos P. Matthaiou and Robert K. Pitt (Athens: Ellēnikē Epigraphikē Etaireia, 2014), 215–40. On the Spartan propensity for brutality, see Rahe, *SSPW*, Chapter 6, note 16. On Clearchus' virtues and defects as a leader, see Xen. *An.* 2.6.1–15. In this connection, note Lawrence A. Tritle, "Xenophon's Portrait of Clearchus: A Study in Post-Traumatic Stress Disorder," in *Xenophon and his World*, ed. Christopher J. Tuplin (Stuttgart: Franz Steiner Verlag, 2004), 325–39.

30. Regarding the timetable, it is telling that Pharnabazus and the ambassadors with him did not learn of the fall of Byzantium until after they had settled down for the winter at Gordium: Xen. *Hell.* 1.4.1. Hellespont pacified, voyage home, reception: Diod. 13.68.1–3, whose sources led him astray by conflating the return of the armada and Alcibiades' return, and Plut. *Alc.* 32, who attempts to reconcile the report found in Ephorus and, possibly, Theopompus with that pro-

vided by Xenophon and who is surely right in rejecting the testimony of Duris of Samos (*FGrH* 76 F70). See Lazenby, *PW*, 215.

31. Theramenes' decree recalling Alcibiades: Thuc. 8.97.3, 98.4; Diod. 13.37.5, 38.2, 42.1–2; Nep. *Alc.* 5.4; and Plut. *Alc.* 27.1. Subsequent decree sponsored by Critias: Plut. *Alc.* 33.1 with Critias 88 B4–5 (DK⁶). Cf. Lazenby, *PW*, 216, and Stuttard, *Nemesis*, 225–26, who suppose that there was only one such decree, with Munn, *SH*, 165–66, who rightly thinks it significant that Critias' decree was passed under the democracy. Note also Rhodes, *Alcibiades*, 68–69.

32. Silver collected in Caria: Xen. *Hell.* 1.4.8 with Kagan, *Fall*, 287; Krentz, *Xenophon*, 127; Lazenby, *PW*, 215; and Stuttard, *Nemesis*, 253–55. Cf. Robertson, "The Sequence of Events in the Aegean in 408 and 407 B.C.," 287, with Munn, *SH*, 165 (with n. 35).

33. Alcibiades, Thrasybulus, Conon elected *stratēgoí* before Thrasyllus and the fleet reach Athens: Xen. *Hell.* 1.4.10 with Hatzfeld, *Alcibiade*, 292 n. 5; Kagan, *Fall*, 287–88; Krentz, *Xenophon*, 128–29; Rhodes, *Alcibiades*, 77–78; and Stuttard, *Nemesis*, 254–55, who underline the significance of the election of the first two on this list. Cf. Kagan, *Fall* 265–68; Krentz, *Xenophon*, 88; Bleckmann, *Niederlage*, 443–60; and Buck, *Thrasybulus*, 40 (n. 112), who conclude on the basis of Lys. 19.52 that the assembly at Athens elected Alcibiades, Thrasybulus, and Theramenes as *stratēgoí* each and every year in the period when they were conducting ongoing operations in the Hellespont and the Sea of Marmara, with Andrewes, "The Generals in the Hellespont, 410–407 B.C.," 2–9; Charles W. Fornara, *The Athenian Board of Generals from 501 to 404* (Wiesbaden: Franz Steiner Verlag, 1971), 68–69; and Ostwald, *Sovereignty*, 427, who recognize the difference between what is *de facto* true and what is *de iure* true. Note also Samons, *Empire of the Owl*, 254–75 (esp. 269–70), who draws attention to the glaring absence in the official records at Athens at this time of any indication suggesting that those in control at Athens provided financial support to the fleet commanded by Alcibiades, Thrasybulus, and Theramenes in the Hellespont. The elections for the *stratēgía* were held in the spring, and those who held that office served from Panathenaea to Panathenaea—i.e., for a one-year term extending from not long after the summer solstice until not long after the subsequent summer solstice: Arist. *Ath. Pol.* 44.4 (with 43.1 and 61.1), read in light of Rhodes, *CAAP*, 517, 535–37, 676–82.

34. Alcibiades' roundabout journey home: Xen. *Hell.* 1.4.11–12 and Plut. *Alc.* 34.1–2 with Hatzfeld, *Alcibiade*, 288–95; Kagan, *Fall*, 285–88, 290; Krentz, *Xenophon*, 129–30; Munn, *SH*, 165–66; Lazenby, *PW*, 215–16; Rhodes, *Alcibiades*, 84–85; and Stuttard, *Nemesis*, 255–59. Cf. Diod. 13.68.1–3 and Plut. *Alc.* 32, who conflate his return with that of the armada. Note, in this connection, Bleckmann, *Niederlage*, 461–72. According to Plutarch (*Alc.* 34), the Plynteria was celebrated on 25 Thargelion, and this date is almost certainly correct—for the date

of 29 Thargelion specified in Photius s. v. *Plyntēría* is a day in which, on a number of occasions, the assembly is known to have met: Jon D. Mikalson, *The Sacred and Civil Calendar of the Athenian Year* (Princeton, NJ: Princeton University Press, 1975), 160–64. The surviving fragments of the Nicomachus calendar appear to situate this festival towards the end of Thargelion: Stephen D. Lambert, "The Sacrificial Calendar of Athens," *ABSA* 97 (November 2002): 353–99 (at 363–64 [F3, col. 1, 1–15] with 374–75). There may have been a separate festival of the same name held a month later month at Thorikos on the eastern coast of Attica: Walter Burkert, *Greek Religion*, tr. John Raffan (Cambridge, MA: Harvard University Press, 1985), 439 n. 5. See Robert Parker *Athenian Religion: A History* (Oxford: Clarendon Press, 1996), 307–8, and *Polytheism and Society at Athens* (Oxford: Oxford University Press, 2005), 160, 162–63, 179 n. 5, 378, 478–79. The date in the Julian calendar can be calculated from the chronological table provided in Benjamin D. Meritt, "The Chronology of the Peloponnesian War," *PAPhS* 115:2 (April 1971): 97–124 (at 114). If Schol. Ar. *Ran.* 1422 claims that Alcibiades' return took place in the archon year of 407/6, it was presumably because the scholiast is speaking loosely with regard to Alcibiades' sojourn in Athens, which stretched through the summer of 407/6, and not with regard to the precise date of his arrival. It is worth noting that, in 407, the Athenians synchronized their two calendars by having them both begin each year on the day of the first full moon after the summer solstice. It is also is worth adding that the summer solstice did not take place in 407 until 28 June in the Gregorian calendar and that, according to skyviewcafe.com, there was not a new moon visible thereafter in Athens until 12 or 13 July—a slight bit later than the day in the Julian calendar mentioned by Meritt.

35. Inauspicious day and significance of veiling: consider Xen. *Hell.* 1.4.12 and Plut. *Alc.* 34.1–2 in light of Douglas L. Cairns, "Anger and the Veil in Ancient Greek Culture," *G&R* 48:1 (April 2001): 18–32, and see Bodil Due, "The Return of Alcibiades in Xenophon's *Hellenica* I.IV, 8–23," *C&M* 42 (1991): 39–53 (at 42); Blaise Nagy, "Alcibiades' Second 'Profanation,'" *Historia* 43:3 (3rd Quarter 1994): 275–85; and Kapellos, *XPW*, 41–43. Cf. Frances Skoczylas Pownall, "Condemnation of the Impious in Xenophon's *Hellenica*," *HThR* 91:3 (July 1998): 251–77 (at 262), who intimates that Xenophon thought the loss at Notium a consequence of Alcibiades' impiety.

36. Alcibiades' reception and sojourn at Athens: Xen. *Hell.* 1.4.13–19; Diod. 13.69; Nepos *Alc.* 7.6; Just. *Epit.* 5.4.9–11; Plut. *Alc.* 32.2–3, 33.2, 35.1; Ath. 12.535c–e with Hatzfeld, *Alcibiade*, 294–99, 302–3; Kagan, *Fall*, 288–90; Krentz, *Xenophon*, 128–32; Due, "The Return of Alcibiades in Xenophon's *Hellenica* I.IV, 8–23," 39–53 (esp. 42–53); Munn, *SH*, 166–69; Lazenby, *PW*, 215–16; Marc D. Gygax, "Plutarch on Alcibiades' Return to Athens," *Mnemosyne* 4th ser., 59:4 (2006): 481–500; Rhodes, *Alcibiades*, 85–87; Stuttard, *Nemesis*, 258–60; and Kapellos, *XPW*, 66–77. For another view, based on a wholesale rejection of the

testimony not derived from Xenophon, see Bleckmann, *Niederlage*, 461–87. *Autokrátōr*: Xen. *An.* 6.1.21 with Hamel, *Athenian Generals*, 201–3; Lazenby, *PW*, 216; Rhodes, *Alcibiades*, 86; and Stuttard, *Nemesis*, 260. Cf. Bleckmann, *Niederlage*, 476–86. Procession antecedent to celebrating the Eleusinian Mysteries: Xen. *Hell.* 1.4.19 and Plut. *Alc.* 34.3–6 with Mikalson, *The Sacred and Civil Calendar of the Athenian Year*, 58–59. See also Hatzfeld, *Alcibiade*, 299–301; Herbert W. Parke, *Festivals of the Athenians* (Ithaca, NY: Cornell University Press, 1977), 55–72; Kagan, *Fall*, 290–92; Krentz, *Xenophon*, 132; Munn, *SH*, 169; Lazenby, *PW*, 216; Rhodes, *Alcibiades*, 87; and Stuttard, *Nemesis*, 265–70.

37. Alcibiades' departure from Athens: Xen. *Hell.* 1.4.21, Diod. 13.69.4, Plut. *Alc.* 35.2 with Hatzfeld, *Alcibiade*, 298–99, 301–7; Lotze, *Lysander*, 19; Moshé Amit, "The Disintegration of the Athenian Empire in Asia Minor (412–405 B.C.E.)," *SCI* 2 (1975): 38–71 (at 67–70); Bommelaer, *Lysandre*, 71; Kagan, *Fall*, 293–94; Krentz, *Xenophon*, 132–33; Lazenby, *PW*, 216–17; Rhodes, *Alcibiades*, 87; and Stuttard, *Nemesis*, 273–74. I take more seriously than do some scholars Pharnabazus' endeavor to keep secret the dispatch of Cyrus.

PART IV. THE MISSION OF CYRUS

Epigraph: Ancient Chinese Proverb

1. Pharnabazus' pledge, departure for Susa prior to Byzantium's capture: Xen. *Hell.* 1.3.8–12, 14, 4.1. In this preface, in the two chapters that follow, and in Appendices 2–8, I draw to some extent on the first two chapters of the unpublished dissertation that I wrote some years ago under the direction of Donald Kagan: Paul A. Rahe, "Lysander and the Spartan Settlement 407–403 B.C." (Ph.D. diss., Yale University, 1977), 1–77. This material I first revised and expanded upon while a Junior Fellow at the Center for Hellenic Studies in 1980–81. I would like to record my debt of gratitude to the late Bernard Knox and to those who were Senior Fellows of that center at that time for their support and encouragement. If, with regard to Cyrus, Lysander, Agesilaus, Agis, Callicratidas, and Sparta's Agiad kings, the story I tell here resembles what is found in Kagan, *Fall*, 293–412, and in Cartledge, *Agesilaos*, 77–82, 139–41, 186–92, it is in part because they both drew to some degree in their books on my dissertation: see ibid. Kagan, *Fall*, 294 n. 4, and Cartledge, *Agesilaos*, 78, 140.

2. Pharnabazus' satrapy: Debord, *AM*, 83–115 (esp. 91–104). Gordium included: *Hell. Oxy.* 24.5–6 (Chambers). Gordium itself: Briant, *CA*, 705–6, 1010–11. Note also Hilmar Klinkott, "The Satrapies of the Persian Empire in Asia Minor: Lydia, Caria, Lycia, Phrygia, and Cappadocia," in *OHANE*, V 592–648 (at 617–27).

3. Pharnabazus and ambassadors winter at Gordium, learn of the fall of Byzantium: Xen. *Hell.* 1.4.1. Course of the royal road from Sardis to Susa: consider Hdt. 5.52–53 and 8.98 in light of 7.26–44, and see Pierre Briant, "De Sardes à

Suse," *AchHist* 6 (1991): 67–82, reprinted in an English translation by Amélie Kuhrt as "From Sardis to Susa," in Briant, *Kings, Countries, Peoples: Selected Studies on the Achaemenid Empire* (Stuttgart: Franz Steiner Verlag, 2017), 359–74, and Pierre Debord, "Les Routes royales en Asie mineure occidentale," in *Dans les pas des Dix-Mille: Peuples et pays du Proche-Orient vus par un Grec*, ed. Pierre Briant (Toulouse: Presses universitaires du Mirail, 1995), 9–97, as well as the secondary literature regarding the royal road system collected in the preface to Part I, note 11, above. Cf., however, David French, "Pre- and Early-Roman Roads of Asia Minor: The Persian Road," *Iran* 36 (1998): 15–43, who thinks that the later Roman road, which bypassed Gordium and the region in which it lay, follows the Achaemenid route. Gordium: Arr. *Anab.* 1.29.5, Just. *Epit.* 11.7.3. Discovery of a packed gravel road running east from Gordium: Rodney S. Young, "Gordion on the Royal Road," *PAPhS* 107:4 (August 1963): 348–64. Fortified check-point: Hdt. 5.52.2.

4. Evidence that, at some point subsequent to 411 and prior to the summer of 407, the Athenians may have entertained an illusion that an alliance with "the king and his allies" was in the offing: consider *IG* I³ 113 = *SEG* X 127 in light of Isoc. 9.54 and [Dem.] 12.10, and see Lewis, *SP*, 129–30. Cf., however, Michael J. Osborne, *Naturalization in Athens* (Brussels: Palais der Academiën, 1981–83), II 23–24 (no. D3), who questions the restoration suggested by Lewis, which forms the basis for supposing that the Athenians entertained this illusion, and Silvio Cataldi, *Symbolai e relazioni tra le città greche nel V sec. a.C.* (Pisa: Scuola Normale Superiore, 1983), 287–314 (no. 10), esp. 301–2, who suggests that the "king" mentioned in the inscription is not *the* King, but the Cypriot monarch Evagoras who is being honored in this decree and awarded Athenian citizenship. That this Evagoras will later play an important role in Athenian–Persian relations as a go-between, however, there can be no doubt: see David M. Lewis and Ronald S. Stroud, "Athens Honors King Euagoras of Salamis," *Hesperia* 48:2 (April–June 1979): 180–93.

5. Encounter with Boeotius, Cyrus to come, three thousand drachmas a month per ship: Xen. *Hell.* 1.4.1–3, 5.5. with Hatzfeld, *Alcibiade*, 307–8, and Lotze, *Lysander*, 10–11. Cf. Rhodes, *Alcibiades*, 82, and Hyland, *PI*, 103–4, who think that Pharnabazus may have hoped for a settlement with the Athenians, with Moshé Amit, "Le Traité de Chalcédoine entre Pharnabaze et les stratèges Athéniens," *AC* 42:2 (1973): 436–57 (at 455), and Kagan, *Fall*, 284–85, 294, who draw attention to the significance of the delays that seem to have been engineered by that satrap. Some scholars suspect that the earlier allusion in Xenophon's text to an embassy to Susa on which Pasippidas served (*Hell.* 1.3.13) is an aside aimed at making his readers aware of the mission headed by Boeotius that was already en route to the ancient Elamite capital: see Chapter 6, note 27, above. Requirement for travel authorization: Hallock, *PFT*, 6, with Richard T. Hallock, *The Evidence of the Persepolis Tablets* (Cambridge: Cambridge Univer-

sity Press, 1971), 11–13, 28–29. On the documents required, see Wouter F. M. Henkelman, "Nakhthor in Persepolis," in *AhW*, II 193–223. Mounted couriers: see note 16, below. The title awarded the younger Cyrus may be derivative from the Old Persian term *kara* for "army assembly": Geo Widengren, *Der Feudalismus im alten Iran: Männerbund, Gefolgswesen, Feudalismus in der iranischen Gesellschaft im Hinblick auf die indo-germanischen Verhältnisse* (Cologne: Westdeutscher Verlag, 1969), 106. Whether the term *káranos* refers to a regional commander, to a commander appointed for the empire's western marches, or to every commander as such is disputed: see Claus Haebler, *"Káranos*: Eine sprachwissenschaftliche Betrachtung zu Xen. *Hell.* I 4, 3," in *Serta Indogermanica: Festschrift für Günter Neumann*, ed. Johann Tischler (Innsbruck: Institut für Sprachwissenschaft der Universität Innsbruck, 1982), 81–90; Thierry Petit, "Étude d'une fonction militaire sous la dynastie perse achéménide (*Káranos*: Xenophon, *Helleniques*, I, 4, 3)," *LEC* 51 (1983): 35–45, and *Satrapes et satrapies dans l'empire achéménide de Cyrus le Grand à Xerxès Ier* (Paris: Les Belles Lettres, 1990), 133–44; Antony G. Keen, "Persian *Karanoi* and their relationship to the Satrapal System," in *Ancient History in a Modern University: I. The Ancient Near East, Greece, and Rome* (Grand Rapids, MI: William B. Eerdmans Publishing Co., 1998), 88–95; and Eduard Rung, "Notes on *Karanos* in the Persian Empire," *IA* 50 (2015): 333–56. That Boeotius was the bearer of a new agreement between Sparta and Persia regarding the Greek cities of Asia Minor, which superseded the third of the agreements negotiated in 411, there is no firm evidence: cf. Lewis, *SP*, 108–25 (esp. 123–25), with Christopher J. Tuplin, "The Treaty of Boiotios," *AchHist* 2 (1987): 133–53, and Cartledge, *Agesilaos*, 189–90.

6. According to Ctesias, Cyrus was born after Darius' accession in 423: *FGrH* 688 F15.51 with Plut. *Artax.* 2.4. His youth at the time of his arrival at Sardis is attested by Diodorus (13.70.3: *neanískon*) and Plutarch (*Lys.* 4.3: *meirákion*). See Kagan, *Fall*, 294–95. and Lazenby, *PW*, 217.

7. On Cyrus' position, see Xen. *Hell.* 1.4.3, *An.* 1.1.2, 9.7; Diod. 14.12.8; Plut. *Artax.* 2.5 with Kagan, *Fall*, 294–95, and Lazenby, *PW*, 218. Cyrus supplanted Tissaphernes both as satrap (Just. *Epit.* 5.5.1) and as military commander of the coastal provinces: cf. Xen. *Hell.* 1.4.3 and *An.* 1.1.2 with Thuc. 8.5.4; Xen. *Hell.* 3.1.3, 2.13; and Diod. 14.26.4, and see Stephen Ruzicka, "Cyrus and Tissaphernes, 407–401 B.C.," *CJ* 80:3 (February/March 1985): 204–11. The two offices were often linked, but could be separated: Hdt. 4.143–44, 5.1–2, 10, 12, 14–17, 23–26, 30, 98, 116, 123, 6.43, 7.135; Thuc. 1.115, 3.31, 34. Lewis (*SP*, 131 with n. 136) draws attention to the fact that Pharnabazus is subordinated to Cyrus (Xen. *Hell.* 1.5.5–7) in a manner in which he does not appear to have been subordinated to Tissaphernes and suggests that Cyrus had "wider supervisory powers." Pharnabazus' docility may, however, have been due to his awareness that Cyrus was much more likely than Tissaphernes to have influence with the younger Darius. Tissaphernes remained in the region after Cyrus' takeover

(Xen. *Hell.* 1.5.8, *An.* 1.1.2), perhaps withdrawing to his estates in Caria: *Hell.* 3.2.12. Lewis (*SP*, 119 n. 78) suggests that he may have been named satrap of Caria which became an independent province at about this time. Regarding Hieramenes, see Appendix 4. On Arsaces' age at this time, see Appendix 6.

8. Alcibiades' advice: Thuc. 8.46.1-2 with the material collected in Chapter 3, note 21, above. Not all of his advice was sensible: he conveniently overlooked Athens' involvement in Egypt (Thuc. 1.104, 109-10; Diod. 11.71.3-6, 74.1-4, 75, 77.1-5; Ctesias *FGrH* 688 F14.36, 38) when he advised Tissaphernes that Persia would be better off if Athens won the war than if Sparta was the victor: Thuc. 8.46.3-4. For a contrary assessment of the value of Alcibiades' advice, see Hyland, *PI*, 104-5.

9. Parysatis' preference for her younger son: Plut. *Artax.* 2.3-4; Ctesias *FGrH* 688 F15.51, 55-56, F15a.2-3, F16.59, 63-66, F17.2.3-5. For the case of Xerxes I and the machinations of his mother Atossa, see Hdt. 7.2-4. Nowhere is Parysatis' responsibility directly asserted in the ancient sources. It is credible because it is the only hypothesis in accord with the surviving evidence concerning the character of the queen and her ambitions for her second son. It has been generally accepted: see Busolt, *Gr. Gesch.*, III:2, 1568; Meyer, *GdA*, IV:2 330; A. T. Olmstead, *History of the Persian Empire* (Chicago: University of Chicago Press, 1948), 369-76; Lotze, *Lysander*, 11; Kagan, *Fall*, 295, 304; and Cawkwell, *GW*, 158-60. Cf. Lewis *SP*, 134-35, and Hyland, *PI*, 106, who place considerably less emphasis on court intrigue than I do below.

10. Great King's wives and concubines: Hdt. 1.135. Cf. 3.1-3 (where we learn that Amasis' daughter's status as an Egyptian ruled out her becoming Cambyses' consort), 31-32, 68-69, 84. See also Ctesias *FGrH* 688 F13a with Briant, *CA*, 277-86. Mother of crown prince King's queen and consort: Esther 1:9-20, 2:1-17. This work, which supplies a faithful representation of the Persian court, is misleading only in that it conveys the impression that a foreign woman could become queen. See also Nehemiah 2:6 and Pl. *Alc.* I 121c1-3, 123b2-d4.

11. Miseducation of the heir apparent: Plato *Leg.* 3.694c-696a. Cf. Hdt. 1.136; Xen. *Cyr.* 1.2.3-16, 5.1, 7.5.71-86, 8.1.34-39 with 8.13-27.

12. Full power attributed to Atossa: Hdt. 7.1-4. Evidence for extent of her influence: Aesch. *Pers.* passim; Hdt. 3.68, 88, 133-34, 7.1-4, 61, 64, 82. Cf. Heleen Sancisi-Weerdenburg, "Exit Atossa: Images of Women in Greek Historiography of Persia," in *Images of Women in Antiquity*, ed. Averil Cameron and Amélie Kuhrt (London: Routledge, 1983), 20-33, with Matthew W. Stolper, "Atossa Re-Enters: Cyrus's Other Daughter in Persepolis Fortification Texts," in *L'Orient est son Jardin: Hommages à Rémy Boucharlat*, ed. Sébastien Gondet and Ernie Haerinck (Leuven: Peeters, 2018), 449-66. Influence of Amestris: Hdt. 7.114, 9.109-12; Ctesias *FGrH* 688 F14.34, 39, 42-46. She may well be the Lady of the Palace mentioned in a Babylonian document dated to the thirty-first year of Artaxerxes' reign: BE IX no. 28 = NBRVT no. 179. She may also be the estate-

owner Amisiri of BE IX no. 39 and CBS no. 5199 or the Am-mi-is-ri of BE X no. 45. Parysatis may ultimately have been granted Amestris' holdings: a woman who held lands belonging to Amisiri (BE IX no. 39) later appears as a tenant of Parysatis (PBS II/1 no. 75): see Stolper, *E&E*, 63–64. As Stolper points out, however, the identification of Amirisi with Amestris is by no means certain. For the view that it is out of the question, see Manfred Mayrhofer, "Alltagsleben und Verwaltung in Persepolis: Linguistisch-onomastische Aufgaben aus neuer-schlossenen Profantexten," *AAWW* 109 (1972): 192–202 (at 201, esp. n. 37).

13. Nature and importance of the Achaemenid harem and the bitterness and politi-cal consequences of the rivalries that arose therein: cf. Maria Brosius, *Women in Ancient Persia, 539–331 BC* (Oxford: Oxford University Press, 1996), and Bri-ant, *CA*, 277–86, who have much of value to report concerning the women of the court but who shy away from a full appreciation of the significance of court intrigue for the regime's operations, with Llewellyn-Jones, *KCAP*, 96–122, 133–48, who brings to his assessment of the Achaemenid harem and of the Persian monarchy as a form of government a broad familiarity with the role that the harem played in the polygynous monarchies of the ancient Near East and of elsewhere in later times, and who errs only in failing to give sufficient emphasis to the fact that the supposedly "Orientalist" picture drawn by Chariton and Plutarch is derivative from Ctesias and Deinon, who had a firsthand knowledge of the Achaemenid court. For his argument with regard to Chariton and Plutarch, cf. Lloyd Llewellyn-Jones, "'Empire of the Gaze': Despotism and Sera-glio Fantasies à la grecque in Chariton's *Callirhoe*," *Helios* 40:1/2 (Spring/Fall 2013): 167–91, wherein we can see, his claims to the contrary notwithstanding, that Chariton's erotic fantasy depicts the institutional reality of the Persian harem as accurately as the Book of Esther and that Plutarch in his *Themistocles* does so as well. Violence and the Persian court: Robert Rollinger, "Herodotus, Human Violence and the Ancient Near East," in *The World of Herodotus*, ed. Vas-sos Karageorghis and Ioannes G. Taiphakos (Nicosia: A. G. Leventis Founda-tion, 2004), 121–50, and "Extreme Gewalt und Strafgericht: Ktesias und Herodot as Zeugnisse für den Achaemenidenhof," in *Der Achämenidenhof/The Achaemenid Court*, ed. Bruno Jacobs and Robert Rollinger (Stuttgart: Harras-sowitz, 2010), 559–666.

14. Conspiracy of Teriteuchmes: Ctesias *FGrH* 688 F15.55.

15. Chosen one of Ahura Mazda: Roland G. Kent, *Old Persian: Grammar, Texts, Lexicon*, 2nd edition, revised (New Haven, CT: American Oriental Society, 1953), 116–157; George G. Cameron, "An Inscription of Darius from Pasargadae," *Iran* 5 (1967): 7–10; and Badri Gharib, "A Newly Found Old Persian Inscription," *IA* 8 (1968): 54–69. Note the religious character of Darius the Great's selection as King: Hdt. 3.85–87. Greek opinion varied. The Achaemenid monarch was said to be descended from god (Xen. *Cyr.* 7.2.24, Pl. *Alc.* I 120e6–10), was regarded as the image of god (Plut. *Them.* 27.4), was accorded "reverence worthy of a

god" (Strabo 11.13.9); but he was not, as far as we can tell, worshipped as a god. See Geo Widengren, "The Sacral Kingship of Iran," in *Studies in the History of Religions: The Sacral Kingship, Numen* Suppl. 4 (1959): 242–57; Richard N. Frye, "The Charisma of Kingship in Ancient Iran," *IA* 4 (1964), 36–54; Clarisse Herrenschmidt, "La Religion des achéménides: État de la question," *StIr* 9:2 (1980): 325–39; Llewellyn-Jones, *KCAP*, 19–30; and Albert de Jong, "The Religion of the Achaemenid Rulers," Jean Kellens, "The Achaemenids and the Avesta," and Manfred Hutter, "Religions in the Empire," in *A Companion to the Achaemenid Persian Empire*, ed. Bruno Jacobs and Robert Rollinger (Hoboken, NJ: Wiley Blackwell, 2021), II 1199–1220, 1285–1302 (esp. 1285–89), as well as the extensive secondary literature cited in Rahe, *PC*, Chapter 1, note 66. For another view, cf. Aesch. *Pers.* 157, 643, 654–55, 711, 856 (which I take to be hyperbole) and Lily Ross Taylor, *The Divinity of the Roman Emperor* (Middletown, CT: American Philological Association, 1931), 247–55. The ostentatious devotion they accorded Ahura Mazda did not prevent the Achaemenids from generously supporting local cults: in addition to the pertinent secondary literature on this subject cited in Rahe, *PC*, Chapter 1, note 66, see Wouter F. M. Henkelman, "The Heartland Pantheon" and "Practice of Worship in the Achaemenid Heartland," in *A Companion to the Achaemenid Persian Empire*, II 1221–70, as well as Hutter, "Religions in the Empire," 1289–1300. Court ceremonials: Llewellyn-Jones, *KCAP*, 42–73, 123–33. One important aspect of this was feasting: see the material collected in Rahe, *PC*, Chapter 6, note 15, to which I would now add Jacob L. Wright and Meredith Elliott Hollman, "Banquet and Gift Exchange," in *A Companion to the Achaemenid Persian Empire*, 1065–74. For the annual peregrinations of the King, see Xen. *Cyr.* 8.6.22; Ath. 12.513e–f; Plut. *Mor.* 78d, 604 c; Dio Chrys. *Or.* 6.1–7; and Ael. *NA* 3.13, 10.6 with Pierre Briant, "Le Nomadisme du Grand Roi," *IA* 23 (1988): 253–73, and *CA*, 186–95, 910; Christopher J. Tuplin, "The Seasonal Migration of Achaemenid Kings," *AchHist* 11 (1998): 63–114; Llewellyn-Jones, *KCAP*, 79–92; and Bruno Jacobs, "The Residences," in *A Companion to the Achaemenid Persian Empire*, II 1005–34. Although the story told is fictional, as I have already observed, the best concise depiction of the workings of the court is the Book of Esther. See also Nehemiah 1–2; Hdt. 1.114, 3.1–3, 34–35, 61–88 (cf. 1.96–100), 118–19, 127–60, 4.43, 84, 5.23–24, 105–8, 6.29–30, 7.1–19, 27–29, 38–41, 101–4, 136, 234–37, 8.85, 103–4, 9.107–13, 122; Ctesias *FGrH* 688 F13.9–F16.65; Plut. *Artax.* passim; Xen. *Cyr.* 4.3.1–2, 5.5.25–34, 7.5.37–72, 8, *An.* 1.6.4, 11, 8.5–6, 21, 25, 28–29, 9.31, 4.4.4; Pl. *Alc.* I 121c, 123c–d, *Leg.* 3.693d–696a with Walther Hinz, "Achämenidische Hofverwaltung," *ZA* 61 (1971): 260–311. For the evidence of the Persepolis reliefs, see Walther Hinz, *Altiranische Funde und Forschungen: Mit Beiträgen von Rykle Borger und Gerd Gropp* (Berlin: de Gruyter, 1969), 63–93. For an admirably detailed comprehensive overview, see Briant, *CA*, 165–354 (esp. 255–354).

For a partial corrective to what Briant has to say, see Llewellyn-Jones, *KCAP*, 30–148.

16. The phalanx of royal officials: Hallock, *The Evidence of the Persepolis Tablets*, 10–31, and Lewis, *SP*, 1–26. In this connection, see Christopher J. Tuplin, "The Administration of the Achaemenid Empire," in *Coinage and Administration in the Athenian and Persian Empires*, ed. Ian Carradice (Oxford: British Archaeological Reports, 1987), 109–66; the essays collected in *L'Archive des Fortifications de Persépolis. État des questions et perspectives de recherches*, ed. Pierre Briant, Wouter F. M. Henkelman, and Matthew W. Stolper (Paris: De Bocchard, 2009); Christopher J. Tuplin, "Managing the World: Herodotus on Persian Imperial Administration," in *Herodot und das persische Weltreich/Herodotus and the Persian Empire*, ed. Robert Rollinger, Brigitte Truschnegg, and Reinhold Bichler (Wiesbaden: Harrassowitz, 2011), 39–64; and the essays collected in *Die Verwaltung im Achämenidenreich: Imperiale Muster und Strukturen /The Administration of the Achaemenid Empire: Tracing the Imperial Signature*, ed. Bruno Jacobs, Wouter F. M. Henkelman, and Matthew W. Stolper (Wiesbaden: Harrassowitz, 2017). See, especially, Bruno Jacobs, "Kontinuität oder kontinuierlicher Wandel in der achämenidischen Reichsverwaltung? Eine Synopse von PFT, *dahyāva*-Listen und den Satrapienlisten der Alexanderhistoriographen"; Wouter F. M. Henkelman, "Imperial Signature and Imperial Paradigm: Achaemenid Administrative Structure and System Across and Beyond the Iranian Plateau"; Christopher J. Tuplin, "Serving the Satrap: Subsatrapal Officials in Greek and Aramaic Sources"; and Michael Jursa and Martina Schmidl, "Babylonia as a Source of Imperial Revenue from Cyrus to Xerxes," in ibid. 3–256, 613–76, 715–40, and note Jan Tavernier, "Persian in Official Documents and the Processes of Multilingual Administration," and Lisbeth S. Fried, "Aramaic Texts and the Achaemenid Administration of Egypt," in *AhW*, III 75–96, 278–90. The older scholarship is by no means without value: see Kenneth G. Hoglund, *Imperial Administration in Syria-Palestine and the Missions of Ezra and Nehemiah* (Atlanta: Scholars Press, 1992), and W. J. Vogelsang, *The Rise and Organisation of the Achaemenid Persian Empire: The Eastern Iranian Evidence* (Leiden: Brill, 1992). For a comprehensive overview, see Briant, *CA*, 114–38, 165–511, and Llewellyn-Jones, *KCAP*, passim (esp. 74–95). Royal roads: Hdt. 5.52–54 with the secondary literature collected in the preface to Part I, note 11, above. Elite guides, couriers, and rations for authorized travellers: Hallock *PFT*, 6 with Hallock, *The Evidence of the Persepolis Tablets*, 11–13, 28–29. Mounted couriers: Hdt. 8.98; Xen. *Cyr.* 8.6.17–18; Plut. *Alex.* 18.7; Esther 6:10, 8:14; and Hallock *PFT*, 6, with Hallock, *The Evidence of the Persepolis Tablets*, 28–29, and Lewis, *SP*, 56–57. Royal secretaries: Hdt. 3.128 and Xen. *An.* 1.2.20, where the scholiast correctly takes *phoinikistḗs* to mean "scribe": see Lilian H. Jeffery and Anna Morpurgo-Davies, "*Poinikastás* and *poinikázen*: BM 1969 4-2.1, a New Archaic Inscription from

Crete," *Kadmos* 9 (1970): 118–54 (esp. 132–33); Lewis *SP*, 25 n. 143; and Kemal Balkan, "Inscribed Bullae from Daskyleion-Ergili," *Anatolia* 4 (1959): 123–28. Royal garrisons and their commanders: Xen. *Cyr.* 7.5.69–70, 8.1.11, 6.1–14, *An.* 1.4.4, 6.6, *Oec.* 4.6 with Christopher J. Tuplin, "Xenophon and the Garrisons of the Achaemenid Empire," *AMI* n.f. 20 (1987): 167–245, and Margaret C. Miller, *Athens and Persia in the Fifth Century BC: A Study in Cultural Receptivity* (Cambridge: Cambridge University Press, 1997), 91–97. More can now be gleaned from İsmail Gezgin, "Defensive Systems in the Aiolis and Ionia Regions in the Achaemenid Period," in *Achaemenid Anatolia: Proceedings of the First International Symposium on Anatolia in the Achaemenid Period, Bandirma, 15–18 August 1997*, ed. Tomris Bakır, Heleen Sancisi-Weerdenburg, Gül Gürtekin, Pierre Briant, and Wouter F. M. Henkelman (Leiden: Nederlands Instituut Voor Het Nabije Oosten, 2001), 181–88; *L'Archéologie de l'empire achéménide: Nouvelles recherches*, ed. Pierre Briant and Rémy Boucharlat (Paris: De Boccard, 2005); Lori Khatchadourian, "The Achaemenid Provinces in Archaeological Perspective," in *A Companion to the Archaeology of the Ancient Near East*, ed. Daniel T. Potts (Malden, MA: Wiley-Blackwell, 2012), II 963–83 (esp. 966–69); and Christopher J. Tuplin, "The Military Environment of Achaemenid Egypt," in *AhW*, III 291–328. We should probably distinguish between the King's Eye (Aesch. *Pers.* 980, Ar. *Ach.* 92–93, Hdt. 1.114, Xen. *Cyr.* 8.6.16, Plut. *Artax.* 12.1), who appears to have been one of the principal officials of the realm and to have made regular inspection tours on the King's behalf, and the Eyes and Ears of the King (Xen. *Cyr.* 8.2.10–12 [cf. Hdt. 1.100.2, 112.1]), who seem to have been paid informers or public accusers of relatively low rank: Wilhelm Eilers, *Iranische Beamtennamen in der keilschriftlichen Überlieferung* (Leipzig: Brockhaus, 1940), 22–23, and Richard N. Frye, "The Institutions of the Achaemenids," in *Beiträge zur Achämenidengeschichte*, ed. Gerold Walser (Stuttgart: Franz Steiner Verlag, 1972), 83–94. The Achaemenids are said to have borrowed these institutions from the Medes (Hdt. 1.100.2, 112.1, 114) who had taken them over from the Egyptians and Assyrians. But Elam, which lay beyond the purview of the Greeks, may well have been the principal source: see Daniel T. Potts, *The Archaeology of Elam: Formation and Transformation of an Ancient Iranian State* (Cambridge: Cambridge University Press, 1999), and the material collected in Rahe, *PC*, preface to Part I, notes 7–8. The Persians apparently passed these practices on to India and China. For a survey of the Oriental evidence, see Adolf L. Oppenheim, "The Eyes of the Lord," *JAOS* 88:1 (January–March 1968): 173–80. Jack M. Balcer, "The Athenian Episkopos and the Achaemenid 'King's Eye,'"*AJPh* 98:3 (Autumn 1977): 252–63, has argued that the Athenians followed Persian practice as well. I see no reason to doubt the existence of an Achaemenid intelligence network. Cf., however, Lewis *SP*, 19–20.

17. National uprisings: Darius' seizure of power in 522 occasioned rebellions in virtually every corner of the empire: DB. For later rebellions, we depend chiefly on

Greek writers who quite naturally knew more about the empire's western marches than about the East. We are best informed concerning Egypt which rebelled in 486 (Hdt. 7.1–2, 4, 7) and again in 460 (3.12, 15, 7.8; Thuc. 1.104, 109–10, 112.3; Ctesias *FGrH* 688 F13.26, F14.35–F36.32–34; Pl. *Menex.* 241e; Philochorus *FGrH* 328 F119; Diod. 11.71.3–6, 74.1–4, 75, 77.1–5), where there was trouble in 411 (Diod. 13.38.4–5, 46.6) and another rebellion not long before 400: *AP* nos. 34–35; Xen. *An.* 1.8.9, 2.1.14, 5.13; Isoc. 5.101; Diod. 14.35.3–5. The second rebellion lasted for a number of years; the last, for decades: Friedrich K. Kienitz, *Die Politische Geschichte Ägyptens vom 7. bis zum 4. Jahrhundert vor der Zeitwende* (Berlin: Akademie Verlag, 1953), 67–112, and Stephen Ruzicka, *Trouble in the West: Egypt and the Persian Empire, 525–332 BCE* (Oxford: Oxford University Press, 2012). Babylon rebelled in 482: cf. Hdt. 1.183, 3.150–60, and Arr. *Anab.* 3.16.4, 7.16.5–17.6 with Ctesias *FGrH* 688 F13.26, whose account gibes with the Babylonian evidence: *BC*, 17. See George G. Cameron, "Darius and Xerxes in Babylonia," *AJSL* 58:3 (July 1941): 314–25. There was a Median rebellion that ended in 409 (Xen. *Hell.* 1.2.19) and another that began in or soon after 407 (2.1.13). If these were the only fifth century uprisings in Babylon and Media, it may be because the Persians pursued a policy of unmitigated brutality in dealing with the rebellious natives of these two provinces: Arist. *Pol.* 1284a37–b4.

18. Transfers of population: Hdt. 4.204, 5.15.3, 98.1, 6.3, 20, 119, with Briant, *CA*, 505–7, 955–56. Lewis, *SP*, 6–7, finds further evidence for this practice in *PFT* nos. 851–53, 1010, 1557, 1823, 1957. For a comprehensive overview, see Chiara Matarese, *Deportationen im Perserreich in teispidisch-achaimenidischer Zeit* (Wiesbaden: Harrassowitz Verlag, 2021). Military colonies—Iranian mercenaries in Syria: P. R. S. Moorey, "Iranian Troops at Deve Hüyük in Syria in the Earlier Fifth Century B.C.," *Levant* 7:1 (1975): 108–17. Hyrcanian cavalrymen in Lydia: Xen. *An.* 7.8.15, Strabo 13.4.13, Diod. 17.19.4. See also Tac. *Ann.* 2.47; Pliny *NH* 5.120; Barclay V. Head, *Catalogue of the Greek Coins of Lydia* (London: British Museum, 1901), 122–26; and Louis Robert, "Hyrcanis," *Hellenica* 6 (1948): 16–26. Assyrian infantry as well: Xen. *An.* 7.8.15. Jews at Elephantine in Egypt: *BP*, passim (esp. 27–63, 100–119). In this connection, see Pierre Briant, "Une curieuse Affaire à Éléphantine en 410 av. n.è. Windranga, le sanctuaire de Khnûm et le temple de Yaheweh," in *Égypte pharaonique: Pouvoir, société,* ed. Bernadette Menu (Paris: L'Harmattan, 1996): 115–35, reprinted in an English translation by Amélie Kuhrt as "A Strange Affair at Elephantine in 410 B.C. Widranga, the Sanctuary of Khnûm and the Temple of Yahweh," in Briant, *Kings, Countries, Peoples: Selected Studies on the Achaemenid Empire* (Stuttgart: Franz Steiner Verlag, 2017), 207–20, as well as Gard Granerød, "The Passover and the Temple of YHW: On the Interaction between the Authorities and the Judaean Community at Elephantine as Reflected in the Yedanyah Archive," and Christopher J. Tuplin, "The Fall and Rise of the Elephantine Temple," in *AhW*, 329–72.

Other such settlements: Muhammad A. Dandamayev, "Politische und wirtschaftliche Geschichte," in *Beiträge zur Achämenidengeschichte*, 15–58. For the military colonies in Babylonia, the system of land tenure, and the attendant military and financial obligations, see Guillaume Cardascia, *Les Archives du Murašû: Une Famille d'hommes d'affaires à l'époque perse (503–455 av. J. C.)* (Paris: Imprimerie nationale, 1951), passim, and "Armée et fiscalité dans la Babylonie achéménide," in *Armées et fiscalité dans le monde antique* (Paris: Éditions du Centre national de la recherche scientifique, 1977), 2–10; Muhammad A. Dandamayev, "Achaemenid Babylonia," in *Ancient Mesopotamia: Socio-Economic History*, ed. I. M. Diakonoff (Moscow: Nauka, 1969), 296–311; and Stolper, *E&E*, 18–35, 70–124 (esp. 98–99, 104–24). Muhammad A. Dandamayev, "Die Lehnsbeziehungen in Babylonien unter den ersten Achämeniden," in *Festschrift für Wilhelm Eilers*, ed. Gernot Wiessner (Wiesbaden: Harrassowitz Verlag, 1967), 37–42, has traced these arrangements as far back as the first year of Cambyses' reign. They were presumably part of the settlement imposed by Cyrus the Great after his conquest of Babylon: Xen. *Cyr.* 7.5.36, 72–73, 8.4.28.

19. For the belt as a symbol of vassalage, see Xen. *An.* 1.6.4–11 and Diod. 17.30.4, which should be interpreted in light of what we know of later practice: Geo Widengren, *Der Feudalismus im alten Iran*, 21–32, and "Le Symbolisme de la Ceinture," *IA* 8 (1968): 133–55, and Thierry Petit, "Xénophon et la vassalité achéménide," in *Xenophon and his World*, ed. Christopher Tuplin (Stuttgart: F. Steiner, 2004), 175–99. See also P. R. S. Moorey and M. L. Ryder, "Some Ancient Metal Belts: Their Antecedents and Relatives," *Iran* 5 (1967): 83–98. For the annual review, see Xen. *Oec.* 4.5–11, *Cyr.* 8.6.16, *An.* 1.9.7, *Hell.* 1.4.3. For other mustering places, see Xen. *Cyr.* 2.1.5, 6.2.11, *An.* 2.4.25.

20. Local magnates: Appendix 5.

21. Honored peers: Xen. *Cyr.* 8.1.6–8, 16–20, 6.4–5. See also Hdt. 3.139.2, 7.40–41, 55, 83, 211, 215–28 (esp., 224.2), 8.85, 113; Xen. *An.* 1.6.4, 8.5–6, 21, 25, 9.31, *Cyr.* 2.1.3, 10, 2.21, 3.4, 11, 3.3.41, 48, 69, 4.2.46, 5.15, 5.3.2, 4.7, 7.5.66–68, 71, 85, 8.5.21; Heracleides of Cumae *FGrH* 689 F1; Clearchus F49 (Wehrli); Diod. 17.20.2, 59; Arr. *Anab.* 3.11.5, 21.1, 23.4.

22. Exhortation regarding the seven: DB IV.80–88. Kingdom said to have been divided into seven parts under the co-conspirators: Pl. *Ep.* 7.332a3–b6, *Leg.* 3.695c3–10. For the groups from which the generals and satraps were ordinarily selected, see Appendix 7. Great magnates: Arsames, for example, became satrap of Egypt in 454 (Ctesias *FGrH* 688 F14.36; Thuc. 1.104, 109.3–110.4; and Diod. 11.71.3–6, 74.1–4, 75, 77.1–5 with Gomme, *HCT*, I 305–7, 321–22) and remained such into the last decade of the century: *AP* nos. 17, 21, 27, 30–32 and *AD*, 8–10, nos. 1–13 = *TADAE* nos. A6.3–16 with D. J. K. Taylor, "The Bodleian Letters: Text and Translation," and Christopher J. Tuplin, "The Bodleian Letters: Commentary," in *AhW*, I 21–49, 61–242. See also Christopher J. Tuplin, "Aršāma: Prince and Satrap," in ibid. III 3–72. Pissouthnes is attested as satrap

of Lydia as early as 440: Thuc. 1.115.4–5, Diod. 12.27.3, Plut. *Per.* 25.3–4, Schol. Ar. *Vesp.* 283, and *ML* no. 55 = *O&R* no. 138 with Gomme, *HCT*, I 349–59. He was still satrap when he rebelled against Darius II in the late 420s: Thuc. 3.31.1, 34.2, 8.5.5, 28.3; Ctesias *FGrH* 688 F15.53. For the quasi-hereditary satrapy based at Dascyleium that Pharnabazus inherited from his father Pharnaces (cf. Ar. *Av.* 1028 with Thuc. 8.6.1), see Thuc. 8.58.1, Xen. *Hell.* 3.4.13, 4.1.15 with Debord, *AM*, 83–115. Artabazus, the first member of this family to be awarded the satrapy (Thuc. 1.129.1), conducted the retreat of the remnants of Xerxes' army following the battle of Plataea: Hdt. 7.66, 8.126–29, 9.41–42, 58, 66, 70, 77, 89; Diod. 11.31.3–32.1, 33.1. Artabazus' father the elder Pharnaces (Hdt. 7.66, 8.126–29, 9.41–42, 58, 66, 70, 77, 89; Thuc. 1.129.1) seems to have been the uncle and was one of the chief financial officers of the elder Darius: Hallock, *The Evidence of the Persepolis Tablets*, 11–14, and Lewis, *SP*, 7–13.

23. Absentee landlords: Xen. *Cyr.* 8.1.6–8, 16–20, 6.4–5. Case of Arsames: Ctesias *FGrH* 688 F15.50; *AD* nos. 1–4, 6–13 = *TADAE* nos. A6.3–5, 8–16; and *CBS* nos. 5205, 12957 with *AD*, 88–90; Stolper, *E&E*, 64–66; and Taylor, "The Bodleian Letters: Text and Translation," 1–27, 33–49, as well as Tuplin, "The Bodleian Letters: Commentary," 61–107, 131–242. Power and wealth of great nobles: Stolper, *E&E*, 52–69, and John Ma, "Aršāma the Vampire," in *AhW*, III 189–208. See also Matthew W. Stolper, "Parysatis in Babylon," in *If a Man Builds a Joyful House: Assyriological Studies in Honor of Erle Verdun Leichty*, ed. Ann Guinan et al. (Leiden: Brill, 2006), 463–72.

24. On the Chiliarchy as an office, cf. Peter J. Junge, "Hazarapatiš: Zur Stellung des Chiliarchen der königliche Leibsgarde im Achämenidenstaat," *Klio* 33 (1940): 13–38, and Émile Benveniste, *Titres et noms propres en Iranien ancien* (Paris: Klinksieck, 1966), 67–71, with the more cautious Oswald J. L. Szemerényi, "Iranica V (nos. 59–70)," *Acta Iranica* 2:2 (1975): 313–94 (at 354–92), and Lewis, *SP*, 17–19; and see Briant, *CA*, 258–62, and Arthur Keaveney, "The Chiliarch and the Person of the King," in *Der Achämenidenhof/The Achaemenid Court*, 499–508. The Persian term *hazarapatiš*, like its Greek translation, means "commander of a thousand" and seems originally to have been used to designate the leader of a division in the Persian army (Aesch. *Pers.* 304 [with 314]; Hdt. 7.81; Xen. *Cyr.* 4.1.4, 7.5.17) or the officer in charge of a royal garrison (8.6.1–3, 9). By the time of Sogdianus (Ctesias *FGrH* 688 F15.49–50), however, one of the commanders bearing this title had—like the praetorian prefect under the Roman principate—taken on important political functions (cf. Szemerényi, "Iranica V," 386–87), presumably those associated with the Chiliarchy in late Achaemenid and Hellenistic times: Nep. *Con.* 3.2 read in light of Diod. 18.48.4–5. At the end of the Achaemenid period, the Chiliarch appears to have been the commander of the royal cavalry: cf. Arr. *Anab.* 3.21.1 with 23.4. I am not inclined to follow Lewis (*SP*, 17) in supposing that this was always so. Sogdianus' Chiliarch was not his cavalry commander: Ctesias *FGrH* 688 F15.49–50. At the time

of Xerxes' expedition, the figure most prominent is the Hydarnes son of Hydarnes who commanded the royal bodyguard dubbed by Herodotus the Ten Thousand Immortals: 7.83.1. See Meyer, *GdA*, IV:1 31; Junge, "Hazarapatiš," 32. One should not suppose that the Chiliarch was ever the court marshal: Szemerényi, "Iranica V," 378–92. For another view of the office, cf. Michael B. Charles, "The Chiliarchs of Achaemenid Persia: Towards a Revised Understanding of the Office," *Phoenix* 69:3/4 (Fall–Winter 2015): 279–303, and "The Achaemenid Chiliarch *Par Excellence*: Commander of Guard Infantry, Cavalry or Both?" *Historia* 65:4 (December 2016): 392–412. Limits on access to the King: cf. Hdt. 3.61–79, 84, 118–19 with 1.96–100. See Esther 4:11, 5:9–15; Xen. *Cyr.* 7.5.37–70; 8.3.9, 19–20; and the evidence collected near the end of note 15, above. The eunuchs served two functions: because of their condition, they could be trusted with the royal harem; because of the contempt aroused by that condition, they had no hope of advancing except in the King's favor and could usually be trusted to protect their royal patron and do his bidding: Xen. *Cyr.* 7.5.58–65. See also 8.4.2 as well as Hdt. 3.77–78, 118, 8.103–4; Esther 1:10, 2:3–4, 21–23, 4:4–11, 6:2–3, 14; Ctesias *FGrH* 688 F13.9, 13, 33, F14.42, F15.51, 54, F19.12.1–6, 15.2, 16.1, 17.5–9; Pl. *Leg.* 3.693e–696a with Briant, *CA*, 268–74, and Lloyd Llewellyn-Jones, "Eunuchs and the Royal Harem in Achaemenid Persia (559–331 BC)," in *Eunuchs in Antiquity and Beyond*, ed. Shaun Tougher (Swansea: Classical Press of Wales, 2002), 19–49. Briant's incredulity regarding the presumption, evident in the ancient Greek sources, that all of the prominent men identified therein as eunuchs were *castrati* (*CA*, 274–77) is ill-founded, as Llewellyn-Jones, *KCAP*, 38–40, has shown. The King's eunuchs performed many of the functions assigned the imperial freedmen of the Roman principate and the imperial eunuchs of the later Roman empire: Keith Hopkins, "Eunuchs in Politics in the Later Roman Empire," *PCPhS* 189, n.s. 9 (1963): 62–80. Cf. Reinhard Pirngruber, "Eunuchen am Königshof: Ktesias und die altorientalische Evidenz," in *Die Welt des Ktesias—Ctesias' World*, ed. Josef Wiesehöfer, Robert Rollinger, and Giovanni B. Lanfranchi (Wiesbaden: Harrassowitz Verlag, 2011), 279–312, who takes the absence of Near Eastern evidence for eunuchs in the Achaemenid court as evidence for their absence, with Shaun Tougher, *The Eunuch in Byzantine History and Society* (London: Routledge, 2008), 20. Occasionally, of course, a eunuch forgot his station. The younger Darius, for example, eventually had trouble with Artaxerxes' favorite eunuch Artoxares: Ctesias *FGrH* 688 F15.54.

25. Treasuries: Hdt. 3.96, 5.49; Diod. 17.66, 70; Curt. 5.2.11, 6.3; Arr. *Anab.* 3.16.6–7, 19.5–8; Plut. *Alex.* 36–37; Strabo 15.3.3, 6, 9, 21; Just. *Epit.* 11.14.9 with Cameron, *PTT*, 1–5, 9–17, and Hallock, *The Evidence of the Persepolis Tablets*, 10–11, 25–28. Resources to be deployed against threats from within and from without: Christopher J. Tuplin, "From Arshama to Alexander: Reflections on Persian Responses to Attack," in *From Source to History: Studies on Ancient Near Eastern*

Worlds and Beyond, ed. Salvatore Gaspa, Alessandro Greco, Daniele Morandi Bonacossi, Simonetta Ponchia and Robert Rollinger (Munster: Ugarit-Verlag, 2014), 669–96.

26. Teritechmes' plot, rebellion squelched, Teriteuchmes and many in his family killed: Ctesias *FGrH* 688 F15.55–56. Rebellion in Media quelled: Xen. *Hell.* 1.2.19.

27. Stateira spared on Arsaces' plea, Darius warns Parysatis against this to no avail: Ctesias *FGrH* 688 F15.56, Plut. *Artax.* 2.1–2. The fact that Arsaces' first act upon succeeding to the throne was the execution of Teriteuchmes' assassin is a sign that Stateira nursed her grievances: Ctesias *FGrH* 688 F16.57–58. Soon thereafter, Tissaphernes accused Cyrus of treason (F16.59, Xen. *An.* 1.1.3, Plut. *Artax.* 3), and another Persian accused Parysatis of adultery: Ctesias *FGrH* 688 F16.60. Parysatis subsequently poisoned Teriteuchmes' son: F16.61. The dispute between the two women ended only when Parysatis poisoned Stateira herself: F27.70, F29a–b = Plut. *Artax.* 6.5–9, 18–19. The ancient sources are silent concerning the origins of the queen's preference for her second son, but they do provide the evidence for this hypothesis: Parysatis and Arsaces were on sufficiently good terms before Teriteuchmes' conspiracy for the latter to be able to plead successfully for his wife, and soon thereafter Parysatis and Stateira were at odds. It makes perfect sense to suppose that Parysatis' hatred of her daughter-in-law was the source of the disdain the mother showed her eldest son: Olmstead, *History of the Persian Empire*, 358–76. Cf. Lewis *SP*, 134 n. 153.

28. Pharnabazus aligned with Arsaces: Diod. 14.11.1–4 = Ephorus *FGrH* 70 F70; Diod. 14.22.1 = Ephorus *FGrH* 70 F208; Nepos *Alc.* 9.4–10.6. Hieramenes also: Xen. *Hell.* 2.1.8–9. Before Cyrus' arrival, Asia Minor was a stronghold of Stateira's allies.

29. Idealized portrait of Cyrus: Xen. *An.* 1.1.2. Cyrus delights in charges lodged against Tissaphernes: Plut. *Lys.* 4.1–2 with Kagan, *Fall*, 304–5. Cf. Lewis *SP*, 84 n. 13, 136 n. 2 who tends in general to give preference to Xenophon's testimony. See also Plut. *Artax.* 3, whose source was Ctesias *FGrH* 688 F16.59, F17.

30. Cyrus executes cousins, Hieramenes' sons: Xen. *Hell.* 2.1.8–9 with Lewis, *SP*, 104 (esp. n. 83); Kagan, *Fall*, 295–96; Briant, *CA*, 262; and Llewellyn-Jones, *KCAP*, 62. For Hieramenes' identity, see Appendix 4.

31. Ceremonial deference as an acknowledgement of a claim to the Persian throne: Xen. *Cyr.* 8.3.10 with Grote, *HG*, VII 180, and Briant, *CA*, 165–354. In this connection, see also Vincent Azoulay, "The Medo-Persian Ceremonial: Xenophon, Cyrus and the King's Body," in *Xenophon and his World*, 147–73. For another view, cf. Arcangela Santoro, "A Proposito del Cerimoniale delle 'Mani Coperte' nel Mondo Achemenide," *RSO* 47:1/2 (April 1972): 37–42. See also Georgina Thompson, "Iranian Dress in the Achaemenian Period: Problems Concerning the Kandys and Other Garments," *Iran* 3 (1965): 121–26, and Pirhiya Beck, "A Note on the Reconstruction of the Achaemenid Robe," *IA* 9 (January 1972):

116–22. The particular practice in question—like many another Achaemenid practice—was probably borrowed from the Medes (Strabo 11.13.9–11) or, I must hasten to add, the Elamites.

32. It is telling that the younger Cyrus found it necessary to act alone in 404 (Plut. *Artax.* 3) and received no substantial support from the high officials of the realm and the military colonists in 401: Ctesias *FGrH* 688 F16.59, 63–64, F19.9.1– 20.5; Xen. *An.* 1.1–9 (esp. 7.6–7); Diod. 14.11.1–4, 12.7–9, 19.2–24.7. In this connection, see Kagan, *Fall*, 296–97.

33. Stages in promotion of Cambyses: Pritchard, *ANET*, 306–7, 315–16; Johannes N. Strassmaier, *Inschriften von Cyrus König von Babylon* (538–529 v. *Chr.*) (Leipzig: Eduard Pfeiffer, 1890) nos. 270, 325; Hdt. 1.208.1 (which should be read in light of the *nómos* requiring the Great King to name a co-regent before leading out the army). One should not suppose that, because Cyrus made Cambyses King of Babylon at this time as well (Waldo H. Dubberstein, "The Chronology of Cyrus and Cambyses," *AJSL* 55:4 [October 1938]: 417–19), Babylon is the kingdom to which Herodotus refers: cf. Peter Calmeyer, "Zur Genese Altiranischer Motive: V. Synarchie," *AMI* n.f. 9 (1976): 63–95 (at 84–85). Cyrus was merely associating the old Assyrian office of the vice-kingship of Babylon with the Persian co-regency: Calmeyer, "Zur Genese Altiranischer Motive: V. Synarchie," 90–93. If Herodotus had had Babylon and not Persia in mind, he would certainly have said so. Cf., however, Briant, *CA*, 522, who doubts whether there could have been a co-regency, with Llewellyn-Jones, *KCAP*, 18–19, 153– 54, who draws attention to the pertinence of PF-NN1657, a recently published text from Persepolis, and to Just. *Ep.* 1.1.1–3 and provides a translation of both.

34. Changing status of Xerxes: Olmstead, *History of the Persian Empire*, 215; Hdt. 7.2–3 (cf. Plut. *Mor.* 488; Just. *Epit.* 2.10.1–11); XPf 27–43. Xerxes is depicted as co-regent in full regalia on the eastern jamb of the southern doorway to the main hall of the Palace of Darius at Persepolis: Erich F. Schmidt, *Persepolis: Structures, Reliefs, Inscriptions* (Chicago: University of Chicago Press, 1953), I Plate 138. Opposite him, on the western jamb, Darius is similarly represented: Plate 139. The figure of Xerxes is identified by the inscription (DPb): "Xerxes, son of the King Darius, an Achaemenid." If the co-regent had a title, it was this. The Babylonian tablets do not indicate whether Xerxes, as co-regent, ever bore the title King of Babylon. In the fifth year of his reign as Great King, the designation was dropped from the royal titulary altogether: Cameron, "Darius and Xerxes in Babylonia," 323–24. It was never employed by the Achaemenids again. Although the *mār šarri* of 498 is not identified by name, it is now clear that it was Xerxes: see PF-NN1657 with Llewellyn-Jones, *KCAP*, 18–19, 153–54. There is also iconographic evidence suggesting that Darius may have had a co-regent as early as 497/6. For Artaxerxes II and his appointment of a co-regent, see Plut. *Artax.* 26.1–4, Just. *Epit.* 10.1–2. In the passage cited, Plutarch provides the description needed for the interpretation of the various depictions of the Great Kings with

their co-regents. There is no literary evidence that Xerxes I appointed his eldest son Darius co-regent (Ctesias *FGrH* 688 F13.33, Diod. 11.69), but there is archaeological evidence. It was long thought (Schmidt, *Persepolis*, I 163–69) that the Persepolis Treasury Reliefs (Plates 119, 121–23) depicted the elder Darius seated and the elder Xerxes as co-regent, standing behind the throne. Subsequent studies demonstrated that the reliefs originally appeared on Xerxes' Apadana (Ann Britt Tilia, *Studies and Restorations at Persepolis and Other Sites of Fārs* [Rome: IsMEO, 1972–78], I 175–208) and that both the seated figure and his crown prince wear the headdress that one finds elsewhere associated only with the representations of Xerxes as Great King: Hubertus von Gall, "Die Kopfbedeckung des Persischen Ornats bei den Achämeniden," *AMI* n.f. 7 (1974): 145–61; Calmeyer, "Zur Genese Altiranischer Motive: V. Synarchie," 76–79; and A. Shapur Shahbazi, "The Persepolis 'Treasury Reliefs' Once More," *AMI* n.f. 9 (1976): 151–56. Where Xerxes is himself represented as co-regent (Schmidt, *Persepolis*, I Plate 138), he wears the same crown as Darius (Plate 139). Each Great King appears to have received a crown peculiarly his own at the time of his succession. In contrast, while serving as crown prince, the heir apparent would wear a headdress modelled on that of his father. It is, then, evident that the Treasury Reliefs depict the elder Xerxes and his co-regent, the ill-fated Darius. Xerxes II was Artaxerxes I's only legitimate son: Ctesias *FGrH* 688 F15.47. As such, he was his only lawful heir: Hdt. 3.2.2. He is presumably the *mār šarri* mentioned in a tablet dated to 437: BE IX no. 15. It has recently become clear that he is depicted as co-regent with his father on the southern jamb of the eastern doorway of the Tripylon at Persepolis: cf. Schmidt, *Persepolis*, I 116–120, Plates 77–81, who identified the two as Darius I and Xerxes I, with Gall, "Die Kopfbedeckung des Persischen Ornats bei den Achämeniden," 145–61, and Calmeyer, "Zur Genese Altiranischer Motive: V. Synarchie," 71–76. The co-regency and this iconographic treatment of it persisted into Sasanian times: Robert Göbl, "Investitur im sasanidischen Iran und ihre numismatische Bezeugung: Zugleich ein Beitrag zur Ikonographie der Göttin Anahit," *WZKM* 56 (1960): 36–51, and *Sasanian Numismatics*, tr. Paul Severin (Braunschweig: Klinkhardt & Biermann, 1971), 7–9.

35. On the relative ages of the two Achaemenid princes, see Appendix 6.

36. Existence of household of the *mār šarri* in Babylon from first year of Darius II's reign: BE X nos. 5, 31, 45, 59, 94–95, 101; PBS II/1 nos. 51, 90, 133, 202. There was evidently never more than one *mār šarri* at a time. The phrase is not attested in the plural, and the *mār šarri* is rarely named. On those rare occasions, the tablets mention Cambyses who is known to have been crown prince: note 33, above. The title alone was apparently sufficient to identify the man. It is perhaps worth noting that those Babylonian tablets (BE IX nos. 72, 82–84) that mention Xerxes' son Artarios, the satrap of Babylon and half-brother of Artaxerxes I (Ctesias *FGrH* 688 F14.41–42), do not call him *mār šarri*. "King's Son" was not

a designation borne by all of the sons of the Great King. Cf. Eilers, *Iranische Beamtennamen in der keilschriftlichen Überlieferung*, I 62–65. In 407, Arsaces not yet named co-regent: Plut. *Artax.* 2.3–5 read in light of 26.1–4. Priority normally given the eldest son: Xen. *Cyr.* 8.7.9–11, Pl. *Alc.* I 121c1–6. Royal robes and other garb: Ar. *Av.* 486; Xen. *An.* 2.5.23, *Cyr.* 8.3.13; Ctesias *FGrH* 688 F15.50; Esther 6:6–9; Plut. *Them.* 29.7; with the evidence collected in note 34, above. The exchange of oaths is evident from Xen. *Cyr.* 8.5.24–27 and from *An.* 1.6.7 (where *pistá* is the operative term). The army assembly may have confirmed the King's choice by acclamation or by some other similar procedure: Xen. *Cyr.* 8.7.9–11 and Pl. *Alc.* I 121c1–6 with Widengren, *Der Feudalismus im alten Iran*, 102–42.

37. *Mana badaka* translated as *doûlos*: DB I.19, II.19–20, 29–30, 49–50, 82, III.13, 31, 56, 84–85, V.8 with *ML* no. 12.4. See Widengren, *Der Feudalismus im alten Iran*, 12–21, 32–34, 38. King and subject supposed master and slave: see, for example, Aesch. *Pers.* 50, 74–75, 234, 241–42, 402–4, 584–97; Hdt. 7.101–4, 135–36; Xen. *An.* 1.7.3, *Hell.* 4.1.34–38; Pl. *Leg.* 3.693d–696a, 698b; Isoc. 4.150–52, 5.107; Arist. *Eth. Nic.* 1160b21–31, *Pol.* 1285a15–29, 1313a34–b32 with Raffaele Cantarella, "La Persia nella Letteratura Graeca," in *La Persia e il Mondo Greco-Romano* (Rome: Accademia Nazionale dei Lincei, 1966), 489–504. Management of polity as household: Ar. *Pol.* 1285b29–33. Mesopotamian notion of stewardship: Thorkild Jacobsen, "Mesopotamia," in *The Intellectual Adventure of Ancient Man: An Essay on Speculative Thought in the Ancient Near East*, ed. Henri Frankfort and H. A. Groenewegen-Frankfort (Chicago: University of Chicago Press, 1965), 125–219. Household model and paternalism: *ML* no. 12, Thuc. 1.129.3, Philochorus *FGrH* 328 F149. According to Aristotle (*Eth. Nic.* 1160b22–31), the Great King treated his children as slaves.

38. Unchanging law of Persia: Daniel 6:5–15. Of the *Basileîai tôn barbárōn*, Aristotle (*Pol.* 1285a17–19 with 20–29, 1285b23–25) writes, "*échousi aûtai ten dúnamin pâsai paraplēsían turannísin, eisi dè katà nómon kaì pátriai.*" The emphasis he places on *patríos nómos* is confirmed by the other available evidence. See DB I.11–26, IV.33–69, V.14–20, DPd, DNa, DNb, DSs, XPa, XPh 35–36; Gharib, "A Newly Found Old Persian Inscription," 54–69; Esther I:8–22, 8:8; Ezra 5:17–6:12, 7:11–26; Hdt. 1.137, 3.31, 5.25; Xen. *An.* 1.9.13; Pl. *Ep.* VII. 332b. See also Olmstead, *History of the Persian Empire*, 119–34, and Christopher J. Tuplin, "The Justice of Darius: Reflections on the Achaemenid Empire as a Rule-Bound Environment," in *Assessing Biblical and Classical Sources for the Reconstruction of Persian Influence, History and Culture*, ed Anne Fitzpatrick-McKinley (Wiesbaden: Harrassowitz Verlag, 2015), 73–126. Cf. Arist. *Eth. Nic.* 1160b26–31. *Dunasteía*: Thuc. 3.62.3–4, 4.78.3; Pl. *Leg.* 3.680a–681d; Arist. *Pol.* 1252b15–27, 1272b10, 1292b10, 1293a31, 1302b18, 1303a13, 1306a24, 1307b18, 1308a18, 1308b8, 1311b26. Progress from clan rule to rule over tribe, then nation: Hdt. 1.125.3–4. See George G. Cameron, *History of Early Iran* (Chicago: University of Chicago

Press, 1969), 170–84; Louis D. Levine, "Prelude to Monarchy: Iran and the Neo-Assyrian Empire," in *Iranian Civilization and Culture*, ed. Charles J. Adams (Montreal: McGill University Institute of Islamic Studies, 1972), 39–45; and Hubertus von Gall, "Persische und Medische Stämme," *AMI* n.f. 5 (1972): 261–83. The tension between *nómos* and royal prerogative is admirably illustrated by Herodotus' description (3.31) of Cambyses' overriding tradition to marry his own sister. The ultimate price for this and other acts of lawlessness was the collapse of his rule (3.32–38, 61–66). King bound by religiously sanctioned custom, law, and covenant: Xen. *Cyr.* 8.5.24–27. Covenant of sorts in Epirus (Plut. *Pyrrh.* 5.5), Macedonia (Polyb. 15.25.11, Curt. 10.7.9, Just. *Epit.* 24.5.14), and Sparta (Xen. *Lac. Pol.* 15.7). Xenophon's claim is supported by what we know of the tradition of kingship common to ancient India and Iran: see Heinrich Luders, "Eine arische Anschauung über den Vertragsbruch," *SPAW* Phil.-hist. Kl. (1917): 347–74.

39. Education in riding, using the bow, telling the truth: Hdt. 1.136.2. Mendacity most shameful of crimes: 1.138.1. Bisitun Inscription on "the Lie": DB I.26–35, IV.2–40, 61–69. Therein, Darius explicitly raises the possibility that he is himself a "lie-follower": IV.61–67. For the sacred character of a Persian noble's oath, see Ctesias *FGrH* 688 F14.37–43. Cf., however, F14.34, Xen. *Cyr.* 8.8.2–4.

40. Breach of faith attack on divine order: Ilya Gershevitch, *The Avestan Hymn to Mithra with an Introduction, Translation and Commentary* (Cambridge: Cambridge University Press, 1959), 75, 125. See Jacques Duchesne-Guillemin, "La Religion des Achéménides," in *Beiträge zur Achämenidengeschichte*, 59–82. It matters little whether one supposes the Achaemenid monarchs to have been Zoroastrians or not. The theology espoused in the Old Persian inscriptions of the first Darius and the first Xerxes verged on monotheism: DB IV.61–63, DPd, DPh, DSp, XPb, XPc. Nonetheless, in Achaemenid Persia, the worship of Mithra is directly attested (Hdt. 1.131.1, Xen. *Cyr.* 7.5.53), and it was ostentatiously embraced by the younger Artaxerxes: A^2Sa, A^2Sd, A^2Ha, A^2Hb, A^3Pa. Moreover, it is indirectly attested by the appearance of theophebe names. Some contend that Darius I built Persepolis at the foot of Mithra's Mountain: A. Shapur Shahbazi, "From Parsa to Takht-i Jamshed," *AMI* n.f. 10 (1977): 197–207. Comparative study has shown that the moral and religious understanding embodied in the passage quoted was the common heritage of the Indian and Iranian peoples: Mary Boyce, *A History of Zoroastrianism I: Early Period* (Leiden E. J. Brill, 1975), 3–5, 22–31. These notions could play a role in Greco–Persian relations and sometimes did: Louis L. Orlin, "Athens and Persia ca. 507 B.C.: A Neglected Perspective," in *Michigan Oriental Studies in Honor of George G. Cameron*, ed. Louis L. Orlin (Ann Arbor: University of Michigan, 1976), 255–66.

41. With regard to the possibility that the younger Darius would follow the example of his namesake, Cyrus was not without hope: Plut. *Artax.* 2.3–5. The precedent was a powerful one. Darius the Great was probably unable to meet his obligation

to appoint a successor (Hdt. 7.2.1) in 520/19 when he marched against Scythia: Jack Balcer, "The Date of Herodotus IV.1: Darius' Scythian Expedition," *HSPh* 76 (1972): 99–132. He was himself only thirty at the time: Hdt. 1.209. None of his sons was then old enough to bear the burden. Darius does seem to have named an heir by 507 when we find a reference to the "King's Son of Elam": *Dar. no. 411*. This can hardly have been Xerxes: he was no older than fourteen at the time. Darius did not marry Xerxes' mother Atossa, the daughter of Cyrus, until after his seizure of power in 522: Hdt. 3.88.2; *BC*, 15–17. The most likely candidate is, therefore, the eldest of the sons of Gobryas' daughter: cf. Hdt. 7.2.2–3, who calls him Artabazanes, with Plut. *Mor.* 488 and Just. *Epit.* 2.10.1–11, who give him the name of Darius' great grandfather Ariaramnes: DB I.5. It is not clear whether the new palace being built at Babylon was intended for this son or for Xerxes. Nor, if one accepts Calmeyer's contention ("Zur Genese Altiranischer Motive: V. Synarchie," 83) that the Shaluf stele of ca. 497/6 depicts Darius I and his co-regent, is it possible to determine who this co-regent was. But, if it is not evident when Atossa had the succession altered in her eldest son Xerxes' favor, it is still virtually certain that she did so at some time. Darius' eldest son by his earlier marriage had certainly expected to succeed his father: Hdt. 7.2, Plut. *Mor.* 488, and Just. *Epit.* 2.10.1–11.

42. In what follows, I restate and refine part of the argument I first presented in Paul A. Rahe, "The Military Situation in Western Asia on the Eve of Cunaxa," *AJPh* 101:1 (Spring 1980): 79–96.

43. Relative weakness of Persian infantry: consider Xen. *An.* 1.8 and *Cyr.* 8.8.23 in light of Aesch. *Pers.* 25, 82, 133, 226, 864; Hdt. 7.41, 61.1, 9.61.3–63.2, and see Eur. *HF* 157–64, 188–205. The Achaemenid kings seem not to have learned the lesson of Marathon (Hdt. 6.109–15; Nep. *Milt.* 4–5; Suidas s.v. *Chōrìs hippeîs* with Rahe, *PC*, Chapter 4), Thermopylae (Hdt. 8.207–33 with Rahe, *PC*, Chapter 6), Plataea (Hdt. 9.12–73 with Hans Delbrück, *History of the Art of War within the Framework of Political History I: Antiquity*, tr. Walter J. Renfroe [Westport, CT: Greenwood, 1975], 111–18, and Rahe, *PC*, Chapter 8), and Mycale (Hdt. 9.94–105 with Rahe, *PC*, Chapter 8). We are not provided with full information regarding the battles of Eurymedon (Thuc. 1.100.1, Plut. *Cim.* 12.5–13.3, Nep. *Cim.* 2.2–3 with Rahe, *SFAW*, Chapter 2) and Cypriot Salamis: Thuc. 1.112.2–4; Diod. 12.3.1–4.6; Nep. *Cim.* 3.4; Plut. *Cim.* 18.1–19.2 (with Phanodemos *FGrH* 325 F23), *Per.* 10.4–5; Aristid. *Panath.* 151f; *Suda* s.v. *Kímōn* with Rahe, *SFAW*, Chapter 6. But it is telling that, in both cases, the infantry on both sides came into play, and the result in each case was a Persian defeat. When deprived of effective cavalry support (and only then), Persian footsoldiers were inferior to Greek infantry—and, in the fourth century thanks to what the Ten Thousand achieved at Cunaxa (Xen. *An.* 1.8) and thereafter (1.10–4.8) and to the absence of obstacles encountered when Agesilaus made his foray into Anatolia in 396–95 (Xen. *Hell.* 3.4.2–4.2.4, *Ages.* 1.6–38; *Hell. Oxy.* 24–25 [Cham-

bers]; Diod. 14.79.1–3, 80.1–8, 83.1; and Plut. *Ages.* 6.1–15.8 with Cartledge, *Agesilaos,* 208–18), some of the Greeks began to reflect on Persian military weakness and even think about what they might accomplish should they cooperate in attacking the Achaemenid empire: Pl. *Leg.* 3.697d–e; Xen. *Cyr.* 8.8.1–27 (esp. 7, 20–21, 26–27), *An.* 1.5.9, *Hell.* 3.4.2, 6.1.10, 7.1.38; Isoc. 4.133–35, 145– 49, 5.90–92, 139. The significance of this can, of course, be exaggerated—for the Persians were by no means bereft of resources, as Christopher Tuplin, "The Sick Man of Asia?" in *Between Thucydides and Polybius: The Golden Age of Greek Historiography,* ed. Giovanni Parmeggiani (Cambridge, MA: Harvard University Press, 2014), 211–38, points out. Nonetheless, as I will be arguing here and argued earlier in the article cited in note 42, above, there were leading Persians who were, in the second half of the fifth century, already giving thought to what could be done in Asia with a military force of Greek hoplites if its flanks were protected by cavalry on the Persian model.

In the four decades that have passed since the publication of that article, it has become an article of faith among many of the scholars working on Achaemenid history that the Greek phalanx was in no way superior to the infantry deployed by the Persians. I think this claim, which requires a thoroughgoing rejection of Hellenic testimony and special pleading regarding the performance of the Persians against the Hellenes on the battlefield in the fifth and fourth centuries, implausible in the extreme. Cf. Briant, *CA,* 783–800, whose critique of what he calls "the Greek thesis" is based on a negative assessment of the Hellenic triumphalism of Diodorus Siculus that has some merit and an extension of that critique to all of the other Greek sources, unsupported by evidence or argument, that has no merit whatsoever; and Jeffrey Rop, *Greek Military Service in the Ancient Near East, 401–330 BCE* (Cambridge: Cambridge University Press, 2019), who acknowledges the inadequacy of Briant's argument and who attempts to reestablish his claim regarding the relative merits of Persia's infantry on another foundation—by dismissing much of the Greek testimony in this regard as a byproduct of the literary strategies adopted by its authors (ibid. 1–29). See, for an example of the special pleading required, his treatment of Xenophon's testimony concerning the battle of Cunaxa: ibid. 30–45, which presupposes that one cannot employ literary devices, as Xenophon does, unless one is playing a con and propagating a lie. Moreover, Rop's rewrite of the Athenian eyewitness' battle narrative (ibid. 45–63) is based on the principle that it is legitimate to choose arbitrarily to believe an eyewitness's testimony when it fits one's own presumptions and to reject that same eyewitness's testimony when it does not. Even, however, if his fanciful reconstruction were correct, it would not demonstrate that on its own, if it was not so numerically superior that it could outflank and envelop its foe, Persian infantry could stand up to the phalanx. As Rop acknowledges at the very end of his disquisition (ibid. 62–63), Cyrus' Greeks "almost certainly would have crushed the royal left wing had its wicker shield-bearing infantry and the archers behind them" actually put up a fight—as, Xenophon reports and Rop denies, they did. Hyland's adherence to what constitutes the new orthodoxy in this regard explains his failure even to consider the possibility explored here—that Cyrus' relations with Lysander were governed from the outset by his desire to acquire a mercenary force of Greek hoplites large enough to enable him to make a bid for the Persian throne: *PI*, 106–18, 123–27.

44. For the various sorts of Persian cavalry, see Hdt. 7.84 (with 61.1), 9.13.3–76.5 (esp. 49.2); Xen. *An.* 1.8, *Hell.* 3.4.13–14, *Cyr.* 6.4.1, 7.1.2, 46. See note 52, in context below: because he neglects the Herodotean evidence for Persian horse archers (9.49.2), Erich R. F. Ebeling, "Die Rüstung eines babylonischen Panzerreiters nach einem Vertrage aus der Zeit Darius II," *ZA* n.f. 50 (1952): 203–13, fails to recognize Gadal-Iama's function: note 52, below. In matters of horsemanship, the Persians appear to have been imitators of the Assyrians: John W. Eadie, "The Development of Roman Mailed Cavalry," *JRS* 57 (1967): 161–63 with Plate IX; J. K. Anderson, *Ancient Greek Horsemanship* (Berkeley: University of California Press, 1961) Plates 3–6; and Yigael Yadin, *The Art of Warfare in Biblical Lands in the Light of Archaeological Study*, tr. Moshe Pearlman (New York: McGraw-Hill, 1963), II 382–87, 402–3, 416–17, 427, 432–33, 442–45, 450–53, 456–59. They may have learned something from the Lydians as well: Hdt. 1.79.3. Cf. J. K. Anderson, "Notes on Some Points in Xenophon's *Perì Hippikês*," *JHS* 80 (1960): 7–8, with Paul Bernard, "Une Pièce d'armure perse sur un monument lycien," *Syria* 41 (1964): 195–212. Ability to defeat the Romans when the cavalry of the latter is inferior: Plut. *Crass.* 17–33.

45. Hoplite phalanx' point of vulnerability: Thuc. 5.71. For the ripple effect, see John Keegan, *The Face of Battle* (New York: Viking Press, 1976), 97–98. In this connection, note Hdt. 6.29; Thuc. 4.96.5, 7.5–6; Polyaen. *Strat.* 5.16.2. For the differences between Greek and Roman infantry, see Delbrück, *History of the Art of War*, I 53–58, 272–77. An imaginative Greek commander could post independent reserve forces near the left and right flanks to meet a cavalry charge head on should it come: Xen. *An.* 6.5.9. See note 48, below.

46. Rough terrain in most of Greece an obstacle to cavalry effectiveness, ancillary function: Xen. *Hipparch.* 1.4, 16, *Eq.* 4.3–5. See Anderson, *Ancient Greek Horsemanship*, 89–92, 111, and Frank E. Adcock, *The Greek and Macedonian Art of War* (Berkeley: University of California Press, 1957), 48. See also Hdt. 9.13.3. One can easily illustrate the ancillary uses of cavalry from Thucydides: 1.111.1, 4.95.2, 96.6–8, 5.73.1, 6.64.1, 66, 68.3, 70.3, 98.3–4, 7.4.6, 11.4, 13.2, 44.8, 78.6, 81.2, 84.1 with Adcock, *The Greek and Macedonian Art of War*, 48–53.

47. Vulnerability of shock cavalry: see R. M. Rattenbury, "An Ancient Armoured Force," *CR* 56:3 (1942): 113–16, who cites Heliod. *Aeth.* 9.15; and note Xen. *An.* 3.2.18–19.

48. Animal behavior as a constraint on the effectiveness of shock cavalry: Keegan, *The Face of Battle*, 94–97, 153–59. This is well illustrated for ancient times by

Hdt. 4.128.2–3, Polyaen. *Strat.* 7.14.3–4, and Procop. *Goth.* 4.8.31–32. Note also Thuc. 1.111.1. In exaggerating the technical advance marked by the introduction of the stirrup, Lynn White attributed to it military, political, and social consequences which it did not have: cf. White, *Medieval Technology and Social Change* (Oxford: Oxford University Press, 1962), 1–38, with critical reviews published by P. H. Sawyer and R. H. Hilton, *P&P* 24:1 (1963): 90–100. Late in the fifteenth century, the Swiss pikemen defeated the Burgundian knights of Charles the Bold in two great battles, employing tactics that differed little from those used by the Greeks in the Persian Wars: Hans Delbrück, *Die Perserkriege und die Burgunderkriege* (Berlin: Walther, 1887), 167–226.

49. Greek cavalry undeveloped as arm: Anderson, *Ancient Greek Horsemanship*, 15–39, 140–54.

50. On Megabyzus, note Ctesias *FGrH* 688 F14.34–43, and see Rahe, *SFAW*, Chapters 5–6, and *SSAW*, Chapter 1 (with note 15), where I cite further evidence and the pertinent secondary literature. Cf. Briant, *CA*, 577–78, who harbors doubts. Hellenic mercenaries long employed in the eastern Mediterranean: Hdt. 3.70, 81–82, 153, 156–60, 4.43, 7.82, 121; Thuc. 1.104, 109–10, 112.3; Ctesias *FGrH* 688 22–43; Diod. 10.19.2–3, 11.74.6–75.2, 77.4, 12.3.2–4, 4.4–5 with Wolf-Dietrich Niemeier, "Archaic Greeks in the Orient: Textual and Archaeological Evidence," *BASO* 322 (2011): 11–32, and Nino Luraghi, "Traders, Pirates, Warriors: The Proto-History of Greek Mercenary Soldiers in the Eastern Mediterranean," *Phoenix* 60:1 (Spring–Summer 2006): 21–47. Employment by Egypt's Saite Pharoahs, see *ML* no. 7; Hdt. 2.152–54, 161–69, 178–82, 3.1–7, 10–13 with Michel M. Austin, *Greece and Egypt in the Archaic Age*, *PCPhS*, Suppl. 2 (1970): 15–22. Pissouthnes, the satrap of Lydia, was employing mercenaries by the time of the Samian rebellion in 440: Thuc. 1.115.2–117.3 and Diod. 12.27–28 with Schol. Ar. *Vesp.* 283, *ML* no. 55 = *O&R* no. 138, and Plut. *Per.* 24–28 (esp. 25.4). Note Hdt. 8.26. For further discussion and a fuller citation of the sources and the secondary literature, see Rahe, *SSAW*, Chapter 1.

51. Use of Greek mercenaries in the rebellions of Artyphius and Pissouthnes: Ctesias *FGrH* 688 F15.52–53 and Thuc. 8.28. See Xen. *Cyr.* 8.8.26.

52. Museum of Anthropology of the University of California no. 9–68: first published by Henry Frederick Lutz, "An Agreement Between a Babylonian Feudal Lord and his Retainer in the Reign of Darius II," *University of California Publications in Semitic Philology* 9 (1928): 269–77. I have adopted the English translation of Robin Lane Fox (*Alexander the Great* [London: Futura Publications, 1975], 159). Cf. Cardascia, *Les Archives du Murašû*, 179–82. The best discussion of this document and of the crisis of Persian feudalism in general is Guillaume Cardascia, "Le Fief dans la Babylonie Achéménide," *Recueils de la Societé Jean Bodin* 1 (1958): 55–88. See also his *Les Archives du Murašû*, 7–8, 29 n. 5, 55–62, 82–83, 98–106; Lane Fox, *Alexander the Great*, 118–20, 126–30, 140–41, 155–60, 514–18, 527–28; and Dandamayev, "Politische und wirtschaftliche Geschichte,"

15–58, "Achaemenid Babylonia," 296–311, and "Die Lehensbeziehungen in Babylonien unter den ersten Achameniden," 37–42. For the role played by the Murašû in Nippur, Stolper's *E&E* is indispensable. See, especially, 18–35, 49–51, 104–56. Situations similar to that of Gadal-Iama pop up elsewhere: cf. Xen. *Hell.* 3.4.15, 6.4.10–11.

53. See Stolper, *E&E*, 104–56. Land appears to have been relatively cheap and draft animals, farm equipment, and water, relatively expensive. From the beginning, the deck was stacked in favor of the entrepreneur and his bureaucratic patrons.

54. Some resolutely deny that there was a decay in foundations of Persian military strength in Babylonia: see, for example, Briant, *CA*, 597–99, 979–80, who rightly insists that the system in place allowed the Great Kings of this period to raise sizable armies but dodges the implications of the evidence cited here for the recruits' military incompetence—which is what I stressed long ago in Rahe, "The Military Situation in Western Asia on the Eve of Cunaxa," and stress again here. Troops untrained in archery, horsemanship, and the management of a chariot are worse than useless.

55. Hoplite core for Cyrus' army in 401: Xen. *An.* 1, Diod. 14.19.2–24.7.

56. Peloponnesus the major source of Greek mercenaries: Herbert W. Parke, *Greek Mercenary Soldiers: From the Earliest Times to the Battle of Ipsus* (Oxford: Clarendon Press, 1933), 14–15 (with notes), 23–42. Hermippus (F63 [Edmonds]) lists mercenaries among Athens' imports from Arcadia. See also Hdt. 8.26; Thuc. 1.115.4, 3.34.2, 7.57.9, 8.3, 28.4; Diod. 12.27.3, 13.51.2; Xen. *An.* 1.1.6, 6.2.10 with James Roy, "The Mercenaries of Cyrus," *Historia* 16:3 (July 1967): 287–323, and "Arcadian Nationality as Seen in Xenophon's *Anabasis*," *Mnemosyne*, 4th ser., 25:2 (January 1972): 129–36.

57. George Grote's judicious remarks (*HG*, VII 220–21) concerning Cyrus have not received the attention they deserve.

58. Conspiracy of Pausanias: Hdt. 5.32, Thuc. 1.126–38, Nepos *Paus.* 2–5, Diod. 11.45–46, and Paus. 3.17.7–9 with Rahe, *SFAW*, Chapters 1–3. Cyrus' need: Kagan, *Fall*, 297–301. Agis on Lacedaemon's "second Pausanias": Ath. 12.543b.

CHAPTER 7. A SECOND PAUSANIAS

Epigraph: Alexis de Tocqueville, *De la démocratie en Amérique*, ed. Jean-Claude Lamberti and James T. Schleifer, I.ii.10, in Alexis de Tocqueville, Œuvres (Paris: Bibliothèque de la Pléiade, 1991–2004), II 395.

1. Lysander at Ephesus, journey to Cyrus at Sardis with Boeotius and the other ambassadors dispatched to Susa from Sparta: Xen. *Hell.* 1.5.1 with Bommelaer, *Lysandre*, 83–86; Kagan, *Fall*, 301–3; and Lazenby, *PW*, 218. The season is a subject of dispute, as Kagan, *Fall*, 297–98, n. 21, points out. The passage cited refers to Lysander's arrival as having occurred "not a great deal of time before these events [*próteron toútōn ou pollộ chrónộ*]." The reference of *toútōn* [these events]

is at issue. Absent compelling evidence to the contrary, it would be natural to assume that it refers to the arrival of Alcibiades at Samos mentioned in the immediately preceding paragraphs (Xen. *Hell.* 1.4.21–23)—particularly since the passage dealing with the meeting of Lysander and Cyrus (5.1–10) is sandwiched in between two discussions of the doings of Alcibiades (4.21–23 and 5.11). Most scholars nonetheless prefer to take *toútōn* as a reference to Alcibiades' decision to return (4.8) to Athens: e.g., Grote, *HG*, VI 361 n. 3; Beloch, *Gr. Gesch.*, II:2 273–74; Antony Andrewes, "The Generals in the Hellespont, 410–407 B.C.," *JHS* (73) 1953: 2–9 (at 2 n. 1); Lotze, *Lysander*, 14; Raphael Sealey, "Die spartanische Navarchie," *Klio* 58:2 (January 1976): 335–58 (at 347); Bommelaer, *Lysandre*, 73–75; and Krentz, *Xenophon*, 134. Some adopt this position without full conviction: Kagan, *Fall*, 297, and Lazenby, *PW*, 217. Those who do take this stand treat the entire discussion of Alcibiades' activities in the summer of 407 as a digression interrupting Xenophon's narrative, but not intervening chronologically between the meeting of Cyrus with the Athenian ambassadors being conveyed by Pharnabazus to Darius (*Hell.* 1.4.4) and the arrival of Lysander at Ephesus (5.1). The latter view has the virtue that it does not leave an unfilled gap of three to five months between Boeotius' meeting with the ambassadors in the spring (4.2–3) and Cyrus' arrival at Sardis in the late summer or early fall (5.1–2), but places both events in the spring. We do not, however, know precisely where the meeting with Boeotius took place, how late in the spring it occurred, when Cyrus left Susa, when he in turn encountered the Athenian ambassadors, and how quickly he is likely to have traveled. Their meeting with Boeotius did not induce the Athenians to give up their hopes of seeing the Great King. In all likelihood, they continued on their journey and encountered Cyrus at a point much closer to Susa. Given the vast distances to be covered and the slowness of travel by land in the ancient world, it is likely that this meeting occurred in the summer at a time when Cyrus still had a great deal of ground to traverse. Note, in this connection Hyland, *PI*, 107, who pays close attention to distances and to the time it takes to travel. The unfilled gap is easily filled. I prefer the former view because it has the virtue of not leaving Lysander inactive at Ephesus (Xen. *Hell.* 1.5.11) during the entire period of Alcibiades' sojourn at Athens. It seems to me incomprehensible that Lysander would not have taken advantage of Alcibiades' absence to take some action. For another argument in favor of the dating scheme followed here, see Chapter 8, note 2, below. The controversy concerning the date at which a Spartiate assumed the office of navarch (cf. Beloch, *Gr. Gesch.*, II:2 269–89, with Sealey, "Die spartanische Navarchie," 335–58, and see Bommelaer, *Lysandre*, 75–79) does not affect the chronological argument above. For the reasons, that I spell out in the text, above, Lysander may well have assumed office some months before he set out for Ionia.

2. Lysander *móthax*: Phylarchus *FGrH* 81 F43 ap. Ath. 6.271e–f, Ael. *VH* 12.43. Helot descent: Isoc. 4.111. Note also Xen. *Hell.* 3.5.12. Rearing: Phylarchus

FGrH 81 F43, Ael. *VH* 12.43, Plut. *Cleom.* 8.1, Harp. s.v. *móthōn*, Schol. Ar. *Plut.* 279, Schol. Ar. *Eq.* 634, Hesych. s.v. *móthakes* and *móthonas*, Etym. M. s.v. *móthōn*, Stobaeus *Flor.* 40.8. See also Hdt. 9.33-36, Xen. *Lac. Pol.* 10.7, Arist. *Pol.* 1270a34-35, Plut. *Mor.* 238e. Some, of course, have been unwilling to believe that a figure as great as Lysander could have come from so vile a social origin: Beloch, *Gr. Gesch.*, II:1 416 n. 1; Busolt, *Gr. Gesch.*, III:2 1569 n. 3; and Bomme-laer, *Lysandre*, 36-38. They have neglected to observe that it is the rarity of the occurrence which caused his origin to be remarked upon: see Grote, *HG* VI 362 (with n. 1); Meyer, *GdA*, IV:2 331 n. 2; Lotze, *Lysander*, 12 n. 4; Kagan, *Fall*, 298-99; Cartledge, *Agesilaos*, 28-29; and Lazenby, *PW*, 217. Some scholars— such as Paul Cartledge—think that the *móthakes* of the fifth century were the sons of Spartiates too poor to pay the requisite mess dues. As I explain in Rahe, *SR*, Introduction and Appendix 1, there are no grounds for supposing the exis-tence of such a class of Spartiates prior to the end of Sparta's third Attic war. On the significance of the demographic crisis produced by the earthquakes of 464 and the subsequent helot revolt for the appearance of the *móthakes*, see Ludwig Ziehen, "Das spartanische Bevölkerungsproblem," *Hermes* 68 (1933): 218-37.

3. Lysander's poverty, his father Aristocritus a Heraclid: Plut. *Lys.* 2.1-2, 8, 18.3, 30.2, 6, *Comp. Lys. et Sull.* 3.6-7 with *IG* II² 1385, line 20; 1388, line 32; 1400, line 15, and Paus. 6.3.14. Aristocritus maintains *xenía* with Libys, name given son: Diod. 14.13.6. For an example of another Spartiate whose claim to descent from Heracles was acknowledged though he was not a member of either royal family, see Diod. 11.50.6. At *Comp. Lys. et Sull.* 2.1, Plutarch seems to intimate that Lysander lacked noble birth. But the fact that it was believed that he had plotted to change the Spartan constitution to allow the selection of the kings from among all of the descendants of Heracles seems to confirm the report that Lysander was Aristocritus' natural son: Plut. *Lys.* 24.4-6. Xenophon (*Hell.* 5.3.8-9) can speak in the same breath of *xénoi tōn trophímōn kalouménōn* and of *nóthoi tōn Spartiátōn*.

4. Lysander a self-made man: Plut. *Comp. Lys. et Sull.* 1.2. I do not share Detlef Lot-ze's suspicion that the Spartans were as yet unaware of the importance of the navarchy and that Lysander might have received the office without having dis-tinguished himself: cf. Lotze, *Lysander*, 13-14.

5. Plato makes much of the Spartan pride of birth [*génous ógkos*] and notes (*Alc.* I 121b4-8) that the ephors kept the wives of the kings under public guard in order to guarantee the purity of the blood of their offspring. For the survival of distinc-tions of this kind at Sparta, see Alcmaeon F49d; Hdt. 4.146.3, 149.2, 7.134.2; Thuc. 4.108.7, 5.15.1, 34.2; Xen. *Lac. Pol.* 8.1-4, 14.4; Plut. *Nic.* 10.8 (with Thuc. 5.34.2, Pl. *Menex.* 242c); Arist. *Pol.* 1270b; Isoc. 6.55. See also Thuc. 1.6.4 and Plut. *Agis* 2.6, 5, *Lys.* 2.3, 19.1, with Franz Kiechle, *Lakonien und Sparta: Unter-suchungen zur ethnischen Struktur und zur politischen Entwicklung Lakoniens und*

Spartas bis zum Ende der archaischen Zeit (Munich: Beck, 1963), 133–41.

6. Lysander and Agesilaus: Plut. *Lys.* 22.6, *Ages.* 2.1. Allied until 396: Xen. *Hell.* 3.3.1–4.20; Plut. *Lys.* 22.3–24.6, *Ages.* 3.4–9, 6.1–8.5 with Cartledge, *Agesilaos*, 20–33, 55, 77–99, 110–15, 211–13, 358–59, 408–9. On the relationship between sex and politics at Sparta, see Pl. *Leg.* 1.636b–c. Regarding the role that love affairs could play in the political arena in that *pólis*, consider the example of Sphodrias: Xen. *Hell.* 5.4.15–23. Cf. Lotze, *Lysander*, 11–14, who harbors a certain skepticism regarding some of the claims of Plutarch that I credit here.

7. Agesilaus' respect for family ties: Xen. *Hell.* 3.4.29, 4.3.10–14, 5.4.25–33, *Ages.* 11.13; Plut. *Ages.* 4.1, 10.11, 17.4–5, 21.1, 25; Paus. 3.9.3. Pronounced penchant for benefitting friends: Xen. *Hell.* 5.3.10–17, 21–24, *Ages.* 1.17–19, 2.22–23, 4.1–6, 6.4, 9.7, 11.3, 8, 10, 12–13, 15; Isoc. 5.86–88; Plut. *Ages.* 5.1–3, 13.4–7, with Cartledge, *Agesilaos*, 139–59.

8. That Agis favored the policy Lysander subsequently pursued is evident from the vigor with which he prosecuted the Deceleian War (Thuc. 8.3, 70–71; Xen. *Hell.* 1.1.33–34), from his eagerness to extend the war to the eastern Aegean and close off the Hellespont (Thuc. 8.3–12, Xen. *Hell.* 1.1.35–36), and from his consistent refusal in and after 411 to entertain terms of peace requiring compromise (Thuc. 8.70–71, Xen. *Hell.* 2.2.11–13). His stance is later confirmed by the proposal that he, with Lysander, submitted after Aegospotami suggesting that Athens be razed (Paus. 3.8.6), and by the hostility to the Agiad king Pausanias that he displayed in the wake of the latter's acquiescence in a restoration of democracy at Athens (Paus. 3.5.1–2). Note Agis' summoning of Alcamenes (Thuc. 8.5), the son of Agis' father's opponent Sthenelaidas (1.79–87), to be the instrument of his policy. By this time, Agis had abandoned his father's caution and had adopted the outlook of Sthenelaidas. Immediately after making a trip to consult with Agis, Lysander departed for the Hellespont to accomplish precisely what Agis, observing the arrival of the grain ships at Athens after the battle of Cyzicus, had sent Clearchus to do: note Xen. *Hell.* 1.1.35, then see Plut. *Lys.* 9.3–6 and Diod. 13.104.8. After the battle of Aegospotami, Lysander moved quickly to cut off the flow of grain from the Hellespont (Xen. *Hell.* 2.2.1–2), following the strategy devised years before by Agis. The only time that the two were together prior to the final settlement in a place where the allies might have held a congress was the occasion described at Xen. *Hell.* 2.2.7–9, Diod. 13.107.3, and Plut. *Lys.* 14.1–2. A number of scholars have concluded that the two were allies: Busolt, *Gr. Gesch.*, III:2 1627; Meyer, *GdA*, V 31 (esp. n. 1), 40; W. G. G. Forrest, *A History of Sparta, 950–192 B.C.*, 2nd edition (London: Hutchinson University Library, 1980), 120; and Cartledge, *Agesilaos*, 29.

9. For the primary evidence focused on the Spartan way of life and the pertinent secondary literature, see Rahe, *SR*, Chapter 1.

10. For the evidence pertaining to the powers accorded the Spartan kings and for

the secondary literature on the subject, see Rahe, *SR*, Chapter 2 (with notes 16–35).

11. Lacedaemon's assault on privacy: Rahe, *SR*, Chapter 1 (with notes 74–81).

12. Plato on the greed and miserliness nonetheless displayed by the Lacedaemonians: *Alc.* I 122e2–123a4, *Resp.* 8.544c, 545a, 548a–b with Rahe, *SR*, Chapter 1 (esp. notes 72–79, where additional evidence is cited).

13. The great wealth of the Spartan kings and its origins: Xen. *Lac. Pol.* 15.3 and Pl. *Alc.* I 123a4–8.

14. Aristotle and Dionysius of Halicarnassus on the defective sumptuary laws at Lacedaemon: Arist. F611.13 (Rose) = Tit. 143.1.2.13 (Gigon) ap. Heraclid. Lemb. 373.13 (Dilts) and Dion. Hal. *Ant. Rom.* 20.13. Aristotle on the Spartans' propensity for greed and on the intemperance and power of their women: *Pol.* 1269b12–1270a33. On the lack of self-control exhibited by Spartan women, see also Pl. *Leg.* 1.637c, 6.780d–781d, 7.804c–806c, and note Dion. Hal. *Ant. Rom.* 2.24.6 and Plut. *Comp. Lyc. et Num.* 3.

15. On the Spartan father's freedom to bestow his daughter on whomever he wished, see Arist. *Pol.* 1307a34–40. The power to oversee adoptions and dispose of heiresses was presumably given to the kings because they had an interest in maintaining the numerical strength of the army. They seem, however, to have lost the latter power by Aristotle's time: *Pol.* 1270a26–28.

16. Agis king by 426: Thuc. 3.89.1.

17. Lysander's winning of his bride: Ath. 13.555c with Plut. *Lys.* 30.2–7. I suspect that Athenaeus is describing the archaic ritual by which the kings disposed of the heiresses. For skepticism concerning this report, see Bommelaer, *Lysandre*, 58. Of modern scholars, Arnold Toynbee seems to have been the first to realize the potential for acquiring clients implicit in the system by which *móthakes* and *hupomeíones* could gain or recover citizenship: *Some Problems of Greek History* (London: Oxford University Press, 1969), 343–46. In this connection, see Paul Cartledge, "The Politics of Spartan Pederasty," *PCPhS* 27 (1981): 17–36, and Kagan, *Fall*, 299–300.

18. Lysander's age can be inferred from the fact that he was the *erastés* of the young Agesilaus. Xenophon indicates (*Ages.* 2.28) that Agesilaus was over eighty and Plutarch (*Ages.* 40.3) that he was eighty-four when he died not long after the second battle of Mantineia, which took place in 362. This means that he was born in about 444. According to Plutarch, Spartan boys took on *erastaí* when they were about twelve: *Lyc.* 16.11–17.1. The context leaves no doubt that the *erastaí* were adults—a conclusion evident also from *Lyc.* 25.1. In light of this, it is clear that Lysander was at least ten years older than Agesilaus. In another context, Plutarch explicitly states that Lysander was substantially older: *Mor.* 805e–f. He can hardly have been younger than forty-seven in the year 407 and may have been in his fifties: see Lotze, *Lysander*, 13 (esp. n. 1–2). Lysander and the *dunatoí*: Plut. *Lys.* 2.4 with Kagan, *Fall*, 300–301. See, in this connection, Polyb.

12.6a.3–4. On the meaning of the term *dunatoí*, see Kiechle, *Lakonien und Sparta*, 133–41, and Pavel Oliva, *Sparta and her Social Problems* (Amsterdam: Hakkert, 1971), 188 n. 3. See also note 5, above: it is clear that an hereditary aristocracy survived at Sparta from the earliest times. Some families no doubt lost the wealth needed to sustain their position. In time, others may, by one means or another, have been recruited, into the *prôtoi oîkoi* and have joined the *dunatoí*.

19. Lysander's melancholia: Arist. *Pr.* 30.1, Plut. *Lys.* 2.5. Alcibiades' *philotimía*: Plut. *Alc.* 2.1–7, 7.4–5, 9.1–10.2, 12.1–3, 16.4, 23.3–9, 27.6, 34.1–7, *Comp. Alc. et Cor.* 2.5, 5.1. That of Lysander: Plut. *Lys.* 2.1–5, 19.1–2, 21.4–6, *Comp. Lys. et Sull.* 4.3– 5. Lysander impervious to the temptations of wealth and luxury: Theopompus of Chios *FGrH* 115 F20 = Ath. 12.543b–c; Plut. *Lys.* 2.6–8, 30.2–7, *Comp. Lys. et Sull.* 3.1–3, 6–8, 5.6. Alcibiades subject to such temptations: Thuc. 6.15.4; Plut. *Alc.* 6.2–4, 8.4–5, 16, 23.7–8, *Comp. Alc. et Cor.* 1.3, 3.1, 5.2.

20. Visit to *parádeisos*: Xen. *Oec.* 4.20–25. Banquet and salary negotiation, four obols a day agreed: Xen. *Hell.* 1.5.1–7; Diod. 13.70.3; Plut. *Lys.* 4.4–6, *Alc.* 35.5 with Lotze, *Lysander*, 15–17; Bommelaer, *Lysandre*, 85–86; Kagan, *Fall*, 303–6; Lazenby, *PW*, 218; Hutchinson, *Attrition*, 189; and Kapellos, *XPW*, 79–83. Persian taste for pederasty: Hdt. 1.135. Tissaphernes' supposed pledge to the Athenians: Thuc. 8.81.3. He had originally contracted to pay a drachma—which is to say, six obols—a day to those crewing the Spartan fleet: 8.45.2. Expense incurred by Cyrus and duration if five hundred talents the limit: Hyland, *PI*, 108–10.

21. Alcibiades on Andros: Xen. *Hell.* 1.4.21–23, Diod. 13.69.5, Plut. *Alc.* 35.2. Cf. Edmund F. Bloedow, *Alcibiades Reexamined* (Wiesbaden: F. Steiner, 1971), 73, with Hatzfeld, *Alcibiade*, 306, and see Moshé Amit, "La Campagne d'Ionie de 407/6 et la bataille de Notion," *GB* 3 (1975): 1–13 (at 2–4). Cf. Bleckmann, *Niederlage*, 91–93. Then, he visits Kos and Rhodes in search of funds: Diod. 13.69.5. On this journey and Alcibiades' aims, see Hatzfeld, *Alcibiade*, 308–9; Kagan, *Fall*, 308–10; and Lazenby, *PW*, 218–19. Abortive embassy to Cyrus: Xen. *Hell.* 1.5.8–9 with Hatzfeld, *Alcibiade*, 309; Lotze, *Lysander*, 17; Amit, "La Campagne d'Ionie de 407/6 et la bataille de Notion," 4–7, 12; Kagan, *Fall*, 307; and Lazenby, *PW*, 219. Cf. Lewis, *SP*, 130–31 (with n. 134), and Munn, *SH*, 179, who leave Alcibiades out of the picture when discussing this embassy. In one passage (*Alc.* 35.5) Plutarch claims that Alcibiades was in Caria at the time of the battle of Notium; in another (*Lys.* 5.1), he follows Xenophon (*Hell.* 1.5.11) in placing him at Phocaea at this time. Considerations of time and geography would suggest that Alcibiades raided Caria en route from Rhodes to Samos and sailed soon after arriving at Notium from there to Clazomenae (*Hell. Oxy.* 7 [Chambers], Diod. 13.71.1) and, then, on to Phocaea. On Athens' need for money, see Plut. *Alc.* 35.4–5.

22. For the purpose of raising the daily pay for mariners above what the Athenians could afford to pay, see Xen. *Hell.* 1.5.4. On the decline in Athenian morale and on their oarsmen turning coat, see Xen. *Hell.* 1.5.8 and Plut. *Lys.* 4.6–8. In this

connection, see Lotze, *Lysander*, 17, and Kagan, *Fall*, 308–11. Clazomenae: Diod. 13.71.1. Phocaea: Xen. *Hell*. 1.5.11 and Plut. *Lys*. 5.1. Cf. Busolt, *Gr. Gesch.*, III:2 1574–75; Hatzfeld, *Alcibiade*, 309; Kagan, *Fall*, 312–14; and Lazenby, *PW*, 219–20, who regard Phocaea as the principal object of the excursion, with Amit, "La Campagne d'Ionie de 407/6 et la bataille de Notion," 8–11, and Krentz, *Xenophon*, 139, who suspect that Chios was the ultimate goal.

23. Battle at Notium: consider *Hell. Oxy*. 8 (Chambers) and Diod. 13.71.2–4 in light of Iain A. F. Bruce, *An Historical Commentary on the Hellenica Oxyrynchia* (Cambridge: Cambridge University Press, 1967), 35–39; Peter Krentz, *The Thirty at Athens* (Ithaca, NY: Cornell University Press, 1982), 139; and Egidia Occhipinti, "The Ships in the Battle of Notion: A New Supplement for Lines 9–12 of the Florence Papyrus (PSI 1304)," *ZPE* 187 (2013): 72–76, and see Paus. 3.17.4, 9.32.6. For a slightly different and, I suspect, less accurate account written from the perspective of a Spartan witness, see Xen. *Hell*. 1.5.12–14, whose version is followed in Plut. *Alc*. 35.6–7 and *Lys*. 5.1–2. Cf. Hatzfeld, *Alcibiade*, 309–12; Hans R. Breitenbach, "Die Seeschlacht bei Notion (407/06)," *Historia* 20:2/3 (2nd Quarter 1971): 152–71 (esp. 168–71); Bommelaer, *Lysandre*, 89–95; Christopher J. Tuplin, "Military Engagements in Xenophon's *Hellenica*," in *Past Perspectives: Studies in Greek and Roman Historical Writing*, ed. Ian S. Moxon, John D. Smart, and Anthony J. Woodman (Cambridge: Cambridge University Press, 1986), 37–66 (at 49–50); Bleckmann, *Niederlage*, 162–80; and Hutchinson, *Attrition*, 190–94, who prefer Xenophon's account, with Kagan, *Fall*, 314–18; and see Lotze, *Lysander*, 19–22; Amit, "La Campagne d'Ionie de 407/6 et la bataille de Notion," 8–13; Antony Andrewes, "Notion and Kyzikos: The Sources Compared," *JHS* 102 (1982): 15–25 (at 15–19); Krentz, *Xenophon*, 139–41; Lazenby, *PW*, 219–22; Rhodes, *Alcibiades*, 88–90; John R. Hale, *Lords of the Sea: The Epic Story of the Athenian Navy and the Birth of Democracy* (New York: Viking Penguin, 2009), 355; Hyland, *PI*, 110–11; and Stuttard, *Nemesis*, 274–76. The view of what Antiochus and Lysander intended that these authors adopt and that I accept is an inference based upon Diodorus' report. For another view of the former's purpose, see Frank Russell, "A Note on the Athenian Defeat at Notium," *AHB* 8:2 (1994): 35–37, and Munn, *SH*, 177–78.

24. Envoys detained by Pharnabazus: Xen. *Hell*. 1.4.4–7. Whether they were held for three years, as we are told in this passage and as Munn, *SH*, 163–64, 176 (with n. 4), 179, believes, or the text needs emending and three months is the correct duration, as Moshé Amit, "Le Traité de Chalcédoine entre Pharnabaze et les stratèges Athéniens," *AC* 42:2 (1973): 436–57 (at 452 n. 16), suggests and most scholars now assume, we do not know. There is, as well, another possibility—unmentioned in the secondary literature as far as I can tell—which is that the unit of time was the week as understood in Babylonia, where it ran for seven days; in Egypt, where it ran for ten days; or in Iran, where it could have been either length. The fact that there was no Greek calendar in which the months

were divided into weeks could help explain the corruption of the text—for the copyist of the original might well have been confronted with a word of Elamite, Babylonian, Egyptian, Aramaic, or Iranian origin which had no analogue in Greek and with which he was not familiar, and he may then have substituted *eniautoí* on the presumption that the non-Greek term he had found was a corruption of this Greek word. At this time, the Zoroastrians of Persia employed a religious calendar of three hundred sixty days supplemented by an additional five days—for which they may to have been indebted to the civil calendar of the Egyptians, which had twelve months of thirty days and tacked on an additional five days: see Sayyid Hasan Taqizadeh, *Old Iranian Calendars* (London: Royal Asiatic Society, 1938), and Willy Hartner, "Old Iranian Calendars," in *CHI*, II 714–92. In this connection, see also Heidemarie Koch, *Achämeniden-Studien* (Wiesbaden: Harrasowitz, 1993), 61–91, and François de Blois, "The Persian Calendar," *Iran* 34 (1996): 39–54, and "Lunisolar Calendars in Ancient Iran," in *Proceedings of the 5th Conference of the Societas Iranologica Europaea*, ed. Antonio Panaino and Andrea Piras (Milan: Mimesis, 2006), 39–52.

25. Minority at Athens profoundly hostile to Alcibiades in the spring of 407: Xen. *Hell.* 1.4.16–17. See also Plut. *Alc.* 34.1–2, 7–35.1. Excessive expectations raised, disappointment the result: 35.3–4. Alcibiades deposed in the wake of Notium: Nepos *Alc.* 7.3, Just. *Epit.* 5.5.4–6.1, and Plut. *Lys.* 5.3–4. Cf. Xen. *Hell.* 1.5.16–20, Diod. 13.73.6–74.4, and Plut. *Alc.* 36.1–4, who summarize the criticism directed at Alcibiades, note the discontent at Samos, and report only that he was not reelected in the early spring of 406. Conon, who had been *stratēgós* for 407/6 (Xen. *Hell.* 1.4.10) and was re-elected for the following year, was dispatched in short order [*tachéōs*] after Notium to relieve Cleinias' now unpopular son: Diod. 13.74.1. I see no reason to doubt the report of Nepos, Justin, and Plutarch that Alcibiades was relieved of duty, but cf. Beloch, *Gr. Gesch.*, II:2 250–52, and Bleckmann, *Niederlage*, 491–503, who also calls into question the reports that there was widespread opposition to him in the fleet, with Busolt, *Gr. Gesch.*, III:2 1578 n. 2. See, in this connection, Hatzfeld, *Alcibiade*, 316, and Rhodes, *Alcibiades*, 91. See also Lys. 21.7 for evidence confirming his deposition. Whether the dispatch of Phanosthenes, who was not a *stratēgós* for 406/5, to take command at Andros (Xen. *Hell.* 1.5.18) when Conon was sent to replace Alcibiades provides further confirmation is a matter of dispute: cf. Jennifer T. Roberts, *Accountability in Athenian Government* (Madison: University of Wisconsin Press, 1981), 224 n. 62, and Kagan, *Fall*, 321–22 n. 120, with Krentz, *Xenophon*, 143–44, and see Lazenby, *PW*, 289 n. 12. Alcibiades' failure to take Andros may well have contributed to breaking the spell. For overviews, see Hatzfeld, *Alcibiade*, 314–18; Lotze, *Lysander*, 22–23; Kagan, *Fall*, 321–22; Munn, *SH*, 177–79; Lazenby, *PW*, 222–24; Hutchinson, *Attrition*, 194; and Luca Asmonti, *Conon the Athenian: Warfare and Politics in the Aegean, 414–386 B.C.* (Stuttgart: Franz Steiner Verlag, 2015), 51–68. Diodorus' account (13.73.3–

74.1) of the role played by Aeolian Cumae in all of this is suspect. Among other things, Cornelius Nepos, who was ordinarily beholden to the same ultimate source as Diodorus, claims that the city was at that time hostile to Athens: *Alc.* 7.1-2. The difference may derive from the fact that Ephorus, who may have been Diodorus' immediate source, was a local booster with a tendency to introduce his native city where it did not belong: see Ephorus *FGrH* 70 F236 ap. Strabo 13.3.6 with Godfrey L. Barber, *The Historian Ephorus* (Cambridge: Cambridge University Press, 1935), 86-88. For a defense of Ephorus against this claim, see Deborah Hobson Samuel, "Cyme and the Veracity of Ephorus," *TAPhA* 99 (1968): 375-88. On the particular question under discussion here, cf. Hatzfeld, *Alcibiade*, 313-14; Kagan, *Fall*, 320-21 (with n. 110); Munn, *SH*, 178; Rhodes, *Alcibiades*, 90, 93; and Stuttard, *Nemesis*, 276-79, who are more favorable to Ephorus' views in this regard, with Bleckmann, *Niederlage*, 488-90. Note, in this connection, Lazenby, *PW*, 222-23, and Kapellos, *XPW*, 65-66, 90-96. Pactyes: *IACP* no. 671. Bisanthe: no. 673.

26. Alcibiades' departure for the Thracian Chersonnesus: Xen. *Hell.* 1.5.17, Diod. 13.74.2-4, Nep. *Alc.* 7.4, Plut. *Alc.* 36.3-5 with Hatzfeld, *Alcibiade*, 318-22; Munn, *SH*, 179; Rhodes, *Alcibiades*, 90-91, 95-96; Stuttard, *Nemesis*, 280-84; and Kapellos, *XPW*, 93-96. Import of loss: cf. Kagan, *Fall*, 323-24, who greatly underestimates Alcibiades' qualities as a *stratēgós*, with Lazenby, *PW*, 223-24, who wrongly suspects that Kagan may be correct on this count but provides a just assessment of Alcibiades' qualities as a diplomat and intriguer, and see Kapellos, *XPW*, 10-36. *Stratēgoí* at Athens elected in the spring of 406: Xen. *Hell.* 1.5.16. Critias forced into exile: Xen. *Hell.* 2.3.15. In exile prior to the battle of Arginusae: 2.3.36. Cleophon lodges charges against him: Arist. *Rhet.* 1375b32. Cleophon vs. Alcibiades: Himer. *Ecl.* 36.15 = Phot. *Bibl.* 377a18. Cf. Buck, *Thrasybulus*, 30, 46-47, who acknowledges that the fate meted out to Thrasybulus and Theramenes at this time derived from their association with Alcibiades, then implies that the judgment of the Athenians with regard to the character of their connection was wrong since their "close professional association implies little about mutual liking or disliking." To substantiate his claim that the ties linking Thrasybulus with Alcibiades were purely professional, he offers no evidence. The fact that the Athenians evidently thought otherwise should be given great weight.

27. The size of the two opposed fleets: Diod. 13.69.4, 70.2-3, 71.4, 76.3, 77.1; Xen. *Hell.* 1.4.21, 5.1, 18, 20, 6.3. Xenophon indicates that Lysander's fleet had increased from seventy to ninety by the time Notium took place (1.5.10) and that his successor's fleet soon grew from one hundred forty to one hundred seventy: 1.6.16. Fifty of the ships in Callicratidas' fleet may have come from Chios and Rhodes (1.6.3), but the odds are that the fifty in question were manned, for the most part, by deserters from the Athenian fleet: 1.5.4, Plut. *Lys.* 4.6-8. In this connection, see Kagan, *Fall*, 326-27, and Lazenby, *PW*, 224. Cf. Asmonti,

Conon the 'Athenian, 69–73, who claims, on no basis whatsoever, that Conon succeeded Alcibiades as *stratēgòs autokrátōr.*

28. For a just appreciation of Lysander's *modus operandi* and his achievement, see Bommelaer, *Lysandre,* 199–206 (esp. 199–202).

29. Iteration in the navarchy prohibited: Xen. *Hell.* 2.1.7, Diod. 13.100.8, Plut. *Lys.* 7.3. Office now held for a defined term: Xen. *Hell.* 1.5.1, 6.1. For the term, cf. Beloch, *Gr. Gesch.,* II:2 269–89, with Sealey, "Die spartanische Navarchie," 335–58, and see Bommelaer, *Lysandre,* 75–79. They all agree that, at this time, the term of office was one year. In this connection, see Kagan, *Fall,* 327, and Lazenby, *PW,* 224. The navarch's sacrifice and consultation of victims: Diod. 13.97.4–5. His command and delegation of responsibilities: 13.98.1–4. His regulation of pay and disposition of booty: Xen. *Hell.* 1.5.1–7, 6.12–14. His negotiations with Persia and arrangements of the affairs of Greek cities: 1.5.1–7 and Diod. 13.65.3–4. Of course, a navarch could sometimes find it difficult to control his subordinates: Thuc. 8.28, 32–33, 38–40, 55, 61. Navarchy almost another kingship: Arist. *Pol.* 1271a40.

30. Macaulay on "noiseless revolutions": see Thomas Babington Macaulay, "History," *Edinburgh Review* 47:94 (May 1828): 331–67 (at 362–63), reprinted in Macaulay, *Critical, Historical and Miscellaneous Essays* (New York: Hurd & Houghton, 1860), I 376–432 (at 425), with Joseph Hamburger, *Macaulay and the Whig Tradition* (Chicago: University of Chicago Press, 1976).

31. Jean-Jacques Rousseau on the mutilation of human nature: see the unpublished first draft of his *Du Contrat social* in Jean-Jacques Rousseau, *Œuvres complètes,* ed. Bernard Gagnebin and Marcel Raymond (Dijon: Bibliothèque de la Pléiade, 1959–95), III 313, with Paul A. Rahe, *Soft Despotism, Democracy's Drift: Montesquieu, Rousseau, Tocqueville, and the Modern Prospect* (New Haven, CT: Yale University Press, 2009), 75–140. *Xenelasía* and prohibition against travel abroad: Xen. *Lac. Pol.* 14.4, Plut. *Lys.* 20.6–21.1. In *The Laws* (1.633a–634c), Plato complains that the Spartan regime does not produce men genuinely endowed with self-control: by depriving them of pleasure, it fails to teach them how to control themselves in the face of temptation.

32. Misconduct of the regent Pausanias drives the Ionians into an alliance with the Athenians: Hdt. 8.3; Thuc. 1.94–97; Plut. *Cim.* 6.1–7, *Arist.* 23.1–7. In the passages cited, Plutarch gives specific examples of Pausanias' excess which included the murder of the Byzantine virgin Cleonice whom he had summoned for purposes of debauchery, and a refusal on his part to allow any of the soldiers of the allied forces to get bedding, fodder, or water before the Spartiates themselves. Pausanias' misconduct causes Lacedaemonians to fear sending Spartiates abroad: Thuc. 1.95, Arist. *Ath. Pol.* 23. Note the manner in which the Spartans, fearful of contamination, quarantined the Spartiate prisoners who had been captured by the Athenians at Sphacteria in 425: Thuc. 5.34.2.

33. Warning issued by the Athenian ambassadors: Thuc. 1.77.6. Subsequent

misconduct by Spartiates sent abroad: 8.20, 23–24, 26, 29, 31–33, 36, 38–42, 45, 50, 61, 63, 68, 78–79, 83–85; Diod. 13.66.3–6. See also 14.12.2–9.

34. Xenophon on the corruption of Spartiates dispatched abroad: *Lac. Pol.* 14.2–7 with Noreen Humble, "The Author, Date and Purpose of Chapter 14 of the *Lakedaimonion Politeia*," in *Xenophon and his World*, ed. Christopher Tuplin (Stuttgart: F. Steiner, 2004), 215–28, and *Xenophon of Athens: A Socratic on Sparta* (Cambridge: Cambridge University Press, 2021), who shows that the harsh critique of Lacedaemon articulated in this particular chapter follows naturally from the analysis and understated critique of the Lycurgan regime presented in the chapters preceding. Also see, in this connection, Leo Strauss, "The Spirit of Sparta or the Taste of Xenophon," *Social Research* 6:4 (November 1939): 502–36; William E. Higgins, *Xenophon the Athenian: The Problem of the Individual and the Society of the Polis* (Albany: State University of New York Press, 1977), 64–82, 115–23; Gerald Proietti, *Xenophon's Sparta: An Introduction* (Leiden: E. J. Brill, 1987); and Christopher J. Tuplin, *The Failings of Empire: A Reading of Xenophon Hellenica 2.3.11–7.5.27* (Stuttgart: Franz Steiner Verlag, 1993).

35. Patron of the new class: Bommelaer, *Lysandre*, 211–15.

36. Extended proconsulships fatal to Roman liberty: Peter A. Brunt, "The Army and Land in the Roman Revolution," *JRS* 52 (1962): 69–86. The army of the late republic included many landless men ultimately dependent for land grants as a compensation for military service on the political skill of their *imperator*. They looked to him for economic benefits while he looked to them for political and, in a crisis, military support. The position of these landless Romans resembled that of the *móthakes* and *hupomeíones* at Sparta. On the willingness of the former to volunteer for service on the campaign against Olynthus in the late 380s, see Xen. *Hell.* 5.3.9.

37. Arrival of Callicratidas on station: Xen. *Hell.* 1.6.1. See also Diod. 13.76.1–2. Xenophon's reference in this passage to the eclipse of 15 April 406 is decisive for the date.

38. Callicratidas' youth: Diod. 13.76.2. His status as a *móthax*: Ael. *VH* 12.43. In this connection, see note 2, above.

39. Rivalry between the two royal houses: Hdt. 6.52.8, Arist. *Pol.* 1275a25–26. The use of the word *stasiázein* in the latter passage suggests that the rivalry between the two houses took the form of strife between factions [*stáseis*] grouped around the two kings. When it comes to the foreign *clientelae* of the two royal houses, the most obvious case in point is Phlius: Xen. *Hell.* 5.3.10–17, 20–25. Note also Diod. 15.19.4. There are indications that this was true at Mantineia as well: Xen. *Hell.* 5.2.1–7. The same can be said for Elis: 3.2.2–31, Paus. 3.8.3–6, Plut. *Mor.* 835f. In each case, one can observe links between the proponents of democracy and the Agiad house and between the supporters of oligarchy and the Eurypontid house. In practice, this probably meant that the Agiad kings favored local autonomy, not democracy, and were therefore tolerant of the democratic

regimes that their Eurypontid colleagues were eager to destroy: see Ronald Legon, "Phliasian Politics and Policy in the Early Fourth Century B.C.," *Historia* 16:3 (July 1967): 324–37; David G. Rice, "Agesilaus, Agesipolis, and Spartan Politics, 386–379 B.C.," *Historia* 23:2 (Second Quarter 1974): 164–82; and George. L. Cawkwell, "Agesilaus and Sparta," *CQ* n.s. 26:1 (May 1976): 62–84, reprinted in Cawkwell, *Cyrene to Chaeronea: Selected Essays on Ancient Greek History* (Oxford: Oxford University Press, 2011), 241–74.

40. Resistance encountered by Callicratidas: Xen. *Hell.* 1.6.4–6.

41. Sharp exchange between Callicratidas and Lysander: Xen. *Hell.* 1.6.2–3, Plut. *Lys.* 6.2–3 with Kagan, *Fall*, 327–29; Lazenby, *PW*, 224–25; and Hutchinson, *Attrition*, 194–95.

42. Lysander returns unused funds to Cyrus: Xen. *Hell.* 1.6.8–11 and Plut. *Lys.* 6.1 with Bommelaer, *Lysandre*, 96, and Hutchinson, *Attrition*, 195. Formation of *het-aireíai* in the Ionian cities: Diod. 13.70.4 and Plut. *Lys.* 5.5–8 with Kagan, *Fall*, 306–7. Diodorus places this before Notium and Plutarch, after. It makes little difference who is right. I prefer Plutarch because it seems to me more plausible to suppose that Lysander could not have accomplished the feat of making these men his clients until after he had shown his tactical prowess at Notium. Hutchinson, *Attrition*, 190, prefers Diodorus.

43. Lysander's partisans: Plut. *Lys.* 13.5–9 with Cartledge, *Agesilaos*, 79–81. The significance of his connection with Cyrus: Bommelaer, *Lysandre*, 218–19. It would be proper to refer to Lysander's Ionian associates as oligarchs—as Lotze, *Lysander*, 17–19, 24, 27–29, does—were it not for the fact that the word often connotes the rich and well-born, as he well knows. Lysander's *dunatótatoi* (Diod. 13.70.4) probably included quite a number of men who, at an earlier time under different circumstances, had been identified with the cause of the *dêmos*. The various revolutions and attempted revolutions on Samos in 412 and 411 are an indication of just how messy allegiances could be, and the same can be said for Athens: see Chapters 2 and 4, above. See, in this connection, Thuc. 6.89.4–6. According to Thucydides (8.66.5), the conspirators of 411 included a number of Athenians whom no one would previously have imagined to be the enemies of the democracy. Peisander himself had been one of the demagogues elected in 415 to the committee of inquiry that looked into the charge that, behind the mutilation of the Herms and the profanation of the Mysteries, lay concealed an oligarchic plot: Andoc. 1.36. One of his colleagues on that board was a man named Charicles (Andoc. 1.36), who later emerged as one of the Four Hundred (Isoc. 26.42, Lys. 13.74) and ultimately as a leading member of the Thirty: Lys. 12.55, Xen. *Hell.* 2.3.2. In both Samos and Athens, the defenders of democracy included a host of opportunists. These were the natural allies of Lysander. Note Plutarch's repeated use of the word *xenía* to describe the connections formed: *Lys.* 5.6, 8.1, 13.7. The parallel institution at Rome was *hospitium*. Ernst Badian justly observed, "Naturally, as Roman power became dominant, *hospitium*, orig-

inally a relationship between equals, developed into a form of *clientela*: the Roman senator would in fact be the patron of the Sicilian *hospes*": Badian, *Foreign Clientelae* (Oxford: Oxford University Press, 1958), 155. The same seems to have been true at this time in Greece. It is this that explains why Nepos (*Lys.* 1.5), in attempting to make sense of Lysander's conduct for a Roman audience, used the terms *hospitium* and *fides* to describe the relationships linking Lysander with his partisans. See, in this connection, Plut. *Lys.* 5.5–9 (esp. 6), 8.1, 13.7. On the role played by personal ties in Greek politics, see Kenneth J. Dover, *Lysias and the Corpus Lysiacum* (Berkeley: University of California Press, 1968), 47–56. This can, of course, be exaggerated: see, for example, Raphael Sealey, "The Revolution of 411 B.C.," in Sealey, *Essays in Greek Politics* (New York: Manyland Books, 1967), 111–32. To assume that personal or factional interest always determined conduct is as absurd as to assume that class interest always did so.

44. Callicratidas tames Lysander's lieutenants: Xen. *Hell.* 1.6.4–6 with Kagan, *Fall*, 329–30; Lazenby, *PW*, 225; and Hutchinson, *Attrition*, 195. Cf. Krentz, *Xenophon*, 146.

45. Callicratidas at odds with Cyrus: Xen. *Hell.* 1.6.7; Plut. *Lys.* 6.5–7, *Mor.* 222c–d, with Lotze, *Lysander*, 24; Kagan, *Fall*, 330–32; Lazenby, *PW*, 225; and Hyland, *PI*, 111–13. Cf. Munn, *SH*, 179, 196, who supposes that, in frustrating Callicratidas, Cyrus is following the advice Tissaphernes was prompted to give him (Xen. *Hell.* 1.5.8–9) and pitting the two Greek powers against one another with an eye to weakening them both. Much has been written regarding the assessment implicit in Xenophon's juxtaposition of Lysander and Callicratidas. For a survey of the scholarship and a reconsideration attentive to the political context, see John L. Moles, "Xenophon and Callicratidas," *JHS* 114 (1994): 70–84. I do not think that Xenophon's only standard for judgment was military leadership, as Vivienne J. Gray, *The Character of Xenophon's Hellenica* (Baltimore: Johns Hopkins University Press, 1989), 14–19, 22–23, 81–83, 146–49, does. For a corrective with regard to Xenophon's assessment of Lysander's conduct, cf. Kapellos, *XPW*, 98–132. In suggesting that Xenophon was a severe critic of Callicratidas' conduct, however, Kapellos is—like Gray and Proietti, *Xenophon's Sparta*, 10–21—insufficiently attentive to the difficulties he faced. Given Lysander's legacy, it is not likely that Callicratidas could have secured Cyrus' support. Nor could he have rallied to his banner his predecessor's partisans. His only option was to assert his authority as navarch, to rely on the fear that this inspired, and to take on the Athenians. Enthusiasm would follow if he was successful in the field.

46. Callicratidas shifts fleet back to Miletus: Xen. *Hell.* 1.6.8–11. Ephesus a center of Persian influence: Plut. *Lys.* 3.3. Lysander and Agesilaus were to make it their base in 396: Xen. *Hell.* 3.4.20. Tissaphernes chose to sacrifice at the temple of Artemis in that city in 411, at a time when he was interested in recovering the goodwill of the Spartans: Thuc. 8.109.2. It was, tellingly, in the name of this goddess that he later summoned the local magnates and their minions to Ephesus'

defense: Xen. *Hell.* 1.2.6. Incident at Miletus: Thuc. 8.84 with Chapter 2, above. On Lysander's selection of Ephesus as his base and Callicratidas' choice of Miletus, cf. Hans Schaefer, "Alkibiades und Lysander in Ionien," *Würzberger Jahrbücher für die Altertumswissenschaft* 4 (1949/50): 287–308 (at 301–2), with Lotze, *Lysander,* 15, 25; Bommelaer, *Lysandre,* 88–89; Kagan, *Fall,* 301–2, 332; and Lazenby, *PW,* 218, 225.

47. Treaty renegotiations: Chapter 2, above. Spartan ambivalence towards Persia was, as we have seen, nothing new: Thuc. 4.50.

48. Callicratidas and Lysander's Milesian partisans: Plut. *Mor.* 222c. Rallies populace against the Mede, secures financial support, sends appeal to Sparta: Xen. *Hell.* 1.6.8–12 with Lotze, *Lysander,* 25; Kagan, *Fall,* 332–33; and Lazenby, *PW,* 225. I see no reason to credit the contention—advanced by Bruce Laforse, "Xenophon, Callicratidas and Panhellenism," *AHB* 12:1–2 (1998): 55–66—that Callicratidas' remarks on this occasion were just a show for Milesian consumption. His subsequent willingness to accept money from Cyrus was a function of necessity.

49. Chian subvention: Xen. *Hell.* 1.6.12. Seizure of Teos and Delphinium: Diod. 13.76.3–4 with Xen. *Hell.* 1.5.15, where I have adopted the emendation suggested by Schneider. Cf. Kapellos, *XPW,* 89, who takes the Xenophon passage as evidence that Lysander captured Delphinium and Eion, which lies on the Strymon river in Thrace. Conquest of Methymna, Thorax dispatched: Xen. *Hell.* 1.6.12–15 and Diod. 13.76.5–6. See Lotze, *Lysander,* 25; Kagan, *Fall,* 333–34; and Lazenby, *PW,* 225–26. Regarding the machinations of Lysander and Callicratidas' predicament and aim, see Bommelaer, *Lysandre,* 86–89, 96 (with 72).

50. Conon to the Hekatonnesoi isles: Diod. 13.77.1–2. Callicratidas' taunt: Xen. *Hell.* 1.6.15. Conon's colleagues: 1.6.16, Lys. 21.8 with Lotze, *Lysander,* 25; Kagan, *Fall,* 334–35; and Lazenby, *PW,* 226. In this connection, see W. James McCoy, "The Identity of Leon," *AJPh* 96:2 (Summer 1975): 187–99 (at 189–93). Note also Asmonti, *Conon the Athenian,* 73–76.

51. Conon's stratagem and its failure: Diod. 13.77.2–78.3. For a much more abbreviated and, in some ways, confusing account, which has Callicratidas, supposedly with a fleet of a hundred seventy triremes, as its focus, and neglects entirely Conon's plans, cf. Xen. *Hell.* 1.6.16–17, whose testimony is preferred by Tuplin, "Military Engagements in Xenophon's *Hellenica,*" 62–65; Vivienne J. Gray, "The Value of Diodorus Siculus for the Years 411–386 BC," *Hermes* 115:1 (1st Quarter 1987): 72–89 (at 80–81, 84–85); Kagan, *Fall,* 355; Bleckmann, *Niederlage,* 93–101; and Hutchinson, *Attrition,* 196–97. Cf., however, Peter Krentz, "Xenophon and Diodoros on the Battle of Mytilene (406 B.C.)," *AHB* 2:6 (November 1988): 128–30; Lazenby, *PW,* 226–27; and Asmonti, *Conon the Athenian,* 75–76. Note also Lotze, *Lysander,* 25–26.

52. The two harbors at Mytilene: Strabo 13.2.2–3 with Nigel Spencer, *A Gazeteer of Archaeological Sites in Lesbos* (Oxford: BAR, 1995), no. 27. I sojourned on the

island of Lesbos from 12 to 18 April 2022 and took the opportunity to examine closely both harbors, the area of Mytilene that had once been an island, and the path along Ermou Street where the channel separating the little island from the rest of Lesbos had once run.

53. The battle over the northern harbor at Mytilene: Diod. 13.78.4–79.7. Cf. Xen. *Hell.* 1.6.16–18. Cf. Tuplin, "Military Engagements in Xenophon's *Hellenica*," 62–65; Gray, "The Value of Diodorus Siculus for the Years 411–386 BC," 85; Kagan, *Fall*, 335; and Bleckmann, *Niederlage*, 102–4, who dismiss Diodorus' testimony, with Krentz, "Xenophon and Diodoros on the Battle of Mytilene (406 B.C.)," 130, who makes a compelling case for the veracity and accuracy of the Sicilian historian's account of this particular engagement. See also Lazenby, *PW*, 228, and Hutchinson, *Attrition*, 197. Death of Archestratus: Lys. 21.8.

54. Cyrus sends funds, Callicratidas refuses offer of *xenía*: Xen. *Hell.* 1.6.18 and Plut. *Mor.* 222e with Kagan, *Fall*, 337–38; Lazenby, *PW*, 227–28; and Hyland, *PI*, 113. Cf. Xen. *Ages.* 8.3–4.

55. Conon's messenger ships: Xen. *Hell.* 1.6.19–22 with Kagan, *Fall*, 337; Lazenby, *PW*, 228–29; and Hutchinson, *Attrition*, 197–98. That Erasinides commanded the vessel that got away is an inference from the fact that he reappears a few weeks later as a commander of the relief expedition dispatched: Xen. *Hell.* 1.6.29. Leon, however, drops out of sight: McCoy, "The Identity of Leon," 192–94.

56. Diomedon's intervention: consider Xen. *Hell.* 1.6.22–23 in light of 1.5.16, and see Lazenby, *PW*, 229, and Hutchinson, *Attrition*, 198, who fails to consider the possibility that Diomedon was at this point unaware of Callicratidas' victory.

57. In 407/6, quite possibly at the instigation of Alcibiades, the Athenians voted to melt down golden dedications from their temples to pay for a crash campaign to produce triremes: Schol. Ar. *Frogs* 720 = Hellanicus *FGrH* 323a F25 with Wesley E. Thompson, "The Golden Nikai and the Coinage of Athens," *NC*, 7th ser. 10 (1970): 1–6, read in light of *IG* I³ 117 = *ML* no. 91 = *O&R* no. 188 with Lazenby, *PW*, 229, and Rhodes, *Alcibiades*, 87. In this connection see Thomas J. Figueira, *The Power of Money: Coinage and Politics in the Athenian Empire* (Philadelphia: University of Pennsylvania Press, 1998), 500–502, 517–21, and Loren J. Samons II, *Empire of the Owl: Athenian Imperial Finance* (Stuttgart: Franz Steiner Verlag, 2000), 281–88. Had the Athenians delayed this crash program until the summer of 406, when word reached them concerning Conon's predicament in Mytilene—as Kagan, *Fall*, 338; Munn, *SH*, 180; and others suppose—there would not have been time for the effort to yield much in the way of triremes.

58. Athenians ready fleet: slave and free, even *hippeîs* called up to serve: Xen. *Hell.* 1.6.24. Freedom and political rights on the Plataean model offered and eventually awarded the slaves who participate: consider Ar. *Ran.* 33, 190–91, 693–702 with the scholia (especially the one for 693–94 that cites Hellanicus *FGrH* 323a F25) in light of Thuc. 3.68.103 and Dem. 59.104, and see Michael J. Osborne,

Naturalization in Athens (Brussels: Palais der Academiën, 1981–83), II 11–16, and Kagan, *Fall*, 338–39, as well as Rahe, *SSAW*, Chapter 3, preface to Part II, and Chapter 4. It is possible that the list of trireme crews found in *IG* I³ 1032 = *O&R* no. 190 pertains to those who departed on this campaign, for the proportion of citizens on the lists is quite high. In the aftermath, there were quite a few new citizens: Diod. 13.97.1. Cf. Ian Worthington, "Aristophanes 'Frogs' and Arginusae," *Hermes* 117:3 (1989): 359–63, and Krentz, *Xenophon*, 152, with Peter Hunt, "The Slaves and the Generals of Arginusae," *AJPh* 122:3 (Autumn 2001): 359–80 (esp. 359–70), who has a compelling case to make in defense of Diodorus' claim; Lazenby, *PW*, 229–30 (with n. 28); and Hutchinson, *Attrition*, 198.

59. Dispute regarding makeup of Athenian fleet, agreement regarding its size: Xen. *Hell.* 1.6.24–25 and Diod. 13.97.1–2 with note 57, above, and with Lazenby, *PW*, 229–30; Hutchinson, *Attrition*, 198; and Debra Hamel, *The Battle of Arginusae: Victory at Sea and its Tragic Aftermath in the Final Years of the Peloponnesian War* (Baltimore, MD: Johns Hopkins University Press, 2015), 42–45. Xenophon apt to have been with the Athenian fleet: Édouard Delebecque, *Essai sur la vie de Xénophon* (Paris: C. Klincksieck, 1957), 24, 44, 58–61.

60. Arrangement of the battle lines at Arginusae: Xen. *Hell.* 1.6.29–32 and Diod. 13.98, which should be read in light of Sosylus *FGrH* 176 F1. Hermon, who may well have been a source for Xenophon, reappears later as Lysander's helmsman: Paus. 10.9.7. Indication that Thrasyllus was the dominant Athenian *stratēgós* on the board: Lys. 21.7. Cf. Tuplin, "Military Engagements in Xenophon's *Hellenica*," 58–59; Gray, "The Value of Diodorus Siculus for the Years 411–386 BC," 85–86; and Bleckmann, *Niederlage*, 104–9, who reject Diodorus' testimony as implausible and even intimate that the Oxyrhynchus historian may have been a bit inventive, and Busolt, *Gr. Gesch.*, III:2 1593–96; Kagan, *Fall*, 339–50; *AT*, 88–91; Lazenby, *PW*, 230–32; and Asmonti, *Conon the Athenian*, 76–79, who in divers ways give that testimony less respect than is its due, with Graham Wylie, "The Battle of the Arginusae: A Reappraisal," *Civiltà Classica e Cristiana* 11 (1990): 234–49, and Hale, *Lords of the Sea*, 224–28, 355–56; then, see Hamel, *The Battle of Arginusae*, 45–50, who provides a compelling defense of the Sicilian historian's account and who rightly follows Hutchinson, *Attrition*, 198–202, in supplying a persuasive analysis of the disposition of the galleys on the two sides. If I prefer the account of the order of battle set out in Hutchinson and Hamel to that proposed by Hale, it is because I believe that the arrangement he has in mind would have left the Athenians' right wing, stretched out between Garipasi and the third and northernmost of the three Arginusae isles, vulnerable to an outflanking maneuver aimed at hitting their galleys from behind, as the map in Hale, *Lords of the Sea*, 226, allows one to see. For an assessment of Callicratidas' conduct, see Bommelaer, *Lysandre*, 96–97. Cf. Kapellos, *XPW*, 125–32, who ignores the disposition of the ships and places far too much emphasis on the fact that the Athenian fleet was the larger of the two forces.

61. Battle of Arginusae: consider Diod. 13.98.5–99.5, 100.1, 3, in conjunction with Xen. *Hell.* 1.6.33–34, and see Wylie, "The Battle at the Arginusae," 241–43, who asks all the right questions, and Hamel, *The Battle of Arginusae*, 50–53, who best answers them. Note also Hutchinson, *Attrition*, 202–3, who anticipates much of what Hamel has to say but errs in supposing that the triremes in the Spartan fleet had reinforced prows of the sort used in the Great Harbor at Syracuse in 413. Cf. Kagan, *Fall*, 350–53; *AT*, 92–93; Lazenby, *PW*, 232–34; and Hale, *Lords of the Sea*, 228. Diodorus errs in only one particular: he situates the Athenian *stratēgós* Pericles on the Athenian right in the north with Thrasyllus, then has Callicratidas, who was stationed, as both Xenophon and Diodorus agree, on the Spartan right in the south, ram his trireme: Diod. 13.98.3, 99.3–4. Xenophon is probably correct in situating the younger Pericles on the Athenian left in the south: *Hell.* 1.6.29. Cf. Bleckmann, *Niederlage*, 109–14, who rejects Diodorus' testimony altogether.

62. Post-battle storm; the escape of Eteonicus' fleet and the retreat of his hoplites; Conon joins the main Athenian force: Xen. *Hell.* 1.6.35–38 and Diod. 13.100.5–6 with Kagan, *Fall*, 352–53, and Lazenby, *PW*, 234. Eteonicus resurfaces on Chios: Xen. *Hell.* 2.1.1. Cf. Hutchinson, *Attrition*, 203–4, whose reconstruction is garbled. Regarding the *kélēs*, see Lionel Casson, *Ships and Seamanship in the Ancient World* (Princeton, NJ: Princeton University Press, 1971), 160–62.

63. Cf. Arist. *Ath. Pol.* 34.1—which mentions the peace offer and dates the battle of Arginusae to the archonship of Callias, which began shortly after midsummer in 406 and extended for a year—with the material concerning the offer made after Cyzicus that is collected in Chapter 6, note 7, above, and see Munn, *SH*, 181–83. As one would expect, there are scholars who dismiss this report, treating it as a doublet of its predecessor: for a list, see Rhodes, *CAAP*, 424, who shares their opinion. That there is no reason to do so, Kagan, *Fall*, 377 n. 1, makes clear. For a half-hearted defense of the Athenian decision to reject the offer, see Lazenby, *PW*, 235–36. Cf. Kagan, *Fall*, 376–79, who has the better argument. Pylos and Nisaea lost in 409/8 (or possibly, in the case of Pylos, a little before): Diod. 13.64.5–7, 65.1–2 and *Hell. Oxy.* 4 (Chambers). Current from the Hellespont: Jamie Morton, *The Role of the Physical Environment in Ancient Greek Seafaring* (Leiden: Brill, 2001), 43–44. Going concern: Halford Mackinder, *Democratic Ideals and Reality* (Singapore: Origami Books, 2018), 4. Neapolis: *IACP* no. 634. Abdera: no. 640.

64. Appeal for Lysander's return; Aracus named navarch; Lysander, *epistoleús*: Xen. *Hell.* 2.1.6–7 and Diod. 13.100.7 with Plut. *Lys.* 7.1–3. Diodorus denies that Lysander held any office: 13.100.8. On the implications, see Busolt, *Gr. Gesch.*, II:2 1610–12; Lotze, *Lysander*, 26; Bommelaer, *Lysandre*, 96–99; Kagan, *Fall*, 379–80; and Lazenby, *PW*, 237.

CHAPTER 8. FROM ARGINUSAE TO AEGOSPOTAMI

Epigraph: Niccolò Machiavelli, *Discorsi sopra la prima deca di Tito Livio* 1.53, ed. Mario Martelli (Florence: Sansoni Editore, 1971), 136.

1. Near mutiny on Chios, request for Lysander's return: Xen. *Hell.* 2.1.1–5 with Kagan, *Fall*, 376; Lazenby, *PW*, 237; Hutchinson, *Attrition*, 205; and Hyland, *PI*, 113–15. Lysander's arrival on the scene: Xen. *Hell.* 2.1.10, Diod. 13.104.3.

2. Lysander visits Cyrus again: Xen. *Hell.* 2.1.11–12, Diod. 13.104.3, Plut. *Lys.* 9.1 with Lotze, *Lysander*, 27; Bommelaer, *Lysandre*, 98–99; Kagan, *Fall*, 380–81; Lazenby, *PW*, 237–38; and Hyland, *PI*, 115. Its timing and that of subsequent events down to the battle of Aegospotami: Appendix 8, below. On the timing of Lysander's meetings with Cyrus, there is more to be said: Cyrus had originally received five hundred talents from his father Darius: Xen. *Hell.* 1.5.3. At sixty · mnai to the talent, one hundred drachmas to the mna, and six obols to the drachma, this came to eighteen million obols. At the new rate of four obols a day paid to each of the two hundred mariners in each trireme, the five hundred talents was enough to support a fleet of one hundred ships for seven and a half months. Cyrus provided financial support for the months stretching from his initial meeting with Lysander to the battle of Arginusae. In the beginning, Lysander maintained a force of seventy ships and, in the end, Callicratidas, a fleet of one hundred forty and, in the last month of his life, thirty more: Chapter 7, above. It would appear that Cyrus supported in the average month about one hundred ships and did so for about seven and a half months. This is further evidence that he first met Lysander in the fall of 407 and not in the spring of that year: Chapter 7, note 1, above. If the two had met in the latter season, Cyrus would have run through the five hundred talents before Callicratidas' arrival in the Greek East.

3. Cyrus summoned to Media by his father or his mother: Xen. *Hell.* 2.1.8–9, 13–15, *An.* 1.1.1–2; Plut. *Lys.* 9.2, *Artax.* 2.3; Diod. 13.104.4 with Kagan, *Fall*, 381, and Hyland, *PI*, 114–15. Xenophon's contention that Cyrus brought Tissaphernes along *hōs phílon* when he made his journey upcountry to see his dying father (*An.* 1.1.2) would, if interpreted as meaning that he regarded him "as a friend," be inconsistent both with what Plutarch (*Lys.* 4.1–2) tells us of Cyrus' initial reaction in 407 to Lysander's complaints against Tissaphernes and with what we know of Cyrus' intentions and of factional politics at the Persian court at this time. It would then be part and parcel of Xenophon's defense of his commander against Ctesias' charge that he really did plot the assassination of Artaxerxes II as, Xenophon reports (*An.* 1.1.3), Tissaphernes charged. The phrase could, however, be interpreted as meaning that Cyrus brought him along "on the pretense that he was a friend." See *Hell.* 1.8.27 for Xenophon's familiarity with Ctesias' *Persika*; *An.* 1.1.1–4 for his canny justification of Cyrus' subsequent rebellion; and Plut. *Artax.* 3 for Ctesias' account of Cyrus' plot. The information related at

Xen. *Hell.* 2.1.8–9 is almost certainly derivative from Ctesias. The inconsistency between the view of Cyrus one gets when reading that passage and that one might get from a naive reading of the first book of the *Anabasis* suggests that the latter, like Xenophon's *Agesilaus*, is a parody of a moralizing biography modelled on a eulogy in which one was traditionally allowed to "attribute to a man a larger number of good qualities than he actually possessed": Isoc. 9.4. See John K. Anderson, *Xenophon* (London: Duckworth, 1974), 167–69, and Munn, *SH*, 196–97.

4. Cyrus summons Lysander, makes arrangements for his support, and departs for Media with Tissaphernes: Xen. *Hell.* 2.1.14–15, Diod. 13.104.4, Plut. *Lys.* 9.2. There is no reason to doubt Plutarch's explicit claim that Lysander was given control of Cyrus' *arché* and of the cities within it. It is confirmed by Diodorus, and Xenophon's silence has no significance. Without political and military authority in the region, the Spartan commander would have been directly dependent for money on Cyrus' enemy Pharnabazus or on Tissaphernes' subordinates: see note 6, below. Some, of course, doubt the testimony of Plutarch and Diodorus: e.g., Busolt, *Gr. Gesch.*, III:1 1613 n. 2; Meyer, *GdA*, IV:2 355; and Lotze, *Lysander*, 27 n. 5. The non-doubters include Grote (*HG*, VI 435), Bommelaer (*Lysandre*, 99–101), Kagan (*Fall*, 381–82), Munn (*SH*, 196–97), Lazenby (*PW*, 238), Hutchinson, (*Attrition*, 205), and Hyland (*PI*, 116–17), who draws attention to the extent of the funds that Lysander has to have spent on the fleet in the months that followed and to the substantial amount of money that, Xenophon (*Hell.* 2.3.8) tells us, remained in his possession thereafter.

5. Massacre at Miletus: Diod. 13.104.5–6, Plut. *Lys.* 8, and Polyaen. *Strat.* 1.45.1 with Lotze, *Lysander*, 28–29; Kagan, *Fall*, 382–8; and Lazenby, *PW*, 238. For another festival massacre, see Xen. *Hell.* 4.4.1–6. There is no reason to suppose that the partisans of Lysander were any wealthier or more respectable than the men they massacred or drove from Miletus. Diodorus (13.70.4) refers to Lysander's friends as the men "most powerful [*dunatótatoi*]" in the cities; Plutarch (*Lys.* 13.7) stresses that they were selected without regard to birth and wealth. At least in Miletus, where there had been a democracy up to the time of the Dionysian festival massacre, Lysander must have chosen his partisans from among the popular leaders: see Chapter 7, note 43, above. It is as erroneous to attempt to explain the revolutions that shook the Greek world in the latter part of the fifth century solely with regard to socioeconomic class as it is to try to account for them without any regard to class at all. It is, of course, highly unlikely that Diodorus' *dunatótatoi* secured the support of the common people in their quest to set up a more narrowly based government and equally unlikely that they were themselves landless thetes. In virtually any regime, the men who devote their lives to public affairs form a very small part of the body politic. Such an expenditure of time requires leisure—a commodity rarer in the ancient democracies than it is today in their modern counterparts, for there were then

fewer men who had the wealth to allow them to spend their time as they wished. Sparta's third Attic war no doubt aggravated class tensions by "depriving men of the power of easily satisfying their daily wants" and by bringing "most people's minds down to the level of their actual circumstances": Thuc. 3.82.2–3. This situation surely encouraged some of those in this narrow political class to contemplate a revolutionary takeover. But, if Thucydides is to be believed, one should not underestimate the role played by the opportunity afforded the rival factions within the political class to call in the Athenians and the Spartans to their aid: 3.82.1.

6. Pharnabazus protects Milesian refugees: Diod. 13.104.6. Location of Blauda: Strabo 12.5.2. Beloch (*Gr. Gesch.*, III:1 30 n. 3), Meyer (*GdA*, IV: 2 355 n. 3), Busolt (*Gr. Gesch.*, III:1 1614, esp. n. 2), Lotze (*Lysander*, 28), and Antony Andrewes ("Two Notes on Lysander," *Phoenix* 25:3 [Autumn 1971]: 206–26 [at 213 n. 15]) all err in substituting Tissaphernes for Diodorus' Pharnabazus. It is true that Diodorus tends to use the name of the latter for both satraps in his thirteenth book, but Tissaphernes had, by this time, departed with Cyrus for Media: Xen. *An.* 1.1.1–2. Earlier Milesian opposition to Tissaphernes: Thuc. 8.84. Tissaphernes, when he returned, apparently restored the exiles to power in Miletus. It became the bastion of those hostile to Cyrus and Lysander: see Xen. *An.* 1.1.6–7, 4.2, 9.9; Polyaen. *Strat.* 7.18.2. See Kagan, *Fall*, 383–84.

7. Iasos taken and razed: Diod. 13.104.7. For its earlier history, see Chapters 2 and 6 (esp. note 12), above. Eteonicus was with Callicratidas at Arginusae (Xen. *Hell.* 1.6.26, 35–38) and may have been with Lysander thereafter: 2.1.6–10, 2.5; Diod. 13.106; Paus. 10.9.10. Cedreia: Xen. *Hell.* 2.1.15. See Kagan, *Fall*, 384, and Lazenby, *PW*, 238–39.

8. Ethic of helping friends, harming enemies: Aesch. *Choeph.* 123; Pindar *Pyth.* 2.83; Theog. 869–72; Soph. *Ant.* 641–47; Eur. *Med.* 807–10, *El.* 807, *Ion* 1045–47; Ar. *Av.* 417–20; Thuc. 2.40, 7.68.1; Lys. 9.20; Pl. *Resp.* 1.332d (and context); Isoc. 1.26; Xen. *An.* 1.3.6, 7.7.46, *Cyr.* 1.4.25, *Hiero* 2.2, *Mem.* 2.3.14, 6.35 (cf. 4.8.11) with Kenneth J. Dover, *Greek Popular Morality* (Oxford: Oxford University Press, 1974), 180–84. One cannot overestimate the role played by the institution of slavery in rendering popular in putatively egalitarian regimes an ethic aristocratic in origin. As Alexis de Tocqueville (*De la démocratie en Amérique*, ed. Jean-Claude Lamberti and James T. Schleifer, II.i.3, in Alexis de Tocqueville, Œuvres [Paris: Bibliothèque de la Pléiade, 1991–2004], II 526) intimates, in antiquity every citizen belonged to "the aristocracy of masters." Panhellenism and the civic tradition so well represented by Sparta stood for an extension of the circle of loyalty, not an abandonment of the aristocratic sense of superiority. Her position as the principal mercantile city of Greece rendered Athens considerably more cosmopolitan than the other cities of Greece: Xen. *Ath. Pol.* 1.10–12. But this should not be exaggerated. It was the democracy of Pericles that tightened up the requirements for citizenship: Arist. *Ath. Pol.* 26.4. As Sir Ernest

Barker (*Greek Political Theory: Plato and his Predecessors* [London: Methuen, 1918], 16) put it long ago, "The [Greek] city was not only a unit of government; it was also a club." Lysander vs. Callicratides: Plut. *Lys.* 5.7–6.3, 7.5 with *Comp. Lys. et Sull.* 2.5–6.

9. Lysander's voyage to meet Agis: Plut. *Lys.* 9.3–4 and Diod. 13.104.8. Silence of Xenophon: *Hell.* 2.1.15–16. Meyer (*GdA*, IV:2 356–57), Lotze (*Lysander,* 29–31), Kagan (*Fall,* 284–85), Munn (*SH,* 197), and Lazenby (*PW,* 239) accept the testimony of Plutarch and Diodorus; Beloch (*Gr. Gesch.,* II:1 423–24), Busolt (*Gr. Gesch.,* III:1 1617), and Bleckmann (*Niederlage,* 589–93) reject it.

10. Failure to recover the quick and the dead after Arginusae: Xen. *Hell.* 1.6.34–35, Diod. 13.100.1–4. If, with regard to the particulars of the subsequent narrative, I do not cite Buck, *Thrasybulus,* 53–60, it is because he rejects the testimony of both Xenophon and Diodorus, then cherry-picks what they have to say for the construction of a narrative consistent with his presumptions regarding the greatness of Thrasybulus and the wickedness of Theramenes.

11. Xenophon's testimony concerning Athens' losses: Xen. *Hell.* 1.6.34 with Diod. 13.100.3. Euryptolemos' testimony: Xen. *Hell.* 1.7.30. On the losses incurred by the Athenians (and their adversaries) in this period, see Victor Davis Hanson, *A War Like No Other: How the Athenians and Spartans Fought the Peloponnesian War* (New York: Random House, 2005), 271–83.

12. The fate of the unburied dead: Hom. *Il.* 23.71–74, *Od.* 11.55–83; Eur. *Hec.* 27–34, *Tro.* 1081–85. Burial a family duty: Soph. *Ant.* 77, 450–55, 745, 749. On this duty's civic dimension, see Pritchett, *GSAW,* IV 235–41, and Pamela Vaughn, "The Identification and Retrieval of the Hoplite Battle Dead," in *Hoplites: The Classical Greek Battle Experience,* ed. Victor Davis Hanson (London: Routledge, 1991), 38–62. Athenian law: Ael. *VH* 5.14 with Schol. Soph. *Ant.* 255 and Philo apud Euseb. *Praep. evang.* 8.358d–359a. For further evidence and a citation of the extensive secondary literature on this question, see Andreas Mehl, "Für eine neue Bewertung eines Justizskandals: Der Arginusenprozess und seine Überlieferung vor dem Hintergrund von Recht und Weltanschauung im Athen des Ausgehenden 5. Hr. v. Chr.," *ZRG* 99 (1982): 32–80 (at 66–79), and Alexander Rubel, *Fear and Loathing in Ancient Athens: Religion and Politics during the Peloponnesian War,* tr. Michael Vickers and Alina Piftor (Durham: Acumen Publishing, 2014), 137–41.

13. Post-battle deliberations of the *stratēgoí* at Garipasi: Xen. *Hell.* 1.6.35 and Diod. 13.100 with Ostwald, *Sovereignty,* 434, and Kagan, *Fall,* 354–62. Import of burying one's dead: Diod. 15.35.1, Plut. *Phoc.* 6, Polyaen. *Strat.* 3.11.2. Indifference of Athens' political class and of the Socratics regarding religious tradition and the reaction to which it gave rise: Mehl, "Für eine neue Bewertung eines Justizskandals," 75–79, with Rahe, *SSPW,* Chapter 3.

14. Claims attributed to Euryptolemos: Xen. *Hell.* 1.7.16–18, 29–31. Report of the *stratēgoí* blames the storm: 1.7.4–6—confirmed by Lys. 12.36. For commentary,

see Ostwald, *Sovereignty*, 434, and Kagan, *Fall*, 362–63. On the relationship between Diomedon and Thrasybulus, see W. James McCoy, "Thrasybulus and his Trierarchies," *AJPh* 112:3 (Autumn 1991): 303–23. There is no compelling reason to deny the historicity of Euryptolemos' speech, as Mehl, "Für eine neue Bewertung eines Justizskandals," 38–41, does. That the speech in some measure reflects the historian's general outlook is clear, and this helps explain why he highlighted and reported it at such great length. But it does not prove or even strongly suggest that he fabricated it himself. Cf. also ibid. 59–79, and Rubel, *Fear and Loathing*, 139–44, who may well be correct in thinking Diodorus right in singling out the failure to collect and bury the dead as the salient issue, but who err in supposing that this operation could have been carried out effectively after the storm had scattered the bodies, with Barry S. Strauss, "Perspectives on the Death of Fifth-Century Athenian Seamen," in *War and Violence in Ancient Greece*, ed. Hans van Wees (London: Duckworth, 2000), 261–84 (at 269–73), who describes in detail what happens to the bodies of the dead consigned to the sea, and John R. Hale, *Lords of the Sea: The Epic Story of the Athenian Navy and the Birth of Democracy* (New York: Viking Penguin, 2009), 229, and Stuttard, *Nemesis*, 285–86, who rightly underline the fact that the pertinent bodies were no longer concentrated where they could be located and collected. The direction of the current in the strait between Lesbos and Anatolia can be inferred from Jamie Morton, *The Role of the Physical Environment in Ancient Greek Seafaring* (Leiden: Brill, 2001), 42–45 (esp. 44), 87–90 (esp. 90), and James Beresford, *The Ancient Sailing Season* (Leiden: Brill, 2013), 81, 83, 101.

15. Arginusae *stratēgoí* deposed and recalled, six return: Xen. *Hell.* 1.7.1–2 with Diod. 13.101.1–5, and see Ostwald, *Sovereignty*, 434–35.

16. Erasinides fined for peculation, then jailed and handed over to the assembly for judgment: Xen. *Hell.* 1.7.2 with Ostwald, *Sovereignty*, 436, and Thomas Hooper, "Archedemus," *CQ* n.s. 65:2 (December 2015): 500–517. Magisterial prerogatives: Edward M. Harris, "Who Enforced the Law in Classical Athens?" in *Symposion 2005: Vorträge zur griechischen und hellenistischen Rechtsgeschichte*, ed. Eva Cantarella (Vienna: Verlag der Österreichischen Akademie der Wissenschaften, 2007), 159–76, and *The Rule of Law in Action in Democratic Athens* (Oxford: Oxford University Press, 2013), 351–52.

17. Arginusae *stratēgoí* accused, jailed, handed over to the assembly: Xen. *Hell.* 1.7.2–3 with Ostwald, *Sovereignty*, 436–37.

18. Xenophon on the appearance of the Arginusae *stratēgoí* and Theramenes before the assembly: *Hell.* 1.7.4–6 with Ostwald, *Sovereignty*, 437–39.

19. Accusation directed at the *stratēgoí*, their misapprehension, and their chosen mode of self-defense at this time, which set Theramenes and Thrasybulus and no doubt the taxiarchs against all of their former commanders—even those hitherto allied with these two trierarchs: consider Diod. 13.101.1–5 in conjunction with Xen. *Hell.* 2.3.35, and see Paul Cloché, "L'Affaire des Arginuses (406 avant

J.C.)," *RH* 130 (1919): 5–68 (esp. 22–23, 37–39), who demonstrates that the *stratēgoí* who wrote the letters imputing responsibility to the two trierarchs initiated the breach and that Theramenes never asserted that they were disingenuous in blaming the storm; Antony Andrewes, "The Arginousai Trial," *Phoenix* 28:2 (Spring 1974): 112–22, who explains why Diodorus' account is to be preferred to that of Xenophon; Ostwald, *Sovereignty*, 434–45, who makes it clear that Theramenes was acting in self-defense and lodged no accusation against the *stratēgoí*; and Kagan, *Fall*, 363–68. Cf. Marta Sordi "Teramene e il processo delle Arginuse," *Aevum* 55:1 (January–April 1981): 3–12, and Bleckmann, *Niederlage*, 509–71 (esp. 539–71), who follow Xenophon in laying the blame on Theramenes, and Kapellos, *XPW*, 140–216, who makes a valiant, if unpersuasive attempt to make sense of these events in light of Xenophon's testimony alone. Also cf. Hatzfeld, *Alcibiade*, 324–29; W. James McCoy, "Thrasyllus," *AJPh* 98:3 (Autumn 1977): 264–89 (at 284–89); Jennifer Tolbert Roberts, "Arginusae Once Again," *CW* 71:2 (October 1977): 107–11, and *Accountability in Athenian Government* (Madison: University of Wisconsin Press, 1982), 64–69; and Munn, *SH*, 181–88, who suspect, on the basis of a dubious claim advanced by Lysias (14.25) that Alcibiades' son was at some point on intimate terms with Archedemus, that the friends of Alcibiades himself were behind the attack launched by men other than Archedemus on the entire body of those who served as *stratēgoí* at Arginusae, with György Németh, "Der Arginusen-Prozess: Die Geschichte eines politischen Justizmordes," *Klio* 66:1 (January 1984): 51–57, who rightly argues that a number of the *stratēgoí* executed were, in fact, associated with Alcibiades; who errs in including Thrasyllus in their number; who wrongly takes at face value Xenophon's claims concerning the role played by Theramenes; and who therefore suggests that Archedemus and the other associates of Cleophon wanted to eliminate Alcibiades' supporters and that Theramenes wanted the same thing because he regarded Alcibiades as an obstacle to his own ambitions. Missing from his analysis is adequate attention both to what Euryptolemos tells us about the stance taken after the storm by Pericles and Diomedon and to what Diodorus has to report. For a highly intelligent, if of necessity at times highly speculative, reconstruction of events: see Hamel, *The Battle of Arginusae*, 71–77.

20. Defense mounted by the *stratēgoí*: Xen. *Hell.* 1.7.5–7 with Ostwald, *Sovereignty*, 438–39, and Hamel, *The Battle of Arginusae*, 77–79.

21. Apaturia held in Panypsion (Schol. Ar. *Ach.* 146) probably on 19–21 or 26–28 of that lunar month: see Jon D. Mikalson, *The Sacred and Civil Calendar of the Athenian Year* (Princeton, NJ: Princeton University Press, 1975), 79. In most years, this would have taken place in October.

22. Callixeinos' *probúleuma* and the mourners, claims made concerning Theramenes and his associates: cf. Xen. *Hell.* 1.7.8–9 and Pl. [*Ax.*] 368d–e with Diod. 13.101.6–7 and Lys. 12.62–78, and cf. Bleckmann, *Niederlage*, 539–71, who fol-

lows Xenophon in blaming Theramenes, with Ostwald, *Sovereignty,* 439–442; Kagan, *Fall,* 368–69; and Hamel, *The Battle of Arginusae,* 79–80. Cf. also Adalberto Giovannini, "Xenophon, der Arginusenprozeß und die athenische Demokratie mit einem Anhang: Die Zahl der athenischen Hopliten im Jahr 431 v. Chr.," *Chiron* 32 (2006): 15–50 (at 15–40), who buys into Xenophon's claims, who completely overlooks the contrast between Xenophon and Diodorus in this regard, who fails to consider what can be learned from Lysias, and who places the chief blame for the condemnation and execution of the *stratēgoí* on Theramenes and his supporters.

23. Religious hysteria arising from the conflict between popular religious sentiment and the religious indifference of the political class: Mehl, "Für eine neue Bewertung eines Justizskandals," 59–79.

24. Euryptolemos and the *graphḕ paranómōn*: Xen. *Hell.* 1.7.12–15, *Mem.* 1.1.18, 4.4.2; Pl. *Ap.* 32b; Arist. *Ath. Pol.* 34.1 with Edwin Carawan, "The Trial of the Arginousai Generals and the Dawn of 'Judicial Review,'" *Dike* 10 (2007): 19–56, who draws a sharp distinction between what counted as *nómoi* before the promulgation of a law code of sorts in 403 and what counted as such after that event. See, more recently, Edwin Carawan, *Control of the Laws in the Ancient Democracy at Athens* (Baltimore, MD: Johns Hopkins University Press, 2020). For the view that what the assembly did was perfectly in accord with prior legal practice and that, with regard to their failure to recover the dead, the *stratēgoí* were, in fact, guilty, see Mehl, "Für eine neue Bewertung eines Justizskandals," 32–80. Cf. also Bleckmann, *Niederlage,* 509–39, who shares Mehl's view with regard to prior legal practice, who emphasizes the failure to save those still alive, and who defends the principle of collective responsibility, and Giovannini, "Xenophon, der Arginusenprozeß und die athenische Demokratie," 25–30, who rightly emphasizes the prominent role played in this drama by the Council of Five Hundred, wherein there was a majority hostile to the *stratēgoí,* but who errs in supposing the council fundamentally at odds with the assembly, wherein there was clearly a similar, if far less stable, majority.

25. Fruitless efforts of Euryptolemos to get the *probotúleuma* amended, condemnation and execution of the *stratēgoí*: see Xen. *Hell.* 1.7.16–34, where I believe, we must—for the reasons laid out by Ostwald, *Sovereignty,* 440 n. 118—accept Bamberg's emendation of the text at 1.7.20, with Diod. 13.101.6, and consider Ostwald, *Sovereignty,* 439–41; Kagan, *Fall,* 370–73; and Hamel, *The Battle of Arginusae,* 80–86. Euryptolemos' proposal that the *stratēgoí* be tried each as an individual in court under the harsh terms stipulated in the Decree of Kannonus: Xen. *Hell.* 1.7.20–21, 34. On this, see Brian M. Lavelle, "*Adikia,* the Decree of Kannonus, and the Trial of the Generals," *C&M* 39 (1998): 19–41. In this connection, see also Ar. *Ran.* 1196 with the scholia (Philochorus *FGrH* 328 F142), Arist. *Ath. Pol.* 34.1, and Plut. *Per.* 37.6.

26. The fate of Callixeinos and his associates: Xen. *Hell.* 1.7.35, Diod. 13.103.1–2.

Theramenes elected *stratēgós*, fails to pass *dokimasía*: Lys. 13.10. Cf. Ostwald, *Sovereignty*, 443, and Rubel, *Fear and Loathing*, 135–36, who fail to recognize the significance of Theramenes' election and mistake the cause of his rejection at the *dokimasía*, and Bleckmann, *Niederlage*, 509–39, who follows Xenophon in laying the blame on Theramenes, who underlines the significance of his election, and who takes it as proof that the Athenians did not in the aftermath react to what they had done with revulsion, with Gabriel Adeleye, "The Arginusae Affair and Theramenes' Rejection at the *Dokimasia* of 405/4 B.C.," *MusAfr* 6 (1977): 94–99; Kagan, *Fall*, 373–75; and Hamel, *The Battle of Arginusae*, 86–89, who take Xenophon's claims regarding Theramenes' responsibility with a large grain of salt and point to his election as proof that the Athenians did not hold him responsible for what happened.

27. On Athens' propensity for treating failure of any sort on the part of her *stratēgoí* in the field as proof of treason, bribery, or some other crime, cf. Roberts, *Accountability in Athenian Government*, 124–41, with Luca A. Asmonti, "The Arginusae Trial: The Changing Role of *Strategoi* and the Relationship between *Demos* and Military Leadership in Late-Fifth Century Athens," *BICS* 49 (2006): 1–21, and see Hamel, *The Battle of Arginusae*, 58–70. For a detailed examination of the evidence pertaining to Athens' punishment of its *stratēgoí* in the late fifth century, see Debra Hamel, *Athenian Generals: Military Authority in the Classical Period* (Leiden: Brill, 1998), 141–46. For the cases where the evidence is dispositive, see nos. 8–9, 12–16, 20–21. For cases where the evidence is merely suggestive, see nos. 5–7, 10–11, 17. For further evidence suggesting that a *stratēgós* was deposed, see nos. 18–19 and perhaps 22. When the orator Demosthenes comments on this propensity half a century later, he indulges in exaggeration: 4.47. But there can be no doubt that this was and remained a prominent feature of Athenian democratic life: Mogens Herman Hansen, *The Athenian Democracy in the Age of Demosthenes* (Oxford: Basil Blackwell, 1991), 215–18, and Pritchet, *GSAW*, II 5–10. The Spartans were far less inclined to treat defeat as a crime: see Fred S. Naiden, "The Crime of Defeat," in *Kállistos Nómos: Scritti in onore di Alberto Maffi*, ed. Barbara Biscotti (Turin: G. Giappichelli, 2019), 103–19. On the failure of Athens' democracy in this particular, Xenophon was in agreement with Thucydides: cf. Dustin Gish, "Defending *Demokratia*: Athenian Justice and the Trial of the Arginusae Generals in Xenophon's *Hellenica*," in *Xenophon: Ethical Principles and Historical Enquiry*, ed. Fiona Hobden and Christopher Tuplin (Leiden: Brill, 2012), 161–212, who thinks otherwise, with Bodil Due, "The Trial of the Generals in Xenophon's *Hellenica*," *C&M* 34 (1983): 33–44, whose analysis of Euryptolemos' speech is especially penetrating; Tim Rood, "Xenophon and Diodorus: Continuing Thucydides," in *Xenophon and his World*, ed. Christopher Tuplin (Stuttgart: F. Steiner, 2004), 341–95 (at 374–80); and Kapellos, *XPW*, 133–216. It is a mistake to suppose that one cannot be a severe critic of the Athenian democracy or of democracy in general without

being a partisan of oligarchy, as does Frances S. Pownall, "Shifting Viewpoints in Xenophon's *Hellenica*: The Arginusae Episode," *Athenaeum* 88 (2000): 499–513, who otherwise has much else of value to say: see Edward M. Harris, "Was All Criticism of Athenian Democracy Necessarily Anti-Democratic?" in *Democrazia e antidemocrazia nel mondo greco*, ed. Umberto Bultrighini (Alessandria: Edizioni dell'Orso, 2005), 11–23, and "Cleon and the Defeat of Athens," in Harris, *The Rule of Law in Action in Democratic Athens*, 305–44. For an impassioned defense of the Athenians' conduct in the course of the Arginusae trial that relies on the presumption rejected here, see Giovannini, "Xenophon, der Arginusenprozeß und die athenische Demokratie," 15–40. To accept Giovannini's claim, one would not only have to suppose Xenophon a bigot and a liar. One would also have to believe that Diodorus' description of the final assembly was derivative from Xenophon and not the Oxyrhynchus historian, a supposition in no way justified; and one would have to avert one's gaze from the desperate plight the Athenians were in before the battle and believe that saving the survivors should without question have taken priority over eliminating Eteonicus' fleet and greatly reducing Lacedaemon's residual strength at sea. If the last-mentioned presumption really were true, it is questionable whether the battle should have been fought in the first place, given the Athenians' poor state of readiness and the risk in lives. The point was to save the city, and a sacrifice of lives was a price that the assembly voted to pay. In the circumstances, the *stratēgoí* made a reasonable decision by dispatching most of the fleet to Mytilene while assigning a squadron to the salvage operation that was more than sufficient for the task. Cf. Gish, "Defending *Dēmokratia*," 161–212, who takes a stand similar to that of Giovannini while vigorously denying that Xenophon was a severe critic of the Athenian democracy. Even, however, if Giovannini and Gish were correct in supposing the procedures followed in the trial acceptable and the verdict just, it would have been lunacy to kill a set of *stratēgoí* who had pulled off such a victory in circumstances so unpromising.

28. On Athens' self-destruction, see Thuc. 2.65.7–12 (esp. 12) with Hanson, *A War Like No Other*, 282–84.

29. Lysander's fleet, not at this time large enough to confront the Athenians, journeys to the Saronic Gulf: Plut. *Lys.* 9.3. Agis repeatedly marshals troops for an attack on Athens: see Chapters 3 and 4, above. On the possibility that Lysander had something of this sort in mind, see Lazenby, *PW*, 239. It is conceivable that the third such attempt, which is mentioned by Diodorus at 13.73.1, has been chronologically misplaced.

30. Agis marches down to confer with Lysander: Plut. *Lys.* 9.4.

31. Agis at Deceleia: Rahe, *SSPW*, Chapter 5, note 1. Imported grain and Agis' maritime strategy: Chapters 4–5, above.

32. Agis and the grain ships after Cyzicus, dispatch of Clearchus; Chalcedon subdued by the Athenians, Byzantium taken: Chapter 6, above.

33. Lysander's purpose in heading for the Hellespont: Xen. *Hell.* 2.1.17 with Meyer, *GdA*, IV:2 356–57; Lotze, *Lysander*, 30–31; Bommelaer, *Lysandre*, 101–2; Kagan, *Fall*, 384–85; and Lazenby, *PW*, 239. See also Plut. *Lys.* 9.4–5 and Diod. 13.104.8.

34. Athenian lack of initiative: Xen. *Hell.* 2.1.16, Plut. *Lys.* 9.3–4. Lysander to Lampsacus: Xen. *Hell.* 2.1.18, Diod. 13.104.8, Plut. *Lys.* 9.4–5. Cf. Kagan, *Fall*, 385, who suspects that Lysander returned by way of Rhodes, with Lazenby, *PW*, 240, who harbors doubts, as do I.

35. Lysander seizes Lampsacus: Xen. *Hell.* 2.1.17–19, Diod. 13.104.8, Plut. *Lys.* 9.5 with Kagan, *Fall*, 385; Munn, *SH*, 198; Lazenby, *PW*, 240; and Hutchinson, *Attrition*, 205–6. Electrum staters of Lampsacus: Aneurin Ellis-Evans, "Mytilene, Lampsakos, Chios and the Financing of the Spartan Fleet (406–404)," *NC* 176 (2016): 1–19.

36. The Athenian camp at Aegospotami: Xen. *Hell.* 2.1.20–21, Strabo 7 F55, Plut. *Lys.* 9.6–7 with Kagan, *Fall*, 385–86; Lazenby, *PW*, 240–41; and Hutchinson, *Attrition*, 206. In telling the same tale, Diodorus Siculus does not specify the location of the Athenian camp: 13.105.1–2. What Alcibiades supposedly saw from the walls of his fort at Pactyes: Xen. *Hell.* 2.1.25. For the Hellespontine shore as the location of the Athenian camp, see Bommelaer, *Lysandre*, 111–12; Barry Strauss, "A Note on the Topography and Tactics of the Battle of Aegospotami," *AJPh* 108 (1987): 741–45; Kagan, *Fall*, 386 n. 33; Munn, *SH*, 198; Lazenby, *PW*, 240–41; Hutchinson, *Attrition*, 206; and Rhodes, *Alcibiades*, 99. I find the case made by John Hale, *Lords of the Sea*, 235–41, 356–59, for the site further north at the mouth of the Sea of Marmara compelling for the reasons spelled out in the text above. For a recent critique of Hale's argument, see Eric W. Robinson, "What Happened at Aegospotami? Xenophon and Diodorus on the Last Battle of the Peloponnesian War," *Historia* 63:1 (2014): 1–16 (at 13–15).

37. The Athenians' difficult situation, Lysander's relative comfort and his caution: Xen. *Hell.* 2.1.22–23, Diod. 13.105.1–2, Nepos *Alc.* 8.1, Plut. *Lys.* 10.1–4 with Kagan, *Fall*, 386–88; Lazenby, *PW*, 341; and Hutchinson, *Attrition*, 206–9. For an overall assessment of the Spartan's conduct as a *stratēgós*, see Bommelaer, *Lysandre*, 199–206. It is impossible to determine the size of the Peloponnesian fleet at Aegospotami. When he came in the late winter, Lysander brought thirty-five ships with him: Diod. 13.104.3. Callicratidas had lost seventy-seven (13.100.3) of the one hundred seventy ships (Xen. *Hell.* 1.6.16) he had commanded on the eve of Arginusae. Thus, before he began building triremes at Antandrus, Lysander had one hundred twenty-eight galleys on hand. After he had captured the Athenian fleet, he manned two hundred ships: 2.2.5. This is rendered meaningless by the fact that he had captured most of Athens' triremes intact on the beach. It would perhaps be best to assume that his fleet was not greatly inferior in size to the Athenian armada before the battle, but one cannot be certain. We have no firm knowledge of the capacity of the boat works at

Antandrus, but the odds are excellent that their efficiency and capacity had greatly grown in the years that had passed since the annihilation of the Spartan fleet at Cyzicus.

38. Our two sources: cf. Christopher Ehrhardt, "Xenophon and Diodorus on Aegospotami," *Phoenix* 24:3 (Autumn 1970): 225–28, who argues for the superiority of Diodorus as a source; Bommelaer, *Lysandre*, 103–15; Barry S. Strauss, "Aegospotami Reexamined," *AJPh* 104:1 (Spring 1983): 24–35; Graham Wylie, "What Really Happened at Aegospotami?" *AC* 55 (1986): 125–41; and Kagan, *Fall*, 390–93, 395. who all, to one degree or another, follow his lead; and Lotze, *Lysander*, 32–38; Christopher J. Tuplin, "Military Engagements in Xenophon's *Hellenica*," in *Past Perspectives: Studies in Greek and Roman Historical Writing*, ed. Ian S. Moxon, John D. Smart, and Anthony J. Woodman (Cambridge: Cambridge University Press, 1986), 37–66 (at 59–60); Bleckmann, *Niederlage*, 115–28; Munn, *SH*, 198–99 (with n. 7); Lazenby, *PW*, 241–44; and Hutchinson, *Attrition*, 207–9, who prefer Xenophon's account, with Robinson, "What Happened at Aegospotami?" 1–16, who shows that there is no need to choose between the two reports.

39. Stalemate at Lampsacus and Aegospotami: cf. Xen. *Hell.* 2.1.22–23 with Diod. 13.105.2. See also Plut. *Lys.* 10.1–4. The fact that, in his extremely compressed narrative, Diodorus makes no mention of the scouts, the time of day when the Athenians presented themselves, and the number of days this stalemate lasted is insignificant.

40. Alcibiades' warning spurned: Xen. *Hell.* 2.1.25–26. His offer of Thracian support rejected: Diod. 13.105.3–4. See also Plut. *Alc.* 36.6–37.3 and *Lys.* 10.5–11.1 as well as Nepos *Alc.* 8.2, and cf. Kagan, *Fall*, 388–90, and Bleckmann, *Niederlage*, 121–22, 586–89, 595–603, with Hatzfeld, *Alcibiade*, 319–37 (esp. 334–37); Bommelaer, *Lysandre*, 107; Rhodes, *Alcibiades*, 95–96, 98–100; and Stuttard, *Nemesis*, 280–84, 287–91; then, see Munn, *SH*, 198–99; Lazenby, *PW*, 241; Hutchinson, *Attrition*, 207; and Hanson, *A War Like No Other*, 284–85. Note also Kapellos, *XPW*, 236–39. Lamachus: Rahe, *SSPW*, Chapter 2, preface to Part II, and Chapter 4. Menander: Rahe, *SSPW*, Chapters 4–6, and Xen. *Hell.* 1.2.16.

41. Lysander's lightning-fast victory at Aegospotami: Xen. *Hell.* 2.1.24, 27–28; Diod. 13.106.1–107.1; Polyaen. *Strat.* 1.45.2; Nep. *Lys.* 1.1–2, *Alc.* 8; Plut. *Alc.* 37.4–5, *Lys.* 11.2–13; Just. *Epit.* 5.6.1–10 (esp. 5–10); and Paus. 3.11.5, 17.4, 9.32.7, 9, 10.9.11 with Aggelos Kapellos, "Philocles and the Sea-Battle of Aegospotami (Xenophon *Hell.* 2.1.22–32)," *CW* 106:1 (Fall 2012): 97–101, and *XPW*, 239–46, as well as Robinson, "What Happened at Aegospotami?" 11–15. Not much value can be attributed to the account of Frontin. *Str.* 2.1.18 and that of Polyaen. *Strat.* 6.27—if, indeed, the latter was written with reference to Aegospotami. If I follow Lotze, *Lysander*, 32–37 (esp. 34), in supposing that Philocles had ordered a withdrawal, it is because that seems to me a proper inference from Diodorus' choice of words, which implies that the commander's conduct of affairs was a

response to Lysander's refusal to engage in a battle and to there being a dearth of food. Cf. Bommelaer, *Lysandre*, 101–15; Strauss, "Aegospotami Reexamined," 24–35; Kagan, *Fall*, 390–93, 395; Munn, *SH*, 199; Lazenby, *PW*, 241–44; Hutchinson, *Attrition*, 207–8; and Robinson, "What Happened at Aegospotami?" 9, who, for one reason or another, think otherwise.

42. Conon's escape and the motive for his flight to Cyprus: Xen. *Hell.* 2.1.28–29; Lys. 21.10–11; Diod. 13.106.6; Plut. *Alc.* 37.4–5, *Lys.* 11.6–8 with Kapellos, *XPW*, 246–47. Cf. Isoc. 5.62, who attributes his failure to head home solely to chagrin. For an attempt to chart his career after the battle of Arginusae, see Luca Asmonti, *Conon the Athenian: Warfare and Politics in the Aegean, 414–386 B.C.* (Stuttgart: Franz Steiner Verlag, 2015), 79–183. Note also Munn, *SH*, 199–200.

43. The fate of Philocles, Adeimantus, and the other Athenian prisoners: Xen. *Hell.* 2.1.30–32; Diod. 13.106.6–7; Plut. *Alc.* 37.4, *Lys.* 11.9–10, 13.1–2; Paus. 9.32.9. If the list of rowers found on *IG* I³ 1032 = *O&R* no. 190 does not pertain to Arginusae, it may pertain to the fleet that fought at Aegospotami, for the proportion of citizens on the triremes is quite high. Cf. Wylie, "What Really Happened at Aegospotami?" 135–41, who rejects Xenophon's testimony altogether, with Gerald Proietti, *Xenophon's Sparta: An Introduction* (Leiden: E. J. Brill, 1987), 30–32, and with Aggelos Kapellos, "Xenophon and the Execution of the Athenian Captives at Aegospotami," *Mnemosyne* 4th ser. 66:3 (2013): 464–72; "Lysander and the Execution of the Athenian Prisoners at Aegospotami (Xenophon, *Hell.* 2.1.31–32)," *Mnemosyne* 4th ser. 71:3 (2018): 394–407; and *XPW*, 247–52, who makes a strong case that the massacre actually took place. I agree with Wylie on one point—that, as Diodorus (13.108.6) asserts, most of the mariners and infantrymen fled and made it to Sestos. Given that thirty-six thousand mariners were present on the Athenian side, the numbers supplied by Plutarch and Pausanias fit well with the notion that only a small proportion were captured. Regarding Xenophon's assessment of Lysander's generalship overall, see Proietti, *Xenophon's Sparta*, 10–11, 21–29.

44. Charges of treason: Xen. *Hell.* 2.1.32; Lys. 14.38; Nep. *Alc.* 8.5–6; Plut. *Alc.* 36.6–37.1, *Lys.* 11.1; Paus. 4.17.3, 10.9.10–11. Cf. Wylie, "What Really Happened at Aegospotami?" 125–35 (esp. 132–33), with Lotze, *Lysander*, 36–37, and Aggelos Kapellos, "Adeimantos at Aegospotami: Innocent or Guilty?" *Historia* 58:3 (2009): 257–75, and *XPW*, 239–47, 251–52, who rightly trace Athens' defeat to the lack of discipline on display at the critical moment and who ask how Adeimantus and Alcibiades or Tydeus could have been personally responsible for what lay within the purview of all of the *stratēgoí*. It is telling that the only commander alert to the danger was Conon, the only one known to have had considerable experience in maritime warfare; and it is no surprise that, upon his return to Athens a decade later, he brought charges against Adeimantus: Dem. 19.191. Someone had to be made the scapegoat—and he certainly did not want to be the one.

45. Majority of Athenian mariners and soldiers flee to Sestos: Diod. 13.106.6.

Lysander takes Sestos, Byzantium, and Chalcedon; Athenians sent home to starve: Xen. *Hell.* 1.2.1–2; Diod. 13.106.8; Plut. *Lys.* 13.3–4, 14.3.

46. Athenian response to news of defeat: Xen. *Hell.* 2.2.3. In this connection, see Peter Krentz, *The Thirty at Athens* (Ithaca, NY: Cornell University Press, 1982), 28–30.

47. Theopompus' arrival at Sparta: Xen. *Hell.* 2.1.30. Xenophon makes him a Milesian and Pausanias (10.9.10) calls him a Myndian, but *ML* no. 95 = *O&R* no. 192 indicates that he hailed from Melos. This explains why Xenophon regarded him as a *lēstēs*. As a man without a country, he may well have made his living from piracy. See Diod. 13.106.7 and Lazenby, *PW*, 244.

48. Lysander after Aegospotami, Athens as well: Xen. *Hell.* 2.2.3–11; Diod. 13.106.8, 107.1–2; Plut. *Lys.* 13.3–14.1 with Lazenby, *PW*, 244–45. The two kings on campaign together: note Hdt. 5.75.2, and see Xen. *Hell.* 5.3.10. Samian revolutions in 412 and 411: Thuc. 8.21, 63, 73 with Chapters 2 and 4, above. The men purged in 404 were presumably those spared in 411. For more detail than is needed here, see Kagan, *Fall*, 395–400.

49. Proposal that Athens be razed, that the men be killed, and that the women and children be sold into slavery advanced by Lysander and Agis: Paus. 3.8.6. See also Diod. 15.63.1. This is—as Charles D. Hamilton, *Sparta's Bitter Victories* (Ithaca, NY: Cornell University Press, 1979), 45, 51–52, and Kagan, *Fall*, 400, recognize—the only possible moment for this event. Lysander departed soon after for the eastern Aegean and did not return to mainland Greece until after Athens had accepted the ephors' peace terms: see Plut. *Lys.* 14.1–5, Xen. *Hell.* 2.2.16–20, Diod. 13.107.3. See also Herbert C. Youtie and Reinhold Merkelbach, "Ein Michigan-Papyrus über Theramenes," *ZPE* 2 (1968): 161–69. It is worth noting that Erianthus, the Theban delegate who later pressed for Athens' destruction (Plut. *Lys.* 15.3), had been the Boeotian navarch at Aegospotami (*ML* no. 95 = *O&R* no. 192, Dem. 19.65, Paus. 10.9.9) and one of the Boetarchs twenty years before at Delium: Thuc. 4.91. Subsequent submissiveness of Lysander and Agis vis-à-vis the ephors: Xen. *Hell.* 2.2.12, 17–18. This should serve to confirm the truth of Pausanias' story which is generally not given credence: see, for example, Munn, *SH*, 408 n. 29.

50. Numbers in 480 and at Plataea: Hdt. 7.234.2, 9.10.1, 29.1. One can estimate the total number of citizens in 371 if one considers the figure of seven hundred which Xenophon gives for Leuctra (*Hell.* 6.4.15) in light of the absence from that battle of two of the six *mórai* (6.1.1, 4.17) and of all of the men over the age of fifty-five (6.14.15). There would have been approximately one thousand fifty Spartiates under fifty-five years and perhaps one hundred fifty more over that age. Population at the time of the first battle of Mantineia: Rahe, *SR*, Appendix 1 (with notes 20–21, where much of the voluminous secondary literature on this vexed subject is cited), and *SSAW*, Chapter 8 (with note 31).

51. Number of *klēroi* said to have been assigned the Spartiates and the *períoikoi*:

Plut. *Lyc.* 8.3, 16.1. Ratio of citizens to helots at Plataea in 479: Hdt. 9.10.1, 28.2, 29.1. Demographic makeup of crowd in Spartan agora in 400: Xen. *Hell.* 3.3.5—where I have taken *tettarákonta* with *állous*. Otherwise, there would have been only forty Spartiates in the marketplace. See Xenophon, *Hellenica*, ed. J. Irving Manatt and Charles E. Bennett (Boston: Ginn, 1888–92), 154.

52. Makeup of the Three Hundred: Hdt. 7.205.2. Great weight accorded the Spartiates captured at Sphacteria: Thuc. 4.15–23, 26–41, 5.15. Murder of ambitious helots: 4.80. Clause anticipating slave revolt in the alliance of 421: 5.23.3. Desire of non-Spartans to "eat the Spartiates raw": Xen. *Hell.* 3.3.4–11 (esp. 6). On the helot hatred of the Spartans see Critias 88 B37 (DK⁶) = Liban. *Orat.* 25.63 as well as Xen. *Lac. Pol.* 12.4.

53. Paus. 8.27 with W. G. G. Forrest, *A History of Sparta, 950–192 B.C.*, 2nd edition (London: Hutchinson University Library, 1980), 74–78. There has for some decades been a modern road through the narrow pass running over Mount Taygetus from Laconia to Messenia. It is cut into the side of the mountain and, in the 1970s, it was regarded as impassable in the winter. I can testify from personal experience that driving it in the summer can be hair-raising. See also D. M. Leahy, "The Spartan Defeat at Orchomenus," *Phoenix* 12:4 (Winter 1958): 141–65 (esp. 162–65). Megalopolis: *IACP* no. 282.

54. For the original articulation of a grand strategy for Lacedaemon, see Rahe, *SR*, Chapter 4.

55. Corinth resists Cleomenes' attempt to establish an empire in central Greece, Sparta's other allies support Corinth: Hdt. 5.55–95 with Rahe, *PC*, Chapter 2. Subsequent disaffection within the Peloponnesus and the consequences: Chapters 4 and 8.

56. Argive ambition sparks a crisis in the Peloponnesus in the 460s: Rahe, *SFAW*, Chapter 3. Argive ambition sparks another crisis in the Peloponnesus following upon the Peace of Nicias: Rahe, *SSAW*, Chapters 7–8. Sparta's wars with Athens: *SFAW*, Chapters 4–6, and *SSAW*, Chapters 3–8.

57. Rise of Thebes in the 420s: Thuc. 3.68.3–4, 4.76.4–77.2, 89.1–101.2, and *Hell. Oxy.* 19.3, 20.3–5 (Chambers) with Paul Cloché, *Thèbes de Béotie: Des Origines à la conquête romaine* (Namur: Secretariat des publications, Facultés universitaires, 1952), 77–86, 90–91.

58. Theban and Corinthian support for razing Athens: Xen. *Hell.* 2.2.19–20, 3.25, 41, 4.30, 3.5.7–8, 6.3.13, 5.35; Andoc. 1.142 (cf. Arrian *Anab.* 1.9.8), 3.21; Isoc. 14.31–32, 18.29; Plut. *Lys.* 15.3–4; Just. *Epit.* 5.8.4. See Geoffrey Ernest Maurice de Ste. Croix, *The Origins of the Peloponnesian War* (Ithaca: Cornell University Press, 1972), 343, and Munn, *SH*, 206.

59. Spartan ephors reject without discussion the Athenians' offer of an alliance on condition that her walls and the Peiraeus fortifications be left intact: Xen. *Hell.* 2.2.10–13 with Hamilton, *Sparta's Bitter Victories*, 45; Krentz, *The Thirty at Ath-*

ens, 30–33; Kagan, *Fall*, 400; Munn, *SH*, 201–2; and Lazenby, *PW*, 245–46. Cf. Thuc. 8.71.3.

60. Ephors advise better counsel, counter-offer requiring only ten stades of the walls to be taken down, Archestratus argues for acceptance: Xen. *Hell.* 2.2.13–15 and Lys. 13.7–9 with Krentz, *The Thirty at Athens*, 32–33; Kagan, *Fall*, 400; Munn, *SH*, 202; and Lazenby, *PW*, 246. The Spartans may even have been willing to let the Athenians keep Lemnos, Imbros, and Scyros: Aeschin. 2.26 with Krentz, *The Thirty at Athens*, 33–34. Cf., however, Andoc. 3.12, 14; Lys. 13.4.

61. Second embassy in 432: Thuc. 1.125–39 (esp. 139) with Rahe, *SSAW*, Chapter 2 (at notes 44–50). Spartan embassies and factional balance: Arist. *Pol.* 1271a4–5. Sellasia: *IACP* no. 343.

62. Cleophon has Archestratus jailed for suggesting acceptance of Spartan counterof-fer: Xen. *Hell.* 2.2.15, Lys. 13.7–9 with Kagan, *Fall*, 400; Munn, *SH*, 202; and Lazenby, *PW*, 246. Cleophon apparently threatened to slit the throat of anyone who spoke of peace: Aeschin. 2.76. See 3.150. In this connection, note also Lys. 30.10. *Stratēgós* Archestratus killed in 406 at Mytilene: Lys. 21.8, Xen. *Hell.* 1.5.16, Diod. 13.74.1 with Chapter 7, above. A close friend of Pericles son of Pericles: Ath. 5.220d. Chaereas son of Archestratus in the upheaval at Samos: Thuc. 8.74, 86 with Chapter 4, above. Works hand in glove with Theramenes, Thrasybulus, and Alcibiades as *stratēgós* at Cyzicus in 410: Diod. 13.49–51 with Chapter 6, above.

63. Theramenes sent to Lysander with full powers to negotiate: Xen. *Hell.* 2.2.16; Lys. 12.68, 13.9–10; and Youtie and Merkelbach, "Ein Michigan-Papyrus über Theramenes," 161–69, with Krentz, *The Thirty at Athens*, 34–41, and Kagan, *Fall*, 402. Cf. Albert Henrichs, "Zum Papyrus über Theramenes," *ZPE* 3 (1968): 101–8, who suspects that the papyrus published by Youtie and Merkelbach derives from a pamphlet written in defense of Theramenes; Antony Andrewes, "Lysias and the Theramenes Papyrus," *ZPE* 6 (1970): 35–38, who thinks that it derives from a later historian who cribbed from Lysias; and Johannes Engels, "Der Michigan-Papyrus über Theramenes and die Ausbildung des 'Thera-menes-Mythos,'" *ZPE* 99 (1993): 123–55, who joins Henrichs and Andrewes in judging it a fragment of a polemical work in which Theramenes is defended, with Raphael Sealey, "Pap. Mich. Inv. 5982: Theramenes," *ZPE* 10 (1975): 279–88. The similarity in phrasing between Lysias' discussion and that in the so-called Theramenes papyrus suggests that the author of the latter drew on the former, but the claim that he was utterly dependent upon Lysias is, as Sealey points out, belied by the fact that, while Lysias has Theramenes travel to Lace-daemon, the papyrus has him journey to Lysander at Samos. There is, moreover, no good reason to suppose that the papyrus is the work of a pamphleteer—much less a partisan of Theramenes. Sealey's ingenious restoration of the fourth fragment ("Pap. Mich. Inv. 5982," 287–88) reinforces the conviction of the first editors ("Ein Michigan-Papyrus über Theramenes," 161–62) that the papyrus is

part of an historical work. The discovery of a new fragment describing later events unconnected with Theramenes confirms this suspicion: Ariel Loftus, "A New Fragment of the Theramenes Papyrus (P. Mich. 5796b)," *ZPE* 133 (2000): 11–20. The author most likely to have written what is found therein is, as Loftus suggests, Ephorus. For the view that the fragments derive from the Oxyrhynchus historian, see Cinzia Bearzot, "Il 'Papiro de Teramene' et *Le Elleniche di Ossirinco*," *Sileno* 27 (2001): 9–32, and Serena Bianchetti, "'Atene sul mare' e la prospettiva delle *Elleniche di Ossirinco*. Avec résumé en Latin," *Sileno* 27 (2001): 33–46. For a fuller citation of the secondary literature on this subject than can be provided here, see Lucia Vannini, "Note sul 'Papiro di Teramene,'" *SEP* 9 (2012): 87–95. Three months later, after Theramenes' return from Samos, he and nine others sent to the ephors at Lacedaemon: Xen. *Hell.* 2.2.16–17 and Lys. 13.10–11 with Kagan, *Fall*, 402–9; Munn, *SH*, 205: and Lazenby, *PW*, 246–47. Note also Hanson, *A War Like No Other*, 286–87.

The chronology I follow here is based on Plut. *Lys.* 15.1, which reports that Athens surrendered on 16 Mounichion in 404 and on Xen. *Hell.* 2.2.16, which asserts that Theramenes returned from Samos to Athens after the passage of three months. At least two weeks—and probably longer—must be reserved for the subsequent journey to and from Sparta and for the negotiations that took place there. Thucydides (5.26) insists that the surrender of Athens took place twenty-seven years and just a few days after the beginning of his war in March 431: consider Thuc. 5.26 in light of 2.2, which should be read with Gomme, *HCT*, II 1–3, III 699–716, and Gomme and Andrewes, *HCT* IV 11–12. With this in mind, Detlef Lotze has argued that 405/4 must have been a leap year with an intercalated month and that, in that year, 16 Mounichion fell in March rather than April 404: Lotze, "Der Munichion 404 v. Chr. und das Problem der Schaltfolge im Athenischen Kalendar," *Philologus* 111 (1967): 34–46. The evidence that we have concerning the reign of Darius II of Persia and concerning that of his successor Artaxerxes II confirms Lotze's hypothesis. The former is said to have died after Athens' surrender: Diod. 13.108.1. He certainly died at about that time: Ctesias *FGrH* 688 F16.57, Xen. *An.* 1.1.1–3, Just. *Epit.* 5.8.7. The Babylonian evidence indicates that he died prior to the beginning of the new year there on 10 April 404—for it treats the Babylonian year 404/3 as the first full year of Artaxerxes II's reign: *BC*, 18–19, 33. The last surviving text from the younger Darius' reign is dated 17 September 405; the earliest surviving text from the younger Artaxerxes' reign dates to April 404: see Matthew W. Stolper, "Mesopotamia, 482–330 B.C.," in *CAH*, VI² 234–60 (at 238), and "Late Achaemenid Babylonian Chronology," *NABU* 1 (March 1999): 6–9 (at 7–9). Had Darius II died in the spring of 405—as Munn, *SH*, 195–97, is inclined to believe—there would be some plausibility to his suggestion that Theramenes, during his three-month sojourn on Samos, was banking on Athens' securing support from the new Great King against his younger brother's associate Lysander (203–5).

64. Mission of Aristoteles: Xen. *Hell.* 2.2.18. Role that Thebes had come to play in Lysander's calculations: Polyaen. *Strat.* 1.45.5. Contemporary evidence that the Theban threat was a matter of concern to the Spartans: Lys. 12.58–61. See also Ael. *VH* 4.6; note Beloch, *Gr. Gesch.*, II:1 428 n. 2; and see Krentz, *The Thirty at Athens*, 40–41, and Kagan, *Fall*, 402–9. The Phocians, who had good reason to fear their neighbor Thebes, were strongly opposed to Athens' destruction: Dem. 19.65, Paus. 3.10.3, Plut. *Lys.* 15.3–4. Role assigned Aristoteles: Xen. *Hell.* 2.3.46, Lys. 12.77. In the passage cited, Lysias claims that, at the time of his trial under the Thirty, Theramenes defended his conduct on this occasion by saying that the restoration of the exiles was due to his efforts and not to the desire of the Lacedaemonians. Whether Lysias' assertion is true or not we do not know. But this much is clear. If Theramenes resorted to such an argument, it did not wash— and for good reason. He had nothing to gain and a great deal to lose from a restoration of the men for whose exile in 411 he had been personally responsible. If he insisted on the inclusion of a clause in the ephors' decree effecting this, it must have been because of an arrangement with Lysander who had his own plans for Athens and, for that reason, an interest in the welfare of Aristoteles and his associates: see Krentz, *The Thirty at Athens*, 41–55. On the role played by Lysander after Aegospotami, see Proietti, *Xenophon's Sparta*, 32–40.

In discussing the making of the peace and what followed—particularly with regard to Theramenes—I have regarded hostile testimony on the part of Lysias as suspect except where another source confirms his account. Lysias' brother Polemarchus was arrested by Theramenes' associate Eratosthenes and executed by the Thirty. Lysias nearly lost his own life in the same fashion. It is hardly surprising that, in discussing the matter, he is given to rhetorical excess. The Attic orators were notorious for this trait anyway (see the anecdote concerning Lysias at Plut. *Mor.* 504c), and blackening the reputation of Theramenes is part of the rhetorical strategy of Lys. 12 and 13. On the conviction that Lysias' claims must resemble the truth in order to be persuasive, I have salvaged as much from him as seems reasonable. Xenophon is also not entirely dependable—particularly with regard to events at Athens. His account of the Arginusae trial is implausible and garbled, as I have suggested above; and his discussion of the aftermath of Aegospotami is incomplete and, in places, inconsistent with contemporary evidence, as Ehrhardt, "Xenophon and Diodorus on Aegospotami," 225–28, demonstrates. For reasons which I have stated above—in cases of conflict, where Xenophon's account makes little sense or is inconsistent with contemporary evidence—I have given preference to Diodorus's account. Unfortunately, Diodorus' discussion of the fall of Athens is very brief, and I have had to depend on the testimony of Xenophon and, where he has no known axe to grind, Lysias. In treating the events leading up to the peace agreement, I have combined Xenophon and that in Lysias which the Theramenes papyrus confirms.

65. Decree of ephors: Plut. *Lys.* 14.7–8. That these were the terms imposed is

confirmed by Andoc. 3.11, 31, 39. They were inscribed on a stele, and this was Andocides' source of information: 3.22. Plutarch presumably had access to the inscription or found it in the collection of Craterus, which we know he consulted: Plut. *Arist.* 26.1–2, *Cim.* 13.5. He quotes it in Doric. See Krentz, *The Thirty at Athens*, 41–43; Munn, *SH*, 206; and Lazenby, *PW*, 247–50. In this connection, see Xen. *Hell.* 2.2.21–22. Razing of walls: 2.2.23, 3.11. Date: Plut. *Lys.* 15.1, 5. Cf. J. A. R. Munro, "The End of the Peloponnesian War," *CQ* 31 (1937): 32–38, with Lotze, "Der Munichion 404 v. Chr. und das Problem der Schaltfolge im Athenischen Kalendar," 34–46. Length of Thucydides' war: 5.26.1 with Hornblower, *CT*, I 236–39. The walls of the city proper were not razed: cf. Andoc. 3.38–39, Lys. 12.63, Xen. *Hell.* 5.1.35, and Plut. *Lys.* 14.9–10, who exaggerate the scope of destruction, with Thuc. 5.26.1, and see David H. Conwell, "What Athenian Fortifications Were Destroyed in 404 BC?" in *Oikistes: Studies in Constitutions, Colonies, and Military Power in the Ancient World*, ed. Vanessa B. Gorman and Eric W. Robinson (Leiden: Brill: 2002), 321–37.

66. Terms of the Athenian–Spartan alliance: Xen. *Hell.* 2.2.20, Diod. 13.107.4. For the autonomy clause, see Diod. 14.3.2, Arist. *Ath. Pol.* 34.3. See also Lys. 12.70, Just. *Epit.* 5.8.3–5. These authors speak as if the treaty of alliance and the guarantee of autonomy were both part of the peace agreement. In one sense, this is true: they were part of the final settlement. But the treaty of alliance with its guarantee of autonomy was not part of the ephors' decree recorded on the stele. It makes sense to suppose that both the terms of alliance and the guarantee of autonomy were included in a subsequent agreement. In 421, the Athenians and Spartans had signed a treaty of peace (Thuc. 5.18) and, only later, a treaty of alliance (5.23). In 417, the Spartans and Argives acted in the same fashion (5.77–79) and included an autonomy clause in both agreements. Cf. 4.118.3. See Busolt, *Gr. Gesch.*, III:2 1635 n. 1, and Ste. Croix, *The Origins of the Peloponnesian War*, 343 n. 2. For another view, see Beloch, *Gr. Gesch.*, II:1 428 n. 3; Meyer, *GdA*, IV:2 365 n. 1; Charles Hignett, *A History of the Athenian Constitution* (Oxford: Clarendon Press, 1952), 285 n. 3; and Alexander Fuks, *The Ancestral Constitution: Four Studies in Athenian Party Politics at the End of the Fifth Century BC* (London:, Routledge and Kegan Paul, 1953), 52–81.

67. Delphic oracle: Ael. *VH* 4.6. Two eyes of Greece: Just. *Epit.* 5.8.4–5. Yokefellows: Plut. *Cim.* 16.10. Cf. Anton Powell, "Why Did Sparta not Destroy Athens in 404, or 403 BC?" in *Sparta and War*, ed. Stephen Hodkinson and Anton Powell (Swansea: Classical Press of Wales, 2006), 287–303, who doubts that Thebes' rising power featured prominently in the thinking of Lysander or in that of his compatriots and who suspects, instead, that the policy ultimately adopted by Lacedaemon was forced on Lysander by those at home wary of his great power.

Epigraph: Carl von Clausewitz, *Vom Kriege* (Hamburg: Severus Verlage, 2016), 20.
1. Flute girls, freedom of Greece expected: Xen. *Hell.* 2.2.23. See also Plut. *Lys.* 15.5.
2. Death of Darius II: Diod. 13.108.1 with *BC*, 16, 32.
3. Athenians issue warning at Sparta in 432: Thuc. 1.77.6.
4. War the norm: cf. George Santayana, "Tipperary," in *Soliloquies in England and Later Soliloquies* (New York: Charles Scribner's Sons, 1923), 99–106 (esp. 102), with Pl. *Leg.* 1.626a.
5. New era: Guido Schepens, "L'Apogée de l'*archè* spartiate comme époque historique dans l'historiographie grecque du début du IVᵉ S. av. J.-C.," *AncSoc* 24 (1993): 169–204.

APPENDIX 1. DATING THE DEATH OF ARTAXERXES SON OF XERXES

1. Ctesias' claim to have been a physician at the court of Artaxerxes II: Ctesias *FGrH* 688 F27.69, F30.72; Xen. *An.* 1.8.4–5; Diod. 2.32.4, 14.26.4, 46.6; Plut. *Artax.* 1.4, 11.1–3, 13.3–7, 18.1–7, 21.1–4. Doubts revived: Marco M. Dorati, "*Ctesia falsario?*" *QS* 41 (1995): 33–52. Charge of Orientalism, and downplaying of harem intrigues: Heleen Sancisi-Weerdenburg, "Exit Atossa: Images of Women in Greek Historiography of Persia," in *Images of Women in Antiquity*, ed. Averil Cameron and Amélie Kuhrt (London: Routledge, 1983), 20–33, and "Decadence in the Empire or Decadence in the Sources? From Source to Synthesis: Ctesias," *AchHist* 1 (1987): 33–46; Pierre Briant, "Histoire et idéologie: Les Grecs et la 'décadence perse,'" in *Melanges Pierre Leveque*, ed. Marie Madeleine Macroux and Evelyne Geny (Besançon: Université de Besançon, 1989), II 33–47, reprinted in an English translation by Antonia Nevill as "History and Ideology: The Greeks and 'Persian Decadence,'" in *Greeks and Barbarians*, ed. Thomas Harrison (Edinburgh: Edinburgh University Press, 2001), 193–210; Jack Martin Balcer, *The Persian Conquest of the Greeks, 545–450 B.C.* (Konstanz: Universitätsverlag Konstanz, 1995); Maria Brosius, *Women in Ancient Persia, 539–331 BC* (Oxford: Oxford University Press, 1996), passim (esp. 1–3); and Yazdan Safaee, "Achaemenid Women: Putting the Greek Image to the Test," *Talanta* 48–49 (2016–17): 101–132.
2. Court intrigue endemic in absolute monarchies: see Lewis, *SP*, 21–22, and Llewellyn-Jones, *KCAP*, 96–122, 133–48, with the preface to Part IV, above.
3. Xenophon's reliance on Ctesias: *An.* 1.8.26–27 and Plut. *Artax.* 13.6–7. Even Eran Almagor, "Ctesias and the Importance of his Writings Revisited," *Electrum* 19 (2012): 9–40 (esp. 28–36), who regards the references to Ctesias in the *Anabasis* as interpolations, acknowledges Xenophon's debt to his predecessor. In this connection, see also Christopher J. Tuplin, "Doctoring the Persians: Ctesias of Cnidus, Physician and Historian," *Klio* 86:2 (February 2004): 305–47, and

"Ctesias as Military Historian," in *Die Welt des Ktesias—Ctesias' World*, ed. Josef Wiesehöfer, Robert Rollinger, and Giovanni B. Lanfranchi (Wiesbaden: Harrassowitz Verlag, 2011), 449–88. Babylonian evidence confirming Ctesias' claims with regard to the transition from Artaxerxes I to Darius II: Chapter 1, note 10, above.

4. Epilycus' treaty and its timing: Rahe, *SSAW*, Chapter 6.

5. Babylonian evidence for dating the death of Artaxeres I and the accession of Darius II: see Matthew W. Stolper, "The Death of Artaxerxes I," *AMI* n.f. 16 (1985): 223–36 (esp. 227, 231), and *E&E*, 116–24, who shows that, in their official documents, the Babylonians treated Artaxerxes as a monarch alive until late December 424, if not beyond that. That Ochus was recognized as Great King in southern Mesopotamia by 10 January 423, even earlier than Stolper supposed, is now clear from a recently studied Babylonian tablet: see Stefan Zawadzki, "The Circumstances of Darius II's Accession in Light of BM 54557 as against Ctesias' Account," *JVEG* 34 (1995–96): 45–49.

6. Babylonian evidence dispositive: Hornblower, *CT*, III 765, and Hyland, *PI*, 42 (with nn. 29–30).

7. For an exception to the rule, see Leo Depuydt, "The Date of the Death of Artaxerxes I," *WO* 26 (1995): 86–96, and *From Xerxes' Murder (465) to Arridaios' Execution (317): Updates to Achaemenid Chronology* (Oxford: BAR, 2008), 13–34.

8. Bēlšunu: see Chapter 1, note 13, above.

APPENDIX 2. COMMERCE WITH THE COMMUNITIES ON THE BLACK SEA, THE CURRENT FROM THE EUXINE TO THE AEGEAN, AND THE GEOSTRATEGIC SIGNIFICANCE OF PROCONNESUS

1. Evidence regarding Proconnesus in the sixth and fifth centuries: Hdt. 4.14.2, 138.1, 6.33.2; Strabo 13.1.2. Tribute of three talents: *IG* I³ 261.iv.17, 271.i.33, 287. ii.14. See *IACP* no. 759.

2. Demosthenes on the grain route: 18.301–2. Convoys: Vincent Gabrielsen, "Trade and Tribute: Byzantion and the Black Sea Straits," in *The Black Sea in Antiquity: Regional and Interregional Economic Exchanges*, ed. Vincent Gabrielsen and John Lund (Arrhus: Arrhus University Press, 2007), 287–324 (esp. 287–97, 308–11).

3. Obstacles to travel by sea from the Aegean to the Euxine: Rhys Carpenter, "The Greek Penetration of the Black Sea," *AJA* 52:1 (January–March 1948): 1–10. I can confirm the strength of the current in the Bosporus, having gone swimming there on a return visit to Istanbul in the late 1980s.

4. Obstacles to moving upstream in the Hellespont and Bosporus: note Hdt. 9.114.1, and see Procop. *Aed.* 5.1.6–16; consider Benjamin W. Labaree, "How the Greeks Sailed into the Black Sea," *AJA* 61:1 (January 1957): 29–33; Alexander John Graham, "The Date of the Greek Penetration of the Black Sea," *BICS* 5

(1958): 25–42; and Askold Ivantchik, "The Greeks and the Black Sea: The Earliest Ideas about the Region and the Beginning of Colonization," in *The Northern Black Sea in Antiquity: Networks, Connectivity, and Cultural Interactions*, ed. Valeriya Kozlovskaya (Cambridge: Cambridge University Press, 2017), 7–25; and then see Jamie Morton, *The Role of the Physical Environment in Ancient Greek Seafaring* (Leiden: Brill, 2001), 40–45, 48–51, 85–90, 152, 237–38, 242–43, 258–61, and James Beresford, *The Ancient Sailing Season* (Leiden: Brill, 2013), 45–52, 79–83, 101.

5. Sizable proportion of the citizen bodies of Tenedos functioning as ferrymen and the implications of this: Arist. *Pol.* 1291b.

6. There is evidence suggesting that Tenedos may have played such a role: note Brian Rutishauser, "Island Strategies: The Case of Tenedos," *REA* 103:1–2 (2001): 197–204, and see Christopher L. H. Barnes, "The Ferries of Tenedos," *Historia* 55:2 (2006): 167–77. Barnes' argument applies with equal force to the ferrymen of Byzantium. Regarding merchant galleys, see Lionel Casson, *Ships and Seamanship in the Ancient World* (Princeton, NJ: Princeton University Press, 1971), 65–76, 157–68.

7. Freighters towed by triremes from Thasos to Stryme on the Thracian coast: Dem. 50.22. Regarding *holkádes* and the other merchant ships that proceeded entirely under sail and, on occasion, required towing, see Casson, *Ships and Seamanship in the Ancient World*, 169–200, 239–45, 270–78, 281–91. Tugboats and barges for use in harbors: ibid. 335–37. Tow path: Tim Severin, *The Jason Voyage: The Quest for the Golden Fleece* (New York: Simon and Schuster, 1985), 132.

8. Sailing up the Hellespont: Severin, *The Jason Voyage*, 107–12. Severin, with a crew of twenty, found rowing up the Bosporus a real challenge: ibid. 130–48.

9. Grain fleet: Hdt. 7.147.2–3, Xen. *Hell.* 1.1.35.

APPENDIX 3. DATING THE CRISES FACED BY DARIUS II

1. The timing of Pissouthnes' rebellion: see Chapter 1, note 18, above.

2. No Arsites found in the Persepolis tablets: Manfred Mayrhofer, *Onomastica persepolitana: das altiranische Namengut der Persepolis-Täfelchen* (Vienna: Verlag der Österreichischen Akademie der Wissenschaften, 1973), 319–42. Elsewhere the name unknown—except with regard to the satrap in Dascyleium in 334: Diod. 17.19.4; Strabo 15.3.24; Arr. *Anab.* 1.12.8, 17.1, 10.16.3; Paus. 1.29.10 with Ferdinand Justi, *Iranisches Namenbuch* (Marburg: Elwert, 1895), 31. Cf. Wilhelm Eilers, *Iranische Beamtennamen in der keilschriftlichen Überlieferung* (Leipzig: Brockhaus, 1940), 125, with Guillaume Cardascia, *Les Archives du Murašû: Une Famille d'hommes d'affaires à l'époque perse (503–455 av. J. C.)* (Paris: Imprimerie nationale, 1951), 7 n. 4, and Stolper, *E&E*, 66, 115–16, who denies that the Arrišittu of PBS II/1 no. 137 and NBRVT no. 189 can be Ctesias' Arsites.

3. Rebellion quelled in Media: Xen. *Hell.* 1.2.19. Ongoing troubles along the west-

ern shore of the Caspian Sea in the south: 2.1.13. The Cadusians did not soon cease to be a problem: Diod. 15.8.5, 10.1. The first Hydarnes recovers Media for Darius and ends up as its satrap: Chapter 1, note 16, above. Quasi-hereditary satrapy based at Dascyleium in Hellespontine Phrygia: Debord, *AM*, 83–115. The other satrapy that passed from father to son was the one based at Damascus and governed by Megabyzus, then Artyphius: Ctesias *FGrH* 688 F14.40, F15.52. Artyphius' possession of a Greek mercenary force is a telltale sign that his satrapy was in the west, and Syria is the only such province not known to have been ruled at this time by someone else.

APPENDIX 4. WHO WAS HIERAMENES?

1. Hieramenes at Caunus: *Tituli Asiae Minoris* I.44c.11–12 with Johannes Friedrich, *Kleinasiatische Sprachdenkmäler* (Berlin: de Gruyter, 1932), 66; and, with regard to the context in which Tissaphernes and Hieramenes are mentioned, note Peter Thonemann, "Lycia, Athens, and Amorges," in *Interpreting the Athenian Empire*, ed. John T. Ma, Nikolas Papazarkadas, and Robert Parker (London: Duckworth, 2009), 167–94 (esp. 176–80).

2. Hieramenes as royal secretary: Meyer, *GdA*, IV:2 277 n. 1; A. T. Olmstead, *History of the Persian Empire* (Chicago: University of Chicago Press, 1948), 362, 370. Hieramenes as sidekick of Tissaphernes: Franz Altheim and Ruth Stiehl, *Die aramäische Sprache under den Achaimeniden* (Frankfurt am Mein: Vittorio Klostermann, 1963), I 151–52.

3. Cilicia semi-independent, ruled by native dynasty: cf. Xen. *Cyr.* 7.4.1–2 with Hdt. 1.74, 5.118, 7.98; Xen. *An.* 1.2.12, 21, 25, 4.4, *Hell.* 3.1.1; Diod 14.19.3–6, 20.2–3, and note the absence of the Cilicians from the various lists of the subject peoples of the empire: Roland G. Kent, *Old Persian: Grammar, Texts, Lexicon*, 2nd edition, revised (New Haven, CT: American Oriental Society, 1953), 116–52.

APPENDIX 5. GREAT MAGNATES IN THE ACHAEMENID EMPIRE

1. See the studies concerning the military colonies in Babylonia that are cited in the preface to Part IV, note 18, above, as well as Geo Widengren, "Recherches sur le féodalisme iranien," *Orientalia Suecana* 5 (1956): 79–182, and *Der Feudalismus im alten Iran: Männerbund, Gefolgswesen, Feudalismus in der iranischen Gesellschaft im Hinblick auf die indogermanischen Verhältnisse* (Cologne: Westdeutscher Verlag, 1969).

2. Land grants after conquests: Hdt. 6.20, 8.85; Xen. *Cyr.* 6.1.17, 7.1.43–45, 5.36, 72, 8.4.28, 6.4–5 with Kathleen M. T. Atkinson, "A Hellenistic Land-Conveyance: The Estate of Mnesimachus in the Plain of Sardis," *Historia* 21:1 (1st Quarter 1972): 45–74; Raymond Descat, "Mnésimachos, Hérodote et le système tribu-

taire achéménide," *REA* 87:1–2 (1985): 97–112; and Gerassimos G. Aperghis, *The Seleukid Royal Economy: The Finances and Financial Administration of the Seleukid Empire* (Cambridge: Cambridge University Press, 2004), 103–4, 137–48, 278–79, 320–23. Asidates: Xen. *An.* 7.8.8–23 with Michael I. Rostovtzeff, "Notes on the Economic Policy of the Pergamene Kings," in *Anatolian Studies Presented to Sir William Mitchell Ramsay*, ed. William H. Buckler (Manchester: The University Press, 1923), 359–90 (at 371–75). Unknown owner of eleven parcels: Georg Kaibel, *Epigrammata Graeca ex lapidibus conlecta* (Berlin: de Gruyter, 1878) no. 335. Mnesimachus: Atkinson, "A Hellenistic Land-Conveyance," 45–74. Castles of a sort: Xen. *An.* 7.8.12–15 with *Cyr.* 4.6.2, 9, 5.2.28, 3.12, 15, 26, 4.2–6, 9, 29, 39; Plut. *Eum.* 8.5; and Josef Keil and Anton von Premerstein, *Bericht über eine Dritte Reise in Lydien und den angrenzenden Gebieten Ioniens* (Vienna: Alfred Hölder, 1914), 102–3. Telltale place-names: Louis Robert, *Noms indigènes dans l'Asie Mineure gréco-romaine* (Paris: A. Maisonneuve, 1963), I 14–16. Serfs: Michael I. Rostovtzeff, *Studien zur Geschichte des Römischen Kolonates* (Darmstadt: Wissenschaftliche Buchgesellschaft, 1970), 240–312, and "Notes on the Economic Policy of the Pergamene Kings," 371–83 with Kathleen M. T. Atkinson, "The Seleucids and the Greek Cities of Western Asia Minor," *Antichthon* 2 (1968): 32–57. Satraps and subordinates: Xen. *Hell.* 3.1.25–27, 2.12, 4.1.15–16, 33, *An.* 4.4.2, 7, *Oec.* 4.5, 20–25; Plut. *Alc.* 24.5 with Christopher J. Tuplin, "Serving the Satrap. Subsatrapal Officials in Greek and Aramaic Sources," in *The Administration of the Achaemenid Empire. Tracing the Imperial Signature*, ed. Bruno Jacobs, Wouter F. M. Henkelman, and Matthew W. Stolper (Wiesbaden: Harrassowitz, 2017), 613–76, and the material collected in *AhW*. See, in particular, John Ma, "Aršāma the Vampire," in ibid. III 189–208.

3. Feudal levy: Hdt. 5.102.1; Xen. *Oec.* 4.5, *An.* 7.8.15, *Cyr.* 8.8.20. Oebazus: Hdt. 4.84. Pythius: 1.34, 7.27–29, 38–39; Plut. *Mor.* 263b. Generosity of the Great King: Hdt. 3.140, 150–60, 8.85, 136, 9.107, 109; Ctesias *FGrH* 688 F15.53 with Pierre Briant, "Dons de terres et de villages: L'Asie Mineure dans le context achéménide," *REA* 87:1–2 (1985): 53–72. For the political economy of the Persian and Hellenistic satrapy, see [Arist.] *Oec.* 1345b19–1346a5. City dwellers who cultivate the King's land: Jonas Crampa, *Labraunda: Swedish Excavations and Researches* (Lund: Gleerup, 1969–72), II:2 no. 42, with M. Çetin Şahín, "Two New Inscriptions from Lagina (Koranza)," *Anatolia* 17 (1973): 187–95 (at 190–91). Demaratus and his descendants: Hdt. 6.70.2; Xen. *Hell.* 3.1.6, *An.* 2.1.3, 7.8.17. Gongylus the Eretrian and his descendants: Thuc. 1.28.6; Xen. *Hell.* 3.1.6, *An.* 7.8.8, 17. For the coins minted by these two great houses, see Ernest Babelon, *Traité des monnaies grecques et romaines* (Bologna: Forni, 1965–76), II:2 79–98. Themistocles: Thuc. 1.138 (with Gomme, *HCT*, I 292, 445), Nepos *Them.* 10.2–5, Plut *Them.* 29. For his coins, see Head, *Hist. Num.*, 581, and P. Gardner, "Coinage of the Athenian Empire," *JHS* 33 (1913): 147–88 (at 165). Holdings of the Persian queen: Pl. *Alc.* I 123b–d2 and Xen. *An.* 1.4.9, 2.4.27 with

Bruno Meissner, "Parysatis," *OLZ* 7 (October 1904): 384–85, as well as Stolper, *E&E*, 62–64, and "Parysatis in Babylon," in *If a Man Builds a Joyful House: Assyriological Studies in Honor of Erle Verdun Leichty*, ed. Ann Guinan et al. (Leiden: Brill, 2006), 463–72. Further examples: Geoffrey Ernest Maurice de Ste. Croix, *The Origins of the Peloponnesian War* (Ithaca: Cornell University Press, 1972), 37–39, 310, 313–14, and Lewis, *SP*, 53–55.

4. For an overview, see Pierre Briant, "Pouvoir central et polycentrisme culturel dans l'empire achéménide: Quelque Réflexions et suggestions," *AchHist* 1 (1987): 1–31, and "Ethno-classe dominante et populations soumises dans l'empire achéménide: Le Cas de l'Egypte," *AchHist* 3 (1988): 137–73, reprinted in an English translation by Amélie Kuhrt as "Central Power and Cultural Polycentrism in the Achaemenid Empire" and as "The Ruling Class and Subject Populations in the Achaemenid Empire: The Egyptian Example," in Briant, *Kings, Countries, Peoples: Selected Studies on the Achaemenid Empire* (Stuttgart: Franz Steiner Verlag, 2017), 43–73, 169–206.

5. Resistance to the Jews' rebuilding their temple: Ezra 4–6 and Nehemiah 2:10, 19–20, 3:33–6:19 with Harold H. Rowley, *Men of God: Studies in Old Testament History and Prophecy* (London: Thomas Nelson, 1963), 211–76.

6. Lydian rebellion early on: Hdt. 1.6–22, 25–28, 69–94, 141–77. Crushed by Cyrus: 1.155.1–157.2. Rebellions nearly everywhere else at the time of Darius' accession: DB. None but the Carians join the Ionian rebellion of the 490s: Hdt. 5.23–38, 97–6.42. Servile rebellion in support of Aristonicus: Wilcken, *RE* 2 (1896): 962–64. Asia Minor pacified and defended: Christopher Tuplin, "The Persian Military Establishment in Western Anatolia: A Context for Celaenae," in *Kelainai-Apameia Kibotos II: Une Métropole achéménide, hellénistique et romaine*, ed. Askold Ivantchik, Latife Summerer, and Alexander von Kienlin (Bordeaux: Ausonius Éditions, 2016), 15–27.

7. Mysian and Pisidian highlanders a threat to the Anatolian gentry: *Hell. Oxy.* 24.1 (Chambers); Xen. *An.* 1.1.11, 2.1, 4, 6.7, 9.14, 2.5.13, 3.2.23, *Hell.* 3.1.13, *Mem.* 3.5.26.

8. Payments for passage from Susa to Persepolis: Strabo 15.3.4 and Arr. *Anab.* 3.17.1–2 with Lewis, *SP*, 55 (esp. n. 36). For an overview, see Pierre Briant, *État et pasteurs au Moyen-Orient ancien* (Cambridge: Cambridge University Press, 1983). In this connection, consider the argument advanced by James C. Scott, *The Art of Not Being Governed: An Anarchist History of Upland Southeast Asia* (New Haven: Yale University Press, 2009).

APPENDIX 6. ARSACES AND CYRUS: RELATIVE AGES

1. Greeks and Romans tend to marry off daughters shortly after puberty: consider Walter K. Lacey, *The Family in Classical Greece* (Ithaca, NY: Cornell University Press, 1968), 71–72, 106–7, 162–63, 212, and M. Keith Hopkins, "The Age of Roman Girls at Marriage," *Population Studies* 18:3 (1965): 309–27, in light of

Darell W. Amundsen and Carol J. Diers, "The Age of Menarche in Classical Greece and Rome," *Human Biology* 41:1 (February 1969): 125–32.

2. Age of menopause in ancient Greece and Rome: Darell W. Amundsen and Carol J. Diers, "The Age of Menopause in Classical Greece and Rome," *Human Biology* 42:1 (February 1970): 79–86.

APPENDIX 7. THE SELECTION OF PERSIAN SATRAPS AND GENERALS

1. Herodotus' catalogue analyzed: Andrew Robert Burn, *Persia and the Greeks: The Defense of the West, 546–478 B.C.*, 2nd edition (Stanford, CA: Stanford University Press, 1984), 333–36. See also Briant, *CA*, 302–54 (esp. 352–54).

2. See the preface to Part IV, note 22, above, where Artabazus' father is identified.

3. The list of satraps known to have been serving under Darius in the late sixth and early fifth centuries is also germane: Wouter F. M. Henkelman, "Nakhthor in Persepolis," in *AhW*, II 193–223 (at 206–11). Gergis was one of their number.

4. Otanes as Xerxes' father-in-law: Ctesias *FGrH* 66 F13.24. Megapanus as satrap of Elam: Henkelman, "Nakhtor in Persepolis," 209.

5. Ardumanish unknown to Herodotus as a conspirator and officeholder: cf. 3.61–88 with DB IV.80–88, which should be read in tandem with DNd.

6. Dascyleium: preface to Part IV, note 22, above.

7. Pissouthnes: Thuc. 1.115.4–5, 3.31.1, 34.2, 8.5.5, 28.3; Ctesias *FGrH* 688 F15.53; Diod. 12.27.3; Plut. *Per.* 25.

8. On Megabyzus, see Rahe, *SFAW*, Chapters 5–6, and Chapter 1, above.

9. Arsames' correspondence in Aramaic is now available in a critical edition with a translation, a commentary, and a series of interpretive essays: see *AhW*, passim. Regarding the letters cited in the text above, see D. J. K. Taylor, "The Bodleian Letters: Text and Translation," and Christopher J. Tuplin, "The Bodleian Letters: Commentary," in ibid. I 21–49 (at 43–45), 61–283 (at 230–45). See also Christopher J. Tuplin, "Aršāma: Prince and Satrap," in ibid. III 3–72. With regard to the Aramaic terminology employed and the Old Persian, Elamite, and Akkadian equivalents employed elsewhere, see Stolper, *E&E*, 53, 59–62.

10. The house of the confederate Hydarnes in the time of Artaxerxes and Darius II: see Chapter 1 and the preface to Part IV, above.

11. Sons of the Royal House: Emile Benveniste, *Titres et noms propres en iranien ancien* (Paris: Klincksieck, 1966), 22–26.

AUTHOR'S NOTE AND ACKNOWLEDGMENTS

This book is the fifth volume in a series dedicated to the study of Sparta and her conduct of diplomacy and war from the late archaic period down to the second battle of Mantineia. Like the series' prelude, *The Spartan Regime: Its Character, Origins, and Grand Strategy*, and its immediate predecessors in the series proper, *The Grand Strategy of Classical Sparta: The Persian Challenge*; *Sparta's First Attic War: The Grand Strategy of Classical Sparta, 478–446 B.C.*; *Sparta's Second Attic War: The Grand Strategy of Classical Sparta, 446–418 B.C.*; and *Sparta's Sicilian Proxy War: The Grand Strategy of Classical Sparta, 418–404 B.C.*, it has been a long time in gestation, and I have incurred many debts along the way. I was first introduced to ancient history by Donald Kagan when I was a freshman at Cornell University in the spring of 1968. The following year, I took a seminar he taught on the ancient Greek city and another seminar on Plato's *Republic* taught by Allan Bloom. After graduating from Yale University in 1971, I read *Litterae Humaniores* at Wadham College, Oxford, on a Rhodes Scholarship. It was there that my ancient history tutor W. G. G. Forrest first piqued my interest in Lacedaemon.

I returned to Yale University in 1974 for graduate study. There, three years later, I completed a dissertation under the direction of Donald Kagan entitled *Lysander and the Spartan Settlement, 407–403 B.C.* In the aftermath, I profited from the comments and suggestions of Antony Andrewes, who was one of my readers, and my interest in Achaemenid Persia, which was already considerable, was increased when David M. Lewis sent me the page proofs of his as yet unpublished *Sparta and Persia*. It was my intention at that time to turn my thesis into a book focused on Sparta, Athens, and Persia, and I carved out of it an article on the selection of ephors at Sparta and penned another in which I discussed the makeup of the Achaemenid Persian army at the time of Cunaxa, the tactics the Persians customarily employed, and the relative strength of Greek hoplites faced with such a challenge. But the book I had in mind I did not write.

Instead, with encouragement from Bernard Knox during the year in which I was a Junior Fellow at the Center for Hellenic Studies, I got sidetracked. I wrote one twelve-hundred-page work entitled *Republics Ancient and Modern: Classical Republicanism and the American Revolution*; then, three shorter monographs—one on Machiavelli and English republicanism, another on the political philosophy of Montesquieu, and a third on modern republicanism in the thought of Montesquieu, Rousseau, and Tocqueville. In the intervening years, I ordinarily taught a lecture course on ancient Greek history in the fall and a seminar on some aspect of that subject in the spring, and I frequently gave thought to Lacedaemon, to questions of diplomacy and war, and to the work I had once done with George Forrest and Don Kagan. This book, like its companions, is a belated acknowledgment of what I owe them both.

I have also profited from the labors of John S. Morrison, John F. Coates, N. Boris Rankov, Alec Tilley, and the others in Britain, in Greece, and elsewhere who, in the 1980s and 1990s, contributed to designing, building, launching, and to rowing and sailing in sea trials a reconstructed trireme that they named the *Olympias*. If we now have a better sense of trireme warfare than scholars did in the past, it is because of the labors and ingenuity of the practitioners of what has come to be called "experimental archaeology" who devised this project and lent a hand.

I would also like to record my debt to the late Patrick Leigh Fermor. Long ago, when Peter Green learned that I was interested in the manner in which the rugged terrain in certain parts of Messenia might have facilitated banditry and resistance on the part of Lacedaemon's helots, he suggested that I contact Paddy, who had learned a thing or two about this sort of resistance while serving on Crete during the Second World War. In the summer of 1983, I followed up on this recommendation. Our meeting over a somewhat liquid lunch at Paddy's home in Kardamyli paved the way for a series of visits, often lasting a week or more, that took place at irregular intervals over the twenty-three years following that memorable repast. On nearly every occasion, our conversations returned to ancient Sparta; and in 1992, when *Republics Ancient and Modern* appeared, Paddy wrote a generous appraisal of it for the *Spectator*.

This volume was produced while I was the Roger and Martha Mertz Visiting Fellow at the Hoover Institution on the campus of Stanford University. This was an invaluable opportunity, and I am grateful for the support I received.

Part of this book was written in years in which I was teaching history at Hillsdale College. I am grateful to the Charles O. Lee and Louise K. Lee Foundation, which supported the chair I held and still hold at the college; to the trustees of the college and to its president, Larry Arnn; and to my colleagues and students there, who were always supportive. I owe a special debt to Jacob Bruns and Benjamin Crenshaw, who helped me check the notes; to Fred S. Naiden, who read and commented on the entire manuscript; and to Maurine McCoury, the director of the Hillsdale College library; Aaron Kilgore, who arranged for the purchase of books; and Pam Ryan, who handled interlibrary loan. Librarians are the unsung heroes of the academic world, and no one knows better than I how much we scholars owe them.

The fact that I was able to finish this book and its predecessors in this series, I owe to Dr. Marston Linehan, Dr. Peter Pinto, Dr. Piyush Kumar Agarwal, and the staff at the Clinical Center of the National Institutes of Health in Bethesda, Maryland—where in the summer of 2012 I was treated for prostate cancer and for complications attendant on surgery and where in and after 2016 I was treated for bladder cancer. Had Dr. Pinto not devised a new method for diagnosing

AUTHOR'S NOTE AND ACKNOWLEDGMENTS

prostate cancer, had he not done my surgery with great precision, and had he and his colleagues not found a way to eliminate the lymphocele that bedeviled me in the aftermath, and had Dr. Agarwal not scraped out the cancer growing in my bladder, I would not now be in a position to write these words.

Throughout the period in which this book was written, my four children were patient, and they and my wife kept me sane. From time to time, they brought me back to the contemporary world from classical antiquity, where, at least in my imagination, I may sometimes have seemed more at home than in the here and now.

INDEX

INDEX

Agesandridas (*cont.*)
 summoned to Hellespont by
 Mindarus, made *epıstoleús* 240,
 250–52
  loses most of fleet in storm off
  Mt. Athos 251–52
 Thraceward region activities 282
Agesilaus, younger son of Archidamus (II), *paıdıká* of Lysander 241,
 321, 328
Agis, elder son of Archidamus (II), late
 fifth-century Eurypontid king 47–50,
 54, 66–68, 93, 101–3, 107–9, 117, 140–
 44, 148–53, 157, 163–64, 182, 186–89,
 196, 224, 272, 281, 287, 318–22, 327–
 28, 370, 381–83, 393–95, 400–403
  Alcibiades at Argos outmaneuvers
  and humiliates 47–48, 142–43,
  149–50
   role in battle of Mantineia
   48–50
  Alcibiades debauches his wife 140–
  42, 151, 328
  maintains fort in Attica at Deceleia
  54–55, 66–68, 102, 107, 115, 138,
  140, 163–64, 182, 186, 188, 211,
  213, 281–83, 287, 360, 381–82,
  400
   alert to Athenian dependence
   on grain imported from the
   Euxine, Hellespontine strategy 102, 221, 224, 230–32,
   263, 281, 382–85, 392
   follows father's stratagem:
   drives wedge between farm-
   ers and salarymen dependent on empire for their
   livelihood 162–64, 178, 265
Ahura Mazda 22, 81, 90–91, 126, 299,
 307–9
Akritas, Cape in southwestern Messenia
 4

Alcamenes son of Sthenelaidas, Spartan
 harmost-designate, enjoys favor of
 Agis 68, 101–4, 327
Alcibiades son of Cleinias, Athenian
 statesman, *stratēgós*, exile, and turncoat 46–58, 93, 97, 104–11, 121, 126,
 139–44, 149–80, 189–202, 212–14,
 222–27, 238–40, 245, 252–96, 319–
 22, 327–35, 353, 360, 371, 375–76,
 380–94, 402–3, 432
  architect of battle at Mantineia, of
  Athens' Sicilian expedition, of
  Sparta's Sicilian proxy war 46–58
  debauches Agis' wife Timaea,
  fathers son 140–42, 151, 328
   later escapes Agis' wrath, joins
   court of Tissaphernes 153–
   54, 166–68
  encourages Spartan cooperation
  with Chios and Tissaphernes,
  engineers Chian revolt 93–94,
  104–8
   deliberately jettisons Agis'
   Hellespontine strategy,
   deflects effort south toward Miletus
   108–20, 123, 157
  forms guest-friendship (*xenía*)
  with Tissaphernes 153–58, 161,
  166–72, 176, 180, 189–90, 194–
  95, 226–27, 256, 280, 329–30
   encourages Tissaphernes to play
   Athens and Sparta against
   one another 154–58, 296
   imprisoned by Tissaphernes,
   escape enabled 256
  maneuvers aimed at forcing compatriots to recall 157–58, 165–78,
  190–98
   foments oligarchic revolution
   at Athens, then overturns
   the oligarchic regime 138,
   157–58, 165–77, 189–214

INDEX

Athens(*cont.*)
    short of triremes, short of money
      61, 96–97, 100, 111–13, 138, 158,
      181, 186, 190, 210, 255–56, 265,
      279, 329, 334, 350–51
    Sicilian disaster shakes confidence
      in institutions 97–98, 138, 158–
      64, 177–78, 210
    wealth classes
      pentakosiomédimnoi 98, 163,
        182–84, 198
      thetes 57, 98, 163, 178, 182
      zeugítai 98, 163, 183–84, 198
    See also Alcibiades son of Cleinias,
      Athenian statesman, *stratēgós*,
      exile, and turncoat; Attica: Ath-
      ens' territory; Cleophon son of
      Cleippides, demagogue; Conon
      son of Timotheos, Athenian
      stratēgós; Peisander, Athenian
      demagogue turned oligarch;
      Phrynichus son of Stratonides;
      Theramenes son of Hagnon;
      Thrasybulus son of Lycus, parti-
      san of Alcibiades; Thrasyllus;
      triremes and trireme warfare
Athos, Mt. on the Acte peninsula in the
    Chalcidice 251, 358, 368
Atossa daughter of Cyrus, wife of Dar-
    ius, mother of Xerxes 84, 297–98
Attica: Athens' territory 17–21, 24–27,
    30–33, 40–42, 54–55, 67, 115, 140,
    149–50, 163–64, 178–79, 203–4, 207,
    212, 222, 368, 381–83, 393–95, 400
    Deceleia on Mt. Parnes: site of
      Peloponnesian fort 54–55,
      66–68, 102, 107, 115, 138–40,
      163–64, 182, 186–88, 211–13,
      281–83, 287, 360, 368, 381–82,
      394, 400
    Eleusis and the Eleusinian Myster-
      ies 55, 159, 171, 204, 287–88, 394

Laurium silver mines 19, 54, 164
Long Walls built to link Athens
    with the Peiraeus 30–31, 34–36,
    40–41, 55, 163–64, 178, 188,
    203, 392–94, 402–4, 407
Marathon, plain of 17–19, 23, 204,
    310, 356, 362, 368, 394, 405
Oenoe , fort on the Attic-Boeotian
    border 55, 211
Oropus, district opposite Euboea
    bordering on Boeotia 55, 204,
    207–9, 394
Peiraeus, the, promontory hosting
    the three harbors constituting
    Athens' port 15, 20, 24, 27–30,
    55–57, 97, 102, 162, 193–210,
    255, 282, 285–86, 368, 382, 392–
    94, 401, 404–7, 418
    commercial harbor Kantharos
      30, 202–4
Prasiae and Thorikos: coastal vil-
    lages 204, 207
Salamis, island of 18–23, 29, 55, 61,
    66, 95, 204, 207, 350, 362, 368–
    70, 394, 405
Sunium, Cape, in Attica 55, 204,
    207, 361, 368, 394

Babylon, Babylonians 13, 76–79, 82–84,
    89, 292–93, 298–307, 313–17, 410–
    16, 424–25, 429–30, 436–37
Bēlšunu, Babylonian dignitary allied
    with Darius II, district governor of
    Babylon and, later, district governor
    or satrap of Syria ("the Land-Across-
    the River") 83, 416
Bisitun inscription 90, 302, 308, 436
Bismarck, Otto von 22
Bithynia, district along the northern
    coast of Anatolia in the north 278,
    292
Black Sea (Euxine) 21–23, 67, 70–71,

INDEX

Lysander(*cont.*)
    genocide at Iasos and Cedreia,
    butchery at Miletus 367–69
    helps friends, harms enemies
    369
    recourse to Agis on Attic coast
    370, 381
    seizes Lampsacus 384–85
    strategic patience again in evi-
    dence 386–89
    victory at Aegospotami: out-
    lasts, outwits, annihilates
    Athenians 385–90
    victory's aftermath
      Athenian prisoners (Philocles
      includes) executed 390–91
      captures Sestos, Chalcedon,
      Byzantium, Lesbos, Samos,
      and the other cities under
      Athenian control, surviving
      Athenians sent home to
      starve 391–93
      flirts, alongside Agis, with
      total destruction of Athens
      394, 400–401
      Theban threat inspires willing-
      ness to preserve Athens as a
      Spartan satellite 400–405
      Theramenes' sojourn, Aris-
      toteles to ephors 403
      oversees razing of Athens'
      walls 404
Lysias, among the *stratēgoí* at Arginusae
351, 374
    victim of the Arginusae trial 379

Macaulay, Thomas Babington, Lord 242,
335
Macedonia, Macedonians 76, 255, 285,
308, 429
Machiavelli, Niccolò 364
Mackinder, Halford J. 3, 95, 362–64

Maeander river in Anatolia 21, 70, 106,
127, 166, 176, 218, 366
Magi of Iran 300, 423
Magna Graecia, region of Greek settle-
ment in Italy 52–53, 115
Magnesia on the Maeander in Anatolia
21, 70, 106, 116, 166, 218, 234, 250,
344, 366, 430
Mahan, Alfred Thayer 43, 112
Malea, Cape, southeastern tip of Laco-
nia 4, 12, 231, 351–52, 358, 370
Malis in Central Greece, Malians 66
Mantineia: battle in 418 pitting Argos,
Mantineia, and Athens against Sparta
46–54, 62–64, 96, 149–50, 187, 396
Mantineia in Arcadia, Mantineians 12,
24, 27, 46–54, 62–64, 96, 149–50,
187, 396–99
Mantitheus, Athenian associate of Alcib-
iades 256, 280–81, 284
Mardonius son of the Gobryas who was
a co-conspirator of Darius 435
Marlborough, John Churchill, duke of 64
Marmara, Sea of (Propontis) 21, 45,
67–71, 101–6, 189, 221, 229, 232–34,
237, 240, 257–63, 274–80, 284, 291–
93, 360, 371, 382–93, 418–21
    length, width, depth, speed of the
    current 232–36
Medizers, medizing 28
Megabyzus (I), co-conspirator of the
first Darius 78–79, 313, 435
    role in Herodotus' Persian Debate
    159–61, 198–99
Megabyzus (II) son of Zopyrus, grandson of like-named co-conspirator of
the first Darius, son-in-law of Xerxes,
protector of Artaxerxes, satrap of
Syria ("The Land-Across-the-River")
79, 86, 310–14, 423, 435–37
    Marshal on Xerxes' march into
    Greece 79, 313

INDEX

INDEX

INDEX

INDEX